Arthur Cox Employment Law Yearbook 2023

Arthur Cox
Employment Law
Yearbook 2023

Bloomsbury Professional

DUBLIN • LONDON • EDINBURGH • NEW DELHI • NEW YORK • SYDNEY

BLOOMSBURY PROFESSIONAL
An imprint of Bloomsbury Publishing plc
Bloomsbury Professional Plc
50 Bedford Square, London, WC1B 3DP, UK
1385 Broadway, New York, NY 10018, USA
29 Earlsfort Terrace, Dublin 2, Ireland

British Library Cataloguing-in-Publication Data

A catalogue record for this book is available from the British Library.

ISBN: PB: 978 1 52652 798 1
ePDF: 978 1 52652 800 1
ePub: 978 1 52652 799 8

Typeset by Compuscript Ltd, Shannon
Printed and bound in Great Britain by CPI Group (UK) Ltd, Croydon, CR0 4YY

MIX
Paper | Supporting responsible forestry
FSC® C013604
www.fsc.org

Practice Areas Involved in the *Arthur Cox Employment Law Yearbook 2023*

Employment and Industrial Relations
Kevin Langford
Cian Beecher
Louise O'Byrne
Séamus Given
Niamh Fennelly
Emma Dunne
Sally Doyle
Sarah Lawn
Rachel Barry
Grace-Ann Meghen
Sarah Faulkner
Hannah O'Farrell
Declan MacQuillan
Ailbhe Moloney
Ciara McDermott
Eamonn Butler
Katie Rooney
Sonam Gaitonde
Aisling Kerins, Arthur Cox Editor
Rosanna McAleese
Melissa O'Sullivan
Aedín McHugh

Tax
Fintan Clancy
Ailish Finnerty
David Kilty
Orlaith Kane
Ciara Fagan
Ciara Murphy
Cristina Susanu
Dearbhla Ní Fhloinn
Edwina Hilton
Elaine Mooney
Isobel D'Arcy
Lebo Motsumi Nkoloti
Mary Dineen
Paulina Serafieva
Rachel Coyle
Ruth O'Sullivan
Simona Prielaidaite

Pensions
Philip Smith
Sarah McCague
Michael Shovlin
Deirdre Cummins
Anne Corrigan
Daniel Watters
Ross Neill
Alan Harney

Technology and Innovation
Rob Corbet
Colin Rooney
Olivia Mullooly
Ian Duffy
Rachel Benson
Aoife MacArdle
Ciara Anderson
Rosemarie Blake
Aoife Coll
David O'Connor
Lorraine Sheridan
Vivian Spies
Dr. Robert Clark
Rory Curtis
Shay Buckley
Laura Dunne

Arthur Cox Belfast
Rosemary Lundy
Chris Fullerton

Introduction

This is the thirteenth volume of the *Arthur Cox Employment Law Yearbook*, which is designed to set out the latest developments and information on employment law and related areas of law in Ireland in 2023. The *Arthur Cox Employment Law Yearbooks* are a unique resource for lawyers, human resource professionals, public and private sector employers, employees, and trade unions, for whom keeping up to date in employment law is an ever-present challenge.

There continues to be a high volume of employment litigation in the WRC and the Labour Court. There have also been many employment cases of note in the civil courts in Ireland, including applications for judicial review and interlocutory injunctions. Key decisions of the Court of Justice of the European Union and of the Employment Appeal Tribunal, the High Court, the Court of Appeal and the Supreme Court in the neighbouring jurisdiction are also noted.

The material for the *2023 Yearbook* has been carefully selected by experienced Arthur Cox lawyers in the fields of employment law, data protection, pensions and taxation.

The line for inclusion in the *2023 Yearbook* was drawn as of 1 December 2023. Work on the *Arthur Cox Employment Law Yearbook 2024* is already in progress.

A particular word of thanks must go to David Hand BL and Shauna Colgan BL who worked with Arthur Cox to put together the internal monthly employment law update briefings on which this Yearbook is based, and to Siobhán Mulholland for her unfailing expertise, guidance and support to the Arthur Cox team.

Others deserving of special thanks are the team at Bloomsbury Professional, in particular Amy Hayes of for her continued guidance and assistance, Andrew Turner for indexing, Caroline Ion for tabling and Compuscript for typesetting.

Sincere thanks also to all those in Arthur Cox LLP who contributed to this Yearbook, in particular our subject matter experts, Katie Rooney the 2022 Yearbook Editor our trainees Claire O'Reilly, Jack Lawlor and Niamh McCarthy and our legal executive Taylor Fowler for their hard work and outstanding efforts in collating the cases for inclusion in the text.

Aisling Kerins, Arthur Cox LLP Editor

January 2024

Contents

Table of Cases

A

B

C

D

E

F

G

H

I

J

K

L

M

N

O

P

Q

R

S

T

U

V

W

X

Y

Z

Table of Statutes

Table of Statutory Instruments

GREAT BRITAIN

C

E

H

I

N

P

R

Table of EU and other Legislation

DIRECTIVES

REGULATIONS

TABLE OF AGREEMENTS, CHARTERS, CONVENTIONS, PROCEDURES AND TREATIES

GUIDELINES, RECOMMENDATIONS AND STATEMENTS

TABLE OF OTHER LEGISLATION

Albania

Bulgaria

Czechoslovakia

Germany

Greece

Italy

Luxembourg

USA

Chapter 1

Contract of Employment

INTRODUCTION

[1.01]

Agency Workers

CM v TimePartner Personalmanagement GmbH was referred to the ECJ by the Federal Labour Court of Germany for a preliminary ruling in relation to the interpretation of art 5 of Directive 2008/104/EC on temporary agency workers. The German Court raised two questions with the ECJ: (1) does Directive 2008/104/EC require a greater level of protection for temporary agency workers than workers generally, and (2) when can a collective agreement which authorises differences in treatment to the detriment of temporary agency workers, be deemed to respect the overall protection of the workers concerned?

In *LD v ALB FILS Kliniken GmbH* the ECJ was asked by the Federal Labour Court in Germany to consider whether Directive 2008/104/EC on temporary agency work applied to an agency worker where their duties were permanently transferred by their employer to a third party.

Bonus Clawback/Restraint of Trade

The High Court of England and Wales considered whether the clawback provisions applicable to a discretionary bonus amounted to an impermissible restraint of trade in *Steel v Spencer Road LLP*.

Suspension

In *Board of Management of Wilson's Hospital School v Burke*, one of two cases between the parties before the High Court this year, the Court considered granting declaratory relief to the employer, affirming it had lawfully suspended the respondent employee and injunctive relief restraining the employee from trespassing on the employer's premises. The second case is discussed in **Chapter 11**.

Intellectual Property

The High Court of England and Wales in *PQ Systems Europe Ltd v Aughton* considered whether an ex-employee used their previous employer's software when starting up their own business, infringing copyright and in breach of the contractual obligation of confidentiality.

Terms of Employment

ESB Networks v O'Grady is a decision of the Labour Court concerning whether the introduction of a new payroll system, which required employees to use an app to lodge overtime claims, amounted to a change in the employee's terms of employment or a change in working practices.

Employee Indemity

See the decision of the Court of Appeal of England and Wales, noted at paragraph 5.02, with reference to claimed obligations to indemnify an employee against losses incurred in the course of employment.

AGENCY WORKERS

[1.02] ***CM v TimePartner Personalmanagement GmbH*[1]*—European Court of Justice—request for a preliminary ruling from Germany—Directive 2008/104/EC,*[2] *art 5—employment and social policy—temporary agency work—principle of equal treatment—collective agreement providing for lower pay than directly-recruited staff—effective judicial protection***

This request for a preliminary ruling concerned the interpretation of art 5 of Directive 2008/104/EC on temporary agency workers (the 'Directive').

The request was made in proceedings between the applicant and the respondent, a temporary-work agency, concerning the amount payable by the respondent in respect of temporary agency work carried out by the applicant as a user undertaking.

The applicant was employed as a temporary agency worker under a fixed-term contract of employment, during which time she was assigned to a retail undertaking in Bavaria, Germany. The applicant received a gross hourly wage of €9.23, in accordance with the collective agreement applicable to temporary agency workers concluded between the German association of temporary agency workers (of which the respondent was a

---

1 *CM v TimePartner Personalmanagement GmbH* (Case C-311/21).

2 Directive 2008/104/EC on temporary agency work.

member) and the German trade union confederation (whose membership included the applicant's trade union).

Comparable workers of the user undertaking to which the applicant was assigned received a gross hourly wage of €13.64.

The collective agreement derogated from the principle of equal treatment under the applicable provisions of Germany's law on temporary agency work (the 'AÜG') by providing for lower pay for temporary agency workers than that granted to workers of the user undertaking.

In proceedings before the Labour Court, Würzburg, Germany, the applicant sought additional pay equivalent to the difference she would have received had she been paid under the collective agreement for retail workers in Bavaria. She argued, unsuccessfully, that the relevant provisions of the AÜG and the collective agreement as they applied to temporary agency workers did not comply with art 5 of the Directive.

On appeal, the matter came before the Federal Labour Court which decided to stay proceedings and refer a number of questions to the European Court of Justice ('ECJ') for preliminary ruling.

By its first question, the referring Court asked, in essence, whether art 5(3) of the Directive, by its reference to 'overall protection of temporary agency workers', must be interpreted as requiring that a greater level of protection specific to temporary agency workers be taken into account than that which applies to workers in general.

Article 5 'lays down the rule that the basic working and employment conditions of temporary agency workers ... are at least those of the user undertaking's own workers'. Derogation under art 5(3) must remain 'within the limits of the overall protection of temporary agency workers'. Its scope must therefore be limited to what is strictly necessary in order to safeguard the need to cope flexibly with labour markets and industrial relations.

The ECJ held that a derogation authorising less favourable treatment of temporary agency workers to those of employees must attract advantages intended to compensate for the effects of the different treatment. Article 5(3) does not, however, require that any account be taken of measures affording greater levels of protection to temporary agency workers than that already afforded under national and EU law.

Accordingly, the first question was answered in the affirmative.

By its second question, the referring Court asked, in essence, under what conditions a collective agreement authorising differences in treatment to the detriment of temporary agency workers may, nevertheless, be deemed to respect the 'overall protection' of the workers concerned. Must the obligation to respect the 'overall protection' of temporary agency workers require the worker concerned to have a permanent contract of employment with a temporary work agency?

On a reading of art 5(1), the EU legislature demonstrated its intention to ensure that temporary agency workers are not 'as a rule' in a less favourable position than that of comparable workers. Temporary agency workers are therefore entitled 'as a rule, to the same basic working and employment conditions [as] those that would apply if the user undertaking had recruited them directly'.

It followed from the limiting scope of art 5(3) that it is appropriate to determine first the basic working and employment conditions which would apply had the temporary agency worker been recruited directly by the user undertaking to occupy the same job. Second, it is necessary to compare those basic working and employment conditions with those resulting from the collective agreement to which the temporary agency worker is actually subject. Third, it must be assessed whether countervailing benefits afforded can offset difference in treatment suffered, ensuring the overall protection of temporary agency workers.

Article 5(2) permits Member States to provide for an exemption to the principle of equal treatment where temporary agency workers under a permanent contract of employment with a temporary work agency continue to be paid between assignments. The derogation, however does not lay down any rule where temporary agency workers are under a permanent contract. Where art 5(2) establishes the actual compensation to be afforded to temporary agency workers with a permanent contract, in return for a derogation from the principle of equal treatment, art 5(3) allows social partners 'to negotiate independently both the exact nature of the derogation … and the advantage deemed capable of compensating for the effects of that derogation, provided that the overall protection of temporary agency workers is respected'.

The ECJ held that it followed from a reading of art 5(3) that the obligation to respect the 'overall protection' of temporary agency workers does not require the worker concerned to have a permanent contract of employment with a temporary work agency.

By its third question, the referring Court asked, in essence, whether art 5(3) of the Directive must be interpreted as meaning that Member States are required to 'lay down the conditions and criteria designed to respect the overall protection of temporary agency workers' in circumstances where social partners are given the option of upholding or concluding collective agreements authorising differences in treatment to the detriment of temporary agency workers.

The Directive permits Member States to allow social partners to define working and employment conditions 'provided that the overall level of protection for temporary agency workers is respected', the purpose being to cope in a flexible manner with labour markets and industrial relations. Under recital 19, the ECJ held it was apparent that this protection for temporary agency workers does not affect the autonomy of social partners to negotiate and conclude collective agreements. Further, Member States are free to adopt the necessary measures, *vis-à-vis* social partners, to ensure compliance with the objective of protecting temporary agency workers. Thus, they are required to respect the overall protection of temporary agency workers, though they need not 'prescribe in detail the conditions and criteria with which collective agreements must comply'.

However, collective agreements must be negotiated and concluded by social partners with the delegated power to do so, 'in compliance with EU law in general and with [Directive 2008/104/EC] in particular'.

By its final question, the referring Court asked, in essence, whether art 5(3) must be interpreted as meaning that collective agreements which authorise differences in treatment to the detriment of temporary agency workers are amenable to judicial review 'in order to determine whether the social partners have complied with their obligation to respect the overall protection of those workers'.

In light of the autonomy afforded under EU law to workers or their respective organisations to negotiate and conclude collective agreements, social partners 'may engage in dialogue and act freely without receiving any order or instruction from whomsoever and, in particular, not from the Member States or the EU institutions'. This broad discretion necessarily extends to defining the measures capable of achieving a particular aim in social and employment policy, albeit within EU law.

While Member States are not required to adopt specific protective legislation, it is for the referring Court to determine, and to do 'everything within its jurisdiction' to ensure, that derogating collective agreements are consistent with the requirements of art 5(3). Accordingly, the final question was answered in the affirmative.

[1.03] ***LD v ALB FILS Kliniken GmbH*[3]*—European Court of Justice—request for preliminary ruling from Germany—Directive 2008/104/EC*[4]*—contract of employment—agency workers—social policy—temporary work—definition of temporary assignment—transfer of functions performed by a worker from the latter's employer to a third-party undertaking—permanent assignment of the worker while maintaining the latter's initial contract of employment***

The applicant entered into employment with the respondent company in 2000. The respondent operated a clinic and the employment relationship was governed by a collective agreement for the public service called 'TVöD'. In 2018, the respondent transferred a number of departments to Company A, which was a wholly-owned subsidiary of the respondent. The duties performed by the applicant and the employment relationship between the applicant and respondent were also transferred to Company A. The applicant exercised his right under the Civil Code to object to the transfer of his employment relationship; accordingly the respondent retained responsibility for his working conditions and the contractual terms in place before the transfer occurred were unchanged. Notwithstanding this, the applicant was required to perform duties for Company A. Under paragraph 4(3) of the TVöD, the respondent had the option to assign the applicant permanently to Company A, which was permitted to issue instructions to the applicant.

The applicant argued that the national legislation contravened Directive 2008/104/EC (the 'Directive') insofar as the legislation allowed the permanent assignment of workers. He sought a declaration that he was not required to carry out work on a permanent basis for Company A, despite the transfer. The applicant's case was dismissed and he appealed to the Federal Labour Court in Germany. The referring Court stayed

3 *LD v ALB FILS Kliniken GmbH* (Case C-427/21).

4 Directive 2008/104/EC on temporary agency work.

proceedings to refer two questions to the European Court of Justice ('ECJ') for a preliminary ruling. In essence, the primary question was: do arts 1(1) and (2) of Directive 2008/104/EC apply if, under the TVöD, an employee must perform their contractually agreed work permanently for a third party, if requested to do so by their current employer.

The ECJ considered whether arts 1(1) and (2) of the Directive, when read in conjunction with arts 3(1)(b)–(e) thereof, must be interpreted as meaning that the Directive applies where a worker's duties are transferred by their employer to a third party undertaking and where the worker, whose employment relationship is retained by the employer following an objection to the transfer, may be required to perform, on a permanent basis, the work contractually owed to that third party and be given technical instructions by that third party.

It was held by the ECJ that, in order for an employment relationship to be caught by the Directive, both where the contract is concluded and when the assignment is made, an employer must intend to assign the worker temporarily to a user undertaking. In this case, it was acknowledged that the worker performed duties in the context of the employment relationship with his employer for a third-party undertaking. In this way he was subject to the undertaking's supervision and direction under art 1(1) of the Directive. However, the ECJ found that the employer did not intend to assign the worker to the third-party undertaking at the time the contract was concluded nor when the worker was assigned, in circumstances where the employment relationship was maintained as between the employer and the worker after the worker exercised his right to object to the transfer of that relationship to the undertaking. The ECJ also noted that a permanent transfer of duties performed by an employee for an employer with whom a contract had been formed, to a third-party undertaking, cannot give rise to a temporary employment relationship with the third-party undertaking. Therefore, the employment relationship here did not fall within the scope of Directive 2008/104/EC. It was added that the literal interpretation of art 1(1) of the Directive supported this.

Accordingly, it was held that art 1(1) of the Directive, read in conjunction with art 3(1)(b) to (e), should be interpreted as meaning that the protection of temporary agency workers, provided for by Directive 2008/104, does not apply to a situation where a worker's duties are transferred permanently by their employer to a third-party undertaking. It was also held not to apply in circumstances where that worker, whose employment relationship has been maintained by the employer, following the worker's exercising their right to object, may be required to perform on a permanent basis the work for the third party undertaking and therefore, be subject to the technical and organisational direction of same.

BONUS CLAWBACK/RESTRAINT OF TRADE

[1.04] ***Steel v Spencer Road LLP*[5]*—High Court of England and Wales—Bacon J—appeal from Insolvency and Companies Court—discretionary***

5 *Steel v Spencer Road LLP* [2023] EWCA 2492 (Ch).

bonus—disincentive to resigning—restraint of trade doctrine—whether 'bonus clawback' provisions in contract of employment were a restraint of trade—whether the trial Judge correctly applied the legal test

The claimant was employed by the respondent. His contract provided for a discretionary annual bonus. This was conditional on the claimant remaining in his employment for three months from the date of payment of any bonus, without giving or being given notice to terminate his employment during that period.

In January 2022, the claimant was paid a bonus of £187,500. In February 2022, he gave notice of termination of his employment. The respondent requested repayment of the bonus under the clawback provisions of the contract of employment. It served a statutory demand for the full amount plus legal costs. The claimant sought to set aside the statutory demand, arguing that the bonus clawback provisions were a restraint of trade, and therefore unenforceable. His application was dismissed by the Insolvency and Companies Court. The claimant repaid the bonus to the respondent but appealed against the Court's decision.

The High Court rejected a submission that an authority[6] relied on by the trial Judge was wrongly decided and should not have been followed. The Court held that the authorities are clear that clawback provisions, such as those in dispute, do operate 'as a disincentive to the employee resigning', but it does not immediately follow that such provisions are a restraint of trade. The bonus clawback provisions did not impose any restrictions on where the claimant could work after leaving the respondent. Accordingly, the trial Judge correctly found that the disputed provisions were not a restraint of trade.

The High Court rejected a submission that the trial Judge wrongly conflated the two stages of the restraint of trade test. The authorities recognise that the first and second stages of the test may in some cases overlap. The analysis is fact sensitive, and in these circumstances the trial Judge correctly concluded that there were no specific facts going to the reasonableness of the disputed provisions. This was of assistance in determining whether the bonus clawback provisions were a restraint of trade in the first place.

The claimant argued that the bonus clawback provisions, combined with his three-month notice period meant that, in reality, he would have to remain an employee for approximately six months in order to retain his bonus. The Court found this submission to be misconceived, given that it had already concluded that the disincentives in this instance were not a restraint of trade.

The Court concluded that the case before it was not a novel one where the issues of law should have been allowed to proceed to trial. Although the doctrine of restraint of trade 'continues to be applied and considered in new contexts', the decision of the trial Judge was based on an established line of authority.

The appeal was, accordingly, dismissed in its entirety.

---

6 *Tullet Prebon (Australia) Pty Ltd v Purcell* [2008] NSWSC 437.

SUSPENSION

[1.05] ***Board of Management of Wilson's Hospital School v Burke[7]—High Court—Owens J—disciplinary process—suspension—employer seeking declaratory and injunctive reliefs***

The applicant board sought a declaration that a decision of 22 August 2022 to put the respondent teacher on paid administrative leave was lawful. The applicant also sought an injunction restraining the respondent from trespassing on school grounds and damages for trespass. The respondent's counterclaim included claims for an injunction preventing continuation by the applicant of his suspension and declarations that the disciplinary process conducted against him was an unlawful interference with his constitutional rights.

The respondent, following the applicant's decision to suspend him, continued to attend at the school in defiance of that decision, and refused to obey an interlocutory injunction which restrained him from entering school premises. The respondent was dismissed from his employment by the applicant on 19 January 2023, with effect from 21 April 2023. He availed of a right to appeal that decision.

On the first day of the trial of the action, the respondent was 'disorderly and in persistent contempt of court'. He was conditionally excluded from participating in the hearing and refused to give an undertaking that he would comply with the Court's directions if allowed back into the courtroom. Accordingly, the respondent's counterclaim was not advanced.

The Court first considered whether the applicant was entitled to a permanent injunction restraining the respondent from entering school premises. On the evidence, it was apparent that mutual trust and confidence between the parties had broken down because of the respondent's actions, which included defying court orders. The Court could not be expected to disregard employee conduct 'calculated to destroy or seriously damage their employment relationships' where such conduct became relevant to the jurisdiction to grant discretionary relief.

Moreover, it was plain that a 'locked-out' employee may not return to the workplace 'unless and until their employer accepts resumption of performance of their service', whether by agreement or by operation of the law. Permission to return to the workplace 'operates prospectively and does not excuse past trespass', irrespective of the employee's view of their 'right' to do so, and the courts are obliged to uphold the right of those in actual occupation or with sufficient possession of the land to exclude trespassers. The Court was thus satisfied that the applicant, being in control of the school during the school day, was entitled to damages for trespass and the injunction sought.

Next, the Court considered whether the applicant complied with its contractual obligations to the respondent in suspending him. The chain of events leading up to the

7 *Board of Management of Wilson's Hospital School v Burke* [2023] IEHC 288.

decision to suspend the respondent were noted. In a letter to the applicant, the principal expressed the view that the respondent's behaviour at the school on a particular day was gross misconduct and a decision was made to invoke stage 4 of the disciplinary process under the Department of Education and Skills Circular 0049/2018 (the 'Circular').

The Court considered that the decision was made in good faith and was rational and consistent with the Circular, which sets out what constitutes gross misconduct by a teacher. The principal's letter demonstrated that the respondent had a case to answer. The applicant acted properly in making its decision in a meeting, held on 15 August 2022, to fix dates for disciplinary and suspension hearings, which were procedural steps, and the attendance of the principal at the meeting did not affect the validity of that decision. The principal was not involved in the subsequent decision to suspend the respondent and did not attend the meeting of 22 August 2022, where that decision was made. Further, the respondent was invited to make submissions in writing ahead of the disciplinary hearing, during which he repeatedly attempted to 'side-track' the process by challenging the validity of the disciplinary procedure.

Judicial oversight would be confined to examining whether any decision of the applicant was 'rational and within the ambit of powers conferred on it by the [C]ircular'. This necessitated a wide margin of appreciation in favour of the applicant, which was entitled to regulate its procedures. The Court found that the applicant had deliberated fully on its decision and had arrived at a consensus without pre-judgement of the result. It further held that the respondent was the author of his own misfortune in failing to make submissions as to why he should not be suspended.

Accordingly, the applicant was granted the reliefs sought.

INTELLECTUAL PROPERTY

[1.06] ***PQ Systems Europe Ltd v Aughton*[8]*—High Court of England and Wales—Zacaroli J—infringement of copyright—breach of confidentiality—software—balance of probabilities***

The claimant company alleged that the defendant former employee 'copied or otherwise made use of' software owned by the claimant. The defendant contended that the software belonged to him because it was written as a 'hobby project' outside the course of his employment with the claimant.

The defendant was employed by the claimant from 1989 as a software developer. He was appointed a director of the company in 1996 but resigned from that position in 2013 and left the company in 2015. Thereafter he founded a company, Factoria, with his wife. During his tenure with the claimant, the defendant worked on a software project, which was abandoned before completion in favour of an alternative version. The defendant was permitted to continue working on his project and he shared it with

8 *PQ Systems Europe Ltd v Aughton* [2023] EWHC 581.

a former employee, Mr Todd, who had been dismissed in 2010. This led to disciplinary proceedings against the defendant, resulting in him being demoted, although he was permitted to continue in employment with the claimant. Following his resignation in 2015, the defendant immediately started work on what he contended was an entirely new programme, and he incorporated Factoria.

The claimant became aware of the defendant's programme in 2017 and, upon review, saw 'significant functional similarities' with their own products. There was no source code available for the defendant's work for the claimant as he had deleted it. Only the object code remained, which the claimant sought to de-compile. It was common case that de-compiled code looks very different to the original source code and the expert evidence was that comparing de-compiled codes was of 'limited' to 'marginal' value when investigating whether copying had occurred. The claimant's case was therefore 'heavily' based on circumstantial evidence.

The Court's conclusion was that it was more likely than not that the defendant 'did copy from at least a substantial part of the source code for [the claimant's product] when writing [the defendant's product]'. Given the deletion of the source code and the lack of any record of how it was created, the Court was unable to conclude whether this copying was done with an automatic translator or whether it was re-written manually by the defendant. However, it was 'sufficient' to establish infringement of copyright and breach of contract that the defendant wrote his programme by copying from the source code of the claimant's product, however this was done.

The Court therefore found that the defendant infringed the claimant's copyright and breached his contractual duties of confidentiality.

TERMS OF EMPLOYMENT

[1.07] ***ESB Networks v O'Grady*[9]*—Labour Court—appeal from Workplace Relations Commission—Terms of Employment (Information) Acts 1994 to 2014, s 8(1)—remuneration intervals—delays to receipt of non-base payments—whether introduction of a new payroll system was a change to terms and conditions of employment***

The claimant was employed as a network technician by the respondent, ESB Networks. The respondent introduced a new payroll system which required employees to submit non-base payment claims (such as overtime) through an online app. The claimant's union was not part of the group of unions recognised by the ESB and therefore was not party to the negotiations leading up to the change. The claimant continued to submit his claims on paper, which resulted in delayed payments.

The claimant submitted that the Terms of Employment (Information) Acts 1994 to 2014 (the 'Acts') require employers to commit to a regular pay interval, in this

9 *ESB Networks v O'Grady* TED239. See also related cases: *ESB Networks v O'Grady* VCD231 and *ESB Networks v O'Grady* PW/23/8.

case fortnightly in arrears. The claimant argued that the respondent had breached this commitment by delaying non-base payments due to him. He alleged that the respondent was also in breach of the Acts by failing to provide formal notice of the changes to the contract to the claimant.

The respondent contended that the introduction of the online payroll system was not a change to the terms and conditions of employment but a change in work practice. A delay caused by the phasing out of the old system did not constitute a change to pay intervals. The claimant was informed of the migration to the online system in advance and any delay in payment was due to his opting to submit his claims manually.

It was clear to the Court that there had been no change to the intervals at which the claimant's salary fell to be paid. A delay arose in respect of particular overtime payments because the claimant eschewed the new payroll system 'in circumstances where he had clearly been advised by the respondent that this would result in a delay to his receiving payment'. The change in question was a change to a work practice, as opposed to a change to a term or condition of employment. The complaints were 'completely misconceived' and the appeal accordingly failed.

Chapter 2

Data Protection/Privacy

INTRODUCTION

[2.01] Throughout 2023 the body of data protection jurisprudence from the European Court of Justice ('ECJ') and the Irish courts continued to grow. Moreover, between November 2022 and the end of October 2023, the Data Protection Commission ('DPC') published 17 decisions in larger-scale inquiries, where orders and fines were considered and/or imposed. Helpfully, it has also produced a booklet that contains 126 of their case studies from the first five years of the General Data Protection Regulation ('GDPR'). These judgments, decisions and case studies are immensely helpful in interpreting data protection legislation and its application in Ireland, not least for employers in navigating their obligations under the law.

2023 also saw the enactment of the Courts and Civil Law (Miscellaneous Provisions) Act 2023, which was signed into law by the President on 5 July 2023. Part 12 of the Act amends the Data Protection Act 2018. Among other amendments, it confers jurisdiction to hear data protection actions on the District Court[1] and broadens the circumstances in which a reprimand can be issued by the DPC. The 2023 Act inserts a new s 26A into the Data Protection Act 2018 to provide a prohibition on disclosure of confidential information by persons engaging with the DPC in connection with certain defined functions, which includes investigations and inquiries.

DATA PROTECTION COMMISSION GUIDANCE

[2.02] The DPC has published new or updated guidance in 2023 on a number of aspects of the GDPR. Below we refer to some of the guidance published by the DPC relevant to employees, employers and employment law generally.

1 Section 77 of the Courts and Civil Law (Miscellaneous Provisions) Act 2023, which amends section 117 of the Data Protection Act 2018 to extend jurisdiction to hear and determine data protection actions to the District Court, came into operation on 11 January 2024. The other sections in Part 12 of the Courts and Civil Law (Miscellaneous Provisions) Act 2023 came into operation on 31 July 2023.

Data Protection in the Workplace: Employer Guidance

[2.03] In April 2023, the DPC updated its Guidance Note on Data Protection in the Workplace: Employer Guidance (the 'Employer Guidance Note').[2] It seeks to draw the attention of employers, in particular, to Chapter IV GDPR, which concerns controllers and processors, and their respective responsibilities and agreements. The Employer Guidance Note illustrates key considerations in relation to an employer's obligations and responsibilities towards their employees.

(i) Personal Data

[2.04] In the Employer Guidance Note, the DPC addresses personal data within the employment context. It looks at the question of whether employee emails are personal data, and those situations in which an email address may be considered to be personal data. Although an individual's name may be identifiable in the email address (eg John Smith@abc.ie), this does not mean that the content of the emails addressed to the identified individual constitute the individual's personal data, as the emails occur within the context of a professional working environment. However, when an employer has received a subject access request, there is an obligation on employers to investigate the content of their commercial or business emails to ascertain if the content of the email to the identifiable individual relates to the personal data of that individual in any way.

The Employer Guidance Note also considers whether an employee's Outlook calendar and job description may be classified as personal data under GDPR. Using a case study, where an employer refused an employee access to his Outlook calendar following a data subject access request, on the basis that information such as details of meetings in the employee's Outlook calendar were work related and not about the data subject, the DPC was satisfied that the job description and Outlook calendar do not fall under the remit of personal data as defined in art 4(1) GDPR.

(ii) General Principles of Data Protection

[2.05] The Employer Guidance Note provides a comprehensive overview as to the general principles of data protection under art 5 GDPR, which provides that the processing of personal data must be lawful, fair, transparent, and comply with the principles of purpose limitation, data minimisation, accuracy, storage limitation, integrity and confidentiality, and accountability. Employers must be able to demonstrate compliance with all of these principles.

In relation to purpose limitation whereby the purpose for the processing of personal data should be explicit and determined at the time of the collection of the personal data, the Guidance refers to a case study in which data relating to the use of car park and building access had been used by a manager to verify employees' time and attendance records, when employees had in fact been informed that the company car park and

2 Employer Guidance was available on the DPC's website as at October 2023 but has since been removed, so readers should consult the DPC website for any updated guidance that may emerge.

building access data was collected for security purposes. The employer also stated that attendance in the building was a security concern. The DPC deemed such processing to be incompatible further processing, as the employees had not been informed that such data would be used to verify their time and attendance. The DPC informed the employer of this and highlighted that it was concerning regardless of the proposed lawful bases relied upon. The DPC recommended the employer consider an alternative way to verify time and attendance.

(iii) Legal Bases for Data Processing

[2.06] The Employer Guidance Note summarises the legal bases for the processing of personal data under art 6 of the GDPR. In addition, if an employer is processing special category data such as health data (eg medical certificates or occupational health reports), the employer will also need to avail of one of the permissible exceptions for processing personal data under art 9 GDPR. Each of the legal bases for processing under art 6 is discussed in the Employer Guidance Note in the employment context. Employers should assess the personal data that is actually necessary for the relevant legal basis and purpose that they are relying upon in processing the personal data.

There is a general prohibition on the processing of special category personal data under art 9(1) GDPR, ie, data that reveals racial or ethnic origin, political opinions, religious or philosophical beliefs, or trade union membership, and the processing of genetic data, biometric data for the purpose of uniquely identifying a natural person, data concerning health, or data concerning a natural person's sex life or sexual orientation. However, there are exceptions to this prohibition, contained under art 9(2) GDPR. The Employer Guidance Note looks at the exception in the case of occupational medicine or evaluating the capacity of an employee within the workplace under art 9(2)(h) of the GDPR.

(iv) Occupational Health

[2.07] Occupational health is the promotion and maintenance of the physical, social, and mental wellbeing of workers. In Ireland, occupational health is underpinned by the Safety, Health, and Welfare at Work Act 2005. Employers have a general duty to ensure the health and safety of their employees. This includes the right to require employees to undergo a medical assessment by a registered medical practitioner, nominated by the employer, of their fitness to perform work activities. The referral of an employee to undergo a medical assessment may give rise to data protection implications, in particular under art 9 GDPR, which relates to the processing of special categories of personal data, such as health data.

Employers must determine, prior to processing, which legal basis they are relying upon to ensure their processing of employee personal data is lawful. Certain lawful bases for processing may apply in an occupational health context, such as in order to comply with a legal obligation to which the employer is subject; to protect the vital interests of the data subject or of another natural person; for the purposes of the legitimate interests pursued by the employer or a third party, except where such interests are overridden by the interests or fundamental rights and freedoms of the data subject which require protection of personal data; or for the purposes of preventive or occupational medicine, medical diagnosis, the provision of health care or treatment or the management of health care systems and services. Consent may also apply as a lawful basis for processing an employee's medical data, although limitations may apply.

An appropriate data protection policy to ensure lawfulness, fairness, and transparency in data processing is equally relevant here. The inclusion of an occupational health policy will allow both the employer and employee to engage with registered medical practitioners to the extent necessary to ensure the employee's fitness to work is guaranteed.

The Data Protection Act 2018 (Access Modification) (Health) Regulations 2022[3] revoked and replaced the Data Protection (Access Modification) (Health) Regulations 1989,[4] which modify how data subject access requests received by employers can be addressed. This modification means that an employer is no longer obliged to consult a medical practitioner before providing health data to the employee in response to their subject access request. The 2022 Regulations provide that where the data controller/employer has reasonable grounds for believing that granting access to the health data concerned would be likely to cause serious harm to the physical or mental health of the data subject, discretion can be exercised by the employer as to whether the data will be released. This refers only to the part of the data that may be 'likely to cause serious harm' and the rest of the data must be released unless the data controller is relying on other lawful exceptions.

(v) Employer Policies and Monitoring Employees

[2.08] Article 24 GDPR requires data controllers to implement appropriate technical and organisational measures ('TOMs') to protect personal data and to comply with the principles of data protection by design and by default. Examples of TOMs in the employment context include: pseudonymisation and anonymisation of personal data; limiting access to personal data to authorised people; encryption of personal data backups and testing of data processing systems; file access audit logs; data protection policies and procedures; data retention and storage policies; internet usage policies; use of personal device policies; and CCTV policies. TOMs should be implemented taking into account the nature, scope, context and purposes of processing and the risks to the rights and freedoms of individuals. Employers should also consider their relationship with any third parties who process employee data on their behalf. Appropriate agreements need to be in place between data controllers and processors, and between joint controllers.

Organisations may monitor their employees using CCTV, internet, email, or phone, but must ensure this is done in a way that protects the employees' data protection rights and right to privacy, ensuring that they have a legitimate interest in monitoring their employees and they are transparent about the use of such monitoring.

Monitoring software should only be used if it is objectively and demonstrably justified and proportionate, and employers should implement other less intrusive means

3 Data Protection Act 2018 (Access Modification) (Health) Regulations 2022 (SI 121/2022).
4 Data Protection (Access Modification) (Health) Regulations 1989 (SI 82/1989).

to monitor employee attendance and productivity first. Covert monitoring software is generally unlawful. Employers should have an Acceptable Usage Policy that clearly sets out their policy on internet usage, including the use of social media on employer-owned devices.

Employers should only monitor employee internet use and private emails if they have a good reason to do so. Their use should be made transparent to employees. The least intrusive methods possible should be used where any monitoring takes place.

Covert surveillance should only be used as a last resort and should be justified on a case-by-case basis. If covert surveillance is used, it should be done in a way that is proportionate and necessary. The organisation should have a written policy that sets out the purpose, justification, procedure, measures, and safeguards that will be implemented. The policy should also set out how the data collected will be used and stored.

Employers should only hold employee data for as long as necessary to achieve the purpose for which it was collected. They must also comply with any statutory obligations or industry guidelines that dictate retention periods. It is recommended that employers should have a data retention policy in place that sets out how long different types of employee data will be held for. This policy should be reviewed regularly to ensure that it is up to date and complies with the law. Once employee data is no longer needed, it should be destroyed securely. This may involve deleting it from electronic systems and shredding paper records.

(vi) Employee Rights

[2.09] Employees have a number of data protection rights, including the right to access and rectify their personal data. Employers must respond within one month to requests to exercise these rights but can extend this by up to two months if the request is complex. In other words, employees have the right to know what personal data their employer holds about them and to have any inaccurate or incomplete data corrected. It is important for employers to be aware of these rights and to ensure that they have procedures in place to respond to requests promptly and accurately.

Employers can lawfully restrict the data protection rights of individuals under certain legislative provisions, such as art 23 GDPR and/or s 60 of the Data Protection Act 2018. If an employer is relying on these provisions to restrict the data protection rights of an employee who has sought to exercise their rights, they must set out which provision is being relied upon.

Records of Processing Activities under Article 30 GDPR[5]

[2.10] Article 30 GDPR requires data controllers and processors to keep records of their processing activities ('ROPAs'). It is important to note in this respect, that

5 DPC Guidance on the Records of Processing Activities (RoPA) under Article 30 GDPR (April 2023), available on the DPC website.

the controller organisation as a whole is responsible for a ROPA and an organisation's DPO should not hold sole responsibility. The GDPR also requires data processors to maintain a record of all categories of processing activities carried out on behalf of each data controller they work with. Article 30 GDPR prescribes the information the records must contain and states that controllers and processors must be in a position to provide such records to the DPC on request. The DPC states that 10 days' notice should be sufficient notice for any organisation in all circumstances.

All data controllers and processors are required to keep a ROPA, unless they employ fewer than 250 employees and their processing activities do not involve:

- processing of special categories of personal data (eg, data relating to health, racial or ethnic origin, or political opinions) or personal data relating to criminal convictions and offences; or
- large-scale processing of personal data.

Certain mandatory information must be included in a ROPA for controllers and processors, respectively. This includes information such as the name and contact details of the controller or processor, the purpose(s) of the processing, the categories of data subjects and personal data processed, the recipients or categories of recipients of the personal data, and the technical and organisational security measures implemented to protect the personal data. Additional relevant extra information should be included as appropriate. Information contained within the ROPA should be granular and meaningful and should specifically detail each category of data subject, category of personal data or processing activity. The Employer Guidance Note requires that the ROPA should reflect the retention period for each specific category of personal data processed.

The DPC recommends that organisations take a systematic approach: ROPAs should be divided up and detailed according to the different business units/functions within an organisation. A data mapping exercise should be conducted involving all relevant units across the organisation. The DPC advises that organisations review their ROPA regularly to ensure that it is accurate and up to date, as ROPAs are deemed a key tool by which to demonstrate GDPR compliance, and as a means of enabling organisations to identify and manage risks to personal data, in addition to facilitating organisations in their response to data requests in a timely and efficient manner.

2022 ANNUAL REPORT OF THE DATA PROTECTION COMMISSION

[2.11] 2022 saw the imposition by the DPC of some high value, high profile fines, with the total value exceeding €1 billion. This figure amounted to over two thirds of the total fines issued by data protection authorities across the EU, EEA and UK. The DPC also received large numbers of consultation requests and had a busy year in terms of engagement with the European Data Protection Board ('EDPB') and other national supervisory authorities. In terms of funding, the DPC received €23.234 million in the budget for 2022, which represents a 21.5% increase on 2021.

Complaints

[2.12] From 1 January 2022 to 31 December 2022, the DPC processed 9,370 new cases (a decrease of 14% compared to 2021 case figures). 6,660 of these cases were in the nature of queries that could be dealt with relatively expeditiously. 2,710 cases progressed to a formal complaint-handling process. The report also shows that the DPC concluded 10,008 cases in 2022 of which 3,133 were resolved through formal complaint handling. It is noted that 42% of the total complaints received under the GDPR in 2022 related to access requests. The DPC received 1,142 new access complaints and concluded 1,255 complaints in 2022.

Data Breach

[2.13] The DPC received 5,828 valid data breach notifications in 2022, a decrease of 12% compared to 2021 figures. Similar to 2021, public sector bodies and banks were within the 'top ten' organisations in terms of the highest number of breach notifications recorded against them, with insurance and telecom companies featuring prominently in the top 20. Notably, 62% of the overall total number of breaches reported to the DPC in 2022 arose from correspondence inadvertently being misdirected to the wrong recipients.

Inquiries and Fines

[2.14] The DPC concluded 17 large scale inquiries (both national and cross-border) in 2022, against various Big Tech and public bodies. Several of these inquiries led to the imposition of serious reprimands and corrective actions. By 31 December 2022, the DPC had progressed nine large-scale inquiries to the point where submissions on a draft decision, statement of issues or inquiry reports were invited from the relevant parties. The Annual Report also contains a chart outlining every art 60 draft decision prepared by the DPC, with a grid of the objecting Member States to each draft decision. Germany was the top objector, objecting to 13 of the 18 draft decisions.

During 2022, the Dublin Circuit Court confirmed six of the DPC's imposed fines, ranging from €1,500 to €17 million. All of these fines have been collected. Many of the larger fines imposed have yet to make their way to the exchequer due to a series of appeals and judicial review proceedings. These appeals potentially will also involve references to the ECJ over matters of interpretation of the GDPR. (As it currently stands, controllers and complainants cannot complain directly against the judgement of the EDPB that informs the DPC's final decisions in cases, but instead must appeal the DPC decision and ask for a preliminary reference to be sent to the ECJ on the validity of the underlying EDPB decision. The Annual Report notes this will lead to procedural delays.)

Ultimately, the DPC notes that the one-stop shop and other cooperation mechanisms with EU supervisory authorities has created a 'legal maze' and an ever more complex landscape for litigators and data practitioners. While there was promising progression throughout 2022, the Annual Report acknowledges that, given the high volume of cases in front of the ECJ on the interpretation of the GDPR, it is likely to be some time before we see clarification on the interpretation of key articles of the GDPR. Further, claims for compensation under the GDPR continue to see very modest awards being issued at the EU level.[6]

DPC DECISIONS AND FINES

[2.15] Some notable inquiries conducted by the DPC in the past 12 months include the following.

An Garda Síochána

[2.16] This inquiry[7] concerned a report by An Garda Síochána to the DPC of a personal data breach, following a data breach at a garda station. The subject of this inquiry concerned the personal data of 'persons of interest' to An Garda Síochána in the context of ongoing investigations. Personal data was posted on an intelligence bulletin board located in a room in a garda station to which any person other than a garda should not have had unaccompanied access. The personal data, which included the names and addresses of 108 data subjects, was accessed by a contractor who was undertaking repair works at the garda station. The personal data was ultimately shared on social media.

The DPC found that there was an absence of specific policies and procedures in the processing of personal data, which failed to satisfy ss 72(1), 75 and 78, and by extension s 71(1)(f) of the Data Protection Act 2018. Specifically, An Garda Síochána failed to implement appropriate technical and organisational measures to protect the personal data An Garda Síochána processed at the time of the breach. The DPC also identified a failure to undertake a risk assessment before processing commenced to determine the appropriateness of security measures *vis-à-vis* the harm that might result from processing. In circumstances where the personal data processed on the bulletin board concerned ongoing investigations and the personal data of vulnerable data subjects, the DPC found that the nature of that personal data was highly sensitive.

6 See **[2.50]** and **[2.53]** below on European Union caselaw.

7 *Inquiry into An Garda Síochána, Decision exercising corrective powers made under the Data Protection Act 2018*, DPC Case Reference: IN-20-1-3.

WhatsApp Ireland Limited

[2.17] This inquiry[8] concerned a complaint made on 25 May 2018 by a German data subject. WhatsApp Ireland Limited ('WhatsApp') updated its Terms of Service and users were asked to click 'agree and continue' to indicate their acceptance of the updated Terms of Service. The services would not be accessible if users declined to do so. The complainant contended that WhatsApp was in fact 'forcing' them to consent to the processing of their personal data for service improvement and security.

WhatsApp considered that, on accepting the updated Terms of Service, a contract was entered into between WhatsApp and the user. It also took the position that the processing of users' data in connection with the delivery of its service was necessary for the performance of that contract, to include the provision of service improvement and security features, so that such processing operations were lawful by reference to art 6(1)(b) GDPR (contract legal basis for processing).

The DPC prepared a draft decision and submitted it to the Concerned Supervisory Authorities ('CSAs') in accordance with art 60 GDPR. Interestingly, the DPC concluded that the GDPR did not preclude reliance on the contract legal basis, but six of the 47 CSAs raised objections (arguing that delivery of service improvement and security features could not be said to be necessary to the core elements of the contract). As no consensus could be found, the case was referred to the EDPB.

The final decision of the DPC reflected the EDPB's determination and concluded that WhatsApp was not entitled to rely on the contract legal basis for the delivery of service improvement and for the WhatsApp service, and that its processing of this data to date, in purported reliance on the contract legal basis, amounted to a contravention of art 6(1) GDPR. This resulted in a €5.5 million fine (for breaches of the GDPR relating to its service) with a direction to WhatsApp to bring its data processing operations into compliance within a period of six months.

Bank of Ireland 365 ('BOI')

[2.18] This decision[9] examined technical and organisational measures in addition to security measures for processing personal data. The inquiry was commenced after BOI notified the DPC of a series of 10 personal data breaches relating to the BOI 365

8 *In the matter of JG, a complainant, concerning a complaint directed against WhatsApp Ireland Limited in respect of the WhatsApp Service, Decision of the Data Protection Commission made pursuant to Section 113 of the Data Protection Act, 2018 and Articles 60 and 65 of the General Data Protection Regulation*, DPC Case Reference: IN-18-5-6.

9 *In the matter of Bank of Ireland Group PLC, Decision of the Data Protection Commission made pursuant to Section 111 of the Data Protection Act, 2018*, DPC Case Reference: IN-20-7-2.

banking app. Four of the 10 data breach notifications concerned individuals gaining unauthorised access to other customers' accounts via the BOI app.

The DPC held that BOI had infringed its obligations under arts 5(1) and 32(1) GDPR as the technical and organisation measures in place at the time were found not to be sufficient to ensure the security of the personal data processed on the BOI app.

The DPC issued a reprimand in respect of the infringements of arts 5(1)(f) and 32(1) GDPR. BOI was ordered to bring processing into compliance with arts 5(1)(f) and 32(1) GDPR. The decision imposed an administrative fine on BOI in the amount of €750,000 in respect of the infringement of art 5(1)(f) GDPR.

Department of Health

[2.19] The DPC launched an inquiry[10] into certain aspects of the Department of Health's processing of personal data in 29 litigation files. The inquiry was commenced following whistleblower allegations in 2021 that the Department had unlawfully collected and processed personal data about plaintiffs and their families in litigation concerning special educational needs. The DPC found that the Department did not infringe data protection law by seeking information from the HSE about the services that were being provided to plaintiffs in relation to cases where there was ongoing litigation: the aim here was to ascertain an appropriate time to settle the cases.

The DPC found that the Department *did* infringe data protection law by asking the HSE broad questions that resulted in the provision of sensitive information about the private lives of plaintiffs and their families. These questions from the Department included broadly worded questions asking the HSE to share 'any other issues HSE feels worth mentioning'.

The DPC found infringements of transparency obligations under the GDPR. The Department's privacy notice did not convey the extent of information sharing that took place between the Department and the HSE. The DPC also found that the Department had infringed the requirements to process personal data securely.

The DPC imposed a fine of €22,500, taking into consideration the cap on fining public authorities. The DPC also imposed a ban on further processing of the sensitive data in the files examined for the purposes of determining an appropriate time to settle a case. A reprimand was imposed for all the infringements.

10 *In the matter of the Department of Health, Decision of the Data Protection Commission made pursuant to Section 111 of the Data Protection Act 2018*, DPC Case Reference: IN-21-3-2.

TikTok

[2.20] The DPC adopted its final decision[11] regarding its inquiry into TikTok Technology Limited ('TTL') in September 2023. The inquiry concerned TTL's processing of children's data in the period of July 2020 to 31 December 2020 and in particular considered:

— platform settings for child users, including the Family Pairing setting;

— methods of age verification; and

— transparency information presented to child users.

The DPC's decision records findings of infringement of arts 5(1)(c), 5(1)(f), 24(1), 25(1), 25(2), 12(1), 13(1)(e) and 5(1)(a) GDPR. In addition to an administrative fine of €345 million, the DPC issued a reprimand and an order for TTL to bring their processing into compliance within three months.

EUROPEAN DATA PROTECTION BOARD GUIDELINES

[2.21] In 2023, the European Data Protection Board ('EDPB') published comprehensive guidelines pertaining to numerous aspects of data protection law. We discuss guidance of interest to employers and employees below.

Guidelines 04/2022 on the calculation of administrative fines under the GDPR[12] **('Guidelines 04/2022')** *and Joint Opinion on the Proposal for a Regulation of the European Parliament and of the Council laying down additional procedural rules relating to the enforcement of Regulation (EU) 2016/679 ('Joint Opinion')*[13]

[2.22] Administrative fines may have been the headline when GDPR became effective in May 2018, however, recent focus has shifted to who is imposing the fines. Lead supervisory authorities ('LSAs') are responsible for supervising the cross-border processing of entities that have their 'main establishment' in the supervisory authority's jurisdiction and ultimately taking enforcement actions against those entities for infringements. Financial impacts of enforcement under the GDPR are becoming significant, with over €1.5 billion of fines issued by the Data Protection Commission, as LSA, in the first half of 2023 alone.

Recent commentary has come from the EDPB, the European Data Protection Supervisor ('EDPS') and the European Commission on the procedural framework that supports the

11 *In the Matter of TikTok Technology Limited, Decision of the Data Protection Commission made pursuant to Section 111 of the Data Protection Act 2018 and Articles 60 and 65 of the GDPR*, DPC Case Reference: IN-21-9-1; available at: *https://www.dataprotection.ie/sites/default/fi les/uploads/2023-09/Inquiry%20into%20TikTok%20Technology%20Limited%20-%20September%202023%20EN.pdf.*

12 Guidelines 04/2022 on the calculation of administrative fines under the GDPR (24 May 2023).

13 Joint Opinion on the Proposal for a Regulation of the European Parliament and of the Council laying down additional procedural rules relating to the enforcement of Regulation (EU) 2016/679 (19 September 2023).

enforcement of the GDPR across the EU with the potential for an interesting reshaping of the roles played by LSAs, CSAs and the parties to enforcement proceedings themselves.

Background

[2.23] In Guidelines 02/2022, the EDPB sets out its views regarding the process for its decision making where there is disagreement between an LSA and CSA on a draft enforcement decision. The European Commission also published a proposal for a regulation which would address the procedural rules relating to the enforcement of the GDPR ('Proposed Regulation').[14] Additionally, the EDPB and EDPS issued a Joint Opinion welcoming the Proposed Regulation and calling for it to be adopted in a timely fashion, noting this as being of 'paramount importance' to improving the efficient and consistency of GDPR enforcement. Some common themes emerge across the guidelines and the proposed regulation, which are drawn out in the Joint Opinion, with the following being notable areas of overlap.

Right to be Heard

[2.24] Both Guidelines 04/2022 and the regulation proposed by the European Commission discuss the procedural rights of affected parties. The guidelines note the right to be heard in particular. The EDPB indicates that this right applies in administrative proceedings of which the outcome is likely to affect a person's interests. As a corollary, the EDPB states that this could involve the EDPB hearing from parties who will be adversely affected by a decision under art 65(1)(a) GDPR and that accommodation of this right is an 'essential element of the procedure, in the absence of which the dispute cannot be settled by the EDPB'.

The Proposed Regulation notes the need for harmonisation of procedural rights of parties, as currently the procedural rights of parties under investigation vary substantially across the Member States. In particular, the European Commission notes elements of these rights that should be harmonised by the Proposed Regulation. The Joint Opinion welcomes these changes and seeks that even greater clarity is provided in the proposed regulation. On the right to be heard, the European Commission notes a lack of clarity around when parties have a right to be heard under the art 65(1) GDPR procedure in particular, as an area that renders findings of the EDPB under this mechanism is more vulnerable to challenge. In order to address this issue, the Proposed Regulation would provide a right for affected parties to be heard at key procedural stages, including in certain circumstances where a draft decision that has been revised by the LSA to incorporate CSA feedback under art 60(5) GDPR, and prior to the adoption of a binding decision by the EDPB under art 65(1)(a) GDPR.

14 Proposal for a regulation laying down additional procedural rules relating to the enforcement of the GDPR (4 July 2023).

Completeness of File Prior to EDPB Decision

[2.25] The completeness of an investigation file is another area where Guidelines 04/2022 and the Proposed Regulation both have points to raise. In Guidelines 04/2022, the EDPB notes the need for the file to be complete. The EDPB may request additional information from the LSAs and CSAs to ensure that all relevant information has been submitted and the file is complete.

Again, with the aim of streamlining procedure, the proposed regulation prescribes requirements for the information to be submitted by the LSA to the EDPB when submitting a matter for dispute resolution. This includes the draft decision, summary of relevant facts, views of the parties under investigation, the complaint, and any relevant and reasoned objections from the CSA not followed by the LSA, along with an explanation from the LSA on why those objections were either not followed or not considered to be relevant or reasoned. Notably, the Joint Opinion urges legislators to go further and provide for exhaustive harmonisation of admissibility requirements, in particular, to pre-empt conflicting national requirements.

Relevant and Reasoned Objections from Concerned Supervisory Authorities

[2.26] Under the art 60 GDPR cooperation process, CSAs can make relevant and reasoned objections ('RROs') to a draft decision of the LSA. Where the LSA has rejected the objections or does not consider them to be relevant or reasoned, the EDPB has competence to adopt a binding decision under art 65(1)(a) GDPR.

In Guidelines 04/2022, the EDPB notes that RROs set the parameters of its competence to adopt binding decisions and clarifies its understanding of this threshold. It notes the definition of 'relevant and reasoned objection' under art 4(24) GDPR, namely whether the objection: (a) relates to a decision on whether the GDPR has been infringed; or (b) whether the envisaged action in relation to the subject of the decision complies with the GDPR, which clearly demonstrates the significance of the risks posed by the draft decision to the rights of the data subject and/or the free flow of data in the EU. The EDPB indicates that it will consider whether each element of this definition has been met and that it will not take a position on the merits of any substantial issues raised by objections that do not meet this threshold.

The Proposed Regulation also notes RROs and envisages these as one area where the process for enforcement could be streamlined. Its Proposed Regulation sets out detailed requirements for the form and structure of these objections with the aim of facilitating effective participation of all CSAs and swift resolution of cases. Notably, the Joint Opinion takes issue with the envisaged scope of RROs, seeing it as unduly narrow and urges that these provisions should be removed from the Proposed Regulation.

Interestingly, RROs are not the only process that the Proposed Regulation targets for streamlining. The Proposed Regulation sets out new requirements that would oblige LSAs to share 'relevant information' with CSAs at an earlier stage in the investigation process. Article 9 of the Proposed Regulation sets out a requirement to share a summary of key issues with CSAs once the LSA has formed a 'preliminary view on the main issues in an investigation' while art 8 of the Proposed Regulation requires the LSA to regularly update CSAs 'at the earliest convenience' with information that may include the opening of an investigation, the envisaged rejection of a complaint, preliminary findings and the responses of parties to the investigation to those findings.

Lead in Name Only?

[2.27] A unifying theme across the EDPB Guidelines, the European Commission proposed regulation and the Joint Opinion is the centralisation of enforcement via cooperation of all supervisory authorities and the decision-making power of the EDPB. Centralisation as an approach aligns with the enforcement framework of new regulations including the Digital Services Act,[15] where the European Commission directly regulates very large online platforms and very large online search engines. While centralised enforcement can lead to efficiencies and streamlining, a potential cost is a substantive lead role for the LSA in enforcement matters. The changes contemplated in the proposed regulation appear to share this substantive effort among the LSAs and CSAs, with a potential impact being the LSA remaining the lead in administrative matters on an enforcement action only.

[2.28] ***Guidelines 8/2022 on identifying a controller or processor's lead supervisory authority***[16]

These guidelines outline the process of identifying a LSA under the GDPR in situations where a controller or processor is carrying out cross-border processing of personal data within the EU.

Article 4(23) GDPR defines cross-border processing as the processing of personal data that occurs within the activities of establishments in multiple Member States, or in situations where the processing of personal data takes place in a single establishment but substantially affects or is likely to affect data subjects in multiple Member States. Although the GDPR does not provide a definition of the concept of 'substantially affects', it is crucial in determining if a processing activity would be deemed to be cross-border processing. The guidelines provide that supervisory authorities will interpret this concept on a case-by-case basis, considering factors such as whether:

— the processing may cause damage, loss or distress;
— the processing may limit rights or deny an opportunity;
— the processing may affect individuals' health, well-being, peace of mind, or financial and economic status;
— the processing may lead to discrimination or unfair treatment;

---

15 https://eur-lex.europa.eu/eli/reg/2022/2065.
16 Guidelines 8/2022 on identifying a controller or processor's lead supervisory authority (17 April 2023).

— the processing involves a wide range of personal data or the analysis of special categories of personal data; and

— the processing has unlikely, unanticipated or unwanted consequences for individuals.

The guidelines can be particularly relevant in employee-related cases. Where an employee can point to a data protection issue that is unique to a particular Member State (eg a works council in Germany objecting to employee monitoring), the employee may be able to claim the matter is not 'cross-border' processing. If the employer has its main establishment in Ireland, the local SA in Germany may have jurisdiction to adjudicate a complaint locally in such cases.

To determine the LSA, the central focus is on the 'main establishment' of an organisation within the EU. This is determined by considering which establishment is responsible for decision making regarding the purposes and means of processing personal data, typically the place of central administration or central control. Accurate identification of the main establishment of an organisation is essential for data controllers and processors, as it offers clarity in relation to which SA they must engage with in respect of GDPR compliance. For multinationals with their EU headquarters in Ireland, it would be unwise to assume that the DPC will necessarily be the LSA in respect of data processing complaints made by employees who are employed by a local entity in another Member State.

In cases involving both a controller and a processor, where the controller is established in the EEA and subject to the one-stop-shop system, the LSA of the controller will also be the LSA of the processor. In cases involving joint controllers, where multiple entities jointly determine data processing, each entity may have its main establishment, but cannot have a common main establishment. Thus, the LSA would be the supervisory authority of the country where the place of central administration is located for each joint controller respectively.

The guidelines emphasise the importance of cooperation between LSAs and CSAs. An authority is deemed to be a 'concerned authority' when:

— a data controller or processor has an establishment on its territory;

— data subjects on its territory are substantially affected, or likely to be substantially affected; or

— when a complaint is received by a particular supervisory authority.

[2.29] *Guidelines 03/2021 on the application of Article 65(1)(a) GDPR*[17]

Article 65(1)(a) GDPR provides a dispute resolution mechanism for cases involving cross-border processing of personal data. The purpose of this mechanism is to ensure that the GDPR is applied correctly and consistently in individual cases. When an LSA issues a draft decision within the meaning of art 60(3) GDPR and either decides

17 Guidelines 03/2021 on the application of Article 65(1)(a) GDPR (24 May 2023).

not to follow a relevant and reasoned objection expressed by a CSA or considers the objection to be not relevant or reasoned, they must attempt to reach a consensus. If they cannot agree, the LSA must refer the matter to the EDPB for dispute resolution. These guidelines provide detailed guidance on the application of the dispute resolution procedure under art 65(1)(a) GDPR, including the legal framework, the role of the EDPB, and the assessment of whether an objection is 'relevant and reasoned' (art 4(24) GDPR).

The EDPB will have the authority to issue a decision when the following conditions are met:

— The submission of a draft decision within the meaning of art 60(3) by the LSA to the CSAs.

— At least one CSA raises one or more objections within the stipulated deadlines, as outlined in art 60(4)–(5) of the GDPR. A mere comment raised by a CSA would not be deemed an objection.

— The LSA disregards or rejects such objections on the basis that they are not relevant or reasoned.

The EDPB will assess the completeness of the file submitted and may request additional information if necessary. Once the file is declared complete, the EDPB assesses the merits of each objection raised and issues a decision. The EDPB decision is legally binding on the LSAs and CSAs and may impact the data processing activities of the relevant controller or processor.

The guidelines highlight that the parties concerned have the right to bring an action before the ECJ under art 263 of the Treaty on the Functioning of the European Union ('TFEU'). The ECJ has jurisdiction to review the legality of the EDPB's decision and may annul or alter the decision if it is found to be unlawful. Additionally, if a final decision produces legal effects concerning a natural or legal person, such person also has the right to seek judicial remedy before the competent national court against the decision (recital 143 GDPR).

[2.30] *Guidelines 05/2021 on the Interplay between the application of Article 3 and the provisions on international transfers as per Chapter V of the GDPR*[18]

The preliminary draft of these guidelines, which underwent a period of public consultation, has been discussed in the *Arthur Cox Employment Law Yearbook 2022.*[19] However, as a result of the public consultation, the final adopted guidelines are more detailed and provide further clarification on the obligations arising from data transfers with a cross-border dimension. Employers and employees must be cognisant of

18 Guidelines 05/2021 on the Interplay between the application of Article 3 and the provisions on international transfers as per Chapter V of the GDPR (final version adopted 24 February 2023).

19 *Arthur Cox Employment Law Yearbook 2022* at **[2.39]** addressed Guidelines 05/2021 on the Interplay between the application of Article 3 and the provisions on international transfers as per Chapter V of the GDPR (18 November 2021).

this guidance and of the critical distinction between the application of art 3 GDPR and Chapter V GDPR.

While art 3 sets out the territorial scope of the GDPR, Chapter V aims to ensure the continued protection of personal data after it is transferred to a third country or to an international organisation. The guidelines provide three cumulative criteria to qualify a processing operation as a transfer subject to Chapter V:

1. a data controller or a processor ('exporter') is subject to the GDPR for the given processing;
2. the exporter discloses by transmission or otherwise makes personal data, subject to this processing, available to another controller, joint controller or processor ('importer'); and
3. the importer is in a third country or is an international organisation, irrespective of whether or not this importer is subject to the GDPR in respect of the given processing in accordance with art 3 GDPR.

If all three criteria are met, a transfer cannot take place unless the personal data is protected in other ways, such as by way of adequacy decision (art 45 GDPR), or through the implementation by the exporter of additional safeguards (art 46 GDPR). If the three criteria are not met, but personal data is being processed outside the EEA, the EDPB stresses that safeguards must nevertheless be implemented. While a certain data transmission may not qualify as a transfer in accordance with Chapter V of the GDPR, the processing may be associated with increased risks which must be considered when taking measures to ensure compliance with the GDPR. Moreover, the guidelines highlight that where a data controller intends to process personal data outside the EEA, the data subject must be informed of this as part of the controller's transparency obligations under art 5 GDPR (recitals 39 and 60 GDPR).

The guidelines provide helpful examples to illustrate the application of art 3 and Chapter V GDPR in the employment context. For example, the transfer of employee data by an EU-based employer, acting as data controller, to a company established outside the EEA will be considered a transfer of personal data. In contrast, where an EU-based employee accesses personal data remotely while outside the EEA, the remote access does not constitute a transfer, as the processing activities are performed by his EU-based employer ie, a controller established in the EU subject to art 3(1) GDPR. However, if such employee sends or makes data available to another controller or processor in the third country, the data flow in question would amount to a transfer under Chapter V GDPR.

[2.31] ***Recommendations 1/2022 on the Application for Approval and on the elements and principles to be found in Controller Binding Corporate Rules (Article 47 GDPR)***

Article 46 GDPR expressly provides for the use of binding corporate rules ('BCRs') for transfers of personal data between a group of undertakings, or a group of enterprises that engages in a joint economic activity. BCRs are essentially a set of internal rules and policies that an organisation develops to ensure the protection of personal data when it is transferred from one entity to another. As per art 47 GDPR, these BCRs must be approved by the LSA for BCRs. These recommendations provide a standard form for the application for approval of BCRs for data controllers and provide a detailed framework for the development and implementation of BCRs.[20] They will be of particular interest to multinationals who host global HR data centrally on systems outside of the EEA and who rely on BCRs to support the free flow of that data.

The form includes information on the data controller's identity, the group structure, the data protection officer (where necessary), the data processing activities, the data subjects and categories of data involved. Additionally, the form includes the requirement to clearly set out how the BCRs apply all the necessary elements and principles to ensure that the personal data transferred is protected to a level essentially equivalent to the one provided by the GDPR. These elements and principles include the identification of the group members involved in the data processing activities, audit and training programmes, the procedures for handling data breaches and complaints and the creation of a network of data protection officers to monitor compliance with the BCRs.

EUROPEAN DATA PROTECTION SUPERVISORY AUTHORITIES' SANCTIONS

[2.32] The European Data Protection Supervisory Authorities (the 'Supervisory Authorities') have continued in 2023 to exercise vigilance in investigating employee complaints as to data breaches by employers in processing the personal data of employees. The following represents a sample of fines imposed by different SAs.

[2.33] *Garante: Access to data for a disciplinary hearing*

On 6 July 2023,[21] the Italian Data Protection Authority, *Garante per la protezione dei dati personali* ('Garante'), fined AcegasApsAmga SpA €10,000, following a complaint by an employee. It found that the company had infringed: art 5(1)(a) GDPR, which requires that data be processed in a fair, lawful and transparent manner; art 12 GDPR, which requires that the information provided to a data subject must be communicated 'in a concise, transparent, intelligible, and easily accessible form'; and art 15 GDPR, which entitles a data subject to obtain from a controller confirmation as to whether or not personal data concerning them is being processed. An employee had filed a complaint with the Garante due to the controller's failure to respond to their requests for access to their personal data. The employee needed this data for their disciplinary proceeding. The Garante highlighted that some of the data that had been unlawfully withheld could have been useful for the exercise of the right of defence.[22]

20 Recommendations 1/2022 on the Application for Approval and on the elements and principles to be found in Controller Binding Corporate Rules (Art. 47 GDPR) (20 June 2023).

21 Garante: Access to data for a disciplinary hearing (Order of 6 July 2023 [9927300]).

22 Provvedimento del 6 luglio 2023 [9927300] – Garante Privacy.

[2.34] *Agencia Espanola Protección Datos: Surveillance of employees*

On 19 June 2023,[23] the Spanish Data Protection Authority, *Agencia Espanola Protección Datos* ('AEPD'), imposed a fine of €50,000 on *Grupo Transaher SL* ('Grupo'), finding that the company had infringed art 6 GDPR by installing video surveillance cameras in employee break areas.

Grupo installed surveillance cameras in workers' rest areas, such as the canteen. An employee claimed that the information notice regarding the cameras was not visible or did not exist and filed a compliant with the AEPD. Grupo replied to the complaint, admitting the installation of the cameras and providing more detailed information about them. First, Grupo argued that it had a logistics park where a large number of people circulated and therefore it was necessary to ensure a high level of security, monitoring and protecting property and people in the building. For this reason, Grupo considered that it was legitimate to use video to survey the entire work centre, including the industrial building and the offices. Second, with regard to the workers' rest area, it argued that it was actually a common area open 24 hours and was not intended for the exclusive rest of the workers. According to Grupo, the room did not have restricted access for the exclusive use of employees; it was also being used by clients, customers, suppliers and freelancers. Third, Grupo pointed out that it performed a proportionality test and implemented mitigating measures such as providing information notices, deleting the recordings after 30 days and limiting the access to the images to only five persons. Finally, Grupo stated that in the employment contract there is a clause informing employees about the use of video surveillance systems for security purposes.

The AEPD found that the use of surveillance cameras in an enclosed room, used as a canteen, was disproportionately invading the employees' privacy. The AEPD highlighted that while a particular Spanish legislative provision allows the use of video cameras for labour control, this control must respect some limitations, such as the workers' dignity. Similarly, another Spanish legislative provision prohibits, in any case, the installation of image recording systems 'in places intended for the rest or recreation of the workers, such as changing rooms, toilets, canteens and the like'. For these reasons, the AEPD found a violation of art 6 GDPR and fined Grupo €50,000.

[2.35] *CNIL: Excessive data collection and lack of cooperation*[24]

On 18 September 2023, the French Data Protection Authority, *Commission Nationale de l'Informatique et des Libertés* (the 'CNIL'), fined SAF LOGISTICS €200,000. An employee reported to the CNIL that the controller had collected data on the private lives of its employees as part of an internal recruitment for a position in the parent company. The CNIL carried out an onsite investigation during which it found that the controller had collected a large amount of information about employees' family members, including their identity, contact details, position, employer and marital status, via a form sent

---

23 Agencia Espanola Protección Datos: Surveillance of employees (Resolution of the Sanction Procedure File No.: EXP20220673 19 June 2023).

24 CNIL: Excessive data collection and lack of cooperation (Decision SAN-2023-013 of 18 September 2018).

to employees. In addition, the forms requested information on blood type, ethnicity and political affiliation. The CNIL found that the controller had no legal basis for processing such sensitive data.

In its finding that there had been an infringement of employees' privacy, the CNIL stated that there were four breaches of the GDPR by SAF LOGISTICS. The first was an infringement of the data minimisation principle under art 5(1)(c) GDPR; the amount and variety of information collected were excessive, infringing the employees' private lives.

The second breach identified was an infringement of the ban on processing sensitive data under art 9 GDPR, as some of the information required on the form was sensitive data, ie, blood type, ethnicity and political affiliation. However, none of the conditions for such processing were met under art 9(2) GDPR.

Thirdly the CNIL found that there was a breach of the ban on processing personal data relating to criminal convictions and offences and related security measures under art 10 GDPR. This related to the maintenance of extracts from the criminal records of employees working in air freight, even though these employees had already been cleared by the relevant authorities following an administrative inquiry.

Finally, the CNIL found that SAF LOGISTICS had not adequately cooperated with the authority as required under art 31 GDPR. When the CNIL asked the company to provide a translation of a form that was written in Chinese, SAF LOGISTICS provided an incomplete translation, in which fields about ethnicity and political affiliation were missing. It was considered that this was intentional to prevent the CNIL from exercising its powers of investigation.[25]

[2.36] ***Norwegian Supervisory Authority: Failure to notify data breach***

On 8 March 2023,[26] the Norwegian Supervisory Authority, Datatilsynet, fined US-based Argon Medical Devices Inc €220,337 for an infringement of art 33(1) GDPR, as the data controller had failed to notify Datatilsynet 'well beyond the statutory deadline', for a data breach that involved personal data of its European employees including one employee in Norway.

ARTIFICIAL INTELLIGENCE

Investigations by European Supervisory Authority

[2.37] The increased prominence of Artificial Intelligence ('AI') in the digital sphere has raised questions throughout Europe, as European Data Protection Supervisory Authorities (the 'SAs') seek to monitor AI developments and assess how AI might

25 Excessive data collection and lack of cooperation: the CNIL imposed a sanction on the company SAF LOGISTICS | CNIL.

26 Norwegian Supervisory Authority: Failure to notify data breach (Administrative Fine 21/03126-13), available at: *https://www.datatilsynet.no/contentassets/c4d1b273cca24eaea43316c2043d9c92/vedtak-om-overtredelsesgebyr---argon-medical-devices-inc.pdf*.

impact the data rights of individuals. Of particular interest, due not least to its rapid development and uptake, is ChatGPT, the software developed by OpenAI, which has been examined by a number of SAs in connection with data processing activities, including:

(i) transparency: considering whether adequate information is provided to users about how their personal data is being collected and used to train ChatGPT;
(ii) consent: considering whether users are giving valid consent to the processing of their personal data for this purpose; and
(iii) data retention: considering whether personal data is retained for longer than necessary.

The Italian SA was the first to proceed with an inquiry into OpenAI in March 2023, with other SAs soon following suit. April 2023 saw the Spanish SA open a preliminary investigation into OpenAI for possible GDPR breaches, while in the same month, the German SA sent OpenAI a questionnaire seeking information as to its data processing practices, including how it collects and uses personal data to train ChatGPT,[27] stating that if ChatGPT did not adequately protect the fundamental and data protection rights of users, the German SA had a wide range of effective tools at its disposal in response. In June 2023, the Dutch SA also voiced their concern 'about the handling of personal data by organisations that use so-called generative artificial intelligence (AI), such as ChatGPT'.[28] Recently, in September 2023, the Polish SA confirmed that it too has opened an investigation into OpenAI following a complaint as to how the technology processes data.

The EDPB has created a task force to 'foster cooperation and exchange information'[29] in relation to handling complaints and investigations into OpenAI and ChatGPT at EU level, demonstrating its concern to ensure the technology is in compliance with the GDPR.

The Garante Investigation

[2.38] On 30 March 2023, the Italian SA (the 'Garante') issued an order compelling OpenAI to stop processing personal data locally in Italy with immediate effect. The Order was issued following an investigation into a reported data breach affecting ChatGPT users, that the processing conducted by OpenAI was in violation of various GDPR articles, specifically:

(a) Article 5: principles relating to processing of personal data. The Garante noted that the processing was misaligned with this article, due to the fact that information

---

27 19 April 2023 Hessian data protection officer demands answers about ChatGPT, available at: *https://datenschutz.hessen.de/presse/hessischer-datenschutzbeauftragter-fordert-antworten-zu-chatgpt*.

28 7 June 2023 AP asks for clarification on ChatGPT, available at: *https://autoriteitpersoonsgegevens.nl/actueel/ap-vraagt-om-opheldering-over-chatgpt*.

29 13 April 2023 EDPB resolves dispute on transfers by Meta and creates task force on ChatGPT, available at: *https://edpb.europa.eu/news/news/2023/edpb-resolves-dispute-transfers-meta-and-creates-task-force-chat-gpt_en*.

provided by the generative AI technology may be incorrect, and not correspond to the real data.

(b) Article 6: lawfulness of processing. The Garante stated that there was an absence of an appropriate legal basis in relation to the mass collection and processing of personal data required to 'train' the AI algorithm.

(c) Article 8: conditions applicable to children's consent in relation to information society services. Although OpenAI's Terms of Service purported to restrict the use of ChatGPT for children under 13, it was noted that there was an absence of any age verification procedures for ChatGPT users. Therefore, the Garante further submitted that the absence of filters may expose children under 13 to inappropriate information, given their degree of development and self-awareness.

(d) Article 13: information to be provided where personal data is collected from the data subject. The Garante noted that no information was provided to users, nor to the interested parties whose data had been collected.

(e) Article 25: data protection by design and default.

Following the imposition of the ban, on 28 April 2023, the Garante confirmed that OpenAI had notified them of its measures to address the issues raised and, on this basis, OpenAI was allowed to resume operations and the processing of Italian users' data. However, the Garante did note that it plans to continue 'its fact-finding activities regarding OpenAI … under the umbrella of the ad-hoc task force that was set up by the European Data Protection Board'.[30]

Considerations from an Employer's Perspective

[2.39] Against the background of the issues raised by SAs, the EU has been working on drafting an AI regulatory structure to ensure that 'systems used in the EU are safe, transparent, traceable, non-discriminatory and environmentally friendly'. A key priority in relation to such regulations is that 'AI systems should be overseen by people, rather than by automation, to prevent harmful outcomes'.[31] Further, it is intended that the proposed AI Regulation will provide AI developers, deployers and users with clear requirements and obligations regarding specific uses of AI.[32] Employers should be vigilant as to whether generative AI products are used in the workplace, and for what purpose, noting that privacy and data protection are not the only legal issues raised by the use of the technology. Further risks may arise in relation to copyright infringement,

30 28 April 2023 ChatGPT: OpenAI reinstates service in Italy with enhanced transparency and rights for European users and non-users, available at: *https://www.garanteprivacy.it/home/docweb/-/docweb-display/docweb/9881490#english.*

31 8 June 2023 EU AI Act: first regulation on artificial intelligence, available at: *https://www.europarl.europa.eu/news/en/headlines/society/20230601STO93804/eu-ai-act-first-regulation-on-artificial-intelligence?&at_campaign=20226-Digital&at_medium=Google_Ads&at_platform=Search&at_creation=RSA&at_goal=TR_G&at_advertiser=Webcomm&at_audience=ai%20eu&at_topic=Artificial_intelligence_Act&at_location=IE&gclid=CjwKCAjw4P6oBhBsEiwAKYVkq_TGsAnxJ-7wlJgiCri3E0dl-SJpCuBaZC3o3Rito4bHVM3V8iPPkxoCBqcQAvD_BwE.*

32 20 June 2023 Regulatory framework proposal on artificial intelligence, available at: *https://digital-strategy.ec.europa.eu/en/policies/regulatory-framework-ai.*

risk of bias and inaccurate results, in addition to other as yet unknown risks. Employers should ensure that all risks are evaluated and assessed, taking account of the application of the proposed AI regulation.

DATA TRANSFERS TO THE UNITED STATES UNDER THE GDPR FOLLOWING ADOPTION OF THE ADEQUACY DECISION ON 10 JULY 2023

[2.40] On 10 July 2023, the European Commission adopted its adequacy decision for the new Trans-Atlantic Data Privacy Framework ('DPF'), concluding that the US provides an adequate level of protection for personal data transferred from public and private entities in the EU/European Economic Area ('EEA') to US organisations participating in the DPF.[33]

Key elements of the DPF

Certification:

[2.41] To be eligible for certification under the DPF, an organisation must be subject to the investigatory and enforcement powers of the Federal Trade Commission ('FTC') or the US Department of Transportation ('DoT').

To certify under the DPF, eligible organisations must publicly declare their commitment to comply with a set of privacy principles issued by the US Department of Commerce ('DoC') (the 'Principles'), make their privacy policies available and fully implement them. They must also submit certain information to the DoC.

Participating organisations must re-certify their adherence to the Principles on an annual basis.

Certified organisations can receive personal data on the basis of the DPF from the date they are placed on the DPF list by the DoC.

The DPF will be administered and monitored by the DoC and compliance will be enforced by the FTC and DoT.

Transfers under the DPF:

[2.42] Personal data transfers from controllers and processors in the EU to DPF certified organisations in the US may take place without the need to obtain any further authorisation.

---

33 Commission Implementing Decision of 10.7.2023 pursuant to Regulation (EU) 2016/679 of the European Parliament and of the Council on the adequate level of protection of personal data under the EU-US Data Privacy Framework.

The DPF applies to any personal data (defined by reference to the GDPR) transferred from the EU to participating organisations in the US, with the exception of data that is collected for publication, broadcast or other forms of public communication of journalistic material and information in previously published material disseminated from media archives.

Principles of the DPF:

[2.43] The Principles generally align to many key obligations and rights under the GDPR. They include, among others, Notice, Choice, Security, Access, Data Integrity and Purpose Limitation Principles. The adequacy decision specifically calls out as a right not addressed in the DPF, the issue of decisions affecting the data subject based solely on the automated processing of personal data. Such decisions, it says, will 'typically be taken by the controller in the Union (which has a direct relationship with the concerned data subject)' as confirmed by a study carried out for the Commission in 2018.

The Principles do not limit privacy obligations that otherwise apply under US law and do not affect the application of the GDPR to the processing of personal data in the EU.

Adequacy Decision:

[2.44] To reach a new decision on adequacy concluding that the US ensures an adequate level of protection, comparable to that of the EU, for personal data transferred from the EU to US companies under the new DPF, the Commission analysed US law, including in particular, two recent US enactments: US Executive Order 14086 on 'Enhancing Safeguards for United States Signals Intelligence Activities' adopted in October 2022, and a Regulation on the Data Protection Review Court issued by the US Attorney General. Executive Order 14086 further particularises the grounds for collection of data and creates additional specifications for 'bulk surveillance'. It establishes further mechanisms for redress to investigate and resolve complaints from European data subjects on access to data by US intelligence authorities, to include a Data Protection Review Court (the second level of a two-tier redress system).

Notwithstanding this decision, the Commission retains the right to evaluate the DPF and suspend, amend or repeal it or limit its scope if it deems that the level of protection afforded by the US is no longer adequate. The DPF will undergo regular reviews, including within one year after its entry into force, to verify whether all relevant elements have been fully implemented and are functioning effectively in practice. Organisations are reminded that opting into the DPF provides one mechanism for the transfer of personal data from the EU/EEA to the US under the GDPR, and they will need to evaluate the different transfer tools available under the GDPR to ascertain which mechanism best suits their circumstances, always bearing in mind that the DPF may be subject to challenge before the ECJ in the same way that its predecessors were.

[2.45] ***Schrems II and the 2023 Meta transfers decision***

In its judgment in July 2020 in *Data Protection Commissioner v Facebook Ireland Ltd and Maximillian Schrems*[34] ('*Schrems II*') the ECJ decided that it was 'impossible to conclude' that the EU-US Privacy Shield could ensure a level of protection essentially equivalent to that guaranteed by the GDPR.[35] Accordingly, the ECJ struck down the predecessor to the DPF, the EU-US Privacy Shield Framework and confirmed, in principle, the validity of the European Commission controller-processor Standard Contract Clauses ('SCCs').

Nearly three years later, but before the establishment of the DPF, in May 2023 the DPC concluded its investigation into the basis upon which upon which Meta Platforms Ireland Limited ('Meta Ireland') transfers personal data from the EU/EEA to the US in connection with the delivery of its Facebook service.[36] Its decision records that Meta Ireland infringed art 46(1) GDPR when it continued to transfer personal data from the EU/EEA to the US following the *Schrems II* judgment. Among other corrective orders, the DPC imposed an administrative fine on Meta Ireland in the amount of €1.2 billion. It held that transfers on the basis of the updated SCCs that were adopted by the European Commission in 2021, in conjunction with additional supplementary measures that were implemented by Meta Ireland, did not address the risks to the fundamental rights and freedoms of data subjects that were identified by the ECJ in its judgment. Importantly, the DPC's decision binds Meta Ireland only. The DPC recalls in its decision that the ECJ in *Schrems II* upheld the validity of the SCCs as a legal instrument, subject to a case-by-case assessment to determine whether, in any given case, data transfers to a third country conducted under their terms are lawful or not.

DATA PROTECTION CASELAW

EU CASELAW

Right of Access to Personal Data

[2.46] ***RW v Österreichische Post AG[37]—European Court of Justice—request for a preliminary ruling from Austria—Regulation (EU) 2016/679 ('GDPR')[38]—information about the recipients or categories of recipient to whom personal data has been or will be disclosed—data subject—right of access to personal data—disclosure of personal data to third parties—restrictions on right of access***

---

34 *Data Protection Commissioner v Facebook Ireland Limited and Maximillian Schrems* (Case C-311/18).

35 See *Arthur Cox Employment Law Yearbook 2020* at **[3.02]** for the decision in *Data Protection Commissioner v Facebook Ireland Ltd, Maximillian Schrems* (Case C-311/18).

36 Inquiry concerning data transfers from the EU/EEA to the US by Meta Platforms Ireland Limited for its Facebook service - May 2023 (IN-20-8-1) Date of Decision: 12 May 2023, available at: *https://www.dataprotection.ie/en/resources/law/decisions/Inquiry-concerning-data-transfers-from-the-EU-EEA-to-the%20US-by-Meta-Platforms-Ireland-Limited-for-its-Facebook-service.*

37 *RW v Österreichische Post AG* (Case C-154/21).

38 Regulation (EU) 2016/679 on the protection of natural persons with regard to the processing of personal data and on the free movement of such data ('GDPR').

This request for a preliminary ruling was made in February 2021 in proceedings between RW and Österreichische Post AG ('Österreichische Post') concerning a request for access to personal data pursuant to art 15(1)(c) GDPR.

On 15 January 2019, RW asked Österreichische Post for access to the personal data concerning him pursuant to art 15 GDPR and, where that data had been disclosed to third parties, for information as to the identity of the recipients. In response, Österreichische Post stated that it uses data, to the extent permissible by law, in the course of its activities as a publisher of telephone directories and that it offers that personal data to trading partners for marketing purposes. It also referred to a website that set out more information and further data processing purposes. However, it did not disclose to RW the identity of the specific recipients of the data.

RW brought proceedings against Österreichische Post seeking an order to require it to provide him with the identity of the recipient(s) of the personal data disclosed. During these proceedings Österreichische Post informed RW that his personal data had been processed for marketing purposes and forwarded to customers, including advertisers trading via mail order and stationary outlets, IT companies, mailing list providers and associations such as charitable organisations, non-governmental organisations or political parties.

The Austrian courts at first instance and on appeal, dismissed RW's action on the ground that art 15(1)(c) GDPR by referring to 'recipients or categories of recipient', provided the controller with the option of informing the data subject only of the categories of recipient, without having to identify by name the specific recipients to whom personal data is transferred. RW brought an appeal on a point of law before the Supreme Court of Austria, the referring Court, which stayed the proceedings pending a preliminary ruling from the European Court of Justice ('ECJ') regarding the interpretation of art 15(1)(c).

The ECJ found that art 15 GDPR lays down a genuine right of access for the data subject, which entitles the data subject to obtain either information about the specific recipients to whom the data have been or will be disclosed, where possible, or information about the categories of recipient. The right of access is necessary to enable the data subject to exercise their rights to rectification, to erasure, to restriction of processing and to object to his or her data being processed, conferred, respectively, by arts 16, 17, 18 and 21 GDPR. To ensure the effectiveness of all these rights, the data subject must have the right to be informed of the identity of the specific recipients where his or her personal data have already been disclosed.

The information provided to the data subject pursuant to the right of access set out in art 15(1)(c) must be as precise as possible. The data subject should be able to obtain from the controller information about the specific identity of those recipients to whom the data has been or will be disclosed or, alternatively, to elect merely to request information concerning the categories of recipient. However, the right to the protection of personal data is not an absolute right. In specific circumstances, it may be accepted that it isn't possible to provide information about specific recipients.

In those circumstances, the right of access may be restricted to information about the categories of the recipient if it is impossible to disclose the identity of specific recipients, eg, where they are not yet known. The ECJ also stressed that under art 12(5)(b) GDPR, the controller may, pursuant to the principle of responsibility, refuse to act on requests from a data subject where those requests are manifestly unfounded or excessive, although it is for the controller to demonstrate that those requests are unfounded or excessive.

[2.47] ***Österreichische Datenschutzbehörde v FF[39]—European Court of Justice—request for a preliminary ruling from Austria—Regulation (EU) 2016/679 ('GDPR'),[40] art 15(3)—data subject's right of access to his or her data undergoing processing—provision of a copy of data—concept***

This request for a preliminary ruling concerned the interpretation of art 15 of Regulation (EU) 2016/679 ('GDPR'). The request was made in proceedings between the applicant, FF, and the respondent, the Austrian Data Protection Authority. The proceedings concerned the respondent's refusal to require the intervening party, a credit rating agency, to send the applicant a copy of documents and extracts from databases containing his personal data undergoing processing.

In December 2018, the applicant applied to the intervening party for access to personal data concerning him. He also asked for copies of emails and database extracts containing his data, or in which that data was reproduced. In response, the intervening party sent him, in summary form only, a list of his data undergoing processing. The applicant complained to the respondent on the grounds that he should have been provided with a copy of all the documents containing his data. By decision in September 2018, the respondent rejected the complaint and found that the intervening party had not in any way infringed the applicant's right of access to his personal data.

The applicant brought proceedings in the referring Court, which was uncertain as to the scope of the first sentence of art 15(3) of the GDPR. The referring Court stayed the proceedings and referred a number of questions to the European Court of Justice ('ECJ') for a preliminary ruling.

By the first three of its four questions, the referring Court asked in essence whether art 15(3) must be interpreted as meaning that the right to obtain a copy of personal data undergoing processing means that the data subject must be given 'not only a copy of [that] data, but also a copy of extracts from documents or even entire documents or extracts from databases which contain, *inter alia*, [that] data'.

The ECJ considered these three questions together and found that the first sentence of art 15(3) states that a controller 'shall provide a copy of the personal data undergoing processing'. Although the GDPR does not define the term 'copy', the usual meaning of that term referred to:

> 'the faithful reproduction or transcription of an original, with the result that a purely general description of the data undergoing processing or a reference to categories of personal data does not correspond to that definition'.

39 *Österreichische Datenschutzbehörde v FF and CREIF GmbH (intervening party)* (Case C-487/21).

40 Regulation (EU) 2016/679 on the protection of natural persons with regard to the processing of personal data and on the free movement of such data ('GDPR').

It was apparent from the wording of the first sentence that the disclosure obligation 'relates to the personal data undergoing the processing in question'.

It was observed that the use of the expression 'any information' in the GDPR's definition of 'personal data' reflects the aim of the EU legislature 'to assign a wide scope to that concept, which potentially encompasses all kinds of information, not only objective but also subjective'. This would include opinions and assessments, provided they 'relate' to the data subject. The ECJ held that 'information' refers to an identified or identifiable natural person 'where, by reason of its content, scope, purpose or effect', it is linked to an identifiable person. 'Identifiable' refers to all reasonably likely means to identify the natural person, directly or indirectly, by the controller or another person. 'Processing', in turn, is accorded a broad scope by the GDPR.

Even applying a literal reading of the first sentence of art 15(3), the ECJ held that the wording does not indicate a right to obtain, *in addition*, copies of extracts from documents, or entire documents or extracts from databases containing that data. In light of art 15(1), which defines the subject and scope of the right of access, art 15(3), which 'sets out the practical arrangements' in respect of controllers' obligations, could not be interpreted as establishing a separate right from that established under art 15(1).

However, a copy of personal data undergoing processing, when provided, must allow the data subject to effectively exercise their right of access. Where contextualisation is necessary to ensure that data is 'intelligible', reproductions or extracts from documents, even entire documents, or extracts from databases, may be essential where they contain, *inter alia*, personal data undergoing processing. The ECJ stated that a balancing exercise is required, and account must be taken of the rights or freedoms of others in the process.

By its final question, the referring Court asked, in essence, whether the third sentence of art 15(3) of the GDPR must be interpreted as meaning that the concept of 'information' relates exclusively to the personal data, a copy of which the controller must provide to the data subject, and whether it goes beyond that, eg in the form of metadata. Having considered the wording and context of the third sentence, the ECJ observed that the 'information' to which it refers 'necessarily corresponds to the personal data of which the controller must provide a copy'. It does not create a right beyond the right to a 'faithful and intelligible reproduction of [that] data'.

Dismissal of Data Protection Officer

[2.48] ***X-FAB Dresden GmbH & Co KG v FC[41]—European Court of Justice—request for a preliminary ruling from Germany—Regulation (EU) 2016/679 ('GDPR'),[42] art 38(3)—data protection officer—prohibition on dismissing data***

[41] *X-FAB Dresden GmbH & Co KG v FC* (Case C-453/21).

[42] Regulation (EU) 2016/679 on the protection of natural persons with regard to the processing of personal data and on the free movement of such data ('GDPR').

protection officer for performing their tasks—requirement for functional independence—national legislation prohibiting the dismissal of a data protection officer without just cause—GDPR, art 38(6)—conflict of interest

This request for a preliminary ruling concerned the interpretation and validity of arts 38(3) and 38(6) of the GDPR. The request was made in proceedings between the applicant employer, X-FAB, and the respondent employee, FC, concerning the respondent's dismissal from his post as data protection officer ('DPO') by the applicant.

The respondent had been employed as chair of the works council of the applicant since 1993, and was appointed its DPO in 2015. In 2017, the respondent was dismissed from the role of DPO with immediate effect at the request of the state officer for data protection and freedom of information. In subsequent communications, the applicant's subsidiaries repeated their dismissal of the respondent, invoking the second sentence of art 38(3) of the GDPR, which in the intervening period had become applicable.

In an action brought before the German courts, the respondent sought a declaration that he retain his position as DPO of the applicant. The applicant submitted that there was a risk of a conflict of interest if the respondent simultaneously performed the functions of DPO and chair of the works council, arguing that the two posts were incompatible. The courts of first instance and of appeal upheld the action and the applicant appealed on a point of law before the Federal Labour Court (the referring Court), which decided to stay the proceedings and to refer a number of questions to the European Court of Justice ('ECJ') for a preliminary ruling.

By its first question, the referring Court asked, in essence, whether the second sentence of art 38(3) of the GDPR precludes national legislation permitting the dismissal of a DPO where there is just cause, even where the dismissal is not related to the DPO's performance of their tasks and duties.

The provision in question states that the DPO 'shall not be dismissed or penalised by the controller or the processor for performing his [or her] tasks'. The provision does not distinguish between a DPO who is a member of staff of the controller or processor and one who is operating on a contract service. Accordingly, the provision applies irrespective of the nature of the relationship between the DPO and its controller or processor.

It was recalled that the objective of art 38(3) of the GDPR is to ensure the 'functional independence' of the DPO. That provision requires that a DPO: 'is not to receive any instructions regarding the exercise of [their] tasks'; is to report 'directly to the highest level of management of the controller or processor'; and is to do so 'bound by secrecy or confidentiality'. Each Member State is free to lay down 'more protective specific measures' in the dismissal of a DPO, provided the objective of 'functional independence' is not undermined. National legislation that would prevent dismissal of a DPO in circumstances where they are no longer in a position to carry out tasks independently, eg, due to a conflict of interest, would undermine that objective. It is for national courts to satisfy themselves as to compatibility with EU law.

Accordingly, the first question was answered in the negative.

By its next question, the referring Court asked, in essence, in which circumstances might the existence of a 'conflict of interest' under art 38(6) of the GDPR be established.

As set out in the second sentence of art 38(6), 'the [DPO] may fulfil other tasks and duties. The controller or processor shall ensure that any such tasks and duties do not result in a conflict of interest'. Thus, there is no fundamental incompatibility between the DPO's duties and the DPO performing other duties within the controller or processor, provided the latter ensures that those other duties do not impair the DPO's functional independence.

It followed that a DPO cannot be entrusted with other tasks or duties 'which would result in him or her determining the objectives and methods of processing personal data on the part of the controller or its processor', in which case a conflict of interest may exist under art 38(6) of the GDPR. The ECJ concluded that it is a matter for the national courts to determine whether a conflict of interest exists on a case-by-case basis.

[2.49] ***ZS v Zweckverband 'Kommunale Informationsverarbeitung Sachsen' KISA, Körperschaft des öffentlichen Rechts*[43]*—European Court of Justice—request for a preliminary ruling from Germany—Regulation (EU) 2016/679 ('GDPR')*[44]*—DPO—dismissal of DPO—independence of DPO—conflict of interests—national legislation prohibiting the dismissal of a DPO without just cause***

This request for a preliminary ruling made in April 2021 concerned the interpretation and the validity of the second sentence of art 38(3) GDPR in proceedings between ZS and KISA, his employers, in the context of the dismissal of ZS from his duties as Data Protection Officer ('DPO') by KISA.

ZS had been employed by KISA since 1 January 2002 and was appointed as DPO on 27 February 2004. By letter dated 15 August 2018, KISA relieved ZS of his duties as DPO, with effect from 31 August 2018, on the basis that there was a conflict of interest between his activities as DPO and his other professional responsibilities. ZS brought an appeal on a point of law to the Federal Labour Court, Germany (the referring Court) against the decision of German Court dismissing ZS' action in relation to his dismissal. The referring Court decided to stay the proceedings and refer certain questions to the European Court of Justice ('ECJ').

By its first question, the referring Court asked, in essence, whether the second sentence of art 38(3) GDPR must be interpreted as precluding national legislation under which a controller or processor may dismiss a DPO, who is a member of staff, only on serious grounds, even if the dismissal is not related to the exercise of the tasks of the DPO. As in its decision in *X-FAB*,[45] the ECJ noted that the objective pursued by the second sentence of art 38(3) GDPR is to ensure that DPOs, whether or not they are employees of the controller or processor, should be able to perform their tasks independently.

---

43 *ZS v Zweckverband 'Kommunale Informationsverarbeitung Sachsen' KISA, Körperschaft des öffentlichen Rechts* (Case C-560/21).

44 Regulation (EU) 2016/679 on the protection of natural persons with regard to the processing of personal data and on the free movement of such data ('GDPR').

45 *X-FAB Dresden GmbH & Co. KG v FC* (Case C-453/21) at [25], see **[2.48]**.

Such independence must enable them to carry out those tasks in accordance with the objective of the GDPR, which seeks to ensure a high level of protection of natural persons within the European Union and the consistent and homogenous application of the rules for the protection of those persons' fundamental rights and freedoms with regard to the processing of personal data throughout the European Union. The second sentence of art 38(3) GDPR protects the DPO against any decision which would terminate his or her duties, or constitute a penalty, where such a decision is related to the performance of the DPO's tasks. As a result, it must be interpreted as essentially seeking to preserve the functional independence of the DPO and, to ensure the effectiveness of the provisions of the GDPR.

The ECJ ruled that each Member State is free, in the exercise of its retained competence, to lay down specific and more protective provisions on the removal of the DPO, provided that those provisions are compatible with EU law and, in particular, with the provisions of the GDPR. Such increased protection cannot jeopardise the attainment of the objectives of the GDPR. That would be the case if it prevented any dismissal, by a controller or processor, of a DPO who no longer possesses the professional qualities required to carry out his tasks in accordance with art 37(5) GDPR, or who does not perform those tasks in accordance with the provisions of the GDPR. It is for the national court to determine whether those domestic provisions are compatible with EU law and, specifically, the provisions of the GDPR.

Compensation for a Data Breach

[2.50] ***UI v Österreichische Post AG[46]—European Court of Justice—request for a preliminary ruling from Austria—Regulation (EU) 2016/679 ('GDPR'),[47] art 82(1)—processing of personal data—right to compensation for damages caused by data processing—compensation for non-material damage—rules for determination of damages by national courts***

This request for a preliminary ruling concerned the interpretation of art 82 of Regulation (EU) 2016/679 ('GDPR'). The request was made in proceedings between the applicant, UI, and the respondent company, Österreichische Post AG. The respondent was an 'address broker' that collected and processed political affinity data from the Austrian population, selling 'target group addresses' to organisations for targeted advertising.

The applicant brought an action seeking compensation for non-material damages claimed as a result of the processing by the respondent of such data, in particular any data concerning the applicant, without his consent. The data in question suggested a 'high degree of affinity' with a certain Austrian political party. The information was not shared with third parties, but with the applicant alone, who felt offended by the

46 *UI v Österreichische Post AG* (Case C-300/21). See *Arthur Cox Employment Law Yearbook 2022* at **[2.45]** for opinion of the Attorney General in *UI v Österreichische Post AG*.

47 Regulation (EU) 2016/679 on the protection of natural persons with regard to the processing of personal data and on the free movement of such data ('GDPR').

affiliation attributed to him. The fact that the data was retained by the respondent caused him 'great upset, a loss of confidence and a feeling of exposure'. The Austrian Regional Civil Court granted the applicant an injunction but rejected the claim for compensation. On considering the issue of compensation, the appellate Court decided to stay proceedings and refer three questions to the European Court of Justice ('ECJ') for a preliminary ruling.

By its first question, the referring Court asked, in essence, whether the mere infringement of the provisions of art 82(1) of the GDPR is sufficient to confer a right to compensation.

The ECJ noted that the GDPR makes no reference to the laws of Member States regarding the meaning and scope of 'material or non-material damage' nor of 'compensation for the damage suffered'. Those terms must be regarded, for the purpose of the GDPR, as autonomous concepts of EU law, to be applied uniformly in all Member States. The ECJ found it clear from the wording of art 82(1) that 'damage suffered' is among the conditions for the right to compensation to be invoked, along with an infringement of the GDPR and a causal link between the two. Infringement on its own does not confer a right to compensation.

By its third question (which it was appropriate to examine before the second), the referring Court asked in essence whether art 82(1) precludes a national rule or practice which provides for compensation for non-material damage reaching 'a certain degree of seriousness'. The GDPR does not define the concept of 'damage' for the purpose of applying that national rule or practice; nor does the context of the provision tend to indicate that the right to compensation is subject to a requirement to reach a threshold of seriousness. Such an interpretation is inconsistent with the objectives pursued by the GDPR and the importance of upholding coherence in its rules. Accordingly, the ECJ concluded that art 82(1) does preclude national rules providing that compensation for non-material damage must reach 'a certain degree of seriousness'.

By its second question, the referring Court asked in essence whether art 82(1) must be interpreted as meaning that, for the purpose of determining the extent of damages payable, national courts must apply domestic rules, with due regard to principles of 'equivalence' and 'effectiveness' of EU law. It was noted that the GDPR does not define rules on the assessment of damages. Therefore, it is a matter for Member States to prescribe safeguarding measures for art 82 rights and, 'in particular, criteria for determining the extent of compensation payable' with due regard to the equivalence and effectiveness of EU law.

Processing of Personal Data

[2.51] ***Hauptpersonalrat der Lehrerinnen und Lehrer beim Hessischen Kultusministerium v Minister des Hessischen Kultusministeriums*[48]*—European***

[48] *Hauptpersonalrat der Lehrerinnen und Lehrer beim Hessischen Kultusministerium v Minister des Hessischen Kultusministeriums* (Case C-34/21).

Court of Justice—request for a preliminary ruling from Germany—Regulation (EU) 2016/679 ('GDPR')[49]—processing of data in the employment context—protection of personal data—regional school system—teaching by videoconference—implementation without the express consent of the teachers

In December 2020, the Administrative Court of Wiesbaden, Germany, made a request for a preliminary ruling concerning the interpretation of arts 88(1) and 88(2) of the GDPR. The request was made during proceedings between the Principal Staff Committee for Teachers at the Ministry of Education and Culture of the Land Hessen, Germany and the Minister for Education and Culture of the Land Hessen. The Minister established a framework for school education during the Covid-19 pandemic that allowed pupils who could not be present in the classroom to attend live classes by video conference. The connection to the video conference service was authorised only with the consent of the pupils themselves or, for those pupils who were minors, with the consent of their parents. The framework did not provide for the consent of the teachers concerned in relation to their participation in the service.

The referring Court stated that the national legislation, which permitted the processing of the teachers' personal data, fell within the category of 'more specific rules', which the Member States are permitted to prescribe in accordance with art 88(1) GDPR to ensure the protection of employees' rights and freedoms regarding the processing of their personal data in the employment context. However, the referring Court questioned whether that national legislation was compatible with the conditions laid down in art 88(2) GDPR and made a reference to the European Court of Justice ('ECJ') for a preliminary ruling.

The ECJ found that the scope of art 88(1) GDPR cannot be determined by reference to the nature of the legal relationship that binds the employee to the employer. The specific features of the processing of personal data in the employment context are explained by the existence of a relationship of subordination between the employee and the employer. As a result, the processing of teachers' personal data during the live streaming, by videoconference, of the public educational classes which they provide, falls within the material and personal scope of art 88 GDPR.

Article 88 GDPR, according to the ECJ, gives Member States the option of adopting 'more specific rules' to ensure protection of the rights and freedoms in respect of the processing of employees' personal data in the employment context. To be classified as a 'more specific rule' within the meaning of art 88(1) GDPR, a rule of law must satisfy the conditions laid down in art 88(2) GDPR. It must comprise normative content specific to the area regulated, which is distinct from the general rules of that Regulation. It must seek to protect employees' rights and freedoms in respect of the processing of their personal data in the employment context and include suitable and specific measures to protect the data subjects' human dignity, legitimate interests and fundamental rights. Particular regard must be had to the transparency of the processing, the transfer

49 Regulation (EU) 2016/679 on the protection of natural persons with regard to the processing of personal data and on the free movement of such data ('GDPR').

of personal data within a group of undertakings, or a group of enterprises engaged in a joint economic activity, and monitoring systems at the workplace.

It is for the referring Court, which alone has jurisdiction to interpret national law, to assess whether the domestic provisions comply with the conditions and limits laid down in art 88 GDPR. If the referring Court were to find that the national provisions do not comply with art 88 GDPR, it would, in principle, be required to disregard those provisions. In accordance with the principle of the primacy of EU law, in the absence of more specific rules that comply with the conditions and limits prescribed by art 88 GDPR, the processing of personal data in the employment context, both in the private and public sectors, is directly governed by the provisions of the GDPR.

The ECJ concluded that art 88(1) and (2) GDPR must be interpreted as meaning that the application of national provisions adopted to ensure the protection of employees' rights and freedoms in respect of the processing of their personal data in the employment context must be disregarded where those provisions do not comply with the conditions and limits laid down in art 88(1) and (2), unless those provisions constitute a legal basis for processing referred to in another article of the GDPR, which complies with the requirements laid down by that Regulation. If that is the case, the application of those national provisions must not be disregarded.

[2.52] ***JM v Apulaistietosuojavaltuutettu, Pankki S (intervening parties)[50]—European Court of Justice—request for a preliminary ruling from Finland—processing of personal data—Regulation (EU) 2016/679 ('GDPR'),[51] arts 4 and 15—scope of the right of access to information—information contained in log data—definition of 'personal data'—definition of 'recipients'—temporal application***

This request for a preliminary ruling concerned the interpretation of art 15(1) of the GDPR and was made in proceedings brought by the applicant, who challenged the decision of Finland's assistant data protection supervisor rejecting the applicant's request that Pankki S, a Finnish bank ('the bank'), be ordered to disclose certain information in relation to the processing of his personal data.

The applicant was an employee and customer of the bank. In 2014, he learned that his own customer data had been accessed by members of the bank's staff on several occasions over a two-month period in 2013. On 29 May 2018, the applicant, who had since been dismissed from his post, asked the bank in its capacity as controller to disclose the identity of those employees who had consulted his customer data, the exact dates of the consultations and the purpose for which his data was accessed. The bank refused to disclose the identity of the employees on the ground that such information was the personal data of those employees. It did, however, explain that the consultation had been directed by its internal audit department in order to clarify an issue and to rule out the suspicion of a conflict of interest on the applicant's part. This had necessitated the

50 *JM v Apulaistietosuojavaltuutettu, Pankki S* (Case C-579/21).

51 Regulation (EU) 2016/679 on the protection of natural persons with regard to the processing of personal data and on the free movement of such data ('GDPR').

processing of the applicant's data and each member of staff involved in the consultation had given a statement to the internal audit department on the reasons for the processing of the data.

The applicant unsuccessfully applied to the data protection supervisor for an order that the bank disclose the information requested. The applicant brought an action against that decision to the Administrative Court of Eastern Finland (the 'referring Court') which decided to stay the proceedings and refer a number of questions to the European Court of Justice ('ECJ') for preliminary ruling.

In the first instance, the referring Court asked, in essence, whether art 15 of the GDPR, read in the light of art 99(2) of the GDPR, is applicable to a request for access to personal data where that data is processed before the date of entry into force of the GDPR (25 May 2018), but the request was made after that date. The European Court of Justice ('ECJ') noted that art 15(1) merely specifies the scope of the data subject's right of access to personal data and does not concern the conditions under which the processing of that personal data is lawful. It follows that art 15(1) 'confers … a procedural right consisting of obtaining information about the processing of [the data subject's] personal data'. Accordingly, art 15(1) applies to requests for access made from 25 May 2018 (such as the applicant's request) and is applicable to processing operations, to which the request for access relates, carried out before that date.

Next, the referring Court asked, in essence, whether information relating to consultation operations carried out on a data subject's personal data, including the dates and purposes of those operations, and the identity of natural persons who carried out those operations, is information which the data subject is entitled to obtain from the controller under art 15(1).

The ECJ noted the use of the expression 'any information' in the definition of 'personal data' contained in art 4 of the GDPR, and stated that this expression reflects the aim of the EU legislature 'to assign a wide scope to that concept', covering not only data collected and stored by the controller, but also including 'all information resulting from the processing of personal data relating to an identified or identifiable person'. The ECJ noted that the definition of 'processing' in art 4 signals a similarly broad scope, covering, 'among other things, collection, recording, storage or also consultation', while 'recipient' means a 'natural person … whether a third party or not'.

Article 15(1) of the GDPR, the ECJ observed, is one of the provisions intended to ensure transparency in the manner in which personal data is processed in relation to the data subject. As regards the information sought by the applicant, the ECJ noted that the dates of the consultation operations—which it was agreed constituted 'processing' within the meaning of art 4—made it possible to verify the lawfulness of that processing. Information relating to the purpose of the processing is expressly referred to in art 15(1)(a), while art 15(1)(c) provides that the controller is to inform the data subject of the recipients to whom personal data has been disclosed. Article 15(3) compels the controller to provide a copy of personal data undergoing processing, which, according to the ECJ's caselaw, refers to 'the faithful reproduction or transcription of an original', meaning that a purely general description or a reference to categories of personal data is insufficient.

The controller's log data containing the information requested by the applicant were 'records of processing activities' within the meaning of art 30 of the GDPR. This log data contained information relating to the identity of persons who carried out the consultation operatives. These were employees of the bank, who acted under its authority and in accordance with its instructions. While the applicant, as the data subject, had the right to obtain from the controller information relating to the recipients to whom the personal data was disclosed, employees of the controller could not be considered 'recipients' within the meaning of art 15(1), provided they were processing personal data under the authority of that controller and in accordance with its instructions. The ECJ emphasised that the right to the protection of personal data is not an absolute right and the right of access 'should not adversely affect the rights or freedoms of others', even if the disclosure is necessary to ensure the lawfulness of the processing of the data subject's personal data.

It was apparent that the applicant did not seek disclosure of the identity of the employees on the ground that they were not acting under the authority and in accordance with instructions of the bank. Rather, the applicant appeared to doubt the truthfulness of the purpose of the operations as explained to him by the bank, in which case it was open to him to lodge a complaint with the national supervisory authority for investigation.

Finally, the referring Court asked, in essence, whether it was relevant for the purposes of defining the scope of art 15(1) that the controller was a banking institution engaged in a regulated activity and that the data subject was an employee of the controller whose personal data was processed in his capacity as a customer of the controller. The ECJ noted no distinction drawn by art 15(1) according to the nature of the activities of the controller or the status of the data subject; and, while art 23 of the GDPR allows Member States to restrict the scope of art 15 by legislative means, it was not apparent that the bank's activity was subject to such legislation. The context in which the data subject requests access to information under art 15(1) cannot have any influence on the scope of that right. Thus, it was immaterial that the applicant was both a customer and an employee of the bank.

[2.53] ***ZQ v Medizinischer Dienst der Krankenversicherung Nordrhein, Körperschaft des öffentlichen Rechts ('MDK')[52]—Opinion of Advocate General Campos Sánchez-Bordona[53]—request for a preliminary ruling from Germany—Regulation (EU) 2016/679 ('GDPR'),[54] art 9—processing of personal data concerning employee health—special category data—assessment of working capacity of employee—right to compensation for damage—degree of fault***

This reference for a preliminary ruling, made in November 2021, concerns the interpretation of the GDPR as regards: (a) the processing of personal data concerning health; and (b) compensation for damage suffered because of an alleged breach of the GDPR.

52 *ZQ v Medizinischer Dienst der Krankenversicherung Nordrhein, Körperschaft des öffentlichen Rechts ('MDK')* (Case C-667/21).

53 Opinion of Advocate General Campos Sánchez-Bordona, delivered on 25 May 2023.

54 Regulation (EU) 2016/679 on the protection of natural persons with regard to the processing of personal data and on the free movement of such data ('GDPR').

ZQ began employment with the MDK in 1991. The MDK is responsible for compiling reports on the capacity for work of persons insured by the relevant health insurance fund (the 'KV') where it is necessary due to the nature, severity, duration or frequency of the illness, or the course of the illness. In certain circumstances, this may include reports concerning the health of the MDK's own employees. ZQ had been continuously ill and incapacitated since 22 November 2017. As from 24 May 2018, ZQ received sickness benefits from the KV which insured him. On 6 June 2018, the KV requested a report from the MDK to remove doubts regarding ZQ's ability to work and on 22 June 2018, a doctor employed by the MDK issued a report containing ZQ's diagnosis, following a telephone call with ZQ.

On 1 August 2018, ZQ contacted a work colleague and at ZQ's request, the colleague took photographs of the report and sent them to ZQ. On 15 August 2018, ZQ unsuccessfully sought compensation from the MDK in the amount of €20,000 based on art 82 GDPR. ZQ brought an action before the Labour Court, Düsseldorf claiming compensation in the amount of lost earnings. During these proceedings, the MDK terminated its employment relationship with ZQ. Both of ZQ's claims were dismissed at first instance and on appeal. ZQ brought an appeal before the Federal Labour Court, Germany (the referring Court), which stayed proceedings and referred certain questions to the European Court of Justice ('ECJ').

Advocate General Campos Sánchez-Bordona delivered his opinion on 25 May 2023 and stated that art 9(2)(h) GDPR includes an exception (to the general prohibition of processing special categories of data) for the processing of personal data 'for the purposes of preventative or occupational medicine, for the assessment of the working capacity of the employee, medical diagnosis, the provision of health or social care or treatment'. Article 9(2)(h), in his opinion, provides sufficient cover for the processing of its employees' health data by the MDK. It is irrelevant that the controller is, at the same time, the data subject's employer, since the MDK is not acting as an employer but as the medical service of a medical insurance fund with which the data subject is insured.

Article 9(3) GDPR lays down the conditions that persons processing personal data concerning health must comply with. The Advocate General stated that the ECJ has made clear that all processing of personal data must also comply with the principles laid down in art 5(1) GDPR and with one of the conditions for lawfulness set out in art 6(1) GDPR. In the present case, the MDK's status as employer of ZQ imposed on it a higher than usual duty of care in relation to the processing of ZQ's health data, as the risks involved were higher. The Advocate General stated that the MDK, as controller or processor, must also implement appropriate technical and organisation measures. The assessment of those measures was held to be a matter for the referring Court, which may decide, after its assessment, that the measures taken were not sufficient.

The Advocate General went on to observe that the GDPR confers on the data subject a right to compensation, the amount of which is to be determined in respect of the actual damage suffered. Article 83 GDPR considers the negligence of the infringer when determining the amount of the fine. Although, the GDPR insists that compensation must be 'full and effective'. The qualification 'full', according to the Advocate General, suggests that there should be no downward revision of the amount of compensation based on the lesser degree of negligence on the part of the controller.

The degree of fault on the part of the controller or processor does not have a bearing on establishing the liability of either of them or quantifying the amount of non-material damage to be compensated on the basis of art 82(1). However, the involvement of the data subject in the event giving rise to the compensation obligation may trigger, depending on the circumstances, the exemption from liability of the controller or processor provided for in art 82(3) GDPR.

[2.54] ***RK v Ministerstvo zdravotnictví[55]—European Court of Justice—request for preliminary ruling from Czech Republic—Regulation (EU) 2016/679[56] ('GDPR')—Regulation (EU) 2021/953[57]—protection of natural persons with regard to the processing of personal data—concept of 'processing'—mobile app—validity of EU digital Covid-19 certificates—processing of personal data and the free movement of such data***

On 29 December 2021, by way of extraordinary measure, the respondent Ministry imposed a series of conditions on access to certain indoor and outdoor premises and participation in organised mass events. These conditions were imposed to mitigate against the spread of the Covid-19 virus. The extraordinary measure required participants in mass events to provide proof of compliance with the conditions of access and required organisers of the events to carry out compliance checks using a mobile app designated for this purpose. Failure or refusal to demonstrate compliance meant that the organiser was prohibited from admitting the individual to the premises or allowing their participation in the event. The mobile app worked by scanning the QR code of EU digital Covid-19 certificates issued under Regulation (EU) 2021/953 and converting the data contained in that code into a format that could be easily read. The information revealed upon scanning included, eg, the surname, first name and date of birth of the certificate holder. The referring Court sought to ascertain whether the conversion and display of the data on a mobile phone constituted 'processing' within the meaning of art 4(2) of the GDPR, being 'any operation or set of operations which is performed on personal data or on sets of personal data, whether or not by automated means'.

The European Court of Justice ('ECJ') noted that it was common case that the obtainable information constituted 'personal data' within the meaning of art 4(1) of the GDPR being 'any information relating to an identified or identifiable natural person'. It was also observed that under Regulation (EU) 2021/953, a vaccination, test and recovery certificate must contain the identity of its holder.

55 *RK v Ministerstvo zdravotnictví* (Case C-659/22).

56 Regulation (EU) 2016/679 on the protection of natural persons with regard to the processing of personal data and on the free movement of such data ('GDPR').

57 Regulation (EU) 2021/953 on a framework for the issuance, verification and acceptance of interoperable Covid-19 vaccination, test and recovery certificates (EU Digital Covid Certificate) to facilitate free movement during the Covid-19 pandemic.

The ECJ noted that art 4(2) of the GDPR provides a non-exhaustive list of examples of what might constitute 'processing', including the consultation and use of personal data. The ECJ held that it is clear from the wording of this provision and, in particular, from the words 'any operation' that the legislature intended 'processing' to have a broad application.

The ECJ found that the verification achieved through the mobile app constituted 'processing' within the meaning of art 4(2). It noted that personal data was subjected to an automated process (scanning) and that the outcome was also automated, in the attribution of a green check mark to the holder of a certificate that complied with the health requirements. This finding accorded with Regulation (EU) 2021/953, which provides that the implementation of the certificate is a form of 'processing' within the meaning of art 4(2) GDPR.

The ECJ held that it would be for the referring Court to decide whether the extraordinary measure observed the principles relating to the processing of data under art 5 GDPR and the principle relating to the lawfulness of processing under art 6 GDPR.

Therefore, the question referred was answered in the affirmative, ie 'processing' within the meaning of art 4(2) GDPR must be interpreted as including the verification, using a national mobile app, of the validity of interoperable Covid-19 vaccination, test and recovery certificates issued under Regulation (EU) 2021/953 and used by a Member State for national purposes.

ECHR—Right to Privacy (Article 6)

[2.55] ***Nikëhasani v Albania*[58]*—European Court of Human Rights—application against the Republic of Albania—ECHR, art 8—private life—reputational damage—justified dismissal of prosecutor from office—vetting process—proportionate lifetime ban from re-entering justice system for serious ethical violation***

The applicant was a prosecutor. Following measures introduced to combat corruption in the Albanian justice system in 2016, a 'vetting process' was introduced to assess serving prosecutors under three headings:

(i) an evaluation of assets,
(ii) an integrity background check, and
(iii) professional competence.

This process revealed financial irregularities relating to the applicant. The body carrying out the vetting process at first instance, the Independent Qualification Commission (the 'IQC'), noted that the applicant had not proven the source of the money she had used to purchase some of the major assets she declared, and had concealed other assets. A hearing took place where the applicant provided explanations for the alleged irregularities.

---

58 *Nikëhasani v Albania* (Application No. 58997/18).

The IQC dismissed the applicant from office and banned her from re-entering the justice system for life, holding that: she had made inaccurate statements in both her annual declarations under the Assets Disclosure Act 2003 and the vetting declaration; she did not prove lawful sources to justify certain assets; she concealed assets; and she attempted to justify the assets retrospectively using recently-drafted documents.

The applicant lodged an appeal with the Special Appeal Chamber, which upheld the IQC's decision that the applicant had declared total assets with a value of more than twice her legitimate income.

The applicant applied to the European Court of Human Rights ('ECtHR') for relief as against the State of Albania. She argued that she had suffered a violation of her art 6 rights under the European Convention on Human Rights (the 'ECHR'), alleging that the vetting bodies were not independent and impartial and that the proceedings were conducted unfairly. The ECtHR referred to its decision in *Xhoxhaj v Albania*,[59] where it had found that the vetting process in question was, on the whole, fair and necessary to combat corruption and to ensure public trust in the justice system. The ECtHR therefore declared the complaint under art 6 inadmissible.

The applicant also alleged that there had been a breach of her art 8 rights under the Convention due to her dismissal from office and subsequent ban.

The ECtHR held that the vetting procedures and applicant's dismissal complied with art 8 of the Convention and pursued legitimate aims of safeguarding security, safety and the rights and freedoms of others, being aimed at combatting corruption among the judiciary. In considering whether the dismissal was necessary in a democratic society, the ECtHR cited *Xhoxhaj* and characterised the provisions as responding to a 'pressing social need'; the ECtHR concluded that the provisions were proportionate to the legitimate aim pursued and found the reasons adduced by the national authorities to justify the provisions to be 'relevant and sufficient'.

In relation to the applicant's alleged loss of reputation, the ECtHR noted that it had previously considered that art 8 could not be relied on in circumstances where any loss of reputation was a foreseeable consequence of her actions.

In relation to the applicant's subsequent ban from practising law as a result of her removal from office, the ECtHR referred to its decision in *Xhoxhaj*, where it held that a lifetime ban in the case of a member of the judiciary, on grounds of serious ethical violations, was 'not inconsistent with or disproportionate to the legitimate objective pursued by the State … to ensure the integrity of judicial office and public trust in the justice system'. The ECtHR found that 'similar compelling considerations apply in relation to the dismissal from the post of prosecutor and the ensuing ban on re-entering the justice system'.

The ECtHR dismissed as inadmissible the applicant's final complaint under art 13 that she was denied an effective remedy due, in particular, to procedural issues at IQC and Special Appeal Chamber level.

---

59 *Xhoxhaj v Albania* (Application No. 15227/19).

Ultimately, the ECtHR held that there had not been a violation of the applicant's art 8 rights under the Convention and declared the remainder of the application inadmissible.

[2.56] ***Sevdari v Albania*[60]*—European Court of Human Rights—application against the Republic of Albania—ECHR, art 8—private life—reputation—ECHR, art 46—disproportionate dismissal of prosecutor—lifetime ban from re-entering justice system—professional error—spouse's tax affairs—absence of bad faith or deliberate violations by the applicant***

The applicant was a prosecutor. Following changes to the Albanian justice system in 2016, a 'vetting process' was introduced to assess serving prosecutors under certain headings:

(i) an evaluation of assets,
(ii) an integrity background check, and
(iii) professional competence.

The vetting process was introduced as a reform in response to widespread corruption. On foot of this process, it was revealed that the applicant had insufficient resources to prove the acquisition of part of her and her spouse's property. In respect of her professional competence, it was revealed that she had missed a deadline for lodging an appeal in one case, which involved wrongdoing of a former government official. The applicant was dismissed from her post and banned for life from re-entering the justice system.

The applicant applied to the European Court of Human Rights ('ECtHR') for relief as against the State of Albania. She argued that she had suffered a violation of her art 6 rights under the European Convention on Human Rights ('ECHR'), alleging that the vetting bodies were not independent and impartial and that the proceedings were conducted unfairly. As in the related case of *Nikëhasani v Albania*,[61] the ECtHR referred to its decision in *Xhoxhaj v Albania*,[62] where it had found that the vetting process in question was, on the whole fair and necessary to combat corruption and to ensure public trust in the justice system. The ECtHR therefore declared the complaint under art 6 inadmissible.

In relation to the applicant's art 8 complaint, the ECtHR found that the dismissal, although amounting to an interference with her private life, had been in accordance with the law and had pursued the legitimate aims of safeguarding national security, public safety and the rights and freedoms of others. The ECtHR again referred to *Xhoxhaj v Albania* in characterising the provisions as responding to a 'pressing social need' of reforming the justice system. It held that the sanctions were proportionate to the legitimate aim pursued and found the reasons adduced by the national authorities to justify the provisions as being 'relevant and sufficient'. The ECtHR then examined whether the dismissal had been proportionate to the aims pursued.

60 *Sevdari v Albania* (Application No. 40662/19).
61 *Nikëhasani v Albania* (Application No. 58997/18), see **[2.55]**.
62 *Xhoxhaj v Albania* (Application No. 15227/19).

The ECtHR noted that all findings concerning the applicant regarding insufficient disclosure of, or failure to justify, assets related to income earned by her spouse from employment abroad. This included income that he had earned when she was not yet married to him and not yet a prosecutor. It also included income that she had been unable to prove that her husband had paid tax on. The irregularities did not relate to the applicant's personal income. The portion of spousal income on which tax had not been proven was negligible when compared to the total amount of spousal income and there were no such difficulties arising in relation to income from domestic sources.

The ECtHR also considered the allegations made against the applicant regarding her professional competence, specifically as a result of her failure to lodge an appeal in a case which concerned a former government official. The ECtHR characterised this as an 'isolated incident in her career as prosecutor notably dealing with economic crimes'.

The ECtHR held that, in the absence of bad faith or intention to do wrong, the applicant's dismissal and subsequent ban was disproportionate to the legitimate aims pursued by the vetting process.

The ECtHR did not consider that the operation of the vetting process in general revealed any systemic problems of compliance with the European Convention on Human Rights. It held that, regarding individual measures, an appropriate form of redress in this case would be to re-open proceedings and review the case in accordance with art 8.

An award of €13,600 as pecuniary damages and €6,000 in respect of non-pecuniary damages was made to the applicant.

IRISH CASELAW

Use of Evidence Obtained for a Different Purpose

[2.57] ***Hyland v Commissioner of An Garda Síochána*[63]*—Court of Appeal—Ní Raifeartaigh J—appeal from High Court—Garda Síochána (Discipline) Regulations 2007*[64]*—disciplinary proceedings—material obtained in course of criminal investigation—whether permissible for An Garda Síochána to use material against a member in disciplinary proceedings where material obtained lawfully in course of criminal investigation—reasonably incidental—public interest***

This appeal raised the question of whether it was permissible for the respondent to use material in disciplinary proceedings against a member of An Garda Síochána where that material was recovered from the member's mobile phone in the course of a criminal investigation.

The appellant faced charges under the Garda Síochána (Discipline) Regulations 2007 (the '2007 Regulations') when concerns were raised as a result of a video clip shared

63 *Hyland v Commissioner of An Garda Síochána* [2023] IECA 278.

64 Garda Síochána (Discipline) Regulations 2007 (SI 214/2007).

by him with colleagues in a WhatsApp group. The appellant's mobile phone was taken and examined on foot of two search warrants obtained under the Child Trafficking and Pornography Act 1998. A file was sent to the DPP, who directed no prosecution.

A disciplinary investigation commenced on the basis of the material recovered from the appellant's phone.

The appellant brought judicial review proceedings seeking, *inter alia*, an order restraining the respondent from relying on any material obtained from his phone other than in the course of a criminal investigation and prosecution.[65]

The trial Judge did not see any difference between a subsequent disciplinary charge and a criminal prosecution on different charges, based on material found in the course of a lawful search. Indeed, it held that the respondent was duty-bound to investigate material suggesting a possible breach of the 2007 Regulations. The High Court held that it was not possible in this case to simply do a 'key word or other limited form of search' when looking for child pornography, and, thus, it was necessary for gardaí to read texts and other messages on the mobile phone (without a time limit) to garner evidence of offences having been committed by its owner under the Child Trafficking and Pornography Act 1998.

The trial Judge held that, although 'in general' the respondent was not entitled to retain property for the purposes of a disciplinary investigation, this did not mean that the respondent was obliged to return 'all of the material from the phone'. The High Court did not accept that the respondent needed to keep the mobile phone as 'best evidence' before a board of inquiry and held that the appellant had a *prima facie* entitlement to the return of his property, following the conclusion of the criminal investigation. The trial Judge found that there had not been a breach of privacy, either by the recovery of the material obtained or by the search of the mobile phone.

The Court of Appeal held that there is a general principle that material compulsorily obtained 'may only be deployed for the purpose for which the power was exercised or for purposes reasonably incidental to it'. This principle, however, 'appears to admit of certain public interest exceptions', allowing for the sharing of the material 'with at least some public bodies in at least some circumstances'. While not well defined in Ireland, common law jurisdictions signal a public interest in 'inter-agency sharing of material', though it is important to examine the precise terms of any relevant legislation.

The Court did not consider garda disciplinary proceedings to be a purpose 'reasonably incidental' to a criminal prosecution in the sense envisaged in the authorities, notwithstanding the public interest in ensuring the integrity of An Garda Síochána.

The Court concluded 'not without some hesitation' that s 9 of the Criminal Law Act 1976 is to be interpreted 'as not merely *authorising* the use' of materials suspected at the time of seizure to be evidence of any criminal offence in certain contexts 'other than those in respect of which the search warrant issued in the first place', but also as

[65] See *Arthur Cox Employment Law Yearbook 2022* at **[13.03]** for decision of High Court in *Hyland v Commissioner for An Garda Síochána* [2022] IEHC 106.

'limiting' the use of any additional material seized to criminal proceedings and prison discipline.

It followed that where the material seized was not likely to fall within the expanded seizure power of s 9 of the Criminal Law Act 1976—in this instance because it did not constitute evidence of any offence at all—it could not be retained and used outside criminal prosecutions or prison discipline proceedings.

Accordingly, the material which incidentally came into the possession of the respondent could not be retained and used in the garda disciplinary proceedings.

The appeal succeeded.

Compensation for Data Breach

[2.58] ***Kaminski v Ballymaguire Foods Ltd*[66]*—Dublin Circuit Court—O'Connor J—Data Protection Act 2018, s 117—Regulation (EU) 2016/679 ('GDPR')*[67]*—data protection policies—clarity and transparency—legitimate interest—CCTV footage containing plaintiff's personal data processed for quality control purposes—non-material damage***

The plaintiff alleged a breach of the Data Protection Act 2018 and/or the GDPR on the part of his employer and sought damages. The complaint arose from the use of CCTV footage in which the plaintiff was identifiable; this, it was alleged, amounted to an unlawful processing of the plaintiff's data, as a result of which he suffered damage and distress in the form of anxiety and embarrassment.

The plaintiff was first employed the respondent in 2009. By March 2019, the plaintiff was a supervisor of 20 employees. Around that time a meeting took place between the quality control manager and several managers and supervisors where CCTV footage was played, the purpose of which was to identify instances of poor food safety practices with a view to implementing corrective measures. During the trial, the respondent formally conceded that the plaintiff was identifiable in one such clip. The meeting did not identify employees by name and did not highlight the actions of specific individuals.

The plaintiff, who was not present at the meeting and who did not know that his image would be used, was later informed of the CCTV clip by colleagues. For two weeks after the incident, the footage was stored on a communal work computer without password protection (though there was no allegation of unlawful processing in that regard). The plaintiff's evidence was that he felt humiliated and mocked by his colleagues.

The Court observed a lack of clarity and transparency in relation to the respondent's data protection policies. Four such policies were in place, each serving a different

66 *Kaminski v Ballymaguire Foods Ltd* [2023] IECC 5.

67 Regulation (EU) 2016/679 on the protection of natural persons with regard to the processing of personal data and on the free movement of such data ('GDPR').

purpose. Indeed, evidence provided by a witness for the respondent confirmed that confusion existed as to the relevant policy. Moreover, the plaintiff's first language was Polish and the Court noted that he would have been expected to navigate the four policy documents through English and identify the relevant one. It was further observed that the respondent had not carried out a 'legitimate interest assessment', and so it could not be shown whether the processing of the data was necessary to achieve a legitimate interest.

The Court was therefore satisfied that there was an infringement of the plaintiff's rights under the GDPR. There was non-material damage resulting from that infringement—taking into account the plaintiff's supervisory role at the time of the incident—and a causal connection between the damage and the infringement. The plaintiff was awarded €2,000 in respect of non-material damage.

[2.59] ***Cunniam v Parcel Connect Ltd t/a Fastway Couriers Ireland*[68]*—Circuit Court—Regulation (EU) 2016/679 ('GDPR')*[69]*—interpretation of art 82 GDPR—data breach—third-party hacker—right to compensation—non-material damage—stay on proceedings***

The plaintiff contended that the defendants, or one of them, had a data breach incident involving a third-party hacker which compromised the personal data of over 450,000 people. The plaintiff claimed that his rights pursuant to the GDPR were infringed and claimed a right to compensation under art 82 GDPR. Notably, the data of the plaintiff which was allegedly accessed by the third party was limited to his name, email address, residential address and mobile number, and the plaintiff effectively confirmed that he had not suffered any material damage nor any interference with his peace and privacy.

The Circuit Court decided to stay the proceedings pending the determination by the European Court of Justice ('ECJ') of the matters referred to it by several European courts (namely Germany, Austria and Bulgaria) in order to fulfil its duty of sincere cooperation, which is provided for under art 4(3) of the Treaty on European Union.

In summary, the relevant issues awaiting judgment by the ECJ (at the time of this judgment) were:

- whether the defendants were liable for the unauthorised disclosure of personal data because of a hacking incident;
- whether the plaintiff was required to establish that his personal data was accessed and misused, or whether loss of control over the personal data in and of itself was sufficient to establish liability;
- whether the degree of fault of the defendants was relevant to the quantification of compensation;

---

68 *Cunniam v Parcel Connect Ltd t/a Fastway Couriers Ireland* [2023] IECC 1.

69 Regulation (EU) 2016/679 on the protection of natural persons with regard to the processing of personal data and on the free movement of such data ('GDPR').

- what was the correct interpretation of non-material damage in art 82(1) GDPR and, in particular, whether anxiety and apprehension alone were capable of constituting non-material damage; and
- what was the appropriate level of damages to be awarded where no material damage was suffered, and the non-material damage allegedly suffered was limited to interference with the plaintiff's peace and privacy and apprehension about the use to which his data had been put?

The defendants argued, and the Court agreed, that refusing a stay would substantially prejudice their defence for a number of reasons, including:

- the value of the plaintiff's claim was so small that even if the plaintiff succeeded in establishing liability, depending on the ECJ's interpretation of art 82, it was possible that the plaintiff would not be entitled to any damages;
- if the proceedings were simply allowed to proceed until such time as they were ready for hearing, the costs that would have been incurred by them would, by far, be in excess of any award of damages the plaintiff might recover; and
- pending receipt of clarification in respect of the correct interpretation of art 82 GDPR from the ECJ, it was impossible to sensibly seek to quantify the sum which might to be lodged with the Court. (This was a particular request from the plaintiffs in this case.) This, it was argued, deprived the defendant of an ability to provide themselves with any meaningful costs' protection.

The plaintiff had suggested alternatives to a stay, including case management or taking a lead case. However, the Court found that it was unrealistic for the Court to exercise a supervisory role over all the cases. Ultimately, the Court decided that refusal to grant a stay in this case risked an irreconcilable judgment being produced by the Court, as well as undue prejudice to the defendant.

The ECJ has since handed down its judgment in *UI v Österreichische Post AG*[70] on 4 May 2023. This judgment was eagerly anticipated by Member States, and data controllers generally, in the hope that it would provide greater clarity on the assessment of claims for non-material damages. On this aspect, the ECJ held that it is for each Member State to determine the assessment of non-material damages in line with domestic practice once the EU principles of equivalence and effectiveness are complied with.

Kaminski[71] was the first written judgment from the Irish courts since the ECJ decision in *UI v Österreichische Post*, where, notably, the Circuit Court awarded the plaintiff €2,000 in damages, along with his legal costs, where his loss exceeded mere upset and created 'an emotional experience and negative emotions of insecurity which did affect him for a short period of time'. This significant decision illustrates the increased role the Irish courts will continue to play in assessing these claims at domestic level and

70 *UI v Österreichische Post AG* (Case C-300/21), at [28]–[59] see **[2.50]**.

71 *Kaminski v Ballymaguire Foods Ltd* [2023] IECC 5.

shines light on the manner in which non-material damage is likely to be interpreted by the Irish judiciary.

[2.60] ***Fox v The Data Protection Commissioner*[72]*—High Court—Heslin J—appeal from Circuit Court—complaint to Data Protection Commissioner***

The plaintiff was a lay litigant who challenged the Circuit Court's dismissal of an appeal against a decision of the respondent Commissioner of 14 November 2019 ('the decision').

The plaintiff was employed by the National Gallery of Ireland as an attendant from 1991. His contract of employment was terminated in November 2011, following allegations that he sent emails containing security-sensitive information to a third party.

In December 2010, the plaintiff submitted a complaint to the respondent, who formed the opinion that it was 'frivolous or vexatious' in nature. This determination was upheld on appeal by the Circuit Court and the High Court.

Prior to the matter being heard by the Court of Appeal, however, the Supreme Court delivered its decision in *Novak v The Data Protection Commissioner*.[73] In the wake of this judgment, the respondent conceded the appeal to the Court of Appeal, and a reconstituted complaint was submitted in October 2016. Most of the issues set out in the complaint were decided in favour of the plaintiff. The balance of these issues (three in total) formed the basis of these proceedings, a statutory appeal to the Circuit Court, which was satisfied that the decision of the respondent 'was carried out fairly and [was] both logical and appropriate, bearing in mind the law and the adjudicative process as a whole'.

On appeal, Heslin J in the High Court concluded that the plaintiff had not 'sufficiently appreciated' the High Court's role in an appeal on a point of law. It appeared to the Court that the plaintiff sought a full re-hearing of the complaints that had not been upheld by the respondent's decision, which was not permissible; nor had the plaintiff identified a point of law in his originating motion.

The Court noted that the respondent had taken the unusual step of issuing her (lengthy) decision in draft form, 'specifically so that both sides could make such submissions as they might wish'. This afforded the plaintiff 'an ideal opportunity to raise any further concerns, issues or evidence which he had not previously raised with the [respondent]'. Rather than identifying any point of law, the plaintiff seemed to be challenging the decision on its merits, while making the case that the trial Judge had erred by not concluding that the decision was wrong. Although the Court did consider each point of appeal in its turn, this did not have a bearing on the Court's conclusion that it did not have jurisdiction to consider a point of law not identified in the plaintiff's notice of motion. Accordingly, the appeal failed.

72 *Fox v The Data Protection Commissioner* [2023] IEHC 529.

73 *Novak v The Data Protection Commissioner* [2016] IESC 18.

Data Breach

[2.61] ***McShane v The Data Protection Commission*[74]*—High Court—Bolger J—Data Protection Act 2018—application for leave for judicial review—data protection—privacy—consent—controller of data—arguable case with a reasonable prospect of success—non-work-related personal data—statutory appeal***

The applicant sought leave to judicially review the respondent's decision on the applicant's complaint that his personal data, which was held by the notice party (the Health Service Executive, his employer), was accessed without his consent. The respondent had found that the notice party was not a controller of the data in question under the GDPR, as the data was stored on the applicant's work phone without its authority or consent. The respondent had focused solely on the applicant's non-work-related personal data.

In support of this leave application, the applicant argued that the respondent did not take account of the work-related personal data on the phone that was processed by the notice party. The respondent argued that the original complaint referred only to the applicant's non-work-related personal data and that he was not entitled to leave for judicial review, in circumstances where there was a statutory right to appeal the decision of the respondent, which the applicant had failed to exercise in time.

The standard of review employed by the Court was whether 'an arguable case with a reasonable prospect of success' existed.

While the Court accepted that, although the default position is that an aggrieved party should avail of the statutory appeal rather than opting to judicially review a decision, there is an exception to the general rule where 'an appeal will not permit the person aggrieved to adequately ventilate the basis of their complaint against the initial decision'. The Court held that there was an arguable case that this exception arose here, in circumstances where the respondent never investigated the applicant's complaint about his work-related personal data. The Court held that the applicant had established an arguable case with a reasonable prospect of success that he had made a complaint about his work-related personal data that was never 'handled' by the respondent, in breach of its statutory function under the Data Protection Act 2018. It was held that the respondent unreasonably and unlawfully focused on the non-work-related data in its determination.

The respondent argued that the applicant failed to bring a statutory appeal in time; however, the Court was satisfied that the applicant had not raised specious points of law in the leave application that could be described as attempting to 'sidestep' the statutory appeal.

The Court held that there was also an arguable case with a reasonable prospect of success that the notice party was a data controller and processed the applicant's personal data and that the respondent should have handled this complaint. The Court noted that

---

74 *McShane v The Data Protection Commission* [2023] IEHC 567.

the definitions of 'data controller' and 'personal data' were wide enough to potentially encompass the applicant's complaint.

Having concluded that the applicant had satisfied the 'not very high standard ... to assert an entitlement to leave', leave was granted.

[2.62] ***Scott v Data Protection Commissioner (No. 2)[75]—Dublin Circuit Court—O'Connor J—appeal from Data Protection Commission—Regulation (EU) 2016/679[76] ('GDPR')—disclosure of personal data—whether the disclosure came within the 'material scope' of the GDPR—legitimate interest***

This was an appeal against a decision of the respondent, the Data Protection Commissioner. The complaint giving rise to the decision concerned the disclosure of information by a barrister to a law firm in determining whether a conflict of interest existed.

The barrister in question previously represented the claimant in an employment dispute before receiving instructions to act against her in an unrelated employment matter two years later. This was disclosed to the instructing law firm, which confirmed the instructions; however, the claimant objected to the barrister's presence at the hearing, believing the barrister to be in possession of potentially prejudicial information obtained from the previous proceedings.

The claimant lodged a complaint with the respondent, stating that a barrister had disclosed private and confidential information, gained through a position of privilege, to a solicitor's firm in breach of her privacy and general data protection rights; specifically, that the barrister had acted for the claimant in a previous, unrelated employment matter two years previously.

The complaint also stated that the solicitor's firm replied that the disclosure was made in the context of a conflict of interest query; that the barrister stated that they no longer held papers in the previous matter and had returned them to the previous instructing firm; and that they had not represented the claimant since.

The respondent decided that the disclosure constituted a disclosure of personal data within the meaning of art 4(1) of the GDPR. However, it decided that the disclosure did not come within the 'material scope' of the GDPR, and that personal data 'must be recorded, in either electronic or manual form' to do so. The respondent found that the disclosure, in this instance, took place verbally and the information disclosed did not form part of a filing system.

The respondent then heard submissions as to a 'legitimate interests' defence. Having heard from the barrister, who relied on art 6(1) as the legal basis for the disclosure, the respondent held, in the first instance, that a 'clear legitimate interest' arose: the barrister was 'a sole trader with a legitimate interest to work and [was] at the same time ...

75 *Scott v Data Protection Commissioner (No 2)* [2022] IECC 5.

76 Regulation (EU) 2016/679 on the protection of natural persons with regard to the processing of personal data and on the free movement of such data ('GDPR').

subject to professional sanction for failing to uphold the obligations placed upon her by the Code of Conduct for the Bar of Ireland'. In the second instance, the disclosure was held to be 'necessary to achieve the legitimate interests of the data controller (the barrister) and the third party (the law firm)'. Finally, the respondent held in balancing the interests of the parties, that the disclosure 'did not pose a risk to the claimant's fundamental rights and freedoms in respect of her personal data and was necessary having regard to the obligations placed on the barrister'. A lawful basis therefore existed for the disclosure and the complaint was accordingly dismissed.

The Circuit Court was asked to determine the following questions:

(a) whether the respondent was correct in finding that verbal disclosure of personal data does not come within the scope of the GDPR; if so,
(b) whether the respondent was correct in issuing a decision on art 6(1) of the GDPR; if not, and the disclosure did come within the scope of GDPR,
(c) whether the barrister had a lawful basis to process the claimant's data; and
(d) whether the respondent was correct to dismiss the claimant's complaint.

The Court, on an assessment of the evidence that was before the respondent at the time of the decision, affirmed the decision and dismissed the appeal. In doing so, the Court held that:

(a) a purely verbal communication, in these circumstances, was not a communication under the GDPR as it could not reasonably be interpreted as falling within its definition of 'material scope';
(b) a barrister's notes, even if disposed of later, are 'insufficient to constitute a filing system for the purposes of GDPR';
(c) the respondent was correct to determine that the disclosure satisfied the legitimate interest test; and
(d) curial deference 'is more circumspect to issues on questions of law' and the Court 'has the right to explore the extent of the specialism attributable to that curial deference' if it covers, eg, legal issues concerning disclosures.

The Court noted that even if a different tribunal were to hold that the barrister did have a conflict of interest, this did not automatically and retrospectively invalidate the legitimate interest test applied to the original disclosure.

Use of CCTV Footage

[2.63] ***McVann v Data Protection Commission*[77]*—Circuit Court—O'Connor J—appeal from Data Protection Commission—Regulation (EU) 2016/679 ('GDPR')*[78]*—Prison (Disciplinary Code for Officers) Rules 1996*[79]*—***

77 *McVann v Data Protection Commission* [2023] IECC 3.

78 Regulation (EU) 2016/679 on the protection of natural persons with regard to the processing of personal data and on the free movement of such data ('GDPR').

79 Prison (Disciplinary Code For Officers) Rules 1996 (SI 289/1996).

privacy—CCTV—disciplinary proceedings—incompatible with original purpose—security—compatibility analysis—prison officer

The appellant was a prison officer employed by the Irish Prison Service (the 'IPS'). In September 2018, the appellant was on duty at Mayo General Hospital (the 'Hospital'), accompanying a prisoner, who had been admitted for treatment. While in the appellant's charge, the prisoner escaped. He was subsequently apprehended by An Garda Síochána. An internal prison investigation followed and the IPS requested CCTV footage from the Hospital for the night in question. The Chief Officer of the prison viewed the footage and referred to it in his findings. The IPS also referred to the footage in subsequent disciplinary proceedings against the appellant. The Governor of the Prison initiated a complaint against the appellant under the Prison (Disciplinary Code for Officers) Rules 1996 and the appellant objected to the use of the CCTV footage to substantiate the complaint. The appellant made complaints to the Data Protection Commission as against the IPS and the Hospital. Among his grounds, the appellant alleged that IPS's use of the material was incompatible with the purpose for which it was collected. The Data Protection Commission rejected both complaints.

The decisions of the Data Protection Commission were appealed to the Circuit Court. The appellant argued that when the CCTV was viewed by the IPS, any threat to security had been neutralised, as the prisoner had been apprehended. The appellant also argued that even if the Court held that the material had been viewed for a permissible reason, ie for the purposes of security, the material was still further processed for the purpose of disciplinary action, which was not permissible.

The Circuit Court referred to *Doolin v The Data Protection Commissioner and Our Lady's Hospice and Care Services*,[80] which concerned the question of whether CCTV footage that was recorded for the purposes of security could be processed for an unrelated employment matter. The High Court in *Doolin* held that the subsequent use of the footage for the purpose of disciplinary action was unlawful as this purpose was different than that for which the CCTV was originally collected. On appeal, the Court of Appeal upheld this decision,[81] stating, however, that the mere fact that data captured is subsequently used for a different purpose does not render it unlawful; it is only where this subsequent use is incompatible with the stated purpose that illegality occurs. The Court of Appeal applied the compatibility test set out by the Working Party on the Protection of Individuals with regard to the Processing of Personal Data, also known as the Article 29 Data Protection Working Party, which encouraged the consideration of a number of key factors including the 'context in which the personal data [has] been collected and the reasonable expectations of the data subjects as to [its] further use'.

In the present case, the Circuit Court noted that the respondent failed to carry out a similar compatibility analysis, despite it being necessary under the circumstances.

80 *Doolin v The Data Protection Commissioner and Our Lady's Hospice and Care Services* [2020] IEHC 90.

81 *Doolin v The Data Protection Commissioner and Our Lady's Hospice and Care Services* [2020] IECA 117.

The Circuit Court held that, unlike in *Doolin*, the use of the CCTV footage for disciplinary reasons in this case would be compatible with the original purpose. It was held that the appellant was aware that CCTV was used for security purposes in the Hospital and that, given the nature of the appellant's occupation, there was a reasonable expectation that the footage could be used in any investigation of a breach of security. The Court held that, insofar as the CCTV footage was used solely to deal with the breach in security at the Hospital, its use was compatible with the original purpose for its collection. It would not be compatible to use the footage for any purpose other than the security breach.

The Circuit Court confirmed the respondent's decision and dismissed the appeal.

Chapter 3

Employment Equality

INTRODUCTION

Age

[3.01] In *BVAEB v BB*, the ECJ considered legislation which retroactively introduced the same treatment in respect of pension rights for different categories of civil servants. The legislation had previously drawn a distinction between pension calculations for those born before 1 January 1995 and those born after that date.

The Labour Court in *Commissioner of An Garda Síochána v Boyle* (maximum age for recruitment) and the UK EAT in *Imperial College Healthcare NHS Trust and Ziprin v Matar* (lack of encouragement to seek a higher qualification), considered cases concerning age-related assumptions which resulted in direct discrimination on the basis of age.

The Labour Court considered a whether the respondent was able to advance any objective justification for its mandatory retirement age in *McLoughlin*.

Civil Status

In *Ellis*, the UK EAT allowed an appeal from the employment tribunal in a case that considered if there was differential treatment on the basis of civil status.

Disability

There were a number of decisions of the Labour Court and the UK EAT that related to reasonable adjustments, differential treatment and proportionality as outlined below.

The Labour Court considered an appeal from the WRC in *G Bruss Gmbh Dichtungstechnik*, this case involved a company that had a mandatory policy to wear a mask in communal areas during the Covid-19 pandemic. The claimant asserted that, due to her disability, she could not wear a mask. The Court considered whether there were objective grounds justifying the existence of the requirement to wear a mask.

The UK EAT considered a number of cases involving reasonable adjustments—in *Riley* the claimant suffered from a disability and claimed he had been unfairly dismissed when his employment had been terminated by way of mutual agreement. In *Davies* the UK EAT considered whether the employer had applied a provision, criterion or practice placing the claimant at a substantial disadvantage, ie, the requirement to work full-time. The provision of reasonable adjustment was also considered in *AECOM Ltd* (requirement to complete an online recruitment form), *Pipe* (the requirement to hold a particular qualification) and *Williams* (the requirement to carry out the full range of duties).

Causation was considered by the UK EAT in *McQueen*, where the claimant alleged he was discriminated against on the grounds of disability when he was disciplined for behaviour he claimed was a result of his disability.

In *Pilkington*, the UK EAT considered an appeal concerning the dismissal of the claimant, who had been long-term absent and intermittently absent for over a year due to chronic pain, where the respondent believed he had engaged in other employment.

The UK EAT considered the meaning of the term 'disability' in *Morris*, in evaluating whether the claimant suffered from a long-term impairment and the cause of said impairment.

In *Greasley-Adams*, the UK EAT considered whether someone was subject to harassment if they were unaware of the unwanted conduct.

The UK EAT in *Boesi* heard an appeal concerning the construction of a hypothetical comparator in a claim of direct discrimination due to disability.

Lingard was an appeal to the UK EAT which related to a claim of disability discrimination where the claimant alleged her employer had constructive knowledge of her condition.

Family Status

Saint John of God Community Services v Doherty was an appeal to the Labour Court concerning a claim of discrimination on the grounds of family status that arose due to the respondent not facilitating the employee's request to work from home.

Gender

In *DX*, the ECJ examined the principle of equal treatment for men and women in relation to Spanish legislation that provided for the right to a pension supplement for women only.

The Labour Court in *Aer Lingus v Barry* examined a complaint of discrimination based on gender in relation to the uniform female cabin crew staff were required to wear.

The Labour Court and the UK EAT assessed whether the claimant was treated less favourably than their male counterparts in *The Housing Sustainable Communities Agency* and *Earl Shilton Town Council*.

The implications of pregnancy in a gender discrimination context were considered by the UK EAT in *Alcedo Orange Ltd* and *Glover*, where the claimant had made a flexible working request at the end of her maternity leave.

In *Thukalil*, the UK EAT considered whether the statutory exception that a 'family worker' was not entitled to the national minimum wage was indirectly discriminatory as women generally make up the majority of domestic workers.

Race

The Labour Court considered an allegation of racial discrimination in the course of an interview process in *Maynooth University*.

The UK EAT considered an appeal from the employment tribunal in relation to a claim of unconscious discrimination in an appraisal grading in *Kohli*, and in *Royal Parks* a claim of indirect discrimination, in relation to a minimum rate of pay.

The UK EAT heard an appeal from the employment tribunal concerning race discrimination in *Edwards* in relation to calculation of a loss of earnings and in *Institute and Faculty of Actuaries* in relation to conferring qualifications as a British national.

Religion

The ECJ in *OP* addressed discrimination on the grounds of religion in relation to a rule which prohibited wearing any philosophical or religious symbol in the workplace.

The Labour Court in *Allpro Services* heard an appeal from the WRC concerning harassment in the workplace on the grounds of the claimant's religion and race, and the employer's vicarious liability for the acts of colleagues.

Covid-19 Vaccination Status

The ECJ considered whether legislation in Italy, which imposed a vaccination obligation on health professionals, resulting in the claimant *DM* being suspended without pay for refusing the vaccine, was discriminatory.

AGE

[3.02] ***Versicherungsanstalt öffentlich Bediensteter, Eisenbahnen und Bergbau (BVAEB) v BB[1]—European Court of Justice—request for a preliminary ruling from Austria—Directive 2000/78/EC[2]—social policy—equal treatment in employment and occupation—prohibition of discrimination on grounds of age—retirement pension—national legislation providing retroactively for treatment in the same way of different categories of civil servants with respect to pension rights***

1 *Versicherungsanstalt öffentlich Bediensteter, Eisenbahnen und Bergbau (BVAEB) v BB* (Case C-681/21).

2 Directive 2000/78/EC on establishing a general framework for equal treatment in employment and occupation.

This request for a preliminary ruling concerned the interpretation of art 2(1) and (2)(a) and art 6(1) of Directive 2000/78/EC establishing a general framework for equal treatment in employment and occupation. The request arose from proceedings between the applicant, Austria's insurance fund for civil servants, public officials, the railways and mining sector, and the respondent, a retired civil servant, who was born in 1946. The dispute concerned the respondent's statutory pension scheme, the gross monthly amount of which was fixed by decision of the applicant in 2012, and thereafter adjusted annually.

Austria's statutory scheme governing civil service pension entitlements made a distinction, broadly, between those recipients born before 1 January 1955 and those born on or after that date, for the purposes of adjustments to pension entitlements. The effect was that the pension adjustments of those born before that date were capped during the first three years of receipt, while those born on or after that date were subject to a statutory 'parallel calculation' when determining their pension entitlements.

In 2015, the respondent challenged an adjustment to her pension entitlements and requested a decision from the applicant, which she challenged while requesting pension arrears. She argued that the law was discriminatory on grounds of age as it put her (older) cohort, ie, those born before 1 January 1955, on a less favourable scheme when compared to those born after that date. This, she argued was incompatible with art 2 of Directive 2000/78/EC. Her action was dismissed by Austria's Federal Administrative Court, which found that the capping of pension adjustments, that applied only to civil servants born before 1 January 1955, was compatible with Directive 2000/78/EC and that the difference in treatment was justified, as civil servants born on or after that date were subject to a 'parallel calculation', which was less favourable.

On appeal, the Supreme Administrative Court set aside that judgment, observing that, under the statutory scheme, the parallel calculation did not apply to all civil servants born after 31 December 1954, resulting in a 'third category' of retired civil servant, who were subject neither to capped pension adjustments nor to parallel calculations. It concluded that the impugned statutory provision constituted 'unjustified direct discrimination on grounds of age for civil servants born before 1 January 1955'. The matter was referred back to the Federal Administrative Court, which subsequently upheld the respondent's appeal.

The law was amended with retroactive effect from 1 January 2011, so that the previously advantaged third category was placed on the same footing as those born before 1 January 1955.

Following a 2019 decision by the applicant in relation to the respondent's pension entitlements in the wake of the judgment, the respondent again appealed to the Federal Administrative Court. She argued that the amended law still contravened art 2 of Directive 2000/78/EC as the position of older civil servants was unchanged, meaning that the discrimination on grounds of age was ongoing. That appeal was dismissed on the ground that the issue was *res judicata*.

The applicant appealed on a point of law to the Supreme Administrative Court (the referring Court), which stayed proceedings and referred a question to the European

Court of Justice (the 'ECJ') for a preliminary ruling, in essence asking whether art 2(1) and (2)(a) and art 6(1) of Directive 2000/78/EC must be read as precluding a national provision which, in order to 'eliminate' discrimination on grounds of age, retroactively removes the civil service pension entitlements of those previously advantaged under the statutory scheme and treats them the same way as those previously disadvantaged.

The ECJ observed that a national legislature is entitled, as a matter of settled European law, to treat recipients in a previously advantaged category in the same way as those within a disadvantaged category—once compliant legislation has been introduced to reinstate equal treatment as appropriate. Notwithstanding the principle of legal certainty, a measure implementing EU law may, exceptionally, have retroactive effect 'where an overriding reason in the public interest so demands'. Accordingly, the ECJ answered the referring Court's question in the affirmative, 'in the absence of an overriding reason in the public interest'.

[3.03] ***Commissioner of An Garda Síochána and The Minister for Justice, Equality and Law Reform v Boyle[3]—Labour Court—appeal from decision of Equality Officer—Employment Equality Acts 1998 to 2021, s 83(1)—discrimination on grounds of age—maximum age limit for recruitment to An Garda Síochána—whether age cap justified under law—whether age cap appropriate or necessary***

This was an appeal by the respondent from a decision of an Equality Officer under the Employment Equality Acts 1998 to 2021 upholding a complaint of discrimination and making an award of €12,700.

The claimant originally applied for a position in An Garda Síochána when he was 25 years of age. On that occasion, he failed the medical examination because of the height requirement in place at the time. Following the abolition of the height requirement, the claimant again applied in 2005, this time aged 48, and was advised that he did not meet the age eligibility requirements.

The respondent accepted that the claimant raised a *prima facie* case of discrimination on grounds of age but submitted that the age cap of 35 years was justified under the Employment Equality Acts 1998 to 2021 and the framework Directive transposed into Irish law by the Garda Síochána (Admissions and Appointments) Regulations 1988[4] concerning admissions and appointments to An Garda Síochána. It was submitted that the age cap was required to achieve the legitimate objective of 'ensuring the operational capacity of An Garda Síochána'.

The evidence before the Court was that all gardaí, regardless of age, must be capable of, and are expected to, carry out the full range of duties from the beginning to the end of their career. There is no facility to place older members on light duties, unless

3 *Commissioner of An Garda Síochána and The Minister for Justice, Equality and Law Reform v Boyle* EDA234.

4 Garda Síochána (Admissions and Appointments) Regulations 1988 (SI 164/88).

recommended by the CMO. On the evidence, the current average age in An Garda Síochána is 41 years of age and there are no roles related to age in its ranks. It was agreed that there is currently no measurement of how physically fit the current force is.

The Court was therefore not persuaded that the objective of safeguarding the operational capacity of An Garda Síochána required exclusive recruitment below the age of 35 and found that the respondent had failed to establish a correlation between the age cap and the requirement of a high fitness level. Existing physical fitness tests as part of the recruitment process could constitute 'an appropriate and less onerous measure' rather than fixing an age cap of 35. In light of medical evidence of individual differences in respect of chronological aging and biological aging, the respondent had failed to establish that the characteristic of a high level of fitness is inevitably related to a particular age. The Court concluded that the age limit of 35 was neither appropriate nor necessary, having regard to the objective of training recruits and the need for a reasonable period to allow those recruits to become effective in the job.

Accordingly, the appeal failed.

[3.04] ***Imperial College Healthcare NHS Trust and Ziprin v Matar*[5]*—UK Employment Appeal Tribunal—appeal from employment tribunal—Equality Act 2010—age discrimination—less favourable treatment due to age—remedy***

These appeals were brought by the respondents against the decision of an employment judge upholding the claimant's complaint of direct age discrimination and making a consequent award of damages.

The claimant was employed by the first respondent NHS trust as a locum consultant. In 2017, the claimant was in his late 50s and intended to retire at age 60. It was became apparent that the claimant's employment was in breach of NHS regulations on the appointment of consultants, as he was not on the specialist register. At the time, the claimant was, separately, the subject of an investigation arising out of clinical concerns and his practice was restricted. In the circumstances, the regulatory matter was not raised with him, however it was raised with younger locum consultants in the same position.

The investigation concluded with no criticism of the claimant's clinical competence and restrictions to his practice were no longer necessary. The claimant was told that he could not continue as a locum consultant as he was not on the specialist register and would have to transfer to the role of specialist doctor and take a pay cut of £35,000. The employment tribunal found that the respondents had, when raising the regulatory issue with the claimant, failed to provide the same support and encouragement to enroll on the specialist register as it had for another younger locum consultant working in the same division. This was found to have arisen from age-related assumptions that the claimant would not accept a lower status position and was nearing his intended retirement in any event.

5 *Imperial College Healthcare NHS Trust and Ziprin v Matar* [2023] EAT 1.

The claimant resigned in 2018, citing inability to return to work at the same level and with the same autonomy.

The employment tribunal found that the claimant had established a *prima facie* case of age discrimination and upheld his claim of constructive, unfair and wrongful dismissal and of direct age discrimination. At a remedy hearing, the tribunal found that, had the claimant not suffered unlawful discrimination, he would have accepted an intended offer from the first respondent to work out his locum consultant contract until his retirement in May 2019 (believing it to be lawful) and the parties' employment relationship would have continued, though he would not have sought specialist registration and would not have accepted a position of lower status.

The UK EAT found that the employment tribunal was entitled to view the claimant's circumstances as materially similar to the comparator, although it had erred in failing to have regard to the respondents' reasons for the difference in treatment. The tribunal had properly applied the burden of proof and had been entitled to find that a *prima facie* case of age discrimination was made out. It had permissibly found that the respondents made assumptions relating to the claimant's age and the award of damages was appropriate to the 'reality of the counterfactual situation'. Further, the result did not offend against public policy.

The appeals were accordingly dismissed.

AGE/MANDATORY RETIREMENT

[3.05] ***McLoughlin & Sons Hardware Ltd v Butler[6]—Labour Court—appeal from Workplace Relations Commission—Employment Equality Acts 1998 to 2021, s 83(1)—discrimination on grounds of age—discrimination on gender ground—mandatory retirement policy—objective justification—flexibility of policy***

This was an appeal by the claimant from two decisions of an Adjudication Officer under the Employment Equality Act 1998. The claimant alleged that she was discriminated against on gender and age grounds in circumstances where the respondent employer sought to compel her to retire on reaching her 65th birthday, having permitted a number of male colleagues to continue in their employment beyond that age.

The claimant was employed by the respondent as a receptionist from 1998 until 2020, working part-time for most of that period. She was placed on temporary lay-off following the onset of the Covid-19 pandemic in March 2020 and did not return to work thereafter. She advised her managing director that she wished to be put forward for redundancy—having learned that redundancy had been offered to a number of her colleagues who were laid off—but was informed that, as she was due to retire on reaching her 65th birthday in September 2020, she would not be made redundant.

6 *McLoughlin & Sons Hardware Ltd/McLoughlins Trading Company v Butler* EDA232.

The respondent subsequently acceded to a request for a six-month extension of the claimant's employment beyond her 65th birthday, though the claimant did not take it up.

The respondent's position was that it operated a policy of mandatory retirement for all employees on reaching the age of 65, though it was accepted that two male comparators named by the claimant had worked beyond that age. The first comparator, a senior sales manager, had agreed to stay on until a suitable replacement could be found. The second, a financial controller, had been absent for a number of months due to illness in the period leading up to his 65th birthday and had agreed to remain in his role to ensure an orderly handover. The Court found these explanations to be clear and cogent. In view of the facts, the claim of less favourable treatment on the gender ground was not well-founded.

The claimant submitted that the respondent's claimed policy of mandatory retirement was manifestly in breach of the Employment Equality Act 1998, there being no reference to such a policy in either the claimant's contract of employment or the respondent's employee handbook.

The respondent was unable to advance any objective justification for its policy of mandatory retirement and the Court found this element of the claimant's case to be well founded. The appropriate level of compensation was measured at €3,000, having regard to the totality of the circumstances giving rise to the appeal.

CIVIL STATUS

[3.06] ***Ellis v Bacon and Advanced Fire Solutions Ltd*[7]*—UK Employment Appeal Tribunal—appeal from employment tribunal—Equality Act 2010—statutory test—unfavourable treatment—discrimination—marital status—fact of marriage as opposed to the identity of spouse***

The claimant was a bookkeeper employed by Advanced Fire Solutions Ltd. She married the managing director and majority shareholder of the company, Mr Bacon. Subsequently she became a director and shareholder of the company. In 2012, Mr Ellis became a director and a 10% shareholder of the company. He became managing director in August 2017. Also in August 2017, the claimant informed her husband that she wished to separate. She was suspended from the company in January 2018 and dismissed in June 2018 by letter signed by Mr Ellis in his role as managing director. A 'wholly baseless' complaint was also made against the claimant to the police.

The claimant brought a claim to the employment tribunal, alleging that she had been treated unfavourably by Mr Ellis as managing director due to her marital status. It was claimed that Mr Ellis was acting on behalf of Mr Bacon.

7 *Ellis v Bacon and Advanced Fire Solutions Ltd* [2022] EAT 188.

The employment tribunal found that Mr Ellis had 'sided with Mr Bacon in relation to the marital dispute and was compliant with him in removing the claimant's directorship, not paying her dividends, reporting her to the police and suspending and dismissing her on spurious grounds'. It was held that Mr Ellis had discriminated against the claimant based on her marital status.

Mr Ellis appealed to the UK EAT on the grounds that the tribunal had erred in law in failing to properly address the statutory test as to the cause of any unfavourable treatment or to consider the appropriate hypothetical comparator.

The EAT set out the relevant sections of the Equality Act 2010, including ss 4, 8, and 13 and referred to *Hawkins v Atex Group Ltd*,[8] which it described as a similar case. *Hawkins* held that the characteristic protected by the Equality Act 2010 is the fact of being married, and that it is essential to establish that the respondents were motivated by that marital status in order to claim protection.

The EAT described the issue as being whether Mr Ellis treated the claimant unfavourably because she was married or whether the unfavourable treatment occurred because she was married to Mr Bacon. The EAT allowed Mr Ellis' appeal on the grounds that the employment tribunal failed to assess whether the treatment in question was because of the claimant's marital status or the identity of the claimant's husband. The employment tribunal also failed to consider an appropriate comparator, i.e., a person in a close relationship with the claimant's husband but not married to him, to discover whether they would be treated differently to the original claimant.

The EAT allowed the appeal.

DISABILITY

[3.07] ***G Bruss Gmbh Dichtungstechnik v Pietrzyk*[9]*—Labour Court—appeal from Workplace Relations Commission—Employment Equality Acts 1998 to 2021—disability—Covid-19—face mask—policy—mandatory mask wearing in communal areas—indirect discrimination***

The claimant worked for the respondent company. In November 2020, the respondent introduced a mandatory requirement to wear face masks for all employees in communal areas, when moving to and from work stations, and when unable to maintain social distancing between colleagues in work stations. The policy was introduced following approval by management, the health and safety committee and the company director. The claimant complained that she had a medical issue which meant that she could not wear a face mask. She was absent from December 2020 to August 2021 on a medically certified absence and thereafter on unpaid absence until the termination of her employment in September 2021. The claimant claimed that her medical condition constituted a disability under the Employment Equality Acts 1998 to 2021. She claimed that she

8 *Hawkins v Atex Group Ltd* [2012] ICR 1315.

9 *G Bruss Gmbh Dichtungstechnik v Pietrzyk* EDA2332.

had proposed alternative accommodations to her having to wear a face covering at work, but that the respondent did not adopt any of these accommodations. The claimant argued that she was effectively denied access to employment and this amounted to discrimination on the grounds of her disability. She brought a claim to the WRC and was successful.

The respondent appealed to the Labour Court. It argued that no discrimination occurred. It pointed to the context in which the policy had been introduced, ie, the global pandemic, and all the relevant national health guidelines issued. It noted that the claimant would not have to wear a face mask at her work station, but only in communal areas and moving to and from her work station. It pointed out that the basis for the policy was the obligation the respondent had to maintain a safe and healthy workplace for all employees. The respondent argued that the claimant did not provide any evidence of her alleged disability until June 2021.

The Labour Court considered both domestic and European caselaw. It held that it was satisfied that the claimant had established a *prima facie* case of discrimination, which shifted the burden to the respondent. The Court considered whether there were objective grounds justifying the existence of the requirement complained of and held that the policy in question was not related to a discriminatory ground; that it responded to a real and legitimate need; and that the means used to respond to that need were appropriate. The Court acknowledged that the claimant had offered alternatives to her having to wear a mask in communal areas, such as staggered start times and the introduction of antigen testing for the claimant, and noted that these were considered by the respondent and the company doctor.

The Court held that it could not conclude that less discriminatory means were available to achieve the real and legitimate need on the part of the respondent at the material time. Accordingly, it was held that the respondent's approach was wholly proportionate to the need of preserving the health and safety of employees.

The appeal, therefore, succeeded.

[3.08] ***Riley v Direct Line Insurance Group plc[10]—UK Employment Appeal Tribunal—appeal from employment tribunal—unfair dismissal—disability discrimination—reasonable adjustments—termination by mutual agreement—refusal to extend time***

The claimant appealed the decision of an employment tribunal rejecting his complaint of unfair dismissal on the basis that his employment was terminated by mutual agreement. He also appealed on the grounds that the tribunal had failed to make reasonable adjustments in the way he was cross-examined at the hearing. Complaints of a failure to make reasonable adjustments were found to have been presented out of time and the claimant also appealed the tribunal's refusal to extend time.

10 *Riley v Direct Line Insurance plc* [2023] EAT 118.

The claimant was employed by the respondent, Direct Line, as a home claims advisor between 2012 and 2018. The claimant was disabled under the Equality Act 2010 by reason of Asperger's syndrome, depression and anxiety. He was enrolled on the respondent's private health insurance scheme which offered support until retirement age in the event of incapacity.

From 2014 until 2017, the claimant was absent from work with anxiety and depression, during much of which he was paid 80% of his normal salary. A rehabilitation specialist proposed a phased return to work with workplace adjustments, including noise-cancelling headphones and Asperger's awareness training for management.

Although the claimant returned to work, on 25 May 2018 he contacted his managers to say that he would not be coming into work due to his mental health. He was assessed as unfit to work because of ongoing anxiety and paranoia. The claimant's health insurer advised the respondent that it was difficult to see the claimant recovering sufficiently to perform his role 'in the near to medium future'.

In August 2018, a meeting took place between the claimant and management. The claimant was advised of the health insurer's 'pay direct' scheme, under which the claimant would cease employment with the respondent and the insurer would 'pick up the payments'. At the claimant's request, the respondent confirmed with the insurer that the claimant would receive payments under the scheme until state pension age. A final meeting took place during which the claimant was advised that the insurer would pay him directly and that his employment would end. He was then informed by letter that he was 'dismissed' with effect from 19 September 2018, on grounds of capability due to ill health.

The claimant's case was that he had not understood what was going on and that he had been tricked or coerced by the respondent.

At a case management hearing, the employment judge directed that, in order to enable the claimant to fully participate in the hearing, cross-examination would be by way of oral and written questions, though the procedure could be 'varied or adjusted' by the tribunal. Over the first two days of the hearing, the claimant was cross-examined in the normal way without being provided with written copies of questions.

The UK EAT was satisfied from the evidence that there had been a discussion about reasonable adjustments before the claimant's cross-examination began and that the claimant had stated that he would not need to have a question written down if it was straightforward and he would indicate if he required the question in writing. The EAT did not accept that the employment tribunal was bound by the case-management direction, which 'would have been rather cumbersome and may have created its own difficulties for [the claimant]' and which, in any event, 'expressly contemplated variation or adjustment' by the tribunal. The claimant had not suffered any substantive unfairness arising from the lack of written questions.

The EAT was further satisfied that it was open to the tribunal to find that the termination came about by 'free mutual consent' of the parties. The tribunal had gone to 'considerable lengths' to support its conclusion that the claimant had not been tricked or coerced.

It observed that the claimant participated in the discussions with management and had made a fully informed decision.

The tribunal found that, although the respondent had failed to issue the claimant with noise-cancelling headphones and had not undergone the recommended Asperger's awareness training, the claimant was unfit to work from 25 May 2018 and the adjustments would not, in the event, have made any difference to the outcome. Any complaint of failure to make reasonable adjustments had to be made within three months of that date. In refusing to extend time, the tribunal found that in August 2018, the claimant decided that he would opt for termination to take up the insurance benefit. A 'change of mind … about an agreement made by both parties in good faith, was not a ground for a just and equitable extension of time'. The EAT was, again, satisfied that the tribunal was entitled to give 'substantial weight' to that finding.

The appeal was, accordingly, dismissed.

[3.09] ***Davies v EE Ltd*[11]*—UK Employment Appeal Tribunal—appeal from employment tribunal—disability discrimination—Equality Act 2010—provision, criterion and practice—whether the tribunal erred in concluding that a PCP was not applied by the respondent***

The claimant was employed as a customer service representative by the respondent in a call centre in Plymouth, until her resignation in February 2020. Her contract provided for an average of 40 hours work per week, with shift patterns to be confirmed by her manager, but falling between core hours of 7.45 am and 10.15 pm Monday to Sunday.

In August 2019, the claimant suffered impairment to her vocal chords, and the respondent conceded that she was disabled at all material times. She was absent from work for a time with pain and discomfort and undertook a phased return to work. In a stage 1 absence procedure meeting, the claimant requested an occupational health assessment (which was granted) and stated that she wanted to work part-time and that her family wanted to see more of her. She was issued a stage 1 warning after the meeting.

The claimant returned to her full-time hours, but it was noted by the tribunal that part-time roles were available, although there were no immediate vacancies at the time. In a medical report, occupational health recommended workplace adjustments and consideration of a reduction in the claimant's hours.

In February 2020, the claimant informed her manager that she had a hospital appointment. Her manager advised the claimant that she would have to use her annual leave or make up the time. The claimant resigned the following day. In response, her manager stated that she wished that there had been a part-time role for the claimant and praised the claimant's past performance.

The employment tribunal did not accept that a PCP requiring employees, including the claimant, to complete a full-time working pattern of 40 hours per week, with each shift approximately 9½ hours in length, was made out on the facts of the case. It found that,

---

11 *Davies v EE Ltd* [2022] EAT 191.

at the time of the claimant's resignation, the respondent had employed some workers on a part-time basis, had acted on the recommendations of the claimant's GP to phase her return to work with reduced hours, had allowed and encouraged the claimant to take occupational health breaks, and had made enquiries about transferring the claimant to part-time work if and when a vacancy arose.

On appeal, the UK EAT held that the tribunal erred in concluding that the respondent had not applied a PCP placing the claimant at a substantial disadvantage in comparison with persons who were not disabled. While it is necessary for a PCP to have a degree of general applicability, it need not apply to the whole of the workforce. The tribunal's findings of fact did not alter the claimant's position of having worked a full-time role of 40 hours per week. This was a PCP, which formed a term of the claimant's contract of employment, and it applied from the point at which the respondent had constructive knowledge of the claimant's disability until the date of her resignation.

The appeal succeeded on this ground and the matter was remitted to a reconstituted tribunal for a fresh hearing.

[3.10] ***McQueen v General Optical Council*[12]*—UK Employment Appeal Tribunal—appeal from the employment tribunal—Equality Act 2010—disability—discrimination—autism spectrum disorder—causation—less favourable treatment—unreasonable conduct***

The claimant was an employee of the respondent. He had dyslexia, left-side hearing loss, was neurodivergent and had experienced some symptoms of Asperger's Syndrome. As a result, the claimant sometimes experienced difficulties interacting with colleagues. Several incidents occurred between the claimant, co-workers and senior colleagues which involved his becoming angry and confrontational in a manner described as a 'meltdown'. Ultimately this culminated in the issuing of warnings to the claimant and the initiation of a disciplinary procedure. The claimant resigned and issued proceedings under s 15 of the Equality Act 2010 for unfavourable treatment, alleging that the respondent had treated him unfavourably in disciplining him for behaviour that arose in consequence of his disabilities.

The employment tribunal held that most of the claimant's claims were out of time. In the case of other claims, the tribunal rejected the allegation that the respondent's treatment persisted over a period of time. It also found that the behaviour in question did not arise as a result the claimant's disabilities but due to his issues with authority and his temper. Accordingly, the claimant had not suffered discrimination 'because of something arising in consequence of' his disabilities as per the test set out in s 15 of the Equality Act 2010.

The claimant brought an appeal to the UK EAT, alleging that the tribunal had erred in its application of the test under s 15 of the Equality Act 2010. He also alleged that the tribunal failed to appreciate that his disabilities could have contributed to, rather than unilaterally caused, his behaviour.

12 *McQueen v General Optical Council* [2023] EAT 36.

The EAT was critical of the way in which the tribunal's decision was structured. Despite this, the EAT held that it was clear that the tribunal had correctly applied the causation test set out in s 15. The tribunal had held that the unfavourable treatment was a reaction to the claimant becoming loud and confrontational with his colleagues. This behaviour, it found, did not arise due to his disabilities. The EAT held that a correct reading of the tribunal's decision was that the claimant's disabilities 'did not play any part in the conduct that led to the unfavourable treatment complained of'. Accordingly, it was not a case where dual or multi-factor causation had to be analysed.

The appeal was therefore dismissed.

[3.11] ***Morris v Lauren Richards Ltd*[13]*—UK Employment Appeal Tribunal—appeal from employment tribunal—Equality Act 2010—disability—discrimination—long-term impairment—error of reasoning—cause of the impairment—anxiety***

The claimant was an employee of the respondent company. She brought a claim for disability discrimination based on events which allegedly occurred up to and including her dismissal. At a preliminary hearing of the employment tribunal, the tribunal held that the claimant was not a disabled person for the purposes of s 6 of the Equality Act 2010 (the '2010 Act'). The tribunal directed itself to Schedule 1 of the 2010 Act and the statutory guidance at paragraph 2 as to what constitutes the long-term effect of an impairment and found that the claimant suffered from a relevant impairment, being anxiety. However, it was held that although it impacted on the claimant's ability to carry out day-to-day tasks, the effect of the impairment was not long term. The tribunal found that the impairment began later than the claimant had argued, having lasted for only three-and-a-half months at the date of dismissal. Further, the tribunal did not consider the impairment was likely to last 12 months, or to persist once she left the respondent and its work environment. It was held that the reasons for the claimant's anxiety were her issues with her workplace and the demands of her work. The tribunal noted that the claimant did not have a pre-existing history of mental health issues, which suggested a particular vulnerability.

The claimant appealed this decision and both parties agreed that the tribunal had made an error of reasoning in taking into account that the causes of the claimant's anxiety were her issues in the workplace and the demands of her work, and that there was nothing to suggest that this anxiety would persist upon leaving the respondent's employ. The UK EAT agreed with this.

The EAT considered whether this error could be said not to have affected the outcome, as the respondent claimed. The EAT held that the tribunal had placed material weight on the fact that the workplace was the source of the claimant's anxiety and, once she left the workplace, this impairment would likely cease. The EAT held that a relevant question for the tribunal to ask itself in assessing the likelihood of persistence would be, if the substantial adverse effect continued, when would it stop and what would make it stop. The EAT found that the tribunal did address that question and concluded that, as the claimant would no longer be in the respondent's employ, the

13 *Morris v Lauren Richards Ltd* [2023] EAT 19.

impairment was not long term. The EAT attempted to review the evidence before the tribunal to reach its own conclusion as to what the outcome of the case should have been. This was, however, impossible, and therefore, the EAT refused to confirm the decision of the tribunal.

The EAT allowed the appeal. The case was remitted to the employment tribunal to determine whether the effect of the impairment as of the date of termination was likely to last for at least 12 months.

[3.12] ***Greasley-Adams v Royal Mail Group Ltd*[14]*—UK Employment Appeal Tribunal—appeal from employment tribunal—Employment Rights Act 1996—Equality Act 2010—autism spectrum disorder—bullying—disability discrimination—drivers—harassment—reasonableness—time limits—victimisation***

The claimant was disabled under s 6 of the Equality Act 2010, having an autistic spectrum disorder. He worked 30 hours per week for the respondent, as an MGV driver. The claimant's terms of employment were confirmed in a COT 3 agreement[15] entered into by the parties following a claim brought by the claimant, which was subsequently compromised. Despite that agreement, the claimant was concerned about his working conditions and felt that he was disadvantaged. He also made disclosures about infringements committed by other drivers in the respondent company, which were the subject of a whistleblowing claim. The claimant was accused of accessing and reading the personal records of a colleague. There was also a separate incident when the claimant suffered an autistic episode leading to a reaction by another colleague. His relationships with his colleagues began to worsen and several bullying and harassment complaints were made against the claimant.

An investigation was initiated by Mr Walker of the respondent company and certain complaints were upheld against the claimant. The claimant complained about Mr Walker's conclusions and recommendations. He submitted a grievance alleging that the investigation had failed to recognise that the claimant had been subject to bullying and harassment also. He alleged that management had bullied him by disclosing confidential information about him; that his colleagues had spread rumours about him; and that he had been the victim of a number of negative comments by his colleagues about his disability and the overtime completed by him under the COT 3 agreement. This grievance was investigated by Ms Stevens of the respondent company and every allegation was rejected by her. Ms Stevens made certain recommendations, including mediation between the respondent and claimant. The claimant challenged Ms Steven's findings and rejected her recommendations by way of text message. This was treated as an appeal and Mr Kelly of the respondent company dealt with the matter. Ultimately, Mr Kelly did not find for the claimant and he too recommended mediation. Mediation was arranged but the claimant refused to participate.

The claimant brought proceedings before the employment tribunal under s 47B of the Employment Rights Act 1996 and ss 26 and 27 of the Equality Act 2010. The tribunal

---

14 *Greasley-Adams v Royal Mail Group Ltd* [2023] EAT 86.

15 A full and final settlement agreement following a dispute resolution process.

dismissed all of the claimant's claims. The claimant submitted an application for reconsideration. The tribunal substituted certain paragraphs of its original decision but otherwise confirmed it. The claimant sought to appeal the amended decision on grounds of harassment, time bar and victimisation.

The claimant's first ground of appeal concerned the significance of his awareness of the unwanted conduct carried out by the respondent. The claimant argued that the tribunal erred in its determination of the question of harassment by not having regard to conduct of which the claimant was not aware. The claimant contended that a person's dignity may still be compromised by conduct even if they are not aware of the unwanted conduct undermining it. The UK EAT looked to the text of s 26 of the Equality Act 2010 and concluded that the test therein was cumulative, i.e., A harasses B if they engage in unwanted conduct which violates B's dignity. In deciding whether this is the case, a number of factors have to be taken into account:

> '(a) the perception of B;
> (b) the other circumstances of the case;
> (c) whether it is reasonable for the conduct to have that effect'.

The EAT concluded that:

> 'In other words, the perception of the person claiming harassment is a key and indeed mandatory component in determining whether or not harassment has occurred'.

Therefore, if the claimant had no awareness of the unwanted conduct, it could not be said that there was any perception.

The second ground of appeal concerned whether the tribunal had erred in determining the question of reasonableness in terms of s 26, having regard to the circumstances in which the conduct came to light, i.e., the bullying and harassment investigation. The claimant argued that this was too narrow an approach, and that it did not consider other factors such as comments made prior to the investigation and the context in which the comments were made. The EAT considered the tribunal's judgment and held that the unwanted conduct and the context of same were relevant factors to be considered, and the tribunal did not misdirect itself on this point.

The third ground of appeal related to the question of time bar in the harassment claim. The EAT held that it failed to establish any error of law on the part of the tribunal.

The final ground of appeal concerned perversity and the judgment of the tribunal. The tribunal held that being subject to a bullying and harassment complaint was a detriment but that the complaints were not submitted because the claimant had carried out a protected act (in this case, exercising his rights under the COT3 agreement, particularly overtime) but because of the effect his behaviour had on his colleagues. The claimant argued that this was perverse having regard to the evidence which, he said, showed a causal link between the claimant carrying out a protected act and the bringing of the complaint. The EAT held that the tribunal had analysed all the evidence before it and that it had ample material to allow it to reach the conclusions it did.

The EAT dismissed the claimant's claim.

[3.13] ***Boesi v Asda Stores Ltd*[16]*—UK Employment Appeal Tribunal—appeal from employment tribunal—UK Equality Act 2010—disability discrimination—hypothetical comparator—relevant circumstances***

This appeal concerned the construction of a hypothetical comparator in a claim of direct discrimination due to disability.

The claimant was employed by the respondent supermarket as a warehouse operative from 2012 until her dismissal in 2019. The claimant was disabled by reasons of a degenerative disc disease in her lower back, of which the respondent was aware. From 2014, the claimant had to take a number of periods of ill-health absence. In March 2018, an initial request for three months' healthcare leave was agreed, then extended to March 2019. When that came to an end, the claimant was again signed off as unfit to work for a further three months. The claimant's role entailed physical activity, including bending and lifting, and the tribunal found that the requirements of her work placed the claimant at a substantial disadvantage. Following a final capability meeting, the claimant was told that she would be dismissed for incapability.

The complaint of disability discrimination was in connection with the respondent's failure to offer the claimant light duties, as well as her dismissal. The tribunal evaluated the claimant's case on the basis of a hypothetical comparator 'who is not disabled … but who has been absent from work for the same length of time, for whom a GP and a physio has provided the same sort of information and who has responded in the same way as [the claimant] has done in various meetings with the respondent'. The tribunal concluded that no less favourable treatment had been demonstrated and the claim of direct discrimination failed.

On appeal, the UK EAT was cognisant that the tribunal had been required to determine whether the claimant's case was one of direct discrimination *because of* disability (the claim having been brought under s 13 of the Equality Act 2010). The tribunal had not concluded that the respondent's failure to offer the claimant light duties was because of her disability *per se*. Rather, it was because the claimant was not fit to return to work.

Similarly, the tribunal had been clear that the respondent's decision to dismiss was because the claimant had been away from work for a year-and-a-half. The medical advice was that she remained unfit for work with no prospect of her returning in the immediate future. Again, the reason for the dismissal was not the claimant's disability as such.

The tribunal 'was bound to impute the relevant circumstances to the hypothetical comparator'. It would have failed in its task 'if it had not discounted that which was at the heart of the case on the facts it had found'. The tribunal had been entitled to find that the reason for the impugned treatment was not the claimant's disability 'as such', though it might have related to something 'in consequence of that disability'. Thus, the tribunal permissibly found that the hypothetical comparator would have been treated in the same way.

The appeal was, accordingly, dismissed.

---

16 *Boesi v Asda Stores Ltd* [2023] EAT 49.

[3.14] ***Pilkington UK Ltd v Jones*[17]*—UK Employment Appeal Tribunal—appeal from employment tribunal—Equality Act 2010—disability—unfavourable treatment—'something arising'—causation—employer's belief that the claimant was engaged in secondary employment during sickness absence***

The claimant had been employed by the respondent, a glass manufacturer, from 1983. He was summarily dismissed in October 2019 for gross misconduct.

Between January and November 2018, the claimant was absent from work due to lasting effects of radiotherapy treatment. The respondent redeployed the claimant to light duties; however, as a result of chronic pain the claimant continued to be absent from work at regular intervals. An occupational health report opined that the claimant's condition was 'very disabling' and that the claimant was not currently fit for work and, indeed, would be permanently prevented from undertaking manual work.

In March 2019, the respondent received information that the claimant had been seen wearing work boots. The claimant was filmed by surveillance agents engaged by the respondent; this produced 'unremarkable' footage of the claimant going to a friend's farm but gave the respondent cause to suspect that the claimant might be working elsewhere. A disciplinary process ensued, on foot of which it was determined that the claimant had undertaken physical activity during sickness absence. The claimant's position was that the purpose of his attendance at the farm was to improve his mental health, which had deteriorated as a consequence of his declining physical health. Accordingly, the misconduct on the claimant's part was as a result of his disability.

The employment tribunal found that the claimant's dismissal was a consequence of the respondent believing him to have engaged in physical activity. There was a causal link between that belief (the 'something arising') and the dismissal, which amounted to unfavourable treatment. The respondent appealed against the decision of the employment tribunal.

The UK EAT conceded that 'at first blush' it might appear surprising that a belief was the 'something arising', given the objective nature of the test. Nevertheless, it was recognised that a subjective state of mind can be 'objectively observed from surrounding facts'. A state of mind which leads to a reaction can be further indicative of a subjective motivation, resulting in unfavourable treatment. In this way, a belief can be properly categorised as 'something arising' from a disability. The respondent's subjective belief resulted from a combination of factors (as opposed to a chain of causation), of which the claimant's absence was a substantial component, and thus it arose from the disability.

Accordingly, the tribunal had correctly identified a causal connection between the respondent's belief and the claimant's disability and the appeal was dismissed.

17 *Pilkington UK Ltd v Jones* [2023] EAT 90.

[3.15] ***AECOM Ltd v Mallon*[18]*—UK Employment Appeal Tribunal—appeal from employment tribunal—Equality Act 2010—disability—discrimination—error or fact—job applicants—perversity—reasonable adjustments—substantial adverse effect—online form—dyspraxia—PCP—reasonableness—genuine applicant***

The claimant had dyspraxia and therefore struggled with written communication. He worked for the respondent in 2017 in its research and development team, but was dismissed during his probationary period due to unsatisfactory performance. In 2018, the claimant sought employment in a research and development role in another office belonging to the respondent. The application process was to take place online. He contacted the respondent's HR manager to explain that he had dyspraxia and would prefer to complete his application over the phone. He received a reply that all candidates were required to fill out the application form online but assistance was available if needed. The HR manager inquired several times in correspondence as to which parts of the form he found challenging to complete. The claimant did not respond to this query, but instead restated his preferences for an oral application.

The claimant argued that the online presentation was a provision, criterion or practice ('PCP') that placed him at a substantial disadvantage and the respondent was therefore required under s 20 of the Equality Act 2010 to make reasonable adjustments for him. The respondent did not accept that the claimant had suffered substantial disadvantage as it contended that he did not genuinely wish to apply for the job. It argued that the new role was the same as the role that the claimant had had in 2017 and that the manager was the same manager that had dismissed him while he was on probation. This evidence was undisputed.

The employment tribunal held that the claimant's intention to apply for the job was a genuine one, despite having been dismissed from a similar role on a similar team in 2017. It noted that the new role represented a fresh start for the claimant and that the claimant would not have considered his being dismissed previously on probation to be a bar to his application for the new role. The tribunal pointed to the respondent's knowledge of the claimant's dyspraxia and his associated issues with written communication and therefore was on notice as to the substantial disadvantage that the online application process had placed on him. It considered the HR manager's attempts to ascertain the particular aspects of the online application process that the claimant found challenging and said that it was unreasonable to expect him to discuss his disability by email, given his written communication issues. The HR manager, it was found, should have contacted him by phone instead. The tribunal held that it should have made reasonable adjustments for him regarding the application process for the new role.

The respondent appealed to the UK EAT on the grounds that: the tribunal had made a perverse finding that the claimant was a genuine applicant for the new role; the tribunal applied the wrong test on knowledge of substantial disadvantage; the tribunal applied

18 *AECOM Ltd v Mallon* [2023] EAT 104. See *Arthur Cox Employment Law Yearbook 2021* at **[4.31]** for previous decision of UK EAT in *Mallon v AECOM Ltd* UKEAT/0175/20/LA, [2021] IRLR 438.

the wrong test regarding the lengths to which the respondent should have gone to make inquiries about the extent of the claimant's difficulties.

The EAT noted that the tribunal had not sufficiently considered the evidence tendered that the role in question was the same role that the claimant had had in 2017, and that the manager was the same manager that had previously dismissed him. It held that the tribunal's finding that the new role would have been a fresh start for the claimant was perverse. The EAT held that this perverse finding was significant in the tribunal's balancing exercise as to whether the claimant was a genuine applicant.

The EAT held that the tribunal had incorrectly approached the question of knowledge as it related to the claimant's alleged substantial disadvantage in asking whether the respondent knew or ought to have known that the claimant had a disability that was likely to place him at a substantial disadvantage. Rather, the tribunal should have considered whether the respondent knew or ought to have known of the particular substantial disadvantage that the claimant was placed under by the alleged PCP. The EAT reasoned, however, that the tribunal had answered the correct questions through its findings that the respondent knew that the claimant found the online application challenging but did not know which specific aspects of it were challenging to him and that they should have phoned him for clarification, given his difficulties in written communication.

The EAT considered whether the tribunal had approached the question of whether the respondent should have correctly made inquiries as to the extent and scope of the claimant's issues by omitting to state that the respondent was only required to make 'reasonable' inquiries about same. Given the fact that the tribunal had used language relating to 'reasonableness' in its dealing with the question, it was held that it had applied the correct test. The EAT held that it was not perverse to find that it was unreasonable of the respondent to expect the claimant to respond to the HR manager with an explanation as to the extent of his difficulties via email, given his dyspraxia diagnosis and the fact that he had asked for an adjustment to avoid applying for the new role via an online form.

The appeal was allowed in part and the case was remitted to the same tribunal to decide whether the claimant was a genuine applicant in light of the EAT judgment.

[3.16] ***Pipe v Coventry University Higher Education Corporation*[19]*—UK Employment Appeal Tribunal—appeal from employment tribunal—Equality Act 2010—sleep disorder—ADHD—disability discrimination—indirect age discrimination—justification—knowledge—proportionality—reasonable adjustments—pathway to progression—PCP***

The claimant was a lecturer in journalism with the respondent university. In 2017, the respondent introduced a framework for internal progression within the university. Applicants were invited to prove that they met the standards required for progression and that there was a business need for their new position. Candidates for a grade 7 position had to 'have attained a PhD or, exceptionally, demonstrate equivalence in

19 *Pipe v Coventry University Higher Education Corporation* [2023] EAT 73.

contribution to professional practice'. It was common cause that the respondent was aware in 2016 that the claimant suffered from a sleep disorder. The claimant applied for a grade 7 position in 2017. His candidacy was rejected by the Head of School as he had not attained a PhD as required and there was not a business case for such a position.

Around the same time, the claimant was formally assessed by a neurologist who concluded that he had a sleep disorder that would make the attainment of a PhD challenging. The claimant submitted a grievance that attached the neurologist's diagnosis, but this was rejected by the respondent. The claimant applied for progression once again on 12 March 2018. He informed the respondent that, as he had a 'declared disability—a long-term sleep disorder that affects memory, focus and organisation, and general health', he had stopped working towards his PhD. His candidacy was rejected. Among the reasons given was that 'budget availability' was not confirmed for such a position. Subsequently, the claimant was diagnosed with ADHD and requested that the respondent reassess his application as a reasonable adjustment under the Equality Act 2010, on the basis that the condition would have had 'a significant impact on my ability to meet the requirements set out in the progression system'. The respondent refused his request.

The claimant made another application in 2019 and asked to be considered for promotion outside the framework process to a non-research teaching role as a reasonable adjustment. This was also refused. In 2020, the claimant made a formal grievance and asked to be promoted outside the framework to a teaching role with no research requirement. A grievance hearing took place where the claimant's abilities to teach and prepare material were found to have met the grade 7 level. Ultimately, however, the respondent refused to appoint the claimant to a teaching-only role as there was no option to create such a role at that time. In June 2020, a further application for a reasonable adjustment to be appointed to a teaching-focused role was refused and the respondent requested that the claimant refrain from making further applications. The claimant resigned in August 2020 and brought a claim to the employment tribunal alleging indirect discrimination (disability and age) and disability discrimination due to a failure to make reasonable adjustments.

The tribunal found that the respondent was not on notice of the full extent of the claimant's disabilities until late 2018. It noted that it was common cause that the framework had been applied as a provision, criterion or practice ('PCP') and examined what it entailed. It held that the PhD requirement had been applied flexibly so that, in practice, a PhD was not strictly required for progression but that a pathway to a PhD had to be established. Flexibility was also applied in relation to the nature of the PhD or equivalent. The tribunal rejected the claimant's submissions on the application of the PCP. As to whether the claimant experienced substantial disadvantage, the employment tribunal noted that the claimant had not established a business case for any role sought. The tribunal held that the adjustments sought were not reasonable and that the respondent had demonstrated that the means of achieving its legitimate aims were proportionate. Accordingly, any unfavourable treatment here was justified. The applicant appealed the matter to the UK EAT.

The EAT found that the tribunal had erred in finding that the respondent could not reasonably have known of the substantial disadvantage suffered by the claimant at the time of his 2018 application. The EAT noted that, by 2018, the full extent of the claimant's disability had become clear. As the tribunal had not had regard to the claimant's indication that he suffered from a disability in his application in March 2018 and the accompanying GP letter, the EAT held that the tribunal did not fully consider the entire picture that had been given to the respondent by that time. This however, became 'academic' given the ultimate conclusion that the tribunal reached, ie, that the claimant had not established a business case for his new role.

The EAT considered ss 19 and 20(3) of the Equality Act 2010 and found that the tribunal had erred in its identification of the PCP in this case. It had focused on the PhD 'requirement'. The EAT held that, even if the framework did not 'require' that an applicant have a PhD or be working towards one, the fact that it provided that others, without the claimant's disability, might have a greater choice of options for progression (because they could demonstrate the skills required to obtain a PhD and justify the contention of a pathway) could be sufficient to show disadvantage. The EAT found that the tribunal had failed to engage with such wider issues in its judgment.

The EAT held that the tribunal had erred in not properly assessing whether a relevant disadvantage arose from the application of a provision within the framework that would have advantaged those who could prove that they had the capability to get a PhD.

With regard to reasonable adjustments, the EAT held that the respondent demonstrated a willingness to consider alternative pathways to progression eg its express consideration of the claimant's request for a lecturing-only role. This was so, despite the respondent's decision that it would not be possible to create such a role without wider negative impact. The EAT found that the respondent was entitled to reach this conclusion. It was also held that the claimant's medical issues had not caused the unfavourable treatment in this case. The fact that there was no proven business case identified and the fact that no pathway for progression had been identified by the claimant were noted by the EAT.

The EAT acknowledged that the respondent's aims to adopt a consistent and transparent approach and establish high standards were legitimate, and held that the tribunal had considered these aims and had considered proportionality also.

It was noted that the tribunal had made no express findings in relation to the claimant's complaint that he had been deterred from applying for progression in 2020. In circumstances where the tribunal had erred in its approach to the identification of the PCP, the EAT allowed the appeal but only in relation to the indirect disability and age discrimination claims arising from the allegation that the claimant was so deterred. These claims were remitted for determination.

[3.17] *Lingard v Leading Learners Multi Academy Trust*[20]*—UK Employment Appeal Tribunal—appeal from employment tribunal—disability—constructive knowledge—occupational health report*

The claimant resigned from her position as head teacher with the respondent school and brought claims of constructive dismissal and disability discrimination in the

20 *Lingard v Leading Learners Multi Academy Trust* [2023] EAT 52.

employment tribunal. She alleged that she suffered from chronic high blood pressure, of which she asserted the respondent had been aware since 2014, when she was diagnosed. She claimed her condition had a 'substantial, adverse and long-term effect on [her] ability to perform her normal day-to-day activities'.

Although her claim for constructive dismissal succeeded, the claimant's claim of disability discrimination was dismissed. The employment tribunal rejected an assertion that the respondent had constructive knowledge of her disability.

The tribunal found that an occupational health report from November 2016 was not sufficient to 'fix' the respondent with the knowledge that the claimant had a disability. This report had expressed optimism that the claimant would soon return to school, and the tribunal found that the respondent would not have had any basis for thinking the claimant's symptoms were long term. There was no further evidence that the respondent would have known the claimant had those symptoms prior to the report.

Further reports were jointly obtained by the parties in the course of the litigation. A consultant cardiologist concluded that none of the claimant's symptoms were the result of hypertension, and that hypertension would not adversely affect her day-to-day life in the manner claimed. A psychiatrist attributed the claimant's symptoms to generalised anxiety disorder, not fulfilling the criteria of disability. Another report, requested by the claimant, led to the respondent conceding that the claimant was disabled, while still denying any knowledge of the disability at the relevant time.

On appeal, the UK EAT rejected an argument that the tribunal failed to direct itself as to the correct legal test for knowledge of an employee's disability, and in so doing had erred in law. Although, read in isolation, the tribunal's reasons did not accurately describe the law as regards knowledge of disability, the grounds of appeal were in reality 'a series of complaints as to findings of fact which the tribunal was entitled to make based on the evidence before it', and were not perverse. Thus, references in the reports to the likely date of knowledge of the disability (in circumstances where a mental health issue was identified for the first time) were matters which were 'plainly relevant' to the tribunal's enquiry; more so given that the claimant was herself unaware of the true nature of her disability. The appeal was dismissed.

The EAT also rejected a cross-appeal in relation to a finding that the claimant had not forged signatures on certain appraisal forms. That allegation had been raised by one witness and was evidence of opinion, not fact. The tribunal was entitled to conclude that the witness was mistaken, despite genuinely holding that belief.

[3.18] ***Williams v Newport City Council*[21]*—UK Employment Appeal Tribunal—appeal from employment tribunal—Equality Act 2010—anxiety—sick leave—reasonable adjustments—disability discrimination—social workers.***

The claimant was a social worker who had worked for the respondent council since 2011. The team that she worked with assessed the suitability of individuals to care

21 *Williams v Newport City Council* [2023] EAT 136.

for children. These decisions were challengeable in court. Although the claimant had not carried out any such assessments, the respondent required her to attend court in 2016 as a representative of the department. The claimant had not been involved in the matter and was unable to answer the Court's questions about particulars. The Judge was critical of her and the incident was a negative experience for the claimant. As a result, when the respondent indicated that the claimant was to commence carrying out assessments as part of her role and to attend court where required, she became anxious and signed off work. After a period of absence, a doctor confirmed that she was fit for work, but only if she was not required to attend court. The respondent refused to make adjustments for the claimant and the claimant remained on sick leave. The respondent dismissed her in August 2018.

The claimant brought a claim before the employment tribunal for disability discrimination and a failure to make reasonable adjustments. The tribunal made a finding that she suffered from anxiety and accepted that she remained unable to go to court. However, it was not satisfied that the impairment had the required substantial effect on her ability to carry out normal day-to-day activities during the period in question sufficient to bring her within s 6(1) of the Equality Act 2010 (the '2010 Act'). Her disability discrimination claim was therefore dismissed.

The UK EAT considered the tribunal's finding that the claimant had suffered from anxiety throughout her period of absence, which meant that she was unable to return to work if she was required to go to court. The EAT noted that medical evidence had been tendered by the claimant in this regard, which had been accepted by both the respondent and the tribunal. It was clear that the anxiety suffered by the claimant about the prospect of having to attend court impacted adversely on her ability to carry out day-to-day activities. In circumstances where the respondent stated that it would not make an adjustment for the claimant so that she did not have to attend court and there was no indication that this requirement was a temporary change or something that could be reconsidered, it followed that the claimant would not be able to return to work at all. The EAT held that the tribunal should have held that the claimant was a disabled person throughout the relevant period, as the effects of her anxiety were likely to last for at least 12 months.

The EAT ordered that the claim be remitted for reconsideration on the basis that the claimant was a disabled person for the period in question. The appeal was allowed.

FAMILY STATUS

[3.19] ***Saint John of God Community Services v Doherty*[22]*—Labour Court—appeal from Workplace Relations Commission—Employment Equality Acts 1998 to 2021, s 83(1)—discrimination on the ground of family status—remote work—redeployment—whether the employer discriminated against the employee in not facilitating her request to work from home***

22 *Saint John of God Community Services v Doherty* EDA2313.

The respondent appealed to the Labour Court against a decision of the WRC upholding a complaint of discrimination on the grounds of family status and awarding the claimant €45,000.

The claimant, who was an experienced social care worker, became employed by the respondent in 2016 and was an instructor in the employment services division. This entailed acting as a job coach to service users with disabilities, assisting them to find employment and supporting them in their roles.

In February 2020, the claimant became aware that she was pregnant with her second child. Her GP advised her to take time off work and issued a medical certificate; which was submitted to the Human Resources department. When the claimant returned to work, she resumed her normal work days until taking pre-booked annual leave, her return from which fell amid the March 2020 Covid-19 restrictions. The claimant advised her coordinator that her preference was to continue working in her role from home as she had no childcare support for her young child and was pregnant again. Her coordinator informed her that it was not possible to facilitate her request, that only pre-agreed annual leave was being granted, and that the only options for the claimant were unpaid leave or redeployment to a residential setting. The respondent's unchallenged evidence to the WRC was that it was prioritising support for its residential services at that time. The claimant decided against redeployment due to unavailability of childcare, nor could she afford to take unpaid leave. Her GP issued a medical certificate for a period of four weeks for pregnancy-related stress and low mood.

During her absence on certified sick leave, the claimant learned of pregnant colleagues who were permitted to work from home. She informed her supervisor, whom she had been assisting throughout her sick leave. Her supervisor replied that she also knew of two pregnant colleagues who were working in residential settings at that time. The claimant repeated her request to her coordinator, who again informed her that it was not possible to facilitate her working from home. The claimant grew concerned that her extended sick leave could impact on her future career. She also formed the view that her supervisor, who did not have children, and another colleague, who was the parent of a teenager, were being treated more favourably than the claimant. However, the Court held these were not appropriate comparators.

The claimant was medically signed off as cocooning. She advised her supervisor that she would not be returning to work before her maternity leave commenced. The claimant then noticed that her pay had been significantly reduced, her supervisor having earlier advised that the system would restore her to full pay. She contacted the respondent's HR officer who advised her as to the relevant HSE pay guidelines and suggested a meeting with the coordinator to discuss the matter further, which the claimant declined. The claimant remained on leave until she gave birth, immediately commencing maternity leave in October 2020 and resigning in 2021.

The Labour Court found that the respondent had taken the decision as early as mid-March 2020 to prioritise support for its residential services over its day-care services, and had redeployed available staff, including some with childcare responsibilities, to residential services. Those with childcare responsibilities for whom redeployment was not suitable were offered only unpaid leave.

A key issue in the case had been the claimant's decision to go on certified sick leave from the date that her pregnancy was confirmed, essentially remaining on leave until she gave birth and immediately taking up maternity leave. The respondent's evidence was that the claimant's absence on medical grounds was the reason she was not offered remote work when the facility to do so was made available.

The Court determined that the claimant's claim that she was discriminated against on grounds of family status was not well-founded and the decision of the Adjudication Officer was set aside. Accordingly, the appeal succeeded.

GENDER

[3.20] ***DX v INSS and TGSS*[23]*—European Court of Justice—request for a preliminary ruling from Spain—social policy—Directive 79/7/EEC,*[24] *art 6—equal treatment for men and women in matters of social security—national legislation providing for the right to a pension supplement for women only—ruling that national legislation discriminatory on grounds of sex—administrative practice to continue to apply the legislation in spite of ruling—pecuniary damages***

This request for a preliminary ruling concerned the interpretation of Directive 79/7/EEC on the progressive implementation of the principle of equal treatment for men and women in matters of social security. The request arose in proceedings between the applicant, DX, a father of two children, and the respondents, Spain's National Institute For Social Security and its General Social Security Treasury. The proceedings concerned a refusal to grant the applicant a pension supplement, which, under Spanish law, was available only to women who had at least two biological or adopted children (the 'pension supplement').

The applicant was awarded an absolute permanent invalidity pension, with effect from November 2018. Relying on *Instituto Nacional de la Seguridad Social*,[25] which held that Directive 79/7/EEC precludes national legislation that reserves the grant of a pension supplement to women only, the applicant applied to the respondent authority for the pension supplement in November 2020, but was refused. The applicant brought an action before Spain's Social Court, which recognised the applicant's right to the pension supplement, although it was limited to the three months preceding his application. It dismissed his claim for damages.

23 *DX v Instituto Nacional de la Seguridad Social (INSS) and Tesorería General de la Seguridad Social (TGSS)* (Case C-113/22).

24 Directive 79/7/EEC on the progressive implementation of the principle of equal treatment for men and women in matters of social security.

25 *Instituto Nacional de la Seguridad Social (Pension supplement for mothers)* (Case C-450/18).

The applicant appealed to Spain's High Court of Justice (the referring Court), where he argued that he was entitled to the pension supplement from November 2018. He submitted that, had he been a woman, he would have been informed of that entitlement from the outset. The respondent argued that the applicant had no right in law to the pension supplement.

The referring Court stayed the proceedings and referred a question to the European Court of Justice ('ECJ') for preliminary ruling. It asked, in essence, whether art 6 of Directive 79/7/EEC must be interpreted as meaning that, in circumstances where a male applicant is refused the pension supplement—the underpinning legislation having already been found by the ECJ to be discriminatory—must a national court hearing the action grant, not only the pension supplement, but award exemplary damages and costs.

The ECJ reasoned that settled caselaw holds that where discrimination contrary to EU law is established, and remedial measures are not adopted, the principle of equality can only be ensured by granting those in the disadvantaged category the same advantages as those considered favoured. A national court must set aside the discriminatory provisions in order to restore equal treatment. Recognition of the right to the pension supplement with retroactive effect, while instrumental, is not appropriate for the purpose of remedying any harm done. Spanish law provides for the possibility of financial compensation for victims of discrimination; to this end, legal costs also cannot be disregarded.

[3.21] ***Aer Lingus v Barry*[26]*—Labour Court—appeal from Workplace Relations Commission—Employment Equality Acts 1998 to 2021, s 83(1)—complaint of discrimination on the ground of gender***

The claimant appealed a decision of the WRC that her complaint of discrimination on the ground of gender was not well-founded.

The complaint arose from elements of the cabin crew uniform the claimant was required to wear. This included the woman's jacket which had three-quarter length sleeves, the requirement to wear pop socks or tights, the design of the female blouse, the requirement to wear high or medium heeled shoes outside of the aircraft and the fact that female staff were provided with handbags while male cabin crew members were provided with satchels (which were much more practical).

The Court identified three distinct issues before it, taking on board that it was not required to look at the uniform 'item by item'. In relation to the provision of a handbag, as opposed to a satchel, to female cabin crew, the evidence had been that when the claimant requested a satchel she was provided with one. The mere provision of a handbag as part of a uniform could not in and of itself be considered discriminatory.

Secondly, the blouse, jacket and pop socks were all uniform items 'that reflect societal norms' and the issues raised by the claimant were about 'individual preferences'. When

26 *Aer Lingus v Barry* EDA2331.

taken as part of the uniform as a whole, these 'did not bear unreasonably more heavily on females than their male counterparts', and were not found to be discriminatory.

Finally, the respondent accepted that there was no functional basis for its requirement for female crew members to wear heels prior to boarding and when departing the aircraft. It was also accepted that a female crew member was required to provide, and carry at all times, an up-to-date medical certificate if she wished to wear flat shoes outside the aircraft. No such requirement applied to male cabin crew and the practice was therefore found to be discriminatory. It was ordered that this practice cease and the claimant was awarded compensation of €6,000.

The appeal was upheld and the decision of the WRC was set aside.

[3.22] ***The Housing Sustainable Communities Agency t/a The Housing Agency v Coombes-Lynch[27]—Labour Court—appeal from Workplace Relations Commission—Employment Equality Acts 1998 to 2021, s 83(1)—discrimination on ground of gender—whether claimant treated less favourably than male colleagues—whether claimant had established a prima facie case of discrimination on gender ground—civil service***

This was an appeal by the respondent from a decision of an Adjudication Officer under the Employment Equality Acts 1998 to 2021. The claimant alleged discrimination on the gender ground.

In 2015, the claimant was assigned to the respondent, initially as a receptionist, before being transferred to the respondent's accounts department. She was promoted to the grades of assistant staff officer, and then to staff officer in the respondent's pyrite department, and made significant contributions in those roles.

The claimant undertook a funded part-time project management course of six months' duration. In 2018, she applied and was placed on a panel for the vacancy of project manager. In post-interview feedback, the claimant was informed that her lack of practical onsite experience impacted on her overall scoring. The same issue again arose in her assessment in January 2019.

The claimant was subsequently assigned onsite visits by her manager on two occasions. She competed for a vacancy at project management level in August 2019 and was placed fifth overall and fourth on the resulting panel. The claimant resigned her position as staff officer grade V in April 2021. She submitted that she was repeatedly treated less favourably than her male colleagues in being denied the opportunity by her managers for meaningful onsite project management experience, while her male colleagues were regularly facilitated in that regard. She alleged that there was a culture of discrimination that favoured the promotion of male candidates over female candidates within the respondent.

The claimant did not take issue with the respondent's conduct of either the 2018 or 2019 competitions. The cognisable period prior to the referral of the complaint commenced

27 *The Housing Sustainable Communities Agency t/a The Housing Agency v Coombes-Lynch* EDA231.

in October 2019 and ended in April 2020. The one event covered by that period was a site visit undertaken by the claimant in December 2019. The claimant alleged that she was asked to attend the site in December, which was a busy time of year for her department, that her project manager had advised her not to wear 'good clothes' onsite, and that on her return to the office she was asked if she had 'enjoyed her day out'.

The Court concluded that the claimant's evidence in relation to the December 2019 site visit did not meet the burden of proof required by s 85(1) of the Employment Equality Acts 1998 to 2021. The claimant had not established a *prima facie* case of discrimination on the gender ground. Her evidence was that from January 2018 onwards, she had actively sought the opportunity to complete onsite visits in order to enhance her chances of securing a position as a project manager. There was no evidence supporting her assertion that a male colleague in a such a situation would not have been required to complete his day job at the same time, as she had. It was unclear why the claimant 'had chosen to interpret what appears to it to be eminently practical advice [not to wear good clothes] as somehow indicative of a male oriented culture in the ... workplace'. The Court saw nothing 'exceptional' in her being asked if she had 'enjoyed her day out' and could see no basis for the allegation of discrimination on the gender ground, such questions being routine regardless of gender.

The respondent's appeal accordingly succeeded.

[3.23] ***Earl Shilton Town Council v Miller*[28]*—UK Employment Appeal Tribunal—appeal from employment tribunal—sex discrimination—adequacy of female toilet facilities—shared facilities—whether the claimant was treated less favourably than male counterparts—whether the employment tribunal erred in law***

This was an appeal by the respondent, Earl Shilton Town Council, against a finding of an employment judge that the respondent directly discriminated against the claimant because of her gender in relation to the provision of toilet facilities from August 2016 until June 2018.

The claimant was employed by the respondent as an office clerk. The respondent operated from a building owned by the Methodist Church, which was also used to host a playgroup. The women's toilets were in the part of the building used for the playgroup and were also used by children. Female employees had to attract the attention of one of the playground staff if they wanted to use the toilets, which was not always easy, and had to wait until the facilities had been checked to see if a child was present.

From May 2017, the respondent's town clerk offered female employees the use of the men's toilets, which consisted of a single cubicle and trough urinal with no sanitary bins. The claimant used the women's toilets where possible but often had no choice but to use the men's toilet. She complained about the lack of a sanitary bin in January 2018. It was not until June 2018 that the church arranged for an internal lock to be fitted to the door to the men's toilets and provided a sanitary bin, which was only emptied at the request of the claimant.

28 *Earl Shilton Town Council v Miller* [2023] EAT 5.

The agreed issues were, first, whether the respondent made inadequate arrangements for the claimant to share male toilets between August 2016 and June 2018, and, second, whether the alleged conduct subjected the claimant to a detriment; if so, whether the respondent treated the claimant less favourably than a hypothetical male comparator in similar circumstances, and, if so, whether that treatment was because of sex.

The UK EAT saw no error of law. The employment tribunal applied 'robust common sense' to find that the treatment complained of constituted direct sex discrimination contrary to the Equality Act 2010. It held that the claimant was treated less favourably than men in not being provided with toilet facilities that were adequate to her needs.

The appeal was accordingly rejected.

[3.24] ***Glover v Lacoste UK Ltd and Harmon*[29]*—UK Employment Appeal Tribunal—appeal from employment tribunal—sex discrimination—provision criterion or practice—appeal of a decision to reject a flexible work request—subsequent decision to accede to the original request—whether the employment tribunal erred in finding that the subsequent decision did not constitute the reversal of a previous decision***

This was an appeal by the claimant against the decision of an employment judge rejecting the claimant's claim of indirect sex discrimination. The first respondent, Lacoste UK Ltd, was the UK retailer of a global fashion brand and the second respondent, Mr Harmon, was a HR business partner employed by the first respondent.

The claimant was employed at the first respondent's shop in Nottingham as an assistant store manager, working full-time on a flexible rota. She commenced maternity leave in March 2020 and originally intended to return in March 2021, but the shop had closed temporarily because of the Covid-19 pandemic. The claimant did not return to work at the end of her maternity leave and took accrued annual leave and was then furloughed.

In November 2020, the claimant requested to work three days a week instead of five. The request was rejected but, on appeal, was upheld in part ('the appeal'). The claimant was offered flexible work four days a week on a six-month trial period. It was indicated to the claimant that this decision was final and that there was no right of further appeal.

In April 2021, the first respondent, having received correspondence from the claimant's solicitors, acceded to the claimant's original request while she was on furlough and she returned to work.

The claimant argued before the employment tribunal that, contrary to what was set out in case-law, 'the statutory tort was *prima facie* completed' when her initial request for flexible working was refused and the repudiatory breach could not be cured by subsequently reversing the offending decision. She argued that the concept of 'disappearing discrimination' has no place in the law.

[29] *Glover v Lacoste UK Ltd and Harmon* [2023] EAT 4.

The employment tribunal considered that for the provision, criterion or practice ('PCP') of flexible working to have been applied, and for the claimant to have suffered a disadvantage or detriment, she would have had to return to work under the arrangement decided on the appeal.

The UK EAT held that the employment tribunal had erred in law. The decision to agree to the claimant's request did not arise from the appeal but only after the claimant's solicitors had sent a letter before the action. On any view, this constituted the reversal of a previous decision, rather than being a final step in the decision-making process.

The matter was accordingly remitted to a freshly constituted employment tribunal with the EAT's finding that the PCP of flexible working was applied at the stage of the determination of the appeal. The issue as to disadvantage or detriment suffered by the claimant was to be left over for the employment tribunal to determine.

[3.25] ***Alcedo Orange Ltd v Ferridge-Gunn[30]—UK Employment Appeal Tribunal—appeal from employment tribunal—Equality Act 2010—Employment Rights Act 1996—gender—maternity rights—pregnancy—discrimination—precedent—composite approach—different roles—automatic unfair dismissal***

The claimant commenced employment with the respondent company on 27 January 2020. During her employment, she had two meetings with Ms Caunt, the registered manager, and Mr Boardman, the managing director of the respondent, about her key performance indicators. Both had concerns about the claimant's performance and her attitude to her work. The claimant discovered that she was pregnant and reported her pregnancy to Ms Caunt on 19 February 2020. On 24 and 25 February 2020, the claimant took two days' leave due to morning sickness and informed Ms Caunt about same. The claimant alleged that Ms Caunt was unsympathetic in her response and made derisive comments about her absence. During the claimant's absence, Ms Caunt informed Mr Boardman that the claimant's job performance was not progressing. On 27 February 2020, the claimant's employment was terminated. The respondent alleged that the claimant was dismissed due to unsatisfactory job performance and inability to meet targets. It was also claimed that she was not receptive to training and was not an appropriate 'fit' for the company.

The claimant brought proceedings to the employment tribunal for pregnancy discrimination under s 18 of the Equality Act 2010 and for automatic unfair dismissal contrary to the Employment Rights Act 1996.

In considering the pregnancy discrimination claim, the employment tribunal was not referred to the decision of *Reynolds v CLFIS (UK) Ltd*,[31] which established that, in a claim for discrimination, the conduct of the person supplying the information must be treated separately from that of the decision maker. Only the motivation of each participant is relevant in determining whether each acted in a discriminatory manner; a composite approach is not appropriate in these circumstances. The tribunal concluded

---

30 *Alcedo Orange Ltd v Ferridge-Gunn* [2023] EAT 78.

31 *Reynolds v CLFIS (UK) Ltd* [2015] ICR 1010.

that the claimant had been discriminated against on the grounds of her pregnancy but had not been automatically unfairly dismissed. The tribunal found that the timing of the claimant's notification to her employer of her pregnancy, her absences for pregnancy-related reasons and her attendance at an antenatal appointment the day before her dismissal all shifted the burden of proof in the claimant's favour. The respondent failed to show that the pregnancy did not factor in the claimant's dismissal.

The respondent appealed to the UK EAT, arguing that the claimant had not been subject to pregnancy-based discrimination. It argued that the tribunal: had misdirected itself or misapplied s 18 of the Equality Act 2010; had failed to properly identify the reason for the claimant's dismissal; had failed to consider *Reynolds*; and had conflated the role of Mr Boardman and Ms Caunt in the process.

The EAT stated that it was 'understandable' that a dismissed employee may conclude that the decisions and opinions of those involved in the process are attributable to the employer itself. This 'composite approach' is not envisaged by *Reynolds*, however. The EAT held that the respondent should have brought the *Reynolds* decision to the tribunal's attention.

The EAT noted the respondent's argument that it was clear that the tribunal concluded that Mr Boardman was the sole decision maker, influenced by Ms Caunt, who was herself motivated by discrimination. The EAT also noted the claimant's contention that her termination was a joint decision by Mr Boardman and Ms Caunt or that the former was knowingly influenced by the latter. The EAT disagreed with both parties' submissions. However, the EAT stated that the tribunal's judgment indicated that *Reynolds* had not been opened to it. The judgment was therefore unsafe.

The appeal was allowed and the claim of discrimination under the Equality Act 2010 was remitted to the same employment tribunal for reconsideration.

[3.26] ***Thukalil v Puthenveettil*[32]*—UK Employment Appeal Tribunal—appeal from employment tribunal—National Minimum Wage Regulations 1999,*[33] *reg 2(2)—Treaty of the Functioning of the European Union, art 157—entitlement to national minimum wage—statutory 'family worker exception'—domestic workers—indirect discrimination on ground of sex***

The respondent appealed against a decision of an employment tribunal that the claimant was entitled to be paid the national minimum wage. The claimant worked as a domestic worker in the respondents' home from 2005 to 2013. She challenged reg 2(2) of the National Minimum Wage Regulations 1999, under which a 'family worker exemption' disqualified her from entitlement to the national minimum wage. The claimant submitted that, as women generally make up the majority of domestic workers, reg 2(2) indirectly discriminated against women contrary to directly effective general principles of non-discrimination in EU law, and was in contravention of her right to equal pay under art 157 of the TFEU.

32 *Thukalil v Puthenveettil* [2023] EAT 47.
33 National Minimum Wage Regulations 1999 (SI 1999/584).

The employment tribunal held that the impugned provision had a 'strong adverse, disparate impact on women', putting them at a disadvantage compared to men, and was indirectly discriminatory on the ground of sex. Nor was it justified; the tribunal considered that reg 2(2) was not a proportionate means of achieving the Secretary of State's stated aims, ie, to reflect 'the unusual working relationship where a living in worker … is treated as a member of the family', and 'to encourage parents to return to work by not imposing unaffordable or deterrent financial burdens on them'. It concluded that reg 2(2) was contrary to the claimant's right to equal pay under art 157 of the TFEU, and accordingly the tribunal was bound to disapply it. The claimant was entitled to the national minimum wage in respect of her period of service with the respondents.

On appeal, the respondent, who was self-represented, argued that the purpose of art 157 of the TFEU is 'not to achieve fair wages but to eliminate discrimination on the ground of sex'. There was no male comparator, because they did not employ one, and there was no 'single source' of the claimed pay disparity, since invariably domestic workers affected by reg 2(2) work for different employers. The UK EAT rejected these arguments and held that reg 2(2) was indirectly discriminatory, putting women generally at a particular disadvantage compared to men. Article 157 of the TFEU can apply where unequal pay is caused by an indirectly discriminatory provision, such as reg 2(2) in this instance. The decision to disapply reg 2(2) had been correct and the appeal was, accordingly, dismissed.

RACE

[3.27] ***Maynooth University v Saad[34]—Labour Court—appeal from Workplace Relations Commission—Employment Equality Act 1998—allegation of discrimination—interview process***

The claimant alleged that he was discriminated against on the grounds of religion and race arising from his unsuccessful application for an assistant professorship with the respondent university. The WRC held that the complaints were not well-founded and the claimant appealed with regard to discrimination on the grounds of race.

The respondent university advertised the role of assistant professor/lecturer for a one-year contract. The claimant applied for the position and was shortlisted by a selection panel. He was interviewed along with five other candidates. Each candidate had to prepare a presentation, the highest-scoring candidate was offered, and accepted, the position.

The claimant was ranked third in the competition. He was informed by the respondent's human resources office that his application had been unsuccessful but that the panel had been impressed by his performance and the claimant was a reserve candidate. At the claimant's request, the respondent gave the feedback on his application; that his presentation had been weak and that this had affected his overall score. The claimant

34 *Maynooth University v Saad* EDA2323.

was dissatisfied with the feedback and the respondent outlined the process used for awarding scores during the interview, explaining why the claimant had been awarded his score. The claimant then requested the feedback and scores of the other candidates and queried the race, ethnicity and skin colour of the permanent staff in the department.

The claimant asserted that he had been asked questions during his interview that were discriminatory. It was noted by the Court that the claimant had made absolutely no reference to the alleged questions until producing a written submission some 40 minutes before the WRC hearing commenced.

The respondent argued that it had discharged its obligations to provide feedback on the application process.

The Court found that the claimant had not established any facts from which an inference that he was treated less favourably on the grounds of race could be made. The appeal was, accordingly, dismissed.

[3.28] ***Kohli v Department for International Trade*[35]*—UK Employment Appeal Tribunal—appeal from employment tribunal—Equality Act 2010—direct discrimination—race discrimination—subconscious discrimination—inferences—pandemic—appraisal grading***

The claimant identified as Indian and joined the respondent in July 2019, working for the Global Strategy Directorate ('GSD') as a Grade 7 civil servant. In October 2019, changes were made to the GSD and the claimant was offered a choice between two roles; she chose the Latin America and Caribbean ('LATAC') role, where she had worked before. Mr Hanna became the claimant's manager and her countersigning manager was Ms Buckingham. The claimant began a temporary voluntary deployment called 'surge' during the pandemic; however, Mr Hanna and Ms Buckingham informed her that there was not much work for the GSD in LATAC and that her role was no longer viable.

The claimant was given a temporary promotion to Joint Deputy Head of GSSEP Strategic Communications and Briefing Unit. This was one of two Grade 6 roles in the department. However, due to a reorganisation following Covid-19, it was decided that instead there would be a Grade 6 and a Grade 7 role created. The claimant was offered the Grade 7 role but changed her mind, intending to return to the GSD. Mr Hanna maintained that there was not a need for a full-time role in the GSD as another department was dealing with the LATAC work.

The claimant underwent an appraisal grading and was graded as 3C. She appealed against this grading, but did not claim that this grading was influenced by race or disability discrimination at the time. Subsequently, the claimant initiated the grievance procedure in which she complained about alleged sex, race, and/or disability discrimination by Mr Hanna. This grievance was not upheld. The role of Head of Africa

35 *Kohli v Department for International Trade* [2023] EAT 82.

subsequently became available, but the claimant was not offered it. Instead, expressions of interest were generally sought. The claimant did not apply for the role and the job went to a male colleague of Afro-Caribbean origin. The claimant brought proceedings before the employment tribunal, alleging direct discrimination against her on race and also on disability grounds.

The tribunal dismissed her claim. She was given permission to challenge the rejection of her direct race discrimination claim and argued that the tribunal failed to consider, expressly or separately, the issue of subconscious discrimination.

The UK EAT acknowledged that the tribunal made findings as to the true reasons for the matters complained of and that there was no suggestion made that the respondent had stereotyped the claimant based on her Indian heritage. The EAT held that, although the tribunal did not refer to subconscious discrimination in its judgment, its findings effectively ruled out that the claimant's race or heritage affected the respondent's decisions. It was also noted that the tribunal found that there were no facts from which it could properly be inferred that the claimant's Indian heritage impacted the respondent's decision making. The tribunal also held that there were no facts established that could lead the tribunal to conclude that the difference in appraisal scores of the claimant were influenced by race.

The appeal was dismissed.

[3.29] ***Edward v Tavistock and Portman NHS Foundation Trust*[36]*—UK Employment Appeal Tribunal—appeal from employment tribunal—Equality Act 2010—race discrimination—compensation—failure to mitigate—future loss—injury to feelings—loss of earnings—perversity—victimisation—loss of chance***

The claimant was an employee of the respondent NHS Trust, working as a 'band 5' data officer. He was demoted to a band 4 data officer in circumstances where he was allegedly not able to complete band 5 work. Rather than provide the claimant with a band 4 post, the respondent dismissed him. The claimant initiated a victimisation claim before the employment tribunal, alleging that he had been redeployed as a result of his having previously brought discrimination grievances against the respondent based on race and age. The claimant was out of work for over two and a half years. By the time of the remedy hearing, he had secured a new job on a fixed-term contract with a higher salary at which he had been working for the previous three months. During his period of unemployment, the claimant had not applied for any band 4 roles in the NHS.

The employment tribunal made a finding that the claimant had been victimised by the respondent. However, it held that, had he been redeployed, there was a 40% chance that he would not have been suitable for the role obtained and would have been forced to leave after the trial period.

36 *Edward v Tavistock and Portman NHS Foundation Trust* [2023] EAT 33.

At the remedy hearing, the tribunal held that, after being unemployed for a certain amount of time, the claimant should have applied for band 4 roles within the NHS. The tribunal reduced his loss of earnings for the remainder of the period of past loss by 50% due to a failure to mitigate by applying for band 4 roles; it awarded six weeks future loss of earnings (as he may not find a new job immediately after his fixed-term contract had expired) and considered pension loss and injury to feelings.

The claimant appealed, and the respondent cross-appealed.

The UK EAT noted that the tribunal's reasons included no direction as to the legal principles to be considered when calculating loss, whether in relation to failure to mitigate or otherwise. The respondent contended that although the tribunal dealt with failures to mitigate on a regular basis, it could not be assumed that the tribunal was applying the correct test in lieu of explicit evidence of consideration in the judgment. The respondent also argued that, by holding that it 'should' have encouraged the claimant to apply for band 4 jobs, the tribunal had made a finding that the respondent had acted unreasonably in its failure. However, it was difficult to ascertain on which party the tribunal had placed the burden of proof when deciding what the parties 'should' have done. It was not clear whether the tribunal considered that the burden be rightly placed on the respondent to prove failure to mitigate or if it had considered whether the claimant had acted unreasonably in failing to take steps to mitigate. The EAT agreed that, given the reasons relied upon by the tribunal, it could not be satisfied that the tribunal applied the correct test. The EAT determined that the tribunal did err in law in its approach to mitigation and that the matter needed to be remitted for rehearing.

The claimant argued that the tribunal had erred in applying the 50% reduction to the relevant period of loss. Instead, it should have made a finding as to when he would have found employment elsewhere and at what rate. *Gardiner-Hill v Roland Berger Technics*[37] was cited. The EAT acknowledged that there may be cases where the 'percentage discount' approach may require further consideration in light of developments in the 'loss of a chance' principles which developed subsequent to the *Gardiner-Hill* decision. However, the EAT held that a departure from *Gardiner-Hill* was not necessary here for the determination of the appeal.

It was held that the tribunal's calculation of future loss of earnings was based on adequate reasoning and was not perverse.

The parties agreed that the tribunal had erred in applying a 40% discount to the sum to be awarded for injury to feelings on the basis that there was a likelihood that the claimant would not have been suitable for the role obtained and would have been forced to leave after the trial period. The UK EAT allowed the appeal on this ground and substituted the award for injury to feelings.

The parties also agreed that the tribunal had erred in calculating pension loss. By consent, appeals and cross-appeals were allowed on this point.

The appeal was allowed and the cross-appeal was allowed.

---

37 *Gardiner-Hill v Roland Berger Technics* [1982] IRLR 498.

[3.30] ***The Royal Parks Ltd v Boohene & Ors*[38]*—UK Employment Appeal Tribunal—appeal from employment tribunal—Transfer of Undertakings (Protection of Employment) Regulations 2006*[39] *('TUPE')—indirect race discrimination—third-party contractors—principal's employees as comparators—minimum rate of pay***

This appeal raised the question of whether, under the UK's equality legislation, workers employed by third-party contractors could rely on the principal's own employees as comparators for the purpose of their claims of indirect race discrimination in relation to minimum rates of pay.

The respondent, The Royal Parks Ltd, is a charity, managing eight of London's royal parks and other open spaces. The 15 claimants were all employees of Vinci Construction UK Ltd ('the third party') which had a toilet maintenance and cleaning services contract with the respondent. More than half of the claimants transferred to the third party under the UK's Transfer of Undertakings (Protection of Employment) Regulations 2006 ('TUPE') when it was awarded the contract, while the others were directly engaged by the third party.

Of the 160 direct employees of the respondent, some 40% were transferred under TUPE from the civil service when the respondent was created in 2017. These employees were paid by the respondent according to their civil service grade and were paid above the London Living Wage ('LLW'). The remaining 60% were either recruited since 2017, or were previously employed by the respondent's predecessor and had chosen to transfer to the new contractual terms. These employees were never paid less than their civil service counterparts.

In 2014, the third party put in a tender for the toilets and cleaning contract at the invitation of the respondent's predecessor. The contract specifications required *inter alia* that TUPE would apply and included a list of staff who would transfer to the contractor. In its tender response, the third party, having reviewed the TUPE information, decided to increase the basic hourly rate from £6.31 to £7 in order to attract and retain staff. It was not in dispute that the respondent's predecessor was also given the option of accepting a bid whereby staff would be paid the LLW rate but had decided not to take that up. The third party was successful in its bid and a contract was signed in November 2014.

In June 2017, two trade unions recognised by the respondent submitted a request that the respondent consider extending the LLW (then £9.75 per hour) to all employees of contractors. Later that year, the chief executive of the respondent recommended to its board members that the respondent 'aspire to the LLW being paid to all of its contractors and concessionaires within ten years'.

In June 2019, the claimants' trade union wrote to the third party pointing out that the vast majority of their cohort was paid below the LLW and asking that the third party respond with a proposal for wholesale implementation of the LLW. In their annual pay claim that year, the trade unions recognised by the respondent submitted that the respondent

---

[38] *The Royal Parks Ltd v Boohene & Ors* [2023] EAT 69.

[39] Transfer of Undertakings (Protection of Employment) Regulations 2006 (SI 2006/246).

should 'extend payment of the living wage to the employees of all its contractors, by incorporating a clause to this effect as part of the procurement process'.

The respondent's position remained unchanged until the third party's contract came up for renewal. At a board meeting in September 2019, it was agreed that the respondent and all of its contractors should pay the LLW to all staff as soon as possible after the contracts came up for renewal and by April 2023 at the very latest. The third party's contract was renewed and it was agreed that the respondent would meet the costs of the LLW.

In a complaint of indirect race discrimination before the employment tribunal, the claimants argued that the contractual arrangements put in place by the respondent for determining the pay of outsourced workers treated them less favourably than the respondent's direct employees. The effect was a 'disparate impact on workers from a black or minority ethnic (BME) background, who are more likely to find themselves in outsourced roles'.

The UK EAT found that the tribunal was entitled to have regard to the higher level of control exercised by the respondent as to the terms on which the claimants would be allowed to work. It had been the choice of the respondent's predecessor as to which option it would accept from the third party. The tribunal found that this choice was determinative of the terms of the minimum level of pay under which the claimants would work. Indeed, it had been the respondent's decision ultimately to move the claimants to LLW rates and to 'require' that its contractors follow suit.

The employment tribunal fell into error in finding that the provision, criterion or practice applied by the respondent was 'that its employees would be paid the LLW as a minimum wage but those working on the cleaning contract with [the third party] would not be paid LLW as a minimum wage'. This was inconsistent with the claimants' pleaded case, that the respondent had maintained a practice of applying a different minimum level of pay depending on whether the staff in question were direct employees or outsourced workers not limited to the third party or to any particular contract. Accordingly, the pool for comparison adopted by the tribunal was incomplete and its analysis was restricted. The appeal was allowed on that basis.

[3.31] ***Institute and Faculty of Actuaries v Davda[40]—UK Employment Appeal Tribunal—appeal from employment tribunal—discrimination on grounds of race—number of opportunities to pass examinations—exemption arrangements with other qualification bodies—whether the tribunal erred in attributing the treatment complained of to the respondent—appropriate comparator***

This was an appeal and cross-appeal against both judgment and remedy of the employment tribunal. The claimant, who was based in Switzerland,was a student member of the respondent qualifications body for actuaries in the UK. The claimant alleged that he had been the subject of direct or indirect race discrimination as a British national in the arrangements that the respondent made for conferring qualifications.

40 *Institute and Faculty of Actuaries v Davda* [2023] EAT 63.

The employment tribunal upheld a complaint of direct race discrimination in respect of the number of opportunities the respondent gave the claimant to pass examinations to qualify as a fellow of the respondent, compared to Indian nationals. Alternatively, there was indirect race discrimination in respect of the respondent's offering only two sittings of its examinations per annum to the claimant, while granting exemptions for recognised examinations set by the Indian Actuarial Institute ('IAI'), membership of which was not available to UK nationals, with the result that a candidate sitting both the IAI's and the respondent's examinations potentially had four opportunities to pass a qualifying examination per annum.

The respondent was also held by the tribunal to have 'subjected the claimant to direct race discrimination by directly or indirectly instructing, causing, inducing and/or aiding the IAI not to admit British nationals as students'. However, the tribunal rejected a complaint of indirect race discrimination on the part of the respondent 'by requiring that, in order to be regarded as a fully qualified actuary of the respondent, a member of the respondent must be appointed as a fellow of the respondent', in circumstances where the claimant alleged that it was easier to pass exams and become a fellow in another European country, eg Switzerland. The claimant was awarded £37,966.27, comprising £15,000 for injury to feeling, and £20,446.27 for future loss of income, and interest.

On appeal, the UK EAT did not accept that the IAI's (or other organisations') exemption arrangements with the respondent was 'treatment afforded by the respondent'. The respondent offered its students two opportunities per year to pass its examinations, irrespective of nationality. Nor was there an 'exact correspondence' between membership or non-membership of the IAI and Indian nationality—a hypothetical student of Indian nationality having been used as a comparator by the claimant. There was nothing to suggest that IAI membership was limited to Indian nationals, even if UK nationals were excluded. In any event, it was not the case that all Indian members of the respondent were also members of the IAI and it was open to UK nationals to obtain exemptions from other organisations with which the respondent had exemption arrangements.

Thus, the tribunal misidentified the treatment afforded to the claimant by the respondent and erred in its identification of a comparator. Accordingly, the appeal succeeded.

In relation to the cross-appeal of the rejected complaint of indirect race discrimination, the tribunal had been entitled to accept the respondent's evidence that its mutual recognition agreement did not entitle overseas actuaries to full fellowship. It had also been entitled to conclude that the claimant was not disadvantaged by any PCP that placed associates at a disadvantage in seeking to obtain fellowship, the claimant having not passed the exams necessary to obtain associate status. Accordingly, the cross-appeal failed.

The claim was remitted to a newly constituted employment tribunal, to include re-determination of whether there was an agreement between the respondent and the IAI that UK nationals would not be permitted to join the IAI.

RELIGION

[3.32] ***OP v Commune d'Ans[41]—European Court of Justice—request for preliminary ruling from Belgium—Directive 2000/78/EC[42]—discrimination on the grounds of religion or belief—public sector—headscarf—visible wearing of any philosophical or religious sign in the workplace—neutrality in contacts with the public***

The applicant worked for the respondent since 2016 as 'head of office'. The applicant did not wear any signs which may have revealed her religious beliefs until February 2021, when she requested to wear a headscarf in work. The municipal board rejected the application until general rules on the wearing of such signs had been adopted by the municipality. In March 2021, the municipal board amended its terms of employment by inserting a requirement that all workers exercise 'exclusive neutrality' when in the workplace. This meant that workers were prohibited from wearing any visible sign which might reveal their religious or philosophical beliefs in the workplace. The applicant brought several proceedings seeking declarations that her freedom of religion had been infringed by this policy, including an injunction before the referring Court, which referred the following questions to European Court of Justice (the 'ECJ'):

> '(1) Can Article 2(2)(a) and (b) of [Directive 2000/78/EC] be interpreted as permitting a public administration to put in place an entirely neutral administrative environment and thus to prohibit all members of staff from wearing [signs which might reveal religious beliefs], whether or not they are in direct contact with the public?
>
> (2) Can Article 2(2)(a) and (b) of [Directive 2000/78/EC] be interpreted as permitting a public administration to put in place an entirely neutral administrative environment and thus to prohibit all members of staff from wearing [signs which might reveal religious beliefs], whether or not they are in direct contact with the public, even if that neutral prohibition appears mostly to affect women, and may thus constitute disguised discrimination on grounds of gender?'

With regard to the first question, the ECJ noted that Directive 2000/78/EC applies to both public and private sectors. It stated that an internal rule, which applies in a general undifferentiated way, does not amount to a difference in treatment, as it treats all workers of the undertaking in the same way. Therefore, it found that, despite the generality of the rule's application, the referring Court would have to decide if the applicant had been treated differently from other workers who had been permitted to practise their religious or philosophical beliefs by wearing a visible sign of these beliefs and, as a result, she suffered direct discrimination. The referring Court would also have to examine whether the rule would put persons having a particular religion or belief at a particular disadvantage, constituting indirect discrimination.

The ECJ noted that if such a rule constituted indirect discrimination it could still be objectively justified by a legitimate aim, if the means of achieving the aim could be said to be appropriate and necessary. It ruled that it was for the referring Court to ascertain

41 *OP v Commune d'Ans* (Case-C148/22).

42 Directive 2000/78/EC on establishing a general framework for equal treatment in employment and occupation.

whether these standards were met. The ECJ noted that it was apparent from Directive 2000/78/EC that the EU legislature did not itself effect the balance between the freedom of religion and the legitimate aims that may justify unequal treatment. Instead it was left to the Member States to reach that balance; there is a margin of discretion for Member States to ensure that the measures taken at a national level are justified and proportionate.

The ECJ therefore held that art 2(2)(b) of Directive 2000/78/EC must be interpreted as meaning that an internal rule of a municipal authority prohibiting members of staff from wearing visible signs, which demonstrate religious beliefs, may be justified in order to promote, having regard to the context in which it operates, an entirely neutral administrative environment in the municipal authority. However, this is subject to the principles of appropriateness, necessity and proportionality and the various rights and interests at stake.

With regard to the second question, the ECJ noted that indirect discrimination on the basis of sex falls within the scope of Directive 2006/54/EC[43] and not within the scope of Directive 2000/78/EC to which the second question related. Accordingly, this question was ruled as inadmissible.

[3.33] ***Allpro Services v Waszkiewicz[44]—Labour Court—appeal from Workplace Relations Commission—Employment Equality Acts 1998 to 2021—harassment in the workplace—name-calling—adequate policies and procedures***

This was an appeal by the respondent of a decision of the WRC upholding a complaint of discrimination against the claimant on the grounds of religion and awarding €15,000.

The claimant was a Polish national and a member of the Catholic Church. He submitted that he was discriminated against when he was subjected to harassment on the grounds of his religion and race in his workplace. The respondent refuted this and submitted that the claimant had not established facts from which a prima facie case of discrimination could be established.

The claimant commenced employment as an industrial cleaner on a construction site in August 2020. He alleged that he was subject to ongoing bullying and harassment in the workplace after notifying a supervisor and HR that another supervisor had 'planned' to have an accident at work to obtain compensation. Subsequently, a colleague made fun of his religion and race at various times. The claimant further alleged that his supervisor did nothing to stop it.

In the Court's view, the name-calling, together with derogatory comments about race and religion clearly constituted conduct 'which can have the effect of violating a person's dignity and creating an intimidating, hostile, degrading, humiliating or offensive environment for that person'. The Court was satisfied that the claimant was subject to harassment on the grounds of his religious belief and his race.

---

43 Directive 2006/54/EC on the implementation of the principle of equal opportunities and equal treatment of men and women in matters of employment and occupation.

44 *Allpro Services v Waszkiewicz* EDA2336.

The legislation fixes an employer with vicarious liability for acts of discrimination carried out by employees during the course of their employment, whether or not those acts are carried out with the employer's knowledge or approval. Thus, the respondent could not rely on its assertion that it was not liable for the actions of employees because it was not on notice.

The respondent did not demonstrate to the satisfaction of the Court that it had adequate policies and procedures in place to protect employees from harassment, and it failed to demonstrate how employees were made aware of the policy. The Court was not satisfied that the respondent had taken 'such steps as were reasonably practicable to prevent the harassment of [the claimant]'. Accordingly, the Court upheld the decision of the WRC, the respondent was vicariously liable for the harassment suffered by the claimant and was ordered to pay the claimant €15,000.

COVID-19 VACCINATION STATUS

[3.34] ***DM v Azienda Ospedale-Università di Padova***[45]***—European Court of Justice—request for a preliminary ruling from Italy—Regulation (EC) 726/2004***[46]***—Covid-19 vaccines—Regulation (EC) 507/2006***[47]***—Regulation (EU) 2021/953***[48]***—public health—national legislation imposing vaccination obligation on health professionals—suspension from duty without pay for personnel refusing vaccine—prohibition of discrimination between vaccinated and unvaccinated persons—inadmissibility***

This request for a preliminary ruling concerned the interpretation art 4 of Regulation (EC) 507/2006, Regulation (EU) 2021/953, and arts 3, 35 and 41 of the Charter of Fundamental Rights of the European Union (the 'Charter'). The request was made in proceedings between DM (the applicant) and the University Hospital of Padua, Italy (the respondent).

The applicant was employed by the respondent as a nurse in its neurosurgery department. In September 2021, the respondent informed the applicant that she was being suspended from her duties with immediate effect, and without pay, on the grounds that she had breached a vaccine obligation for health professionals under Italian law and that it was impossible to assign her to other duties.

The applicant sought interim reliefs from the District Court of Padua (the referring Court), applying to be reinstated to her post. She argued, *inter alia*, that the national law was contrary to EU law. She also argued that she had acquired a natural immunity as a

---

45 *DM v Azienda Ospedale-Università di Padova* (Case C-765/21).

46 Regulation (EC) 726/2004 laying down Community procedures for the authorisation and supervision of medicinal products for human and veterinary use and establishing a European Medicines Agency.

47 Regulation (EC) 507/2006 on the conditional marketing authorisation for medicinal products for human use falling within the scope of Regulation (EC) No 726/2004.

48 Regulation (EU) 2021/953 on a framework for the issuance, verification and acceptance of interoperable Covid-19 vaccination, test and recovery certificates (EU Digital Covid Certificate) to facilitate free movement during the Covid-19 pandemic.

result of having previously recovered from Covid-19. The referring Court decided to stay the proceedings and to refer a number of questions to the European Court of Justice ('ECJ') for preliminary ruling.

By the first of its questions, the referring Court asked, in essence, whether the conditional marketing authorisations granted for Covid-19 vaccines were valid in light of art 4 of Regulation (EC) 507/2006, read with arts 3 and 35 of the Charter, 'on the ground that alternative treatments which were effective against Covid-19 and less harmful to health had [by the date of the reference for a preliminary ruling] already been approved in several member states'.

In its order for reference, the referring Court did not identify the authorisations at issue, nor did it address their content with reference to the validity requirements in art 4. It merely expressed doubts 'without going into the specific nature of those doubts in any way whatsoever'. Moreover, the referring Court did not explain how a challenge to the validity of the conditional authorisations could affect the standing of the vaccination obligation for health professionals. In the absence of a statement of reasons which led the referring Court to question the validity of those provisions of EU law, as well as the link established between the provisions and the national legislation applicable to the main proceedings, the question was held to be inadmissible.

Next, the referring Court asked, in essence, whether Regulation (EU) 507/2006 must, for the purpose of satisfying a vaccine obligation for health professionals under national law, be interpreted as precluding the use of vaccines which have been the subject of a conditional authorisation under art 4, 'even in a situation where those professionals have developed immunity to the virus causing that disease and the health authority has not specifically established that there are no contraindications to that vaccination'. The referring Court also asked whether a penalty consisting of suspension of a health professional from their duties without pay for non-compliance with a vaccine obligation was consistent with art 41 of the Charter and principles of proportionality and *audi alteram partem*.

The ECJ observed, as a starting point, that art 168(7) TFEU does not set any requirement for Member States concerning compulsory vaccinations of certain categories of persons, since EU law does not affect the competence of Member States to define national health policy. The referring Court's question appeared to be based on the premise that Regulation (EU) 507/2006, or the conditional authorisations granted under that Regulation, governs the conditions for the imposition of an obligation to vaccinate under domestic law and the consequences that may follow for non-compliance with that obligation. The ECJ stressed that the grant of such authorisation does not impose an obligation on potential recipients of vaccines to take them. The referring Court did not explain the link it drew between art 4 of Regulation (EU) 507/2006 and the national legislation imposing the vaccine obligation for health professionals in the context of the main proceedings. Nor did the referring Court explain how art 41 of the Charter (the right to good administration) related to the implementation of an obligation to vaccinate, having made no finding that the national legislation constituted an implementation of EU law. Again, these questions did not comply with the ECJ's rules of procedure and were held inadmissible.

Finally, the referring Court asked, in essence, whether Regulation (EU) 2021/953, 'read in conjunction with the principles of proportionality and non-discrimination', must be interpreted as precluding national legislation which imposes an obligation on health professionals to be vaccinated against Covid-19.

The referring Court did not specify what provisions of Regulation (EU) 2021/953 it was referring to and the details contained in the order for reference did not make it possible to determine 'with any accuracy' what was sought to be interpreted for the resolution of the dispute in the main proceedings. It was not apparent that there was a connecting link between Regulation (EU) 2021/953 and the main proceedings and these questions, too, were inadmissible.

Chapter 4

Employment Litigation

INTRODUCTION

[4.01]

Abuse of Process

In *FKJ*, the High Court of England and Wales considered whether the claimant's employer had improperly acquired WhatsApp messages used as evidence in an employment tribunal hearing.

Anonymity Order/Reporting Restrictions

The High Court heard an interlocutory application for anonymisation in *RM* in the context of a claim of wrongful dismissal. See also CMA notes at Chapter 11. In *Clifford*, the Court of Appeal of England and Wales considered whether to restrict public reporting on a whistleblowing case.

The UK EAT considered an application for an anonymity order in *F v J*.

Bias

Alleged bias on the part of the deciding tribunal featured in a number of cases. In *Department of Enterprise, Trade and Employment*, the Labour Court considered a request for the recusal of an ordinary member of the Court. The UK EAT also heard a number of such claims. In *Mohammed* it overturned the decision to strike out a claim on its entirety for the claimant's failure to provide certain information within a prescribed timeframe. *Veizi, Higgs* and *Aspect Windows (Western) Ltd* all concerned applications to recuse members or the entirety of the employment tribunal on the grounds of bias.

Concurrent Claims

An application for a stay on employment tribunal proceedings where there were concurrent High Court proceedings was considered by the UK EAT in *Onea*.

Dismissal Injunction—Costs

In *Nesbitt*, the High Court considered an application for costs in a claim for an interim injunction.

Delay

The High Court considered an application to dismiss proceedings for an inordinate and inexcusable delay in *Lane*.

Privilege

The Court of Session of Scotland considered the scope of legal professional privilege in *University of Dundee v Chakraborty*.

Employment Status

Employment status featured in a number of cases in 2023. There was a significant decision of the Supreme Court concerning delivery drivers in *Karshan*. *PBR Restaurants Ltd* was an appeal to the Labour Court under the Unfair Dismissal Acts 1977 to 2015 where the issue was whether the applicant was self-employed or an employee. The UK Supreme Court also considered the question of employment status in *Independent Workers Union of Great Britain*. The UK EAT also dealt with employee status in *Ter-Berg*, *United Taxis Ltd*, *Plastic Omnium Automotive Ltd*, *Manning*, and *Anglian Windows Ltd*.

Isaac Wunder *Order*

Morgan v Labour Court concerned an application to the High Court for an Isaac Wunder order restricting the applicant from initiating any further proceedings in relation to their employment.

Judicial Immunity: Labour Court

In *A Legal Representative v Chairman of a Division of the Labour Court* the WRC considered whether the Labour Court was immune from litigation.

Norwich Pharmacal Orders

The Court of Appeal considered an application for a *Norwich Pharmacal* order in *Blythe*.

Fraud

Tinkler concerned an application to set aside a judgment for fraud.

Settlement Agreements

The Court of Appeal of England and Wales had to consider disputes about settlement agreements in two cases. In *Warburton*, the Court considered whether the appellant's case amounted to a retrial of proceedings previously settled between the parties. *Arvunescu* concerned an appeal to determine the proper interpretation of a settlement agreement.

Territorial Jurisdiction

In *ROI Land Investments Ltd*, the ECJ considered a question referred from Germany regarding the application of the Rome I Regulations and the concept of 'trade or profession'/'professional activities'.

The Rule in Henderson v Henderson

In *Munnelly*, the Supreme Court considered whether the rule in *Henderson v Henderson*, which prohibits two sets of proceedings with overlapping facts and claims running, can be invoked by parties that were not party to the first set of proceedings.

Time Limits—Point of Law Appeals

In *Marino Camarasa*, the applicant issued a notice of motion within the required 42-day time limit but had to amend it; the amended notice of motion issued outside the required time limit. The High Court considered whether it could extend the time limit and allow the application to appeal.

Time Limits Appeals

In *Hanlon* Labour Court considered the time limit on appeals from the WRC. See also the decision of the Labour Court in Acorn Brokerage, noted at Chapter 19, where the appellant used the incorrect Labour Court Appeal form.

The UK EAT heard a number of cases relating to the time limits on bringing an appeal, including in *Anghel*, *Hawkes* and *Elhalabi*.

Time Limits—Claims

The UK EAT also dealt with a number of cases where claims were made out of time. Note the decisions in *Meaker*, *Owen*, *Fernandes* and *The Sports PR Company Ltd.*

Without Prejudice Privilege

In *Garrod* the UK EAT considered whether evidence that was referenced as being 'without prejudice' was privileged and was inadmissible for the hearing.

ABUSE OF PROCESS

[4.02] ***FKJ v RVT*[1]*—High Court of England and Wales—Master Davison—abuse ofprocess—hacking—Henderson v Henderson rule—malicious prosecution—misuse of private information—Rules of Court—striking out—summary judgment—text messaging***

The claimant was a solicitor employed by the second and third respondent law firms. The first respondent was the managing partner of the firms. After the claimant's dismissal for falsifying a timesheet, she brought a claim to the employment tribunal alleging that the first respondent had sexually harassed her. The respondents used the claimant's private WhatsApp messages against her at trial. The authors of these messages were the claimant, her husband and her best friend. The messages included intimate conversations and pictures shared between the claimant and her husband. The claimant ultimately failed in her employment tribunal claim. It was noted that some of the messages used at the trial had 'undermined her credibility'.

The claimant brought a claim for misuse of private information in the High Court, alleging that the respondents had acquired the WhatsApp messages illegally or improperly, by hacking into her account. The respondents claimed that a substantial quantity of the messages was found on the claimant's work computer after she was dismissed. The rest, it was alleged, were received via letters from an anonymous source. The respondents issued a counterclaim for malicious prosecution and abuse of process as well as harassment under the Protection from Harassment Act 1997.

The respondents sought to strike out the High Court proceedings or an order granting summary judgment on the claim and counterclaim. In the alternative, the respondents

1 *FKJ v RVT* [2023] EWHC 3 (KB).

sought an order making the claimant's defence of the counterclaim contingent on her being able to lodge monies in court.

The respondents contended that the claimant's claim was either: (1) an example of *Jameel* abuse;[2] (2) an example of *Henderson* abuse;[3] or (3) an abuse because it breached the implied undertaking arising from CPR, r 31.32 (ie disclosed documents can only be used in the proceedings in which they are disclosed). The respondents also argued that the claimant's case had 'significant problems' and that the claimant could not have had a reasonable expectation of privacy or confidence in relation to the messages which had been either saved or downloaded to her work computer during her employment.

The High Court of England and Wales held that this was not an example of *Jameel* abuse, as it could not be said that 'no real or substantial wrong' had been committed or that 'litigating the claim will yield no tangible or legitimate benefit to the claimant proportionate to the likely costs and use of Court procedures'. The suggestion that this was *Jameel* abuse was said to be 'unrealistic' given the volume of messages and the intimate nature thereof. The claim appeared to represent a very serious breach of the claimant's privacy rights which may attract a substantial damages if she were to be successful.

The Court also did not consider this claim to be an example of *Henderson* abuse, sufficient to strike out the proceedings. The Court acknowledged that the claimant could have challenged the admissibility of the messages during the employment tribunal hearing. However, it was not incumbent on the claimant to do so. The Court held that even if the claimant had obtained an order from the employment tribunal excluding the evidence, this would not have prevented her from bringing a misuse of private information claim in the High Court. It was noted that the tribunal did not have jurisdiction to deal with a misuse of private information claim.

With regard to the respondents' claim that the proceedings represented an abuse based upon a breach of CPR, r 31.32, the Court held that the claimant did not need the permission of the Court to disclose her own documents to her instructed solicitors for the purpose of prosecuting her misuse of private information claim. The messages were disclosed voluntarily and therefore fell outside the implied undertaking under the rule. Further, it was emphasised that the messages were deployed at the tribunal hearing, which was held in public.

The Court stated that the respondents' arguments relating to the claimant's not enjoying a reasonable expectation of privacy could not apply to those messages which were received from an anonymous source. It was also noted that no authority had been offered to support the argument that material downloaded to a work computer loses its private character.

2 *Jameel v Dow Jones & Co Inc* [2005] EWCA Civ 75, where the Court of Appeal of England and Wales held that if an action involves no or minimal damage to the claimant's reputation, then the action itself may be an interference with the right to freedom of expression.

3 *Henderson v Henderson* [1843–60] All E.R. 378, [1843] 7 WLUK 87, the rule states that if a party could have pleaded an issue in earlier proceedings between the parties, it cannot plead the issue in subsequent litigation between the parties.

The Court noted that, as the date of discovery and/or receipt of the messages pre-dated the employment tribunal proceedings, there was no justification for the messages' retention or use. It was also noted that, of the thousands of messages in the respondents' possession, only 40 were relevant to the employment tribunal proceedings in any event. The Court observed that the receipt of the messages was not brought to the claimant's attention or nor were they returned to her. Finally, the Court stated that even if the proceedings were in being at the time of the respondents' discovery and/or receipt of the messages, the retention thereof would still have been *prima facie* actionable, as it would have been an impermissible kind of self-help. The appropriate approach would have been to return the messages to the claimant, who may then have been answerable to the principles of disclosure.

The High Court refused the respondents' application.

The Court also refused the respondents' application for an interim payment or the lodging of monies in court, citing the claimant's financial circumstances and the concern that doing so would stifle her claim.

As regards the respondents' summary judgment applications, the Court held that the respondents had not demonstrated that the claimant had no real prospect of successfully defending the counterclaim. Due to the novelty of the points that arose in this case and also to the requirement to make a ruling as to the claimant's state of mind and motivation, the claims for malicious prosecution and abuse of process were deemed to be unsuitable for summary judgment.

ANONYMITY ORDERS/REPORTING RESTRICTIONS

[4.03] ***RM v SHC*[4]*—High Court—Roberts J—interlocutory application—Civil Law (Miscellaneous Provisions) Act 2008, s 27—anonymisation order—evidence concerning respondent's medical condition***

The employer sought an order under s 27 of the Civil Law (Miscellaneous Provisions) Act 2008 (the '2008 Act') prohibiting the publication or broadcast of any matter relating to the proceedings 'which would, or would be likely to, identify the respondent or any medical condition from which she is suffering or any information relating to the identification, gender, occupation, profession, practice and/or place of work or location with the state of the respondent'.

The interim application was brought in the context of proceedings in which the plaintiff was claiming that their employment with the employer was unlawfully terminated. The plaintiff exhibited a consultant psychiatrist's report to an affidavit which set out in detail the plaintiff's medical history and made a diagnosis of an acute generalised anxiety disorder in response to the proceedings. In particular, it was reported that the plaintiff was particularly stressed 'by the prospect of being identified as suffering from

4 *RM v SHC* [2023] IEHC 252.

a psychiatric disorder'. The author of the report expressed concern that the identification of the plaintiff in the proceedings was 'likely to cause a significant deterioration' in the plaintiff's condition.

While the employer was willing to consent to an order prohibiting any publication of the plaintiff's medical condition, it was argued that the fact of the medical condition did not entitle the plaintiff to anonymisation under s 27 of the 2008 Act. It was further argued that the plaintiff's medical condition was not a central aspect of the proceedings.

An unusual feature of the case was that correspondence which emanated from the plaintiff, and which led to the plaintiff's dismissal, made liberal reference to the plaintiff's medical condition. That correspondence was an important feature of the proceedings and would form a part of the evidence. The Court was of the view that the plaintiff's medical condition was a matter that would have to be opened to the Court. Indeed, that correspondence was already exhibited to the plaintiff's affidavit.

In the circumstances, the Court did not consider a limited order to be workable, as the evidence was 'likely to be somewhat intertwined and overlapping', leaving open the possibility of a breach of reporting restrictions, even inadvertently. The simpler alternative was to make an order protecting the identities of the parties.

The Court, being satisfied that the making of a s 27 order would not be prejudicial to the interests of justice granted the application in the terms sought.

[4.04] ***Clifford v Millicom Services UK Ltd*[5]*—Court of Appeal of England and Wales—Lewis, Elisabeth Laing & Warby LJJ—appeal from UK Employment Appeal Tribunal—Employment Tribunals (Constitution and Rules Procedure) Regulations 2013,*[6] *Schedule 1, paragraph 50—employment litigation—reporting restrictions—derogations—disclosure—freedom of expression—open justice—public interest—right to fair trial—right to respect for private and family life***

The appellant was employed as global investigations manager by the first-named respondent, a group of companies that provided digital services to emerging markets in Latin America and Africa. The appellant was dismissed in 2019 and he alleged that this was because of whistleblowing activity on his part. This activity concerned staff at a subsidiary company of the first-named respondent who had allegedly tracked the mobile phone of a customer in another country and shared their findings with a government agency in that country. This customer was later the victim of a serious crime. The appellant brought a case to the employment tribunal as against the first-named respondent and three other employees (second to fourth respondents).

The respondents applied for an order under the Employment Tribunals (Constitution and Rules Procedure) Regulations 2013, Schedule 1, paragraph 50 preventing the

5 *Clifford v Millicom Services UK Ltd* [2023] EWCA Civ 50. For decision of UK EAT in *Millicom Services UK Ltd and Ors v Clifford* [2022] EAT 74, see *Arthur Cox Employment Law Yearbook 2022* at **[4.27]**.

6 Employment Tribunals (Constitution and Rules Procedure) Regulations 2013 (SI 2013/1237).

public disclosure or reporting of certain sensitive details relating to the claim, including: the identity of the customer; the details of the attack; and identification of the staff that allegedly tracked the phone. The respondents argued that this order was necessary, in the interests of justice, to safeguard rights under arts 3, 5, 6 and 8 of Protocol 12 of the European Convention on Human Rights (ECHR), and because the appellant was subject to a contractual duty of confidence. The second-named respondent, who was the vice president of legal, indicated that he would not act as a witness if the order was not granted and that the first-named respondent would not defend the proceedings.

The employment tribunal dismissed the application. It ruled that it did not have the requisite jurisdiction under paragraph 50 or under the common law to protect the Convention rights of those who were not within signatory states. Secondly, the tribunal held that the respondents had not established that there was no 'objective evidence' underlying the claim that there were risks to the safety and security of staff and, therefore, they had not satisfied the requisite threshold. The employment tribunal was not convinced that the appellant's contractual duty of confidence offset the open justice principle. Finally, it was held that the respondents' refusal to defend proceedings or to call the vice president of legal as a witness in proceedings was not legally relevant.

The respondents appealed to the UK EAT, which upheld the employment tribunal's first and second findings above. However, it found that the tribunal erred by limiting its review of the case to a consideration of rights under arts 3, 5 and 8 without discussing whether an order was appropriate under art 6 or whether the interests of justice demanded that it be made. Further, the employment tribunal erred in failing to consider whether the second-named respondents' subjective concerns may have triggered art 8. In addition, it was held that the tribunal erred by failing to conduct a fact-specific balancing test and by failing to consider whether it was in the public interest for the duty of confidence alleged to be breached by disclosure within the proceedings. The EAT ordered the re-determination of the matter under all three limbs of paragraph 50, being whether it was necessary to ban the public disclosure of the information outlined: (1) because the interests of justice demanded such an order; (2) in order to protect the second-named respondent's art 8 rights; and/or (3) in order to safeguard confidentiality.

The appellant appealed to the Court of Appeal, arguing that the EAT was wrong to interfere with the tribunal's conclusion that art 8 was not triggered and that, accordingly, a balancing exercise was not required. The appellant also argued that the EAT should not have found that the tribunal should have carried out a further or different balancing test with regard to the confidentiality clause. The appellant argued that these points would be enough to dispose of the appeal because everything turned on whether art 8 was triggered and if not, there would be no interests of justice issue to be determined.

The respondents cross-appealed, arguing that the EAT should have held that the company's fears had such a clear objective basis that the tribunal was wrong to find otherwise and that said fears were enough to trigger art 8. They argued that a party's willingness to take part in proceedings had to be legally relevant.

The Court of Appeal emphasised that the principle of open justice is qualified by the interests of justice. Derogations from the principle to protect the right to security, or to ameliorate a risk to life and limb, for example, applied. In order to ascertain whether a derogation could be granted, the Court emphasised the need for evidence of a real and immediate risk of harm. It stated that there was still a possibility that a derogation might be granted if this evidence did not demonstrate a risk to life, limb or security.

The Court held that the EAT was correct to order the re-determination. The Court noted that the second-named respondent's subjective fears had not been considered by the tribunal, which had limited its evaluation to the Convention issue. It emphasised that no balancing exercise had been carried out by the tribunal, which was a flawed approach. Rather, the tribunal should have considered the harm that disclosure could cause and whether and to what extent the order sought would undermine the open justice principle. The Court held that although a threat not to defend proceedings if an order is not made is not enough to justify the making of said order, there was no authority that stated that a decision maker should always ignore such stated intentions. The decision maker should consider the effect that publicity might have on a party or witness' willingness to participate in a trial. It was held that any decision to refuse a derogation should be examined for compatibility with any other Convention rights that were properly relied on in order to protect the information.

Regarding the tribunal's finding that there was no 'objective evidence' supporting the claim that there were risks to the safety and security of staff, the Court held that the tribunal had misdirected itself. The evidence supporting the claim was more than mere subjective fears. Rather, the evidence suggested that disclosure would materially increase, for example, the threat of vigilante action and this was to be taken as objective evidence.

The Court held that the tribunal should have employed a fact-specific analysis to determine whether limiting the disclosure of confidential information was compatible with open justice, regardless of the rights of confidentiality under contract in this case.

The Court of Appeal dismissed the appeal but allowed the cross-appeal.

[4.05] *F v J[7]—UK Employment Appeal Tribunal—appeal from employment tribunal—anonymity order—litigant in person—error of fact—fair procedure—unfair inferences*

The claimant applied for an anonymity order ahead of a multi-day hearing of a complaint of disability discrimination before the employment tribunal. The claimant, who was a litigant in person, expressed fears concerning the impact on his future employability if his application for anonymity was refused. The application was refused by an employment judge at a preliminary hearing and the claimant appealed that decision.

The UK EAT observed that the employment judge proceeded on the erroneous understanding that a claim passes into the public domain by virtue of it's having been

7 *F v J* [2023] EAT 92.

presented. This had a bearing on the judge's assessment of the claimant's submissions, as the judge proceeded on the basis that the claimant's art 8 rights under the European Convention on Human Rights would be infringed, in any event, by the fact of his disability going public.

The EAT also noted that fairness would also have required that the tribunal take 'proactive steps' to explain to the claimant, at the start of the hearing, the onus on him to provide cogent evidence of the potential harm, and to afford him the opportunity to provide that evidence.

The judge was found to have unfairly drawn an inference from the claimant's submissions that the claimant 'would not wish to tell his future employer that he was disabled', and that he would be 'less than candid' if asked that direct question by a prospective employer. The claimant had made neither point in submissions and had not had the opportunity to give sworn evidence.

The appeal was allowed and the tribunal's decision not to grant the anonymity order was quashed.

BIAS

[4.06] ***Department of Enterprise, Trade and Employment v McCarthy*[8]*—Labour Court—appeal from Workplace Relations Commission—Industrial Relations Act 1946—recusal of ordinary member of the Court—allocation of the Labour Court hearings—actual bias—objective bias—objective bystander test—ordinary reasonable person test***

The claimant had been an ordinary member of the Labour Court, employed by the respondent Government Department. A decision was made to reject his statutory claims in the WRC and the claimant appealed the decision to the Labour Court. A Labour Court case management meeting took place regarding a number of issues.

In the first instance, the claimant revealed that he had obtained information through a Freedom of Information request which attributed a statement to the Chairman of the Labour Court, responsible for assigning the division to hear his case. This statement allegedly indicated that the claimant's right to a fair hearing, free from bias, was at risk.

Separately, the respondent made a recusal request against an ordinary member of the Labour Court, who was nominated to the Court by the Irish Congress of Trade Unions ('ICTU'). The respondent noted that, in his submissions, the claimant made assertions concerning the processes within the ICTU which ultimately led to that person's appointment. It was argued that this might lead to the risk of potential objective bias on the part of that person, which might be raised by the claimant at a later stage.

8 *Department of Enterprise, Trade and Employment v McCarthy* EDA2324.

The Labour Court considered the relevant provisions of the Industrial Relations Act 1946 concerning the Chairman's role in assigning to each division the business to be transacted by it. The Court noted that the claimant's application arose from an apprehension that the Chairman might express a view detrimental to his case while assigning it to the relevant division. The Labour Court held that the sitting division was assigned this case in accordance with the Industrial Relations Act 1946. It was noted that the Chairman was not a member of the division assigned to hear the case and that the division had had no interaction or discussion with the Chairman in respect of the case. The information relied on was held not to relate to any member of the current division. The Court applied the reasonable person test and determined that the claimant's argument did not meet the test for objective or actual bias.

With regard to the respondent's request for recusal, the Court considered the claimant's submissions where he stated:

> 'It is the [claimant's] belief and understanding that internal developments [arose] in one of the member unions of the Irish Congress of Trade Unions which it is understood presented a difficulty for management of that Union in respect of its internal leadership structure. As a means of resolving this internal difficulty, the Irish Congress of Trade Unions nominated an individual to the Court notwithstanding that there was no vacancy at that time'.

The Court noted that the assertion did not relate to the member personally, nor was it supported by documentary or testimonial evidence. The Court noted that the apprehension of bias is a fair procedure matter and that there has to be a nexus between the case and the relevant factor. Here, however, the only relevant factor was a bald assertion made about a third party.

It was noted that the member concerned was among two other nominees by the ICTU. It was this process that the claimant had criticised and not that member's ultimate appointment to the Court by the Minister. The Court noted that the respondent did not elaborate on how this could give rise to objective bias.

The Court held that an objective bystander, who was informed of all relevant facts, would not consider that any member of the division would be incapable of hearing the case due to bias.

Accordingly, the Court held that no member had to recuse themselves and the division would reschedule the case management conference before hearing the substantive case.

[4.07] ***Veizi v Glasgow City Council*[9]*—UK Employment Appeal Tribunal—appeal from employment tribunal—bias—recusal application refused—whether the employment judge showed actual or apparent bias towards the claimant—scope of pleadings***

The claimant was employed as a temporary accommodation development officer by the respondent until his dismissal for gross misconduct in April 2019. The claimant, who

9 *Veizi v Glasgow County Council* [2022] EAT 182.

was of Albanian origin with British nationality, brought claims for unfair dismissal, race discrimination and victimisation.

In his role, the claimant was responsible for managing the respondent's properties so that temporary furnished accommodation could be brought into service for homeless people. He was suspended and an investigation by the respondent's corporate fraud team alleged that he had been double ordering white goods for his own personal gain and using his council email for personal purposes. A disciplinary hearing led to the claimant's summary dismissal by the respondent.

In the course of the employment tribunal hearing, and before his cross-examination had concluded, the claimant made an application asking that the tribunal recuse itself on grounds of bias. The tribunal refused the recusal application, setting out written reasons for several decisions it had made in the course of the hearing. The substantive hearing was stayed while the claimant brought an appeal to the UK EAT challenging various procedural aspects of the tribunal's ruling. These related chiefly to matters concerning evidence given or to be given, admissibility of documents, and amendments to pleadings.

The EAT found that the tribunal's decision to disallow part of a proposed amendment to the respondent's pleadings, and to make a small adjustment of its own so that what was pleaded made grammatical sense, did not exceed the tribunal's powers and did not 'cross the line of acting as an advocate for one party so as to render the hearing unfair'. The tribunal was not required to either accept the amendment application in its entirely or to reject it in its entirety.

The EAT also found that the tribunal was entitled, in the course of the claimant's examination-in-chief, to admit a document (in this instance, a High Court judgment tendered by the respondent on the basis that it purportedly went to the claimant's credibility) on a precautionary basis, and to decide at a later stage, based on what was put to the claimant in cross-examination, whether it was in fact relevant.

The EAT did not consider that the tribunal's decision to play back a recording of a part of the claimant's evidence in order to settle a point of dispute between the parties gave rise to an inference of bias, apparent or actual, against the claimant.

It also found that in giving his evidence-in-chief, the claimant gave what was arguably conjectural evidence of the dismissing officer's state of mind that went beyond his pleaded case. Accordingly, the respondent had been entitled to put to the claimant in cross-examination what the evidence of that officer would be on that particular point. The parties were required only to set out the 'essence' of their case in pleadings, 'and not every fact and evidential matter in support of it'.

While the above grounds failed, the EAT allowed an appeal and cross-appeal on one point which arose from the approach taken by the tribunal to the respondent's application to supplement further and better particulars. That application was refused owing to the prejudice it would have caused the claimant. However, during the claimant's cross-examination, a dispute arose as regards what could or could not be put into evidence as a result of that refusal. The tribunal permitted a particular question because 'there was a foundation for it in the case as pleaded, notwithstanding the exclusion from the further and better particulars of the proposed information'. That decision was challenged by both parties and the EAT held that the tribunal had erred in permitting the respondent to present the evidence, having already refused the application to supplement. It had also erred in failing to consider prejudice to the respondent in its refusal to permit the supplemented information.

The appeal was allowed in part.

[4.08] ***Higgs v Farmor's School and The Archbishops Council of England*[10]*—UK Employment Appeal Tribunal—appeal from employment tribunal—preliminary application—claimant seeking recusal of lay member—reasonable apprehension of bias—membership of a trade union in senior role***

The claimant appealed against the decision of an employment tribunal. Her claim related to her sharing of social media posts, which the respondent school concluded (reasonably, in the view of the tribunal) could be read as homophobic or transphobic. The claimant argued that the tribunal's finding was perverse.

The claimant called for the recusal of a certain lay member of the UK EAT from hearing her appeal. This lay member had formerly held the position of assistant secretary of the National Education Union (the 'NEU'), and had publicly expressed clear views in opposition to those held by the claimant, in the context of a heated debate.

The EAT, while agreeing that it will not always be appropriate for certain lay members to sit in on certain appeals, found that, in this case, none of the material relied upon by the claimant had been published or communicated by the lay member, nor could the material be associated with them in that role.

In considering whether public statements made by the NEU gave rise to a reasonable apprehension of bias, the EAT found that while that lay member had not personally expressed any public view on either side of the debate, the NEU itself campaigned on a platform that opposed the views held by the claimant. The lay member would inevitably be associated with NEU's views, irrespective of their own views.

The EAT was therefore satisfied that there was 'real ground for doubt', so that the application should be resolved in favour of recusal.

[4.09] ***Aspect Windows (Western) Ltd v Retter*[11]*—UK Employment Appeal Tribunal—appeal from employment tribunal—apparent bias—social media post by tribunal member***

The respondent appealed against a decision of the employment tribunal involving a complaint of a sham redundancy in which the claimant was successful.

---

10 *Higgs v Farmor's School and The Archbishops' Council of England* [2023] EAT 45.

11 *Aspect Windows (Western) Ltd v Retter (As representative of the Estate of Mrs C McCrorie)* [2023] EAT 95.

The appeal concerned a LinkedIn post by one of the tribunal members, which appeared following the publication of the tribunal's decision. The post had a link to a Mail Online article about the case and the tribunal member replied to comments beneath the post. The respondent submitted that the LinkedIn posts showed apparent bias.

The UK EAT found that, whatever the wisdom or appropriateness of the tribunal member posting the link, the impartial, informed observer would not infer that she had done something indicating a real possibility that she had been biased in favour of the claimant. The main post only referred to the fact that she had sat on the case and that it has been reported in the Mail Online. She did not comment on the outcome or substance of the tribunal's decision.

The appeal was, accordingly, dismissed.

CONCURRENT CLAIMS

[4.10] ***Onea v Contingent and Future Technologies Ltd*[12]*—UK Employment Appeal Tribunal—appeal from employment tribunal—appeal of refusal to grant a stay—concurrent High Court proceedings—relevant considerations***

The claimant appealed an order of the employment tribunal refusing his application for a stay of the tribunal proceedings.

The claimant was a co-founder and a director of the respondent company with two others. The claimant resigned on 11 October 2021, asserting a breakdown of trust and confidence in the respondent. The respondent did not accept his resignation and the claimant was purportedly dismissed for gross misconduct the following day. As a result of the purported dismissal, the claimant was deemed a 'bad leaver,' with adverse consequences for his shareholding.

In a complaint of unfair dismissal, the claimant alleged that he had made protected disclosures concerning another of the co-founders of the respondent and that he had been automatically dismissed. He also complained of 'ordinary' unfair dismissal and wrongful dismissal.

A stay was sought by the claimant pending the determination of two sets of proceedings in the High Court of England and Wales: one in which the respondent sought injunctive relief against the claimant in respect of alleged misuse of confidential information and the other was an unfair prejudice petition filed by the claimant against the respondent and the other co-founders.

The claimant submitted that the tribunal had erred in refusing the stay on the basis that there was no 'considerable overlap' between the High Court proceedings, 'when the overlap was in fact very substantial'. If the employment tribunal claim were heard

12 *Onea v Contingent and Future Technologies Ltd* [2023] EAT 125.

first, it was argued that the binding decisions of fact and law would result in issue estoppels, which could 'embarrass' the High Court Judges hearing those proceedings. In the second instance, the claimant argued that the tribunal erred in taking into account the delay to the full hearing of the claim if the stay were granted. Thirdly, the tribunal erred in taking into account 'the liberty of the claimant to seek a direction from the High Court on whether the … claim should be stayed'. Finally, the claimant argued that the tribunal erred in deciding that it was not in the interests of justice overall to grant the stay.

The UK EAT held that the employment tribunal failed to ask the correct question when refusing the application for a stay. The tribunal had stated that the claimant was 'required to establish a very real risk of considerable embarrassment to the High Court'. While this was no doubt relevant, the correct approach was one involving 'a weighing up of all relevant considerations', rather than meeting a 'threshold criterion' of the kind apparently identified by the tribunal. This was a material error of law which invalidated the tribunal's exercise of its discretion.

Accordingly, the appeal succeeded on most of its grounds and the tribunal claim was stayed pending the outcome of the High Court proceedings.

DISMISSAL INJUNCTION—COSTS

[4.11] ***Nesbitt v Kefron*[13]*—High Court—O'Moore J—costs—mootness—costs for defined period—injunctive relief—disciplinary proceedings—admission of wrongdoing—appeal upheld***

The plaintiff was an employee of the defendant; and following an investigation on foot of a number of allegations against her, she was dismissed on 14 February 2023. The plaintiff was advised that she had five days to appeal this decision, which she did. The plaintiff wrote to the defendant and listed a number of concerns she had about the fairness and legality of the disciplinary process and asked for certain undertakings. She indicated that if she did not receive said undertakings by a specific date, she would seek injunctive relief.

On 9 March 2023, the plaintiff issued a motion seeking injunctive relief restraining the taking of any steps in the determination of her appeal and requiring the continuation of her salary payments during the interim time. On 15 March, the managing director wrote to the plaintiff and informed her that her appeal would be upheld, other than in relation to the wrongdoing that she had admitted during the course of the disciplinary process. The managing director stated that, on review, this was not a case that should result in dismissal and that the wrongdoing concerned did not amount to gross misconduct or grossly indecent behaviour.

---

13 *Nesbitt v Kefron* [2023] IEHC 619.

The plaintiff applied to the High Court for her costs in the injunction application. It was agreed that the action became moot shortly after it was initiated on 9 March 2023. The proceedings were served on the date of issue. The plaintiff argued that she was entitled to her costs for a defined period being 17 January 2023 to 17 April 2023.

The Court held that the decision of the managing director was not something that arose from the bringing of the application for injunctive relief. It found that the proceedings were effectively at an end when the managing director gave his decision on 15 March 2023, allowing the plaintiff's appeal. While there was some activity after this date it was not sufficient to permit her to seek her costs. The Court held that if the proceedings had been initiated after the 15 March 2023, they would have been difficult to justify. It was equally difficult to justify any claim for costs for the prosecution of the proceedings after that date. The Court held that the plaintiff was not entitled to her costs and made no order as to costs.

DELAY

[4.12] ***Lane v Enterprise Ireland*[14]*—High Court—Heslin J—inordinate and inexcusable delay—want of prosecution—harassment—bullying—intimidation—breach of contract—oral testimony—balance of justice—degradation of witness memory—moderate prejudice—unfair trial—passage of time***

The plaintiff complained that she was harassed and bullied by servants or agents of the defendant on dates between 2008 and 2012. She brought personal injuries proceedings. The plaintiff lodged a PIAB application in 2013 and issued the personal injury summons in 2014. In 2022, the defendant brought a motion to dismiss the plaintiff's claim for inordinate and inexcusable delay.

The Court noted that, in order to make findings as to the plaintiff's claims concerning particulars of incidents of harassment, bullying and intimidation, and breach of contract, it would have to rely on the oral testimony of those present at the time of these incidents. The Court held that 'it is a statement of the obvious that 2008 is 15 years ago and … the case is nowhere near being ready for trial'.

The Court noted that, despite the antiquity of the claim (the alleged incidents first occurred in 2008), the plaintiff allowed a further two years to lapse since the last incident of the impugned behaviour before issuing proceedings. It held that, due to this 'late start' the plaintiff was under a greater obligation to prosecute her claim in a timely manner. The Court acknowledged the positive steps that the plaintiff had taken to further her claim eg, furnishing replies to particulars in 2016 and updated particulars in 2021 and calculated her delay at five years and three months.

---

14 *Lane v Enterprise Ireland* [2023] IEHC 527.

The Court considered the plaintiff's reasons for the delay, including: her limited access to supporting documentation; delay in acquiring an expert's report; the fact that she was missing documentation relating to her employment; her seeking counselling for the alleged harassment suffered, which took considerable time; housing, employment and stress issues; and family bereavement and sickness. The Court found that while it had sympathy for the plaintiff, the grounds relied on were not sufficient to excuse the delay.

The Court characterised the substantive case as not being a 'documents case', stating that it 'is utterly unlike, for example a dispute in relation to the proper interpretation of words in a contract'. Here, there were a number of impugned incidents claimed and therefore, in order to determine the issues in dispute, oral testimony was vital.

The Court held that the evidence before it disclosed no excuse for the plaintiff's delay and that it was inordinate in nature. The Court then turned to the balance of justice and focused on the potential degradation of relevant witnesses' memories. It also held that moderate prejudice arose here, and that the defendant had established that there was a significant risk of an unfair trial or unjust result, due to the passage of time.

The Court dismissed the plaintiff's claim for want of prosecution on the basis of inordinate and inexcusable delay and ruled that costs should follow the event.

PRIVILEGE

[4.13] ***University of Dundee v Chakraborty*[15]*—Court of Session of Scotland—Lord Carloway—appeal on a question of law from UK Employment Appeal Tribunal—report produced at the outcome of a grievance procedure—scope of privilege arising from legal confidentiality—whether an original version of a document became confidential when the final version was issued because comparison between them would permit an inference about what legal advice had been tendered—doctrine of waiver***

The appellant university issued a policy document providing for an independent 'Dignity at Work and Study' ('DAWS') investigation panel. The respondent was a post-doctoral research assistant to a professor at the university and was employed by the appellant until his resignation in December 2021. In November 2021, he raised a grievance against the professor in question under the appellant's DAWS procedure, alleging racial abuse, harassment, bullying and discrimination. The appellant appointed a member of its academic staff to chair the investigation panel.

In December 2021, prior to the outcome of the grievance procedure, the respondent lodged a claim with the employment tribunal for unfair and/or constructive dismissal and racial discrimination against the appellant and the professor.

15 *University of Dundee v Chakraborty* [2023] CSIH 22. See *Arthur Cox Employment Law Yearbook 2022* at **[4.10]** for EAT decision in *University of Dundee v Chakraborty* [2022] EAT 150.

The appellant issued its report on foot of the DAWS procedure in February 2022. This report was amended by the appellant's legal advisors in March and June 2022. The author of the report agreed to the changes and added some of her own. In all, there were five versions of the report before it was finalised in June 2022. A footnote in the final report explained that the document had been 'amended and reissued ... following independent legal advice'.

At the employment tribunal hearing, the respondent sought discovery of the original report. He expressed suspicion that the appellant had altered the original version in order to assist the professor who was the subject of the grievance procedure. The appellant contended that a comparison between the original report and the final version would reveal the legal advice that had been tendered. The employment tribunal rejected the appellant's argument and ordered that it produce the original document.

The appellant appealed to the UK EAT, where it conceded that the original report was not protected by privilege when it was created as it was not a communication between a client and a lawyer for the purposes of giving or receiving legal advice. The appellant appealed on a question of law to the Court of Session, which was asked to determine whether confidentiality attached to the original version of the appellant's report.

The central question was whether the original version of the report was made confidential by the issue of the final version because comparison between the two would permit an inference about what legal advice had been given. If the appellant was correct, the Court observed, the respondent would be prevented from seeing what the author of the report had said in her original version and would be unable to cross-examine her on the validity of her findings. The Court noted that this was not a case concerning 'material which would allow the reader to work out whether legal advice had been given'. Rather, the appellant itself 'had revealed [in the footnote] the existence of such advice as having influenced the content of the final version'.

Privilege was probably abandoned when the advice that was obtained by the appellant was revealed to the person 'who was carrying out what was supposed to be an impartial investigation' and the Court found that waiver had been established.

Accordingly, the appeal was refused.

EMPLOYMENT STATUS

[4.14] ***Revenue Commissioners v Karshan (Midlands) Ltd t/a Domino's Pizza[16]—Supreme Court—Murray J—appeal from Court of Appeal—employment status of***

16 *Revenue Commissioners v Karshan (Midlands) Ltd t/a Domino's Pizza* [2023] IESC 24. See *Arthur Cox Employment Law Yearbook 2022* at **[18.33]** for decision of Court of Appeal in *Karshan v The Revenue Commissioners* [2022] IECA 124.

delivery drivers for the purposes of taxation—contract of service or contract for services

This was an appeal from the Court of Appeal, which set aside an order of the High Court in a consultative case stated by the Tax Appeals Commissioner ('TAC'). The decision of the TAC had determined that pizza delivery drivers engaged by Karshan ('Domino's Pizza'), who had worked during the years of assessment 2010 and 2011, had done so under contracts of service, and as such were taxable under the Taxes Consolidation Act 1997. The High Court upheld this decision. The Court of Appeal allowed the appeal and set aside the order of the High Court and the decision of the TAC on the grounds that there was no mutuality of obligation in the contractual arrangements between Domino's Pizza and the drivers, and therefore, the drivers worked under contracts for services as self-employed, independent contractors. The Revenue Commissioners appealed to the Supreme Court.

Overturning the decision of the Court of Appeal, the Supreme Court held that, on the facts of the case, the delivery drivers were properly categorised by Revenue as employees and not as independent contractors as was contended for by Domino's Pizza.

Importantly, the Supreme Court rejected the contention that 'mutuality of obligation' was a prerequisite for concluding that a person is rightly categorised as an employee, as distinct from a self-employed person. Specifically, the Court concluded that it was not essential that an agreement 'impose an obligation to provide work and to complete that work on an ongoing basis' for it to be classified as an employment contract.

Domino's Pizza engaged the drivers on what was referred to as an overarching 'umbrella' contract. Under this contract, the drivers would confirm to Domino's Pizza their availability for work one week in advance. Only then would they be rostered for work.

The Supreme Court found that single stints of work (in this instance, the rostered work) can comprise contracts of employment, even if not accompanied in an umbrella contract by a commitment by an organisation to actually give any work in advance of these stints.

The Supreme Court, having found the term mutuality of obligation to be 'a wholly ambiguous label', disposed of the fallacy that there is a requirement for mutuality of obligation on an ongoing basis, went on to consider the tests that should be applied when determining the status of a worker. Those tests are as follows:

1. Does the contract involve the exchange of wage or other remuneration for work?

At the outset, the decision maker must satisfy itself that the parties have entered into a valid contract in the first place and then identify the precise terms of the alleged contract. For there to be a valid contract, there must be consideration, ie, a wage or other remuneration.

To qualify as an employment contract, the consideration must involve a promise of some kind by the worker to work for the alleged employer.

2. Has the worker agreed to provide their services to the employer personally?

For a contract to be a contract of employment the agreement must be one for personal service by the worker. This is the essence of an employment contract.

Some limited degree of substitution is permissible. An agreement may provide for a right of substitution only where the worker is unable to carry out the work, or with the consent of another person who has an absolute and unqualified discretion to withhold consent. The Supreme Court observed that these scenarios are consistent with a requirement for personal service.

However, an unconditional or unfettered right to substitute is inconsistent with an undertaking to provide the work or service personally. A right of substitution limited only by the need to show that the substitute is qualified to do the work is not consistent with personal performance.

In every case it is necessary to decide if the agreement is just one for personal services or whether it is an agreement that enables such unconditional delegation that it is not a contract for personal services at all.

3. A Framework of Control vs Day-to-Day Control

There must be a minimum level of control over a worker before a relationship is found capable of being an employment contract. However, the control arising at this point of the enquiry does not itself determine the issue of employment. The legally minimum element of control is a framework of control in the sense of ultimate authority rather that the concept of day-to-day control which has been a focus in previous cases.

The question is whether there is a right of control over what is to be done; at least generally the way in which it is to be done, the means to be employed in doing it, and the time when, and the place where, it shall be done.

For skilled work, the alleged employer will not be expected to be able to direct the worker as to how to achieve the prescribed objective. However, if the alleged employer does not have the power to direct the type of work the worker is required to do, the relationship will not be capable of constituting an employment relationship. The Supreme Court noted that there is an expectation that the organisation retain some residual authority over workers carrying out skilled work.

Similarly, if the services are provided to an organisation that does not have an entitlement to prescribe times by which the work is to be done, no power to determine where or in what conditions the work is to be done or, within an enterprise, the persons who are to do particular work, the Supreme Court found that it is difficult to see how there can be said to be any requisite control.

4. All the circumstances of the employment

The Court concluded that the first three questions set out above should be applied as a filter, in the form of preliminary questions, which, if any are answered negatively, means there can be no contract of employment.

However, if they are all answered affirmatively, the next step it to examine the facts and circumstances to ascertain the true nature of the relationship.

The Supreme Court reframed an existing test as follows:

> *'Are the terms of the contract between employer and worker interpreted in the light of the admissible factual matrix and having regard to the working arrangements between the parties as disclosed by the evidence, consistent with a contract of employment, or with some other form of contract having regard, in particular, to whether the arrangements point to the putative employee working for themselves or for the putative employer'*

In this regard, the Court noted;

- The contract must be interpreted in the light of the factual matrix in which it was concluded.
- The Court must take into account the actual dealings between the parties.
- Where the agreement seeks to characterise the status of the parties, that description does not prevent the Court from determining what, as a matter of law, the agreement actually is.
- Furthermore, 'it is clear that the court in ascertaining the true nature of a working relationship is not analysing an ossified arrangement: a person who begins to work on their own account—perhaps casually—may as time passes become, by reason of the frequency of their work or absorption into the employer's undertaking, an employee'.
- This fourth stage of the assessment does not depend on any presumption arising from the previous three parts. It is freestanding, the onus of proof being on the party who asserts any proposition of fact, law or mixed fact and law, having regard to the statutory processes in which the decision is made.
- The capacity to profit in a material way from their own skill, the need for the employee to invest significantly in their ability to undertake the work, and the requirement to bring tools or equipment to the task, all lean against the existence of a contract of employment.

What depends on the particular facts is the place of those positives and negatives and the weight to be given to them in the balancing exercise undertaken in any case.

5. Is there anything in the particular legislative regime under consideration that requires the Court to adjust or supplement any of the foregoing?

In relation to the first three questions, the Court examined the TAC's earlier decision and noted that:

1. there were binding legal relations between the parties involving the exchange of consideration characteristic of an employment agreement;
2. the right of substitution or delegation was limited such that personal service was required; and
3. Domino's Pizza exercised control over the operation of rosters, allocation of work, drivers' manner of dress, number of deliveries, particularities in relation to insurance, preparation of invoices, and directions to the drivers while on the premises etc.

On the basis of the above, the first three limbs of the test were satisfied.

In relation to all the circumstances of the working arrangements, the Court noted that drivers did not take calls from customers; did not employ their own labour; took no credit or economic risk; worked exclusively from Domino's Pizza's premises; had limited ability to maximise profits; did not advertise their services; and did not scale their delivery business. Additionally, the drivers were required to wear uniforms, carry branding, and deliver as instructed by managers. On that basis, they could not be said to have been engaged in their own business.

The Supreme Court therefore found that the TAC was correct to determine that the drivers were employees of Domino's Pizza for the purposes of tax assessment.

[4.15] ***PBR Restaurants Ltd v Hanley[17]—Labour Court—appeal from Workplace Relations Commission—Unfair Dismissal Acts 1977 to 2015, s 8A—length of service—whether the claimant was an employee—protected disclosure—appellate jurisdiction to hear new claim***

The claimant appealed against the decision of the WRC that he was not an employee of the respondent company prior to 9 December 2019 and did not, therefore, have the 12 months' required service under the Unfair Dismissal Acts 1977 to 2015.

In 2008, the claimant set up, and was managing director of a business which was acquired in 2019 by the respondent company, following a period of examinership. From 9 December 2019, the claimant was appointed managing director of the respondent company. In August 2020, the claimant's contract was terminated on grounds of redundancy.

On a hearing of preliminary issues, the claimant argued that he had been dismissed due to having made a protected disclosure (something that had not been argued at

17 *PBR Restaurants Ltd v Hanley* UDD2320.

first instance) and that the required 12 months' of service under the Unfair Dismissal Acts 1977 to 2015 was not applicable. The respondent objected to the claimant raising the issue of a protected disclosure, having made no reference to one at any stage in the former hearing.

The Court, having regard to the entitlement of the respondent to the opportunity to defend itself against the new allegation, and remarking that the claimant could not rectify his failure to provide that opportunity by seeking to enlarge his claim on appeal, was satisfied that it did not have jurisdiction to hear the protected disclosure claim.

On the issue of length of service, the claimant argued that the WRC erred in only considering the Revenue criteria for self-employment without considering the criteria used to assess if an individual is an employee, 'which needs a careful and flexible understanding of relationships'. The respondent argued that under the code of practice on employer status, someone who owns more than 50% of a company cannot be classed as an employee for PRSI purposes, and is classed as self-employed.

The Court observed that no decisive evidence supported the assertion that the claimant was obliged to carry out work for an employer prior to 2019. Indeed, the claimant was part owner of the company with a substantial share, acting as managing director. The existence of a board did not alter the fact that the claimant was a 'beneficial owner running the business day to day and with all the de facto authority to do so on his own behalf'. The fact that the claimant was classed as self-employed by the Revenue during that period was not, of itself, determinative. Finally (for completeness), the claimant never issued himself with a contract of employment in the relevant period.

The Court was therefore satisfied that the claimant was not an employee prior to 9 December 2019 and the Court did not have jurisdiction to hear the appeal. The decision of the WRC was upheld.

[4.16] ***Independent Workers Union of Great Britain v Central Arbitration Committee[18]—UK Supreme Court—Lloyd-Jones & Rose LJJ—appeal from High Court of England and Wales—European Convention on Human Rights, art 11—Trade Union and Labour Relations (Consolidation) Act 1992—refusal to require an employer to recognise trade union for collective bargaining purposes—employment relationship—power of workers to appoint a substitute***

The appellant trade union appealed against the dismissal of its application for judicial review of the decision of the Central Arbitration Committee ('CAC'), which refused to require the food delivery company, Deliveroo, to recognise the appellant for collective bargaining purposes.

A substantial number of delivery riders, who worked in a particular London zone, had joined the appellant and had asked it to negotiate with Deliveroo on their behalf to improve their conditions of service. Deliveroo refused a formal request from the appellant in November 2016 to enter into collective bargaining negotiations with it.

---

18 *Independent Workers Union of Great Britain v Central Arbitration Committee* [2023] UKSC 43.

Refusing an application to order Deliveroo to recognise the appellant and to engage in collective bargaining, the CAC, a quasi-judicial body, accepted Deliveroo's position that the delivery riders were not 'workers' within the meaning of the Trade Union and Labour Relations (Consolidation) Act 1992. The CAC rejected the alternative argument that refusal to recognise the appellant would constitute a breach of the delivery riders' freedom of association rights under art 11 ECHR. A judicial review challenge brought by the appellant was dismissed and the dismissal was upheld in the Court of Appeal.

The Supreme Court observed that the art 11 right to form and join a trade union is a smaller subset of the general right to freedom of peaceful assembly and freedom of association. The rights on which the appellant sought to rely could only arise in an employment relationship, an autonomous concept applying across all Member States and not dependent on definitions of 'workers' or 'employees' in domestic law.

In determining whether there was an employment relationship within art 11, the Court had to consider, *inter alia*, recommendations of the International Labour Organisation, which were incorporated into the ECHR test for identification of an employment relationship under art 11. The correct approach required the application of 'a multi-factorial test, focusing on the practicalities of the relationship and how it operates in reality'.

The appellant argued for a 'purposive construction' of art 11. A key feature of the relationship was that the delivery riders were 'in a subordinate position with unequal bargaining power as regards the setting of their occupational interests'. It argued that collective bargaining was needed to establish fair working conditions. The Court found that the appellant's approach was not supported by the authorities; many situations exist whereby persons in a position of unequal bargaining power are offered contractual terms on a 'take it or leave it' basis. It does not follow that they are entitled to band together and require the counterparty to negotiate with them collectively.

The issue was whether the relationship between Deliveroo and the riders was an employment relationship consistent with art 11. In this regard, the preceding Courts had correctly focused on the power to appoint a substitute. Delivery riders were genuinely not under an obligation to provide their services personally. The power to appoint a substitute was 'virtually unlimited', making it, *prima facie*, 'totally inconsistent' with an obligation for personal service, which is essential to the existence of an employment relationship within art 11. The Court was satisfied that the CAC had 'rigorously scrutinised' the substance of the relationship. Of particular significance were its findings that there was no policing by Deliveroo of appointments of substitutes, and riders were not subject to criticism or sanction for doing so. The CAC found that Deliveroo did not terminate riders' contracts for failure to accept a certain percentage of orders or failure to make themselves sufficiently available. Moreover, Deliveroo did not object to riders working for competitors simultaneously. The CAC was entitled to conclude that this arrangement reflected the true relationship.

This was determinative of the issue and, accordingly, the appeal was dismissed.

[4.17] ***Ter-Berg v Simply Smile Manor House Ltd, NHS England Midlands and East, Malde and Hancock*[19]*—UK Employment Appeal Tribunal—appeal from employment tribunal—employment status—protected disclosure***

The claimant claimed that he was unfairly dismissed by the first respondent for having made a protected disclosure, and that the third and fourth respondents were co-liable as directors of the first respondent. The employment tribunal determined that the claimant was not an employee of the first respondent and dismissed the claim. The claimant appealed against that determination, which pre-dated the UK Supreme Court decision in *Uber v Aslam*.[20]

The claimant argued that, in light of *Uber*, the tribunal made the error of treating the terms of the written contract as its starting point, and placing emphasis on the parties' common intention as to the claimant's status when they signed the agreement; in essence, limiting the scope if its inquiry. The claimant urged upon the UK EAT the need to have regard to the purpose of legislation protecting whistleblowers, of which the claimant would not be entitled to avail if he was not treated as an employee or a worker.

It appeared to the EAT that the tribunal had considered 'all of the wider circumstances and context' relating to the relationship that were raised before it, and in doing so had looked beyond the written terms of the agreement, and had not confined itself to 'the application of conventional contract law principles'. These included the fact that the claimant had reminded the first respondent more than once that he and his colleagues were not employees, 'but, as he put it, independent contractors paid at a piece rate, supporting the inference that he was entirely cognisant of the contents and significance of what he had signed'.

The EAT did not accept that the tribunal had placed undue emphasis on what it had found to be the parties' intentions on signing the agreement, but had properly considered 'a range of aspects of the working relationship, and whether the terms of the written agreement did or did not reflect that reality'.

Nor did the EAT accept that the tribunal had treated a clause in the written agreement, which stated that the agreement did not create a contract of employment, 'as providing a determinative and complete answer by itself'. Rather, the tribunal had 'surveyed the circumstances' and concluded that the clause was a genuine reflection of the parties' true intentions as to the nature of their relationship.

The EAT did, however, accept that the tribunal fell into error by focusing on clause 36 of the agreement—the opening words of which appeared to negate the requirement of personal service on the part of the claimant—and concluding that it was inconsistent with a contract of employment. This was 'an erroneous reading of the

---

19 *Ter-Berg v Simply Smile Manor House Ltd, NHS England Midlands and East, Malde and Hancock* [2023] EAT 2.

20 *Uber v Aslam* [2021] UKSC 5; [2021] ICR 657, see *Arthur Cox Employment Law Yearbook 2021* at [5.08].

natural meaning' of the opening words, which obliged the claimant to use 'best endeavours' to make arrangements for the use of the clinical facilities by a locum in the event of his absence for more than 20 days 'through ill health or other cause'. This aspect of the appeal was upheld and remitted to the employment tribunal for determination.

[4.18] ***United Taxis Ltd v Comolly, Tidman v United Taxis Ltd*[21]*—UK Employment Appeal Tribunal—appeal from employment tribunal—Employment Rights Act 1996—Equality Act 2010—employment litigation—employment status—worker—employee—control—mutual obligation—Ready Mixed Concrete test—dual employment—substituted findings***

The claimant was a taxi driver who was registered with the respondent, United Taxis Ltd through one of its shareholders, Mr Parkinson, using his taxi. Subsequently, after his relationship with Mr Parkinson ended, he performed taxi services for the company through another one of its shareholders, Mr Tidman, using his taxi. When that relationship ended, the claimant brought a number of complaints to the employment tribunal, arguing that he was either an employee or worker of United Taxis Ltd or Mr Tidman. Mr Tidman argued that the claimant was self employed and United Taxis Ltd argued that it and the claimant had no contract relationship whatsoever.

The tribunal made several preliminary findings including that the claimant was a worker of United Taxis from July 2014 to March 2020 and also an employee of Mr Tidman during that period.

United Taxis Ltd and Mr Tidman both appealed the decision. United Taxis Ltd raised three grounds of appeal. First, that the tribunal had erred in finding that the claimant was at the same time an employee of Mr Tidman and a worker of United Taxis Ltd in respect of the same work. Second, that the tribunal had erred by implying that there existed a contract between United Taxis Ltd and the claimant in circumstances where it was not necessary to do so in order to give effect to the arrangements between the parties. Finally, it was argued that the tribunal erred in finding that any contract between the claimant and United Taxis Ltd created a worker relationship in circumstances where, for example, the company did not retain any part of the fares paid to the claimant and had no interest or control over the arrangements made by the shareholders and the claimant.

Mr Tidman also contended that the tribunal had erred in finding that the claimant was at the same time an employee of Mr Tidman and a worker of United Taxis Ltd in respect of the same work. Second, that the tribunal had erred in its characterisation of the legal and factual nature of the contract between Mr Tidman and the claimant insofar as it described the contract as one by which the claimant provided services for which Mr Tidman paid him. In actuality, it was argued, a different arrangement was reached whereby the claimant hired Mr Tidman's taxi and paid him a hire fee of 50% of the income he generated using it. Finally, Mr Tidman argued that even if the tribunal did

21 *United Taxis Ltd v Comolly and anor, Tidman v United Taxis Ltd and anor* [2023] EAT 93.

not err in finding that the claimant provided services to him, the tribunal erred in finding that the contract between them was one of employment.

The UK EAT found that the tribunal properly concluded that a contract existed between Mr Tidman and the claimant, under which the claimant provided taxi services, and that Mr Tidman paid for those services. It was held that United Taxis Ltd contracted out the task of taxiing its passengers to Mr Tidman and this was sub-contracted to the claimant.

The EAT concluded, however, that the tribunal erred in finding that Mr Tidman had a contract with United Taxis Ltd under which he also did work for the company. There was no necessity to imply such a contract, despite the fact that he had registered with United Taxis and was required to adhere to their rules as a sub-contractor. Further, the EAT underscored the dual employment point which was advanced by the respondents. It was held that the tribunal could not make a finding that the claimant was simultaneously an employee and/or worker of two employers in respect of the same work.

The tribunal also erred in finding that the claimant's contract with Mr Tidman was a contract of employment. With regard to the *Ready Mixed Concrete* test, the EAT held that the tribunal did not err in concluding that there was an obligation of personal service. However, the tribunal's finding that there was an uninterrupted mutuality of obligation during the relevant period was not made out. The EAT also took issue with the tribunal's findings regarding the level of control exercised by Mr Tidman over the claimant.

The EAT allowed both appeals. A finding was substituted that the claimant was neither a worker nor an employee of United Taxis Ltd but was a worker for Mr Tidman.

[4.19] ***Plastic Omnium Automotive Ltd v Horton*[22]*—UK Employment Appeal Tribunal—appeal from employment tribunal—Employment Rights Act 1996—whether the claimant had employee status—whether the claimant was a worker—parties to the contract***

Between 2011 and 2016, the claimant worked on certain automotive component manufacturing projects for the respondent through a service company ('ProMan') which he operated and with which he had a written contract. The claimant acted as programme manager on a number of projects awarded to the respondent and was required to report to the respondent's programme director. The respondent determined the number of days on which the claimant's services would be provided.

In September 2018, the claimant established a new service company ('ProManOne') which invoiced the respondent in the same manner as ProMan had previously done.

The respondent provided the claimant with an access card for the respondent's premises, a laptop and a company email address. On his first day of work, the claimant 'was introduced and treated in exactly the same way' as any other newly employed

22 *Plastic Omnium Automotive Ltd v Horton* [2023] EAT 85.

programme manager. The employment tribunal accepted that the claimant was 'fully integrated' into the respondent's business for in excess of eight years.

The claimant worked regular hours, attended training days and had the same holiday entitlements as employees, with the same level of autonomy as employed programme managers. The only difference was that the claimant did not have to clock in and out. He was not appraised on an annual basis (or any basis), nor was he subject to any disciplinary procedure.

In November 2019, the respondent terminated the contract through which the claimant provided his services and ProManOne invoiced the respondent in respect of work purportedly undertaken by the claimant in November 2019. The respondent never made any payments directly to the claimant but to the service companies.

The claimant alleged that he was an employee of the respondent under s 230(1) of the Employment Rights Act 1996 or alternatively a worker. The respondent submitted the claimant was neither an employee nor a worker and further that the contract between them was void for illegality.

The tribunal found that the 2011 agreement reflected the true agreement between the parties. That contract was 'plainly inconsistent with there being a contract of employment' between the parties. It was 'clearly regarded by [the claimant] as beneficial and both parties complied with its terms throughout'. However, the tribunal was persuaded that the claimant was 'in a subordinate or dependent position' in regard to the respondent and was therefore a worker and not an employee. The tribunal also concluded that the contract was not illegal and found that the respondent had unlawfully deducted wages from the claimant. The respondent appealed these findings.

The UK EAT held that, while the tribunal found there was a contract of employment, it had not considered who the parties to the 2011 agreement were. The contract had not been between the claimant and the respondent, but rather the service companies and the respondent, therefore the tribunal had erred in law by failing to engage with a 'real issue' in the case, ie, that the contract was not between the parties at all.

The EAT allowed the appeal and substituted a finding that the claimant was not a worker.

[4.20] ***Manning v Walker Crips Investment Management Ltd[23]—UK Employment Appeal Tribunal—appeal from employment tribunal—Employment Rights Act 1996—Working Time Regulations 1998[24]—employee status—implied term—self-employed—mutuality of obligation—contract—salaried employee—personal service—independent contractor—implied term was not necessary for business efficacy nor was it so obvious that it went without saying***

The respondent engaged two different types of investment managers: those that were considered salaried employees and those that were engaged as 'self-employed'

23 *Manning v Walker Crips Investment Management Ltd* [2023] EAT 79.

24 Working Time Regulations 1998 (SI 1998/1833).

managers, who were paid commission. The claimant fell into the latter designation. The claimant complained that he had not been paid his entitlement to annual leave contrary to the Working Time Regulations 1998. He contended that this was a detriment which was unlawfully imposed on him, contrary to the Employment Rights Act 1996, on foot of his making protected disclosures.

The employment tribunal held that the claimant did not fall within the definition of 'worker' under the Employment Rights Act 1996 or reg 2 of the Working Time Regulations 1998. It held that the claimant owed no obligation of personal service to the respondent because his employment contract contained a substitution clause that allowed him to substitute another person on his behalf to carry out tasks, subject to the respondent's approval of that person. This was despite the claimant's evidence that he had never exercised this clause. The tribunal held that, on its face, the clause did not appear to nullify personal service and the approval requisite was in fact subject to an implied term that the respondent's approval would not be unreasonably withheld. The tribunal also listed a number of factors which suggested that the claimant was in business on his own account and that the respondent was his client, eg the fact that the contract of employment designated him as an independent contractor and the fact that the claimant was entitled to engage in personal trading during business hours.

The claimant appealed to the UK EAT on several grounds. Among them was his argument that the tribunal had erred in holding that the claimant did not owe the respondent an obligation of personal service. In support of this ground, the claimant argued that the tribunal erred in implying a term into his contract of employment that the respondent could not unreasonably withhold its approval of a substitute. The claimant submitted that contrary to the principle established in *Braganza v BP Shipping Ltd*,[25] the implied term here was not being relied on to protect the worker against an abuse of power or a conflict of interest. Rather, the respondent sought to rely on it to circumvent the claimant's statutory rights.

The EAT found that the tribunal had erred in holding that the claimant owed no obligation of personal service to the respondent. As a result of its decision, the tribunal had implied a term into the contract of employment that was not necessary for business efficacy nor was it so obvious that it went without saying. It was also held that the tribunal had failed to consider the fact that the claimant had never used the substitution clause in practice.

The EAT held that the tribunal had also erred in concluding that the claimant was in business on his own account and that the company was his client. This decision, it was held, was made with reference to irrelevant factors, such as the description of the claimant in the contract and the fact that he was permitted to execute personal trading during business hours. In the latter case, it was noted by the EAT that the respondent permitted all of its investment managers (workers and 'self-employed' alike) to trade on personal investments during working hours.

The appeal was allowed in part.

---

25 *Braganza v BP Shipping Ltd* [2015] 1 WLR 1661.

[4.21] ***Anglian Windows Ltd v Webb[26]—UK Employment Appeal Tribunal—appeal from employment tribunal—application to strike out claim as having no reasonable prospect of success—employment status—whether a pre-existing partnership precluded the existence of contract of employment***

The claimant and his wife operated as a partnership, through which the claimant provided services as an 'area sales leader' to the respondent company and was paid through the partnership. The partnership was a pre-existing one, which was accepted to be genuine.

The claimant lodged a complaint of unfair dismissal. The respondent applied to have the claim struck out as having no reasonable prospect of success, arguing that the claimant was not an employee but in partnership with his wife. The employment tribunal refused the respondent's application, on the basis that the pre-existing partnership 'did not preclude the possibility of the existence of a contract of employment between the claimant and respondent', and, thus, did not prevent the claimant from being able to establish employee status. It reasoned that a traditional partnership is not a separate legal body or an entity distinct from its partners. The respondent appealed that decision.

The UK EAT held that the employment tribunal had erred in seeking to draw a distinction between this case and *Firthglow Ltd v Descombes*,[27] which held that 'a two-man partnership could not be an employee'. The tribunal ought to have considered itself bound by that authority.

Although it is open to the EAT to depart from its previous decisions, none of the circumstances warranting this course of action applied here. Furthermore, the agreed facts of the case meant that the possibility of the existence of a contract of employment between the claimant and the respondent was precluded in any event. Therefore, the claimant's claim of unfair dismissal had no reasonable prospect of success, and the tribunal ought to have allowed the respondent's strike-out application.

The appeal therefore succeeded.

ISAAC WUNDER ORDERS

[4.22] ***Morgan v Labour Court[28]—High Court—Phelan J—Employment Equality Act 1998, s 97(2)(b)—employment litigation—*****Isaac Wunder** ***orders—seeking leave to apply for an order—whether the notice of motion which the applicant sought leave to issue was affected by the doctrine of*** **functus officio**

The applicant was employed as an art teacher by one of the notice parties, Kildare and Wicklow Education and Training Board. Ultimately, the applicant was dismissed by the Board and she initiated a series of largely identical claims challenging her dismissal.

26 *Anglian Windows Ltd v Webb* [2023] EAT 138.
27 *Firthglow Ltd v Descombes* UKEAT/0916/03.
28 *Morgan v Labour Court* [2023] IEHC 122.

One such set of proceedings related to an appeal on a point of law against a determination of the Labour Court made on 1 April 2020. In an ex tempore judgment of 22 March 2022, Ferriter J dismissed this appeal in circumstances where the applicant had failed to point to any error of law in the Labour Court's determination. On 23 October 2021, and in the context of these proceedings, the Board bought a motion seeking an order to restrict the applicant from bringing further proceedings. Despite being afforded the opportunity to file a replying affidavit in response, the applicant did not do so.

In June 2022, an Isaac Wunder order was made by Ferriter J restricting the applicant from initiating any further proceedings concerning, in particular, any matter relating to her employment with the Board, without prior leave of the Court. The applicant appealed the order to the Court of Appeal.

In the present proceedings, the applicant applied to Phelan J in the High Court for leave to issue a motion seeking the grant of an order under s 97(2)(b) of the Employment Equality Act 1998 (the '1998 Act') for the disclosure of certain information. The motion was to bear the record number of the appeal proceedings which had been dismissed by Ferriter J.

Phelan J noted that the proceedings in question were now spent and that the applicant was pursuing a similar application for disclosure before the Court of Appeal by way of motion. The Court emphasised as a 'fundamental question' whether the High Court retained any jurisdiction to make an order such as that sought where the substantive proceedings had already been finally determined.

Ultimately, the Court held that it was *functus officio*. In so deciding, Phelan J noted that the applicant was afforded an opportunity to move an application on foot of s 97(2) of the 1998 Act at the hearing on 22 March 2022, before Ferriter J ultimately dismissed the proceedings. Therefore, it was held that it was not now open to the applicant to change her mind and apply to re-litigate the matter.

In circumstances where appeals were now pending before the Court of Appeal and Supreme Court, the High Court held that it should be left to the appellate courts to decide whether further evidence may be adduced under s 97(2)(b) of the 1998 Act.

Phelan J stated that even if there were no *Isaac Wunder* Order in place, the Court could not consider the applicant's application where the substantive proceedings had been dismissed. In circumstances where an *Isaac Wunder* Order was in place, the Court was satisfied that it could not grant leave to issue the intended notice of motion.

The application for leave was therefore refused.

JUDICIAL IMMUNITY: LABOUR COURT

[4.23] ***A Legal Representative v Chairman of a Division of the Labour Court*[29]*—Workplace Relations Commission—Equal Status Act 2000, s 21—disability—whether***

29 *A Legal Representative v Chairman of a Division of the Labour Court* ADJ-00042833.

the Adjudicator had jurisdiction to hear the complaint—judicial immunity from litigation

The claimant, who appeared as a legal representative at a hearing of the Labour Court, alleged that she was discriminated against on the disability ground by the respondent Chair of the Court, who failed to make reasonable accommodation for her disability.

The claimant submitted that the respondent made a show of her because of her disability, ignored requests for accommodation that she had made in advance, then rejected a subsequent written complaint made by the claimant against him.

The respondent contended that the case was misconceived and should be struck out in advance of the hearing. It was argued that the Labour Court is engaged in the administration of justice and is immune from litigation.

The WRC determined that, when hearing the case that led to the complaint, the Labour Court was engaged in the administration of justice and the respondent was entitled to judicial immunity. The complaint was therefore misconceived and was dismissed.

NORWICH PHARMACAL ORDERS

[4.24] ***Blythe v The Commissioner of An Garda Síochána*[30]*—Court of Appeal—Collins J—appeal from High Court—Norwich Pharmacal orders—disclosure—defamation—speculation—costs—good arguable case—standard of proof***

The respondent was a member of An Garda Síochána. He applied for promotion and was interviewed, but was informed that he had been unsuccessful. He sought an administrative review of this decision but this was not done. In September 2018, at the conclusion of the promotion competition, the respondent brought proceedings against the Garda Commissioner in the High Court.

At the time he initiated these proceedings, but before the proceedings became public knowledge, the respondent became aware of 'grossly defamatory and scandalous comments and photographs' relating to him that were circulating on WhatsApp and Facebook groups, which included members of An Garda Síochána. The respondent was sent screenshots of these messages by friends and put An Garda Síochána on notice of the material. The appellant undertook to conduct an investigation into the material. The respondent resigned in July 2019 and in August 2019 requested the identities of 'the person(s) who created, shared, distributed, published or forwarded the defamatory material' which might have come to the appellant's attention during its investigation, with a view to initiating defamation proceedings against the wrongdoers. The respondent was successful in the High Court in securing a Norwich

30 *Blythe v The Commissioner of an Garda Síochána* [2023] IECA 255.

Pharmacal[31] order against the appellant; however, the appellant's response to the order was that the investigation carried out by An Garda Síochána had failed to identify the senders of the WhatsApp messages, and the Commissioner was never in a position to provide meaningful assistance to the respondent. The Commissioner appealed the High Court order to the Court of Appeal.

A preliminary application was made by the respondent before the Court of Appeal indicating that he had not been aware of this previously, but the information disclosed in response to the High Court order rendered that order moot, involving hypothetical arguments and issues. Any appeal, it was argued, opened the respondent to the hazard of 'severe costs'. The Court rejected this preliminary application, holding that while the '*practical* consequences of the Order may be spent, it continues to have potential *legal* consequences for the Commissioner'.

The Court held that the applicant for a Norwich Pharmacal order must establish that it has a cause of action against the alleged wrongdoer. As regards the standard of proof to be applied, the Court rejected the approach favoured in England and Wales (being 'a good arguable case'). Instead, the Court held that applicants must establish a 'strong case' of actionable wrongdoing, the standard of 'strong *prima facie* case' having been applied in *Megaleasing UK Ltd v Barrett*.[32] This requires that the Court must be satisfied that the applicant's claim is 'likely to succeed at trial'.

The Court also held that such an order would not be made unless the information requested is likely to be in the possession of the defendant and that the information is necessary for the purpose of bringing proceedings. It is also imperative that the applicant show that it has no other more appropriate means of obtaining the information sought.

Once the Court is satisfied that a strong case exists against the alleged wrongdoer, the Court must engage in a balancing exercise as between the right to access the courts and the right to privacy.

Finally, the Court noted that the applicant seeking a Norwich Pharmacal order is subject to an implied undertaking, similar to that which applies to discovery. The cost of a Norwich Pharmacal order was also considered.

The Court of Appeal concluded that the High Court Judge was correct to hold that the wrongdoing requirement was satisfied on the material before him. The Judge was also entitled to conclude that An Garda Síochána had failed to demonstrate that there was some other means by which the respondent could obtain the information necessary to commence his intended proceedings. The appeal was dismissed and a costs order was made against the appellant.

---

31 *Norwich Pharmacal Co v Customs and Excise Commissioners* [1974] AC 133; a Norwich Pharmacal order requires an innocent third party possessing information concerning unlawful activity by a wrongdoer to disclose that information to the party suffering damage as a result of the wrongdoing.

32 *Megaleasing UK Ltd v Barrett* [1992] 1 IR 219.

SETTING ASIDE A JUDGMENT FOR FRAUD

[4.25] ***Tinkler v Esken Ltd*[33]*—Court of Appeal of England and Wales—Snowden LJ—appeal from High Court of England and Wales—refusal to set aside a judgment—fraud—new evidence—whether the original findings were impugned***

This appeal concerned a failed application to set aside a judgment for fraud. The appellant was the former CEO of the respondent company. The substantive case concerned a boardroom dispute between the appellant and other leading board members. The appellant was summarily dismissed for alleged gross misconduct in June 2018. Although re-elected as a director by the respondent's shareholders, the appellant was again removed from office by his fellow directors under its articles of incorporation in July 2018. In an action in which the validity of the respondent's actions was disputed, the respondent's claim was upheld and the appellant's cross-claims dismissed.

The appellant subsequently applied before another judge (the 'trial Judge') to have the initial judgment set aside, claiming that new evidence, which would have been highly material to the issues decided upon, and which would have supported the appellant's claim of a pre-meditated effort to oust him, had been deliberately withheld from the initial trial Judge. That application was rejected.

The Court of Appeal rejected the appellant's complaint that the trial Judge failed to treat the claim as an independent cause of action in fraud. It was quite clear from a reading of the judgment that the trial Judge 'understood quite clearly that he was dealing with a free-standing cause of action'. The trial Judge repeatedly said that his task was to 'hear and evaluate the new evidence and then decide whether [the findings] could stand in the light of it'. The trial Judge had been correct to focus his attention on whether the alleged concealment was an 'operative cause' of the initial judgment, thus impugning it. Nor had it been shown that the trial Judge had only considered the new evidence to the exclusion of the old. Clearly, the trial Judge had to look at some of the old evidence alongside the new in order to understand how the new evidence supported the allegation of fraud, and he did so appropriately. The trial Judge had not considered himself bound by the earlier findings, and, although he used the material findings as a 'starting point', he would have had to consider them anyway. In the event, no harm was done.

The Court of Appeal found that the trial Judge applied the correct legal test of materiality.

The appeal was dismissed in its entirety.

SETTLEMENT AGREEMENTS

[4.26] ***Warburton v The Chief Constable of Avon and Somerset*[34]*—Court of Appeal of England and Wales—Philips LJ—appeal from High Court of England***

---

33 *Tinkler v Esken Ltd* [2023] EWCA Civ 655.

34 *Warburton v Chief Constable of Avon and Somerset* [2023] EWCA Civ 209.

and Wales—Data Protection Acts 1998 to 2018—amended pleadings—settlement talks—abuse of process—whether claimant entitled to issue fresh proceedings on the back of amended pleadings having accepted an offer in full and final settlement

The appellant claimed damages and injunctive reliefs against the respondent police force for alleged breaches of the Data Protection Acts 1998 to 2018 (the 'Acts').

In February 2005, the appellant applied to become a special constable for the respondent. His application was refused after a vetting check revealed allegations recorded against him in 1998, when the appellant was a probationary constable with the West Midlands, including that he had performed a striptease dance in a student bar and that he had racially abused Muslims, including a police colleague. A separate allegation of putting inappropriate pictures on a colleague's desk was recorded against him while in the respondent's employ. These allegations were recorded in a log and were held in an intelligence file by the respondent's Counter Corruption Unit ('CCU'). A 2008 incident in which the appellant posted a complaint on social media against a sergeant employed by the respondent was also added to the CCU file.

In 2017, the appellant passed vetting for a constabulary post with the Hertfordshire force; however, the offer was withdrawn when the respondent disclosed the CCU files to the Hertfordshire force.

The appellant brought defamation proceedings against the respondent. These were struck out in December 2018 for being out of time and for deficiencies in the pleadings. In April 2019, an appeal was allowed and the proceedings, including an application for leave to amend the pleadings, were restored and transferred to the High Court. In draft amended pleadings, which were served on the respondent, the appellant also sought compensation for breach of his data protection rights.

In settlement talks, the appellant sought permanent deletion of all of the evidence logs. The respondent accepted that there were some data protection breaches, albeit not in respect of the racial abuse allegations. In July 2019, the appellant accepted a Part 36 offer 'to settle the whole of the claim' and the defamation proceedings settled, though the respondent retained the CCU file relating to the West Midland allegations.

Fresh proceedings issued in August 2020, essentially advancing the same data protection claims and seeking the same reliefs. The respondent applied to strike out the proceedings as an abuse of process under the rule in *Henderson v Henderson*.[35] The trial Judge rejected the appellant's argument that it was enough to simply 'raise' an issue in correspondence or settlement talks, without pleading it as alternative cause of action, to avoid the effects of *Henderson*. It would have been an abuse of process to allow the appellant to pursue a data protection claim up to and including the defamation settlement talks in July 2019 and the trial Judge summarily dismissed that aspect of the claim. The appellant appealed.

35 *Henderson v Henderson* [1843–60] All E.R. 378, [1843] 7 WLUK 87, the rule states that if a party could have pleaded an issue in earlier proceedings between the parties, it cannot plead the issue in subsequent litigation between the parties.

The Court of Appeal dismissed the appeal. It held that to remove 'raised but not brought' from the scope of *Henderson* 'would create an unnecessary and unprincipled exception'. This would enable parties to bring second claims 'with impunity, no matter how obviously abusive and contrary to the clear public interest they might be'. The principles of *res judicata* and *Henderson* allow the courts to identify and prevent duplicative litigation and to apply a broad merits-based test. There was 'no room for a "third" type of duplicative litigation ("raised but not brought")'.

The Court held that the offer was undoubtedly one that had been made in settlement of 'the whole of the claim' and was to be construed as referable to the pleaded case only. Any other claims were excluded, even if set out in draft amended pleadings which had been served but not yet approved by the Court. The trial Judge had been entitled to consider the negotiations leading up to the settlement of the defamation proceedings as part of this broad merits-based test and had correctly concluded that the parties had been negotiating on the basis that they would settle all claims.

The appeal was, therefore, dismissed.

[4.27] ***Arvunescu v Quick Release (Automotive) Ltd*[36]*—Court of Appeal of England and Wales—Lewis, Laing & Warby LJJ—appeal from UK Employment Appeal Tribunal—discrimination on grounds of race—settlement agreement—whether a subsequent claim against the respondent was within the scope of the earlier settlement agreement***

This appeal concerned the proper interpretation of a settlement agreement. The claimant was employed by the respondent between 4 May and 6 June 2014, when his employment was terminated. The claimant brought proceedings alleging discrimination on grounds of race and, on 1 March 2018, a settlement agreement ('COT3 agreement') was reached between the parties.

In January 2018, the claimant unsuccessfully applied for a post with a company in Germany, which was a wholly-owned subsidiary of the respondent. Alleging victimisation, the claimant submitted that he was rejected for that post because of the earlier claim against the respondent.

This appeal concerned the question of whether the second claim came within the scope of the COT3 agreement on its proper interpretation, the employment judge having held that it did, and so could not therefore be the subject of fresh proceedings.

The claimant, appearing as a litigant-in-person, submitted that the COT3 agreement was ambiguous, and therefore should have been interpreted narrowly to exclude employment in Germany. In the alternative, if unambiguous, there was no link between the conduct giving rise to the second complaint and the first employment. In essence, the claimant's claim alleged that the respondent 'knowingly helped' the German company to victimise the claimant because of his claim for racial discrimination against the respondent.

36 *Arvunescu v Quick Release (Automotive) Ltd* [2022] EWCA Civ 1600.

The Court of Appeal of England and Wales found that the second complaint did fall within the wording of the agreement. The complaint arose in connection with, or was linked to, the claimant's 2014 employment with the respondent, albeit not arising directly or indirectly out of that employment. The COT3 agreement was expressed 'widely' and included claims arising 'indirectly ... in connection with the employment'.

The purpose underlying the COT3 agreement was to settle claims the claimant may have had against the respondent as at the date of agreement, ie, 1 March 2018. The context in which the agreement was reached, and its wording, indicated 'an intention to settle claims connected with the claimant's employment which existed as at 1 March 2018, whether or not they were known about at that date'. The claim of January 2018 was connected with the claimant's employment with the respondent and existed at the date of the settlement. The Court found that 'the purpose underlying the settlement agreement was to settle all such existing claims'.

While the relevant words of the COT3 agreement: 'arising ... indirectly ... in connection with the claimant's employment' could be difficult to interpret, this did not mean that the agreement was ambiguous. On a proper interpretation of the COT3 agreement, the second claim fell within the scope of the settlement. There was no ambiguity capable of giving a different interpretation and the UK EAT had applied the correct approach, construing the agreement objectively in accordance with contract law.

Accordingly, the claim that the respondent breached the Equality Act 2010 did not arise indirectly in connection with the claimant's employment with the respondent. The claim was therefore settled by the COT3 agreement and the EAT was correct to strike it out.

The appeal was accordingly dismissed.

TERRITORIAL JURISDICTION

[4.28] ***ROI Land Investments Ltd v FD*[37]*—European Court of Justice—request for a preliminary ruling from Germany—Rome I,*[38] *art 6(1)—Regulation (EU) 1215/2012,*[39] *arts 6, 17, 21—judicial cooperation in civil matters—respondent not domiciled in a Member State—jurisdiction over consumer contracts—concept of 'trade or profession'/'professional activities'***

This request for a preliminary ruling concerned the interpretation of arts 6(1) 17(1) and 21(1)(b)(i) and (2) of Regulation (EU) 1215/2012 on jurisdiction and the recognition and enforcement of judgments in civil and commercial matters, and of art 6(1) of Regulation (EC) 593/2008 on the law applicable to contractual obligations ('Rome I Regulation'). The request was made in proceedings where the applicant refused to pay

37 *ROI Land Investments Ltd v FD* (Case C-604/20).

38 Regulation (EC) 593/2008 on the law applicable to contractual obligations ('Rome I Regulation').

39 Regulation (EU) 1215/2012 on jurisdiction and the recognition and enforcement of judgments in civil and commercial matters (recast).

claims arising from a contract of employment between the respondent and a subsidiary of the applicant. Under a 'letter of comfort' the applicant was liable to the respondent for the obligations under that contract.

In 2015, the parties agreed to transfer their contractual relationship to a Swiss company (not yet created) and, accordingly, to retroactively terminate the contract of employment between them. On 14 January 2016, the company R Swiss AG, of which the applicant was a parent company, was created under Swiss law. The respondent, who was based in Germany, subsequently entered into a contract of employment with R Swiss ('the contract of employment at issue') under which the respondent was engaged as a director. The parties entered into an agreement where the applicant was directly liable to the respondent for the obligations under the contract of employment with R Swiss ('the letter of comfort').

On 11 July 2016, R Swiss dismissed the respondent. The dismissal was challenged in the Labour Court, Stuttgart, Germany, which found the dismissal to be ineffective and awarded damages.

In March 2017, insolvency proceedings were brought against R Swiss under Swiss law but were discontinued due to lack of assets. The respondent brought an enforcement action in Germany to recover the monies owed to him under the Labour Court judgment. The respondent relied on the letter of comfort.

The Labour Court dismissed the action as inadmissible on the ground that it did not have international jurisdiction to hear the matter. This decision was overturned by the Higher Labour Court, Baden-Württemberg, Germany.

The applicant in turn appealed on a point of law before the Federal Labour Court, Germany ('the referring Court'), which was uncertain whether the German Courts had jurisdiction to rule on the respondent's appeal and, if they did, which law was applicable. The question was referred to the European Court of Justice ('ECJ') for preliminary ruling.

By its first question, the referring Court asked, in essence, whether art 21(1)(b)(i) and (2) of Regulation (EU) 1215/2012 must be interpreted as meaning:

> 'that an employee may bring proceedings before the courts for the last place where or from where he or she habitually carried out his or her work, against a person, whether or not domiciled in a Member State, with whom he or she does not have a formal contract of employment but who is, under a letter of comfort that was a prerequisite for conclusion of the contract of employment with a third party, directly liable to that employee for performance of the obligations of that third party'.

In that regard, it was to be borne in mind that, for disputes relating to contracts of employment, the relevant provisions of Regulation (EU) 1215/2012 lay down a series of rules 'to protect the weaker party to the contract by means of rules of jurisdiction that are more favourable to his interests'. Under art 21, which must be interpreted 'autonomously', an employer 'not domiciled in a Member State may be sued in a Court of a Member State'; an employer may also be sued 'in the courts of the place where or from where the employee habitually carries out his work or in the courts for the last place where he did so'.

Notwithstanding the absence of a formal contract, the letter of comfort did not preclude 'out of hand' a hierarchical relationship between the parties and it was for the referring Court to have regard to all relevant factors to determine whether there was an employment relationship, characterised by the existence of a hierarchical relationship. This assessment was to include the circumstances surrounding the conclusion of the letter of comfort and the contract of employment at issue. The conclusion of those contracts did not affect the nature of the work that the respondent performed, first for the applicant and then for a wholly-owned subsidiary of the applicant.

By its second question, the referring Court asked, in essence, whether art 6(1) of Regulation (EU) 1215/2012 must be interpreted as meaning that the reservation in respect of the application of art 21(2) 'precludes a court of a Member State from relying on the rules of jurisdiction of that state even where those rules would be more favourable to the employee'.

Article 6(1) provides, in principle, that the national rules of jurisdiction apply where the respondent is not domiciled in a Member State. However, the words 'subject to' mean that situations falling within certain listed provisions are excluded from the application of national law. Accordingly, certain rules of jurisdiction should apply 'regardless of the respondent's domicile'.

It followed that, where the jurisdiction of the courts of a Member State is not derived from a specific provision of the regulations referred to in art 6(1), Member States are at large to apply national legislation in order to determine jurisdiction. In contrast, where the jurisdiction of the courts is derived from one of those specific provisions, that specific provision will take precedence over the national rules for determining jurisdiction, even where those rules are more favourable to employees.

By the third and fourth questions, examined jointly, the referring Court asked, in essence, whether art 17(1) of Regulation (EU) 1215/2012 and art 6(1) of the Rome I Regulation must be interpreted as meaning that

> 'the concept of "trade or profession" includes not only self-employed activities but also paid employment and, if the answer to that question is in the affirmative, whether, where in the context of that paid employment an agreement has been concluded between the employee and a third party other than the employer referred to in the contract of employment, under which that third party is directly liable to the employee for the obligations of that employer under the contract of employment, that agreement constitutes a contract concluded outside and independently of any trade or professional activity or purpose'.

According to the ECJ's settled case-law, only contracts concluded 'solely for the purpose of satisfying an individual's own needs in terms of private consumption', are covered by the special rules laid down by those regulations to protect the consumer, as the 'weaker party'. Such protection is unwarranted in the case of contracts for the purpose of a 'trade or professional activity'.

Paid employment falls within the concept of 'trade or profession' under art 17(1) of Regulation (EU) 1215/2012 and art 6(1) of the Rome I Regulation.

In the present case, the letter of comfort was 'inextricably linked' to the professional activities carried out by the respondent, since he would not have concluded the contract of employment at issue without the letter of comfort. It could not be found that it was concluded outside and independently of any trade or professional activity or purpose.

In the light of the foregoing, the answer to the third and fourth questions should be that art 17(1) of Regulation (EU) 1215/2012 and art 6(1) of the Rome I Regulation must be interpreted as meaning that the concept of 'trade or profession' includes not only self-employed activities but also paid employment. Furthermore, an agreement concluded between the employee and a third party other than the employer referred to in the contract of employment, under which that third party is directly liable to the employee for the obligations of that employer under the contract of employment, does not, for the purposes of applying those provisions, constitute a contract concluded outside and independently of any trade or professional activity or purpose.

THE RULE IN *HENDERSON V HENDERSON*

[4.29] ***Munnelly v Hassett, Cremin and Anor*[40]*—Supreme Court—O'Donnell CJ—appeal from High Court—bullying and harassment—two sets of proceedings with overlapping facts and circumstances—whether parties who were not parties in earlier set of proceedings could invoke Henderson v Henderson***

The respondent commenced working with City Learning Ltd (the 'company') in September 2012. She left the company in May 2015 following a series of incidents involving her and Ms Hassett, who was the managing director of the company between 1998 and 2019.

One such incident resulted in the commencement of two sets of Circuit Court proceedings, in 2016 and 2019. The 2016 proceedings issued against the company alone and were dismissed. The 2019 proceedings concerned allegations of bullying and harassment and issued against the company, Ms Hassett and Mr Cremin, who was a director of the company between 1998 and 2016 (collectively the appellants). The appellants argued that the proceedings offended the rule in *Henderson v Henderson*,[41] and that the respondent had not sought the authorisation of PIAB prior to the commencement of the proceedings. The 2019 proceedings were struck out on those bases.

On appeal, the High Court reversed the decision of the Circuit Court. The appellants sought leave to appeal to the Supreme Court, which granted leave on the issue of

40 *Munnelly v Hassett, Cremin and Anor* [2023] IESC 29.

41 *Henderson v Henderson* [1843–60] All ER 378, [1843] 7 WLUK 87, the rule states that if a party could have pleaded an issue in earlier proceedings between the parties, it cannot plead the issue in subsequent litigation between the parties.

whether the proceedings offended the rule in *Henderson v Henderson*, in particular whether the rule applied in the matters pleaded, and whether the rule could be invoked by parties who were not parties to the 2016 proceedings.

The Supreme Court held that the rule in *Henderson v Henderson* was applicable and there was no reason that it should not apply 'at least' in respect of the company, which had successfully defended the 2016 proceedings. The Court held that to permit the 2019 proceedings to proceed to trial 'would inevitably put the company to the cost and inconvenience of defending a further set of proceedings, arising from essentially the same facts and circumstances as were the subject of the 2016 proceedings'.

The Court held that while the reliefs sought by the respondent in this instance may have differed from those sought in the 2016 proceedings (although, with some overlap), all of those reliefs ought to have been sought in the earlier proceedings, but were not. This was precisely what the rule in *Henderson v Henderson* was intended to avoid.

There was 'an unusual degree of identity between [Ms Hassett] and the company in the two claims which was … more than sufficient to render it just that Ms Hassett should be entitled to rely on the existence of the earlier proceedings against the company to invoke the rule in *Henderson v. Henderson*'. Ms Hassett was a central witness in those proceedings, which had involved, 'almost exclusively', complaints made by the respondent in respect of the conduct of Ms Hassett on behalf of the company, including incidents which were central to the 2019 proceedings against her personally.

Accordingly, the appeal was allowed.

TIME LIMITS—APPEALS—POINT OF LAW

[4.30] ***Marino Camarasa v Labour Court and Tyco Ireland Ltd*[42]*—High Court—Phelan J—appeal from Labour Court—Workplace Relations Act 2015—Unfair Dismissals Acts 1977 to 2015—point of law appeals—time limits—appeal period—Eire Continental—power to extend time to appeal—no stateable error of law identified***

The plaintiff was employed by the notice party from 2015. He was advised in June 2020 that his unit was being dismantled and that there would be redundancies. He was subsequently informed that his position was being made redundant. He was furnished with a draft agreement which reflected the termination and provided for an enhanced redundancy package upon agreement to provide certain waivers and enter into restrictive covenants. The plaintiff did not sign the agreement. He was made redundant, together with 11 other members of his unit, and thereafter received statutory redundancy entitlement. The plaintiff brought a claim to the WRC under the Unfair Dismissals Acts 1977

42 *Marino Camarasa v Labour Court and Tyco Ireland Ltd* [2023] IEHC 471.

to 2015, arguing that, because he did not receive his letter of redundancy, his social protection benefits were delayed.

In the WRC, the notice party argued that the plaintiff had been at all times legally represented and had never sought said letter. The WRC decided that the plaintiff's employment was legally terminated by reason of a *bona fide* redundancy and he was not unfairly dismissed. The plaintiff appealed to the Labour Court. Before the Labour Court, the plaintiff advanced further grounds to justify a finding of unfair dismissal, namely that: he was unsure of his final termination date as a result of the notice party's failure to issue a redundancy certificate; he did not receive the same *ex gratia* terms as other employees in the past; and he was not offered alternative roles within the company. The plaintiff did not raise any issue with regard to notification in the appeal. The Labour Court upheld the finding of the WRC that the dismissal was not unfair.

The plaintiff sought to appeal to the High Court by way of Notice of Motion which was sent to the Central Office on 5 May 2022, within the 42-day appeal window. An unissued copy was served on the notice party. The Central Office requested that the plaintiff make changes to the Notice of Motion, namely that the notice party be correctly identified as such. An amended version of the Notice of Motion was issued on the 27 May 2022, outside the 42-day period. Phelan J therefore had to determine whether the time limit provided under s 46 of the Workplace Relations Act 2015 was absolute or whether the Court had the power to extend time.

The Court examined caselaw, including *Aherne v National Council for Special Education*,[43] which, it was argued, bore factual similarities to this case. It was noted by the Court, however, that the question as to whether the Court had the power to extend time was not contested in this case and accordingly the trial Judge did not hear any argument as to it. The Court consulted the principles set down in *Re Worldport Ireland Ltd (In Liquidation)*[44] and determined that it was appropriate to depart from the implicit underlying rationale that the Court has the jurisdiction to extend the 42-day limitation period under s 46 of the 2015 Act as held in *Aherne*.

The Court also considered the question under the *Eire Continental* principles and was satisfied that the plaintiff would satisfy the first limb thereof, given that the intention to appeal was clearly formed during the 42-day period. However, it was held that the plaintiff did not satisfy the other two limbs, ie the existence of mistake and an arguable ground of appeal; and therefore it was not in the interests of justice to extend time. In this regard, the Court considered whether the plaintiff had a stateable ground of appeal in accordance with the third limb of the test. The Court concluded that there was no clear point of law identified by the plaintiff and that it could not decide questions of fact that had not been put before the Labour Court.

The appeal was struck out.

43 *Aherne v National Council for Special Education* [2023] IEHC 143.

44 *Re Worldport Ireland Ltd (In Liquidation)* [2005] IEHC 189.

TIME LIMITS—APPEALS

[4.31] ***Cavtat Taverns 3 Ltd v Hanlon*[45]*—Labour Court—appeal from Workplace Relations Commission—application for extension of time to bring appeal—whether the circumstances relied upon to explain the delay were exceptional***

The respondent appealed from a decision of the WRC finding against it in a complaint of discrimination and harassment on the gender ground. The respondent did not attend at the WRC hearing.

The respondent's appeal was made almost two years after the WRC's decision, by which time the claimant had issued enforcement proceedings in the District Court. The respondent sought an extension of time in which to bring an appeal. There was no appearance by the claimant at the appeal, though she filed a written submission opposing the application.

In refusing to extend time, the Labour Court was satisfied that the WRC's decision was clearly sent to the address of the respondent's office at Dublin Airport where it carried on business, notwithstanding that the named recipient had by then ceased his employment with the respondent. There was 'no doubt that the intended ultimate recipient was the respondent'.

No evidence was proffered by the respondent in support of the claim that it had no access to Dublin Airport due to Covid-19 restrictions. The Court held that it was not permissible to allow the respondent to rely on its own failure to take appropriate steps to have its correspondence redirected.

The Court stated that a prudent solicitor would have advised the respondent to immediately refer an appeal to the Labour Court on receipt of the claimant's notice of motion to enforce the WRC's award. Instead, a delay of five weeks followed, during which time the respondent submitted that it needed to 'investigate the circumstances surrounding its lack of knowledge in relation to the first instance hearing' in order to determine whether it had a basis for seeking an extension of time.

The circumstances relied upon by the respondent, 'albeit unusual and uncommon', were not exceptional and the respondent did not act expeditiously to refer its appeal.

[4.32] ***Anghel v Middlesex University*[46]*—UK Employment Appeal Tribunal—appeal from employment tribunal—extension of time—late filing—limitation periods***

The claimant appealed as a litigant-in-person against the order of the registrar of the UK EAT refusing to extend time to lodge her appeal from the employment tribunal. Her notice of appeal and attachments were submitted within the time limit, but the attachments were missing the document containing detailed grounds of claim, which was submitted after the time limit had expired.

---

45 *Cavtat Taverns 3 Ltd v Hanlon* EDA2320.

46 *Anghel v Middlesex University* [2022] EAT 176.

As the written judgment of the employment tribunal, and its reasons for refusing reconsideration, were sent to the parties on 5 January 2021, the final day for an appeal to be instituted was 16 February 2021, no later than 4pm. The claim form referred the reader to 'attached grounds of claim'. This was an essential document that needed to be provided to the EAT in order for the claim to be properly instituted. That document was not provided until 17 February 2021 at around 13.49 and the appeal was, accordingly, instituted out of time.

The claimant 'plainly' made the assumption that the document was included with the email attachments accompanying the ET1 form without checking. It was incumbent upon her to do so and 'an error of this sort, and the fact that the error was not intentional, are not sufficient excuse to justify an extension of time'. Nor was there any other 'sufficient exceptional reason' to extend time.

Accordingly, the appeal against the registrar's order, and the underlying substantive appeal, were dismissed.

[4.33] ***Hawkes v Oxford Economics Ltd*[47]*—UK Employment Appeal Tribunal—appeal of Registrar's order—claim time limits—extension of time—notice of appeal—judgment—bounce-back email—default of procedure—Covid-19—unfair dismissal—defence force***

The claimant was an employee of the respondent and at the same time was in the Royal Marine reserve force. The claimant was summarily dismissed by the respondent in 2019 and brought a claim for unfair dismissal under the Defence Reform Act 2014, which provides that the usual two-year qualifying period for initiating an unfair dismissal claim does not apply to cases which concern membership of a reserve force.

After the hearing in October 2020, the tribunal delivered a judgment on 29 December 2020, where it held that the dismissal was not connected with his membership of a reserve force, and accordingly, the employment tribunal did not enjoy the requisite jurisdiction to hear the claim. The claimant decided to appeal this decision to the UK EAT. The deadline for appealing was 9 February 2021. In order to appeal, the claimant was required to lodge a notice of appeal, a copy of the judgment, and copies of the ET1 and ET3. During the period from 29 December 2020 to 9 February 2021, the claimant focused on liaising with the respondents in relation to a so-called 'subject access request' for notes relating to the matter. This was despite the fact that no such notes were required to lodge an appeal of the tribunal's decision. On the last day of the 42-day appeal period, the claimant emailed the necessary documents to the EAT. Ultimately, unbeknownst to the claimant, the EAT did not receive the notice of appeal on time. This was due to the fact that, although the claimant sent a separate email to the EAT attaching these documents, it was never received. In the absence of a bounce-back email, the claimant assumed that the documents had been received.

47 *Hawkes v Oxford Economics Ltd* [2022] EAT 179.

In April 2021, the EAT wrote to the claimant to inform him that he was out of time to lodge his appeal but that he could apply to extend the time for this purpose. The claimant did so, justifying his claim by citing internet service issues which had caused his email attaching the notice of appeal and judgment not to send. This was evidenced by an email from the claimant's internet service provider acknowledging issues with the claimant's internet connection resulting in inconsistencies in sending and receiving emails that day. The claimant also referred to the fact that he had been suffering from Covid-19 symptoms from 28 January 2021 to 10 February 2021 and, as a result, was confined to his home and unable to effect personal service on the EAT.

The EAT considered the test for extending time for an appeal being:

> '(a) what is the explanation for the default? (b) does it provide a good excuse for the default? (c) are there circumstances which justify the [EAT] taking the exceptional step of granting an extension of time?'

In relation to the first limb of the test, the EAT was critical of the claimant's subject access request attempt which it termed both 'misguided and unnecessary' to lodge an appeal. It noted that the claimant was not so ill during this time that he could not have lodged the appeal and despite his being confined to his home, he could have served the documents electronically. The EAT was also critical of the fact that the claimant waited until the final day of a 42-day appeal period to attempt service of the necessary documents. It noted that the main explanation for the default was that the email attaching the notice of appeal and judgment did not deliver due to some technical issue and ultimately held that, absent a bounce-back email, it was reasonable for the claimant to assume that the email, having been properly sent, had been received. The EAT held that this was a good excuse for the claimant's default, and the fact that the claimant waited until the final day to attempt service did not affect this finding.

The EAT held that there was no evidence of procedural abuse, deliberate default or prejudice in this case. On the latter point, it was clear that the respondent was well aware of the claimant's intention to appeal. Although the EAT held that the claim was not bound to succeed, it held that it was not doomed to fail either.

Therefore, the EAT allowed the appeal and extended time.

[4.34] ***Elhalabi v Avis Budget UK Ltd*[48]*—UK Employment Appeal Tribunal—appeal of registrar's interim orders—Employment Appeal Tribunal Rules 1993—appeal notices—delay—employment—extensions of time—late filing***

The claimant had his claims for unfair dismissal and race discrimination dismissed by the employment tribunal. The claimant and the respondent employer requested reasons for this decision. Under the Employment Appeal Tribunal Rules 1993, the period within which an appeal could be lodged was 42 days from the date on which written reasons were given. The claimant did not wait for receipt of the reasons and instead, lodged his

48 *Elhalabi v Avis Budget UK Ltd* [2022] EAT 185.

notice of appeal. He explained to the UK EAT that he had not yet received the tribunal's written reasons but that they had been requested. The claimant attached copies of his emails requesting the tribunal's reasons.

The employment tribunal subsequently furnished the reasons for its decision. The claimant did not send these reasons to the EAT upon receipt. After being informed that a copy of said reasons was required to appeal, he complied. However, at this stage, it was in excess of 42 days from the date the written reasons were furnished.

The registrar decided that the claimant had not appealed in time and refused the request to extend the time required to lodge the appeal. The claimant did not receive a hard copy of this decision. Instead, a soft copy was sent to him by email, which went to his spam folder. Upon becoming aware of the registrar's decision, the claimant appealed, albeit outside of the time limit for doing so. The registrar refused the requested extension of time to appeal.

The claimant argued that, as his first appeal was properly lodged in time, he did not require an extension. However, he argued, if such an extension was required, he should be given one under the circumstances. The respondent maintained that the first appeal had been premature.

The EAT considered r 37(1) of the Employment Appeal Tribunal Rules 1993, which provides the power to extend time for an appeal, and referred to *United Arab Emirates v Abdelghafar*,[49] where it was held that adherence to time limits is crucial for certainty and finality, and that there is no guaranteed right to an extension.

The EAT considered whether the appeal against the registrar's second order was out of time under r 37(1). The time for appealing against the registrar's order was within five days of the date of the decision. The claimant was more than a month out of time. The EAT held that the guidance set out in *Abdelghafar* also applied to decisions of the registrar which were not concerned with case management but with whether an appeal should be permitted at all.

The EAT then considered whether the claimant's explanation for the delay amounted to a good excuse. The EAT emphasised that the registrar had used the contact details on file for the claimant and that it was the claimant's responsibility to ensure that any correspondence sent to these addresses came to his attention and that he did not miss any appeal deadlines. The fact that the emails were redirected to the claimant's spam folder did not, in the EAT's opinion, provide a good excuse for not complying with the time limits set.

The EAT held that even where there was no good excuse for not complying with time limits for appeal, there was the possibility to extend time where some exceptional reason necessitated this.

The fact that the claimant had first sent his notice of appeal with an accompanying explanation as to why the tribunal's written reasons were not attached, and where there

49 *United Arab Emirates v Abdelghafar* [1995] ICR 65.

had been timely requests of the tribunal for these reasons, the EAT should have taken the appeal as being properly instituted. This was especially so, given the EAT's powers under r 39(2) and (3). In the alternative, it was held that exceptional circumstances existed here to extend the time to appeal the registrar's first order, despite not having a good excuse for missing the deadline.

Both appeals against the registrar's orders succeeded.

TIME LIMITS—CLAIMS

[4.35] ***Meaker v Cyxtera Technology UK Ltd*[50]*—UK Employment Appeal Tribunal—appeal from employment tribunal—unfair dismissal complaint out of time—effective date of termination—'without prejudice' dismissal letter—whether tribunal correctly identified the effective date of termination***

The claimant appealed against the decision of an employment tribunal dismissing his claim for unfair dismissal for being out of time. The claimant challenged the tribunal's decision on the effective date of termination of employment with the respondent.

The claimant was employed by the respondent as a data centre operations technician. This was a manual role involving heavy lifting and lone night shifts. The claimant suffered back injuries in August 2016 and November 2018. In 2019, an occupational health assessment concluded that the claimant's physical limitations were likely permanent. An application for income protection payments was refused and an appeal was dismissed in January 2020.

In a meeting with a HR manager for the respondent, it was indicated that the respondent was considering terminating the claimant's employment and the possibility of a settlement agreement was raised. Thereafter, the claimant received a letter headed 'without prejudice' from the respondent to say that a mutual termination of employment had been agreed. It stated that the claimant's last date of employment was to be 7 February 2020.

For his part, the claimant had mistakenly believed that further information about alternative employment would be forthcoming, and the tribunal found that the respondent had not made it clear to him that it would not. The letter offered an *ex gratia* payment in addition to the claimant's contractual entitlements, which was conditional on the claimant signing a settlement agreement. The claimant rejected the settlement offer, and the HR manager emailed him to accept his decision and to explain that the respondent could not allow him to return to work. The claimant received a payment on 14 February, which he was informed was his payment in lieu of notice and outstanding holiday pay.

50 *Meaker v Cyxtera Technology UK Ltd* [2023] EAT 17.

The 'without prejudice' letter was sent on 5 February 2020 and received by the claimant on 7 February. The tribunal found that this letter was a dismissal letter, that the effective date of termination of employment was 7 February, and the claim was out of time.

The UK EAT held that the tribunal had not erred in deciding that the effective date of termination of employment, for the purpose of an unfair dismissal claim (as distinct from in contract law), fell on the date of receipt of the letter. Nor had the tribunal erred in construing the letter as a dismissal letter. The tribunal had correctly held that, notwithstanding references to an 'agreement', the letter unambiguously communicated that the respondent would be unilaterally terminating the claimant's employment with effect on 7 February 2020.

Finally, the claimant had not shown that it was not reasonably practicable for him to present his unfair dismissal claim in time, and the tribunal was also correct in this conclusion.

All grounds of appeal having failed, the appeal was dismissed.

[4.36] ***Owen v Network Rail Infrastructure Ltd*[51]*—UK Employment Appeal Tribunal—appeal from employment tribunal—Equality Act 2010—employment litigation—time limits—sex discrimination—prejudice—delay—direct discrimination—discretion of the court—extension of time—reasoning—clarity of reasoning—explanation for delay***

The claimant was a railway signaller and was employed by the respondent from 2012. She was allegedly subject to numerous incidents of direct sex discrimination until she went off sick in 2017. The claimant submitted a grievance in this regard but was unsuccessful. She issued a claim in the employment tribunal relating to 25 allegations against 22 of the respondent's workers, along with complaints about the grievance procedure. None of the 22 individuals were called as witnesses by the respondent.

The tribunal found that the claimant had been treated as she had alleged by her male colleagues. However, it noted that the claim was out of time; nor had the claimant provided any evidence why it would be just and equitable to extend time in this case. In order to save the discrimination claims, they would have to be linked to the allegations about the grievance procedure, as an ongoing act of discrimination. While the tribunal criticised the grievance procedure, it held that the issues with it were unrelated to the claimant's sex. The tribunal noted that the time for bringing a sex discrimination claim could be extended under Equality Act 2010 if there were equitable reasons to do so. However, in circumstances where the claimant provided no explanation for the delay in bringing the claim, the tribunal refused to exercise its discretion in extending the time. This decision was also based on the length of time that had elapsed since the incidents complained of had allegedly occurred and the risk of prejudice to the respondent in this regard.

---

51 *Owen v Network Rail Infrastructure Ltd* [2023] EAT 106.

The claimant appealed to the UK EAT on the grounds that there was no rule of law that dictated that a satisfactory explanation for delay was a prerequisite to an award extending time. She also argued that, as the respondent had chosen not to call any of the individuals who were subject to the allegations as witnesses, the delay caused the respondent no prejudice.

The EAT considered whether the tribunal had erred in its decision not to use discretion to extend time because the claimant had provided no explanation for her delay. The EAT considered conflicting caselaw on the topic and referred with approval to *Concentrix GVC Intelligent Contract Ltd v Obi*.[52] It concluded that there was no rule of law that rendered the tribunal bound to refuse discretion to extend time in circumstances where there was no such explanation. It was held that the lack of explanation was relevant but not dispositive of the matter.

The EAT also held that the tribunal had not erred in considering the passage of time and associated risk of prejudice to the respondent when assessing whether to exercise discretion to extend time. However, the EAT was critical of the reasoning given in this regard and the clarity of the judgment.

The appeal was allowed and the matter was remitted to the same tribunal to decide whether it would be equitable to extend time.

[4.37] ***Fernandes v Department for Work and Pensions[53]—UK Employment Appeal Tribunal—appeal from employment tribunal—Equality Act 2010—disability—indirect discrimination—time limits—reasonable adjustment—limitation periods—PCP—notional date where time begins to run***

The claimant was an employee of the respondent. She was also a trade union health and safety representative. The claimant was disabled by reason of depression, anxiety and back pain. Prior to taking maternity leave she had been given a special chair to ease her back pain at work. When she returned to work after maternity leave, the chair was not provided. Occupational Health advised that an ergonomic assessment of the claimant's working area should be carried out. This did not occur. From July to November 2020, the claimant worked from home and requested an ergonomic assessment of her home-working area. She claimed that this did not occur. While working from home there was a problem with her smart card, which was required to access the respondent's IT system. The respondent requested she attend the office to resolve this issue. This request came at the same time as the hospitalisation of the claimant's child. She complained that the ergonomic assessment had not been completed and the respondent explained that it would be completed upon her return to work. From November 2020 until January 2021, the claimant was absent due to severe anxiety and depression. She returned briefly to work in January, before a further sickness absence.

52 *Concentrix GVC Intelligent Contract Ltd v Obi* [2022] EAT 149.
53 *Fernandes v Department for Work and Pensions* [2023] EAT 114.

The claimant argued that several PCPs applied in her case: a requirement to work from home without appropriate equipment; not providing the equipment quickly enough; and requiring her to attend the office to remedy the problem with the smart card access. She brought a case to the employment tribunal based on indirect disability discrimination and a failure to make reasonable adjustments. These claims were brought outside the time limit provided and the tribunal found that it was not just and equitable to extend time.

In so finding, the tribunal considered a number of factors, including: the length of delay in bringing the claim; her lack of knowledge of tribunal time limits; her role as a trade union health and safety representative; her emails to the respondent reiterating her rights; and the fact that she had contacted ACAS on two occasions. The claimant appealed to the UK EAT.

The EAT held that the tribunal had misdirected itself in finding that time began to run for the purpose of the limitation period for bringing a claim when a respondent would be expected to make a reasonable adjustment to allow for an employee's disability. Rather, the EAT stated, the tribunal should determine both when a respondent would have made the adjustment and then also consider when the reasonable employee, based on the facts known to that employee, would conclude that the duty has not been complied with. This did not require the tribunal to ascertain the claimant's subjective state of mind but rather an objective view as to when the employee, who was vested with the relevant facts, would have reached the conclusion that the employer had not complied with its duty to make reasonable adjustments.

The appeal was allowed.

[4.38] ***The Sports PR Company Ltd v Cardona[54]—UK Employment Appeal Tribunal—appeal from employment tribunal—Employment Rights Act 1996—employment litigation—time limits—conciliation—extension of time—pro bono costs order—wages—statutory sick pay—ACAS certificate—notice period—interests of justice—respondent names did not match—claim form***

The claimant was employed as a press assistant by the respondent from 30 March 2020. Her employment came to an end and she began ACAS early conciliation in September 2020. She received an ACAS early conciliation certificate, correctly naming the respondent in October 2020. The claimant issued a claim to the employment tribunal for unpaid wages. The claim form, in box 2, requested the respondent's details and read: 'Give the name of your employer or the person or organisation that you are claiming against'. The claimant filled out that box with the name of the director of the respondent company. The claimant also provided the respondent's address, its phone number and her ACAS early conciliation certificate number. Elsewhere on the form, she referred to 'the company' and the name of the company. In November 2020, via letter, she was informed that the judge had rejected her claim because, although she had given an early conciliation number, the name of the prospective respondent on the certificate (being

54 *The Sports PR Company Ltd v Cardona* [2023] EAT 110.

the respondent's company name) did not match the name that she provided in box 2 of the claim form, ie the name of the director of the respondent company. In the letter, the tribunal noted that: 'The judge has considered if the error is minor and has decided that it is not; it would be in the interests of justice to reject the claim'. On 8 December 2020, the claimant emailed the tribunal and indicated that she would like to change the name of the respondent in box 2 of the claim form to the respondent company name. In May 2021, she was informed that after reconsideration, the judge had decided to accept the claim as having been received on 8 December.

At the hearing, the employment tribunal decided that, having been treated as presented on 8 December 2020, the claim was *prima facie* out of time. However, the tribunal held that it was not reasonably practicable for the claimant to have presented the claim in time given the circumstances. The claimant was not notified of her original mistake in filling out box 2 of the claims form until after the preliminary time period had expired. It also emphasised the fact that she had been a lay litigant at this point. The tribunal further held that the claim had been presented in a subsequent reasonable period and upheld the wages claim.

The respondent appealed to the UK EAT. The grounds challenged the employment tribunal's conclusions on the time point and on the merits of its decision. The latter ground was dismissed as not arguable at sift stage, on a paper review of the appeal. The EAT wrote to the respondent informing it of the EAT's decision on the merits point and referring it to r 3(10) of the EAT Rules of Procedure which provides a r 3(10) hearing in respect of the merit ground. By the time the respondent applied for a r 3(10) hearing, it was out of time. It applied for an extension but the Registrar refused that application.

At the full hearing on the time point, the EAT found that the tribunal was entitled to reach the conclusion that the error of the claimant was a reasonable one. It was noted that the respondent had not sought an appeal of either of the Judge's decisions and accordingly, the tribunal could not look behind those decisions, in particular the second decision to accept the claim as having been submitted on 8 December 2020. The EAT considered the reasons given for the decision that the claim could not have been presented in time and considered them adequate. The EAT emphasised one of the respondent's arguments that had 'given me pause', which related to the question of whether the tribunal could conclude that it was not practicable for the claim to have been presented in time when the judge had previously said that the error was not minor and that it would be in the interests of justice to reject the claim. The EAT held that while it might be that the practical effect of the tribunal's decision was to reverse the Judge's decision, it did not indicate an error of law in the tribunal's decision. The tribunal considered a very different legal test to the judge, ie, that which was set out in s 23 of the Employment Rights Act 1996.

The respondent was permitted to raise a challenge as to the calculation of the wages award by amendment and this was upheld. The EAT held that in calculating the award, the tribunal failed to consider the three-day waiting period at the start of a period of sickness before an entitlement to statutory sick pay arose.

The matter was remitted to the tribunal to recalculate its award.

WITHOUT PREJUDICE PRIVILEGE

[4.39] ***Garrod v Riverstone Management Ltd*[55]—*UK Employment Appeal Tribunal—appeal from employment tribunal—without prejudice communication—offer of severance payment—admissibility—whether a meeting between the parties formed part of negotiations genuinely aimed at settling the dispute—whether circumstances of unambiguous impropriety existed***

The claimant appealed against a preliminary decision of an employment tribunal that a reference in her pleadings to settlement proposals made by the respondent in a meeting, that had taken place before the claim issued, should be removed. The employment tribunal held that the reference fell within the scope of 'without prejudice' privilege and was inadmissible in evidence.

At the meeting in question, a representative of the respondent invited the claimant to have a 'without prejudice discussion'. It was assumed that the claimant, who was unrepresented at the meeting, but who had legal qualifications, understood what this meant (and she did not ask). The employment relationship was described as 'fractured' and 'problematic' and the possibility of a severance payment was raised. The employment tribunal accepted that the claimant had been taken by surprise by the discussion and had felt 'ambushed'. However, it was also found that the claimant understood the meaning of 'without prejudice' and her evidence that the meeting had been 'overbearing and aggressive' was exaggerated.

The EAT found that there was 'no reliance on the meeting as an unlawful act giving rise to a head of claim'. At a case management hearing, the claimant tried unsuccessfully to amend her claim to add an express allegation of victimisation arising from that meeting. The claim was therefore not based 'to any significant extent' on the allegedly without prejudice meeting and the employment tribunal was entitled to conclude that the dispute, the subject of the claim, already existed at the time of the meeting. The contents of the grievance, which corresponded closely with the particulars of claim, were 'clear signposts' to the possibility of litigation. The claimant's legal training was also a reasonable basis to conclude that these signposts were genuine.

The employment tribunal had therefore reached a reasonable conclusion and was entitled to conclude that the meeting was part of negotiations genuinely aimed at settling the dispute. There was no failure to apply the relevant law and this ground was dismissed.

The claimant argued that a settlement proposal based on termination 'could not have been a genuine attempt to resolve a dispute in which [the claimant], in her grievance, had expressed the wish to remain in her employment'. If there was an extant dispute at the meeting, it did not involve termination of the claimant's employment.

The EAT rejected this ground of appeal, repeating that this was not a claim in which the 'termination proposal' was the alleged misconduct. The grievance, the meeting and

55 *Garrod v Riverstone Management Ltd* [2022] EAT 177.

the tribunal claim 'all concerned the same subject matter' and the employment tribunal was entitled to come to the conclusion that the dispute discussed at the meeting was the same dispute which would form the claim.

Finally, the claimant argued that the employment tribunal erred in not finding that excluding the evidence would be an abuse of the without prejudice principle in circumstances of 'unambiguous impropriety'. It was submitted that responding to the claimant's grievance by proposing termination was an act of victimisation and that the termination offer was 'probative generally'.

The EAT observed that the claimant was seeking to place a 'discriminatory interpretation' on the act of proposing a 'consensual termination'. It seemed to the tribunal that any criticism which might be made against the respondent fell far short of the conduct typified by 'unambiguous impropriety' (for example, blackmail and perjury). The employment tribunal had correctly identified the law and had rightly concluded that this was not 'the very clearest of cases' of unambiguous impropriety.

Even if the claimant was correct that evidence of the termination offer could provide support for her claim, it did not follow that it should be admitted. The point of the exclusion rule, the EAT concluded, 'is that the policy aim of encouraging settlement of disputes outweighs the competing aim of allowing all relevant material to be placed before Court and tribunals'. The rule can only be displaced by 'very clear and very serious wrongdoing'.

The appeal was accordingly dismissed.

Chapter 5

Employment-Related Torts

INTRODUCTION

[5.01]

Duty to Avoid Risk of Being Convicted of a Criminal Offence

Credit Suisse (Securities) Europe Ltd was an appeal to the Court of Appeal of England and Wales, where the Court considered whether the High Court had erred in its decision that the appellant's employer had not breached their duty of care to the appellant by failing to protect them against exposure to a criminal conviction, as well as whether the appellant's contract of employment contained an implied indemnity against economic loss arising from the performance of their duties.

Personal Injury Claims

A number of personal injuries cases came before the Irish High Court—the issue of delay was considered in *Bowen*; the adequacy of damages was considered in *Joe Curran Commercials Ltd*; and the apportionment of liability as agreed by the parties was examined in *Peter Leonardi and Virginia Park Lodge Ltd. Queally Pig Slaughtering Ltd* concerned a workplace injury and the mitigation of loss by the plaintiff. The permissibility of the plaintiff amending the particulars of their claim was considered in *Deering Transport Ltd.* In *Dealey and Health Service Executive* the use of a medical consultant appointed by the plaintiff's solicitor was at issue. Renewing a personal injuries summons was considered in *Swords Barbers Ltd.*

Personal Injuries Assessment Board and Mater Misericordiae Hospital was a personal injuries case before the Irish Court of Appeal concerning the assessment of injuries falling within two different sub-categories in the Personal Injuries Guidelines and the obligation of the Personal Injuries Assessment Board to give reasons.

There were also a number of personal injuries cases before the High Court of England and Wales—*Lewin* concerned claims of negligence as well as breaches of statutory duty including occupiers' liability and *Brands Transport Ltd* concerned the negligent actions of an independent contractor and the non-delegable duties of the employer.

Vicarious Liability

In *Trustees of the Barry Congregation of Jehovah's Witnesses*, the UK Supreme Court held that, although the relationship between an elder and the organisation of the Jehovah's Witnesses was akin to employment, the offence committed by the elder did not satisfy the close connection test for vicarious liability to apply.

The High Court of England and Wales also considered the vicarious liability of employers in personal injuries cases involving sexual assault in *MXX*.

DUTY TO AVOID RISK OF BEING CONVICTED OF A CRIMINAL OFFENCE

[5.02] ***Benyatov v Credit Suisse (Securities) Europe Ltd*[1]*—Court of Appeal of England and Wales—Underhill, Bean & Singh LJJ—appeal from High Court of England and Wales—duty to avoid risk of being convicted of a criminal offence—bankers—breach of duty of care—consequential loss—employees' rights—foreign convictions—foreseeability—indemnity—loss of earnings—implied terms***

The appellant was an employee of the respondent investment bank from 1996 to 2015. In 2006, the appellant was arrested by the Romanian authorities on suspicion of criminal activity relating to a consultancy project he was working on for the respondent. He was found guilty and received a sentence of ten years' imprisonment. Ultimately, this was overturned and replaced by another charge which attracted a lesser sentence. Before his sentence commenced, the appellant moved to the United States. His Financial Conduct Authority approval was revoked and the respondent terminated the appellant's employment in 2015.

The appellant initiated negligence and breach of contract proceedings against the respondent in the High Court of England and Wales for career-loss earnings. He alleged that the respondent breached its duty of care not to expose him to criminal conviction in the carrying on of his duties. He also claimed that there was an implied term in his employment contract with the respondent that they would indemnify him against any economic loss arising from the performance of his duties.

The High Court dismissed the appellant's case. It held that, as Romania was not a high-risk country and the appellant was not involved in a high-risk transaction, his conviction was not reasonably foreseeable. Therefore, a duty of care did not arise. The High Court also found against the appellant with regard to the implied indemnity claim.

---

1 *Benyatov v Credit Suisse (Securities) Europe Ltd* [2023] EWCA Civ 140. For decision of the High Court of England and Wales in *Benyatov v Credit Suisse Securities (Europe) Ltd* [2022] EWHC 135, see *Arthur Cox Employment Law Yearbook 2022* at [5.03]. See *Arthur Cox Employment Law Yearbook 2021* at [6.02] for related case *Benyatov v Credit Suisse Securities (Europe) Ltd* [2021] EWHC 1318 (QB) concerning duty to indemnify.

The appellant appealed to the Court of Appeal, arguing that the High Court had erred in applying a subjective rather than an objective approach to the issue of foreseeability and had failed to consider whether the respondent had tacitly assumed responsibility for that risk.

The Court of Appeal held that the trial Judge had not taken a subjective approach. Rather, he had considered what the bank knew and what it ought to have known in order to assess foreseeability. The Court cited *Caparo Industries plc v Dickman*[2] and the three factors to be considered when assessing whether a duty of care exists: foreseeability; proximity; and fairness, justice and reasonableness. The Court held that the High Court had duly considered these factors and did not err in their application. It was held that an assumption of responsibility analysis was not appropriate here. The respondent was not aware of the risk of a criminal conviction in this case and therefore could not be said to have assumed the responsibility to indemnify the appellant against this risk.

With regard to the contractual claim, the Court held that it would not be appropriate to extend any contractual indemnity to losses of any kind suffered by an employee as a result of carrying out his employment duties. To hold otherwise would mean that employers may be found liable for loss of earnings where harm is caused to an employee during the course of his work by a third party, which had nothing to do with the employer. No general indemnity could be implied in these circumstances, based on the location or nature of the work being inherently high risk, as the trial Judge had found that neither were high risk.

Ultimately, it was held that the respondent owed no duty of care to safeguard the appellant against a criminal conviction and any economic loss arising on foot of same. Nor was there an implied indemnity in his contract with the respondent.

The appeal was therefore dismissed.

PERSONAL INJURY CLAIMS

[5.03] ***Bowen v H&M Hennes and Mauritz (Ireland) Ltd & Otis Elevator Ireland Ltd*[3]*—High Court—Simons J—personal injuries—third-party notice—delay—application to set aside third-party notice—whether the defendant failed to serve the third-party notice within a reasonable time***

The plaintiff was employed by the defendant company as a sales assistant. On 11 October 2016, she was trapped for a period of time in a lift in the workplace and claimed damages for psychiatric and physical injury. A personal injuries summons issued on 28 March 2019.

2 *Caparo Industries plc v Dickman* [1990] 2 AC 605.
3 *Bowen v H&M Hennes & Mauritz (Ireland) Ltd* [2022] IEHC 658.

The defendant issued a motion on 10 May 2021, seeking leave to serve a third-party notice on Otis Elevator Ireland Ltd ('the third party'). The third party subsequently issued a motion to set aside the third-party notice on the grounds of delay. That application was refused by the Circuit Court and the application came before the High Court on appeal. In the interim, the main proceedings settled and were struck out.

The question of whether the defendant served the third-party notice as soon as reasonably possible 'fell to be assessed by reference to events subsequent to the issue of the personal injury summons' on 28 March 2019. The Court concluded that it was reasonable for the defendant to 'hold off' delivering its defence—and thereafter applying to join the third party—until receipt of replies to particulars on 10 September 2019. However, once replies had been received, the application for leave to serve the third-party notice should have issued 'no later than December 2019'. In fact, the motion did not issue until 10 May 2021, some 20 months after replies to particulars were delivered.

The Court held that none of the reasons offered by the defendant amounted to a reasonable justification for the delay. It would have been immediately obvious from the circumstances of the claim that some consideration would need to be given as to whether liability attached to the party responsible for servicing and maintaining the lift. It was unreasonable for the defendant to delay until February 2020 before obtaining maintenance records relating to the lift. Similarly, a delay in locating paperwork detailing the contractual arrangement between the defendant and the third party was unreasonable and could not legitimately be attributed to 'logistical difficulties' caused by the Covid-19 pandemic. There should have been 'ample time' to locate the paperwork before the restrictions were implemented in March 2020.

It was 'telling' that the defendant was able to articulate a claim against the third party in its defence delivered on 20 November 2020. In spite of this, the motion for leave to serve the third-party notice was not issued for another six months, without reasonable justification.

Accordingly, the defendant failed to serve the third-party notice as soon as reasonably possible and the appeal against the Circuit Court order was allowed.

[5.04] ***Lyttle v Joe Curran Commercials Ltd*[4]*—High Court—Barr J—personal injuries—damages—quantum—whether it was appropriate to proceed to assess damages notwithstanding the failure of the defendant to appear at the hearing of the action***

The plaintiff worked at the defendant company. In October 2019, the plaintiff suffered severe personal injuries when using a sandblasting machine in the course of his employment. The sandblaster operated by firing shards of glass onto a surface to remove rust. The plaintiff had been holding a pipe on the machine when the bracket broke, causing his hand to receive the force of the blast from the machine. The plaintiff suffered a

4 *Lyttle v Joe Curran Commercials Ltd* [2022] IEHC 665.

deep laceration to his left hand as a result. The plaintiff alleged that he had never been trained to work with a sandblasting machine by his employer and had not been given any protective equipment to wear while using the machine.

The plaintiff initiated High Court proceedings against the defendant, and when no appearance was entered by the defendant, the plaintiff obtained judgment in default of appearance in November 2021.

A notice of trial was served on the plaintiff in May 2022 and in November 2022, the defendant was informed of the hearing date. An affidavit of service was sworn in relation to the service of this correspondence. The defendant did not appear at the hearing. The plaintiff gave evidence which the Court was 'impressed' by, and which it found was 'consistent with the evidence given by his medical consultant'. The Court was satisfied, given the existence the order for judgment in default of appearance and the affidavit of service, that it was appropriate to proceed to assess damages in the company's absence.

In relation to general damages, the Court was referred to the Book of Quantum. The Court awarded the plaintiff €25,000 for pain and suffering to date and €22,500 for pain and suffering and disablement into the future. The Court referred to the special damages pleaded and awarded the €1,680 sought. The Court also found that the plaintiff was unfit for work for a period of one year after the accident which, net the deductible social welfare benefits, amounted to a loss of earnings of €14,924. This meant a total award for special damages of €16,604.

The High Court found that the plaintiff was entitled to judgment as against the defendant in the total sum of €64,104.

[5.05] ***Wilson v Peter Leonardi and Virginia Park Lodge Ltd*[5]*—High Court—Barr J—Social Welfare (Consolidation) Act 2005, Part 11B—practice and procedure—post-hearing—judicial orders—apportionment of liability—RBA certificate***

The plaintiff was employed by the second-named defendant in its hotel. In 2017, she was involved in a road traffic accident, having been struck by a vehicle driven by the first-named defendant.

These proceedings were eventually settled between the parties, who requested that the order of the Court include an agreed term that liability be determined on a 50/50 basis between the plaintiff and second-named defendant. This term was sought by the defendants so as to relieve them of the obligation to pay the Minister for Social Protection the entire amount of the benefit included in the Recoverable Benefits and Assistance ('RBA') certificate issued in respect of the plaintiff.

The Court considered whether it was appropriate to accede to this application and noted the conflicting judgments of the High Court on this issue, which it sought to address.

5 *Wilson v Peter Leonardi and Virginia Park Lodge Ltd* [2022] IEHC 670.

The Court considered the relevant provisions of the Social Welfare (Consolidation) Act 1993, which provides that certain social welfare benefits, paid to a plaintiff as a result of their having suffered personal injuries, were deductible from the compensation to be paid by a culpable defendant. The intent of the legislature in this regard was to prevent the plaintiff being compensated twice: once by social welfare payments and subsequently by receiving compensation for the same loss in damages awarded in Court. This arrangement was carried over by ss 96 and 286 of the Social Welfare (Consolidation) Act 2005. The effect of this deductibility meant that the culpable defendant and/or their indemnifier did not have to pay a portion of compensation, because that head of loss had been catered for by way of social welfare benefits.

The Court noted that the Law Reform Commission recommended that this arrangement should be changed, so that a culpable defendant should pay the value of such benefits to the State. This recommendation was adopted in the form of Part 11B of the 2005 Act, as inserted by s 13 of the Social Welfare and Pensions Act 2013, which repealed and replaced s 96(1) and (2) and s 286 of the 2005 Act.

The Court set out the text of s 343R, which provides for the obligation to pay recoverable benefits to the Minister. The effect of the change is that if parties settle personal injury proceedings, the compensator is liable to repay the full amount of benefits set out in the statement of recoverable benefits.

In order to avoid this, compensators must bring themselves within s 343R(2), obtaining an order from the Court apportioning liability between parties or making certain declarations in relation to the extent or duration of the plaintiff's loss of earnings claim. The effect is to limit or modify the obligation to pay the amount of benefits specified in the RBA certificate.

The Court cited conflicting decisions on the topic, including: the joined cases of *Condon v Health Service Executive and Szwarc v Hanford Commercial Ltd*,[6] *Matthews v Eircom*,[7] *Fahy v Padraig Fahy Tiling Contractors Ltd*,[8] *Kuczak v Treacy Tyres (Portumna) Ltd (No 1)*[9] and *Kuczak v Treacy Tyres (Portumna) Ltd (No 2)*.[10] It noted in particular, that Twomey J took the view in *Kuczak (No 1)* that an apportionment of liability could only occur after a judge had heard evidence and ruled on liability. Twomey J held that the Court could not make consent orders regarding apportionment of liability merely at the request of parties in the terms dictated by them.

In these proceedings, the High Court held that, while the doctrine of horizontal precedent ordinarily requires that a judge follow a judgment given by a colleague of the same hierarchal jurisdiction, where there are conflicting decisions at that same level, a subsequent judge is permitted to follow whichever line of authority they deem most persuasive.

6 *Condon v. Health Service Executive and Szwarc v Hanford Commercial Ltd* [2021] IEHC 474.
7 *Matthews v Eircom* [2021] IEHC 456.
8 *Fahy v Padraig Fahy Tiling Contractors Ltd* [2021] IEHC 682.
9 *Kuczak v Treacy Tyres (Portumna) Ltd (No 1)* [2022] IEHC 181.
10 *Kuczak v Treacy Tyres (Portumna) Ltd (No 2)* [2022] IEHC 619.

The Court held that it was appropriate to include consent terms in relation to either the loss of earnings claim maintained by the plaintiff or the apportionment of liability, so long as there was 'some rational and fair basis' for said inclusion.

The Court was not convinced by the report that there had been a shortfall to the Minister of €20 million due to such consent orders being made by the courts in the past. Despite this figure being relied on in some of the previous case-law, the Court characterised this as 'triple hearsay' as it could not be verified. The Court noted that if the Minister believed the Department had been short-changed in this regard, the Minister could have taken steps to address this, eg, by amending the legislation, bringing judicial review proceedings, or in an application to be joined into any proceedings which the Minister felt an inappropriate determination had been made.

The Court went on to state that a court should not 'blindly rubberstamp' a request for such an order. In much the same way as with infant rulings, the Court held that it would be appropriate for it to be given 'sufficient information' to satisfy itself that the determination requested is properly to be included in the order.

Having considered the submissions of the parties as they pertained to causation and liability and the likely evidence which would have been given if the proceedings had not been compromised, the Court made a determination of liability on a 50/50 basis between the plaintiff and second defendant.

[5.06] ***Ryan v Queally Pig Slaughtering Ltd[11]—High Court—O'Connor J—loss of earnings—general damages—facet joint dysfunction—minimising losses—health and safety—summary judgment***

The plaintiff was an employee of the defendant and suffered a facet joint dysfunction injury while at work in the 'vac pac' area of the defendant's premises, lifting bags of pork. The plaintiff brought personal injuries proceedings in the High Court.

It was contended by the defence that the plaintiff suffered from historic issues with his back and that due to the degeneration of his lumbar discs and adjoining facet joints, the pain which he currently suffered was an eventuality. The question as to the fact and degree of mitigation by the plaintiff of his losses was also submitted for consideration.

Medical evidence was submitted that the work undertaken by the plaintiff while employed by the defendant contributed to the arthritis in the plaintiff's spine. Accordingly, the Court held that 'the facet joint dysfunction and the contribution of some 20% to the plaintiff's arthritis from the work required, combined to have an overwhelming effect on the plaintiff's lumbar spine'. The Court held that a 'more automated system of work for that undertaken by the plaintiff before April 2017' would have allowed the plaintiff to persist even with his 'bad back'. The Court held it was reasonable to conclude that the plaintiff would have continued in employment until 65 or 66, had the injury not occurred.

11 *Ryan v Queally Pig Slaughtering Ltd* [2022] IEHC 732.

The defendant suggested that the plaintiff could have returned to some different manual work after the injury and that it was for the plaintiff to identify a task which he could do. The Court held that the onus of proof lay on the defendant to establish that the plaintiff had not taken steps to mitigate his loss. In this case, it was held that the defendant did not meet this threshold. Further, the Court held it was unlikely that any step which the plaintiff might have taken could have mitigated his losses to any great extent, as the evidence submitted to the Court made it clear that the plaintiff was not able to work.

Past loss of earnings was calculated to amount to €130,000. The Court considered the judgment of Noonan J in *Twomey v Jeral Ltd*,[12] which it characterised as clarifying that the 'controversial' *Reddy v Bates* discount was between 15% and 25%. The Court arrived at a sum of €150,000, which represented a figure for cessation of work when aged between 65 and 66, minus a 20% discount, resulting in €120,000 for future loss of earnings.

The Court noted that although a 'facet joint dysfunction' in the lumbar spine was not mentioned in the Book of Quantum, the 'back injuries and spinal fractures' section at Part 3A was instructive. The Court decided that the description offered under the sub-heading 'severe and permanent' most closely reflected the plaintiff's injuries. General damages were awarded in the sum of €55,000. An identical sum was awarded for future suffering. Agreed special damages were ruled in the sum of €5,536.

An order was made in favour of the plaintiff, together with his costs against the defendant in the sum of €365,536.

[5.07] ***Behan v Deering Transport Ltd*[13]*—High Court—Ferriter J—damages—amendment—plaintiff seeking permission to amend particulars of claims contained on his personal injury summons—whether amendments would cause prejudice***

The plaintiff was a truck driver working at the first-named defendant's haulage company. In October 2014, the plaintiff suffered personal injuries in the course of his duties. In the plaintiff's personal injury summons, he alleged that he suffered an injury when he alighted from the truck he was driving and slipped on the wet floor of a warehouse which was owned by the second, third and fourth-named defendants. This sequence of events was consistent with the plaintiff's accident report form and PIAB application.

The plaintiff sought permission from the High Court under Order 28 RSC to amend the personal injury summons to claim that his injuries were caused, not by the wet floor of the premises, but by a defect in the ridges on the lowermost step of the cab of the truck he was alighting from. The plaintiff also sought to amend his particulars of negligence and breach of duty as against the first-named defendant to reflect this sequence of events. The plaintiff discontinued the claims against the other defendants.

12 *Twomey v Jeral Ltd* [2022] IECA 177.

13 *Behan v Deering Transport Ltd* [2023] IEHC 64.

The first-named defendant opposed the application given the prejudice that it might suffer, including by depriving it of a defence under the Statute of Limitations. It was argued that the plaintiff had consistently identified that the cause of the accident was the wet floor of the warehouse, in the accident report form, PIAB application, and summons. It was submitted that the introduction of wholly new facts at this stage would be unfair.

The Court rejected the suggestion of actual prejudice. It was noted that the first-named defendant was on notice from 2016 of a factual case made by the other defendants to the effect that the injury was caused by a fall from the steps on the truck and not the wet floor. It also had asked its engineering expert to examine the truck to meet this case.

The Court held that the proposed amendments did not alter the originally pleaded claim and accordingly, to permit the amendments would not deprive the first-named defendant of a Statute of Limitations defence. The amendments did not introduce any new cause of action. It was the factual basis underpinning the existing cause of action that was sought to be amended.

It was held that any delay in this application was explained by way of affidavit and did not persuade the Court to refuse the application.

The Court held that the amendments sought were necessary to determine the real issue of contention, being causation in this case. The Court also held that there was no prejudice to the defendant that could not be addressed by appropriate terms, including terms as to costs. Therefore, the Court made an order allowing the amendments of the personal injury summons, subject to certain conditions, ie, that the first-named defendant remain entitled to raise any ground of defence it wished in circumstances where the claim was now based on different facts from those in the PIAB authorisation; and that the plaintiff pay the first-named defendant the costs of having to amend the defence and the costs of raising any particulars. The Court reserved to the trial judge the issue of unnecessary or additional costs incurred to date arising from the amended case (other than the costs of amending the defence and raising particulars).

The application was therefore granted.

[5.08] ***McLaughlin v Dealey and Health Service Executive*[14]*—High Court—Ferriter J—personal injuries—assessment of damages—medical witnesses—expert evidence—weight to be attached to medical evidence where plaintiff was referred directly to consultant—workplace accident***

The plaintiff worked as a full-time healthcare assistant for the second-named defendant. She injured her back in the course of employment, lifting a patient onto a trolley. Her injury impacted her ability to continue working in her chosen profession. The plaintiff brought personal injuries claims against both defendants. The proceedings against the first-named defendant settled. The second-named defendant ultimately admitted

14 *McLaughlin v Dealey and Health Service Executive* [2023] IEHC 106.

liability during the trial and the matter subsequently proceeded as an assessment of damages only.

The plaintiff relied on expert evidence from an orthopaedic surgeon to substantiate her claim. The consultant, in his report, stated that the plaintiff would likely suffer recurrent symptoms from her injuries into the future due to her lack of progress in rehabilitation. One of the defendant's experts seemed to support this view. However, a second expert for the defendant took the view that the plaintiff's soft tissue injuries would eventually completely resolve themselves and did not accept that her ongoing symptoms were linked to the original injury suffered.

The defendant argued that less weight should be placed on the evidence of the plaintiff's expert in circumstances where the plaintiff had been referred directly to this expert for examination by her solicitor and had not been the subject of a referral from the plaintiff's GP. A point was also made regarding the fact that, on the date of the examination, the consultant had not reviewed the plaintiff's medical records and therefore was not adequately informed of her history to make an accurate diagnosis or prognosis. The plaintiff argued that the evidence was not of less relevance simply because the expert had been engaged directly by the plaintiff's solicitor. The plaintiff rejected any suggestion that the consultant lacked objectivity or independence as a result of how he was engaged.

The High Court held that it was a matter for the Court to assess the strength of the evidence provided by any medical expert, the quality of their opinions, and their objectivity. In evaluating the case-law, the Court noted that none of the authorities establish a rule that a plaintiff may not engage an expert, separate from their GP, in order to elicit an opinion from them or to call them at trial. Rather, a plaintiff is entitled, subject to the Rules of Court, to engage medical experts in personal injuries proceedings in the same way as they are entitled to engage and call experts in other forms of civil litigation. The Court noted that there is no provision in Irish law that requires that a medical witness be subject to a GP referral.

It was therefore permissible for a solicitor to directly engage a medical expert for the purposes of acquiring expert evidence, so long as they are properly informed of all relevant information about the patient's medical history and have had an appropriate opportunity to examine the plaintiff and to prepare their report in accordance with their overriding duties to the court.

The Court held that the consultant had been adequately briefed by the plaintiff herself on her medical history, but did note that it would have been preferable for the consultant to have been given the plaintiff's official GP record. However, it was held that, in the absence of this record, the consultant was not hindered in the making of his report.

The Court therefore applied the appropriate weight to the evidence and awarded €57,500 in general damages, and €2,772 in special damages, but did not award any damages for loss of opportunity.

The total award to the plaintiff was therefore €60,272.

[5.09] ***Rajauskiene v Swords Barbers Ltd*[15]*—High Court—Bolger J—personal injuries—renewal of summons—application to set aside renewal—delay—prejudice***

The defendants applied to set aside an order of the High Court renewing the plaintiff's personal injury summons for a period of three months.

The plaintiff admitted to an inadvertent delay in serving the defendants, which efforts were then thwarted by the onset of Covid-19. The Court noted that there was a considerable further period of delay following the Covid-19 lockdown. Nevertheless, the defendants waited some time from when they were made aware of the plaintiff's intention to renew the summons and the making of the High Court order before bringing this application.

In balancing the interests of justice and the respective prejudice for each side, the Court was not satisfied of a 'sufficiently specific' prejudice to the defendants 'such as would outweigh the prejudice to the plaintiff in being statute barred'. The application was therefore refused.

[5.10] ***Wolfe v Personal Injuries Assessment Board and Mater Misericordiae Hospital*[16]*—Court of Appeal—Binchy J—appeal from High Court—Personal Injuries Assessment Board Act 2003—Judicial Council Act 2019—assessment of damages—sufficient reasons—multiple injuries—two sub-categories—Personal Injury Guidelines—ambiguity***

The appellant was a catering assistant who suffered personal injuries at work. She claimed she suffered injuries to her left shoulder, lower back and right leg. She made an application to the respondent for an assessment of damages under s 11 of the Personal Injuries Assessment Board Act 2003 (the '2003 Act'). The respondent assessed general damages at €11,000. It indicated what it considered the most dominant injury and 'where appropriate' the presence or absence of other less significant injuries. It referred to the Personal Injury Guidelines adopted by the Judicial Council under the Judicial Council Act 2019. The respondent identified the dominant injury in the appellant's case as being her back, and that the category was minor. Under 'sub-category' the respondent noted 'substantial recovery 1–2 years'.

The appellant argued that her solicitor had difficulty in advising her whether or not to accept the assessment owing to the absence of sufficient reasons as to how the sum was calculated. In the High Court, the appellant sought: an order of certiorari quashing the assessment; an order remitting the matter to the respondent for an assessment with all necessary details; a declaration that an assessment must contain reasons in writing, based on the Personal Injury Guidelines; and costs.

15 *Rajauskiene v Swords Barbers Ltd* [2023] IEHC 349.

16 *Wolfe v Personal Injuries Assessment Board and Mater Misericordiae Hospital* [2023] IECA 245.

The High Court noted that while the 2003 Act requires the respondent to 'have regard' to the Personal Injury Guidelines, there is no statutory provision which mandates the provision of reasons for an assessment, and nothing in the Personal Injury Guidelines that requires the provision of reasons in relation to the application of same. Accordingly, the Court assessed the matter based on the constitutional principles of fair procedures and natural justice. The High Court held that the appellant's application must be rejected, having regard to: the information provided by the appellant (eg, medical reports); the nature of the process (it being a mere assessment); the fact that the decision of the respondent was not binding; and the fact that there was no statutory obligation to state reasons.

The Court of Appeal noted that, in other contexts, the importance of adequate reasons for a decision might assist in deciding to appeal or take judicial review proceedings. While the type of assessments made by the respondent were administrative in nature, it was noted that: 'A person in receipt of an assessment from the respondent has an important decision to make'. The Court noted that the 2003 Act was introduced to reduce legal costs in personal injuries cases and inadequate reasons may lead a claimant to issue personal injuries proceedings and open themselves to the legal costs incurred by the defendant in those proceedings if unsuccessful. The Court held therefore that claimants are 'entitled to be given information sufficient to understand the basis of its calculation of general damages without having to resort to guesswork'.

The Court noted that if the appellant had suffered only injury to her back, the respondent's description of the injuries in the body of the assessment and description of the relevant category and sub-category applicable, 'read together with the medical reports and the Guidelines would constitute a sufficiently reasoned decision'. In that scenario, the appellant would have had ample information available to her to understand in a general way the basis of the assessment and whether to accept or reject it. What complicated the appellant's case was that she suffered from other more minor injuries and that her main injury, being her back, straddled two different sub-categories. The Court noted that, given the level of damages recommended in the assessment, there were two possibilities: that the respondent had considered the lesser injuries to be so minor as to not merit additional compensation over and above that assessed for her back; or that the respondent had, in taking the lesser injuries into account, assessed general damages at the higher end of the sub-category in which it considered the dominant injury was located than it would have done if there had not been lesser injuries at play. Due to this ambiguity, the Court rejected the High Court's conclusion that an 'objective observer' would be aware of the reasons for the assessment having regard to all the information available to them.

An order was made quashing the assessment and referring the matter back to the respondent for reconsideration and the provision of adequate reasons to explain the assessment of general damages.

The appeal was allowed.

[5.11] ***Lewin v Gray*[17]*—High Court of England and Wales—Robinson J—Occupiers' Liability Act 1957—Construction (Design and Management) Regulations 2015*[18]*—Health and Safety at Work Act 1974—accidents at work—breach of duty of care—causation—construction sites—occupiers' liability—fall from roof—failure to ensure construction phase plan completed by contractor***

The claimant was a self-employed builder who had been contracted to install guttering on the roof of a barn located on a farm, which was run by the defendant. While installing the guttering, the claimant fell through the roof and suffered severe injuries. The claimant brought a personal injuries claim, grounded in negligence and breaches of statutory duty, including duties under: the Occupiers' Liability Act 1957, the Work at Height Regulations 2005,[19] and the Construction (Design and Management) Regulations 2015 (the '2015 Regulations'). It was alleged that the defendant: had failed in the selection of the claimant as an appropriate contractor; had failed to supervise the claimant in his work; and had failed to ensure that he had completed a construction phase plan before commencing the work. A number of these allegations fell away at trial.

The Court held that, under s 2(3)(b) of the Occupiers' Liability Act 1957, it was reasonable for the defendant to expect that the claimant would understand and safeguard against the risks associated with undertaking the guttering work.

The Court noted that according to s 47 of the Health and Safety at Work Act 1974, as amended, no breach of duty imposed by the 2015 Regulations would be civilly actionable except insofar as the 2015 Regulations explicitly provided. Therefore, no civil liability arose in this case in respect of the facts giving rise to the defendant's breach of reg 4(5), which required him to ensure that before the construction commenced, a construction phase plan was drawn up by the claimant.

Accordingly, the Court considered whether the defendant owed a duty of care to the claimant to ensure that he produced a construction phase plan in compliance with the 2015 Regulations and, if so, whether the defendant in failing to ensure that the claimant had produced a construction phase plan had caused or materially contributed to the accident. This was so, notwithstanding the facts that the defendant could have been criminally liable in respect of his breach of reg 4(5) and that this could be used as evidence against him in a civil trial (albeit only to prove that the offence had been committed).

The Court found that the defendant was not liable for the injuries on the grounds offered. The Court noted that even if a construction phase plan had been produced by the claimant, it would not have prevented the accident from happening.

The Court dismissed the claim.

---

17 *Lewin v Gray* [2023] EWHC 112 (KB).
18 Construction (Design and Management) Regulations 2015 (SI 2015/51).
19 Work at Height Regulations 2005 (SI 2005/735).

[5.12] ***Carr v Brands Transport Ltd*[20]*—High Court of England and Wales—Knowles J—personal injuries—negligence—duty of care—non-delegable duty—nature of relationship between claimant and defendant***

The claimant was loading cars on to the top deck of a double-deck car transporter. The car transporter consisted of a tractor cab and trailer unit with decks that could be raised for the loading of cars. Safety rails were welded to the unit to prevent people from falling from the decks. Although no one witnessed the tragic accident, it was inferred that when the claimant leaned back or otherwise put pressure on the safety rail, he fell some 14 feet onto concrete, suffering catastrophic and permanent injuries.

It was common case that the safety rail failed because of corrosion in a particular guard pillar, which snapped. The transporter was owned by the first defendant, Brands Transport Ltd, of which the claimant was sole director, 80% shareholder and (the Court was satisfied) an employee. The claimant sued the first defendant for negligence. A third party, Trax (Coventry) Ltd, carried out safety checks on large vehicles and had since ceased trading. It had inspected the car transporter in October and November of 2017 and deemed it roadworthy.

Because the car transporter worked at a height, it was subject to health and safety regulations and required a thorough inspection at least every six months. The Court was satisfied that the next inspection was due more than five months before the date of the accident. Had that inspection been carried out, it would have identified the corroded guard pillar and prevented the accident.

It was agreed that as the health and safety regulations were not actionable, the claimant's remedy lay in common law negligence, though the regulations were helpful for determining the scope of the duty of care.

The High Court of England and Wales found that the transport manager engaged by the first defendant, whose evidence was frank and honest, had undertaken in his role to ensure that 'vehicles and trailers are kept in a fit and roadworthy condition', and on the evidence had failed to exercise reasonable care and skill in the exercise of his functions. It was negligent of the transport manager not to have scheduled an inspection of the car transporter in the circumstances, and not to have familiarised himself with the transporter's manuals.

Although the transport manager was an independent contractor, the first defendant owed a non-delegable personal protective duty to the claimant, who was an employee, and the first defendant was thus liable. The first defendant's claim against the third party failed on the clear evidence that the agreement between those parties did not include inspection of the upper deck safety rails.

The claimant's claim succeeded and the first defendant's claim against the third party was dismissed.

---

20 *Carr v Brands Transport Ltd and Trax (Coventry) Ltd* [2022] EWHC 3167 (KB).

VICARIOUS LIABILITY

[5.13] ***Trustees of the Barry Congregation of Jehovah's Witnesses v BXB*[21]*—UK Supreme Court—Burrows LJ—appeal from Court of Appeal of England and Wales—psychiatric injury—vicarious liability—relationship akin to employment—close connection—test for vicarious liability***

The appellant appealed the Court of Appeal of England and Wales' dismissal of their appeal against a finding of vicarious liability by the High Court.

In 1990, the respondent was raped by an 'elder' of the Barry Congregation of Jehovah's Witnesses, with whom she had established a close personal friendship. She reported the rape to the other congregation elders in 1993 on learning of an allegation by a minor against that same elder. She did not report the matter to police at that time. An ecclesiastical judicial committee was formed, and it found the allegation against the elder in question unproven. In 1994, that elder was expelled from the congregation for unrelated conduct. Sometime thereafter, the respondent ceased her involvement with the Jehovah's Witnesses. In 2013, having learned of another allegation made against the former elder, she reported the rape to the police. There followed a criminal trial and the former elder was convicted and sentenced to 14 years' imprisonment.

In 2017, the respondent brought personal injury proceedings in the High Court against the appellant, alleging vicarious liability for the rape. The trial Judge, having determined that it was equitable to allow the claim to proceed, found the appellant vicariously liable for personal injuries, including psychiatric harm, to the respondent. The Court of Appeal dismissed the appellant's appeal against that decision, holding that both stages of the test for vicarious liability were satisfied.

On appeal, the UK Supreme Court was satisfied that the relationship between the convicted elder and the Jehovah's Witnesses organisation was indeed akin to employment and that the lower courts were correct in their analysis. The fact that there was no payment for the work of an elder was not decisive of the issue, other considerations were relevant such as: the convicted elder carried out work on behalf of, and assigned to him, by the Jehovah's Witnesses; he performed duties in furtherance of, and integral to, the aims and objectives of the organisation; and there was an appointment process, a removal process, and a hierarchical structure in which he fitted.

However, the Supreme Court identified a number of errors at the 'close connection' stage of the test applied by the lower courts. The correct test that should have been applied was whether the rape 'was so closely connected with acts that the tortfeasor … was authorised to do, that the rape can fairly and properly be regarded as committed by him while acting in the course of his quasi-employment as an elder'.

The respondent failed to satisfy the close connection test. The rape was committed in the elder's own home at a time when he was not engaged in any work connected with his role in the organisation. The elder was not exercising control over the respondent

---

21 *Trustees of the Barry Congregation of Jehovah's Witnesses v BXB* [2023] UKSC 15.

in the context of his position as an elder, but rather as a close personal friend of the respondent. It was not realistic to suggest, as the respondent had done in the course of submissions, that the convicted elder 'never took off his "metaphorical uniform" as an elder'. While it was accepted that the tortfeasor's role as an elder was a 'but for' cause of the respondent's friendship with the elder, the Court recalled that 'but for' causation is insufficient to satisfy the close connection test. The Court did not accept that the elder's increasingly flirtatious behaviour towards the respondent was analogous to a grooming relationship, but was, rather, a shocking 'one-off' attack owing more to their friendship than to his role as an elder in the organisation.

The appeal was, accordingly, allowed.

[5.14] *MXX v A Secondary School*[22]*—Court of Appeal of England and Wales—Davies LJ—appeal from High Court of England and Wales—personal injuries—sexual assault—vicarious liability—relationship akin to employment—close connection*

This was an appeal against the dismissal of a personal injuries action, in which the appellant had sought damages for recognised psychiatric illness consequent on sexual assaults committed by a tortfeasor—a former pupil who had undertaken workplace experience at the respondent school—while the claimant was a pupil at the school.

The claim was dismissed in the High Court of England and Wales on a finding that the respondent was not vicariously liable for the torts committed by the tortfeasor. The trial Judge found that there was not a relationship akin to employment between the respondent and the tortfeasor, who had undertaken one week's work experience at the school. It was held that the tortfeasor's role was not integral to the respondent's business and the very limited role he played in the school 'barely went beyond his own learning'. It was 'artificial' to describe the tortfeasor as performing a teaching role 'or even that of a classroom assistant', and he had 'no independent responsibility for any aspect of the respondent's undertakings', including the entrusting of pupils to his care. It would be neither fair, just nor reasonable to impose vicarious liability, the entirety of the wrongdoing having been committed 'many weeks after' the work experience placement ended. This decision was appealed.

The Court of Appeal held that the trial Judge was wrong to find that the relationship between the school and the tortfeasor was not akin to employment. The trial Judge's reliance on a finding that the school treated the tortfeasor's request for work experience as a 'favour' was inconsistent with the position in law, 'that there need not be an alignment between the objectives of the defendant and the tortfeasor'. It was not a fair representation to describe the tortfeasor's work as 'minor ancillary tasks', as the trial Judge had done. The tortfeasor was subject to the school's close direction and control, which was suggestive of an employment-type relationship. The trial Judge did not lend sufficient weight to the fact of the school's requirement that the tortfeasor understand

22 *MXX v A Secondary School* [2023] EWCA Civ 996.

and accept its safeguarding policy. The tortfeasor's role, to undergo training, was 'not inconsistent' with employee status. He assisted with PE classes and after-school sports clubs and pupils were told to treat him as a member of staff.

The Court of Appeal also differed from the High Court in its finding that grooming behaviour commenced when the tortfeasor was at the school, where his role was akin to employment. Here, however, the Court of Appeal agreed with the trial Judge's assessment as to the limited nature of the tortfeasor's role at the school. He had 'no caring or pastoral responsibility' for pupils, was kept under close supervision at all times and held no position of authority over the pupils. It was not until the tortfeasor left the school that any communication took place with the appellant on Facebook. Thus, the close connection test was not satisfied. The grooming behaviour was not 'inextricably woven' with the carrying out of the tortfeasor's work during his week at the school such that it would be fair and just to hold the respondent vicariously liable for his acts.

Accordingly, the appeal was dismissed.

Chapter 6

European Law

INTRODUCTION

Professional Qualifications

[6.01] The Supreme Administrative Court of Finland referred *Opetushallitus* to the ECJ for a preliminary ruling in relation to Directive 2005/36/EC on the free movement of workers. The case concerned the recognition of professional qualifications in other Member States.

Social Security

In *Caisse nationale d'assurance pension*, the Cour de Cassation, Luxembourg requested a preliminary ruling from the ECJ regarding the application of arts 18, 45 and 48 of the Treaty on the Functioning of the European Union and art 7 of the Regulation (EU) 492/2011 on the freedom of movement for workers within the Union in the context of Social Security.

Public Service Employment

In *Ministero dell'Istruzione, dell'Università e della Ricerca (MIUR)*, the ECJ made a preliminary ruling in relation to art 45 of the TFEU in a case concerning national legislation that did not allow professional experience gained in other Member States to be taken in account when applying for a role in the Public Service of Italy.

PROFESSIONAL QUALIFICATIONS

[6.02] ***A v Opetushallitus*[1]*—European Court of Justice—request for preliminary ruling from Finland—Directive 2005/36/EC*[2]*—freedom of movement for***

---

1 *A v Opetushallitus* (Case C-270/21).

2 Directive 2005/36/EC *on the recognition of professional qualifications.*

workers—recognition of professional qualifications in a Member State—right to exercise the profession of nursery school teacher—regulated profession—right of access to the profession on the basis of a diploma issued in the home Member State

The applicant applied to the Finnish National Agency for Education (the 'EDUFI') for formal recognition of her qualifications as a nursery school teacher. The requirements for the carrying on of this profession in Finland were a higher education qualification and certain other competences.

To support her application, the applicant referred to her relevant qualifications including: an Early Childhood Education qualification (received in 1980) and a Professional Teaching Certificate (received in 2017) from her home Member State of Estonia. In Estonia, the law leaves it to the employer to assess a nursery school teacher's ability to occupy the post and compliance with the qualification requirements. The applicant's professional experience included working as a nursery school teacher in what was then the Estonian Soviet Socialist Republic from 1980 to 1984 and working in a creche in Finland from 2016–2017.

Her application for recognition was rejected by the EDUFI and this was upheld by the Administrative Court of Helsinki in circumstances where the applicant's experience did not meet the threshold for recognition under Finnish law. The applicant brought an appeal to the Supreme Administrative Court of Finland, which referred questions to the ECJ for preliminary ruling. These questions concerned the correct interpretation and applicability of art 3(1)(a) and art 3(3) of Directive 2005/36/EC in circumstances where:

(a) a profession that is subject to legislation which imposes qualification requirements for access but leaves a measure of discretion to the employer to decide whether the requirements are met can be considered a regulated profession within the meaning of that article and;
(b) there is evidence of formal qualifications which were obtained within another State, which was not at the time of the attainment of the qualifications, a Member State.

The ECJ underscored the fact that Directive 2005/36/EC, which pertains to the recognition of professional qualifications, only applies if the profession is regulated in the host Member State. The ECJ reiterated the text of art 3(1)(a) of Directive 2005/36/EC, which describes a 'regulated profession' as meaning:

> 'a professional activity or group of professional activities, access to which, the pursuit of which, or one of the modes of pursuit of which is subject, directly or indirectly, by virtue of legislative, regulatory or administrative provisions to the possession of specific professional qualifications'.

The ECJ noted that Finnish law did dictate the minimum requirements for access to the profession of nursery school teacher. The ECJ also observed that under art 13(1) of Directive 2005/36/EC, if the profession in question is also regulated in the home Member State, the host Member State must allow access to that profession under the same conditions as its own nationals if an applicant has documentation attesting their formal qualifications in their home Member State. Otherwise, art 13(2) applies.

In circumstances where there was a measure of discretion given to employers in Estonia to assess whether the qualifications of an applicant entitle him/her to access the profession of nursery school teacher, the ECJ held that the law in this home country did not guarantee that access to and pursuit of the profession were only permitted to those who held certain qualifications. Accordingly, the profession could not be said to be a 'regulated profession' in Estonia. In answering the first referred question, the ECJ held that art 3(1)(a) of Directive 2005/36/EC must be interpreted as not including a profession in respect of which national legislation imposes certain qualification prerequisites to access or pursue the profession, but gives employers discretion in assessing whether those prerequisites are met.

In circumstances where the profession was not regulated in Estonia, the ECJ held that art 13(2) therefore applied and that access to and pursuit of the profession must be permitted if the applicant had pursued the profession on a full-time basis for one out of the previous 10 years in another Member State and held an attestation of competence or evidence of formal qualifications from the home State. In this case, however, the applicant practised her profession in Estonia from 1980–1984, a period of time which was not in the past 10 years. Article 13(2) also provides that the aforementioned requirement falls away if the applicant can show evidence of formal qualification which attests regulated education and training. The ECJ considered whether the Early Childhood Education qualification that the applicant had received in 1980 in Estonia satisfied this.

The ECJ noted that under art 3(3) of Directive 2005/36/EC, evidence of formal qualifications attained in a third country are to be considered sufficient evidence if the holder has three years professional experience in the State which recognised that evidence in accordance with art 2(2) and certified by that State. It was held that art 3(3) must be interpreted as meaning that the provision is not applicable where the evidence of formal qualifications was obtained in a State that was not a Member State at the time and where the evidence was regarded by that State as evidence of formal qualifications after it gained its independence. Such evidence, it was held, had to be considered as having been attained in a Member State and not a third country. Therefore, the qualification that the applicant received from the Estonian Soviet Socialist Republic could not be considered as having been issued by a third country.

The application was not successful.

SOCIAL SECURITY

[6.03] ***Caisse nationale d'assurance pension[3]—European Court of Justice—request for preliminary ruling from Luxembourg—TFEU, art 45—Regulation***

[3] *Caisse nationale d'assurance pension* (Case C-731/21).

(EU) 492/2011,[4] art 7(1) and (2)—equal treatment—social advantages—survivor's pension—members of a civil partnership

The applicant and her partner were both French nationals living in France and working in Luxembourg. In 2015, they registered a joint declaration of a civil solidarity pact in the Metz District Court in France (the 'PACS'). In 2016, the applicant's partner died as a result of an accident at work. The applicant applied to the national pension insurance fund in Luxembourg (the 'CNAP'), for the grant of a survivor's pension. This application was rejected in 2017 because the PACS, despite being registered in France, had not been recorded in the Luxembourg Civil Records Registry when the applicant's partner was alive, in accordance with the Social Security Code of Luxembourg. Accordingly, it could not be relied upon to bind third parties.

In 2020, the Social Security Arbitration Board, Luxembourg dismissed proceedings taken by the applicant against CNAP's decision refusing to grant her a survivor's pension. This decision was subsequently upheld by the Higher Social Security Board, Luxembourg. An appeal was brought before the Cour de Cassation, Luxembourg. The applicant argued that the Luxembourg legislation concerning the provision of survivors' pensions infringed arts 18 and 45 TFEU, relating to the prohibition of discrimination on grounds of nationality and freedom of movement for workers. She also alleged an infringement of art 7(2) of Regulation (EU) 492/2011. The Cour de Cassation held that legislation did not discriminate directly between Luxembourg partners and partners who were nationals of other Member States. In relation to indirect discrimination, the Court was unsure as to whether the relevant law affected disproportionately those cross-border workers who had already registered their partnership in another Member State. The Court therefore referred the following question to the European Court of Justice ('ECJ') for a preliminary ruling:

> 'Does EU law, in particular Articles 18, 45 and 48 [TFEU], and Article 7(2) of Regulation [No 492/2011], preclude provisions of the law of a Member State … which make the grant, to the surviving partner of a partnership properly entered into and registered in the Member State of origin, of a survivor's pension, due as a result of the exercise by the deceased partner of a professional activity in the host Member State, subject to the condition that the partnership was recorded in a register kept by that State for the purposes of verifying compliance with the substantive conditions required by the law of that Member State in order to recognise a partnership and ensure its effectiveness vis-à-vis third parties, whereas the grant of a survivor's pension to the surviving partner of a partnership entered into in the host Member State is subject to the sole condition that the partnership has been properly entered into and registered there?'

The ECJ noted that although arts 18 and 48 TFEU formed part of the question referred, these provisions were not relevant to the dispute at hand. This left a single question: whether art 45 TFEU and art 7(2) of Regulation (EU) 492/2011 should be interpreted as precluding domestic legislation, which provides that the grant of a survivor's pension, to the surviving partner of a partnership that was validly entered into and registered in

4 Regulation (EU) 492/2011 on the freedom of movement for workers within the Union.

another Member State, is subject to the condition that the partnership was first recorded in the register kept by the legislating State.

The ECJ cited *Sotgiu*[5] and *Gemeinsamer Betriebsrat EurothermenResort Bad Schallerbach*[6] in stating that art 45 TFEU and art 7(2) of Regulation (EU) 492/2011 preclude both direct discrimination and covert forms of discrimination which, through the application of other distinguishing criteria, have the same result.

The ECJ also cited *O'Flynn*[7] as authority for the principle that even if national law applies regardless of nationality, it must be held to be indirectly discriminatory if it is liable to affect workers who are nationals of other Member States more than workers who are nationals of the legislating Member State, unless the effect is objectively justified and proportionate to the aim pursued.

The ECJ noted that according to the Social Security Code of Luxembourg, a partnership entered into abroad may be registered in the Luxembourg Civil Records Registry. While a partnership entered into and declared in Luxembourg is also required to be recorded in the Luxembourg Civil Records Registry, the law places responsibility for this registration on the registrar before whom the partnership was declared. That registration is therefore carried out automatically for the couple. The ECJ found this as amounting to unequal treatment indirectly based on nationality. The ECJ therefore had to determine whether this treatment was objectively justified and proportionate to the aims pursued by the Code.

The ECJ noted that the Code is aimed at allowing the Luxembourg authorities to verify that the partnership can be relied upon against third parties. This was held to be a legitimate aim. However, it was noted that according to *Hartlauer*,[8] national legislation is only appropriate for attaining the aim sought if it genuinely reveals 'a concern to attain it in a consistent and systematic manner'.

It was held that a refusal to grant a survivor's pension on the sole ground that the partnership was not registered in Luxembourg goes beyond what is necessary to achieve the aim sought. This was because, firstly, according to the ECJ's caselaw, the production of an official document by an authority of a Member State in which a partnership was entered into should be sufficient to ensure that that partnership can be relied on in another Member State, which is responsible for payment of survivors' benefits. This is so, unless there is doubt as to the accuracy of the document. Secondly, it was held, that where there is no condition in the national legislation relating to a deadline for registration of a partnership, there should be nothing to stop registration of a partnership in the Member State responsible for paying the benefits being carried out on the date on which the survivor's pension is sought. The ECJ noted that this was not a possibility in this case.

5 *Sotgiu* (Case 152/73).
6 *Gemeinsamer Betriebsrat EurothermenResort Bad Schallerbach* (Case C-437/17).
7 *O'Flynn* (Case C-237/94).
8 *Hartlauer* (Case C-169/07).

Accordingly, the ECJ held that the answer to the question referred was that art 45 TFEU and art 7 of Regulation (EU) 492/2011 must be interpreted as precluding such domestic legislation.

PUBLIC SERVICE EMPLOYMENT

[6.04] ***BM and NP v Ministero dell'Istruzione, dell'Università e della Ricerca (MIUR)*[9]*—European Court of Justice—request for a preliminary ruling from Italy—freedom of movement for workers—art 45 TFEU—Regulation (EU) 492/2011,*[10] *art 3(1)—obstacle—equal treatment—procedure for compiling lists for awarding posts in certain national public institutions—requirement for admission linked to prior professional experience gained at those institutions—national legislation not allowing professional experience gained in other Member States to be taken into account—whether justified—objective of combating job insecurity***

This request for a preliminary ruling concerned the interpretation of art 45(1) and (2) TFEU and art 3(1)(b) of Regulation (EU) 492/2011 on the freedom of movement for workers within the Union. The applicants were Italian nationals who had gained professional experience in Member States other than Italy. The respondent was Italy's Ministry of Education, Universities and Research.

The underlying proceedings concerned the lawfulness of a ministerial decree only permitting candidates 'who have gained a certain amount of professional experience at Italian public higher-education institutions for the fine arts, music and dance' to be included in lists compiled for the recruitment of staff in those institutions. Professional experience gained in other Member States could not be taken into account.

By separate actions, the applicants sought annulment of the ministerial decree, arguing that it infringed art 45 TFEU and art 3 of Regulation (EU) 492/2011 on the freedom of movement for workers. The respondent argued that the decree was based on a law introduced to address job insecurity in the sector of higher education in the arts. That law did not provide for a difference in treatment based on the nationality of candidates and the procedure was open to both Italian citizens and foreigners.

The referring Court decided to stay the proceedings and refer a question to the European Court of Justice ('ECJ') for a preliminary ruling, asking in essence whether art 45 TFEU and art 3(1)(b) of Regulation (EU) 492/2011 must be interpreted as precluding national legislation such as that in issue in the main proceedings.

It was noted that the relevant provisions of the TFEU preclude measures which might place nationals of Member States at a disadvantage in the pursuit of economic activity in another Member State. Recruitment conditions for public service posts, subject to art 45(4), fall within the scope of that provision.

---

9 *BM and NP v Ministero dell'Istruzione, dell'Università e della Ricerca (MIUR)* (Case C-132/22).

10 Regulation (EU) 492/2011 on freedom of movement for workers within the Union.

National laws which preclude or deter a national of a Member State from exercising the right to freedom of movement constitute 'restrictions' on that freedom within art 45(1), even if they apply without regard to the nationality of the workers. Article 45 is intended 'in particular' to prevent less favourable treatment of workers who have exercised their right to freedom of movement. Legislation which does not take into consideration 'in full' previous periods of equivalent activity completed in another Member State is likely to breach art 41(1) by rendering the exercise of the right to freedom of movement less attractive for workers. Further, the ECJ's caselaw has held that public bodies of Member States may not distinguish candidates based on whether previous employment was carried out in those Member States or others.

The legislation in issue laid down conditions requiring a minimum period of professional experience for a candidate to be included on lists compiled for recruitment purposes. Thus, the legislation was 'liable to deter a worker from exercising his or her right to freedom of movement' under art 45 TFEU. It was liable to affect migrant workers more than national workers and was therefore capable of creating 'a difference in treatment indirectly based on nationality'.

The restriction at issue in the main proceedings did not appear to be appropriate to the objective of addressing job insecurity in institutions for the arts. Nor did it appear to be necessary 'to promote the elimination of job insecurity' as the procedure allowed institutions to recruit both permanent and temporary workers. The aim of increasing the proportion of permanent workers in that sector could be achieved just as effectively without reserving permanent posts for 'long-term' temporary workers. Italy would not be prevented from addressing job insecurity in the sector by opening up the recruitment procedure to candidates in the applicants' position. In those circumstances, the restriction on the freedom of movement for workers created by the national law at issue was unjustified.

Chapter 7

Fixed-Term Work

INTRODUCTION

[7.01] The ECJ considered the fixed-term work entitlement to a contract of indefinite duration, in the context of Directive 1999/70/EC concerning the framework agreement on fixed-term work, in the Italian case of *Presidenza del Consiglio dei Ministri ea (Chercheurs universitaires)*.

CONTRACT OF INDEFINITE DURATION

[7.02] ***Presidenza del Consiglio dei Ministri ea (Chercheurs universitaires)*[1]*—European Court of Justice—request for a preliminary ruling from Italy—Directive 1999/70/EC*[2]*—Framework Agreement—social policy—fixed-term work principle of non-discrimination—measures to prevent abuse of successive fixed-term employment contracts—public-law fixed-term employment relationship—university researchers***

In these joined cases, a number of university researchers had executed fixed-term contracts for a period of three years with the University of Perugia under art 24(3)(a) of Law No. 240/2010. These contracts were extended for a further period of two years. The researchers wished to transform their contracts into contracts of indefinite duration or to submit to an appraisal so that they may be added to the list of associate professors.

The researchers relied on art 20(1) of Legislative Decree No 75/2017, entitled 'Overcoming job insecurity in employment with public authorities', to petition the university to transform their contracts into contracts of indefinite duration or to initiate the recruitment procedure with a view to engaging them for an indefinite duration. Legislative Decree No 75/2017 provided that in order to overcome job insecurity in employment and to reduce the reliance on fixed-term contracts, authorities could, between 2018–2020, recruit certain non-managerial staff and offer them contracts of indefinite duration.

---

1 *Presidenza del Consiglio dei Ministri ea (Chercheurs universitaires)* (Cases C-40/20 and C-173/20).

2 Directive 1999/70/EC concerning the framework agreement on fixed-term work.

The university refused the researchers' request on the basis that, under Circular No 3/2017, the rules contained in art 20 of Legislative Decree No 75/2017 did not change the employment relationship of university researchers and professors whose public-law contracts were not subject to procedures for stabilising insecure jobs.

The applicants initiated proceedings before the Regional Administrative Court, Umbria, Italy, arguing that Legislative Decree No 75/2017 did not prevent university researchers under fixed-term contracts from availing of the procedure for stabilising insecure jobs. If that were the case, it was argued, that provision would be unconstitutional and contrary to EU law, in particular the Framework Agreement on fixed-term work which was annexed to Directive 1999/70/EC.

The Regional Administrative Court dismissed the actions. The researchers appealed to the Council of State, which referred several questions for preliminary ruling. The questions concerned the interpretation of clauses 4 and 5 of the Framework Agreement.

The European Court of Justice ('ECJ') described the rationale for the Framework Agreement as: firstly, to improve the quality of fixed-term work by safeguarding the application of the principle of non-discrimination; and secondly, to create a framework to prevent the abuse by employers of the use of back-to-back fixed-term contracts.

The ECJ ruled that clause 5 of the Framework Agreement should be interpreted as allowing for national legislation that permits universities to conclude three-year fixed-term contracts with researchers, which can be extended for a maximum of two years, without making the creation or extension of these contracts conditional upon there being objective temporary or exceptional requirements. It was also held that clause 5 should be interpreted as allowing for national legislation that sets a maximum total duration of successive fixed-term employment contracts at 12 years, regardless of whether these contracts are concluded as between the researcher and different universities and whether the period of employment is continuous or not.

However, the ECJ noted that impermissible unequal treatment of two categories of fixed-term workers is not envisaged by the Framework Agreement. The ECJ noted that such impermissible unequal treatment arose in this case, where researchers who were employed under a fixed-term contract, and who had the appropriate national academic qualifications, were not permitted to undergo a specific appraisal procedure with a view to being added to the list of associate professors. In this way they were treated differently to those researchers who had a contract of indefinite duration, who had the same qualifications and who were carrying out the same services. In order for such treatment to be permissible, it must be objectively justified by a genuine need to treat them differently. It was held that clause 4(1) of the Framework Agreement should be interpreted accordingly.

Chapter 8

Health & Safety

INTRODUCTION

[8.01] The Labour Court in *Blacklough Construction Ltd* considered a claim of penalisation under the Safety, Health and Welfare at Work Acts 2005–2014.

The Labour Court considered whether an employee was duly appointed as a safety representative within the meaning of the Safety, Health and Welfare at Work Acts 2005–2014 in *Board of Management of Clonkeen College.*

The UK EAT considered in *Driver and Vehicle Standards Agency* a claim brought by an employee who refused to return to work due to safety concerns following the Covid-19 pandemic.

PENALISATION

[8.02] ***Blacklough Construction Ltd v Kealy*[1]*—Labour Court—appeal from Workplace Relations Commission—Safety, Health and Welfare at Work Acts 2005–2014, s 27—penalisation—dismissal—complaint relating to safety, health and welfare at work—previous complaints—redress***

The claimant was employed as a tower crane operator by the respondent company. As part of his work, the claimant was required to work with a banksman. The role of the banksman was to direct the claimant from the ground. The availability of a suitable banksman to work with the claimant was a persistent issue throughout his employment and the claimant raised with this issue with the foreman on multiple occasions. Ultimately, on 11 October 2021, when the claimant was instructed to work without a banksman, he refused. After refusing, the claimant left the premises to go to lunch. The claimant alleged that during his lunch break, he was phoned by the foreman who advised him not to return to work after lunch. The claimant did return to work 15 minutes later and found the gates of the respondent's premises had been locked.

It came to the claimant's attention that the next day the respondent had sought to replace him with another crane driver through an agency. The claimant attempted to contact

---

1 *Blacklough Construction Ltd v Kealy* HSD231.

the health and safety officer, who responded via text message to inform him that the matter would be investigated. The claimant received no further communication from the respondent. The claimant sought employment elsewhere and brought a WRC claim, alleging that he had been penalised contrary to s 27 of the Safety Health and Welfare at Work Act 2005 (the '2005 Act'). Ultimately, the claimant was unsuccessful and sought to appeal to the Labour Court.

The respondent, in written submissions, rejected any suggestion that a complaint had been made on 11 October 2021 regarding the absence of a banksman. It was maintained that the claimant was not dismissed. Rather, he had walked off the site. It was submitted that the gates were locked after lunch as part of the usual course of dealings.

Before the Labour Court hearing, the respondent advised the Court that it had gone into examinership and its legal representatives came off record. A letter was furnished to the Court requesting that the Court notify the respondent of the outcome of the appeal and informing the Court that the respondent would not be attending the hearing.

The Court made a finding of fact that the claimant had made several complaints to his employer regarding the absence of a banksman onsite, including on 11 October 2021. These complaints constituted a protected act within the meaning of the 2005 Act.

The Court also found that the phone call between the foreman and the claimant did occur and that the gates were locked upon the claimant's return to work in order to deny him access to the premises. A finding of fact was made in the claimant's favour regarding the sequence of events which occurred as between the claimant and the health and safety officer.

The Court therefore found that the actions of the respondent constituted a dismissal and penalisation under the 2005 Act and awarded the claimant €20,000 in compensation.

The appeal succeeded and the decision of the WRC was set aside.

[8.03] ***Board of Management of Clonkeen College v Cassidy*[2]*—Labour Court—appeal from Workplace Relations Commission—Safety, Health and Welfare at Work Acts 2005–2014, s 29(1)—safety representative—complaint of penalisation—whether employee was duly constituted a safety representative within the meaning of s 25(1)***

The claimant was employed as a geography teacher by the respondent board of management and was a member of the ASTI. He submitted that, at a meeting of his trade union colleagues in November 2018, he was appointed 'safety representative' within the meaning of the Safety, Health and Welfare at Work Act 2005 (the '2005 Act'). Thereafter, he sought to introduce the Health and Safety Authority's 'Work Positive' programme in the school and conducted an online survey of staff for that purpose.

2 *Board of Management of Clonkeen College v Cassidy* HSD236.

The claimant alleged that the results generated by this survey were not welcomed by school management, and that the principal took steps to remove him from his role as safety representative. In the WRC, he submitted that this amounted to penalisation within the meaning of the 2005 Act, which was rejected and he then appealed to the Labour Court.

The Labour Court was satisfied from the evidence that the claimant was not duly appointed as the school's safety representative within the meaning of s 25(1) of the 2005 Act. It was accepted that the respondent was the relevant employer, and the Court heard no evidence to suggest that the respondent had agreed to the selection of multiple safety representatives, although it was open to the respondent's employees to select a single safety representative 'from among their number'.

The evidence had been that the claimant was commonly regarded by ASTI members in the school as the ASTI safety representative. There was nothing to suggest that the claimant was regarded by his peers as the 'whole-school' representative and the meeting of November 2018 was attended solely by ASTI members. The plain meaning of the 2005 Act does not envisage a 'sub-group' of employees selecting one of themselves to act as safety representative.

Accordingly, there was no basis for the complaint of penalisation for being the safety representative, and the decision of the WRC was upheld.

[8.04] ***Miles v Driver and Vehicle Standards Agency*[3]*—UK Employment Appeal Tribunal—appeal from the employment tribunal—Employment Rights Act 1996—driver—health and safety representative—reasonable belief—Covid-19—detriment—unfair constructive dismissal***

The claimant was an employee of the respondent, working as a driving examiner. The claimant was diagnosed with chronic kidney disease in 2018. In March 2020, all but the most essential driving tests were cancelled as a Covid-19 precaution. The tests reconvened in July 2020 and the respondent required driving examiners to return to work unless they were considered extremely vulnerable. The claimant refused to return to work, and his pay ceased. The claimant resigned and brought disability discrimination, health and safety detriment, and unfair constructive dismissal proceedings to the employment tribunal under the Employment Rights Act 1996 (the '1996 Act').

The tribunal stated that, although the claimant reasonably believed that there were circumstances associated with his work that he considered harmful or potentially harmful to his health or safety, there was a health and safety representative available, with whom he could have raised his concerns, although this representative was not based in the same office as the claimant. The tribunal was critical of the 'blinkered approach' that the claimant took regarding social distancing and other safety measures, which he insisted on as contingents to his returning to work. The tribunal also noted that the claimant did not seek occupational health advice. The tribunal differentiated between a belief

3 *Miles v Driver and Vehicle Standards Agency* [2023] EAT 62.

that something may be harmful to one's health and a belief of serious imminent danger. Ultimately, the tribunal held that the claimant did not hold a reasonable belief that returning to work posed a serious and imminent danger to his health and safety under s 44(1)(d) and s 100(1)(d) of the 1996 Act.

Separately, although the tribunal accepted that the claimant had a physical impairment, the claimant was able to reduce the risk of his impairment having a substantial adverse effect on his normal day-to-day activity, eg by shopping online rather than in person. The tribunal ultimately held that the claimant was not 'disabled'; his reasons for not coming back to work could not be attributed to his impairment but were based on his 'unreasonable belief'.

The UK EAT held that, in evaluating what was reasonable for the claimant to believe, the tribunal did not place an excessive burden on him to investigate matters. The EAT held that it did not matter that the health and safety representative was not at the office where the claimant worked. The EAT also stated that, in order to satisfy s 44(1)(d) and s 100(1)(d) of the 1996 Act, it was only required that the claimant reasonably believed that there existed circumstances of danger that were serious and imminent. This belief could be subjective and had to be considered at the point of his exiting from the workplace. It was held that the tribunal did not err in holding that the claimant did not have a reasonable belief in the existence of a serious and imminent risk to his health or safety.

The EAT found that the tribunal was entitled to conclude that, by changing his behaviour, the claimant was able to reduce the impact that his impairment had on his day-to-day activity. However, it considered that the tribunal did err in its approach to the claimant's decision not to return to work. The tribunal had found that the claimant did not return to work due to an 'unreasonable belief' but did not elaborate as to what this was or why it was unreasonable. The EAT held that the tribunal's reasoning was not sufficient to support the conclusion that the claimant's not returning to work was not a substantial effect on his day-to-day activities as a result of his impairment. Although the claimant could not establish that his refusal to return to work resulted from a reasonable belief in a serious and imminent danger to health or safety, this did not necessarily mean that if he reasonably believed a return could be harmful to his health, he could not show that the effect on his day-to-day activities resulted from his impairment. The EAT upheld the appeal because of the inconsistency that existed between the tribunal's finding that the claimant did have a genuine belief about a risk to his health and safety and the finding that he did not return to work due to an 'unreasonable' belief.

The matter was remitted for the tribunal to consider whether there was a break in causation that prevented the claimant's decision not to go back to work being a substantial adverse effect which resulted from his impairment.

The appeal was allowed in part.

Chapter 9

Immigration

INTRODUCTION

[9.01] In *Staatssecretaris van Justitie en Veiligheid e.a.*, the ECJ considered the proportionality of withdrawing a right of residence from three Turkish nationals residing in the Netherlands.

The High Court considered a number of immigration-related judicial review applications: *LK* concerned an international protection applicant's right to access the labour market; *A (A minor suing by his mother and next friend), AA and NA* concerned a parent's entitlement to exercise a right to access the labour market vicariously on behalf of their child; *Imran* related to a decision to revoke the applicant's permanent residence card by reason of a claimed marriage of convenience; and *Singh* concerned the refusal of critical skills employment permits to the applicant.

RIGHT OF RESIDENCE

[9.02] ***Staatssecretaris van Justitie en Veiligheid e.a. (Retrait du droit de séjour d'un travailleur turc)[1]—European Court of Justice—request for a preliminary ruling from the Netherlands—Decision No 1/80,[2] arts 6, 7, 13, 14—Turkish nationals already integrated into the labour market of a host Member State and enjoying an associated right of residence—decisions of national authorities withdrawing the right of residence from Turkish nationals who have been lawfully resident in the Member State concerned for more than 20 years—present, genuine and sufficiently serious threat to a fundamental interest of society—public policy—proportionate—immigration***

1 *Staatssecretaris van Justitie en Veiligheid e.a. (Retrait du droit de séjour d'un travailleur turc)* (Case C-402/21).

2 Decision No 1/80 of the Association Council of 19 September 1980 on the development of the Association between the European Economic Community and Turkey.

A request for a preliminary ruling was made concerning the interpretation of arts 6, 7, 13 and 14 of Decision No 1/80 of the Association Council on the development of the Association between the European Economic Community and Turkey.

This request arose from two sets of proceedings between the State Secretary for the Netherlands and S, in the first instance; and E and C and the State Secretary in the second instance. Both sets of proceedings concerned the decision of the State Secretary to withdraw the right of residence of S, E and C, who were all Turkish nationals, and to deport them from the Netherlands.

The Association Agreement between the EEC and Turkey is aimed at promoting economic ties between the signatories. The Decision No 1/80 concerning the EEC and Turkey, deals with, among other things, employment and free movement of workers for Turkish nationals within Member States and the residence of their family members. Article 3.86 of the Decree on foreign nationals of 2000 (the '2000 Decree'), which amended the existing law on foreign nationals, provides for the revocation of an application for an extension of a residence permit, for example, 'where the foreign national has been sentenced, by a judicial decision which has become final, in connection with at least five offences'. Article 3.9 of the 2000 Decree states that an ordinary residence permit of unlimited duration may be revoked where 'the foreign national concerned has been sentenced, by a judicial decision which has become final, in connection with an offence punishable by a term of imprisonment of three years or more'. This Decree represented a so-called 'tightened sliding scale'.

In the cases of S, E and C, all three were Turkish nationals, lawfully living in the Netherlands. In all cases, the individuals had been lawfully resident in the Netherlands for over 20 years. The individuals had been convicted of multiple criminal offences during that time. The State Secretary withdrew the residence permits of all three individuals on foot of the tightened sliding scale. The State Secretary described each of the three individuals as representing a 'genuine, present and sufficiently serious threat affecting one of the fundamental interests of society'. This had the effect of directing S, E and C to leave the Netherlands and banning them from re-entering.

It was argued that the workers enjoyed rights under arts 6 and/or 7 of Decision No 1/80. Article 6 includes the entitlement of a worker to free access in a Member State, in which he is duly registered, to any paid employment after four years of legal employment. Article 7 includes the entitlement of the worker's family members to enjoy free access to any paid employment of their choice if they have been legally resident in the Member State for at least five years.

The referring Court in both sets of proceedings referred three questions to the European Court of Justice ('ECJ'):

'(1) Can Turkish nationals who have the rights referred to in Article 6 or Article 7 of Decision No 1/80 still rely on Article 13 of Decision No 1/80?

(2) Does it follow from Article 14 of Decision No 1/80 that Turkish nationals can no longer rely on Article 13 of Decision No 1/80 if, due to their personal conduct, they represent a genuine, present and sufficiently serious threat affecting one of the fundamental interests of society?

(3) Can the new restriction whereby the right of residence of Turkish nationals may be terminated even after 20 years [of lawful residence] on grounds of public policy be justified by reference to the changed social perceptions which gave rise to that new restriction? Is it sufficient that the new restriction serves the public policy objective, or is it also required that the restriction be suitable for achieving that objective and not go beyond what is necessary to attain it?'

With regard to the first question, the ECJ noted that art 13 of Decision No 1/80 contains a standstill clause, which prohibits Member States from introducing new restrictions that affect the access of workers and their families to employment applicable to them. The ECJ emphasised the direct effect of such a standstill clause and the rationale underpinning same, being to prohibit Member States 'from taking measures likely to compromise the attainment of the objective of Decision No 1/80, which is to allow freedom of movement for workers'. The standstill clause also prohibits the introduction of national law that imposes more restrictive conditions on free movement for Turkish nationals than those which applied when Decision No 1/80 entered into force in that Member State. Accordingly, new laws, which restrict the conditions of access to the first professional activity of a Turkish worker or members of their family and which, once that worker or family members benefit from rights under arts 6 or 7 of Decision No 1/80, restrict their access to paid employment guaranteed by those rights, are not permitted, due to the standstill clause. It was noted that in S, E and C's cases, the national legislation in question (the 2000 Decree) postdates the coming into effect of Decision No 1/80 in the Netherlands.

Accordingly, the ECJ answered the first question by holding that art 13 of Decision No 1/80 must be interpreted as meaning that it could be relied on by Turkish nationals who enjoyed the rights under arts 6 or 7 thereof.

With regard to the second and third questions, the ECJ noted that art 14(1) of Decision No 1/80 allows Member States to derogate from same where they are justified on grounds of public policy, public security or public health. The ECJ held that in the present cases, the tightened sliding scale was allegedly introduced on public policy grounds. It was noted that this is not sufficient in itself and that the measures must also be deemed to have not gone beyond what is necessary in order to attain the objective pursued and must comply with the principle of proportionality. In order to determine whether the national legislation so complies, the ECJ listed a number of factors which it was for the referring Court to consider, including: whether the authorities implementing a withdrawal have taken into account the duration of residence in the Netherlands; whether the authorities considered if the worker had made positive changes to their conduct since the conviction; and whether expulsion was automatic upon the worker being convicted of a crime.

With regard to the second and third questions, the ECJ held that art 14(1) must be interpreted as meaning that workers that allegedly represent a 'genuine, present and sufficiently serious threat to one of the interests of society' may rely on art 13 to oppose the 'new restriction' from being applied. The authority may rely on art 14 and argue that such a derogation is justified on the grounds of public policy. However, the derogation must be necessary and proportionate.

ACCESS TO THE LABOUR MARKET

[9.03] ***LK v IPAT and the Minister for Justice[3]—High Court—Heslin J—judicial review—international protection applicant—right to access labour market—Directive 2013/33,[4] art 15(1)—implementing Regulations—Francovich damages***

This was a 'modular' hearing referable to a challenge to the refusal of a labour market access permit to the applicant, LK, who had applied for international protection.[5] In its earlier judgment, the Court found that there was a failure by the State to properly transpose Directive 2013/33/EU (the 'Directive'), the objective of which is to lay down standards for the reception of international protection applicants. This resumed hearing dealt with the issue of *Francovich* damages, which followed the Court's original finding.

The respondents initially sought to advance new arguments asserting that there had not been a failure to properly transpose the Directive, while signalling an intention to appeal the earlier judgment. The Court was of the view that the appellate Court was the proper forum in which to raise those new arguments and that it was not open to this Court to do so at a resumed hearing of the substantive matter.

The Court did not accept the respondents' argument that the Directive 'does not vest individuals with rights in the *Francovich* sense'. It held that it was plain 'on any first principles analysis' of art 15(1) of the Directive that it confers on relevant individuals the right to access the labour market.

The Court was, in the second instance, satisfied that the failure to properly transpose the Directive constituted 'a serious and manifest error which was at the heart of the decision impugned'. While conscious that the right of labour market access is not unqualified, the Court contrasted the words used in art 15(1) with those used in the implementing Regulations. The Court noted that the Regulations contain additional wording entitling the State to deny labour market access where the delay 'can be attributed, *or can be attributed in part* to the applicant' (emphasis denoting additional wording). It concluded that, while this was not indicative of an intention to deprive applicants of rights, the seriousness of this failure to properly transpose spoke 'to the effect on the individual, not the motivation for the breach'. In this instance, the effect on the applicant 'was of the starkest sort', depriving him of the right to work which art 15 otherwise conferred upon him.

---

3 *LK v International Protection Appeals Tribunal, the Minister for Justice and the Attorney General* [2023] IEHC 210.

4 Directive 2013/33/EU laying down standards for the reception of applicants for international protection (recast).

5 *LK v International Protection Appeals Tribunal, the Minister for Justice and the Attorney General* [2022] IEHC 441.

In the third instance, the Court was satisfied that the applicant had established a causal link between the breach and the damage sustained by him.

However, the Court's factual findings were that, despite the applicant being in possession of a labour market access certificate since 8 June 2022, and despite being an experienced labourer on construction sites, the applicant did not secure employment in Dublin until 6 February 2023, and that since receiving labour market access permission, the maximum he appeared to have earned was €420.72 per week. Accordingly, damages were quantified on the basis of those findings.

[9.04] ***A (A minor suing by his mother and next friend), AA and NA v International Protection Appeals Tribunal[6]—High Court—Simons J—application for judicial review—International Protection Act 2015—Directive 2013/33/EU[7]—European Communities (Reception Conditions) (Amendment) Regulations 2021[8]—right to access the labour market—derived right to work—whether parents were entitled to exercise a right to access the labour market vicariously on behalf of their child—vulnerable persons***

The applicants were a minor aged under two years old and his parents, who were non-EU nationals. The parents had sought and failed to obtain international protection in Ireland under the International Protection Act 2015. While the child's application for international protection was pending, the parents applied for access to the labour market on his behalf. Article 15 of Directive 2013/33/EU states that Member States must ensure that applicants have access to the labour market no later than nine months after the date of an application for international protection. In Ireland, this has been shortened to a six-month period by the European Communities (Reception Conditions) (Amendment) Regulations 2021. The parents submitted that they were entitled to exercise their child's right to access the labour market vicariously on his behalf. This application was refused.

Subsequently, on 30 September 2022, the parents were both given 'Stamp 4' permissions to continue to reside in the State and work for a period of three years. The applicants initiated judicial review proceedings prior to 30 September 2022, when the parents had not been permitted to work lawfully within the Irish State and, during which time, they contended they should have been permitted to access the labour market on their child's behalf. The trial Judge had to consider whether the proceedings were moot, given the change to their immigration status that had occurred on 30 September 2022. Further, the Court had to consider whether the parents were permitted to work vicariously on behalf of the child in order to give effect to his right to access the labour market. The Court had to also decide whether the parents had a derived right to work on behalf of the child.

6 *A (A minor suing by his mother and next friend), AA and NA v International Protection Appeals Tribunal* [2023] IEHC 141.

7 Directive 2013/33/EU laying down standards for the reception of applicants for international protection (recast).

8 European Communities (Reception Conditions) (Amendment) Regulations 2021 (SI 52/2021).

The Court did not consider it proper to dismiss the proceedings for mootness. It was noted that the application for international protection was initiated on behalf of the child on 26 July 2021 and that, as of the date the judicial review proceedings were initiated that international protection application had not been decided. The Court noted that an entitlement to access the labour market accrued six months after the application for international protection is made and expires upon the refusal of said application. The lead time for judicial review proceedings is often longer than this period. The Court held that an overly rigid application of the mootness doctrine in such cases might result in legal issues being 'timed out'. Further, it was considered, that in the instant case, the issue of damages was also still live and fell to be determined by the Court.

The Court noted that, save in exceptional circumstances, a child under the age of 14 years does not have a right to work lawfully in the Irish State. Accordingly, the child did not enjoy a right to work under domestic employment law. There was therefore no right that the child enjoyed which the parents could exercise vicariously on his behalf. The Court held that Directive 2013/33/EU did not change domestic law in this respect; art 15 was personal to the individual applicant for international protection and did not create a right for a minor to access the labour market where that did not exist domestically.

The Court considered whether the parents had a derived right to work given the fact that the child had a right to reside in the Irish State pending his application for international protection and to enjoy an appropriate standard of living. It was acknowledged that Directive 2013/33/EU imposes an obligation on Member States to ensure that specific standard of living requirements or the special reception needs of 'vulnerable persons', including children, are met. This is to be assessed in the best interests of the minor applicant. It was held that the obligation to provide for a child who is an applicant for international protection lies with the Member State. If parents are unable to provide for such a child due to their not being entitled to work, then it is the Member State that must ensure an adequate standard of living for the child as a 'vulnerable person'. Therefore, it was held that there was no derived right to work that the parents enjoyed in order to provide for their child.

The application for judicial review was dismissed.

MARRIAGE OF CONVENIENCE

[9.05] ***Imran v The Minister for Justice*[9]*—High Court—Barr J—application for judicial review—Directive 2004/38/EC*[10]*—European Communities (Free***

9 *Imran v The Minister for Justice* [2023] IEHC 338.

10 Directive 2004/38/EC on the right of citizens of the Union and their family members to move and reside freely within the territory of the Member States.

Movement of Persons) Regulations 2015[11]—permanent residence card—submission of false and misleading information—employment—revocation of immigration documentation—allegation of fraudulent documents—proportionality assessment

The applicant was a Pakistani national and had lived in Ireland since 2003, having entered the country on a student visa. He married a Hungarian national in January 2011. In 2016, the applicant obtained a permanent residence card due to his being a qualified family member of his wife, an EU national, who was exercising her right to work in the country. In support of his application, the applicant submitted that his wife was self-employed in her own childminding business. The marriage broke down in 2016 and the applicant's wife returned to Hungary. The applicant claimed that his wife left Ireland in August 2016.

In 2018, the respondent wrote to the applicant informing him of a proposal to revoke his permanent residence card. It was alleged that his marriage had been a marriage of convenience and that the information he had submitted regarding his wife's childminding services on various dates between December 2015 and May 2016 did not match the records of the Department of Employment Affairs and Social Protection, which indicated that the applicant's wife only worked for one week in 2016. The applicant submitted vouching material for his wife's employment: a receipt book which contained approximately 92 receipts from the period of December 2015 to May 2016.

In her first instance decision, the respondent found that the applicant's marriage was one of convenience and that the documentation submitted in support of his application had been fraudulent and/or misleading. Ultimately, the respondent issued a decision, revoking the applicant's permission to remain in Ireland. The applicant sought a review of this decision.

In 2021, the applicant made submissions in furtherance of this review. As part of these submissions, his solicitor indicated that the applicant's wife left Ireland in January 2016. The respondent, in her review decision, stated that she was not satisfied that it had been adequately established that the applicant's marriage had been one of convenience under Directive 2004/38/EC (the 'Citizens' Rights Directive'), nor that there were sufficient grounds to make a finding under reg 28(1) of the European Communities (Free Movement of Persons) Regulations 2015 (the '2015 Regulations'). Accordingly, the respondent held that that element of the first instance decision should be set aside.

However, the respondent highlighted the fact that the applicant had indicated that his wife left Ireland in January 2016. The respondent noted that the receipt book had to, therefore, be either false or misleading. The respondent's decision also pointed to the discrepancy between the information held by the Department of Employment Affairs and Social Protection and the information submitted by the applicant. The respondent held that she was satisfied that the applicant had submitted information that he knew to be false and/or misleading in order to acquire a derived right of free movement

11 European Communities (Free Movement of Persons) Regulations 2015 (SI 548/2015).

and residence under EU law. This, it was held, was contrary to reg 27 of the 2015 Regulations. His permanent residence card was revoked and he applied to the High Court to have the decision of the respondent set aside.

In January 2022, the applicant submitted a fresh application for a permanent residence card and the applicant's solicitor wrote to the respondent, claiming that the applicant had made an error in his original instructions and that, while he could not remember the exact date of his wife's return to Hungary, he believed it was the middle of 2016. The letter requested that the respondent review her decision to revoke the applicant's permanent residence permit. The respondent again refused the application. The applicant's solicitor wrote to the respondent seeking a re-assessment of his application once the High Court proceedings had concluded.

In the High Court, the applicant contended that the respondent had not carried out a proportionality assessment in her decision to revoke his permanent residence card, as required by the Citizens' Rights Directive and the 2015 Regulations. However, the applicant did not disclose to the Court that he had made the second application for a permanent residence card in January 2022 and the respondent applied to have the application struck out *in limine* for failure to comply with the duty of candour in this regard. The Court however, accepted that the applicant's omission had been explained, on affidavit, to be an administrative error.

The Court acknowledged that the wording of art 35 of the Citizens' Rights Directive and reg 27 of the 2015 Regulations make it necessary for the respondent to carry out a proportionality assessment in circumstances where: the applicant has been found to have had a valid marriage to an EU citizen that had been exercising her EU rights by living and working in Ireland; the applicant had been living and working in Ireland for nearly 20 years himself; and the applicant had been tax compliant and had not come to the attention of the gardaí. The Court held that the respondent had not carried out an assessment to take account of the applicant's personal circumstances, in particular his tax compliance, as against the finding that the information he submitted was fraudulent or misleading. Further, it was noted that the respondent did not consider any other, lesser sanction such as reporting the offence of submitting false or misleading information to the gardaí.

The Court also concluded that to base a serious allegation of fraud on a single sentence in submissions made by the applicant's solicitors, was 'somewhat harsh' and that it was in the interests of justice that the applicant be allowed to correct the statement. The Court noted that the receipt book was furnished in answer to the assertion that the applicant's claims about his wife's employment did not tally with records kept by the Department of Employment Affairs and Social Protection. It was not put to the applicant that the receipt book was forged and therefore, the Court found that it was also in the interests of justice to give the applicant an opportunity to confront this allegation.

The Court made an order setting aside the decision of the respondent and remitting the matter for further consideration.

CRITICAL SKILLS EMPLOYMENT PERMITS

[9.06] ***Singh v The Minister for Business, Enterprise and Innovation; Ahmad v The Minister for Business, Enterprise and Innovation*[12]*—High Court—Mulcahy J—application for judicial review—Employment Permits Act 2006—Employment Permits Regulations 2017*[13]*—Standard Occupational Classification 2010—immigration—critical skills employment permit***

The applicants in both proceedings sought critical skills employment permits under the Employment Permits Act 2006 (the '2006 Act'). Regulation 18 of the Employment Permits Regulations 2017 (the '2017 Regulations') uses occupational codes corresponding to particular job descriptions and related job titles, which are sorted into either Schedule 3 or 4. The Standard Occupational Classification 2010 ('SOC 2010') forms the basis of these codes.

The applicant in the first proceedings had been offered a position with KPR Pizza Ltd trading as Apache Pizza Leixlip, as a business and financial project manager. The position attracted a gross salary of €32,500. His application for an employment permit was refused as the renumeration was too low for Schedule 4, and the job did not correspond with the Critical Skills Occupation List in Schedule 3. The applicant opted for a review of this decision under s 13 of the 2006 Act and requested that the position be taken as falling under SOC number 2424, which relates to 'Business and Financial Project Management Professionals'. This review was refused. The respondent noted that the occupation in question appeared to correspond more readily to SOC number 3534, being 'Finance and Investment Analysts and Advisers' and therefore, the role was not on the Critical Skills Occupation List.

The applicant in the second set of proceedings was offered a job with RJC Retail Ltd for the position of business and financial project manager with a salary of €33,800 per year. He made an application for a critical skills employment permit but was refused by the respondent for the same reasons as the applicant in the first set of proceedings. The applicant sought a review of this decision, indicating that the application should be considered under SOC number 2424. This review was refused for the same reasons that were given in the first set of proceedings.

The applicants sought orders of certiorari quashing the decisions of the respondent to refuse their applications for critical skills employment permits. It was argued in both cases that the respondent acted irrationally in holding that critical skill employment permits could not be obtained for the positions to which the applicants had applied. In relation to the first set of proceedings, the respondent averred on affidavit that, on reflection, SOC code 3545 was a more appropriate code than 3534, which had been applied.

---

12 *Singh v The Minister for Business, Enterprise and Innovation; Ahmad v The Minister for Business, Enterprise and Innovation* [2023] IEHC 332.

13 Employment Permits Regulations 2017 (SI 95/2017).

The Court stated that if the respondent had decided that neither of the applicants' positions fell within SOC number 2424, or were not otherwise on the Critical Skills Occupation List, it would have been open to him to reject the applications. However, it was held that this was not the basis upon which the respondent refused to grant critical skills employment permits to the applicants. Rather, the respondent seemed to conclude that the positions fell within SOC number 3534 and therefore were not on the Critical Skills Occupation List. This conclusion was, it was held, irrational. There was no obligation to assign an SOC number to a position in order to decide whether it was on the Critical Skills Occupation List. The Court stated that it could not identify any reason for the positions falling within SOC number 3534, nor was any given by the respondent. The Court noted the respondent's averment on affidavit that there was a more appropriate code to describe the positions in question. The Court stated that had the respondent's decisions that the positions were not on the Critical Skills Occupation List been arrived at separately from his decision that they more properly fell within SOC number 3534, it would have ruled that any error in the applicable code did not render the entire decisions unlawful. However, here it was evident that the decision that the positions were not on the Critical Skills Occupation List 'flowed from the irrational minor premise—that the jobs fell under SOC Code 3534'.

The Court made orders quashing each decision and remitting them to different review officers for review.

Chapter 10

Industrial Relations and Trade Unions

INTRODUCTION

[10.01]

Trade Union Deductions

In *Secretary of State for the Home Department*, the Court of Appeal of England and Wales considered an employer's right to unilaterally withdraw from 'check-off arrangements' used to pay trade union subscriptions as agreed in a collective agreement.

The High Court of England and Wales considered whether the individual claimants had accepted a variation of their contracts of employment with reference to trade union deductions in *Smith.*

European Works Council

In *easyJet European Works Council*, the Court of Appeal of England and Wales considered whether the appellant's European Works Council subsisted following the UK's withdrawal from the EU.

Verizon Ireland Ltd related to a complaint concerning expert fees and training that arose following the respondent's European Works Council moving to Ireland.

In *Olsten* the UK EAT considered the claimant's obligations under the European Works Council agreement with the respondent to inform and consult with the respondent's employee representatives in relation to collective redundancies.

Information and Consultation

The ECJ considered a request for a preliminary ruling from Greece in *Ethnikos* relating to two questions on the interpretation of Directive 2002/14/EC, on informing and consulting with employees.

Victimisation—Trade Union Action

In *ESB Networks*, the Labour Court considered the right of the claimant to bring a victimisation complaint under s 8 of the Industrial Relations Act 2004, where the respondent employer engages in collective bargaining.

CHECK-OFF ARRANGEMENTS

[10.02] ***Secretary of State for the Home Department v Cox[1]—Court of Appeal of England and Wales—Underhill, Stuart-Smith & Lewis LJJ—appeal from High Court of England and Wales—Contracts (Rights of Third Parties) Act 1999—government administration—civil servants—collective arrangements—trade unions—check-off arrangements—deductions—employees rights—enforcement—intention—subscriptions deducted from salary—third-party enforcement of a contractual term***

The appellants appealed against three judgments of the High Court of England and Wales in favour of their employees and a trade union about the use by the employees of 'check-off arrangements' to pay their trade union subscriptions.[2] These arrangements saw the deduction of sums from the employees' wages and the payment made to the trade union. The arrangements had been agreed in collective agreements which were concluded between the Government and the relevant trade union.

The appellants indicated in 2014 that they wished to withdraw from the arrangement. The trade union objected. The appellants withdrew and the trade union initiated separate proceedings (the '*Cavanagh* proceedings')[3] on behalf of two employees of the Department for Work and Pensions, arguing that, as the check-off arrangements made up part of the employees' contracts, the trade union had a right to said term. The trade union succeeded.

Subsequently the instant proceedings were initiated in the High Court (the '*Cox* proceedings'), seeking declarative relief that the appellants' withdrawal from the check-off arrangement amounted to a breach of contract. The trade union sought to rely on the Contracts (Rights of Third Parties) Act 1999 (the '1999 Act') to argue that the contracts of employment purported to transfer a benefit to it, and it could not be shown that the term was not intended to be enforceable by the trade union as a third party.

The High Court, in the *Cox* proceedings, held that the check-off arrangements amounted to a term of the employees' contract and the trade union was entitled to enforce said provision as a third party. It was held that the employees had not accepted any variation of their contract by their employer's actions, and they had not waived any previous breaches of their contractual rights by continuing in the appellants' employ.

1 *Secretary of State for the Home Department v Cox* [2023] EWCA 551.

2 See *Smith and others v Commissioners for HM Revenue & Customs* [2022] EWHC 3188 at **[10.03]**.

3 *Cavanagh v Secretary of State for Work and Pensions* [2016] EWHC 1136 (QB).

The appellants appealed, arguing that, as the employees continued to work after the check-off facility had been withdrawn, this indicated agreement to a variation and waiver of any past breaches of contract.

The Court of Appeal held that the trial Judge was entitled to hold that the employees had not accepted any variation of their contract and that they had not waived any previous breaches of their contractual rights. The Court noted that the trade union had operated on its members' behalf by objecting to the proposed withdrawal initially and also had brought proceedings on behalf of members in the *Cavanagh* proceedings. This, it was held, was a good indication that the employees did not accept the withdrawal. The Court held that the trial Judge was entitled to have regard to the fact that the appellant had not pointed out the withdrawal as a change in the terms of the employees' contract, nor had it been made clear that by continuing to work for the appellants, this constituted acceptance of the changes.

The Court then set out its interpretation of s 1 of the 1999 Act.[4] It considered s 1(b) and s 1(2) of the 1999 Act together and noted that the question to be determined was whether the parties to the contract intended that a contractual term should be enforceable by a third party. This context, the Court held, was relevant and the trial Judge had erred in not taking this into account. The Court placed emphasis on the way that the check-off arrangement provision came into being, the nature of the term—in that it offered a facility to employees—and the likelihood that parties had intended that the term was to be enforceable by all possible recipients of authorised deductions, eg saving schemes, social clubs, etc. Therefore, the Court allowed the appeal on this ground.

The Court of Appeal allowed the appeal in part.

[10.03] ***Smith v Commissioners for HM Revenue & Customs*[5]*—High Court of England and Wales—Freedman J—contractual right—collective agreement—reasonable notice—third-party right of enforceability—removal of a 'check-off' facility for union subscriptions—whether the individual claimants had by their conduct accepted a variation of their contracts of employment***

The claimants were employed by the respondent, HMRC. The respondent was established by an Act of Parliament in 2005, merging the departments of Inland Revenue and HM Customs and Excise. Prior to this, the first and second claimants were employed by Inland Revenue, while the third and fourth claimants were employed by HM Customs and Excise. All four individual claimants were members of the Public and Commercial Services Union (the 'PCS'), which was the fifth claimant.

Prior to 1 May 2015, union subscriptions were deducted from each individual claimant's pay and forwarded to the PCS by the respondent. The respondent notified the union of its intention to remove this 'check-off' facility with effect from the end of April 2015.

4 Of union there is no equivalent in Irish law.

5 *Smith and others v Commissioners for HM Revenue & Customs* [2022] EWHC 3188.

The individual claimants sought a declaration that the termination of their right to avail of the check-off system amounted to a continuing breach of their contracts. At issue was whether there was a contractual right to insist that the respondent continue to implement the check-off system, or whether the individual claimants had accepted a variation of their contracts of employment, removing any such right by their conduct.

Also at issue was whether the PCS, which was not a party to each individual claimant's contract of employment, was entitled to enforce the contractual right and, accordingly, whether it was entitled to damages for breach of contract in respect of the individual claimants, and those non-party PCS members whose circumstances were materially identical.

The claimants contended that it had, for many decades, been a term of all contracts of employment of HMRC employees (and those of predecessor departments) that employees had the right to deduction of their PCS subscriptions by check-off. The term was agreed collectively by HMRC's predecessors with trade unions, and was incorporated by express reference into individual contracts. It had never, the claimants contended, been removed by either collective or individual agreement.

The respondent maintained that by its formation in 2005, the individual claimants agreed to new terms and conditions set out in the 'Blue Book', which followed collective negotiations and did not mention the right to check-off. The respondent submitted that check-off was not a contractual entitlement and was removed by consultation in 2015. Policy documents which post-dated the Blue Book and made reference to the right to check-off had not, in the respondent's submission, been expressly incorporated by the Blue Book and there was no reason why they should be so treated, by implication or otherwise. The standard written terms and conditions for HMRC employees, the respondent argued, drew a distinction between terms and conditions (as set out in the Blue Book) and 'policies and procedures', with voluntary pay deductions falling under the latter category.

The High Court was satisfied that there was a contractual right to the deductions. Thus, the check-off-related paragraphs in the policy documents were intended to have contractual effect. These were mirrored in the applicable Civil Service Codes, which regulate terms and conditions on which civil servants are employed. The Court held the check-off paragraphs were: 'expressed in language apt for incorporation in individual contracts of employment'; they 'formed part of a set of documents including provisions intended to have contractual force'; and they created an arrangement which was 'of importance to the contractual relationship'.

There was no express or implied removal of the right to check-off during the 2005 merger. Indeed, the right was 'expressed in clear unequivocal terms' in numerous documents, before and after the merger. The Court rejected the respondent's case that such a contractual obligation could be removed by the respondent giving reasonable notice and found there was no basis for concluding that the respondent had an implied right to terminate the check-off facility unilaterally. Such a reading would be inconsistent with policy documents which limited the circumstances in which the respondent could withdraw check-off to official industrial action.

Next, the Court addressed the respondent's argument that the individual claimants accepted the removal of the right to check-off by their conduct, whether viewed as affirmation, waiver, estoppel, acquiescence, or express/implied acceptance. The respondent submitted that it had notified its intention to change the terms without protest from the individual claimants, and that protest by the PCS was 'faint'. The individual claimants continued to be employed by the respondent without check-off, which had 'immediate and monthly effect' on their salaries. They also availed of the respondent's assistance setting up a direct debit to PCS in lieu of check-off. Finally, the first claimant was promoted on two occasions without check-off. Even if acceptance was not initially unequivocal, the respondent argued that there must have come a time in the five-and-a-half years prior to the issue of proceedings that the individual claimants had accepted the removal of check-off.

The Court concluded that there was no agreement to the change; on the contrary, the change was 'in the face' of a statement of the PCS of 12 January 2015 that the check-off arrangement was contractual and that its removal would require specific agreement. A letter from the claimants' solicitors of 15 April 2015 referred to an 'anticipatory breach of contract' by the removal of check-off. Even when it was removed and the individual claimants continued to work, there was 'no evidence of an agreement or unequivocal conduct capable of giving rise to an acceptance or a waiver of any breach or acquiescence or the like'. There would have been serious consequences in terms of loss of pay had the individual claimants stopped working. It was also known to the individual claimants that the PCS had threatened legal action against the respondent (at the time, the similar case, *Cavanagh v Secretary of State for Work and Pensions*[6], was being pursued by the PCS). The making of direct debits in favour of the PCS 'was not clear and unequivocal acceptance' of the removal of check-off; rather, it could be treated as 'mitigation of the position' so that union representation could be retained for payees.

With regard to the enforceability of the term by the PCS as a third party, it was found that the PCS benefited from the check-off facility in a manner coinciding with the benefit conferred on the employees. Check-off provided 'greater and more secure funding for the union' and made it more likely that members would join, without compelling them to do so. The benefit did not have to be the 'predominant purpose or intent' behind the term and was not negated by the fact that there was also a benefit to parties to the contract. There was nothing express or implied in the terms of the contracts of employment to suggest that the parties had not intended check-off to be enforceable by the PCS.

Accordingly, the issues were determined in favour of the claimants.

---

6 *Cavanagh v Secretary of State for Work and Pensions* [2016] EWHC 1136 (QB).

EUROPEAN WORKS COUNCILS

[10.04] ***easyJet Plc v easyJet European Works Council[7]—Court of Appeal of England and Wales—Bean, Coulson & Davis LJJ—appeal from UK EAT—Transnational Information and Consultation of Employees Regulations 1999[8]—Employment Rights (Amendment) (EU Exit) Regulations 2019[9]—Directive 2009/38/EC[10]—trade union and industrial relations—European Works Council—Brexit—Central Arbitration Committee—statutory interpretation—jurisdiction—EU legislation—exit day—whether EWC subsisted after the completion day of UK's withdrawal from the EU***

The appellant airline company operated across Europe. The respondent European Works Council ('EWC') was established under the Transnational Information and Consultation of Employees Regulations 1999 (the 'TICER'), to provide information to, and engage in, consultation with employees' representatives on transnational issues. The TICER were amended by the Employment Rights (Amendment) (EU Exit) Regulations 2019 (the '2019 Regulations').

In March 2021, the respondent made a complaint to the Central Arbitration Committee, which was situated in the UK. The appellant argued that the enactment of the 2019 Regulations meant that the EWC did not survive the completion day of the UK's withdrawal from the EU and, therefore, the Central Arbitration Committee had no jurisdiction to hear the complaint. The committee maintained that the EWC continued to exist. The UK EAT agreed. The appellant appealed the EAT decision that the respondent EWC continued to exist post-Brexit.

In the Court of Appeal of England and Wales, the appellant argued that the amendments to regs 4 and 5 of the TICER meant that the EWC did not survive the UK's withdrawal from the EU. It also argued that the EAT erred in its interpretation of reg 4 and, in doing so, created an anomalous situation whereby the company was obliged to answer to two EWCs, one in the UK and one in Europe, contrary to Directive 2009/38, which envisaged a single EWC.

Both reg 4 (which, in its unamended form, dealt with the procedure for setting up an EWC and the way it should be conducted) and reg 5 (which in its unamended form, created a duty to establish an EWC) were the focus of discussion in this case.

---

7 easyJet *Plc v* easyJet *European Works Council* [2023] EWCA Civ 756. See *Arthur Cox Employment Yearbook 2022* at [10.08] for decision of UK EAT in *easyJet PLC v easyJet European Works Council & Secretary of State for Business Energy and Industrial Strategy* [2022] EAT 162.

8 Transnational Information and Consultation of Employees Regulations 1999 (SI 1999/3323).

9 Employment Rights (Amendment) (EU Exit) Regulations 2019 (SI 2019/535).

10 Directive 2009/38/EC on the establishment of a European Works Council or a procedure in Community-scale undertakings and Community-scale groups of undertakings for the purposes of informing and consulting employees.

It was common case that the effect of the 2019 amendments to the TICER were that, subject to any transitional provisions, no new EWC could be established after 31 December 2020. Regulation 4 was otherwise unamended. The following excerpt of reg 4 is of particular import: '[the TICER shall apply] only where, in accordance with regulation 5, the central management is situated in the United Kingdom'. The Court noted that the 2019 Regulations repealed reg 5(1)(a) which had provided that reg 5 applied where 'the central management is situated in the United Kingdom'. The new reg 5 was now a deeming provision with regard to undertakings where central management was not in a country within the EEA or the UK. The appellant argued that the critical words outlined above were clear and unequivocal. It was argued that, due to the changes made to reg 5, central management situated in fact in the UK was excluded and the TICER was restricted to cases where central management was deemed to be in the UK only. The EAT had held that the appellant's interpretation of reg 4 did not make sense. In its view, the words 'in accordance with regulation 5' did not exclude undertakings where the central management in fact was situated in the UK. These words simply meant 'in agreement or harmony with' the terms of reg 5. Therefore, the TICER applied to cases where central management was deemed to be in the UK as well as where central management was, in fact, in the UK.

The Court of Appeal considered the interpretation of reg 4 of the TICER. It acknowledged the 'opacity' of the provision and held that a wider view had to be taken of it, taking the whole context of the Regulations into account. The Court noted that reg 18, as amended, provided for: the composition of an EWC; how its members were to be chosen by ballot; the competence of an EWC; and the procedures relating to an EWC. Regulation 18 assumed that an existing EWC would continue to operate post 31 December 2020. The Court of Appeal concluded that, were it otherwise, there would be no reason to include the express reference made. Regulation 23(6), the Court noted, was restricted to circumstances where central management was situated in the UK. This was not amended. The Court inferred from this that, if existing EWCs were to cease to exist, reg 23(6) would be rendered redundant.

The Court considered the 2019 Regulations' transitional provisions, which permitted the creation of a new EWC where the process had begun before 31 December 2020. The Court held that it would be inconsistent with the idea that any existing EWC would cease to exist for it to be possible for a new EWC to be established where the process had begun by 31 December 2020.

Given the above, the Court held that the appellant's interpretation of reg 4 was incorrect and that EWCs that were established prior to exit day continued to exist post that date. This interpretation, it was said, accorded with the 2019 Regulations' explanatory memorandum.

Accordingly, it was held that the respondent EWC which was in being prior to exit day subsisted for all purposes set out in the TICER as amended. The Central Arbitration Committee therefore had jurisdiction to hear the original complaint.

The Court of Appeal dismissed the appeal.

[10.05] ***Charpentier v Verizon Ireland Ltd*[11]*—Workplace Relations Commission—Directive 2009/38/EC*[12]*—Transnational Information and Consultation of Employees Act 1996—industrial relations—expenses—spirit of cooperation—information and consultation—expert—training***

The claimant was the chair of the Verizon European Works Council ('EWC'). He was located in France and his direct employer was Verizon France SAS. After the UK left the EU, Verizon Ireland became the location of central management of the respondent company. The Verizon EWC Agreement (the 'Charter') expired on 20 October 2020 and thereafter the EWC operated under the subsidiary requirements as provided for in the Annex to Directive 2009/38/EC.

Following the movement of the EWC to Ireland and the expiration of the Charter, a 'vacuum' arose and an expert was required to provide input on a number of matters, including on the subsidiary requirements and on an information and consultation procedure, which ultimately did not transpire. The EWC sent an invoice for this expert to the respondent in the sum of €11,220. The respondent expressed surprise at having received this invoice, especially since the information/consultation procedure did not take place. It was argued by the respondent that this was a unilateral decision of EWC and in the 'spirit of cooperation' they should have alerted central management before engaging an expert. The respondent proposed training to focus on the subsidiary requirements and online training was provided to the staff in Dublin by the respondent. The claimant did not think this was 'appropriate and necessary training'. The respondent provided an additional conference in Hamburg, which the claimant attended; he acknowledged that he knew he would not be reimbursed for the costs of going to the Hamburg conference.

The claimant brought two complaints to the WRC under s 17 of the Transnational Information and Consultation of Employees Act 1996, which transposes art 10 of Directive 2009/38/EC. The first complaint concerned the respondent's failure to discharge the invoice of €11,220 for professional services provided by the expert engaged. The second related to the costs of attending the training conference in Hamburg which was hosted by the Verizon EWC.

The WRC decided that, but for the situation faced by the EWC after the Charter lapsed, it would have found that the EWC had not complied with the 'spirit of cooperation' required of all parties by engaging the expert unilaterally. However, given the circumstances, the WRC found it appropriate that the respondent should discharge part of the invoice. A portion of the total sum was disregarded in light of the aborted information and consultation process.

The WRC noted that Directive 2009/38/EC provides an explicit right to training without loss of pay and the respondent had a training obligation under art 10(4) thereof.

11 *Charpentier v Verizon Ireland Ltd* ADJ-00034402.

12 Directive 2009/38/EC on the establishment of a European Works Council or a procedure in Community-scale undertakings and Community-scale groups of undertakings for the purposes of informing and consulting employees.

This obligation should be assessed over the course of a year. It decided that the online training in Dublin did qualify as 'training'. The WRC then considered whether this training was insufficient, as claimed by the claimant and whether additional training was required that year in Hamburg. The WRC decided that the training in Dublin satisfied the respondent's obligations under Directive 2009/38/EC for that year. This was despite the fact that the training in Hamburg was also valuable. It also emphasised that the claimant acknowledged that he would not be recompensed for the costs of attending the Hamburg conference.

The WRC decided that the first complaint was, in part, well founded and, under s 17(1A) of the Transnational Information and Consultation of Employees Act 1996, it held that the respondent should pay the claimant €5,610 towards the expert's fees.

In relation to the second complaint, the WRC decided that this was not well founded due to the fact that there was no breach in respect of the provision of training by the respondent.

[10.06] ***Olsten (UK) Holdings Ltd v Adecco Group European Works Council*[13]*—UK Employment Appeal Tribunal—appeal from Central Arbitration Committee—Directive 2009/38/EC*[14]*—collective redundancies—Covid-19—limitation periods—penalties***

The claimant was the UK representative of the Adecco Group, a multinational group of companies based in Switzerland. The respondent was a European Works Council ('EWC') established by the Adecco Group in accordance with Directive 2009/38/EC (the 'Directive'). The EWC agreement between the parties limited information and consultation with the respondent's members to 'transnational' matters.

This case concerned the claimant's obligations under the EWC agreement to inform and consult the respondent's employee representatives in relation to collective redundancies in at least two EEA states. The claimant contended that the Central Arbitration Committee ('CAC'), whose decision was the subject of this appeal, misdirected itself on the meaning of a 'transnational' matter requiring the Adecco Group to convene an 'extraordinary meeting' to discuss the collective redundancies.

The claimant submitted that there was no overall collective redundancy process with a 'common rationale'. Rather, the redundancy decisions were made locally, for reasons 'peculiar to those countries, unconnected with each other and not dictated by the central management of the Adecco Group'. Accordingly, the collective redundancy decisions were a 'purely national affair', taken by local management and governed by each country's national legislation. This meant that the decisions fell under an exclusion clause in the EWC agreement relating to 'staffing levels', and were not transnational.

13 *Olsten (UK) Holdings Ltd v Adecco Group European Works Council* [2022] EAT 183.

14 Directive 2009/38/EC on the establishment of a European Works Council or a procedure in Community-scale undertakings and Community-scale groups of undertakings for the purposes of informing and consulting employees.

A transnational matter, it was submitted, typically involved a decision made in one EEA State having consequences for at least one other EEA state. Employment events in two or more EEA states which were otherwise unrelated did not make a matter transnational merely because they were concurrent. A finding to the contrary would be unduly burdensome on management.

The respondent defended the CAC's interpretation of 'transnational' but cross-appealed the decision that part of the respondent's complaint to the CAC was out of time.

The respondent also sought a penalty notice against the claimant; firstly, for failure of the Adecco Group to convene an extraordinary meeting with the steering group established under the EWC agreement to engage in dialogue on the collective redundancies (the 'redundancy complaint'); and secondly, for refusing to provide business sales performance data broken down on a country-by-country basis at the annual plenary meeting of 2020 (the 'sales data complaint'). The sales data complaint was admitted to be well-founded by the claimant, which pleaded for leniency.

On the first issue, the UK EAT upheld the CAC's reading of a 'transnational' matter under the EWC agreement. In doing so, it rejected the claimant's contention that the relevant decision must be taken in one EEA state, affecting employees in at least two other EEA states. Neither the language of the Directive, its transposing regulations, nor the EWC agreement supported such a 'gloss'. Moreover, decisions to make redundancies taken in one EEA State were 'inherently likely to have indirect or knock-on effect' on employees of the same group in another EEA State 'without the need to search on each occasion for a direct link, common cause or decision; particularly because there is free movement of workers between those states'.

Collective redundancies were expressly covered by the definition of transnational matter and could not therefore be captured by the 'staffing levels' exclusion. This definition meant that redundancies must significantly affect Adecco employees in 'each of at least two EEA countries', indicating that the effect in each of the two countries need not be the same.

Finally, it was inherent in a group structure that central management has 'at least oversight of country based units of management and the ability to impose its will'. The information and consultation rights conferred by the EWC agreement would be difficult to secure if they could be defeated simply by requiring local management to take sole responsibility for redundancies. The claimant did not dispute the Adecco Group's supervisory oversight role, setting budgets and parameters influencing local management in the usual way.

Accordingly, the appeal failed.

In relation to the cross-appeal, there was clearly an obligation to convene an extraordinary meeting of the EWC within five working days of the 'last relevant redundancies' being made, but the meeting need not take place within that period. The Court found that combined redundancies in the Netherlands and Hungary, and the lapse of five working days, all occurred outside the six-month limitation period for the making of a complaint to the CAC, and so the CAC decision on timing was correct and the cross-appeal failed.

On the issue of penalties, the claimant submitted that both complaints attracted penalties at the bottom end of the scale, from £0.01 to £100,000. The grounds of appeal, its mistakes notwithstanding, were 'genuinely advanced' and 'provided strong mitigation'. The failure to convene an extraordinary meeting occurred over a short time, affecting a relatively small number of employees. The sales data complaint was referable to a single failure at the 2020 annual plenary meeting and was 'limited and short-lived', though the respondent submitted that the data had been sought after and refused on several occasions.

The EAT found the failings of the Adecco Group to be of medium gravity. In relation to the redundancy complaint, the group did not have a record of CAC findings against it. However, it was found to have deliberately adopted a 'self-serving and expedient' interpretation of 'transnational', knowing that it was challenged, and relying on its mistaken belief as a reasonable excuse up to the time of the oral hearing, leaving no room for evidence of contrition. The penalty in respect of the redundancy complaint was set at £20,000.

In relation to the sales data complaint, the EAT again took into consideration the group's lack of previous offending in this regard. The Adecco Group accepted that it was liable for penalisation but called no evidence in support of a plea in mitigation. Accordingly, there was no contrition or assurances about future conduct. Regionally-based information was given to the EWC, though some of this was publicly available already. The EAT held the mistake was genuinely made but, again, was a deliberately taken risk. The penalty in respect of the sales data complaint was set at £5,000.

INFORMATION AND CONSULTATION

[10.07] ***Ethnikos Organismos Pistopoiisis Prosonton & Epangelmatikou Prosanatolismou (Eoppep) v Elliniko Dimosio*[15]*—European Court of Justice—request for preliminary ruling from Greece—Directive 2002/14/EC*[16]*—information and consultation—scope—meaning of 'undertaking carrying out an economic activity'—private law entity operating in the public sector—removal of workers appointed to managerial positions—no prior information or consultation of employee representatives***

The applicant was considered a legal person subject to private law within the broader public sector and carried out a number of vocational guidance tasks for the Greek

15 *Ethnikos Organismos Pistopoiisis Prosonton & Epangelmatikou Prosanatolismou (Eoppep) v Elliniko Dimosio* (Case C-404/22).

16 Directive 2002/14/EC establishing a general framework for informing and consulting employees in the European Community.

Ministry of Education, Religious Affairs, Culture and Sports and the Ministry of Labour, Social Security and Welfare, as well as professional training bodies, businesses and employees' or employers' associations. In 2012, an individual, PM, was made acting head of the applicant's qualifications certification department and another individual, DM, was made acting deputy director of the directorate of administrative and economic services and acting head of the finance department. Subsequently, DM became acting director of the directorate of administrative and economic services.

In 2018, the board of directors of the applicant agency made the decision to have DM continue to perform the duties as acting head of the directorate of administrative and economic services pending the appointment of a director. However, ultimately, DM was released from her duties because, it was claimed, of a failure to perform the role satisfactorily. DM remained assigned to the administrative services department.

Also in 2018, the board of directors released PM from her duties as acting head of the qualifications certification department but had her continue to work in the unit as an employee.

Both DM and PM challenged these decisions before the Labour Relations Inspectorate. The Inspectorate held that the applicant had disregarded the Presidential Decree 240/2006 by failing to inform and consult the representatives of the employees concerned before changing their posts. A fine was imposed on the applicant.

The applicant challenged this decision before the referring Court. It argued that it was not an 'undertaking' carrying on an 'economic activity' under the Presidential Decree 240/2006 and Directive 2002/14/EC (the 'Directive'). The decisions, rather, fell within the applicant's managerial powers. Accordingly, it was argued that the applicant did not fall within the scope of either the Presidential Decree or the Directive. It noted that DM and PM were aware that the posts they were appointed to were temporary in nature.

Two questions were referred to the European Court of Justice ('ECJ') for preliminary ruling. The first related to whether art 2(a) of Directive 2002/14/EC must be interpreted as meaning that the provision refers to a legal person governed by private law which acts as a legal person governed by public law and exercises public powers while also providing, for remuneration, services which are in competition with those provided by market operators.

The ECJ noted that art 2(a) of the Directive provides that the word 'undertaking' means a public or private undertaking carrying out an economic activity, regardless of whether it operates for gain. The ECJ referred to case law where the term was taken as covering any entity engaged in an economic activity, regardless of its legal status or how it is financed. The ECJ noted that the Directive does not define 'economic activity', but that caselaw has defined it as 'any activity consisting in offering goods or services on a given market'. Activities that concern the carrying out of public powers are *prima facie* excluded from the definition. However, services which are carried out in the public interest and are not for profit and which are in competition with those of other entities which are for profit have been taken to be economic activities. The ECJ considered the objective of the Directive and held that this definition of economic activity could be implied.

The ECJ considered whether the applicant carried on an economic activity, as defined. It looked at the services it provided and concluded that these services did not *a priori* come within the exercise of public powers. It was noted that the agency's activities were finance, not only by the fees and supervision costs, but also by income and revenue from the performance of work and the supply of services. The ECJ held that it was for the referring Court to determine whether this revenue could be considered remuneration for services rendered, normally agreed upon between the provider and recipient of the services. Subject to the ruling of the referring Court on this point, the ECJ held that the applicant carried on, in part, an activity of offering services on a given market, and that it therefore could be considered an undertaking within the meaning of art 2(a) of the Directive.

Given the above, the ECJ held that art 2(a) of the Directive must be interpreted as meaning that the provision may refer to a legal person governed by private law which acts as a legal person governed by public law and exercises public powers where it also provides, for pay, services which compete with those provided by market operators.

The second question was, in essence, whether art 4(2)(b) of Directive 2002/14 must be interpreted as meaning that the information and consultation obligation laid down therein applies in the event of a change of post for a small number of employees appointed on an interim basis to management roles, where that change is not capable of affecting the situation, structure or probable development of employment within the undertaking concerned, or place employment more generally under threat.

The ECJ noted that the Directive was aimed at establishing information and consultation of employees where employment in general is under threat in order to offset the adverse effects of the negative development of the situation for the employees involved. The ECJ found that here, while DM and PM were removed from their posts, there was no threat to employment generally. Further, these employees were not removed from the employ of the agency but remained in its service.

The ECJ therefore held that art 4(2)(b) of the Directive must be interpreted as meaning that the information and consultation obligation does not apply in the event of a change of post for a small number of employees that are appointed on an interim basis to management roles, where that change is not capable of affecting the situation, structure or probable development of employment within the company or threatening employment more generally.

VICTIMISATION—TRADE UNION ACTIVITIES

[10.08] ***ESB Networks v O'Grady*[17]*—Labour Court—appeal from Workplace Relations Commission—Industrial Relations (Miscellaneous Provisions) Act 2004—investigation and recommendation—victimisation—collective bargaining—preliminary issue—standing***

The claimant was employed by the respondent as a network technician. He made a complaint against his employer, alleging contravention of s 8 of the Industrial Relations (Miscellaneous Provisions) Act 2004 (the '2004 Act'), which prohibits victimisation. The complaint was linked to other complaints.[18]

The claimant appealed the recommendation of the WRC.

In the appeal, a preliminary point was raised on behalf of the respondent, regarding the claimant's standing. It was argued that, as the respondent had a practice of engaging in collective bargaining, the claimant could not make a complaint under s 8 of the 2004 Act. The claimant accepted that the employer engaged in collective bargaining.

The Labour Court considered s 8 of the 2004 Act, particularly s 8(1): 'This section applies where it is not the practice of the employer to engage in collective bargaining negotiations'.

The Labour Court held that for a party to rely on the protections afforded under s 8 of the 2004 Act, it must not be the practice of employer to engage in collective bargaining. As it was common cause that the respondent did engage in collective bargaining the appeal was dismissed and the decision of the Adjudication Officer was upheld.

17 *ESB Networks v O'Grady* VCD231.

18 *ESB Networks v O'Grady* PW/23/8 and *ESB Networks v O'Grady* TED239.

Chapter 11

Injunctions

INTRODUCTION

[11.01]

Disciplinary Process

Board of Management of Wilson's Hospital School first came before the High Court on foot of an application by an employee teacher for an interlocutory injunction restraining their employer from holding a disciplinary hearing. The employer subsequently sought an interim injunction preventing the employee from attending the school's premises and teaching classes. The case ultimately came before the Court of Appeal, which affirmed the decision of the High Court. See also Chapter 1.

The High Court also considered whether to grant an interlocutory injunction restraining an employer from continuing its disciplinary procedure in *Dunne, Hennigan* and *QQ*.

In *Royal United Hospital Bath NHS Foundation Trust*, the High Court of England and Wales considered an application for an interim injunction compelling witnesses in a disciplinary investigation to attend a disciplinary hearing to be cross-examined and the disclosure of the full investigation report.

Dismissal

Commissioner of An Garda Síochána and Minister for Justice, which was on appeal to the Court of Appeal, concerned an application for an interlocutory injunction restraining the employee's dismissal. This case also concerned a claim of victimisation under the Protected Disclosures Act 2014.

Three Irish High Court cases are noted. In *CMA* the applicant argued she had been unlawfully dismissed outside her probationary period. In *Oak Fuel Supermarket*, the applicant was dismissed only a number of weeks into the probationary period. In *RM*, the applicant argued the dismissal process was not in accordance with fair procedures.

Non-Compete

There were also a number of cases involving the enforcement of restrictive covenants post-employment. The Court of Appeal of England and Wales considered this in *Boydell*, and the following cases came before the High Court of England and Wales: *Jump Trading International Ltd*, *Waste Managed Ltd*, *Hine Solicitors Ltd* and *Evrythng Ltd.*

DISCIPLINARY PROCESS

[11.02] ***Board of Management of Wilson's Hospital School v Burke[1]—High Court—Dignam J—injunction—disciplinary meeting—gender identity—breach of court orders—undertaking as to damages***

Mr Burke was a teacher employed at the Wilson's Hospital School. The principal of the school informed staff of a student's request to be addressed by a different name and by the identifying pronouns 'they/their' as part of their making a social transition in their gender identity. Mr Burke objected to this instruction. Eventually, after a number of exchanges between parties, the board of management of the school met to consider a report drafted by the principal outlining certain allegations of serious misconduct against Mr Burke. The Chair of the board wrote to Mr Burke and informed him that the principal had initiated the disciplinary procedure at Stage 4 and that a meeting would be arranged on 14 September 2022 for Mr Burke to respond to the allegations against him. After a meeting in August 2022 to discuss the possibility of suspension, to which Mr Burke was invited, the Chair wrote to Mr Burke, placing him on paid administrative leave. Mr Burke took issue with this decision and argued that the initiation of the disciplinary process was 'unreasonable, unjust and unlawful'. Mr Burke continued to attend the school despite the school's decision to suspend him being communicated to him.

Mr Burke applied to the Court for certain orders, including an injunction to prohibit the school from holding the disciplinary meeting on 14 September 2022. On the return date of 11 September 2022, the school gave an undertaking that no meeting would be held without three days' notice to Mr Burke. Due to this undertaking, it was not necessary for the Court to determine the application on that date.

Notice was given to Mr Burke in December 2022 of a disciplinary meeting to be held in January 2023. The school initiated proceedings by plenary summons and applied for interim relief so as to enforce the suspension. Stack J in the High Court granted an interim order prohibiting Mr Burke from attending the school or teaching any classes or students. Mr Burke continued to attend at the school despite this order. The school sought an order for attachment and committal due to Mr Burke's continued breaches of the High Court order. Ultimately, Mr Burke was committed to Mountjoy Prison. Interlocutory orders were made by Barrett J in the High Court including an order prohibiting

1 *The Board of Management of Wilson's Hospital School v Burke* [2023] IEHC 22.

Mr Burke from attending the school premises during his paid administrative leave and from trespassing on the property of the school. Mr Burke refused to purge his contempt and refused to indicate whether he would comply with the orders of Barrett J.

Mr Burke brought an application to the High Court for interlocutory injunctive relief to restrain the disciplinary process, to prevent the board of management from dismissing him, and to restrain the holding of the planned disciplinary meeting.

The Court set out the legal principles in respect of interlocutory injunctions in a disciplinary context and considered whether Mr Burke had established a strong case that he was likely to succeed at trial, while being aware of the 'requirement to prove at trial that the process had gone irremediably wrong'. Mr Burke offered a number of grounds upon which he claimed that the disciplinary process was 'unconstitutional, flawed and invalid'. The Court held that the threshold for the application was met on the basis of a combination of Mr Burke's grounds that: the principal's report contained findings and conclusions that had been made without giving Mr Burke the chance to respond, in contravention of natural justice and fair procedures; and the report was read and discussed at a board meeting to which Mr Burke was not invited, in contravention of natural justice and fair procedures.

The Court concluded that damages were not an adequate remedy due to the risk of damage to Mr Burke's reputation. The Court noted that Mr Burke did not give an undertaking as to damages. However, it also acknowledged that no authorities were opened as to the consequences of such a failure. The Court stated that its understanding was that failure to give an undertaking will not always be fatal. Rather, it is a matter of judicial discretion. The Court declined to refuse the reliefs sought on this point alone.

The Court considered a number of other factors in assessing where the balance of convenience lay, including, but not limited to: the effect that a dismissal would have on Mr Burke's reputation; the desirability of bringing the disciplinary proceedings to a conclusion; the disruption that the proceedings were causing to the students of the school; the anticipated expediency of a trial in circumstances where the proceedings were being case managed; and Mr Burke's stated intention to continue to attend the school in breach of court orders. The Court described as an 'incongruity' a situation whereby the school would be bound to comply with any injunctions granted, prohibiting them from continuing with a disciplinary procedure while at the same time, Mr Burke continued to breach orders restricting him from attending at the school premises. The Court stated that if it was wrong to consider the latter 'incongruity' in its assessment of where the balance of convenience lay, it could take it into consideration while exercising its discretion. The fact that Mr Burke refused to give an undertaking as to damages also was considered by the Court in the exercise of its discretion.

The Court stated that it had 'no doubt' that Mr Burke's conduct and stated intentions to continue to defy court orders meant that he had come to the proceedings with unclean hands.

The Court stated that while Mr Burke satisfied the first limb of the test for an injunction, the balance of justice favoured the refusal of his application, given his stated intention to continue to breach court orders. Rather than simply refuse the relief sought, however, the Court allowed Mr Burke time to consider whether he would comply with the orders, even on a without prejudice basis.

The matter was listed for mention on a future date.

[11.03] ***Board of Management of Wilson's Hospital School v Burke*[2]*—Court of Appeal—Birmingham P, Whelan & Edwards JJ—appeal from the High Court—interim injunction—interlocutory suspension—balance of convenience—transgender recognition—length of judgments—religious rights—conscientious objection***

In August 2022, Stack J made an order restraining Mr Burke from attending at the school premises until after 7 September 2022. In September 2022, this was followed by interlocutory relief granted by Barrett J restraining Mr Burke from attending the school pending the determination of the disciplinary action. Mr Burke sought injunctive relief with a view to pausing the disciplinary process and lifting his suspension. This application was unsuccessful before Dignam J. Finally, Mr Burke sought to overturn his suspension before Roberts J, but this was refused. Mr Burke sought to appeal the decisions of Stack J and Barrett J to the Court of Appeal. He did not seek orders in relation to the decisions of Dignam J and Roberts J, but did request a 'review' of these judgments.

The Court of Appeal noted that the proceedings before Stack J had been 'quite brief'. However, the Court emphasised that the trial Judge had been 'very attentive' to all matters at issue. The Court held that the trial Judge had not made any errors in deciding the matter and commented that it was 'inconceivable that any judge would not have concluded that this was a case for an interim injunction'.

With regard to the appeal of Barrett J's decision, the Court of Appeal held that the trial Judge had considered all aspects of the test for an interlocutory injunction. Again, notwithstanding the brevity of the proceedings, the decision of the trial Judge was sound. A distinction was drawn by the Court between judgments given immediately following oral argument and those which are reserved, the latter usually include a 'recap' of the facts and areas of dispute. This is as a result of the passage of time between the proceedings and the judgment and to provide context for the submissions. As to the balance of convenience, the Court highlighted that Barrett J had weighed the impact of the suspension on Mr Burke against the impact of his refusing to adhere to the strictures of his suspension and not attend at the school. It was acknowledged that the impact of suspension would be 'very grave indeed, and may not be easily or at all remedied' but that, in this case, Mr Burke had demonstrated his intent to continue to act in a manner that gave rise to the suspension and that this was a significant contributing factor in the trial Judge's decision.

Birmingham P in the Court of Appeal also emphasised that the transitioning student's perspective should be considered in order to ascertain where the balance of convenience lay. He noted that, although accommodation satisfactory to all parties might have been reached, where that was not possible, the wishes of the child must prevail in this particular case.

Birmingham P considered Mr Burke's claim that there had been an attack on his religious beliefs. The Court noted that it was significant that the school had decided that

2 *Board of Management of Wilson's Hospital School v Burke* [2023] IECA 52.

the student would be supported in their transition, in line with the school's ethos. The Court held that this decision was 'in no sense an outlier' given the wider public policy in this area and the Gender Recognition Act 2015.

Whelan J and Edwards J also delivered judgments in this case.

Whelan J noted that the school and Mr Burke, as a teacher, acted in *loco parentis* to each student, including the student in question. Accordingly, it was important to gauge how Mr Burke intended to engage with the student going forward. Mr Burke failed or refused to provide a direct answer as to his intentions, contending that this was of no relevance. This failure, Whelan J stated, created 'uncertainty' and justified the concerns of the school in circumstances where Mr Burke lacked 'all insight' into his behaviour; he also failed to appreciate that it was 'inappropriate, undermining, intimidating, contumelious towards and demeaning of the school Principal'. The school could not 'reasonably countenance the risk that a student would be exposed to harm in respect of their social and personal development' contrary to statutory obligations. The Court considered Mr Burke's arguments concerning freedom of religion and held that the law does not automatically protect any one belief system in circumstances where the belief is 'calculated to deny, diminish or even destroy the personal and fundamental rights of another, in particular a child'.

Edwards J detailed the State's history of transgender recognition in his judgment. The Court considered Mr Burke's conscientious objection in supporting the student's choice to transition and stated that no one had a monopoly on rights, and freedom of conscience and expression were not unqualified. It was held that the school's support of the student did not necessarily trespass on Mr Burke's constitutional rights. The Court acknowledged, however, that this did not arise for consideration in Mr Burke's appeal.

All three judges upheld the High Court decisions and the appeal was dismissed.

[11.04] ***Dunne v Board of Management of Little Angels Special School*[3]*—High Court—Butler J—interlocutory injunction—applicant seeking to restrain disciplinary hearing—fair question to be tried—fair procedure in disciplinary process—impartiality—conflict of interest—delay***

The applicant was the principal of a national school and sought an interlocutory injunction restraining a disciplinary hearing into seven complaints made against her by the chairperson of the respondent, the board of management of the school. The school in question had been founded by the chairperson's father and both men were directors of the company that was the school patron.

The first complaint alleged that the applicant sought to retrospectively change the interview score of a teacher following interviews in August 2019. This was denied by the applicant, who presented a different narrative and complained that the chairperson frequently crossed the line between the management of the school and the 'day-to-day management' of the school, which was the preserve of the principal. The second

3 *Dunne v Board of Management of Little Angels Special School* [2023] IEHC 312.

complaint alleged that the applicant, when questioned directly by the chairperson, did not give the respondent full information in relation to a special-needs assistant who had been the subject of an anonymous complaint. The third complaint, similarly, alleged that the applicant had not been forthcoming with information relating to an incident on a school outing in which a child got into difficulty at a local swimming pool when left unattended and had to be rescued.

The fourth complaint concerned the applicant's alleged 'lack of leadership' during the running of a July provision scheme in 2020, a time of significant public health restrictions which was not acknowledged in the chairperson's report. The fifth complaint alleged a 'lack of engagement' from the applicant in relation to a grievance procedure instigated by the deputy principal against the applicant which was ongoing at the time of these proceedings. The sixth complaint alleged that the applicant had accused a parent nominee on the respondent board of 'leaking' information to a local radio station. This was denied by the applicant and the evidence pointed to there being particularly poor relations between the applicant and the parent nominee in question. The final complaint alleged that the applicant did not bring tenders for a cleaning contract to the attention of the respondent.

The chairperson instigated a stage 4 disciplinary process against the applicant. This is the final and most serious stage of the process, and provides for the potential for dismissal. The applicant argued that she had been deprived of the benefit of the earlier stages and that the chairperson had usurped and bypassed the role of the board of management in forming the view (without the board's involvement) that commencement at stage 4 was appropriate. She argued that most of the allegations against her dated back to 2019—a year or more before the disciplinary process commenced—and should have been dealt with as they arose, rather than cumulatively.

The Court was not convinced that the commencement of the disciplinary process at stage 4 excluded the board from a role that it would otherwise have. It observed that the relevant circular issued by the Department of Education seemed to envisage the indirect involvement of the board of management for the purpose of exercising appellate or decision-making functions at various stages of the disciplinary process, including stage 4. The Court therefore did not regard this issue as having reached the threshold of a fair question to be tried.

However, the circular undoubtedly envisaged that the process 'move through a number of informal and formal stages before reaching the ultimate stage when the most serious sanction of dismissal becomes a possibility'. If the 2019 complaints were of substance, then the applicant was not afforded the opportunity 'to improve in response to any warning which might have been issued to her'.

The Court stressed that 'the mere fact that the circular allows for disciplinary proceedings to be instituted at stage 4 does not necessarily mean it is appropriate to do so and, indeed, it is probably inappropriate to do so in most instances'. Normally, such an approach would follow a particularly serious incident involving an allegation of gross misconduct. It was 'difficult to understand' how a number of the complaints, which were not considered serious enough to merit disciplinary action at the time, could suddenly be 'grouped together' at stage 4.

The Court was not convinced by the respondent's reliance on *prima facie* compliance with the circular and the ongoing nature of the disciplinary process. The chairperson had a 'clear conflict of interest', in that he was both complainant and prosecutor in presenting his report to the respondent. Many of the incidents complained of involved interactions between the applicant and the chairperson. Accordingly, someone else should have prepared the report on which the disciplinary process was based.

The report itself was observed to be neither fair nor balanced in its treatment of the facts. Nor could the report be described as comprehensive—with seven separate complaints spanning a little over six pages—it largely comprised the chairperson's view of events and made findings of fact against the applicant.

On the strength of the above, the applicant had established a fair question to be tried in relation to the continuation of the disciplinary process.

The Court was not persuaded that the applicant's action should be barred *in limine* for failure to comply with the three-month time limit for the bringing of judicial review proceedings (it being accepted that the institution of plenary proceedings could not be used to circumvent the time limits for judicial review). The delay defence was not sufficiently conclusive to change the Court's view that the applicant had raised a fair question to be tried. Nor did that defence, when weighed in the balance of convenience, persuade the Court that the applicant should not have the opportunity to raise her issues in court for determination before participating in the disciplinary hearing.

The Court found that the balance of convenience favoured the restraint of the disciplinary process until the High Court had the opportunity to determine the issues between the parties. Accordingly, the injunctive reliefs were granted.

[11.05] ***Hennigan v An Coimisiún Le Rincí Gaelacha[4]—High Court—Roberts J—disciplinary procedure—suspension clause—interlocutory reliefs—mandatory injunctions—applicant seeking to lift her suspension—applicant seeking to halt disciplinary process—whether there was prima facie evidence of gross misconduct***

The applicant was an Irish dancing teacher and adjudicator. The respondent ran and regulated Irish dancing competitions at national and international levels.

From July 2022, the respondent's investigation committee received an unprecedented volume of complaints against a number of named individuals, including the applicant, alleging corrupt activity. These complaints consisted of screenshots of historic text exchanges. It was alleged that the applicant was involved in influencing the result of dance competitions. The allegations generally received significant publicity and media attention following the leaking of documents online. This was linked closely in time to the respondent issuing a statement, on 26 September 2022, to the effect that it had received allegations with supporting documentation of several grievous breaches of its code of conduct.

4 *Hennigan v An Coimisiún Le Rincí Gaelacha* [2023] IEHC 87.

The applicant was first advised by the respondent, on 10 October 2022, that the respondent had received a complaint in relation to her; that an independent investigator had been appointed to establish the facts; and that the applicant would be informed in writing of the outcome of that investigation. The applicant was also advised that she would be invited to attend a formal disciplinary hearing if it was found that she had a case to answer and that a finding of serious or gross misconduct could result in the removal of her registration. She was directed to the respondent's disciplinary procedure policy for further information.

The independent investigator produced his report on 11 October 2022. In the report he recommended a disciplinary hearing to deal with a '*prima facie*' (for the purpose of that preliminary investigation) case of gross misconduct, though he did not reference suspension. The applicant was advised the following day that, by operation of a clause in the respondent's disciplinary procedure policy, she was automatically suspended pending the conclusion of the inquiry. That suspension clause was not in place at the time of the text exchange and was only introduced two years later.

The applicant brought these proceedings challenging the lawfulness of her suspension. She sought mandatory injunctive reliefs against the respondent on an interlocutory basis. Broadly, she sought to lift her suspension and/or prevent the disciplinary procedure from continuing until the full hearing of the action.

Having heard submissions, the Court found there was a strong case that the applicant had not been afforded fair procedures in relation to her suspension. It noted no clear evidence of a *prima facie* finding of gross misconduct against the applicant and no certainty that the text exchange involving the applicant, on its face, met the threshold of gross misconduct; none of which was to say that such a finding could not follow from the inquiry. The complaint against the applicant was considered 'not as a standalone complaint', but rather, 'in the eye of a media storm, in tandem with multiple other complaints of a different and more explicit character'. Accordingly, there was a concern that the manner in which her complaint was amalgamated with others may have tainted the complaint against the applicant.

The Court also found that the applicant was not afforded an opportunity to explain or comment on the text exchange prior to her suspension. It was not sufficient that an explanation could be given at a future disciplinary hearing, the date for which was indeterminate.

In the absence of *prima facie* evidence of gross misconduct, the suspension clause did not apply and, in any event, was not likely to satisfy the requirements of natural justice.

In considering where the balance of convenience lay, the Court was satisfied that the applicant would not be adequately compensated by an award of damages were she to succeed at trial. The Court was mindful of ongoing prejudice and damage to the applicant's health, reputation and well-being arising from her suspension. Accordingly, the Court granted the interlocutory reliefs as they related to the applicant's suspension by the respondent.

The applicant did not, however, make out a strong case to halt the disciplinary process against her, no matter how valid her complaints. The applicant now had the complaint materials and there was no evidence that the leaking of the materials online was due to any failure on the respondent's part. The Court did not believe that the proposed introduction of a new disciplinary procedure, in itself, invalidated the process at that stage (though it could become salient if the applicant were dissatisfied with the outcome of the disciplinary process). Thus, the proper course was to allow the disciplinary process to proceed and continue to conclusion.

The application for interlocutory reliefs was therefore granted in part.

[11.06] ***QQ v Board of Management of a School[5]—High Court—Dignam J—application for injunction—disciplinary proceedings—interlocutory relief—restraining disciplinary process—irreparably flawed—disciplinary process already commenced—sanctions—bias***

The applicant was an Irish teacher in the defendant school. By email on 27 May 2021, the principal of the school initiated Stage 4 disciplinary proceedings against the applicant under the Department of Education Circular 0049/2018. These proceedings were commenced by delivering the principal's report on serious issues of alleged misconduct on the applicant's part. The allegations against her pertained to her allegedly trying to gain unfair advantage for her son (who attended the school) in respect of the 2020 Leaving Certificate, contrary to Circular 0037/2020.

The applicant applied to the High Court for interlocutory relief to restrain disciplinary proceedings against her, which she argued were irreparably flawed. The interlocutory relief sought included injunctions restraining the defendant from: commencing and/or continuing the proceedings based on a report attached to the defendant's letter of 28 May 2021 (relief number 2); proceeding with the hearing on 3 and 4 of November 2021 (relief number 3); dismissing the applicant or imposing sanctions upon her in reliance on 'findings', 'conclusions', or 'facts', which were set out in the report (relief number 4); commencing or continuing with the process involving any decisions made or to be made with the participation of the chair or the board of management who participated in the decision of 27 May 2021 and/or based on any report made by the principal of the defendant school (relief number 5); investigating or disciplining the applicant under Circular 37/2000 or otherwise (relief number 6); and dismissing the applicant or imposing sanction as required by Circular 49/2018 (relief number 7).

The Court noted that relief number 2, as it was originally drafted, was ill-conceived in circumstances where the disciplinary process had been commenced by delivery of the principal's report. Accordingly, the Court granted an amended version of relief number 2: an interlocutory injunction restraining the defendant, its servants or agents from continuing with any disciplinary process based on the report, pending the determination of the proceedings.

---

5 *QQ v Board of Management of a School* [2023] IEHC 302.

The Court held that where relief number 3 related to a disciplinary hearing on 3 and 4 of November 2021, the relief was redundant.

The Court held that relief number 4 was not necessary at this early stage, given that a sanction could only be imposed following the conclusion of the disciplinary process. In circumstances where the process was now restrained from continuing (under amended relief number 2), there was no current need to grant the relief.

The Court noted that there were a number of limbs in relief number 5. Again, the Court noted that what was sought was an injunction restraining the commencement of a disciplinary process that had already commenced. The Court noted that the chair of the defendant board had previously indicated that he would not participate in the process. Therefore any injunction restraining his participation was redundant. The third limb of this relief was an order restraining any disciplinary process involving any decision made, or to be made by the board based on the report. The Court held that this was 'far too open-ended'. The Court noted that the reasoning behind this limb seemed to be an allegation of bias against the board in circumstances where there was no serious question to be tried relating to these matters; therefore, an order could not be made.

The Court held that no fair issue was established in respect of the defendant's entitlement to discipline the applicant in respect of the matters contained in the report. Therefore, there was no basis for an order in terms of relief number 6.

Relief number 7 was also refused for the same reasons as relief number 4. The Court concluded that proceedings for trial should be prepared as expeditiously as possible.

[11.07] ***Colbert v Royal United Hospital Bath NHS Foundation Trust*[6]*—High Court of England and Wales—Squires KC—contract of employment—interim injunctions—redactions—compelling witnesses—disclosure of unredacted copy of report***

The applicant was a consultant working with the respondent Trust (the 'Trust'). The Trust held an external review of the department where the applicant was stationed, in response to allegations of inappropriate workplace behaviour. A report was generated on foot of the review and it recommended that the Trust investigate the applicant for alleged intimidation and bullying of colleagues. An investigation was initiated, the investigator interviewed a number of witnesses and made several findings against the applicant. The matter proceeded before a disciplinary panel. At the hearing, the panel wished to call the investigator as a witness instead of the employee witnesses interviewed by her. The applicant was furnished with a copy of the investigator's report and a redacted copy of the initial department report, which contained allegations about other individuals. The applicant argued that his contract of employment incorporated Trust policies which gave him a contractual right to compel the employee witnesses to attend the hearing for the purpose of cross-examining them and also gave him the right to see the unredacted version of the initial report. He submitted that the Trust had breached express contractual obligations in dealing with the allegations made against

6 *Colbert v Royal United Hospital Bath NHS Foundation Trust* [2023] EWHC 1672 (KB).

him. He sought an interim injunction compelling the witnesses and the disclosure of the unredacted report.

On the compulsion point, the Court stated that the applicant had to show a real prospect of success in demonstrating that he had a contractual right to compel the witnesses. He argued that the 'Managing Conduct Policy' gave him the right to require the attendance of witnesses employed by the Trust where it could not be agreed how their evidence would be questioned. He claimed that this policy was incorporated into his contract of employment. The Court did not accept that this policy provided the applicant with an unqualified right to compel the witnesses. Upon examination of the policy, it was revealed that the right to compel witnesses was actually reserved for the Trust and not the employee. There was a separate section in the policy which dealt with the rights of employees facing disciplinary action and the Court held that if it was intended that the employee would have the right to compel witnesses, it would have been explicitly listed there. The Court concluded that the applicant's interpretation of the policy would have unworkable consequences, which would considerably lengthen proceedings.

The Court added that it was not its role to become involved in the supervision of disciplinary proceedings in the way sought. It was held that there was unlikely to be a breach of contract if the disciplinary process was capable of 'ironing out' any unfairness via the appeal procedure.

With regard to disclosure, the applicant argued that the Trust's failure to furnish the unredacted document was a breach of the Trust's own policy, 'Maintaining High Professional Standards in the Modern NHS', which required the applicant to be permitted to view correspondence relating to his case. The Court held that the applicant had no real prospect of success with this argument either. It rejected the submission that an internal investigative report could be construed as 'correspondence'. It was also noted that the redacted material did not relate specifically to the applicant or his case. However, even if the material did relate to the applicant and his case, the Court noted that he did not have an unqualified right to the unredacted version of this report and that the confidentiality of the other individuals, to whom the material referred, must be safeguarded.

The interim injunction was refused.

DISMISSAL

[11.08] ***Barrett v Commissioner of An Garda Síochána and Minister for Justice*[7]*—Court of Appeal—Ní Raifeartaigh J—appeal from High Court—refusal of interlocutory reliefs—fair procedure—delay in seeking interlocutory***

7 *Barrett v Commissioner of An Garda Síochána and Minister for Justice* [2023] IECA 112. See *Arthur Cox Employment Law Yearbook 2022* at [11.07] for the decision of the High Court in *Barrett v Commissioner for An Garda Síochána & Minister for Justice & Equality* [2022] IEHC 86 and at [11.09] for the decision in *Barrett v Commissioner for An Garda Síochána and Minister for Justice and Equality (No 2)* [2022] IEHC 153.

reliefs—Protected Disclosures Act 2014—detriment—burden of proof—standard of proof

The appellant appealed against the High Court's refusal of an interlocutory injunction. The appellant was the Human Resources director for An Garda Síochána. He was the subject of a disciplinary process, which commenced in May 2018 and was expanded by the first respondent, in October 2018. The process had reached an advanced stage when, in July 2020, the appellant withdrew from the investigation. In December 2020, a recommendation was made by the first respondent to the second respondent, the Minister, that the appellant be dismissed.

It was at this stage that the appellant sought interlocutory reliefs from the High Court, restraining further continuance of the disciplinary process.[8] His complaints centred 'loosely' on fair procedure grounds, though he maintained that the process itself amounted to victimisation for his having made seven alleged protected disclosures, and was indicative of a personal *animus* within An Garda Síochána towards him. The reliefs were refused, the High Court not being satisfied that the first four communications—even if presumed to be protected disclosures—were connected to the disciplinary process, while finding that the remaining three communications did not amount to protected disclosures. The High Court added that it would, in any event, have refused the reliefs on the grounds of delay on the part of the appellant in bringing the application.

The respondent gave an undertaking allowing him to remain in his position, albeit suspended on full pay, pending determination by the Court of Appeal.

The Court of Appeal was satisfied that the matter could be disposed of solely on the basis of delay on the part of the appellant and took the view that the High Court had been to correct to refuse relief on that basis. The appellant's challenges to the disciplinary process 'were not merely procedural but ... existential'. His position throughout was that the process was 'fundamentally illegal, unfair and utterly incapable of being rectified'. The appellant was therefore not entitled 'to sit back and allow the process to unfold ... until the very final stages'. On the contrary, it was incumbent on him to move with reasonable expedition in seeking interlocutory relief.

The Court of Appeal nevertheless went on to address the protected disclosure argument. In doing so, it found that the High Court had erred insofar as it appeared to consider that the burden of proof fell on the appellant 'to establish all matters to the *Campus Oil* standard'. Its analysis did not factor the statutory presumption that a communication in issue is a protected disclosure within the meaning of the Protected Disclosures Act 2014, unless the presumption is displaced on the balance of probabilities. This error did not affect the High Court's conclusion in respect of some of the appellant's communications, which lacked sufficient informational content to amount to protected disclosures in the first place.

8 See *Arthur Cox Employment Law Yearbook 2022* at [11.07] for the decision of the High Court in *Barrett v Commissioner for An Garda Síochána & Minister for Justice & Equality* [2022] IEHC 86.

However, in relation to other communications, the High Court's analysis had not included whether the respondents had proved, on the balance of probabilities, that the appellant did not hold a 'reasonable belief' that the information tended to show 'one or more relevant wrongdoings'. In this respect, it had fallen into error. Nevertheless, the High Court's factual findings were correct in that the appellant failed to show a connection between the first four communications and the alleged detriment.

In light of the Court of Appeal's findings on delay, the appeal was dismissed.

[11.09] ***CMA v K*[9]*—High Court—Roberts J—Irish Human Rights and Equality Commission Act 2014—dismissal—termination of employment—interlocutory injunction restraining the termination of employment or removal from position pending further order of the court—whether the applicant was unlawfully dismissed outside probationary period***

The applicant was an employee of the respondent until her employment was terminated for unacceptable job performance on 26 January 2023 with immediate effect. The applicant was paid two weeks' wages in lieu of notice. In the substantive proceedings, the applicant claimed damages for breach of contract and wrongful dismissal. The applicant argued that she was unlawfully dismissed outside of her probationary period.

The applicant's employment contract included a clause which related to an 11-month probation period, which read: 'For the first eleven months of this contract you will be on probation'. The applicant interpreted this as meaning that the first 11 months of her contract ran from the date of execution of the contract, being 21 February 2022. She argued that her probation therefore ended on 20 January 2023. The applicant submitted that, as her employment was not terminated until 26 January 2023, she was dismissed outside of her probation period and was entitled to all the protections of natural justice and fair procedures that an employee would be entitled to. The applicant argued that, under contract, she was entitled to two weeks' notice of her termination. She noted that the only mention of payment in lieu of notice in the contract pertained to termination outside the probationary period as set out in clause 14.

The respondent claimed that the applicant was dismissed while on probation. It argued that the initiation date for the probation period could only be read as beginning when the applicant's employment commenced, being 16 March 2022. The respondent argued that it was nonsensical for a probation period to start prior to the commencement of employment. It stated that it was entitled to pay the applicant payment in lieu of notice and that clause 14 should not be interpreted strictly. It argued that even if two weeks' notice was required, the expiry of that period was still within the applicant's probationary period.

It was the applicant's case that she was a disabled person within the meaning of the Employment Equality Acts 1998 to 2021 and that, although she disclosed her medical condition to the respondent, it did not make reasonable accommodation for her. The applicant also claimed that the respondent, as a public body within the meaning of s 42 of the Irish Human Rights and Equality Commission Act 2014 had a statutory duty to

9 *CMA v K* [2023] IEHC 96.

have regard to the need to avoid discrimination, promote equality of opportunity and treatment of staff and safeguard the human rights of its personnel.

The applicant sought interlocutory injunctive relief against the respondent: to prohibit the termination of her employment; to prohibit the respondent from commenting on her work performance; and to compel the respondent to continue paying her salary and benefits, including her pension contributions, pending a further order. The applicant also sought certain orders preserving her anonymity until a further order was made. She sought declaratory relief that the respondent failed to have regard to its s 42 duties.

The respondent objected to these applications and highlighted the applicant's delay in seeking injunctive relief as well as her failure to give an undertaking as to damages.

The Court held that the applicant's case, as it pertained to her probation period starting date and her arguments regarding being paid in lieu of notice, was not so strong as to raise a reasonable expectation that she was more likely than not to succeed at trial. Further, she had not established a strong case on which she was likely to succeed in relation to whether she was entitled to, or had been denied, fair procedures. The Court held that the applicant did not meet the standard for mandatory injunctive relief in relation to the declaratory relief sought.

The Court reasoned that reinstatement would not be appropriate since the applicant's performance was not acceptable during her probationary period and trust and confidence was now lost between the parties. The Court held that, in such a wrongful termination case, damages should be an adequate remedy. It noted that the applicant had not given an undertaking as to damages and that there was a likelihood that damages may not be an adequate remedy for the respondent if injunctive relief was granted at an interlocutory stage and where the respondent was ultimately successful at trial.

Given the conclusions of the Court regarding the applicant not having met the threshold for injunctive relief, consideration of the respondent's points on delay were not necessary.

While the Court refused most of the reliefs sought, it granted the applicant an order under s 27 of the Civil Law (Miscellaneous Provisions) Act 2008, which provided that her anonymity should be preserved in any publication or broadcast concerning the proceedings. The Court did so in circumstances where the publication of the applicant's identity might adversely affect her in circumstances where she had a medical condition.

The application was therefore refused.

[11.10] ***Buttimer v Oak Fuel Supermarket*[10]*—High Court—Dignam J—interlocutory reliefs—injunctions—employee seeking interlocutory reliefs against employer—applicant seeking to compel respondent to bring applicant back to work***

The applicant commenced employment with the respondent, Oak Fuel Supermarkets, as a supervisor at its fuel station in Rathcormac, Cork. She was promised that, subject to her performance, she would be promoted to store manager after one month (she

10 *Buttimer v Oak Fuel Supermarket t/a Costcutter Rathcormac* [2023] IEHC 126.

commenced in March 2022). Meanwhile, she performed the duties of a manager and was treated as one by other staff. The applicant did not have any experience as a manager.

An employee made allegations against the applicant about her conduct, which the applicant maintained were made as part of a staff effort to have her removed. In the course of an independent investigation into the allegations, the applicant stated that this was her first managerial position and that she accepted having made mistakes, but denied allegations of bullying or harassment.

The applicant was formally promoted to store manager on 25 April 2022. Further complaints were received and the investigation was still ongoing when, on 17 May, the applicant was told her employment was being brought to an end. The applicant raised the possibility of being given another position in another of the respondent's stores. A meeting was arranged, which the applicant was unable to attend, and the respondent informed the applicant the following day that the purpose of the meeting was to offer her a position as trainee manager in the other store. The respondent attempted to follow up with the applicant but there was no further communication from her directly.

The applicant sought interlocutory orders restraining the respondent from: treating her 'as otherwise than employed' and 'as otherwise than continuing to be employed' by the respondent; appointing someone else to her position; re-assigning her duties or otherwise terminating her employment; and requiring the respondent to continue to pay her salary and other benefits.

The respondent argued that the applicant was estopped from obtaining relief or should be refused on the basis that she did not come with 'clean hands'. It was submitted that the applicant had not informed the respondent of her view of the offer of another position before instituting proceedings (though she had communicated a refusal of the offer through her solicitor).

The Court did not accept that the applicant's conduct amounted to 'that type of conduct', nor was it convinced that the reliefs should be refused *ab initio*. The Court was satisfied that the applicant had established a strong case that her employment was brought to an end due to alleged misconduct, and that she was not given the opportunity to address the allegations of misconduct.

The Court was not satisfied that the balance of convenience favoured an order compelling the respondent to bring the applicant back to work, there being sufficient evidence of difficulties in the relationship between the parties. However, it was satisfied that the balance of justice required some relief in order to avoid 'irredeemable harm to the applicant in the event that she is ultimately successful at trial', and interlocutory orders were granted in limited terms.

[11.11] ***RM v SHC*[11]*—High Court—Mulcahy J—interlocutory relief—disciplinary process—summary dismissal—fair procedures—fair case to be tried***

[11] *RM v SCH* [2023] IEHC 424.

The applicant applied for an injunction to restrain the respondent from terminating her employment on the grounds of gross misconduct. The applicant claimed that the dismissal process was not in accordance with fair procedures. The respondent submitted that there had been a mutual loss of trust and confidence and the employment relationship had been irretrievably tainted, making the application inappropriate.

The applicant worked for the respondent for over 20 years, in positions of increasing responsibility. In 2022, on her return from a period of sick leave, the applicant was contacted by the respondent, who enquired about an issue that had arisen while the applicant was out of office. The respondent lost her temper on the call, following which the applicant left the office and was certified unfit for work. During her absence, the applicant wrote a letter setting out 'in direct terms' a large number of issues which, in her view, had caused difficulties within the office. The letter was highly critical of the respondent. The applicant delivered the letter to the respondent at her home. The manner of the delivery of the letter, its contents, as well as concerns of breaches of confidentiality, gave rise to the allegation of gross misconduct.

Shortly after she was certified to return to work, the applicant was advised that she was being suspended with pay pending a disciplinary investigation. An independent investigator was appointed by the firm. The investigator's report was sharply critical of the applicant and although the investigator had not investigated the applicant's complaints about the respondent, she would consider the applicant's actions inappropriate even if the complaints in the letter were well-founded. The report concluded that the applicant had not intended the letter to be read as a threat to commit breaches of confidentiality.

The financial controller, as 'nominated company representative', informed the applicant that the report's findings were sufficiently serious to potentially amount to gross misconduct. The applicant put in a written response rejecting the allegation. By letter, from the financial controller, the applicant was informed that she was summarily dismissed. The applicant intended to appeal but said that the timeframe was unrealistic. The financial controller allowed the applicant an extension of two working days. When the applicant emailed to ask for further time, the financial controller replied on a Saturday, before the extension had lapsed, to inform the applicant that no further time extensions would be granted and that any written appeal received thereafter would be considered 'strictly without prejudice'. When contacted by the applicant's solicitors, the respondent rejected allegations of breach of fair procedure and refused to give undertakings.

The Court found that the applicant established a strong case likely to succeed that there had been a breach of fair procedures, both in the initial decision to dismiss and the appeals process. It would be premature to conclude that damages would be the only remedy available. The least risk of injustice warranted the grant of injunctive relief on terms, pending the trial.

NON-COMPETE

[11.12] ***Boydell v NZP Ltd*[12]*—Court of Appeal of England and Wales—Macur, Bean & Coulson LJJ—appeal from High Court of England and Wales—injunction—non-compete—*American Cyanamid *principles—interim injunction—enforcement of contract—restrictive covenants***

The respondent was a company specialising in the development, production, and sale of bile acid derivatives to pharmaceutical companies. The appellant was an employee of the respondent, working as head of commercial speciality products. Upon resignation, he stated his intention to work for the respondent's main competitor to head their bile acid business. The appellant's employment contract included a non-compete clause which stated that, for a period of 12 months after the termination of his employment, he would not be involved in any activity that benefited a company that competed with the respondent, or any of its affiliates, including each entity in a group. The activities in question were listed in the clause and included 'any activities relating to the supply chain [manufacturing or use of] bile from various animals'.

The respondent sought an interim injunction to enforce this term. The trial Judge granted the injunction, albeit severing some words from the clause in question, including the reference to 'affiliates' or 'group' companies and 'supply chain' of bile. The Judge also granted injunctions to enforce the non-solicitation and non-dealing provisions which occurred elsewhere in the contract.

The appellant sought permission to appeal on various grounds, including that: the trial Judge erred in not finding the clause to be unenforceable; the Judge erred in failing to hold that the clause was too wide; and the Judge erred in his approach to severance. The respondents argued that all they needed to establish was a serious question to be tried to be awarded an injunction under the principles in *American Cyanamid Co v Ethicon Ltd.*[13]

The Court of Appeal of England and Wales compared the *American Cyanamid* case, which it characterised as 'a large and complex patent claim', with this case, which was a straightforward employment case. In cases such as this, it was held that it may be unjust to limit the Court's consideration to simply to whether there is a serious question to be tried. The Court noted that the statutory test for an injunction is whether it is just and convenient to grant it. Caselaw was outlined which stated that where a trial could not be held until after the period of a restrictive covenant had expired, it was permissible for a Court to form at least a preliminary view on the applicant's prospect of success and to consider this when assessing where the balance of convenience lies.

The Court commented that if, even assuming any disputes of fact would be resolved in an applicant's favour, a clause, on its proper construction including any severance, is plainly unenforceable, the Court should say so. In such circumstances, there would not be a serious issue to be tried.

12 *Boydell v NZP Ltd* [2023] EWCA Civ 373.
13 *American Cyanamid Co v Ethicon Ltd* [1975] AC 396.

The Court noted that on the principles of construction, if there is only one interpretation of a clause (rather than two competing interpretations which affect the contract's validity) then that interpretation must be adopted.

With regard to severance, the Court noted that the deletion of references made were reasonable and that the trial Judge was entitled to sever the words and grant an injunction on a more limited basis. It was not plain and obvious that the clause was incapable of severance, nor that having been severed, the clause was too wide to be enforced.

The Court refused permission to appeal against the trial Judge's decision to include both the non-solicitation and non-dealing clauses in the injunction.

The Court noted that, in accordance with the impugned clause, the respondent had offered to pay the appellant his full salary during the period prior to the trial, when he was unable to start work with his new employer. Accordingly, the appellant was facing no loss. On the other hand, it was held that the inadequacy of damages to the respondents if they were refused the injunction but succeeded at trial was 'entirely obvious'. The balance of convenience therefore favoured the grant of the injunction.

The appeal was dismissed.

[11.13] ***Jump Trading International Ltd v Couture[14]—High Court of England and Wales—Simler & Laing LJJ—contract of employment—non-compete clause—interim injunction—employer seeking to restrain employee from commencing employment with a competitor—enforceability of clause—prejudice caused by delay***

The applicant, Jump Trading International Ltd, a leading trading and investment firm, sought an interim prohibitory injunction restraining commencement of the first respondent, Mr Couture's, employment with the second respondent, Verition Advisors (UK Partners) LLP, until the end of a non-compete period.

The first respondent worked as a quantity researcher in the applicant's trading team in London from June 2016 until his resignation, giving the one year's notice required under his contract of employment on 30 March 2022. The second respondent, a global hedge fund, recruited the first respondent on 23 March 2022 to commence employment on the expiry of his notice period.

The first respondent's contract of employment with the applicant contained a 'garden leave' clause, by which he could be required not to work during his one-year notice period. A non-compete covenant also restrained the first respondent from 'directly or indirectly engaging in competitive activity' during his employment and any notice period, garden leave or non-compete period. The non-compete period was defined as the 0–12 month period after the termination date 'as elected by the company' within 20 business days following the notice of termination.

The first respondent was placed on garden leave from 30 March 2022 with his termination date being 30 March 2023. The following day, he received legal advice saying that

14 *Jump Trading International Ltd v Couture and Verition Advisors (UK Partners) LLP* [2023] EWHC 1305 (KB).

the non-compete covenant was unenforceable. That same day, the applicant informed the first respondent that the full 12-month non-compete period was being imposed on him after the termination date and would expire on 30 March 2024.

In July 2022, the first respondent informed the applicant for the first time that he intended to join the second respondent, commencing on 3 April 2023. The first respondent was advised by the applicant that this would be considered competing.

By letter dated 17 November 2022, the first respondent informed the applicant that he did not believe the restrictions on him were enforceable and that a minimum of 12 months in his new role would be spent writing software, rather than trading, and that he did not believe that he would be in competition with the applicant. A response did not come until 6 March 2023, in which the applicant disagreed with the first respondent's assertions. Thereafter, proceedings issued.

The High Court of England and Wales accepted the applicant's submission that the non-compete covenant could, in principle, be justified as a legitimate business interest owing to the difficulty in policing the use of confidential information and the difficulty in 'drawing the line' between confidential information and other information without such a mechanism. While the temporal extent of the non-compete covenant would not have been known at the time the contract was entered into, it did not necessarily follow that the covenant went further than was reasonably necessary to protect the applicant's interests. The length and breadth of the covenant were matters which the Court did not consider it could appropriately address at an interim stage. Accordingly, the Court could not rule out there being a serious issue to be tried.

It was not contested that damages would not be an adequate remedy for the applicant, nor for the first respondent.

The applicant accepted that the period of almost four months' delay on its part, having received the first respondent's letter dated 17 November 2022, amounted to an unreasonable delay for which there was no explanation. The Court noted that, had an application been made earlier, an expedited trial could have been arranged before the first respondent started work for the second respondent. This would have resolved the issue of the enforceability of the non-compete covenant without the need for interim relief at all. The matter could also have proceeded to arbitration without the need to join the second respondent as a party.

The Court accepted that the first respondent would suffer prejudice if unable to start work as expected and that his skills in a market would atrophy while waiting for a trial. The second respondent would also suffer prejudice if it were to lose the benefit of a new recruit. Thus, the delay in itself was a sufficient reason, on the balance of convenience, to refuse the application for interim reliefs.

[11.14] ***Waste Managed Ltd v Wilce[15]—High Court of England and Wales—Murray J—interim injunction—serious issue to be tried—misuse of confidential information—balance of convenience***

15 *Waste Management Ltd v Wilce* [2023] EWHC 1456.

The applicant sought an interim injunction against the respondents. The proceedings concerned former employees of a waste removal service owned by the applicant, acting in concert with others to set up a competing waste management company. The applicant alleged, among other things, misuse of confidential information.

It was alleged that the respondents had spearheaded a team that replicated the applicant's confidential business model, obtaining a significant unlawful advantage. The applicant sought to restrain the use or disclosure of certain confidential information as well as the delivery of certain listed items from the respondents.

The High Court of England and Wales was not persuaded that the respondents had misused the applicant's confidential business model or that there was a serious issue to be tried. The applicant made a 'highly inferential case, with a number of gaps … to be filled by disclosure and by evidence at trial'. At that interim stage, it was a case based on suspicions 'supported by alleged correlations', not necessarily indicative of causation.

The Court also refused the application on the basis of the balance of convenience. While it was accepted that damages would not be an adequate remedy for the applicant, nor would the respondents be adequately compensated by damages if their business were to become insolvent as a result of the granting of the injunction; the Court was not persuaded by the applicant's evidence that it would become insolvent if the injunction were not granted. The Court also noted that the applicant had failed to justify a delay in bringing its application, which weighed heavily against granting the relief. This delay increased the potential adverse impact on the respondents' company, which, as a result of the injunction, would be prevented from operating on the business model it had followed since its inception. Accordingly, there would have been a greater risk of injustice against the respondents if the injunction were granted than if it were refused.

The application was therefore refused.

[11.15] *Hine Solicitors Ltd v Jones and Blaser Mills LLP*[16]*—High Court of England and Wales—Constable J—Employment Rights Act 1996—contract—fidelity clause—interim injunction—resignation—repudiation—restrictive covenants—solicitor—enticement of clients—serious issue to be tried—implied term*

The applicant was a solicitors firm that had employed the respondent in their family law department. The employment contract, which was entered into in February 2022, provided for a fixed term of employment of 36 months, after which the respondent could terminate the relationship by giving three months' notice. This clause, clause 9.1, expressly stated that the respondent could not give notice during the fixed-term period. The respondent provided three months' notice just a year into the fixed-term period and joined the second respondent firm, Blaser Mills LLP.

The applicant argued that the first respondent was not at liberty to terminate the employment relationship until May 2025. It sought injunctive relief preventing the first

16 *Hine Solicitors Ltd v Jones and Blaser Mills LLP* [2023] EWHC 1708 (KB).

respondent from enticing away, or attempting to entice away, its clients until the end of the fixed term period. It was argued that the contract subsisted in circumstances where the alleged act of repudiatory breach by the first respondent was not accepted by the applicant. The justification for the relief sought was grounded on an implied duty of fidelity which the applicant alleged existed in this case.

At the hearing, the first respondent argued that s 203 of the Employment Rights Act 1996 (the '1996 Act') prevented the applicant from contracting out of the operation of s 86(2) of the 1996 Act, which provided that: 'The notice required to be given by an employee who has been continuously employed for one month or more to terminate his contract of employment is not less than one week'. The respondent also alleged that the applicant had accepted her resignation and therefore, the termination had been executed by mutual agreement. She argued that there was no evidence of unlawful competitive activity in her case.

The High Court of England and Wales was not convinced by the first respondent's claim regarding s 203 of the 1996 Act, as to hold with her submission on this point would have far-reaching consequences. It was noted that there were no caselaw to support the contention that any clause which prevents an employee from working for a minimum term before the right to notice arises is ineffective.

Nevertheless, the Court stated that in this case, all it had to consider was whether there was a serious issue to be tried as regards the validity of the non-compete clause. It was held that it was plainly arguable that the clause was valid.

The Court examined the issue of repudiation and the first respondent's allegation that the applicant had accepted her resignation. It stated that any acceptance of repudiatory conduct must be clear. This was usually done by express communication but could also be shown by some unequivocal act which was inconsistent with the contract of employment. The Court noted that when deciding whether inconsistent actions constitute acceptance of repudiation, the Courts apply an objective test. The Court observed that the first respondent's line manager seemed to accept her resignation (a leaving dinner was held for her and gifts had been presented); it was not until her penultimate day of work that the applicant advised her that it was invoking clause 9.1.

However, the Court accepted again that it need only decide if there was a serious issue to be tried. In order to hold that there was no serious issue to be tried here, the Court noted that it would have to be able to conclude summarily that repudiation was accepted by the applicant. The Court refused to do so and held that there was a serious issue to be tried as to whether the contract continued to exist.

The Court considered the applicant's argument that there was an implied term in the contract of employment which imposed a duty of fidelity on the first respondent to not compete with the applicant, to act honestly, and to safeguard its confidential information. The Court noted that it was common cause that the second respondent was not a 'competing business' under the contract. There was also no suggestion that the first respondent had acted dishonestly. With regard to safeguarding the confidential information, the Court assessed whether the first respondent had enticed away any of the applicant's clients. Evidence was tendered that two clients had followed the respondent to her new place of work but there was no evidence that the first respondent had enticed these clients. It was held that the migration of these clients, without more, was insufficient to establish a breach of any implied duty of fidelity. Accordingly, there was no serious issue to be tried in this aspect of the case.

The Court held that damages would not be an adequate remedy in this case but held that the balance of convenience weighed against granting the injunction. Of particular note to the Court was the fact that the applicant had delayed invoking clause 9.1 and bringing its claim.

The application for injunctive relief was refused.

[11.16] ***Evrythng Ltd v Gilbert-Rolfe*[17]*—High Court of England and Wales—Henshaw J—injunctions—non-compete—breach of covenant—interim injunction—contract of employment—executive service agreement—share purchase agreement—restrictive covenant agreement—confidentiality—damages not adequate remedy***

The applicant provided information technology services to consumer product manufacturers. The respondent was employed by the applicant as the managing director for EMEA and Oceania. His contract, the executive service agreement ('ESA'), contained a 12-month non-competition covenant which was justified in the contract by virtue of the respondent's access to confidential information and/or contacts of the applicant during his employment. The clause applied to the respondent acting directly or indirectly on his own behalf or with any company or firm in any capacity. In January 2022, the applicant was taken over by a US company and the respondent, in return for having his share options converted into equity in the company, was required to sign a share purchase agreement and a restrictive covenant agreement ('RCA'). In June 2022, the applicant's employment was terminated with three months' notice. In October, the applicant learned that the respondent was working for a competitor, albeit in a sales role, in an alleged breach of the non-competition clause. The applicant sought an interim injunction requiring the respondent to comply with the clause. This injunction was scheduled to last until 13 June 2023, pending trial.

The respondent argued that he was not privy to the degree of confidential information claimed and that much of it was in the public domain. He also argued that his new employer would not keep his position open if he was not available to work for up to six months.

The High Court referred to the tests in *American Cyanamid Co v Ethicon Ltd*,[18] that there be a serious issue to be tried, that damages must not be an adequate remedy, and finding where the balance of convenience lies.

The Court considered whether the non-competition covenant was enforceable, and acknowledged that a covenant constricting trade is *prima facie* against the public interest

17 *Evrythng Ltd v Gilbert-Rolfe* [2023] EWHC 7 (Comm).

18 *American Cyanamid Co v Ethicon Ltd* [1975] AC 396.

and is unenforceable if it is not proved that it is in the interests of the parties and the public interest. It was also noted that covenants in employment contracts are construed more strictly than say, in vendor/purchaser agreements. Further, it was understood that the utility of non-competition clauses is for the protection of employers against exploitation of legitimate business interests, which include confidential information, client connection and workforce stability. The Court noted that if such a covenant is to be upheld, the clause must be no stricter than reasonably necessary for the safeguarding of these business interests. The reasonableness of the covenant is to be calculated at the time that the contract was entered into and includes an examination of the parties' intentions.

The Court held that the ESA, which contained the 12-month non-compete clause was on the outer limits of acceptability. Although the company mitigated its length by the garden leave available, which took up the first three months, there was no justification for its breadth and duration. The functional restriction put on the clause, which limited it to activities of the kind that the respondent performed for the applicant supported the argument in favour of its enforceability. The Court therefore held that there was a serious issue to be tried as it pertained to the enforceability of the ESA covenant.

The Court considered whether the RCA superseded the ESA and noted that the RCA included a number of covenants which cut across the ESA. It was noted that the periods of application overlapped. It was also noted that the ESA non-compete clause contained an explicit reference that none of the covenants should prevent the respondent from being engaged in any business concern which related solely to activities that he had not been engaged in before termination. The RCA, however, if it applied, would prohibit the respondent from doing just that. It was concluded that it would be necessary for the trial Judge to decide whether the RCA superseded the ESA at the hearing of the matter.

It was held that damages were not likely to be an adequate remedy for the applicant. The applicant would suffer harm from the potential misuse of confidential information if the injunction was not awarded. However, the respondent's new position would be at risk if the injunction was awarded. The respondent had also given undertakings relating to non-solicitation and release of confidential information. The Court refused the application.

Chapter 12

Judicial Review

INTRODUCTION

[12.01]

Civil Service—Probation

In *Whelan* the High Court reviewed a decision of the Minister of Transport not to extend the probationary period of a principal officer and considered whether a probationary period could be extended beyond 12 months

Consultants Contracts—Suspension

The Supreme Court decision in *O'Sullivan* concerned an appeal against the decision of the Court of Appeal to grant an order of mandamus terminating the respondent's suspension and reinstating him to his position as a consultant.

Defence Forces Promotion

The Court of Appeal considered the terms of a promotion competition in the context of the defence forces in *Robinson.*

Disciplinary Proceedings—Legal Representation

The High Court considered the legality of not permitting an employee to have legal representation at a disciplinary meeting in *Governor of a Prison.*

Garda Discipline

The Court of Appeal heard an appeal of the decision to quash the suspension of a garda in *Hegarty*.

Garda Síochána Probation Dismissal

The dismissal of a garda on probation was considered by the Irish Court of Appeal in *Murphy*.

CIVIL SERVICE PROBATION

[12.02] ***Whelan v Minister for Transport*[1]*—High Court—Simons J—application for judicial review—Civil Service Regulation Act 1956—Terms of Employment (Information) Act 1994—civil service promotion—Civil Service Appeals Board—extension of probationary period—termination of appointment—order of certiorari***

The applicant was promoted to the position of principal officer within the defendant government department, subject to a probationary period of 12 months (ie to December 2022). In October 2022, on foot of a negative review from his manager, the applicant requested that the probationary period be extended in order for him to improve. The probationary period was extended until 9 January 2023. On 10 January 2023, the applicant was informed that his position would revert to assistant principal officer. A review was carried out by the Civil Service Appeals Board, which recommended that the probationary period be extended for a further six months. The Minister noted that no extension beyond the probationary period of 12 months could be granted. Ultimately, on 13 July 2023, the Minister decided that no extension was to be given. The applicant sought to review this decision.

The High Court considered whether a probationary period could be extended beyond 12 months under s 6D of the Terms of Employment (Information) Act 1994 (the '1994 Act'), implementing Directive 2019/1152/EU.[2] Although the Court acknowledged that by way of derogation, public servants are excluded from the transitional provisions of the 1994 Act, it held that the defendant was correct that it did not have the power to extend the probationary period beyond 12 months.

The Court held that, on a literal and purposive interpretation of s 7 of the Civil Service Regulation Act 1956, the defendant could not terminate the appointment of the applicant after the expiration of the probationary period as the decision to terminate must have been reached 'during' the probationary period. A civil servant who has completed his probation without incident is entitled to continue in his appointment.

The Court considered the defendant's argument that an appointment cannot become permanent by default, according to s 5A of Civil Service Regulation Act 1956 and held that this interpretation was 'misplaced'.

It held that the probationary period came to an end in December 2022, the applicant's permanent appointment as principal officer took effect at that point and the Minister's decision to revoke the appointment subsequently was unlawful.

The Court granted the order of certiorari, quashing the Minister's decision of 13 July 2023.

---

1 *Whelan v Minister for Transport* [2023] IEHC 586.

2 Directive 2019/1152/EU on transparent and predictable working conditions in the European Union. Implemented in Ireland by SI686/2022. See 13.33 below.

CONSULTANT CONTRACTS—SUSPENSION

[12.03] ***O'Sullivan v Health Service Executive*[3]*—Supreme Court—Dunne J—appeal from Court of Appeal—contract of employment—misconduct—disciplinary procedure—employee put on administrative leave—whether the employer was justified in deciding that the employee presented an immediate and serious risk to patients—whether a reasonable decision-maker would have allowed the employee's suspension to continue on receipt of new information***

The appellant appealed against the Court of Appeal's decision to grant the respondent an order of mandamus terminating his suspension and reinstating him to his position as a consultant in St Luke's Hospital, Kilkenny with immediate effect.

The respondent was employed as a consultant obstetrician and gynaecologist at the hospital since 2006 under a consultant contract, clause 3 of which provided as follows:

> 'Where it appears to the [CEO of the HSE] that by reason of the conduct of a consultant, there may be an immediate and serious risk to the safety, health or welfare of patients ... the consultant may apply for or may be required and shall, if so required, take immediate leave with pay for such time as may reasonably be necessary for the completion of any investigation into the conduct of the consultant'.

In September 2018, while carrying out surgical procedures on five female patients, the respondent conducted a 'feasibility study', involving the insertion of a small balloon catheter into the vaginas of the patients to measure the internal pressure on the vaginal wall. None of the patients consented to this part of the procedure, nor was ethical approval sought. Hospital authorities were not informed in advance and the equipment used was not hospital equipment, but had been purchased by the respondent from a recognised supplier.

The matter was reported to senior hospital management by a member of the nursing staff. An external review was directed, on foot of which two experts concluded that the feasibility study had not been carried out ethically and in accordance with good clinical practice. The review did not suggest that the respondent presented a risk to patient safety, though it was critical of his behaviour.

An open disclosure was made to each of the patients affected and they were advised to undergo infection screening tests. Although not physically harmed, the patients suffered considerable psychological distress upon discovery of the procedure.

A further, more in-depth report was commissioned (the 'SAR report'), the purpose of which was to identify 'any possible significant ongoing patient safety issues'. This report recommended that the respondent undertake accredited clinical practice training within three months and that he undertake consent training with the Irish Medical

3 *O'Sullivan v Health Service Executive* [2023] IESC 11. See *Arthur Cox Employment Law Yearbook 2022* at [13.07] for the decision of the Court of Appeal in *O'Sullivan v Health Service Executive* [2022] IECA 74; see also *Arthur Cox Employment Law Yearbook 2021* at [14.03] for the decision of the High Court in *O'Sullivan v Health Service Executive* [2021] IEHC 93.

Council. The respondent complied with the recommendations and the SAR report identified no ongoing patient safety concerns.

Senior management at the hospital subsequently sought the views of, the clinical director of the National Women and Infants Health Programme, furnishing him with the SAR report for that purpose. In a letter, the clinical director concluded that he had 'significant reservations' about the respondent's continued involvement in the clinical director's clinical practice until certain issues were fully resolved. The SAR report, along with the clinical director's letter, and the respondent's contract of employment, were forwarded to the CEO of the appellant, who informed the respondent that he was commencing the disciplinary procedure provided for in the respondent's contract of employment. In August 2019, the respondent was informed that he was required to take immediate administrative leave with pay, pending the completion of the investigation.

The CEO obtained a report from a clinician's perspective, having notified the respondent's solicitors of his intention to do so. This report concluded that, while the respondent's overall conduct had fallen below the standard of conduct expected among doctors, it had not fallen 'seriously below' that standard. The report was forwarded to the respondent's solicitors but, owing to a technical error, was not adverted to by them.

In December 2019, the appellant communicated its decision that, as a result of the respondent having 'seriously misconducted' himself, it was to be proposed that he be removed from office. In January 2020, having heard submissions from the respondent, the appellant confirmed its decision and stated its intention to notify the Minister so that the proposal could be considered by a statutory committee.

Before the committee was set up, the disciplinary process was stayed pending a judicial review challenge by the respondent, which was dismissed.[4] The respondent appealed to the Court of Appeal, which found that there was no basis for the CEO to conclude that the conduct of the respondent represented an immediate and serious risk to patients. While it overturned the decision to suspend the respondent, the Court of Appeal did not interfere with the disciplinary procedure, which continued.[5]

The Supreme Court considered whether there was any basis for challenging the CEO's decision. The Court noted that, in his letter to the respondent of August 2019, the CEO referred expressly to the fact that he was not reassured that the respondent understood the seriousness of the concerns raised or the nature of his ethical and legal obligations as a doctor in his field. The letter also referred to the patients' distress on learning that the additional procedures had taken place without their informed consent, and that the respondent had appeared to question the need for the open disclosures.

The Supreme Court found it 'hard to accept' the views of the Court of Appeal 'to the effect that there was no evidence that could be relied upon to justify the CEO in reaching

4 See *Arthur Cox Employment Law Yearbook 2021* at **[14.03]** for the decision of the High Court in *O'Sullivan v Health Service Executive* [2021] IEHC 93.

5 See *Arthur Cox Employment Law Yearbook 2022* at **[13.07]** for the decision of the Court of Appeal in *O'Sullivan v Health Service Executive* [2022] IECA 74.

a conclusion that [the respondent] presented an immediate and serious risk to the safety, health and welfare of patients'. Certainly, the question of informed consent was 'one of critical importance', as was the question of patient welfare, which was clearly 'to the fore of the CEO's mind'. The Supreme Court found that there was significant evidence available to the CEO supporting issues of patient safety, health and welfare and he was entitled to reach the conclusion that he did.

The Court then considered whether, in light of the written opinion secured by the CEO reasonable decision maker would have allowed the suspension to continue. It disagreed with the conclusion of the Court of Appeal that the CEO was required, as a matter of law, to immediately review the continuation of the suspension upon receipt of the report. The key test was not whether there *had* been serious misconduct on the part of the consultant concerned, but whether it *appeared* to the CEO that there *may* have been serious misconduct. In view of the information available to the CEO at the time, the decision was not unreasonable, arbitrary, capricious or irrational, and that was the test that should be applied here, following the decision in *Braganza v BP Shipping Ltd.*[6]

The Court noted that, in his letter of December 2019, the CEO had set out his reasons for disagreeing with the views of the doctor from whom he had commissioned a report and that his position did not change upon hearing submissions from the respondent. Also of note was the fact that the CEO provided further opportunities for the respondent to make submissions when it became apparent that the report had not been received by the respondent's solicitors.

Accordingly, the decisions to suspend the respondent and to recommend his dismissal were lawful and the appeal was allowed.

DEFENCE FORCES PROMOTION

[12.04] ***Robinson v The Minister for Defence, the Attorney General and Ireland[7]—Court of Appeal—Edwards J—appeal from High Court—Defence Acts 1954 to 2007—promotion competition document—industrial relations—defence forces promotion—refusal to consider for promotion—fixed and inflexible policy—legitimate expectation***

The appellant was an air corps sergeant with 21 years of experience. He applied for promotion to flight sergeant, which was a non-commissioned officer ('NCO') role. Under the Defence Acts 1954 to 2007, a promotion competition document was issued in relation to the role, which dictated that promotion was subject to either an applicant completing a senior NCO training course, or the applicant being certified by a corps director as having completed a particular standard of training.

---

6 *Braganza v BP Shipping Ltd* [2015] 1 WLR 1661.

7 *Robinson v The Minister for Defence, the Attorney General and Ireland* [2023] IECA 88. See *Arthur Cox Employment Law Yearbook 2021* at **[14.08]** for High Court decision in *Robinson v The Minister for Defence, the Attorney General and Ireland* [2021] IEHC 672.

The appellant contended that he had achieved the standard of training required for promotion. However, his application was refused on the grounds that the appellant did not meet the requirements for promotion as he had not completed the NCO course. The General Officer Commanding refused to certify him for the role as it was his policy that all service members should complete the NCO course unless the 'exigencies of the service' required otherwise.

The Ombudsman for the Defence Forces noted the two paths for promotion and recommended that a suitably-qualified officer provide the appellant with information as to which aspects of his training did not meet the standard of training. The complaint generally was dismissed. The appellant initiated judicial review proceedings in the High Court but was unsuccessful in his application. The appellant appealed to the Court of Appeal.

The Court of Appeal stated that, regardless of the General Officer Commanding's preferred policy, he was obliged to apply the promotion competition document which provided an alternative route to promotion, that of an assessment as to whether an applicant had completed a satisfactory standard of training. The Court held that the document provided for promotion either by completing the NCO course or by having reached said standard of training. It was held that effect must be given to the words used in the document and that it had to be presumed that said words of limitation ('either' and 'or') included in the document were not superfluous. Further, it was held that there was nothing in the document that indicated that the second route was dependent on whether 'the exigencies of the service require it'. It was held that the General Officer Commanding misinterpreted his discretion by refusing to engage with this second route. In this way, the respondents acted *ultra vires* their powers under the Defence Acts 1954 to 2007.

The Court held that the General Officer Commanding's approach was a 'fixed and inflexible policy', which amounted to an unlawful fettering of discretion. It was held that the trial Judge placed too much significance on the fact that the appellant made no representations to the General Officer Commanding regarding his qualifications. The General Officer Commanding did not refuse promotion on foot of this lack of insight, he did so on foot of his inflexible policy.

The Court held that the terms of the promotion competition document induced in the appellant a legitimate expectation that an assessment would be carried out to ascertain whether he had reached a satisfactory standard of service. The General Officer Commanding's refusal to consider this was a breach of that legitimate expectation.

The Court allowed the appeal and requested submissions concerning which of the reliefs claimed should be included in the final order.

DISCIPLINARY PROCEEDINGS/LEGAL REPRESENTATION

[12.05] ***H v Governor of a Prison*[8]*—High Court—Barr J—judicial review—disciplinary meeting—legal representation—employee challenging employer's decision***

8 *H v Governor of a Prison and The Irish Prison Service* [2023] IEHC 262.

to refuse a request to be legally represented at a disciplinary meeting—whether as a matter of justice the applicant required the assistance of a legal representative to answer charges against him

The applicant, a serving prison officer, challenged a decision of the first respondent, the Governor of the prison, not to permit the applicant to have legal representation at a disciplinary meeting.

In December 2020, the spouse of an inmate in the prison where the applicant worked (the 'first complainant') sent an email to the first respondent in which she alleged inappropriate contact in the form of WhatsApp messages and images from the applicant. The telephone number from which the messages emanated was recognised as being that of the applicant. In an email, the applicant was informed of the allegations made against him and that it was intended to establish a number of investigations. A decision was subsequently reached to suspend the applicant from duty pending the conclusion of the investigations.

In March 2020, a prisoner (the second 'complainant') made a statement in which he made a number of allegations against the applicant, including that the applicant had brought contraband into the prison and had arranged to place bets for prisoners. The applicant was provided with a copy of the statement.

By letter in August 2020, the applicant was informed that a formal investigation was to commence under the Civil Service Disciplinary Code (the 'Code') in relation to matters raised by the two complainants. An investigating officer was appointed for that purpose, though neither complainant cooperated with the investigation. The applicant attended for interview by the investigating officer but, on the advice of his solicitor, refused to answer any questions—the applicant having some months earlier been informed that the allegations of the first complainant had been referred to An Garda Síochána. In fact, the first complainant did not make a criminal complaint to gardaí, and a criminal investigation did not proceed.

The investigating officer's report found that, on the balance of probabilities, it could be shown that the applicant had made inappropriate contact with the spouse of a prisoner, that this contact had included threats to have a prisoner killed or seriously assaulted, and that there had been a breach of trust by the applicant in contacting a member of a prisoner's family without business need. Due to the lack of cooperation of the second complainant, the contraband allegations were not taken any further.

The first respondent decided to hold a disciplinary meeting under step 4 of the Code and the applicant was so informed. The applicant was also informed that he had a right to be represented at the disciplinary meeting by a serving prison officer or by an official from the Prison Officers Association (it would be contended by the applicant that the latter had refused to represent him because the matter was the subject of a criminal investigation). The first respondent refused the applicant's request to be represented by his solicitor. The applicant was informed that he was not entitled to legal representation at a scheduled disciplinary meeting and that such an entitlement would only arise in very complex or 'exceptional' cases.

An Garda Síochána subsequently confirmed that there was no ongoing criminal investigation concerning any conduct of the applicant. This being the case, the Court was satisfied that 'any perceived obstacle to the involvement of [an official from the Prison Officers Association] on behalf of the applicant, had been removed'. The Court was further satisfied, having examined the tone and the context of the words used by the applicant in the WhatsApp thread provided by the first complainant, that no threats were made by the applicant. The words used amounted to 'empty bravado' on the applicant's part and were plainly intended to impress their recipient.

The Court next considered whether, as a matter of justice, the applicant required the assistance of a legal representative to answer the charges that he had brought the prison service into disrepute by having inappropriate contact with the spouse of a prisoner. It considered that, while disciplinary investigations 'must always adhere to the requirements of a fair hearing, they are not to be saddled with the rigorous requirements of a criminal trial'. In a disciplinary inquiry in an employment context, there is an obligation on the employee 'to be proactive in putting forward his or her answer, to the allegations made against him or her'. The Court was satisfied that it would be possible for the applicant to adequately defend himself against the remaining allegations with the help of an experienced trade union representative from the Prison Officers Association, and that there was no need for legal representation.

Accordingly, the Court refused the reliefs sought by the applicant.

GARDA DISCIPLINE

[12.06] ***Hegarty v The Commissioner of An Garda Síochána[9]—Court of Appeal—Noonan J—appeal from High Court—Garda Síochána Act 2005—Garda Síochána (Discipline) Regulations 2007[10]—civil service promotion—garda disciplinary process—cross-examination of decision maker—suspension—pure issue of law—misconduct—dismissal—order of certiorari***

The respondent member of An Garda Síochána was accused of two breaches of conduct, following a complaint from a member of the public. A board of inquiry considered the accusation and recommended that, with regard to the first accusation, the respondent should be asked to resign from his position as an alternative to dismissal. In the event that the respondent did not resign, it was recommended that he be dismissed. Regarding the second accusation, a sanction of temporary reduction of pay for two weeks was imposed. The respondent exercised his right to appeal to an independent appeal board. He appealed both the determination and the disciplinary action to be taken. Pending the outcome of the appeal, he was suspended from duty.

In relation to the first breach, the independent appeal board substituted a less serious sanction, being 'a temporary reduction in pay of 4 weeks'. The board left in

9 *Hegarty v The Commissioner of An Garda Síochána* [2023] IECA 266.

10 Garda Síochána (Discipline) Regulations 2007 (SI 214/2007).

place the second sanction. Notwithstanding these determinations, the respondent was suspended. The initial reason provided to him was that the suspension was justified to allow the Commissioner to consider the position of the respondent under s 14 of the Garda Síochána Act 2005 (the '2005 Act'). He received a further notice justifying his continued suspension as follows: 'The decision of the Commissioner to require [the applicant] to resign from An Garda Síochána as an alternative to dismissal on or before midnight on 16th November 2018'. It was subsequently acknowledged by the appellant that this reasoning was erroneously expressed. The suspension was renewed from time to time. The respondent wrote to the appellant advising that the appellant had failed to abide by the Garda Síochána (Discipline) Regulations 2007 (the '2007 Regulations') and therefore the respondent's suspension was unlawful. The respondent warned that he would avail of the protections of the High Court if he was not reinstated to duty.

The respondent obtained leave to apply for judicial review of the decision to suspend him. Ultimately, the High Court granted an order of certiorari quashing the decision of the appellant to invoke s 14 of the 2005 Act where the respondent's conduct had already been the subject of a determination and sanction under Part 3 of the 2007 Regulations.

The appellant appealed to the Court of Appeal. The central question of the appeal was whether it was lawful for the appellant to seek the dismissal of the respondent for certain conduct under s 14 of the 2005 Act (as indicated in the letter suspending him) in circumstances where the respondent had already been the subject of a disciplinary process for the same conduct.

The Court held that in circumstances where the appellant had elected for and instigated the disciplinary procedure provided for in Part 3 of the 2007 Regulations, he was not permitted to invoke s 14 of the 2005 Act and try to effectively overturn the ultimate decision of the appeal board. The Court stated that s 14 of the 2005 Act, could not be invoked 'in a vacuum'. The original sanction of resignation/dismissal had been overturned and substituted for a lesser sanction. This could not be ignored. The Court held that the appellant had no lawful basis for invoking s 14 and accordingly, the appeal was dismissed. A costs order was made in favour of the respondent.

GARDA SÍOCHÁNA PROBATION DISMISSAL

[12.07] ***Murphy v The Commissioner of An Garda Síochána*[11]*—Court of Appeal—Donnelly J—appeal from High Court—Garda Síochána (Admissions and Appointments) Regulations 2013*[12]*—Garda Síochána probation dismissal—premature proceedings—presumption of innocence—fair procedures—judicial review—probationer garda***

11 *Murphy v The Commissioner of An Garda Síochána* [2023] IECA 92. See *Arthur Cox Employment Law Yearbook 2021* at [14.05] for High Court decision in *Murphy v The Commissioner of An Garda Síochána* [2021] IEHC 354.

12 Garda Síochána (Admissions and Appointments) Regulations 2013 (SI 470/2013).

The respondent was a member of the Gardaí who was on probation. Regulation 12 of the Garda Síochána (Admissions and Appointments) Regulations 2013 (the '2013 Regulations') allows the Commissioner of An Garda Síochána to dispense with the services of a member who is on probation, based on a consideration of the suitability of that probationer garda to carry out his/her functions.

On 17 December 2019, the appellant wrote to the respondent, under Regulation 12 of the 2013 Regulations, giving notice of his proposal to dispense with his services as a probationer garda following an allegation of commission/omission on the respondent's part. At the time, a District Court case was pending against the respondent pertaining to the offence of intoxication in a public place, under s 4 of the Criminal Justice (Public Order) Act 1994. The notice expressly stated that, before deciding whether to dispense with the respondent's services, the respondent would have an opportunity to make any submissions regarding the proposal within 28 days as provided for in the 2013 Regulations. This would give the respondent until 14 January 2020 to make submissions.

On 8 January 2020, the respondent's solicitor replied to the appellant. The letter sought confirmation that the appellant would not take any further steps pending the District Court prosecution until the respondent was furnished with all the material to be relied upon by the appellant in the making of his final decision. Further time was also sought to make submissions. The letter noted, under the heading 'Innocent until proven guilty', that the only factors that the appellant considered relevant were subject to District Court prosecution. It argued that the appellant had presented statements made in his letter to be facts and had already made a decision to dispense with the respondent's services. It was contended that findings made by the appellant were made without due process and in breach of the respondent's constitutional rights. The appellant failed to respond to this letter. Ultimately, however, the materials requested were furnished to the respondent.

The respondent initiated judicial review proceedings for an order of certiorari of 'the determination of the [Commissioner] to dispense with the [respondent's] services as a probationary member of An Garda Síochána'. The High Court held that no such determination was made. Rather, the Court noted the use in the appellant's notice of the word 'allegations'.

Despite this finding, however, the trial Judge ultimately decided to grant an order of certiorari quashing the decision to notify the respondent of the appellant's decision to issue the notice under Regulation 12 of the 2013 Regulations. This order was made because the respondent was not provided with a copy of the materials on which the appellant intended to rely in reaching any ultimate decision as to whether or not to dispense with the respondent's services. Further, the High Court questioned the manner in which the appellant proposed to proceed, holding that it breached the respondent's presumption of innocence in criminal proceedings. The appellant appealed to the Court of Appeal.

The Court of Appeal had to determine whether or not the respondent's judicial review proceedings were premature when the suitability process had only just commenced; whether the appellant had proceeded in a manner which impinged the respondent's presumption of innocence; and whether the failure of the appellant to provide the respondent with materials at the first stage of proceedings breached the respondent's right to fair procedures.

The Court of Appeal considered the respondent's argument that the determination of the appellant, insofar as it was based on evidence alleged against him in the District Court proceedings, was made in breach of his constitutional rights to natural justice and fair procedures or, in the alternative, the presumption of innocence. The Court did not agree that the appellant had *already* breached the presumption of innocence and noted that the respondent had never put on affidavit any evidence that demonstrated that there was a real risk of prejudice to the presumption of innocence if the matter was to be proceeded with. In circumstances where the High Court had held that no formal determination had been made by the appellant in the issuance of the notice, this argument 'evaporated'.

Regarding the 'prematurity' issue, the appellant argued that the respondent had come to Court at the beginning of the suitability process to prevent the Commissioner from continuing with the process until the determination of the criminal proceedings in the District Court and until he had been provided with the material he felt he was entitled to. The appellant argued that Regulation 12 of the 2013 Regulations did not require such material to be forwarded with a notice. The Court considered the principles set out in *Rowland v An Post*[13] and whether they were applicable to judicial review proceedings. It noted that, as the *Rowland* case was a decision after a plenary hearing, it could be applied to cases other than interlocutory relief cases and extended to ongoing employment disciplinary procedures.

The Court considered the respondent's arguments that he was at imminent risk of having his services dispensed with but held that this would only have happened if the appellant had failed to engage at all with the respondent's submissions. It was noted that the respondent ultimately received the materials sought, that the process was at its infancy, and it could not be said that the process had gone 'irremediably wrong' at the time that the judicial review proceedings were initiated.

Therefore, the appeal was allowed.

13 *Rowland v An Post* [2017] 1 IR 355.

Chapter 13

Legislation 2023

INTRODUCTION

[13.01] The key legislative developments in 2023 were the adoption of the EU Pay Transparency Directive, the enactment of the Work Life Balance and Miscellaneous Provisions Act 2023, the enactment of the Regulated Professions (Health and Social Care) (Amendment) Act 2023 and the publication of the Guidance for Public Sector Bodies with reference to Protected Disclosures.

DIRECTIVE (EU) 2023/970[1]—EU PAY TRANSPARENCY DIRECTIVE

[13.02] On 17 May 2023, Directive (EU) 2023/970 (the 'Directive') was published in the *Official Journal of the European Union* after it was adopted by the European Parliament and European Council. The deadline for transposing the Directive into Irish law is 7 June 2026.

The aim of the Directive is to 'strengthen the application of the principle of equal pay for equal work or work of equal value between men and women through pay transparency and enforcement mechanisms'. To this end, there are three key elements of the Directive:

(i) reporting measures;
(ii) transparency obligations; and
(iii) remedies and enforcement.

(i) Reporting Measures

[13.03] The Directive will require employers to report on the gender pay gap in their organisation. Gender pay gap reporting has been mandatory for large companies in Ireland since 2022, but further legislation will be required, as the Directive requires gender pay gap reporting among 'categories of workers'. In general terms, a 'category of workers' is made up of workers performing the same work or work of equal value.

---

1 Directive (EU) 2023/970 to strengthen the application of the principle of equal pay for equal work or work of equal value between men and women through pay transparency and enforcement mechanisms.

This information must be provided to employees and their representatives and may have to be provided to the Workplace Relations Commission ('WRC') and the Irish Human Rights and Equality Commission ('IHREC'), subject to the implementing Irish legislation. It will not have to be reported publicly.

These obligations will initially target organisations with more than 250 employees, which will have to report annually from 2027, and organisations with 150–249 employees, which will be obliged to report every three years from 2027. From 2031, the threshold will fall and companies with between 100–249 employees will be subject to reporting every three years.

Joint pay assessments

[13.04] Currently, large Irish employers must calculate and report on the gender pay gap in their organisations. The data must be accompanied by an explanation of the reason for the difference in pay and the measures they are taking, or will take, to remedy the difference.

The Directive introduces a more onerous 'joint pay assessment' for employers whose pay reporting reveals a gender pay gap of 5% or more between any category of worker that cannot be justified on a gender-neutral basis. A joint pay assessment must include the following:

(a) an analysis of the proportion of female and male workers in each category of workers;
(b) information on average female and male workers' pay levels and additional pay levels;
(c) any gender pay gap in each category of workers;
(d) the reasons for any gender pay gaps based on objective, gender-neutral criteria, if any, as established jointly by the workers' representatives and the employer;
(e) the proportion of female and male workers who benefited from any improvement in pay following their return from maternity or paternity leave, parental leave or carers' leave, if any improvement occurred among a category of workers during the period in which the leave was taken;
(f) measures to address differences in pay if they are not justified on the basis of objective, gender-neutral criteria; and
(g) an evaluation of the effectiveness of measures from previous joint pay assessments.

The employer must make the joint pay assessment available to employees and their representatives as well as to the WRC and the IHREC. The employer is obliged to implement measures to remedy any unjustified gender pay gap identified in the joint pay assessment in close cooperation with employees' representatives.

(ii) Transparency Obligations

[13.05] The Directive also provides for a raft of new information rights with corresponding obligations related to transparency.

Transparency prior to employment

[13.06] Prior to any employment, employers will have to provide information about salary levels or salary ranges to 'ensure an informed and transparent negotiation on pay', without a candidate having to ask. In practice, employers will be required to include pay rates when advertising jobs or to provide this information ahead of an interview. Further, an employer cannot ask an applicant about their pay history in past or current jobs.

Pay-setting criteria in employment

[13.07] Employers will have to make the objective and gender-neutral criteria used to determine employees' pay, pay levels, and pay progression easily accessible to employees. Member States will have the option to exempt employers with fewer than 50 employees from this obligation.

Right to information

[13.08] The Directive will give employees a right to information. More specifically, this provision will oblige employers to disclose to employees, at their request, information about their level of pay and average pay, broken down by sex, for categories of workers performing the same work as them or work of equal value to theirs. Employers will have at most two months to provide this information. Employers will be obliged to remind their employees annually of their right to make such a request. Employers will be able to ensure that employees do not use information acquired pursuant to this right to information for any purpose other than exercising the right to equal pay.

Pay confidentiality

[13.09] The Directive obliges Members States to introduce legislation to prohibit contractual terms that restrict employees from disclosing information about their pay.

(iii) Remedies and Enforcement

Intersectionality in pay discrimination

[13.10] The Directive seeks to clarify concepts such as 'pay', 'discrimination' and 'work of equal value'. To this end, pay discrimination under the Directive will encompass discrimination where gender is a factor, alongside another protected ground such as age or disability. It remains to be seen whether this will give employees further protection in practice, but it will not mean that employers must gather data related to protected grounds other than sex.

Burden of proof

[13.11] Currently, an employee must prove facts from which a presumption of discrimination can be drawn in order to raise a claim for pay discrimination. The burden of proof then shifts to the employer to show that no discrimination occurred. Under the Directive, in a scenario where an employer has not complied with its pay transparency obligations, the burden of proof will be on that employer to show there is no discrimination in relation to pay.

Comparators

[13.12] Equality claims are generally based on comparators. As such, currently a claimant in a pay discrimination claim must be able to identify a real comparator performing like work but receiving more favourable treatment to ground a claim. The Directive will change this position significantly in relation to gender pay discrimination—where claimants cannot establish a real comparator, they will be empowered to raise a hypothetical comparator or use other evidence to substantiate their claim instead.

Penalties and compensation

[13.13] In implementing the Directive, Member States must introduce 'effective, proportionate and dissuasive' penalties for infringements of the rights and obligations relating to the principle of equal pay. This will necessitate a departure from the current equal pay regime in Ireland, which is enforced by pay claims by individuals. It remains to be seen how Ireland will opt to implement this requirement, but it is notable that the recitals of the Directive steer Member States to include GDPR-like fining mechanisms based on employers' gross annual turnover or total payroll.

In terms of compensation for individual claimants, the Directive provides that employees who have suffered damage due to an infringement of the principle of equal pay should have a right to obtain full compensation with no upper limit. This will allow for a recovery of back pay and related bonuses or payments in kind, compensation for lost opportunities, non-material damage, and interest on arrears.

REGULATED PROFESSIONS (HEALTH AND SOCIAL CARE) (AMENDMENT) ACT 2023

[13.14] On 6 June 2023, the Regulated Professions (Health and Social Care) (Amendment) Act 2023 (the '2023 Act') was signed into law. The 2023 Act amends the Medical Practitioners Act 2007, certain un-commenced sections of the Regulated Professions (Health and Social Care) (Amendment) Act 2020, and most substantially the Health and Social Care Professionals Act 2005 (the '2005 Act'). The key changes to the 2005 Act are summarised below.

Social care is a designated profession under the 2005 Act. Ireland's multi-profession health regulator, CORU, encompasses the Social Care Workers Registration Board which opened the Social Care Workers Register on Thursday 30 November 2023. Two years after the register is opened, the title of 'social care worker' will be protected and individuals will be required to be registered with CORU to practise in the profession.

The 2023 Act amends the 2005 Act to create a two-year grandfathering period for registration of existing practitioners. This will be available to individuals who have worked in the profession for two years by the end of the period and:

(a) hold a qualification specified in Schedule 3 of the 2005 Act;
(b) hold a professional qualification deemed to be sufficiently relevant and attesting to a standard of proficiency comparable to a specified Schedule 3 qualification;
(c) complete an assessment of professional competence; or
(d) have been determined by their employer to meet the standards of proficiency for the profession in accordance with guidelines issued by CORU.

The minimum of two years' experience in social work required for registration under the grandfathering provision must have occurred in the five years leading up to an application and may include experience garnered during the grandfathering period. The experience need not be continuous. The 2023 Act sets out that CORU must equally recognise work experience obtained in Ireland, EU and EEA Member States, and in the United Kingdom.

The 2023 Act provides that during the grandfathering period, social care workers can apply for registration based on their employer's opinion as to their proficiency. The 2023 Act therefore expands the Social Care Workers Registration Board's powers to enable it to determine the competence of an employer or former employer to form an opinion as to an individual's proficiency and as to the duration of any employment relationship.

Separately, the 2023 Act amends the Minister's powers under the 2005 Act to make regulations. The Minister may, following consultation with the relevant registration body or other organisations, by regulation prescribe further qualifications which attest to an individual having achieved the standard of proficiency required for registration in a designated profession. The designated professions under the 2005 Act are as follows: clinical biochemist, dietitian, medical scientist, occupational therapist, orthoptist, physiotherapist, podiatrist, psychologist, radiographer, social care worker, and social worker, and speech and language therapist. The Minister may also amend the reference to a qualification in the 2005 Act that becomes inaccurate.

WORK LIFE BALANCE AND MISCELLANEOUS PROVISIONS ACT 2023

[13.15] The Work Life Balance and Miscellaneous Provisions Act 2023 (the '2023 Act') transposes the EU Directive on work-life balance for parents and carers[2] and

2 Directive (EU) 2019/1158 on work-life balance for parents and carers.

introduces new rights for employees in Ireland to support them in balancing family life, work life and caring responsibilities. The 2023 Act introduces a number of new rights and protections for employees. These provisions are due to take effect on different dates.

The 2023 Act introduces a right to leave for medical purposes for employees who have dependants. This provision is effective from 2 July 2023. The 2023 Act provides that all employees will have an entitlement to five days of unpaid leave per year where the employee needs to provide personal care or support to persons specified in the 2023 Act who need significant care or support for serious medical reasons. The list of specified persons is:

(i) a person of whom the employee is the relevant parent;
(ii) the spouse or civil partner of the employee;
(iii) the cohabitant of the employee;
(iv) a parent or grandparent of the employee;
(v) a brother or sister of the employee;
(vi) a person, other than one specified in any of subparagraphs (i) to (v), who resides in the same household as the employee.

The leave cannot be taken in periods of less than one day and shall not exceed five days in any period of 12 consecutive months. An employee availing of this leave must, as soon as is reasonably practicable, confirm to their employer in writing that they have taken or intend to take this leave, the date of commencement, duration and a statement of the facts entitling the employee to the leave.

Also effective from 3 July 2023 is the extension of breastfeeding breaks under the 2023 Act. The 2023 Act extends the period in which an employee is entitled to paid time off work to breastfeed from 26 weeks post-birth to 104 weeks (two years) post-birth.

The 2023 Act introduces a right to request remote working arrangements. It is due to be commenced by the Minister for Enterprise, Trade and Employment in conjunction with the Department publishing a Code of Practice. Under the 2023 Act an employee who has completed six months' continuous service has the right to request approval from his or her employer for a remote working arrangement. The request must be in writing, specify the details of the remote working arrangement, reasons why the employee is requesting approval, details of the proposed remote working location and the suitability of the location. The employer in considering the request must either approve or refuse the request within four weeks of receipt or provide a notice in writing to the employee extending the period. Where an employer is having difficulty assessing the viability of the request, the employer may extend the four-week period by a further period not exceeding eight weeks.

The 2023 Act also introduces domestic violence leave. This section came into effect on 27 November 2023, with the commencement of Pt 3. It provides that any employee or relevant person who has experienced in the past, or is currently experiencing, domestic violence will have an entitlement to take paid leave for the purposes of seeking medical attention, to obtain services from a victim services organisation, psychological or other professional counselling, relocating temporarily/permanently, legal assistance, or any other relevant services that they may require. This entitlement also extends to employees to take domestic violence leave for the purposes of supporting certain defined people who are dependent on that employee to seek such services. The entitlement is for one or more days but shall not exceed five days paid leave in any 12 consecutive months. The employer shall pay an employee a prescribed daily rate of pay (referred to as 'domestic violence leave pay'). The Government has announced that employees who avail of domestic violence leave will be entitled to their full pay. Ireland is one of the first EU countries to introduce paid domestic violence leave.

The 2023 Act also introduces a right to request flexible working arrangements for parents and carers. It provides that employees who have six months' continuous service with their employer, and who have caring responsibilities in respect of specified persons, will have the right to request flexible working arrangements. This right will only come into effect once a corresponding Code of Practice is published by the WRC.

PROTECTED DISCLOSURES (AMENDMENT) ACT 2023: STATUTORY GUIDANCE FOR PUBLIC BODIES AND PRESCRIBED PERSONS

[13.16] In November 2023, the Minister for Public Expenditure and Reform published new Statutory Guidance for public bodies and prescribed persons on the handling of reports made to them under the Protected Disclosures Act 2014 (the '2014 Act'). While the Guidance is intended to support public sector bodies in meeting their obligations under the Protected Disclosures Act 2014, as amended by the Protected Disclosures (Amendment) Act 2022 (the '2022 Act'), regarding the establishment and operation of internal and external reporting channels, private sector employers coming within the remit of the 2022 Act may also find some of the material in the Guidance helpful.

The Guidance is 150 pages long and is quite detailed. Some of the key information contained in the Guidance is summarised below and will help inform what constitutes best practice for employers when dealing with reports made under the updated protected disclosures regime.

General Guidance

[13.17] The Guidance states that overall responsibility for procedures for internal reporting should rest with the head of the public body. Oversight of the procedures should rest with the board of the public body (or equivalent), while day-to-day responsibility should be delegated to an appropriate function of the public body with the requisite authority, independence, knowledge and expertise to operate the procedures correctly.

Public bodies should also consider appointing a senior individual in the organisation to 'champion' the protected disclosures process and to promote and drive cultural change and a change in attitudes to protected disclosures among all employees of the body. Training and awareness on protected disclosures, and on the procedures, should be provided to all employees, and be regularly refreshed.

Bodies should ensure that the procedures are easily available to all categories of workers (including current and former employees, independent contractors, trainees, agency staff, volunteers and job candidates) and have regard to accessibility considerations such as language and disability. In addition to providing a copy of the procedures to its workers, it is also recommended that the public body communicates the existence of the procedures appropriately.

Senior management should be kept appraised of protected disclosures received by the public body. The level of detail needed to be provided may vary from case to case; however, for a disclosure that raises serious issues for the public body, senior management may need to be provided with all details of the disclosure. Only where it is absolutely necessary should this information include the identity of the reporting person.

The Guidance also contains a template internal reporting policy for public bodies. Most (although not all) of this suggested structure and wording is relevant for employers more generally. This is found at Appendix B of the Guidance.

Internal Reporting Channels and Procedures

[13.18] The Guidance recommends that the following information be included in the internal reporting channels and procedures and a specific process is included in the guidance:

- A succinct policy statement confirming the board's commitment to creating a workplace culture that supports the making of protected disclosures and provides protection for reporting persons. These policy statements should, where relevant, make reference to, and be aligned with, any corporate policies pertinent to the workplace culture already in place in the organisation, such as: mission statements; strategy statements; people strategies; codes of governance/behaviour/ethics; and environmental and social and governance ('ESG') policies.
- Encouragement of workers to provide specific factual information in any disclosure to allow the appropriate assessment and investigation of the disclosure; but workers should be informed that they are not required or entitled to investigate matters themselves to find proof of their suspicion and should not endeavour to do so.
- Confirmation that no reporting person will be penalised simply for getting something wrong, so long as the reporting person had a reasonable belief that the information disclosed showed, or tended to show, wrongdoing, along with confirmation that motivation is irrelevant when determining whether or not a report is a disclosure protected by the 2022 Act. The procedures should also state that a report made in the absence of a reasonable belief will not be entitled to the protections of the 2014 Act and could result in disciplinary or legal action being taken against the reporting person.
- Information setting out what types of report may not qualify as a protected disclosure, such as where: (i) the report concerns interpersonal grievances; (ii) it is the

function of the worker or employer to detect the wrongdoing; (iii) it is mandatory for a worker to make such a report due to mandatory obligations in other legislation; and (iv) the report is made by a non-worker or the general public.

— A statement that the worker must make a report in the manner set out in the 2022 Act to gain the protections of the 2022 Act and that higher standards apply when the protected disclosure is made externally.

— A clear statement that it is solely the responsibility of the worker to satisfy themselves that they and their report meet the criteria for protection under the 2014 Act. To this end, the procedures should signpost the worker to places where they can seek further information.

— Confirmation that it is preferable in most circumstances to disclose to the employer and, if that is not appropriate, to use one of the options of either prescribed persons, the Minister, or the Protected Disclosures Commissioner. The procedures should explain that there are specific—and more onerous—conditions that must be met for a worker to receive protection if they report to a person other than their employer, a responsible person, a prescribed person, the Commissioner, a legal adviser or a Minister.

— Information in relation to the external remedies available to workers who believe they have been penalised for making a protected disclosure.

— A dedicated email address for receiving written reports or a dedicated phone number/voicemail system for receiving oral reports, or both, as appropriate. Access to the email inbox or voicemail system used must be restricted solely to persons designated to receive and handle reports. Other methods for receiving reports can include online forms, mobile applications, postal addresses and internal mailboxes, as well as in-person reporting. In determining the avenues through which reports can be made, the Guidance suggests that due consideration should be given to the nature and distribution of the workforce and the workplace.

— The information that should be included in the initial acknowledgement. The acknowledgment should endeavour to set expectations early as to what will happen—and when—after the report is made, and to set the boundaries for the reporting person's involvement in the follow-up process. In particular, the acknowledgement should provide further information about the protected disclosures process and attach/enclose, or link to, the procedures that will apply to the handling of the report. Information should be provided in relation to the protection of the identity of the reporting person and protection from penalisation. The acknowledgement should signpost the reporting person to any advice or support services that may be available to them (eg the Transparency International Ireland helpline, any employee assistance services, their trade union, etc).

— Confirmation that an initial assessment or screening process must be undertaken when a report is made. This need not be solely carried out by the designated person, but can be delegated to another authorised person, as appropriate.

— Information in relation to feedback; namely, the type of feedback that will be provided, as well as the type of feedback that will not be provided, and that the reporting person may request in writing further feedback at three-month intervals.

— The measures that will be taken to protect the identities of reporting persons and persons concerned. The measures should address such matters as document security, IT, digital and manual filing in the context of fulfilling the confidentiality obligation in the individual public body and within its systems.
— The definition of penalisation in the 2022 Act, which is very comprehensive (but not exhaustive).
— A clear statement that the organisation will not tolerate any form of penalisation or threat of penalisation against a worker who has made a protected disclosure (or any person connected with the reporting person). This statement should include a commitment that the organisation will take an appropriate action—including disciplinary action, if required—against any worker who penalises a reporting person.
— How and to whom a complaint of penalisation should be made and the process by which such complaints would be handled.

Information which Should Be Included in a Report

[13.19] The Guidance recommends at Appendix A that the following information should be included in a report (and that such recommendation be contained in the procedures):

— that the report is a protected disclosure and is being made under the procedures;
— the reporting person's name, position in the organisation, place of work and confidential contact details;
— the date of the alleged wrongdoing (if known) or the date the alleged wrongdoing commenced or was identified;
— whether or not the alleged wrongdoing is still ongoing;
— whether the alleged wrongdoing has already been disclosed and if so, to whom, when, and what action was taken;
— information in respect of the alleged wrongdoing (what is occurring/has occurred and how) and any supporting information;
— the name of any person(s) allegedly involved in the alleged wrongdoing (if any name is known and the worker considers that naming an individual is necessary to report the wrongdoing disclosed); and
— any other relevant information.

Dealing with a Protected Disclosure Informally

[13.20] The Guidance states that public bodies should recognise that workers may raise concerns informally at first rather than immediately using the formal internal channels. Where the line manager is comfortable doing so, the Guidance states that these concerns can be addressed by the line manager in the first instance. It states that, should a worker raise such concerns with a line manager, there is no obligation to follow the requirements in the 2022 Act regarding formal acknowledgement, follow-up, feedback, etc, since these reports are not being made through the formal channel. The line manager may need to follow up on the concern and provide feedback to the worker, but this can be done in a more informal manner. However, despite a concern being raised in an informal manner with a line manager, the worker may still be entitled to the protections of the 2022 Act. Line managers should have basic awareness of the 2022 Act and the protections it provides, and should be able to direct a worker to the formal internal reporting channel if necessary.

Interpersonal Grievances

[13.21] The Guidance notes that care should be taken when assessing whether a potential protected disclosure concerns the worker exclusively. If the potential protected disclosure refers to information that could also apply to other workers, or other workers could also be affected, then it may be a relevant wrongdoing for the purposes of the 2022 Act. If a body is unclear as to whether a report is an interpersonal grievance exclusively affecting a reporting person, a complaint concerning the worker exclusively, or a protected disclosure, they should consider seeking legal advice.

Keeping Records

[13.22] The Guidance states that any person to whom a report is made or transmitted must keep a record of every report made to them, including anonymous reports. Records management policies may need to be reviewed and updated to ensure that records related to protected disclosures are held and managed in a manner compatible with the requirements of the 2022 Act.

If a recorded telephone line or voice messaging system is used, a recording or transcript of the report may be kept, with the consent of the reporting person. If the call is not recorded, minutes of the call may be made. If a meeting takes place in person, subject to the consent of the reporting person, a recording of the meeting may be made by the person receiving the report. If the meeting is not to be recorded, accurate minutes should be taken. The reporting person should be given the opportunity to check, rectify and agree by way of signature the transcript or minutes of the call or meeting.

For anonymous disclosures, the person receiving the report shall record in a manner they deem appropriate, the receipt or transmission of the disclosure, and such information relating to the disclosure that the person receiving the report considers necessary and appropriate for the purposes of the 2022 Act, should the person making the report be subsequently identified and penalised.

Records should be retained for no longer than is necessary and proportionate to comply with the provisions of the 2022 Act or any other legislation. Public bodies are obliged to consult with the National Archives as regards appropriate practices for the retention, disposal and archiving of records relating to protected disclosures.

Designated Persons

[13.23] The Guidance states that it is important that the designated person has sufficient seniority, authority and autonomy within the organisation to be able to effectively follow-up on reports independently and impartially. This is a matter for individual public bodies but it is recommended that the role of designated person be assigned to a person or persons in an area of the organisation responsible for internal corporate governance, compliance etc.

An alternative designated person or point of contact should also be provided in case circumstances arise such that it is inappropriate that the primary designated person be involved in the process. Specific training in the receipt, handling and follow-up of reports of disclosures, as well as the requirements of the 2022 Act, should be provided to designated persons.

The designated person should always ensure that the identity of the reporting person is only ever shared on a 'need to know' basis and only where it is necessary to carry out proper follow-up of a report. Where action is to be taken following a protected disclosure, it is recommended that a process is put in place for consulting with the reporting person and, where possible, for gaining the informed consent of the reporting person, prior to any action being taken that could identify them.

Investigations

[13.24] The Guidance states that if an investigation is required, the public body should consider the nature and extent of the investigation. This could consist of an informal approach for less serious wrongdoings, a detailed and extensive investigation of serious wrongdoings, or an external investigation by another body. The assessment process should also consider the extent to which the reporting person may be at risk of penalisation because of their report and what actions may need to be taken to mitigate this risk.

It is important to note that some matters may be of such seriousness that the investigation will more appropriately be carried out externally or by professional experts in a particular area. In some cases the matter may need to be reported to, and investigated by, An Garda Síochána or another body with the statutory power and function of investigation of particular matters.

The Guidance states that the incorporation of a detailed and prescriptive investigative process in the procedures may impede the public body's ability to respond flexibly and in a responsive way to reports of wrongdoing. Specific timeframes as part of the investigation process may also create a difficulty as the nature of protected disclosures are such that they will range from being quite simple and relatively easy to assess/investigate to being quite complex and cumbersome, thus requiring a much more substantial period of time to carry out an investigation.

Provision of Feedback

[13.25] The 2022 Act defines "feedback" as the provision to the reporting person of information on the action envisaged or taken as follow-up and the reasons for such follow-up. "Follow-up" is defined as meaning any action taken by the recipient of a report, or a person to whom the report is transmitted, to assess the accuracy of the information and, where relevant, to address the wrongdoing reported. Therefore, follow-up includes the assessment and investigation of the report of a disclosure and actions taken to address the wrongdoing. The Guidance states that the overriding requirement when providing feedback is that no information is communicated that could prejudice the outcome of the investigation or any action that ensues, by undermining the right to fair procedures enjoyed by the person against whom a report or allegation is made.

The extent of the feedback will depend on the report itself.

Confidentiality

[13.26] In order to comply with the obligation to protect the identity of the reporting person under the 2022 Act, the Guidance cautions that it is generally unlikely to be permissible for the identity of the reporting person to be disclosed to an individual who is the subject of an allegation. The designated person will need to consider this when determining whether a protected disclosure can be investigated and the nature of any investigation. Internal reporting channels must be designed in such a way so as to protect not only the confidentiality of the identity of the reporting person but also any third party mentioned in a report.

Bodies under the Aegis of Government Departments

[13.27] In relation to opening up internal channels to subsidiary organisations, the Guidance suggests that government departments may wish to consider whether workers in bodies under their aegis should be able to make protected disclosures concerning wrongdoing in the aegis body to the parent department. Careful consideration should be given to this on a body-by-body basis. Departments should bear in mind that the purpose of the Act is not only to allow for the reporting of wrongdoing but also that said reports should be received only by those in a position to determine if an alleged wrongdoing has indeed occurred and take corrective action to address the wrongdoing. In particular, bodies that are statutorily independent from their parent should consider implementing their own internal channels as, in such situations, the usefulness of making the department's internal channel available to staff in such bodies may be questionable.

Outsourcing of Internal Reporting Channels

[13.28] The 2014 Act provides that internal reporting channels can be 'provided externally by a third party authorised in that behalf by an employer'. It is a matter for individual public bodies to decide if their reporting channels should be outsourced or not.

Regardless of whether the internal channel is operated in-house or by an external provider, it remains the statutory responsibility of the public body to ensure its internal reporting channel is designed, established and operated in a secure and confidential manner and handles all reports in accordance with the provisions of the 2014 Act.

Preventing and Dealing with Penalisation

[13.29] The Guidance sets out that public bodies should be proactive in their approach to protecting reporting persons from penalisation. Protection of the reporting person should begin as soon as their report is received and continue throughout the assessment and follow-up process and following the closure of the report.

In practical terms, the Guidance calls on bodies to: (i) have appropriate policies and procedures for dealing with penalisation; (ii) ensure that senior management and the board (where one exists) implement policies and procedures for dealing with penalisation; (iii) provide training on protected disclosures and internal procedures; (iv) implement a process for assessing reports, including risk assessments of the potential exposure of the reporting person to penalisation; (v) protect the identity of reporting persons; and (vi) promptly address complaints of penalisation.

Annual Reporting

[13.30] The 2014 Act imposes statutory obligations on public bodies, prescribed persons and the Commissioner to provide a certain information to the Minister every year by 1 March. These reports must include information on the number of reports made under the Protected Disclosures Act 2014 in each preceding calendar year.

The Guidance set out the format that public bodies and prescribed persons respectively must use when reporting to the Minister. The Minister will subsequently publish the information reported by public bodies, prescribed persons, and the Commissioner in aggregate form. The Guidance provides templates and instructions to assist those under an obligation to provide information to the Minister.

BILLS

[13.31] ***The Employment (Collective Redundancies and Miscellaneous Provisions) and Companies (Amendment) Bill 2023***

The Employment (Collective Redundancies and Miscellaneous Provisions) and Companies (Amendment) Bill 2023 (the '2023 Bill'), was previously known as the Plan of Action on Collective Redundancies following Insolvency Bill 2023.

The Head of Terms of the Bill proposes to make the following changes to the 1977 Act:

(a) The insertion of a new definition of the 'person responsible for the affairs of the business' as 'in the case of an employer whose business is being terminated following the commencement of bankruptcy or winding up proceedings or for any other reason as a result of a decision of a court of competent jurisdiction, the person who has assumed full responsibility for the management of the business concerned'. This new definition is intended to capture appointees such as liquidators and receiver managers but will exclude examiners, receivers where the directors retain control of the businesses management, and process advisors under Small Companies Administrative Rescue Procedure ('SCARP').

(b) Section 9 of the 1977 Act will be amended to allow liquidators or receivers to continue consultation which had been commenced by the employer but not concluded prior to the appointment of the liquidator or receiver. In the absence of this provision, the appointment of a liquidator or receiver interrupts the 30-day period, necessitating a fresh 30-day consultation period. An additional provision will explicitly state that the obligations of an employer in respect of consultation and provision of information will apply to any such liquidator or receiver.

(c) Section 11 of the 1977 Act will be amended such that a prosecution may be brought against a liquidator or receiver where the employer is insolvent, they have been appointed to wind up the company and are wholly responsible for managing the collective redundancies process as part of the wind-up and they fail to fulfil their obligations concerning consultation and provision of information. The penalty is a fine not exceeding €5,000 on summary conviction but it is possible for a person responsible to plead the defence that, having exercised all reasonable professional care, they had reasonable grounds for believing that the employer had complied with consultation and information obligations. Section 13 will be similarly amended to provide that such prosecutions may be brought against liquidators or receivers where they fail to notify the Minister of proposed collective redundancies and the same defence may be made.

(d) It also includes a new ground of complaint upon which an employee may refer a case to the WRC. An employee will be able to refer a dispute to the WRC where an employer makes them redundant prior to the expiry of the 30-day period following notification to the Minister.

(e) The removal of the exemption, which applies in cases of collective redundancy arising from bankruptcy or winding up of a business, that the person responsible is obliged to comply with the requirement to notify the Minister only if the Minister so requests. As such all collective redundancies will need to be notified to the Minister. This exemption will also be deleted from s 14, which exempts fines in cases of bankruptcy or winding up where redundancies were carried out prior to the expiry of the 30-day period following notification to the Minister.

(f) The Minister will be given the power to prescribe that notices may be submitted by electronic means. The existing section provides that notices are to be delivered by registered post to the head office of the Department.

The 2023 Bill also proposes to establish a statutory body known as the Employment Law Review Group to review and advise the Minister concerning employment and redundancy enactments, judgments of the courts concerning employment and redundancy law, EU employment and redundancy law, international developments in employment and redundancy law and such other related matters.

The 2023 Bill details the proposed membership of the review group and is to include those persons appointed by the Minister. Members shall hold office for a period not exceeding four years and may be reappointed by the Minister. Chairpersons of the review group, where reappointed, will not hold office for periods the aggregate of which exceeds 10 years. The Minister is required to determine once in every two years the programme of work to be undertaken by the review group, subject to any subsequent amendments to the programme by the Minister. Within three months of the end of each year the review group is required to make a report to the Minister on its activities during the year and the Minister must lay such copies before each House of the Oireachtas within two months of receipt of the report. The review group may also be requested by the Minister to provide a report on any matter concerning the activities of the group or any matter referred by the Minister to the review group for their advice.

The Heads of Terms propose to make the following changes to the Companies Act 2014:

(a) The Bill will amend section 571 of the 2014 Act by inserting section 571(1A) and (1B), which will provide that where a petition for winding up the company is presented, the directors of the company shall notify the employees at the time the winding up petition is presented or as soon as practicable. In deciding whether an order should be made under section 572 the court may have regard to the compliance of the directors in notifying the employees of the winding up petition.

(b) Section 573 will be amended such that the court may appoint a liquidator provisionally at any time after the presentation of a winding up petition before the first appointment of a liquidator. The court will direct that the appointed provisional liquidator will inform the employees or their representatives of their appointment, explain the process and invite them to provide information they have which they would deem to provide a complete overview of the company's affairs.

(c) Section 593 shall be amended to provide that where a Statement of Affairs is served on the liquidator, they must in turn notify the employees of this fact not later than eight working days after they are served. The amendment provides for such notice to be given by way of email but, where electronic delivery is not possible, delivery may be made by way of post. An employee may request that a copy of the Statement of Affairs is delivered to them, and a liquidator must comply. A failure on the liquidator's part to comply with any of these requirements shall constitute a category 3 offence. Subsection 9 of the section is also amended such that any creditor can continue to request a copy of the Statement of Affairs on the payment of a fee to the court.

(d) Section 599 provides that a related company may be required to contribute to the debts of the company being wound up. The Heads of Terms propose to amend the section such that the court could have regard to the extent to which the circumstances that gave rise to the winding up are attributable to the acts or omissions of the related company. Additionally, the court may consider other factors it sees fit, which would in turn lower the test required to make a contribution order under section 599.

(e) Section 604 concerning unfair preference and transaction made prior to winding up. The Heads of Terms propose to amend the section to enable the court to exercise its discretion to make an order, where just and equitable to do so, should a transaction fall outside the relevant six-month period, or two-year period in the case of connected persons.

(f) Section 608 concerns the power to return company assets where they have been improperly transferred and the effect has been to defraud the creditors or members of the company. The amendment to section 608 provides that this section shall not apply to any transactions or payments made in the ordinary course of business, ie, the payment of wages.

(g) Section 610, concerning civil liability for fraudulent or reckless trading of a company, is to be amended such that the relevant test for reckless trading is made an objective one. Further to this, subsequent (3) would be amended to enable the court to give a wider consideration of the particular facts of the case and the threshold that an individual ought to have known such actions 'would' cause loss to the creditors would be amended to 'was likely to' and subsection (8) would be substituted such that the relevant defence to reckless trading is converted from a subjective to objective defence, requiring the person to take reasonable steps where they knew or ought to have known that there was no reasonable prospect that the company would avoid insolvency.

[13.32] *Civil Service Regulation and Public Service Management (Amendment) Bill 2023*

The main purpose of the Civil Service Regulation and Public Service Management (Amendment) Bill (the '2023 Bill'), previously known as the Civil Service Regulation (Amendment) Bill 2018, is to amend the Civil Service Regulation Acts 1956 to 2005 and the Public Service Management Act 1997, to provide that disciplinary action up to and including dismissal, in the civil service can be assigned below the level of the head of the organisation.

The Government agreed the General Scheme and Heads of Bill on 11 April 2018. Pre-legislative scrutiny was held on 28 June 2018.

The Heads of the Bill also include: enabling the introduction of a binding internal appeal for civil servants; facilitating a two-stage appeals process for the most serious disciplinary sanctions, ie, an internal and external appeal; reducing delays related to the current structure of disciplinary and appeals processes; bringing the civil service disciplinary and appeals process in line with external practice; empowering civil service managers to manage their staff effectively by providing access to a fuller range of discipline management tools; and allowing for more flexibility in the management and reform of the civil service disciplinary process and related appeals process.

STATUTORY INSTRUMENTS

EU Regulations

[13.33] *SI 686/2022 European Union (Transparent and Predictable Working Conditions) Regulations 2022*

The European Union (Transparent and Predictable Working Conditions) Regulations 2022, ('the Regulations') transpose into Irish law Directive (EU) 2019/1152 on transparent and predictable working conditions in the European Union, which replaces Directive 91/533 EEC. The Regulations amend the Terms of the Employment (Information) Act 1994 (the '1994 Act'), the Organisation of Working Time Act 1997, and the Protection of Employees (Fixed-Term Work) Act 2003.

Scope and Time Limits

[13.34] The Regulations apply to all employees in Ireland with limited exceptions, such as employees who have less than four consecutive weeks' service (previously one month) and working hours that amount to an average of three hours or less per week (previously eight hours or less). New employees are entitled to a written statement of all terms and existing employees can request that the employer provide a statement containing the new mandatory terms in accordance with the Regulations. The written statement of terms of employment (set out in s 3(1) of the 1994 Act) which previously had to be provided within two months of commencement of employment with the employer is now required to be provided not later than one month after commencement of employment. In addition, the terms to be provided within five days and one month have been amended to include additional requirements.

Probation

[13.35] The Regulations provide that a statement furnished by an employer must be: (a) signed and dated by the employer; (b) in writing; and (c) transmitted on paper or, provided that the information is accessible to the employee, that it can be stored and printed, and that the employer retains proof of transmission or receipt, in electronic form.

Whenever there is a change to any of the particulars furnished to the employee, the employer must notify the employee in writing of this no later than the day on which the change takes effect. Employers previously had one month from the change taking effect to notify the employee. The Regulations provide that a probationary period must not exceed six months but that this period may, on an exceptional basis, be longer where such longer period: (a) does not exceed 12 months; and (b) would be in the interest of the employee. If an employee is absent from work during the probationary period, the period may be extended by the duration of such absence. It further provides that the probationary period of a public servant must not exceed 12 months. The Regulations also amend the Protection of Employees (Fixed-Term Work) Act 2003 and provide that where a fixed-term employee is subject to a probationary period, the length of this period should be proportionate to the duration of the fixed-term contract and the nature of the work. Renewed or extended fixed-term contracts (for the same work) must not be subject to a new probationary period.

Parallel Employment

[13.36] In relation to parallel employment, the Regulations provide that an employer must not prohibit an employee from taking up employment with another employer, outside the work schedule established with the first employer, or subject an employee to adverse treatment for taking up employment with another employer. An employer may restrict an employee from taking up employment with another employer where the restriction is proportionate and is based on objective grounds. Where an employer imposes an 'incompatibility restriction', details of the incompatibility restriction (including details of objective grounds on which it is based) must be included in the contract or the employer must provide a statement in writing setting out the incompatibility restriction. The list of objective grounds provided for in the Regulations includes health and safety, the protection of business confidentiality, avoidance of conflicts of interests, etc.

Posted Worker

[13.37] The Regulations also contain a new obligation in relation to information to be provided to posted workers. Where an employee is a posted worker (within the meaning of the European Union (Posting of Workers) Regulations 2016[3]), the employer must give the employee the following additional particulars: (1) the remuneration to which the employee is entitled in accordance with the applicable law of the host Member State; (2) any allowances specific to posting and any arrangements for reimbursing expenditure on travel, board and lodging; and (3) the link to the single official national website (Internal Market Information System) developed by the host Member State pursuant to the IMI Regulation (Regulation (EU) 1024/2012[4]).The Regulations also increase the information that must be provided to employees who are required to work outside the State for a period of not less than one month. The employer must also now give the employee details of the country or countries in which the work outside the State is to be performed.

Predictable and Secure Working Conditions

[13.38] An employee who has been in the continuous service of an employer for not less than six months and has completed their probationary period (if any) may once, in any 12-month period, request a form of employment with more predictable and secure working conditions where available. An employer must provide a reasoned

3 European Union (Posting of Workers) Regulations 2016 (SI 412/2016).

4 Regulation (EU) 1024/2012 on administrative cooperation through the Internal Market Information System.

written reply within one month of receipt of any such request. Employers may provide an oral reply where a subsequent similar request is submitted by the same worker where the situation of the worker remains unchanged.

Mandatory Training

[13.39] In relation to mandatory training, the Regulations provide that where an employer is required by law or by a collective agreement to provide training to an employee so that they can carry out their role, such training must be: (a) provided to the employee free of cost; (b) count as working time; and (c) where possible, take place during working hours.

Collective Agreements

[13.40] Where an employee is party to either: (i) a collective agreement approved of by the Labour Court; or (ii) a registered employment agreement, and such agreement provides for probationary periods, the right to seek additional employment, the right to request transfer to employment with more predictable and secure working conditions, and work-related training, the provisions of the Regulations on these matters will not apply.

[13.41] ***SI 375/2023 European Union (Protection of Persons Who Report Breaches of Union Law) Regulations 2023***

These Regulations amend the Protected Disclosures Act 2014 (the '2014 Act') and the Protected Disclosures (Amendment) Act 2022. The 2014 Act is amended to include, at section 7B, an additional channel of disclosures, namely: 'Disclosure to relevant institutions, bodies, offices or agencies of European Union'. It further provides that a disclosure has been made in the manner specified if the worker has reasonable grounds to believe that the information on breaches reported was true at the time and that such information fell within the scope of the Directive. It amends section 10 of the 2014 Act, which provides for disclosure to third parties, to include when a worker has previously made a disclosure of substantially the same information in the manner specified in s 7B.

Industries

[13.42] ***SI 317/2023 Industrial Training (Agricultural and Horticultural Industry) Order 2023***

This Order defines the activities of the agricultural and horticultural industry in relation to which An tSeirbhís Oideachais Leanúnaigh agus Scileanna (Solas) shall exercise its functions in the creation of statutory apprenticeships. This Order specifies the activities that are to be designated industrial activities for the purposes of the Industrial Training Act 1967 and includes:

(a) the husbandry and reproductive management of animals on a farm for the production of products, horses for purposes including equestrian sports, transportation and recreation etc; and

(b) cultivation, planting, inspection, maintenance and reproductive management of plants fungi or algae on a farm for the production of products or for the purposes of conservation, recreation, sale or enjoyment etc.

[13.43] *SI 318/2023 Industrial Training (Civil Engineering Industry) Order 2023*

This Order defines the activities of the civil engineering industry in relation to which An tSeirbhís Oideachais Leanúnaigh agus Scileanna Solas shall exercise its functions in the creation of statutory apprenticeships. The following activities are declared to be industrial activities for the purposes of the Industrial Training Act 1967:

(a) design of construction projects;
(b) management and supervision of construction projects;
(c) the review of all aspects of construction projects for compliance with applicable specifications and requirements, including, but not limited to, client, industry, technical and/or legal requirements; and
(d) the use of testing and measurement methods, including, but not limited to, instrumentation and software, to gather and analyse data relating to construction projects, for the purpose of any of the matters at (a)–(c).

[13.44] *SI 319/2023 Industrial Training (Quantity Surveying Industry) Order 2023*

This Order defines the activities of the quantity surveying industry in relation to which An tSeirbhís Oideachais Leanúnaigh agus Scileanna Solas shall exercise its functions in the creation of statutory apprenticeships. It specifies the following activities to be designated industrial activities for the purposes of the Industrial Training Act 1967:

(a) the conduct of costs and/or valuation analyses relating to construction projects, including, but not limited to, the preparation of budgets;
(b) the management and supervision of matters relating to costs and/or valuation aspects of construction projects;
(c) the provision of advice and assistance on matters relating to costs and/or valuation aspects of construction projects;
(d) the management and supervision of tendering and procurement processes, in so far as such management and supervision relates to the costs and/or valuation aspects of construction projects; and
(e) the provision of advice and assistance on tendering and procurement processes, in so far as such provision of advice and assistance relates to the costs and/or valuation aspects of construction projects.

[13.45] *SI 424/2023 Employment Regulation Order (Security Industry Joint Labour Committee) 2023*

These Regulations give effect to terms of employment that apply to security operatives that are employed by a security firm and hold a security guard employee licence issued by the Private Security Authority. The terms of the order provide that workers shall be entitled to €12.50 per hour from the date of signature of the order and €12.90 per hour from 1 February 2023. Where employees receive composite rates of pay higher than the rates of pay noted prior, employers shall have to provide employees with a breakdown of the elements included in their pay and confirm that the above rates are being complied with. The Regulations further provide for a premium to be paid for hours worked between 21:00 and 07:00. Provision is also made for the rates of pay where a worker has not attained the age of 18, turns 18 during the course of their employment or has undergone a course of study or training authorised by the employer in the workplace. Overtime is at a rate of time-and-a-half for all hours worked in excess of an average 48 hour week.

Annual leave and public holiday requirements are brought in line with the Organisation of Working Time Act 1997 (the '1997 Act') and the Regulations provide that employees are exempt from subsections 11, 12 and 13 concerning rest periods in the 1997 Act. It is required that rosters will set out hours for a minimum period of one week, which shall be made available in writing to employees within three days of commencement. Shifts comprising of less than four hours will attract a minimum of four hours pay but scheduled hours may constitute less than four hours where an employee is employed on a part-time basis. After six months' service, employees are entitled to a contract of employment with a required minimum of 24 hours a week but contract hours of less than 24 hours a week shall be permissible where necessary for operational purposes.

Security firms are to provide employees with appropriate facilities to ensure their safety, health and welfare at their place of employment. These shall include protective clothing, shelter, toilet facilities, heat, light and access to canteens or means to cook/heat food, communication equipment and first aid. The employer will also ensure there are appropriate monitoring procedures.

The Regulations also provide that a death-in-service benefit, personal-attack benefit, and sick-pay-scheme benefit will be provided to employees, depending on their length of service. Employers are responsible for the provision of uniforms and where employees leave the organisation within six months of the issuance of the uniform, they may make certain deductions. Similarly, the Regulations provide for deductions to be made where an employee leaves within a specified time after the provision of training. The Regulations have also introduced disclosure of information requirements in respect of termination and transfer of contracts.

[13.46] *SI 207/2023 Sectoral Employment Order (Construction Sector) 2023*

This Order was enacted following a recommendation by the Labour Court to amend the Sectoral Employment Order for the construction sector (SI 598/2021). This recommendation came after five trade unions submitted a s 14 request under the Industrial Relations (Amendment) Act 2015 (the '2015 Act') to the Labour Court in December 2022, to carry out an examination in relation to persons employed in the construction sector as craftspersons, construction operatives and apprentices. The Order came into effect on 18 September 2023.

The Order sets new minimum hourly rates of basic pay for the sector which will increase further from 5 August 2024. It also establishes minimum pension contributions for the sector.

[13.47] ***SI 229/2023 Registered Employment Agreement (Overhead Powerline Contractors Group) Order 2023***

This Order confirms the terms of an employment agreement registered by the Labour Court on 17 January 2023 between the Overhead Powerline Contractors Group and Connect Trade Union. The purpose of the agreement is to set out terms of employment, to promote co-operation and good industrial relations between the parties and to develop an orderly, harmonious relationship to the mutual advantage of the parties and all employees/members. The agreement is binding only on the parties to the agreement.

Immigration

[13.48] ***SI 346/2023 Employment Permits (Amendment) Regulations 2023***

These Regulations amend regulation 30(4) of the Employment Permits Regulations 2017[5] (as amended by regulation 7 of the Regulations of 2022[6]). The Regulations substitute paragraph 4 to include the maximum number of general employment permits that may be granted in respect of employment as a vehicle roadworthiness tester is 100 and the period during which it may be granted is 30 June 2023 and ending when the maximum number of permits have been granted.

[13.49] ***SI 439/2023 Employment Permits (Amendment) (No 2) Regulations 2023***

These Regulations amend the Employment Permits Regulations 2017[7] (the 'Principal Regulations') by providing that the maximum number of general employment permits that may be granted in respect of employment as a line worker is 100. The period in which these permits shall be granted is from the beginning of these Regulations and ending when the maximum number of permits are granted. These Regulations also amend the Principal Regulations by the substitution of a new Schedule 4, setting out employments in respect of which an employment permit shall not be granted.

[13.50] ***SI 442/2023 Immigration Act 2004 (Visas) (Amendment) Order 2023***

These Regulations come into operation on 12 September 2023 and amend the Immigration Act 2004 (Visas) Order 2014[8] by removing 'Bolivia' from Schedule 1 which lists the classes of members which are not required to be possession of a valid Irish Visa upon landing in the State. 'Bolivia' is added to Schedule 5 by these Regulations, requiring Bolivian nationals to be in possession of a valid Irish transit visa upon arrival to the State.

---

5 Employment Permits Regulations 2017 (SI 95/2017).

6 Employment Permits (Amendment) (No. 2) Regulations 2020 (SI 510/2020).

7 Employment Permits Regulations 2017 (SI 95/2017).

8 Immigration Act 2004 (Visas) Order 2014 (SI 473/2014).

Social Welfare

[13.51] *SI 128/2023 Social Welfare (Consolidated Claims, Payments and Earnings) Regulations 2023*

These Regulations amend the Social Welfare (Consolidated Claims Payments and Control) Regulations 2007 to 2023.

Social welfare recipients can apply to receive an increase to their personal rate of payment where they have an adult dependent spouse, civil partner, or cohabitant meeting the definition of a 'qualified adult' for the legislation. One of the criteria that must be met for a successful claim for such an 'increase for a qualified adult' is that the income of the dependent adult must meet the requirements of section 7 of the 2007 to 2023 Regulations. It was previously the case that a recipient of jobseeker's allowance, pre-retirement allowance, disability allowance, or farm assist would by default be regarded as a qualified adult.

This provision has been amended by the Social Welfare (Consolidated Claims, Payments and Earnings) Regulations 2023 to provide that a person entitled to, or in receipt of, jobseeker's allowance, whose spouse, civil partner, or cohabitant is a participant in the Community Employment Scheme, will not by default be deemed to have a dependent adult. The Community Employment Scheme seeks to enhance the employability of disadvantaged and long-term unemployed people by providing work experience and training opportunities on a temporary fixed-term basis.

To complement this, Social Welfare (Consolidated Claims, Payments and Earnings) Regulations 2023 also amend section 5 of the 2007 to 2023 Regulations, concerning the assessment of the earnings of a spouse, civil partner, or cohabitant of a recipient of jobseeker's allowance, pre-retirement allowance, disability allowance, or farm assist. The value of money derived by the spouse, civil partner, or cohabitant from the Community Employment Scheme will be assessed as half value. This is less than the 60% at which earnings from insurable employment are assessed.

The insertion of section 153(4)(f) sets out that increases in social welfare payments to spouses, civil partners, or cohabitants who are participants in the Community Employment Scheme, received for an increase for a qualified child, are among the sources of income deducted in the calculation of average weekly earnings.

[13.52] *SI 129/2023 Social Welfare (Consolidated Claims, Payments and Control) (Amendment) (No 3) (Domiciliary Care Allowance) Regulations 2023*

These Regulations amend the Social Welfare (Consolidated Claims Payments and Control) Regulations 2007.[9]

The Regulations in effect expand the class of 'qualified persons' for s 186D of the Social Welfare and Pension Act 2008 entitled to receive the domiciliary care allowance in respect of a qualified child. A 'qualified child' must have 'a severe disability

9 Social Welfare (Consolidated Claims Payments and Control) Regulations 2007 (SI 142/2007).

requiring continual or continuous care and attention substantially in excess of the care and attention normally required by a child of the same age'. A qualified person includes *inter alia* a person with whom the child normally resides.

Sub-article 5 is inserted into art 140C of the 2007 Regulations. As result, a qualified child will be regarded as residing with and being cared for by the qualified person in circumstances where, (as set out in article 140E substituted by the Regulations) the qualified child: (i) immediately after birth, being a child born on or after 1 January 2023, remains in hospital or is transferred to another hospital for medical or other treatment; or (ii) the qualified child is admitted to an institution on a full-time basis for the purpose of receiving medical or other treatment of a temporary nature.

The qualified person is entitled to the payment for not more than 26 weeks in a 12-month period.

[13.53] ***SI 324/2023 Social Welfare (Consolidated Claims, Payments and Control) (Amendment) (No 6) (Circumstances in which carer is to be Regarded as Providing Full-time Care and Attention) Regulations 2023***

These Regulations amend the Social Welfare (Consolidated Claims Payments and Control) Regulations 2007.[10]

Article 56A is inserted and sets out that, for the purposes of the domiciliary care allowance, a carer may be regarded as providing full-time care and attention for a period not longer than 26 weeks in a 12-month period where the relevant person for whom they are a carer is a person to whom article 140E applies. Article 140E applies where a qualified child: (i) immediately after birth, being a child born on or after 1 January 2023, remains in hospital or is transferred to another hospital for medical or other treatment; or (ii) the qualified child is admitted to an institution on a full-time basis for the purpose of receiving medical or other treatment of a temporary nature. This is notwithstanding situations where, as set out in article 56(a), a carer is regarded as providing full-time care and attention and therefore can still qualify for the payment of carer's benefit, in circumstances where the carer or the relevant person is undergoing medical or other treatment of a temporary nature in an institution for a period of not longer than 13 weeks.

In article 136, sub-article (1A) is substituted. The revised sub-article sets out that a carer may be regarded as providing full-time care and attention for a period not longer than 26 weeks in a 12-month period where the relevant person is a person to whom article 140E applies. This is notwithstanding that a carer may continue to be regarded as providing full-time care and attention to a relevant person where he or she would qualify for payment of an allowance but for the fact that either the carer or the relevant person is undergoing medical or other treatment of a temporary nature in an institution for a period not longer than 13 weeks.

Article 167A is also inserted into the 2007 Regulations. This sets out that a carer may be regarded as providing full-time care and attention for a period not longer than 26 weeks in a 12-month period where the relevant person is a person to whom art 140E applies.

10 Social Welfare (Consolidated Claims Payments and Control) Regulations 2007 (SI 142/2007).

This is notwithstanding that a carer may continue to be regarded as providing full-time care and attention to a relevant person where the carer is undergoing medical or other treatment of a temporary nature in an institution for a period or periods amounting to not more than 13 weeks.

[13.54] ***SI 160/2023 Social Welfare (Consolidated Claims, Payments and Control) (Amendment) (No 4) (Income Disregard) Regulations 2023***

These Regulations form part of a suite of legislation enacted to extend the 'rent a room' tax relief to some social welfare recipients by amendment of the Social Welfare (Consolidated Claims Payments and Control) Regulations 2007 to 2023.

To this end, in article 8, which deals with the calculation of income limits allowable to receive social welfare, paragraph 3(i) is amended to include a sunset clause until 17 March 2025 on the exception for income (subject to a maximum of €269.23 per week) arising to a person in respect of the lawful rental of living accommodation of a room, or rooms, in his or her home to another person or persons, where that other person, or persons have the use of the room or rooms for a period of not less than 28 consecutive days.

Article 155 is also amended by the insertion of a similar sunset clause in paragraph (i) to ensure that certain means calculations do not take into account income derived under the rent a room by a person or his or her spouse, civil partner or cohabitant.

Similarly, article 174(o) is amended to include a sunset clause to ensure that rent a room income is disregarded for the purposes of determining weekly family income for relevant payments.

[13.55] ***SI 161/2023 Social Welfare (Consolidated Supplementary Welfare Allowance) (Amendment) (No. 1) (Calculation of Means) Regulations 2023***

These Regulations form part of a suite of legislation enacted to extend the 'rent a room' tax relief to some social welfare recipients by amendment of the Social Welfare (Consolidated Claims Payments and Control) Regulations 2007 to 2023.

Article 36(i) of the Social Welfare (Consolidated Supplementary Welfare Allowance) Regulations 2007 is amended to include a sunset clause until 17 March 2025 for an exception from the calculation of means, for the purposes of certain social welfare payments, of income (subject to a maximum of €269.23 per week) arising to a person in respect of the lawful rental of living accommodation of a room, or rooms, in his or her home to another person or persons, where that other person, or persons have the use of the room or rooms for a period of not less than 28 consecutive days.

[13.56] ***SI 162/2023 Social Welfare (Consolidated Claims, Payments and Control) (Amendment) (No 5) (Income Disregard) Regulations 2023***

These Regulations insert s 155A into the Social Welfare Consolidated Claims Payments and Control Regulations 2007.[11]

[11] Social Welfare (Consolidated Claims Payments and Control) Regulations 2007 (SI 142/2007).

This insertion sets out that the schemes prescribed for the purposes of r 1(2)(b)(ix)(I)(W) of Pt 2 and r1(2)(b)(x)(I)(W) of Pt 3 of Schedule 3 of the Social Welfare Consolidation Act 2005 are:

(a) the Sheep Improvement Scheme;
(b) the Agri-Climate Rural Environment Scheme ('ACRES');
(c) the Organic Farming Scheme;
(d) the Reconstitution of Woodland Scheme (Frost) 2022;
(e) the Afforestation Grant and Premium Scheme;
(f) the Forestry Grants and Premium Schemes.

The effect of this Regulation is that income derived from the agri-environmental schemes listed (a)–(f) is disregarded calculating in a person's means for the purposes of jobseeker's allowance, pre-retirement allowance, disability allowance and farm assist, and the non-contributory state pension.

[13.57] ***SI 234/2023 Social Welfare (Consolidated Claims, Payments and Control) (Amendment) (No 2) (Qualifying Conditions) Regulations 2023***

These Regulations amend the Social Welfare (Consolidated Claims Payments and Control) Regulations 2007.[12]

Sub-article (4) is inserted into art 26 of the 2007 Regulations. Article 26 sets out qualifying conditions for illness benefit claimants. As a result, where a claimant becomes entitled to illness benefit by virtue of qualifying contributions built up solely from their receipt of certain social welfare payments made to address the effects of Covid-19, that claimant is deemed to have had average weekly earnings of €300 or more in the contribution year 2021. Such a claimant is therefore entitled to the maximum rate of illness benefit in 2023, as 2021 is the relevant contribution year.

Article 45B is inserted and sets out that where a claimant becomes entitled to jobseeker's benefit by virtue of qualifying contributions built up solely from their receipt of certain social welfare payments made to address the effects of Covid-19, that claimant is deemed to have had average weekly earnings of €300 or more in the contribution year 2021. Such a claimant is therefore entitled to the maximum rate of jobseeker's benefit in 2023, as 2021 is the relevant contribution year.

Article 52HA is inserted and sets out that where a claimant becomes entitled to jobseeker's benefit (self-employed) by virtue of qualifying contributions built up solely from their receipt of certain social welfare payments made to address the effects of Covid-19, that claimant is deemed to have had average weekly earnings of €300 or more in the contribution year 2020 or 2021. Such a claimant is therefore entitled to the maximum rate of jobseeker's benefit (self-employed) in 2023, as 2021 is the relevant contribution year.

12 Social Welfare (Consolidated Claims Payments and Control) Regulations 2007 (SI 142/2007).

[13.58] *SI 325/2023 Social Welfare (Temporary Provisions) (No 2) Regulations 2023*

These Regulations put on a legislative footing the Government's decision to provide a one-off increase of €100 to the child benefit payment for June 2023. The measure was introduced to assist families with high energy prices and the increases in the cost of living.

[13.59] *SI 355/2023 Social Welfare (Consolidated Claims, Payments and Control) (Amendment) (No 7) (One Parent Family Payment) Regulations 2023*

These Regulations amend the Social Welfare (Consolidated Claims, Payments and Control) Regulations 2007[13] (the '2007 Regulations') by substituting new provisions for arts 124, 125, 125A, and 126 which set out the: (a) circumstances in which a person is to be regarded as being a separated spouse (art 125); (b) circumstances in which a civil partner is to be regarded as a civil partner who is not living with the other civil partner of the civil partnership (art 125A); and (c) circumstances in which a person is to be regarded as being an unmarried person (art 126).

(1) A person is to be regarded as being a separated spouse for the purposes of the 2007 Regulations if he or she and his or her spouse have lived apart from one another for a continuous period of at least three months immediately preceding the date of his or her claim for one-parent family payment and continue to so live apart. This will not be the case for a person who continues to maintain a spousal relationship with his or her spouse, notwithstanding the fact that, for certain periods, they may live apart for a continuous period of at least three months.
Separately, a person is to be regarded under the 2007 Regulations as being a separated spouse if he or she and his or her spouse are living apart from one another other due to the fact that the person is currently resident in Ireland under the Council Directive 2001/55/EC[14] on inter alia the minimum standards for giving temporary protection in the event of a mass influx of displaced persons (the 'Council Directive') in so far as it relates to Council Implementing Decision (EU) 2022/382 which establishes the existence of a mass influx of displaced persons from Ukraine for the purposes of the Council Directive, and having the effect of introducing temporary protection for those displaced persons.

(2) A person is to be regarded under the 2007 Regulations as being a civil partner who is not living with the other civil partner of the civil partnership if he or she and his or her civil partner have lived apart from one another for a continuous period of at least three months immediately preceding the date of his or her claim for one parent family payment and continue to so live apart. This will not apply to a person who continues to maintain a civil partnership relationship with his or her civil partner, notwithstanding the fact that, for certain periods, they may live apart for a continuous period of at least 3 months.

(3) A person is to be regarded under the 2007 Regulations as being an unmarried person if not being a married person or a party to a civil partnership, he or she is the parent of a relevant child and is living apart from the other parent. For the purposes of this provision, a parent shall include, in the case of a child who has been adopted under an adoption order within the meaning of the Adoption Act 2010, or under such other form of adoption as the Minister considers appropriate in the circumstances, the adopter.

---

13 Social Welfare (Consolidated Claims Payments and Control) Regulations 2007 (SI 142/2007).

14 Directive 2001/55/EC on minimum standards for giving temporary protection in the event of a mass influx of displaced persons and on measures promoting a balance of efforts between Member States in receiving such persons and bearing the consequences thereof.

[13.60] ***SI 512/2023 Social Welfare (Consolidated Claims, Payments and Control) (Amendment) (No 10) (Days Not to Be Treated as Days of Unemployment) Regulations 2023***

These Regulations amend the wording of art 44(1)(b)(iii) (inserted by art 2 of the Social Welfare (Consolidated Claims, Payments and Control) (Amendment) (No. 8) (Days not to be treated as days of unemployment) Regulations 2023 (SI 362/2023)) of the Social Welfare Consolidated Claims Payments and Control Regulations 2007 which considers what days are not deemed days of unemployment. The 13-week limitation which applies where an individual is subject to an agreement of the WRC or Labour Court and is retained in their occupation by their employer without taking any gainful employment for that employer, is amended such that this period may be extended by a further period not exceeding 13 weeks by the Minister.

Public Service

[13.61] ***SI 12/2023 Teaching Council (Registration) (Amendment) Regulations 2023***

These Regulations amend the Teaching Council (Registration) Regulations 2016 to enable the Teaching Council to register extra teachers to assist with teacher supply challenges in the context of the public health situation. The amendment now facilitates the acceptance of applications from primary teachers and post-primary teachers who have qualified outside of Ireland (in states which, in the opinion of the Council, would be assessed as equivalent), but who have not completed the required period of induction in the country in which they qualified. Applications will be accepted until 1 February 2024.

[13.62] ***SI 230/2023 Teaching Council (Information to be Furnished by Employer in Case of Dismissal or Resignation of Registered Teacher) Regulations 2023***

These Regulations provide that when a registered teacher is dismissed or resigns and resignation follows either: (i) the making of a complaint under s 42 of the Teaching Council Act 2001; or (ii) invoking procedures under s 24 of Education Act 1998, the employer shall, as soon as possible furnish in writing to the Council the information set out in reg 3. Regulation 3 states the information to be provided is the name and address of the employer and the registered teacher concerned; the resignation number of the registered teacher; and where the teacher has been dismissed: (i) reasons for dismissal; (ii) documentation relating to the disciplinary process; (iii) all complaints made in relation to the teacher etc.; circumstances surrounding the dismissal or resignation, ie, any investigations or civil proceedings and, where known, the current employment status and place of employment of the registered teacher.

The Regulations then provide how the Council will protect the legitimate interests of a third-party data subject where the information provided under reg 2 contains or discloses their personal data (within the meaning of article 4 of the Data Protection Regulation) by conducting rick assessments, using secure storage, passwords, encryption etc.

[13.63] ***SI 30/2023 Public Service Pay and Pensions Act 2017 (Section 42) (Payments to General Practitioners) (Amendment) Regulations 2023***

In accordance with the 2019 GP Agreement on Contractual Reform and Service Development, the Chronic Disease Management programme's Opportunistic Case Finding and Preventative components are to be extended from 1 January 2023 to General Medical Services patients aged 45 years and older.

[13.64] ***SI 407/2023 Public Service Management (Sick Leave) (Amendment) Regulations 2023***

These Regulations amend the Public Service Management (Sick Leave) Regulations 2014[15] (the 'Primary Regulations'). The main amendment is to introduce a three-day waiting period for temporary rehabilitation remuneration ('TRR') such that if individuals are eligible for TRR they shall not be paid TRR for the first three days of a period of sick leave. This shall not apply where the relevant persons' entitlement to be paid sick leave has been exhausted or where they satisfy the criteria in regulation 14(2) but are not entitled to sick leave remuneration as a result of this entitlement ceasing under Pt 4 of the Primary Regulations.

The Regulations introduce the requirement that a relevant person must have two years' service in a public service body to be eligible for TRR and such remuneration shall be paid at 37.5% of the whole amount of remuneration that would otherwise accrue to the relevant person concerned. Otherwise, where a relevant person is employed in a public service body and the rate at which ill-health retirement pension would be paid to the relevant person is higher than the rate of TRR, then TRR shall be paid at the same rate at which the ill-health retirement pension is.

The maximum period of 183 days' paid sick leave, by reference to the preceding four-year period, includes TRR and excludes from the four-year calculation a period that is not less than six months, is not reckonable as a period of service for the purposes of the calculation of the superannuation entitlements of the relevant person, is unpaid, and not a period in respect of which annual leave accrues. Similar exclusions have been provided for in respect of the maximum period of paid sick leave for critical illness or injury.

Equality

[13.65] ***SI 405/2023 Employment Equality Act 1998 (Section 12) (Reservation of Vocational Training Places) Order 2023***

This Order sets out that Dublin City University may reserve 32 places for the Church of Ireland community in its vocational education courses leading to the degree of

15 Public Service Management (Sick Leave) Regulations 2014 (SI 124/2014).

Bachelor of Education and commencing in the academic years 2023/2024, 2024/2025, 2025/2026, 2026/2027 and 2027/2028, being such number of places as seem reasonably necessary to the Minister for Education to meet the purposes set out in s 12(4) of the Employment Equality Act 1998.

Health and Safety

[13.66] *SI 255/2023 Safety, Health and Welfare at Work (General Application) (Amendment) Regulations 2023*

These Regulations amend the Safety, Health and Welfare at Work (General Application) Regulations 2007 to 2023, and provide that an employer must take appropriate actions, in accordance with the relevant Health and Safety Authority code of practice, to provide sufficient fresh air circulating in enclosed spaces within a place of work. The Regulations also provide for the introduction of the concept of a 'relevant code of practice' under the General Application Regulations.

Minimum Wage

[13.67] *SI 260/2023 National Minimum Wage Act 2000 (Amendment of Schedule 1) Regulations 2023*

The Regulations re-classify service charges as a non-reckonable component in the calculation of the average hourly rate of pay. This re-classification will only apply to the sectors in the economy to which the Payment of Wages (Amendment) (Tips and Gratuities) Act 2022 applies. This will have the effect of ensuring that service charges are not used by employers in those sectors when calculating an employee's hourly rate of pay for the purposes of the National Minimum Wage Act 2000.

Pensions

[13.68] *SI 455/2023 Superannuation (Designation of Approved Organisations) Regulations 2023*

These Regulations designate the Approved Housing Bodies Regulatory Authority, the Charities Regulatory Authority, and the Digital Hub Development Agency as approved organisations for the purposes of section 4 of the Superannuation and Pensions Act 1963 which details those provisions relevant to employees concerning the transfer of pensionable service within approved organisations.

Work Life Balance

[13.69] *SI 341/2023 Work Life Balance and Miscellaneous Provisions Act 2023 (Commencement) Order 2023*

This Order confirmed the coming into effect of Pt 1; Pt 2 (other than ss 7, 8, 12 (a), 13 and 14); and ss 32 to 39 of the Work Life Balance and Miscellaneous Provisions Act 2023 as of 3 July 2023.

Following the commencement of these provisions, employees are entitled to up to five days unpaid leave (in any period of 12 consecutive months) for medical care purposes to provide personal care or support to certain specified persons, including: a child, spouse/civil partner, cohabitant, parent or grandparent, brother or sister or a person who resides in the same household as the employee, where any of those persons is in need of significant care or support for a serious medical reason. For the purposes of the Act, a person is considered to be 'in need of significant care or support for a serious medical reason', where, owing to a person's disability, injury or illness, they require such care and support that includes the presence of the employee at the place where the person is. There is no service requirement needed to avail of this leave and the leave must be taken in periods of at least one day.

An employee who has taken or intends to take leave for medical care purposes must as soon as reasonably practicable provide a signed confirmation of this to their employer. This confirmation must specify the date and duration of such leave and a statement of the facts entitling the employee to the leave. Their employer, on receipt of such confirmation, can request that the employee provide further information in relation to the employee's relationship with the person who required care, the nature of the care required and relevant evidence relating to the need for significant care.

This order also brings into effect changes to the Maternity Protection Act 1994. There has been an increase in the number of weeks from 26 to 104 weeks during which mothers are entitled to take paid time off work and have reduced working hours for breastfeeding purposes. This change will also lead to an extension of the period during which health and safety leave may need to be considered for a breastfeeding employee. Secondly, transgender men who have given birth can now access maternity leave.

[13.70] *SI 342/2023 Maternity Protection (Protection of Mothers Who Are Breastfeeding) (Amendment) Regulations 2023*

These Regulations came into operation on 3 July 2023 and amend the Maternity Protection (Protection of Mothers who are Breastfeeding) Regulations 2004 (S.I. No. 654 of 2004) by expanding the definition of 'employee who is breastfeeding' to include an employee who gave birth up to 104 weeks earlier, who is breastfeeding and who has informed her employer of her condition.

[13.71] *SI 573/2023 Work Life Balance and Miscellaneous Provisions Act 2023 (Commencement) (No 2) Order 2023*

These Regulations commence s 7 of the Work Life Balance and Miscellaneous Provisions Act 2023, which provides statutory leave for employees who are victims of domestic violence.

[13.72] ***SI 574/2023 Parental Leave Act 1998 (Section 13Aa) (Prescribed Daily Rate of Domestic Violence Leave Pay) Regulations 2023***

These Regulations detail the prescribed daily rate of domestic violence leave pay payable to an employee for the purposes of s 13AA(5) of the Parental Leave Act 1998, as inserted by the Work Life Balance and Miscellaneous Provisions Act 2023.

The Regulations provide that an employee who is paid:

(a) a fixed wage or salary or fixed hourly time rate for a set number of hours, will receive 100% of the sum paid to them in respect of their normal daily hours last worked by them before the day on which they are absent;
(b) a fixed wage or a variable number of hours per week or month, will be paid 100% of the sum that would have been payable to them had they worked on that day; or
(c) if not paid in reference to either of the above, they will receive a sum that is equal to 100% of the average hourly rate of pay.

Protected Disclosures

[13.73] ***SI 359/2023 Protected Disclosures Act 2014 (Digital Markets Act) (Amendment) Regulations 2023***

This order amends the Protected Disclosures Act 2014 ('the 2014 Act') in Pt 1 of Schedule 6 by the insertion of the following in point J:

> '(iv) Regulation (EU) 2022/1925 of the European Parliament and of the Council of 14 September 2022 on contestable and fair markets in the digital sector and amending Directives (EU) 2019/1937 and (EU) 2020/1828 (Digital Markets Act) (OJ L 265, 12.10.2022, p. 1)'.

This insertion gives effect to article 43 of Regulation (EU) 2022/1925 on contestable and fair markets in the digital sector (the 'Digital Markets Act'), which provides that Directive (EU) 2019/1937 (the 'EU Whistleblowing Directive'),[16] shall apply to the reporting of all breaches of the Digital Markets Act and the protection of persons reporting such breaches.

Schedule 6 of the 2014 Act sets out the Annex to the EU Whistleblowing Directive. Breaches of the 2014 Act include acts or omissions that are unlawful and which fall within the scope of European Union Acts set out in the Annex of the EU Whistleblowing Directive. The Acts included in the Annex concern the following areas: (I) public procurement; (II) financial services, products and markets, and prevention of money laundering and terrorist financing; (III) product safety and compliance; (IV) transport safety; (V) protection of the environment; (VI) radiation protection and nuclear safety; (VII) food and food safety and animal health and welfare; (VIII) public health; (IX) consumer protection; and (X) protection of privacy and personal data, and security of network and information systems.

16 Directive (EU) 2019/1937 on the protection of persons who report breaches of Union law.

As a result of the insertion brought about by this statutory instrument, Schedule 6 of the 2014 Act is brought in line with the Annex to the EU Whistleblowing Directive in respect of the Digital Markets Act.

[13.74] ***SI 524/2023 Protected Disclosures Act 2014 (Disclosure to Prescribed Persons) (Amendment) Order 2023***

These Regulations make a number of amendments to the Schedule to the Protected Disclosures Act 2014 (Disclosure to Prescribed Persons) Order 2020 (SI 367/2020) to update references to various bodies and legislation to align the Schedule with recent updates.

Chapter 14

Part-Time Work

INTRODUCTION

[14.01] In *Lufthansa CityLine GmbH*, the ECJ considered the Framework Agreement on part-time work and the principle of non-discrimination against part-time workers.

PRO RATA TEMPORIS

[14.02] ***MK v Lufthansa CityLine GmbH*[1]*—European Court of Justice—request for preliminary ruling from Germany—Directive 97/81/EC*[2]*—part-time work—pro rata temporis—social policy—Framework Agreement on part-time work—principle of non-discrimination of part-time workers—pilots—remuneration for additional flying duty hours—difference in treatment***

The Framework Agreement, attached to the Directive 97/81/EC, provides that part-time workers shall not be treated in a less favourable way than comparable full-time workers simply because they work part-time. Comparable full-time workers are defined as being a full-time worker in the same establishment having the same type of employment contract or relationship and who is engaged in the same or similar work as the part-time worker.

The applicant in the main proceedings had been employed by the respondent airline as a pilot. He had been working part-time since 2010, his working hours being 90% of full-time hours. In accordance with the relevant collective agreements, pilots received remuneration for additional flying duty hours in excess of the basic remuneration when they worked a certain number of flying duty hours in a month and therefore exceeded the trigger thresholds for additional remuneration. There were three hourly rates for this purpose. However, the collective agreements made no provision for those trigger thresholds to be reduced according to their part-time percentage for part-time workers. The applicant contended that he would have been entitled to additional renumeration if the trigger thresholds were reduced in line with his part-time hours.

---

1 *MK v Lufthansa CityLine GmbH* (Case C-660/20).

2 Directive 97/81/EC concerning the Framework Agreement on part-time work concluded by UNICE, CEEP and the ETUC—Annex: Framework agreement on part-time work.

The question was referred to the European Court of Justice ('ECJ') as to whether clause 4.1 of the Framework Agreement should be interpreted so that national legislation, which made the payment of additional remuneration for both part-time workers and full-time workers contingent on the same number of hours being exceeded for flight duty, equated to 'less favourable' treatment of part-time workers.

The Court stated that the aim of clause 4.1 is the elimination of discrimination between part-time and full-time workers. It acknowledged that the part-time pilots did the same work as the full-time pilots and the two types of workers were comparable. The Court noted that, without the threshold being lowered in a manner proportionate to the length of a part-time pilot's individual working time, part-time pilots often did not reach the trigger thresholds required to be entitled to additional remuneration, or were much less likely to do so than full-time pilots. Accordingly, a part-time pilot with the respondent company was held to be subject to 'less favourable' treatment within the meaning of the Framework Agreement.

The Court noted that remuneration of part-time workers must be equivalent to that of full-time workers, subject to the principle of pro rata temporis under clause 4.2, unless any differences are justified on objective grounds. The Court referred to caselaw relating to the meaning of 'objective grounds'. It emphasised that this standard is not met simply because the difference is provided for in law or by collective agreement. Rather, it has to be justified by:

> 'the presence of precise and specific factors, characterising the employment condition to which it relates, in the specific context in which it occurs and on the basis of objective and transparent criteria, in order to ensure that that difference in treatment in fact responds to a genuine need, is appropriate for achieving the objective pursued and is necessary for that purpose'.

In this case, the Court noted that the threshold for triggering flying hours laid down in the collective agreements was not based on objective, scientific values or data, relating, for example, to the effects of accumulating monthly flying hours. Therefore, the Court held that there were no objective and transparent criteria for ensuring the difference in treatment here responded to a genuine need.

It was also noted that, in order to prove that the difference responds to a genuine need, it must be such as to make it possible to attain the objective and be necessary in order to do so.

The ECJ found that clause 4.1 of the Framework Agreement must be interpreted as meaning that the national legislation making the payment of additional remuneration for part-time workers and comparable full-time workers contingent on the same number of working hours being exceeded in a given activity (eg flight duty) constituted 'less favourable' treatment of part-time workers.

Chapter 15

Pensions

INTRODUCTION

[15.01] Various changes to Irish legislation in respect of pensions are outlined below, including changes to the tax treatment of pensions, occupational pension schemes, the proposed reform of the State pension system and the introduction of an automatic enrolment retirement savings system. Changes under EU legislation are also noted, as well as updates from the Pension Authority.

There were a number of significant cases before the courts in Ireland and the UK concerning pensions in 2023. Cases noted related to: the dissolution of a pension scheme, the rights under an Irish scheme in a UK Bankruptcy, environmental, social and governance ("ESG") investment, auto-enrolment penalties in the UK, the power of the courts to force pension draw-down to satisfy a debt, an actuary's discretion to set contributions for an occupational pension scheme, the right to marry, and the power to amend a trust deed.

There were also some notable decisions of the UK Pensions Ombudsman this year. The decisions noted related to a trustee's delay in transferring a member's fund, the liability of a trustee for dishonest breach of trust and maladministration, and the power of a trustee to return surplus to an employer on the winding-up of an occupational pension scheme.

BUDGETS

Budget 2023

[15.02] Budget 2023 (the 'Budget') was announced on 27 September 2022. The Budget did not include any policy change announcements in respect of private pensions. Announced some weeks earlier than usual, the Budget statements and policy initiatives were formed against an inflationary environment and material cost of living pressures. Measures announced included provision for double payment of the €253-per-week state pension payment in October 2022 and again in December 2022. It was announced that the core rate of the state pension itself will then increase by €12 to €265 per week in 2023. It was also announced that pensioners in receipt of the living alone allowance are to receive a separate once-off €200 lump sum payment.

Budget 2023—Finance Act 2022

[15.03] The Finance Act 2022 (the '2022 Act') was signed into law on 15 December 2022 and implements a number of taxation changes which were announced in the budget in September 2022. The 2022 Act includes the following pension tax measures:

(a) amending the tax treatment of employer contributions to a PRSA on behalf of an employee so that such contributions:
  - (i) no longer count towards the Revenue limits for the maximum tax relieved contributions that an employee or employer can make to a PRSA in a single year; and
  - (ii) are no longer considered a benefit-in-kind for the employee;

(b) bringing the tax relief available to employees for employer contributions to a PRSA in line with the relief available for employer contributions to an occupational pension scheme;

(c) introducing a new chapter into the Taxes Consolidation Act 1997 to set out the tax treatment of contributions to and payments out of pan-European pension products, a new form of personal pension product introduced by Regulation (EU) 2019/1238[1]; and

(d) providing that Irish tax residents can receive a tax-free lump sum of up to €200,000 from a foreign pension (see further below).

Budget 2024

[15.04] Budget 2024 was announced on 10 October 2023. The 2024 Budget includes an across-the-board permanent increase to weekly welfare and pension payments of €12. The 2024 Budget also introduces, from 1 October 2024, an increase in PRSI contribution rates of 0.1%, which is expected to raise €240m in a full year, to secure State pension entitlements now and for the future.

IRISH UPDATES

[15.05] ***SI 114/2023 Occupational Pension Schemes (Revaluation) Regulations 2023***

The Minister for Social Protection has signed the Revaluation Regulations in respect of the revaluation year 2022 and has prescribed an increase of 4% in the amount of preserved benefits. Administrators will need to update the records of deferred members with entitlements to preserved benefits to take the revaluation into account.

[15.06] ***SI 499/2023 Occupational Pension Schemes (Preservation of Benefits) (Amendment) Regulations 2023***

---

1 Regulation (EU) 2019/1238 on a pan-European Personal Pension Product ('PEPP').

On 17 October 2023, the Occupational Pension Schemes (Preservation of Benefits) (Amendment) Regulations 2023 came into force. The main changes introduced by these Regulations are:

(a) Increase in the threshold for transfers without member consent: s 35 of the Pensions Act 1990 permits trustees of occupational pension schemes to make a transfer payment in respect of a member without the member's consent, instead of providing a preserved benefit from the scheme, where the amount available for transfer is below a certain threshold set out in Regulations. The Regulations increase this threshold from €10,000 to €20,000.
(b) Statutory member notifications may be made by electronic means: trustees are required to notify members at least 30 days before any transfer payment is made in accordance with s 35 of the Pensions Act 1990. The Regulations provide for such notifications to be made by means of any electronic medium.
(c) Revised list of schemes exempt from the provisions of Part III of the Pensions Act 1990: the Regulations update the list of schemes that are exempt from the preservation requirements in the Pensions Act 1990. The Single Public Service Pension Scheme has been included in the list of exempt schemes, and a number of other schemes have been added to, or removed from, the list.

[15.07] *Automatic Enrolment Retirement Savings System Bill (the 'AE Bill')*

In 2022, the introduction of a pensions automatic enrolment retirement savings system was announced. The proposed new system is intended to be designed to simplify pensions decisions for workers and to make it easier for employers to offer a workplace pension. Employees will have access to a workplace pension savings scheme which is co-funded by their employer and the State.

It is expected that 750,000 employees will be initially enrolled in the scheme once it is operational, and the numbers are expected to increase over time.

Under the proposed automatic enrolment scheme outlined in the AE Bill:

(a) Employees between 23 years and 60 years of age, earning over €20,000 per annum (who are not already in a qualifying occupational pension scheme), will be automatically enrolled.
(b) Employees will be required to make certain fixed minimum contributions starting at 1.5% of gross earnings initially (increasing to 3% in year 4, 4.5% in year 7 and 6% in year 10).
(c) The employer contributions will match the employee contributions.
(d) The State will top up employee and employer contributions (state contributions to range from 0.5% to 2% on a phased basis); i.e., for the State, contributions will be levied as a percentage of the employee's gross earnings, at the following rates: (i) 0.5% from years 1 to 3; (ii) 1% from years 4 to 6; (iii) 1.5% from years 7 to 9; (iv) 2% from year 10 onwards.
(e) Contributions will be calculated on the gross earnings of an employee up to €80,000 [per annum].

(f) Employees will be able to opt-out or suspend their contributions after six months' mandatory participation. However, they will be automatically re-enrolled after two years, after which they may opt-out or suspend their contributions after six months' mandatory participation.
(g) The Central Processing Authority will be established to oversee the automatic enrolment system and will act for participants.
(h) Commercial investment companies will compete through an open tender for the role of 'registered provider' and will invest contributions on behalf of the participants.
(i) Participants will have a range of funds to choose from, including a default fund, for those who prefer not to choose, or an alternative choice of funds for those who wish to make a more active choice.
(j) There will be limited scope to access retirement funds before retirement—draw-down will be aligned with the state pension age.

While it was initially expected that auto-enrolment would be introduced in 2023; it now appears that the start date has been pushed back well into 2024, not least because the Pensions Council has commenced research into certain aspects of the proposed system.

[15.08] ***Reform of State Pension System (Contributory)***

On 20 September 2022, the Minister for Social Protection announced 'landmark' reforms to the state pension system in Ireland, in response to recommendations by the Pensions Commission. These include the following:

(a) Maintaining the state pension age at 66 years and introducing a new flexible pension age model.
(b) From January 2024, people will be given the option to continue working until they reach 70 years of age in return for a higher pension.
(c) From January 2024, there will be a move to a 'Total Contributions Approach' for the calculation of individual pensions entitlements on a phased basis over 10 years.
(d) From January 2024, there will be enhanced state pension provision for long-term carers. People who have to give up work over a long duration (over 20 years) to look after a loved one will have their time spent caring recognised in the pension system. This will be accomplished by attributing the equivalent of paid contributions to long-term carers of incapacitated dependants to cover for gaps in their contribution record, and by establishing a register of family carers for this purpose. These 20+ years of attributed contributions can be used to access the state pension (contributory) even for those without 10 years of paid contributions, as is currently required.
(e) The Department of Enterprise, Trade and Employment will introduce measures that allow, but do not compel, an employee to stay in employment until the state pension age.
(f) Employees will be provided with access to a PRSI contribution statement service each year in a manner that enables them to understand their entitlements.

(g) The long-term sustainability of the state pension system will be addressed through, incremental increases in social insurance rates over time.

(h) A commitment to explore the design of a scheme that would modify the current benefit payment for 65-year-olds, to provide a benefit payment for people who, following a long working life, (40 years or more), are not in a position to remain working in their early 60s.

[15.09] ***SI 86/2023 European Union (Sustainability—Related Disclosures in the Financial Services Sector) (Occupational Pension Schemes) Regulations 2023 (the 'SRD Regulations')***

The Sustainable Finance Disclosure Regulation ('SFDR')[2] requires 'financial market participants' to publish information on the extent to which they take into account sustainability factors in their decision-making processes. The SFDR also requires certain additional disclosures in respect of 'financial products' that promote environmental and social characteristics. Occupational pension schemes fall within the definition of both 'financial market participants' and 'financial products' under the SFDR.

On 7 March 2023, the Minister for Social Protection published the SRD Regulations. The SRD Regulations amend the Pensions Act 1990 to require trustees of pension schemes to comply with specified articles of the SFDR. The SRD Regulations also give the Pensions Authority (the 'Authority') express powers to: (i) monitor compliance by the trustees of schemes with the specified parts of the SFDR; and (ii) request trustees to provide such information as the Authority may require in relation to compliance with same.

The SRD Regulations address specific parts of the SFDR by requiring certain information to be disclosed in trustees' 'pre-contractual disclosures' (i.e., IORP II remuneration policies, member booklets/investment booklets, statements of investment policy principles ('SIPPs'), statements of investment governance and 'periodic reports' (i.e., trustee annual reports)). The disclosure requirements relate to financial products that promote sustainable objectives (i.e., 'greener' financial products) and enable end-investors to verify the sustainability of the product by covering matters such as policies on the integration of sustainability risks in investment decision-making processes and due diligence policies in relation to the adverse impacts of investment decisions on sustainability factors. The information required to be disclosed to members and prospective members must also be made available by electronic means, including by means of a website.

In order to comply with SFDR, investment managers are requiring trustees of occupational pension schemes to certify the nature of their pension scheme as regards ESG investment. It appears that the classifications outlined in that certification process have been taken directly from EU templates and as such, are not entirely aligned with the nature of an occupational pension scheme where ESG factors are not one of the many factors considered when in making investment decisions.

2 Regulation (EU) 2019/2088 on sustainability-related disclosures in the financial services sector.

To date, the Authority has not published any guidance on how it expects Irish pension schemes to address the SRD Regulations or SFDR Level 2 requirements (see below).

EUROPEAN LEGISLATION

[15.10] *SFDR Level 2 Requirements*

Since 1 January 2023, financial market participants must comply with the SFDR Level 2 requirements, which expand and build upon the Level 1 requirements introduced on 10 March 2021.

The practical steps required to comply with the SFDR Level 2 requirements are set out in the Regulatory Technical Standards ('RTS') published by the European Commission in April 2022. The RTS set out a template adverse sustainability impacts statement to be completed by financial market participants and published on their website by 30 June each year, covering the period from 1 January to 31 December in the preceding year. If financial market participants do not complete an adverse sustainability impacts statement, they must instead publish a statement on their website stating that they do not consider the adverse impacts of their investment decisions on sustainability factors.

The RTS also set out template pre-contractual disclosures and periodic reporting disclosures for financial products falling within art 8 or art 9 of the SFDR, namely products that promote, among other characteristics, environmental or social characteristics (eg, so-called 'article 8' investment fund options) or products that have sustainable investment as their objective (eg, 'article 9' investment fund options).

[15.11] *Digital Operational Resilience Directive*

Regulation (EU) 2022/2554 on digital operational resilience for the financial sector ('DORA') and Directive (EU) 2022/2556 ('DORA Amending Directive') form part of the EU's Digital Finance Package. DORA creates a harmonised, regulatory framework strengthening the information and communication technology ('ICT') security of financial entities (which includes pension schemes). Its objective is to achieve a high common level of digital operational resilience across all EU Member States.

DORA and DORA Amending Directive came into force on 16 January 2023 and will be directly effective from 17 January 2025.

Exemptions apply for pension schemes which do not have more than 15 members in total, and certain derogations apply to pension schemes which have fewer than 100 members in total.

DORA requires financial entities to:

(a) have in place an internal governance and control framework that ensures effective and prudent management of ICT risk;

(b) use and maintain updated ICT systems, protocols and tools that meet specified requirements;
(c) monitor and control the security and functioning of ICT systems and tools and to minimise the impact of ICT risk on ICT systems;
(d) put in place a comprehensive ICT business continuity policy;
(e) include certain prescribed, key contractual terms in contracts with third-party ICT providers; and
(f) report major ICT-related incidents to the relevant competent authority.

To date, the Pensions Authority has not published any guidance on how it expects Irish pension schemes to address the requirements of DORA. In the absence of such guidance, there would appear to be two ways to address compliance: either to include a 'DORA policy' alongside the existing IORP II[3] policies; or incorporate appropriate DORA additions into each of the relevant IORP II policies.

[15.12] *Expiry of the Final EMIR Clearing Exemption for Pension Schemes*

On 18 June 2023, the exemption for pension schemes from the central clearing obligations of the European Market Infrastructure Regulation ('EMIR') expired. The EMIR central clearing obligation requires pension schemes to clear over-the-counter derivative contracts with a central clearing party. The exemption had previously been extended on a number of occasions to allow further time to finalise the operational measures required for central clearing to operate efficiently. The UK has taken a different approach in this area, extending the exemption for pension schemes from the central clearing obligation under the UK equivalent of EMIR until 18 June 2025.

PENSION AUTHORITY UPDATES

[15.13] *Authority Settles Legal Proceedings to Remove Professional Trustee*

On 28 March 2023, the Authority announced that it had settled legal proceedings in relation to an application to the High Court under s 63 of the Pensions Act 1990 to remove the professional trustee of seven small, self-administered pension schemes ('SSAPs').

The Authority resolved to suspend the legal proceedings on the basis that the professional trustee agreed that they would: (a) cease to act as trustee of the seven sample SSAPs and would co-ordinate the appointment of a replacement professional trustee within six weeks; (b) cease to act as trustee of all other SSAPs within 12 months; (c) not accept any new appointment to act as a pension scheme trustee for a five-year

3 Directive (EU) 2016/2341 on the activities and supervision of institutions for occupational retirement provision (IORPs) (recast).

period; and (d) communicate with impacted scheme members and employers to inform them of the process by which they would cease to act as trustee and a replacement appointed.

The Authority stated that the resolution achieved was the 'best outcome for members by avoiding legal proceedings, minimising costs and reducing the risk of disorderly transfer'. The case nonetheless demonstrates that the Authority is willing to use its powers under the Pensions Act 1990 to seek the removal of trustees where the Authority considers that they are failing to act in members' best interests, in particular where the Authority perceives a conflict between the interests of members and the personal or financial interests of trustees.

[15.14] *Pensions Authority Annual Report and Accounts for 2022*

On 4 September 2023, the Authority published its annual report and accounts for 2022,[4] accompanied by a statement from the Pensions Regulator.

The report noted that the Authority concluded five prosecutions in 2022, resulting in one conviction in relation to non-remittance of employee contributions under s 58A(1) of the Pensions Act 1990. The four other prosecutions were struck out due to payment of arrears, or the underlying matter being resolved advance of the court date.

In 2022, the Authority also opened 15 new investigations into various alleged breaches of the Pensions Act 1990, while 17 investigations were finalised and closed. The majority of new investigations opened related to suspected non-remittance of contributions or a suspected failure to pay benefits.

The Pensions Regulator's (the 'Regulator') statement highlighted a number of points that may be relevant for defined benefit ('DB') schemes:

(a) As a result of the transposition of IORP II, the Authority is now obliged to apply a system of forward-looking, risk-based supervision to pension schemes. The Regulator stated that this system would be implemented 'in the coming months and years as the IORP II transition is completed'.
(b) The Regulator noted that trustees and their advisers have been looking to the Authority for guidance on risk assessment and other IORP II-related matters. The Regulator acknowledged that the provision of guidance is part of the Authority's responsibilities and that the Authority will continue to provide such guidance where appropriate, but noted that trustees' responsibilities are not limited to merely following guidance and that the Authority expects trustees to be pro-active in addressing the interests of members and beneficiaries of their schemes.
(c) The Authority considers that there are lessons to be learned from the issues that arose in the UK pensions market regarding liability driven investments ('LDI') in

4 Available at: *https://pensionsauthority.ie/wp-content/uploads/2023/10/the_pensions_authority_annual_report_and_accounts_2022.pdf* [last accessed 8 November 2023].

autumn 2022. The Authority is reviewing this area and is considering issuing guidance on this topic later in 2023.

(d) The Regulator also noted that the Authority has concerns regarding unlisted, unregulated investments and whether these are appropriate for scheme members in all cases. The Authority will address this point further as part of its forward-looking, risk-based supervision/approach.

[15.15] *Pensions Authority Statistics for Funded Defined Benefit Schemes*

On 31 October 2023, the Pensions Authority published its annual defined benefit ('DB') scheme statistics. These statistics are compiled from the annual actuarial data returns ('AADRs') that are required to be submitted by funded DB schemes to the Authority under reg 23 of the Occupational Pension Schemes (Disclosure of Information) Regulations 2006,[5] as amended.

The 2023 publication is presented in a time series format. It includes statistics for previous years based on data from AADR submissions with effective dates up to and including 31 December 2022. The data excludes AADR submissions for single large pension schemes subject to the funding standard, in which members build up retirement benefits exclusively on a defined contribution basis. In addition, small schemes that are in wind-up in any given year are also generally excluded from the statistics, given that such schemes are not required to submit an AADR.

The Authority noted that the statistics in the 2023 publication are not directly comparable with figures published in previous years, previous reports aggregated the data of the most recent AADR submitted by each scheme at the publication date. Therefore, past figures for any year were based on AADRs spread across more than one calendar year.

[15.16] *Pensions Authority Own-Risk Assessment Guidance for Trustees*

On 11 October 2023, the Pensions Authority published its guidance for trustees on the own-risk assessment ('ORA') that is required under s 64AL of the Pensions Act 1990. Both s 64AL and Chapter 3 of the Pensions Authority's Code of Practice for trustees outline the requirement for trustees to complete and document an ORA at least once every three years; and without delay following any significant change in the risk profiles of a pension scheme or trust retirement annuity contract.

The guidance states that the purpose of the ORA is to provide an objective assessment of risk by identifying the actions needed to effectively manage and, where appropriate, mitigate the risks identified; it is not merely a rationalisation of the scheme's current position. Its overall purpose is to ensure members' benefits are well protected and that

---

5 Occupational Pension Schemes (Disclosure of Information) Regulations 2006 (SI 310/2006).

the scheme delivers good member outcomes. Therefore, the ORA must be a periodic, structured, and thorough assessment of the risks a scheme faces by its trustees.

Notably, the guidance also states that the quality and integrity of the ORA is the responsibility of the trustees. While trustees may engage professional advice to ensure that the ORA is fit for purpose, the trustees remain responsible for the design of the ORA process and the delivery of the ORA itself. Furthermore, the guidance reminds trustees that the ORA process should not be mechanistic and that it should be sufficiently considered by the trustees and flexible to work within a scheme's individual risk profile.

In the Appendix to the Authority's guidance, there are six areas of consideration listed which trustees can check. These include: governance and process; risk identification; measurement and evaluation; risk mitigation; monitoring and review; and documentation and reporting.

[15.17] *Updated Pension Benefit Statement Projection Assumptions*

Under reg 33 of the European Union (Occupational Pension Schemes) Regulations 2021[6] (the 'IORP II Regulations'), the trustees of a funded scheme must provide active and deferred members with an annual pension benefit statement ('PBS') which contains key information prescribed in the IORP II Regulations in relation to their pension benefits.[7]

A PBS must include a projection of the estimated value of a member's benefits at retirement. On 10 March 2023, the Authority published its updated guidance on the assumptions to be used in preparing these projections. Many of the changes in the updated guidance reflect the persistence of high inflation and the rapid increase in interest rates since the Authority's original guidance was published in July 2022. These changes include:

(a) an increase in the assumed maximum, gross investment return for equities and property from 4% p.a. to 5.75% p.a.;
(b) an increase in the assumed maximum, gross investment return for fixed interest securities from 1% p.a. to 2.5% p.a.;
(c) an increase in the assumed salary inflation rate or benefit deflation rate from 1.5% p.a. to 3% p.a.; and
(d) an increase in the assumed maximum interest rate for annuity calculations from 0.5% p.a to 2% p.a.

The updated guidance must be applied to any PBSs being prepared with an effective date on or after 1 May 2023.

---

6 European Union (Occupational Pension Schemes) Regulations 2021 (SI 637/2021).

7 Trustees of unfunded schemes continue to be required to provide an "Annual Benefit Statement" under Regulation 13 of the Occupational Pensions Scheme (Disbursement of Information) Regulations, 2006.

[15.18] *Pensions Authority Membership and PRSA Data as at 31 December 2022*

Alongside its summary of regulatory activity, the Authority also published a summary of occupational pension scheme membership and PRSA data as at 31 December 2022. The data shows that:

(a) the total number of DB schemes decreased from 658 to 636 in the course of 2022 (with a further 183 of these 636 schemes labelled as 'frozen' and 14 labelled as being 'in wind-up');
(b) the total number of defined contribution schemes decreased from 85,964 to 85,228 in the course of 2022; and
(c) the number of PRSA contracts increased by 19,175 in the course of 2022, so that the total number of PRSAs at 31 December 2022 was 349,326 with total assets under management of €8.9 billion.

[15.19] *Pensions Authority Engagement and Audit Findings Report 2022*

On 15 December 2022, the Authority published its Engagement and Audit Findings Report[8] for 2022. The purpose of the report is to share observations on the key findings identified during the Authority's engagement and audit activity in 2022. The engagement programme included face-to-face meetings with the trustees of a number of large defined benefit and defined contribution schemes. The Authority also conducted a series of compliance audits on one-member arrangements and an audit of pension scheme trustees' obligation to prepare the 2021 annual compliance statement.

The report found that most schemes the Authority reviewed appeared to be taking steps to address the significantly enhanced governance standards introduced in 2021, but the pace of change is slow and needs to be accelerated. The Authority found instances of non-compliance among the majority of schemes it looked at. Areas for improvement identified by the Authority included:

(a) The structure of trustee boards: the Authority found that few trustee boards had reviewed their composition to assess whether their mix of skills, knowledge and experience was adequate for good governance of the scheme. Many trustee boards relied heavily on one individual who was considered to have superior knowledge or experience. The Authority expects all trustees to play an active part in scheme stewardship.
(b) Outsourcing: the Authority identified a lack of scrutiny by trustees over their outsourced service providers, in particular, scheme administrators. Trustees should regularly review the performance of service providers and evidence of such reviews should be documented and available for inspection by the Authority.
(c) Scheme policies: the Authority noted that, while plans for the completion of written scheme policies by the IORP II compliance deadline were in place, many schemes

8 Available at: *https://pensionsauthority.ie/wp-content/uploads/2022/12/engagement_and_audit-findings-report-2022.pdf* [last accessed 8 November 2023].

were adopting template policies without sufficient consideration of content and scheme-specific appropriateness.

(d) Investment: the Authority noted that it did not see enough evidence of trustees reviewing investment information and evaluating fund performance, fund managers and their investment advisers. The Authority expects trustees to be active in assessing their investments, probing the investment information presented to them and considering value for money.

The Authority noted that it expects all trustee boards and their advisers to consider its findings and evaluate their own practices to establish if any improvements are required.

REVENUE UPDATES TO PENSIONS MANUAL

[15.20] Throughout 2023 a number of updates were made to the Pensions Manual (the 'Manual') including:

[15.21] *Chapter 10 Benefits on Death in Service*

On 27 July 2023, the Revenue updated Chapter 10 of the Manual to clarify that where a pension scheme member dies in service, the balance of the deceased member's benefits (after taking a tax-free lump sum) can be paid as an annuity or transferred into an Approved Retirement Fund, but cannot be paid as a taxable lump sum to the surviving spouse, civil partner or dependant.

[15.22] *Chapter 25 Limit on Tax-Relieved Pension Funds and Lump Sums*

On 1 February 2023, Chapter 25 of the Manual was updated to include detail on the method to be used to calculate the present value of the pension lump sum for the purposes of the Standard Capital Superannuation Benefit calculation.

[15.23] *Chapter 27 Taxation of Retirement Lump Sums*

On 6 July 2023, the Revenue updated Chapter 27 of the Manual to provide further information on the payroll notification and filing requirements for excess lump sums. This update will primarily be of relevance to scheme administrators required to process retirement lump sums that exceed statutory tax-free limits.

[15.24] *Chapter 29 Dual Private/Public Pension Scheme Encashment Option*

On 5 September 2023, the Revenue updated Chapter 29 of the Manual to clarify who can qualify for the encashment option, how to submit declarations to Revenue and how to update the Revenue contact address.

CASELAW

[15.25] ***Re Trustees of the Meadowvale Pension Scheme[9]—High Court—Roberts J—trust assets—dissolution of pension scheme—failure of trustees to divest themselves of trust assets before purporting to wind up pension scheme—whether the trust assets remained vested in the trustees following the purported winding up***

The applicants were trustees of the Meadowvale Pension Scheme (the "Scheme"). The Scheme was the registered owner of shares in African Gateway Convention and Exhibition Precinct Proprietary Ltd, the notice party, having acquired the shareholding in December 2005. The applicants conceded that the trustees had failed to properly divest themselves of the shareholding before purporting to wind up the scheme in 2011.

The question before the Court was whether the notice party's shareholding continued to be vested in the trustees following the purported dissolution of the Scheme. The notice party argued that the shareholding was *prima facie* property to which the State was entitled as *bona vacantia*. The applicants argued that the shares never left the hands of the trustees.

The Court found that the deed of wind-up was incorrectly predicated on the understanding that all of the trust assets of the scheme had been disposed of by the date of dissolution. The deed of wind up did not provide for the divestiture of assets inadvertently held by trustees and was fundamentally flawed. As the shares in the notice party had not been effectively transferred prior to the purported wind up, there was no divestiture of the shares by the trustees. Accordingly, the shares never validly parted from the trustees, despite the deed of wind-up, and remained subject to a trust.

The Court did not consider that the notice party's shares could be equated to a 'surplus' of trust funds. There had been no redistribution of assets. Further, the winding up was not accepted as a valid by Revenue and, in practical terms, the Scheme continued to be treated as live.

[15.26] ***Wilson v McNamara[10]—Court of Appeal of England and Wales—Lewison, Newey & Baker LJJ—appeal from High Court—Treaty on the Functioning of the European Union, art 49—rights in Irish scheme in UK bankruptcy—indirect discrimination—objective justification***

This was an appeal in relation to whether pension schemes recognised for tax purposes in an EU Member State are protected in UK bankruptcy proceedings by the operation of art 49 of the Treaty on the Functioning of the European Union (the 'TFEU'). The Court of Appeal of English and Wales unanimously upheld the High Court judgment but also stated that although the decision sets a precedent, it will not preclude anyone in further

---

9 *In the matter of an application by O'Rourke and Anor as Trustees of the Meadowvale Pension Scheme* [2023] IEHC 148.

10 *Wilson v McNamara* [2023] EWCA Civ 20. See *Arthur Cox Employment Law Yearbook 2022* at **[16.41]** for decision of High Court of England and Wales in *Wilson and another (joint trustees in bankruptcy of Michael Bernard McNamara) v McNamara* [2022] EWHC 243 (Ch).

proceedings from arguing that the indirect discrimination as it occurred in this case is in fact objectively justified.

The case involved Mr McNamara, an Irish national with rights in an Irish pension scheme (the Simcoe Scheme), who was made bankrupt in England. The underlying issue was whether his entitlement under a pension scheme established in Ireland formed part of his bankruptcy estate in the UK. Mr McNamara argued that the UK legislation, which on its face did not exclude his entitlement under the Simcoe Scheme from forming part of his bankruptcy estate, was incompatible with EU law, as the Simcoe Scheme was governed by Irish law and it was not registered under s 153 of the UK Finance Act 2004. However, his trustees in bankruptcy argued that his entitlement under the Simcoe Scheme did form part of his bankruptcy estate.

In November 2019, Nugee LJ ruled that the preliminary issue was that the UK legislation which, on its face differentiates between UK pension schemes and foreign schemes may be incompatible with EU law. The case was therefore referred to the CJEU to decide whether the UK legislation was contrary to EU law.

In November 2021, the CJEU held that the exemption placed migrant workers at a particular disadvantage because most migrant workers would have their pension rights in schemes established outside the UK, which would not in general be approved for tax purposes in the UK. The CJEU found that UK law was indirectly discriminatory on this point, unless it can be found to be objectively justified and proportionate. The CJEU stated that it was a matter for the High Court to rule whether there was an objective justification.

The matter was referred back to the High Court to decide whether the question of justification should be considered. Nugee LJ rejected the request from the trustees to consider the justification, primarily because the justification had not been raised when he heard the initial preliminary issue in November 2019 and it would not be procedurally appropriate to raise it at this stage. Therefore, Nugee LJ held that, on the basis that the indirect discrimination was not justified, the bankruptcy exemption under the UK Finance Act 2004, should be interpreted as including assets in a scheme established in another EU Member State that was recognised for tax purposes.

In January 2023, the Court of Appeal unanimously upheld the decision of Nugee LJ to decline to consider the question of justification. However, the judgment also noted that it would not preclude anyone in further proceedings from arguing that the indirect discrimination was in fact objectively justified.

[15.27] *McGaughey v Universities Superannuation Scheme Ltd*[11]*—Court of Appeal of England and Wales—Sir Flaux, Chancellor of the High Court, Asplin & Snowden LJJ—appeal from High Court—ESG investment—breach of directors' duties—members' ethical survey*

11 *McGaughey v Universities Superannuation Scheme Ltd* [2023] EWCA Civ 873. See *Arthur Cox Employment Law Yearbook 2022* at [16.39] for decision of High Court of England and Wales in *McGaughey v Universities Superannuation Scheme* [2022] EWHC 1233.

The Court of Appeal of England and Wales (upholding an earlier decision of the High Court) dismissed a claim brought by two members of the Universities Superannuation Scheme (the 'Scheme') against the directors of the Scheme's trustee company (the 'Directors'). The Scheme was administered by its corporate trustee, Universities Superannuation Scheme Ltd (the 'Company').

The appellants sought to continue several multiple derivative claims on behalf of the Company against its Directors and former Directors. The appellants alleged that the Scheme continued to invest in fossil fuels when its Directors had no divestment plan, despite the Company's stated ambition to be carbon neutral by 2050, thereby cause a breach of the Directors' duties under ss 171 and 172 of the UK Companies Act 2006. They also claimed that, in failing to have a divestment plan, the Directors failed to take account of a number of relevant considerations, including the results of a members' ethical survey.

However, the Court of Appeal ruled that the claim did not meet the requirements of a derivative action, as there was no *prima facie* loss to the Company as a result of the alleged breaches of the Directors' duties, meaning that the claim fell at the first hurdle.

In July 2023, the Court of Appeal upheld the August 2022 decision of the High Court, ruling that the appellants failed to justify their allegation that the trustee Directors had breached their duties under the Investment Regulations in relation to their power of investment. Although the Court of Appeal dismissed the claim, primarily on procedural grounds, the Court nonetheless noted that, even in the absence of such procedural factors, it was doubtful that the appellants would have a *prima facie* case for breach of duty against the Directors. The Court held that the trustee Directors had ensured a proper diversification of assets and had taken appropriate professional advice, which had informed them that immediate divestment from fossil fuel companies was not the most effective way to reach its carbon neutral target. Nor did the Court consider it relevant that a 'members' ethical survey' completed by less than 1% of the Scheme's membership had indicated a desire for the Scheme to divest from fossil fuel companies. Furthermore, the appellants were unable to show they had suffered loss due to the alleged breaches by the Directors of their duties. The Court held that there was no evidence that the Directors had 'furthered their own interests' or that they had 'put their own beliefs with regard to fossil fuels' above the interests of the Scheme members. In these circumstances, the Court concluded that 'this was a claim which was bound to fail'.

[15.28] *Finishing Touches Cheltenham Ltd v The Pensions Regulator*[12]*—UK First-tier Tribunal—Pensions Act 2008, s 40—Employers' Duties (Registration and Compliance) Regulations 2010*[13]*—auto-enrolment penalties*

The First-tier Tribunal dismissed a challenge brought by the appellant, to a fixed-penalty notice issued by the Pensions Regulator under s 40 of the UK Pensions Act 2008 (the '2008 Act').

12 *Finishing Touches Cheltenham Ltd v The Pensions Regulator* [2023] UKFTT 457 (31 May 2023).
13 Employers' Duties (Registration and Compliance) Regulations 2010 (SI 2010/5).

The appellant was required to provide a Declaration of Compliance to the Pensions Regulator within five months of their staging date under the Employers' Duties (Registration and Compliance) Regulations 2010 (the 'Regulations'). The appellant did not declare by the deadline and thereafter the Pensions Regulator issued a compliance notice under s 35 of the 2008 Act. The notice required the appellant to comply with specified steps to remedy its contravention. The appellant did not take these steps and, as a result, the Pensions Regulator issued the appellant with a penalty notice under s 40 of the 2008 Act. The appellant applied to the Pensions Regulator for a review of the penalty notice and thereafter applied to the Pensions Tribunal.

In making the appeal, the appellant asserted that it had delegated its obligations to comply with the Regulations to its accountant. The appellant further stated that it was the accountant's responsibility to provide notice of re-declaration on behalf of the appellant and to ensure that the terms of the compliance notice were followed. The appellant asserted that the accountant had failed in all respects.

In its decision, the Tribunal noted that the timely provision of information to the Pensions Regulator is crucial to the effective operation of the automatic enrolment scheme. If the Pensions Regulator is not supplied with the relevant information, it cannot effectively ensure that employers are complying with their duties. This is the justification for the provision of a specified timeframe as a mandatory requirement in the Regulations. Unless there is an issue with receipt of the compliance notice, or there is some other reasonable excuse for the failure to comply, a penalty notice must be issued.

In this case, the Tribunal deemed that there was no reasonable excuse for a failure to comply. Ultimately, the requirement for the appellant to meet its pensions obligations is the responsibility of the appellant and it would not be relieved of that responsibility if an accountant is instructed to act on its behalf, although the appellant could seek a remedy against the accountant in other respects.

The Tribunal further considered the requirement to pay £400. It noted that it is a significant burden for a small business. However, the amount was prescribed because it reflects the importance of complying with employer duty provisions. The Tribunal also does not have the power to direct substitution of a lesser penalty. Accordingly, the challenge was dismissed.

[15.29] *Manolete Partners Plc v Ian Russell White*[14]*—High Court of England and Wales—Deputy Master Teverson—power of court to force pension draw down to satisfy judgment debt*

The Court made an order that the respondent exercise such rights as he may enjoy under the relevant pension scheme rules to draw down his pension benefits to satisfy a substantial outstanding judgment debt to the applicant and thereby, indirectly, the creditors of Lloyds British Limited (the 'Company').

14 *Manolete Partners Plc v Ian Russell White* [2023] EWHC 567 (Ch).

The applicant was a specialist insolvency litigation funder and the assignee of claims asserted on behalf of the Company and its liquidators against the respondent. The core issue that arose in the proceedings was whether the Court could compel the respondent to draw down his benefits under an occupational pension scheme financed by his employer to satisfy a substantial outstanding judgment debt in favour of the assignee of claims for breach of director's duties. If recovery was available, significant sums could be paid back to the Company in liquidation, with the prospect of a substantial benefit to its creditors. It was held that the applicant had established that the respondent held sufficient power to exercise draw down rights under the Scheme Rules and that the respondent could be directed to draw down his pension.

[15.30] ***Railways Pension Trustee Company Ltd v Atos IT Services UK Ltd*[15]*—High Court of England and Wales—Sir Flaux, Chancellor of the High Court—scope of actuary's discretion over contributions***

This claimant was the sole trustee of the Railways Pension Scheme ('RPS') that sought the directions of the High Court on a number of questions arising in the administration of the RPS, an industry-wide defined benefit occupational pension scheme, established on the privatisation of the railways for those employed in the railways industry. The defendants were the participating employers for the Atos section, which is one of the 106 sections that comprise the RPS.

A particular feature of the scheme is that it is a shared cost scheme, i.e., the contributions payable by participating employers and active members are normally payable in the ratio 60:40.

The deficit contribution rule provided that if an actuarial valuation uncovered a shortfall and there were no agreed arrangements between the trustee and the employer to make it good, the shortfall was to be made good by increasing normal contributions 'as determined by the Actuary' (up to the 130% cap), and by reducing future service benefits as agreed between the employer and the trustee or, in default of agreement, as 'the Actuary shall determine'.

The employers argued that the deficit contributions to be 'determined by the Actuary', should be calculated on the 60:40 ratio (up to the 130% cap), and that the future service benefit reduction, as the 'Actuary shall determine', should reduce the remaining deficit as much as possible by way of mathematical calculation, which would mean reducing future benefit accrual to zero. Therefore, the small number of active members would have to pay increased contributions for no benefit accrual.

The trustee argued that the actuary had a discretion when determining by how much to increase contributions and reduce future service benefits, having regard to matters such as affordability and collectability of contributions. Therefore, the actuary was not obliged to set contribution increases or reductions in benefit in such a way that would lead to active members opting out.

15 *Railways Pension Trustee Company Ltd v Atos IT Services UK Ltd* [2022] EWHC 3236 (Ch) (16 December 2022).

The High Court agreed and found that the rule did not provide an exhaustive and comprehensive regime for eliminating the shortfall, since one of the ways in which it would not be 'practicable' to do so would be if issues concerning affordability and value for money were ignored, it would lead to active members opting out, so that the shortfall would not be addressed, or only to a limited extent.

The Court accepted the trustee's arguments and held that the actuary had a discretion when determining the contribution increases and benefit reductions.

This judgment was handed down in December 2022, however there was a hearing fixed for December 2023 following a successful appeal application by the employers (Atos) to the Court of Appeal.

[15.31] ***Green v Commissioner of Police of the Metropolis Court of Appeal (Civil Division)[16]—Court of Appeal of England and Wales—Bean, Jackson & Asplin LJJ—Metropolis Court of Appeal—Police Pensions Regulations 1987[17]—European Convention on Human Rights, art 12—right to marry***

This was an appeal concerning the question of whether reg C9 of the UK Police Pensions Regulations 1987 (as amended) was compatible with the appellant's right to marry under art 12 of the European Convention on Human Rights. The provision provided that a deceased member's widow or civil partner would receive a pension for life, unless they remarried, formed a new civil partnership or cohabited with a new partner, in which case it would cease to be payable. The Court dismissed the appeal, holding that the trial Judge had not erred in finding that this provision did not impair or injure the essence of the right to marry.

[15.32] ***BBC v BBC Pension Trust Ltd[18]—High Court of England and Wales—Johnson J—amendment power***

The BBC brought a referral seeking clarification regarding the interpretation of the amendment provisions of the trust deed and rules in relation to its defined benefit scheme (the 'DB Scheme'). The application was brought against the background of a review by the BBC, with the aim of reducing future costs associated with the DB Scheme.

Rule 19 of the DB Scheme vested in the trustees the power to amend the trust deed or rules, with the consent of the BBC, subject to certain qualifications/limitations or provisos. The third proviso stated that no such amendment or modification would take effect with respect to active members where those members' interests were certified by the actuary to be affected, unless certain criteria were met, including the provision of adequate alternative benefits or by agreement of the active members in a duly convened meeting.

16 *Green v Commissioner of Police of the Metropolis Court of Appeal (Civil Division)* [2022] EWCA Civ 1686, 21 December 2022.

17 Police Pensions Regulations 1987 (SI 1987/257).

18 *BBC v BBC Pension Trust Ltd* [2023] EWHC 1965 (Ch).

Two interrelated questions were put before the Court. The first question concerned the scope of what was included in the term 'interests' of active members in the third proviso. While the parties agreed that the concept of 'interests' included past service, they disagreed regarding the breadth of the scope of 'interests'. The BBC argued that the term was limited to rights earned by past service and possibly any linkage of the value of past service rights to final salary, while the representative beneficiary argued that the concept of 'interests' was sufficiently broad to also include the ability to accrue future service benefits on the same terms as before the amendment, among others.

The second question concerned the 'separate domains under a pension scheme', that is of the employer and the DB Scheme trustees. The representative beneficiary argued that any change regarding future service benefits was within the domain of the employer, not the trustees, as it is the role of the employer to design the scheme and that of the trustees to manage and administer it. In the context of the trust deed and rules, the representative beneficiary argued that, given that there are established procedures governing the manner in which the employer can alter the benefits enjoyed by employees involving consultation and consensus either by agreement or collective bargaining, should the trustees seek to bring amendments affecting the future service benefits without such procedures being observed, this would amount to an improper purpose of the trustee.

In relation to the first question, the Court held that the 'natural focus' of the inquiry was to look at the position of active members under the trust deed and rules, before any proposed amendment, compared to their 'intended position' were the proposed amendment to come into effect. The Court held that if the position is different, then the 'inescapable conclusion' is that the interests are affected, and the protections afforded in the third proviso come into play. The purpose of the protections in the third proviso, is to give assurance to active members that, although their position will be different after the proposed amendment, they will not be 'substantially prejudiced'; or if they are prejudiced, the scheme actuary deems the change appropriate.

On the second question, the Court held that the amendment power in the deed would not be exercised for an improper purpose, due to the fact that employer consent was required, and that the trustees were required to comply with the safeguards provided in the third proviso which included either certification that the interests of the member were not substantially prejudiced, confirmation of substantially equivalent benefits, or approval at a duly convened meeting. The Court held, therefore, that there was no separate precondition that active member consent was required in order for any amendment to take place.

UK PENSIONS OMBUDSMAN DECISIONS

[15.33] ***Gala Coffee and Tea Group Pension Scheme[19]—UK Pensions Ombudsman determination—trustee's delay in transferring a member's transfer unreasonable—financial loss in investment***

19 *Gala Coffee and Tea Group Pension Scheme* (CAS-56752-R2J6).

In this UK Pensions Ombudsman determination, the Deputy Pensions Ombudsman found the trustee's delay in processing a member's transfer request to be unreasonable. Miss I was a member of the Gala Coffee and Tea Group Pension Scheme (the 'Scheme'), a money purchase scheme administered by Clerical Medical (the 'Administrator'). The Scheme's trustee was Gala Coffee Ltd, which later merged into UCC Coffee UK Ltd (the 'Trustee'). The Deputy Ombudsman partly upheld Miss I's complaint concerning the Scheme trustee's delay in processing a request to transfer to a self-invested personal pension ('SIPP').

In February 2018, Miss I had informed the trustee that she wanted to make two separate withdrawals of her Scheme benefits, with the initial withdrawal on, or immediately after, her selected retirement date in the 2017/18 tax year; and the second withdrawal a few days later in the 2018/19 tax year.

However, after a lack of communication from the Trustee, in November 2019 Miss I decided to transfer her benefits to a SIPP. In December 2019, Fidelity (the SIPP provider) contacted the Trustee requesting a transfer value illustration and transfer forms. However, the Trustee did not send this request to the Administrator until June 2020. In July 2020, Miss I's benefits were transferred to the SIPP.

Among other complaints, Miss I argued that she had suffered a financial loss of around £3,786 due to the delay in the transferred funds being available for reinvestment. She argued that some of her other pension investments had shown positive growth by 13.1% on average from January to July 2020. On this basis, she believed that if the transfer had proceeded in a timely manner, her funds in the SIPP would have been invested in a similar way.

The Deputy Ombudsman held that the transfer delay had been unreasonable, using a notional timescale, he considered that on receipt of Fidelity's request, the Trustee should have contacted the Administrator within a working week, by 19 December 2019. However, factoring in the further 13 working days that it took the Trustee to sign and return the forms and for the transfer to be completed, the Deputy Ombudsman was satisfied that 29 January 2020 would have been the notional date for completion of the transfer.

On this basis, he ordered the Trustee to make a comparison between Miss I's entitlement in the SIPP and what her entitlement would have likely been had a transfer value been paid on the notional date. He also held that the redress for any financial loss that Miss I suffered should be paid directly to her instead of to the SIPP, due to her fixed protection status. It was also held that the Trustee's delay in completing the transfer forms and its failure to respond to communications in a timely manner amounted to severe distress and inconvenience to Miss I as a result of the Trustee's maladministration. The Trustee was directed to pay £1,500 to Miss I.

It is worth noting that the Irish Financial Services Ombudsman cannot award financial redress that exceeds 'any actual loss of benefit under the scheme concerned' and accordingly does not have the power to award compensation.

[15.34] ***The Positive Retirement Potential Plan*[20]*—UK Pensions Ombudsman determination—liability of trustee for dishonest breach of trust and maladministration—undue influence—personal liability***

In this UK Pensions Ombudsman determination, three occupational pension scheme members, Mr A, Mr S and Mrs S, made complaints on identical issues against the trustee of the Positive Retirement Potential Plan (the 'Plan') and PR Potential Ltd ('PRP Ltd'). The Deputy Pensions Ombudsman found the trustee personally liable for dishonest breaches of trust and maladministration. The members argued that the trustee had invested the Plan's funds inappropriately, which resulted in the loss of their pension benefits.

The Plan was established in May 2013. Between May 2013 and April 2015, a total of 42 individuals, including the three members, transferred funds into the Plan. After April 2015, the Plan did not accept any new members, due to the absence of its administrator.

The Deputy Ombudsman upheld the members' complaints against the trustee and PRP Ltd and found that the trustee had committed several breaches of trust and maladministration by failing to have regard to the need for diversification and to carry out meaningful due diligence in relation to the investments. It was also held that the trustee had failed to obtain and consider proper advice in writing as to the suitability of the investments. Furthermore, the Deputy Ombudsman held that the trustee failed in his equitable duty to exercise due skill and care in the performance of his investment functions, as well as the statutory requirement to operate an effective system of governance, including internal controls.

The Deputy Ombudsman also took into consideration the circumstances in which the members had joined the Plan which, according to them, had been introduced to them by individuals with a clear interest in them joining. Additionally, none of the three members had any prior investment experience. Therefore, the Deputy Ombudsman held that, on the balance of probabilities, the members lacked the full knowledge of the facts of the investment of their funds under the Plan and had been unduly influenced by the individuals that introduced them to it when they made their decision to transfer funds into the Plan.

The Deputy Ombudsman held that the trustee committed breaches of trust and maladministration dishonestly and that, on this basis, he was not relieved from liability for these breaches under s 61 of the Trustee Act 1925. He was also not excused from personal liability under s 33 of the Pensions Act 1995, nor by the terms of the Plan's exoneration and indemnity clause.

The trustee was directed to pay into the Plan, to be held on trust for the benefit of all members, the amount of £200,163.09 (representing the total amount of funds transferred by the members in this complaint), less £14,000 paid to Mr A from Group First, including simple interest at the rate of 8% per annum to the date of payment.

---

20 *The Positive Retirement Potential Plan* (PO-28532).

The trustee was also ordered to pay £10,000 to Mr A and £7,000 each to Mr S and Mrs S for the exceptional distress and inconvenience caused by its maladministration. PRP Ltd was also directed to pay £3,000 to each applicant for its exceptional maladministration, in its failure to provide a proper system of administration.

The Irish Financial Services Ombudsman cannot award financial redress that exceeds 'any actual loss of benefit under the scheme concerned' and accordingly does not have the power to award compensation.

[15.35] ***Water Companies Pension Scheme – Bristol Water plc Section[21]—UK Pensions Ombudsman determination—power of trustee to return surplus to sponsoring employer on winding up of occupational pension scheme***

The UK Pensions Ombudsman dismissed a complaint by the applicant, Mr S, concerning a trustee's decision to return a surplus of approximately £12 million to the sponsoring employer on the winding up of an occupational pension scheme.

Mr S was a pensioner member of the Bristol Water section of the Water Companies Pension Scheme (the 'Scheme'), a segregated pension scheme with Bristol Water plc as its sponsoring employer (the 'Employer') and the Water Companies Trustee Company as the Scheme's trustee (the 'Trustee').

Under the Scheme rules, the trustee was required to secure member benefits through the purchase of individual insurance policies or annuity contracts and comply with the winding up provisions of s 76 of the Pensions Act 1995. The rules also clearly described the Trustee's power to augment the members' benefits as discretionary: i.e., it 'may' increase 'all or any' of the benefits 'to any extent that it considers it just and equitable'. This discretion was to be exercised 'in consultation with' the employer. Thereafter, any remaining assets would be returned to the Employer. In this case, after consulting with the Employer and the members, the Trustee decided that all the surplus assets, less tax, should be returned to the Employer on the completion of the wind up. Mr S contended that the Scheme funds were only to be used for the benefit of its members, and that the surplus (which included monies paid in by the membership) was a result of increases in members' contributions and investment returns. Therefore, it was 'morally indefensible' for the Employer to benefit from the surplus.

The Ombudsman was satisfied that the Trustee had followed the requirements of the Scheme rules. Minutes from Trustee Council meetings showed that there had been ongoing communication with the employer, in relation to the allocation of the surplus on the winding up of the section, which was consistent with the consultation process, and that the Trustee's decision not to augment the benefits was taken after considering a correct interpretation of the requirements of the Scheme rules. The Ombudsman noted that it is generally accepted in law that trustees are able (and may in fact be under a duty) to take account of a sponsoring employer's interests when exercising its powers under a pension scheme, provided that those interests are relevant.

21 *Water Companies Pension Scheme – Bristol Water plc Section* (CAS-92093-N4D9).

The Trustee recognised that the Employer had endured all the downside risk for the duration of the operation of the Scheme, as well as the fact that the Employer had paid significant additional contributions (amounting to over £16 million between 2005 and 2016) to try and mitigate some of the downside risks until the members' benefits were secure. On this basis, the Ombudsman dismissed the complaint, as it was deemed that the trustee acted properly in determining that it was fair and reasonable to return the surplus to the Employer.

Chapter 16

Redundancy

INTRODUCTION

[16.01]

Statutory Redundancy

In *Roadbridge Ltd*, the claimant had transferred from Ireland to the UK and received a statutory redundancy payment when the respondent went into receivership. However, the claimant had been informed by the employer that they would have the same entitlements as employees in Ireland and brought a claim seeking the balance. The Labour Court upheld the claim.

The UK EAT considered what constitutes suitable alternative work, and whether it was reasonable for the claimants to refuse the roles offered to them, in *Mid and South Essex NHS Foundation Trust*.

Collective Redundancy

There were a number of cases concerning collective redundancies this year. *MO* and *EI* were both before the ECJ and concerned the application and interpretation of Directive 98/59/EC relating to collective redundancies.

Debenhams Retail (Ireland) Ltd was a significant decision of the WRC which concerned whether the respondent engaged in meaningful consultation with its employees as required under Directive 98/59/EC and the Protection of Employment Act 1977.

The UK Supreme Court considered whether an administrator appointed under insolvency legislation could be held criminally liable for failure to comply with collective redundancy obligations in *Northern Derbyshire Magistrates' Court*.

STATUTORY REDUNDANCY

[16.02] ***Roadbridge Ltd v Cuffe*[1]*—Labour Court—appeal from Workplace Relations Commission—Redundancy Payments Acts 1967 to 2022—terms of contract—redundancy entitlements—transfer to international company***

The claimant worked for the respondent since 2011. The respondent went into receivership and the claimant was made redundant in April 2022. The claimant had by that time been transferred from Ireland to the UK, and was paid statutory redundancy of £5,440 under UK legislation, which was less than he would have been entitled to in Ireland. The claimant brought a complaint to the WRC seeking payment of the balance but failed to attend the hearing.

On appeal, the respondent was not in attendance; however, the Court was satisfied that it was aware of the hearing.

The Court found that employees of the respondent were assured in writing that 'all entitlements enjoyed by Roadbridge employees in Ireland will be exactly the same as employees who transfer to international companies. This formed the basis on which employees transferred and formed a part of the contract with the respondent. It was therefore incumbent on the respondent to take whatever steps were necessary to ensure that this undertaking was met. The claimant was not afforded a reasonable opportunity by the respondent to be present in the State on the date of the dismissal. The appeal succeeded.

[16.03] ***Mid and South Essex NHS Foundation Trust (previously Mid Essex Hospital Services NHS Trust) v Stevenson*[2]*—UK Employment Appeal Tribunal—appeal from employment tribunal—Employment Rights Act 1996—suitable alternative work—reasonableness—redundancy—redundancy payments—refusal***

The claimants were employed as heads of the HR department of the respondent trust. Their roles were made redundant on foot of a restructure. They were offered alternative employment in the role of senior HR lead. The claimants refused the roles, viewing them as less autonomous, and were made redundant. The respondent refused to pay redundancy payment to the claimants, arguing that they had unreasonably refused offers of suitable employment.

The claimants brought claims to the employment tribunal for unfair dismissal, breach of contract and redundancy payments. The employment tribunal held that the alternative positions offered to the claimants were, in fact, suitable; however the claimants had not unreasonably refused the offers of 'suitable employment' as their view that they would not have the same autonomy was not groundless, and therefore they were not excluded from their entitlement to redundancy payments.

The respondent appealed to the UK EAT. The appeal pertained to the entitlement to redundancy payments and the respondent argued that the tribunal erred in concluding that

---

1 *Roadbridge Ltd v Cuffe* RPD2310.

2 *Mid and South Essex NHS Foundation Trust (previously Mid Essex Hospital Services NHS Trust) v Stevenson* [2023] EAT 115.

the claimants did not unreasonably refuse the offer of suitable employment, misdirecting itself that its findings on suitability were not relevant to reasonableness and failing to consider, as a result, that was not how the facts 'ought to have appeared' to the claimants.

The respondent pointed to the fact that, although the line management might have changed in the alternative role posited, the day-to-day duties at the trust would not have changed and that it was not reasonable to anticipate reduced levels of autonomy or status. The tribunal had held that the claimants were not justified in considering any lack of autonomy or status in their contemplation of the offer of senior HR lead role. In this way, it was clear to the EAT that the tribunal had considered that the role was 'suitable'.

The EAT noted that, after a very detailed analysis, the tribunal found that while the role was suitable in relation to the claimants, there were sufficient grounds for the claimants' perceptions of the role such that they had not acted unreasonably in refusing it.

In considering whether the tribunal failed to consider how the facts 'ought to have appeared' to the claimants, the EAT noted that there is no requirement that an employment judge in every case specifically asks that question of himself. The words were guidance only as to how to apply the statutory test of whether the role was unreasonably refused. The EAT did not consider that the respondent established an error of law in the decision of the tribunal.

The appeal was dismissed.

COLLECTIVE REDUNDANCY

[16.04] ***MO v SM as liquidator of G GmbH[3]—European Court of Justice—request for preliminary ruling from Germany—Directive 98/59/EC[4]—redundancy—collective redundancy—social policy—information and consultation—obligation of employer contemplating a collective redundancy to forward to the competent public authority a copy of the information communicated to the workers' representatives***

The applicant in the substantive proceedings had been an employee of G GmbH. The respondent had been appointed as insolvency administrator for the company. On 17 January 2020, it was decided that G GmbH would cease business operations by April 2020 and that more than 10% of its workers would be made redundant from 28 to 31 January 2020. On the same date, 17 January 2020, a consultation procedure was started with the works council, which acted as the workers' representative. In accordance with Art 2(3)(b) of Directive 98/59/EC (the 'Directive'), certain information was communicated to the works council in writing. However, no copy of this communication was forwarded to the Osnabrück Employment Agency as required by the Directive. On 22 January 2020, the works council concluded that it did not see any way in which the proposed redundancies would not be made.

---

3 *MO v SM as liquidator of G GmbH* (Case C-134/22).

4 Directive 98/59/EC on the approximation of the laws of the Member States relating to collective redundancies.

The applicant brought an action in the local German Labour Court seeking non-termination of his employment relationship. He claimed that the respondent breached the second subparagraph art 2(3) of the Directive and paragraph 17(3) of the German Law on protection against unfair dismissal by failing to forward a copy of the communication sent to the works council to the employment agency. The respondent argued that the dismissal was valid. It maintained that paragraph 17(3) of the Law on protection against unfair dismissal was not intended to protect workers against collective redundancy or to avoid redundancies. The respondent submitted that the purpose of forwarding a copy of the requisite communication to the employment agency was merely to inform that agency of the proposed redundancies. The action could not protect the workers against collective redundancy. The action was dismissed at first instance and on appeal. The applicant appealed on a point of law to the Federal Labour Court of Germany, which referred to the European Court of Justice ('ECJ') for a preliminary ruling on what the purpose of the second subparagraph of art 2(3) of Directive 98/59 was.

The ECJ noted that the information referred to in point (b) of the first subparagraph of art 2(3) of the Directive could be provided during the consultations and not necessarily when the procedure organising them began. This was underscored by the purpose of the obligation, being, it was held: 'to enable the workers' representatives to participate in the consultation process as fully and effectively as possible'. It was also noted that the information supplied to the workers' representatives may develop and change over time.

It was held that the forwarding of information to the employment agency serves only to give the authority an indication of the reasons for the proposed redundancies, the number and types of workers to be made redundant, the number and types of workers employed and when the redundancies are proposed to be made.

It was acknowledged that the employment agency would not be given any active role in the consultation procedure and the second subparagraph of art 2(3) of the Directive merely designates it as a recipient of certain information for preparatory purposes. In light of this purpose and the fact that the failure to supply the documentation was at a stage where redundancies were merely contemplated, it was clear that the Directive did not provide personal protections for individual workers.

Therefore, the answer to the question referred was that the Directive must be interpreted as meaning that the obligation to forward the communication is not intended to confer individual protection on the workers affected by collective redundancies.

[16.05] ***EI v SC Brink's Cash Solutions SRL*[5]*—European Court of Justice—request for a preliminary ruling from Romania—social policy—approximation of the laws of the Member States relating to collective redundancies—Directive 98/59/EC,*[6] *art 1(1)(b) & art 6—procedure for informing and consulting workers in the event of projected collective redundancies—no workers' representatives appointed—national legislation allowing an employer not to inform and consult the workers concerned individually***

5 *EI v SC Brink's Cash Solutions SRL* (Case C-496/22).

6 Directive 98/59/EC on the approximation of the laws of the Member States relating to collective redundancies.

This request for a preliminary ruling concerned the interpretation of art 1(1)(b), art 2(3) and art 6 of Directive 98/59/EC on the approximation of the laws of the Member States relating to collective redundancies. The request arose in proceedings between the applicant, EI, and his former employer, SC Brink's Cash Solutions SRL.

The applicant was employed as a cash-in-transit agent for the respondent, having commenced employment in August 2014. In the midst of the Covid-19 pandemic, and an associated state of emergency in Romania between March and May 2020, the respondent initiated a collective redundancy procedure to cut 128 jobs. On various dates in May 2020, it notified the relevant national authorities of its intention to initiate the procedure, and that the redundancies would take place between May and July 2020. Neither the workers' representatives (whose terms of office had expired without renewal in April 2020), nor the affected workers were notified.

The applicant, who was one of 128 workers made redundant, brought an action against the decision to dismiss him. This was unsuccessful in the first instance and the applicant appealed to the referring Court, arguing that the respondent was under a 'mandatory obligation to inform and consult workers individually … even in the absence of a trade union or representative appointed to protect their interests'. The appellant argued, further, that it was for the respondent to inform the workers concerned of the need to appoint new representatives for the purposes of the redundancy procedure.

The respondent countered that, owing to the failure to renew the terms of office of the workers' representatives, it found itself in the 'atypical situation of having no social partner' with whom to consult and inform. In so far as the transposing national legislation provided that the collective redundancy procedure was be carried out with the relevant trade union or workers' representatives, it was argued that the respondent was 'exempted' from having to inform and consult the workers individually.

The referring Court noted that other workers had challenged the respondent's collective redundancy procedure before the Romanian courts. In circumstances where the referring Court found itself at odds with other courts in Romania as to the interpretation of Directive 98/59/EC, it decided to stay the proceedings and refer two questions to the European Court of Justice ('ECJ') for a preliminary ruling.

The ECJ considered the referring Court's questions, the first of which asked, in essence, whether the first subparagraph of art 1(1)(b), art 2(3) and art 6 of Directive 98/59/EC must be interpreted as precluding national legislation which does not require an employer 'to consult individually the workers affected by projected collective redundancies'.

The ECJ stated that the main objective of Directive 98/59/EC is to ensure that collective redundancies are subject to prior consultation with the workers' representatives, and prior notification to the competent national authorities. It observed that the ECJ's caselaw has 'repeatedly held' that the right to information and consultation is intended for workers' representatives, and not for workers individually. Moreover, it was apparent from art 3 of Directive 98/59/EC that only the workers' representatives must receive a copy of the employer's notification to the competent national authorities. Accordingly, it was held that the provisions of Directive 98/59/EC do not require an employer to inform and consult affected workers individually before a collective redundancy. It followed that the provisions of Directive 98/59/EC must not be interpreted as precluding national legislation which does not require an employer to consult individually the workers affected by projected collective redundancies.

By its second question, the referring Court asked whether the first subparagraph of art 1(1)(b), art 2(3) and art 6 of Directive 98/59/EC, read in the light of its preamble, must be interpreted as meaning that, in circumstances such as this case, the employer is required to inform and consult the affected workers.

While true that Directive 75/129/EEC[7]—the predecessor of Directive 98/59/EC—does not make provision for situations where there are no workers' representatives in an undertaking contemplating collective redundancies, its provisions require Member States 'to take all measures necessary to ensure that workers are informed, consulted and in a position to intervene through their representatives in the event of collective redundancies'. National legislation permitting an employer to 'circumvent' or 'frustrate' the protection of workers' rights guaranteed by Directive 98/59/EC 'manifestly fails to satisfy those requirements'.

The ECJ observed, firstly, that the national legislation at issue in the main proceedings granted workers the right to appoint representatives, and an employer could not preclude the existence of worker representation. Secondly, the national legislation did not impose an obligation on workers to appoint representatives. Although Directive 98/59/EC does not impose such an obligation on workers, it is for the Member States 'to ensure the effectiveness of the provisions' of Directive 98/59/EC.

Thus, the ECJ held, it is for the Member States:

> 'to adopt all appropriate measures to ensure that workers' representatives are appointed and to ensure that workers are not in a situation in which, for reasons beyond their control, they are prevented from appointing those representatives'.

It is a matter for the referring Court to determine the adequacy of the national provisions in that regard, specifically (in this instance) those governing the appointment of workers' representatives and limiting the duration of their term of office, in circumstances where it is impossible, for reasons beyond the workers' control, to appoint new representatives.

[16.06] *Cox v Debenhams Retail (Ireland) Ltd[8]—Workplace Relations Commission—Workplace Relations Act 2015—Protection of Employment Act 1977 as amended—Directive 98/59/EC[9]—collective redundancy—good time—meaningful consultation—relevant information*

The claimant was an employee of the respondent company, working as a catering assistant. She was made compulsorily redundant when the respondent company ceased to trade. She argued that the respondent breached ss 9 and 10 of the Protection of

7 Directive 75/129/EEC on the approximation of the laws of the Member States relating to collective redundancies.

8 *Cox v Debenhams Retail (Ireland) Ltd* ADJ-00039722.

9 Directive 98/59/EC on the approximation of the laws of the Member States relating to collective redundancies.

Employment Act 1977 as amended. She complained that the consultation that should have taken place took place late; that her representatives were not provided with the information required and requested and, accordingly, that they could not formulate meaningful proposals to mitigate the impact of redundancy on her; and that the consultation was not meaningfully engaged with by the respondent.

The WRC noted that, under art 2 of Directive 98/59/EC, a consultation shall begin 'where an employer is contemplating collective redundancies'. Section 9 of the Protection of Employment Act 1977 as amended states that consultation shall begin 'where an employer proposes to create collective redundancies'. It was clear from the evidence before the WRC that an emergency board meeting of the respondent company took place on 24 March 2020, wherein the company was confronted with projected losses of €9.5 million. Options were discussed to limit the impact on cash flow and liquidation was considered. It was argued by the claimant that, as liquidation would have naturally led to redundancies, the company could be said to have contemplated redundancies at this time. A decision was made by the UK parent company on 8 April 2020 that it was not in a position to continue to fund the respondent. The respondent argued that, based on that notice from its parent company, the 'decision' triggering the consultation process was 14 April 2020, when the parent company adopted a resolution to wind up the respondent. The WRC was critical of the respondent's delay until 17 April 2020 to commence consultation as, at this time, the parent company had withdrawn financial support and liquidators had already been appointed. The second consultation was on 28 April 2020 and there was no discussion about reducing or avoiding collective redundancies. The third consultation was on 7 May 2020 and the workers were informed that, without the support of the UK, the Irish branches could not trade and redundancies would be a reality in the absence of alternatives.

The claimant argued that the respondent had an obligation to supply all relevant information and specific information that would allow her representatives to make alternative proposals to redundancy. The specific information sought was provided seven days into the consultation process. By 7 May 2020, the date on which the liquidator informed the workers that there were no alternatives to redundancy, a significant amount of information requested had not been provided.

The WRC held that the date on which the consultation should have started was 8 April 2020, when the UK parent company indicated that it would not be in a position to continue to fund the respondent. It did not matter that not all relevant information was to hand at this time. The WRC noted that, under the Directive, the consultation must commence in 'good time' having regard to the facts of the case, including the impact of Covid-19, which existed as a backdrop to the dispute. However, the WRC notes that financial vulnerability required consultation to commence at an early stage and this was no later than 9 April 2020.

The WRC was critical of the respondent's failure to provide the necessary information sought by the claimant.

With regard to whether the respondent engaged in a meaningful consultation, the WRC decided that the consultation process should have begun no later than 9 April 2020 and that commencing the consultation on 17 April 2020 was not in good time. The WRC also noted that relevant information sought was not provided to the claimant. It was also noted that there was no material change in the redundancy proposal as detailed at the outset of the consultation process and the decision to engage in collective redundancy at the end.

The WRC decided that the respondent breached ss 9 and 10 of the Protection of Employment Act 1977 as amended; however, it found that the case for the maximum award was not made out and instead awarded four weeks compensation in the amount of €1,800.

The complaint was upheld.

[16.07] ***R (Palmer) v Northern Derbyshire Magistrates' Court[10]—UK Supreme Court—Richards LJ—appeal from High Court of England and Wales—Trade Union and Labour Relations (Consolidation) Act 1992—administrator appointed under insolvency legislation—criminal liability for failure to give statutory notice of a collective redundancy—whether an administrator is an 'officer'—statutory construction***

The appellant, a joint administrator of a company, appealed against a decision of the Magistrates' Court that he was an 'officer' of the company within the meaning of the Trade Union and Labour Relations (Consolidation) Act 1992 (the '1992 Act'). The appellant was one of three joint administrators appointed under the insolvency legislation. After the company went into administration, a collective redundancy situation arose, and certain employees were dismissed with notice.

The company failed to notify the Secretary of State of its intention to make the redundancies, thereby committing an offence under the 1992 Act. The appellant was charged on the basis that he was a director, manager, secretary 'or other similar officer' of the company within the meaning of the 1992 Act, and that the failure to notify had taken place 'with his consent or connivance, or as a result of his neglect'. He argued that he could not have committed the offence because an administrator was not an 'other similar officer'. The Magistrates' Court addressed this as a preliminary issue, rejecting the argument.

The High Court dismissed the appellant's claim for judicial review of the Magistrates' Court's decision. It held that it was clear that an administrator had 'day-to-day conduct of the company's affairs ... including the power to make employees redundant', and was therefore an 'officer' for the purposes of the 1992 Act.

On appeal, the Supreme Court found that the 1992 Act does not define 'officer'. Moreover, none of the references to a company's officers in the Insolvency Act 1986 suggest that an administrator is an officer.

10 *R (Palmer) v Northern Derbyshire Magistrates' Court* [2023] UKSC 38.

The Court held that there was no scope for giving the phrase 'other similar officer' an extended meaning so as to encompass an administrator; nor was there any policy justification for doing so. The High Court had applied a 'functional test', holding that Parliament must have intended that anyone with day-to-day management and control of a company, carrying out the same types of functions as officers, should be capable of being fixed with personal liability for failure to give statutory notice. However, had this been its intention, Parliament would have used words such as 'or other person concerned in the management', rather than 'or other similar officer'. In the context of the legislation, an 'officer' is someone who holds an office within the 'constitutional structure' of the company. Officers with functions similar to directors, managers and secretaries could potentially be liable under the 1992 Act; however, an administrator appointed under the Insolvency Act 1986 would not.

The appeal was therefore allowed, and the decision of the Magistrates' Court quashed.

Chapter 17

Taxation

INTRODUCTION

[17.01] The various changes to the Irish tax regime that affect employers and employees are noted below, including changes relating to employer-provided benefits, flat-rate expenses, share incentive schemes and pensions.

Employment tax cases are also noted. Cases in 2023 involve the deductibility of employee expenses; recovery of underpaid tax from employees; and the conditions to qualify for the Special Assignee Relief Program ('SARP'), with a particular focus on the administrative filing requirements. In this respect, the Tax Appeal Commission ('TAC') is the first-tier tribunal whose role is to adjudicate, hear and determine appeals against decisions and determinations of the Revenue Commissioners concerning taxes and duties. Appeals from the TAC can be made on a point of law to the High Court from which another appeal on a point of law can be made to the Court of Appeal and to the Supreme Court. This appeals process is highlighted in *The Revenue Commissioners v Karshan Midlands Ltd t/a Dominos Pizza* which is noted in chapter 4.[1]

REVENUE eBRIEF UPDATES

[17.02] Revenue eBriefs are short articles produced by the Irish Revenue Commissioners which highlight the latest changes and updates to the Irish tax regime and Tax and Duty Manuals ('TDM'). Tax and Duty Manuals are documents that contain the rules, guidelines, procedures and practices that cover the whole range of Revenue activities.

The various changes to the Irish tax regime that affect employers and employees are noted below, including changes relating to PAYE, remote working relief, expenses of travel, provision of staff awards, income tax and pensions.

Special Assignee Relief Programme

[17.03] On 26 September 2023, Revenue published *eBrief 200/23* confirming TDM Part 34-00-10 has been amended in paragraph 15 to provide updated guidance on the

1 *The Revenue Commissioners v Karshan Midlands Ltd t/a Dominos Pizza* [2023] IESC 24. see [4.14] above.

certification requirements of a relevant employer or associated company in respect of a relevant employee.

Paragraph 15.2—COVID-19 Concession-SARP 1A Form, provides that in light of the unique circumstances arising due to Covid-19, the 90-day employer filing obligation was extended in March 2020, to afford employers a further 60 days to file this form. In exceptional cases, and on a request basis, a further extension was permitted. This concessionary measure ceased to apply on 31 December 2020. From 1 January 2021, all SARP 1A forms must be filed within the 90-day timeframe in the usual manner.

This amendment deleted the concession for late submission of the Form SARP 1A (outside 90 days) due to issues wholly outside the employer's control, for example the imposition of Covid-19 restrictions, or delays in an employee providing a PPSN. Previously if there were such extenuating circumstances wholly outside the control of the employer, the relevant employer or associated company would have completed the form with all other required information included and have submitted this form to Revenue within the required 90-day filing deadline. In such circumstances, at the time of submission of the form, a brief note to explain the reason would be sent to Revenue.

Share Schemes Manuals

[17.04] On 4 August 2023, Revenue published *eBrief 178/23* stating that Chapter 3 of the Share Schemes TDMs has been amended.

Chapter 3—Unapproved Share Options

Updated section 3.6.3—Interest on late payment of RTSO.

The normal provisions relating to assessments, appeals, collection and recovery of income tax apply also to the assessment, collection, and recovery of RTSO.

Where relevant tax on share options ('RTSO') is paid late, there is provision for the imposition of interest at 0.0219% per day or part of a day (from 1 January 2023). The rate that applied prior to this was 0.0322% per day or part of a day. Interest is payable from the date when the RTSO becomes due and payable until the actual date of payment.

Inserted section 3.6.4—Penalties for the non-filing of the Form RTSO1.

The Finance Act 2022 introduced a technical amendment to Schedule 29 of the TCA 1997 which provides for the imposition of a penalty for the non-filing of a return or for the deliberate, careless, fraudulent or negligent filing of an incorrect return. Where a Form RTSO1 has not been filed there is provision for the imposition of a penalty of €3,000. Where an incorrect return has been filed there is provision for the imposition of penalties up to €5,000.

Employers' Guide to PAYE

[17.05] On 26 June 2023, Revenue published *eBrief 146/23* confirming TDM Part 42-04-35 has been amended. Appendix 2: List of forms used by employers/agents, has been updated to remind customers that, as part of the reform and modernisation of the PAYE reporting system on 1 January 2019, the forms P30, P45, P46 and P35 (end-of-year return) have been abolished and replaced by new procedures. Accordingly, these forms are not available for filing in ROS—online or offline.

Pensions Taxable in Ireland (OECD and Other International Organisations)

[17.06] On 8 June 2023, Revenue published *eBrief 141/23* announcing TDM Part 04-04-03 has been created.

This manual explains:

— The tax treatment of pensions received by retired employees resident in Ireland in respect of service in OECD, including certain other international organisations, and how these pensions are dealt with in accordance with international agreement.

— The verification process and Revenue's interaction with the International Service for Remunerations and Pensions ('ISRP'), the arm of the OECD that coordinates communications on behalf of the Co-Orgs.

— The need for Revenue to perform compliance checks, to ensure that the pension and FPA received by each pensioner resident in Ireland are returned and taxed appropriately.

Remote Working Relief

[17.07] On 24 May 2023, Revenue published *eBrief 122/23* which noted that TDM Part 05-02-13 has been amended. Section 5—Treatment of Employer Reimbursed Remote Working Expenses, now clarifies conditions relating to the €3.20 per diem payment. These are:

1.1 there is an agreement in place between the employer and employee under which the employee works from home,

1.2 the employee performs substantive duties of his/her employment at home, and

1.3 performs his/her duties for substantial periods at home.

Credit in Respect of Tax Deducted from Emoluments of Certain Directors and Employees

[17.08] On 2 May 2023, Revenue published *eBrief 108/23* confirming TDM Part 42-04-59 has been amended so as to update section 6.

The update explains that the non-Schedule E liabilities must be paid when filing the tax return. Warehousing of Schedule E liabilities for a self-assessed director or employee was available for income tax payments which fell due on 31 October 2020 and 31 October 2021 ie, 2019 income tax year balancing payment, preliminary tax and balancing payment for the 2020 income tax year and preliminary tax for 2021 income tax year. It was not possible to warehouse Schedule E liabilities that were due to be paid by 31 October 2022 (16 November 2022, where the ROS extension applied).

Tax Treatment of the Reimbursement of Expenses of Travel and Subsistence to Office Holders and Employees

[17.09] On 18 April 2023, Revenue published *eBrief* 097/23 which noted TDM Part 05-01-06 has been amended.

The main changes are as follows:

Section 2.5.1—Remote Working

Section 2.5.1—Remote Working, has been created to clarify that employees who work part-time at home and part-time in the office cannot claim expenses for travelling between the two. The section also states that expenses of travelling between an individual's home and place of work may not be reimbursed tax-free. Likewise, subsistence expenses for periods spent in an individual's home may not be paid without deduction of tax.

New Civil Service Rates

The guidance has been updated in respect of the new civil service rates as provided for in DPER circulars 16/2022 and 17/2022.

For example

Appendix 1: Current civil service rates for travel and subsistence

— Has updated A: Domestic subsistence rates effective from 1 September 2022

— Standard domestic subsistence rates—effective from 1 September 2022

— Update to overnight rates:

Overnight rates		
Normal rate	**Reduced rate**	**Detention rate**
€167.00	€150.30	€83.50

— Vouched accommodation ('VA') domestic subsistence rates (for use in Dublin only)—effective from 1 September 2022:

Vouched accommodation ('VA') rate	**Accommodation**		**Meals**
VA Rate	**Vouched** Cost of Accommodation up to €167	Plus	€39.08

— B: Standard motor travel rates effective from 1 September 2022

— Motor travel rates per kilometre:

	Engine capacity		
Distance Bands	**Up to 1200cc**	**1201cc to 1500cc**	**1501cc and over**
Band 1: 0–1,500 km	41.80 cent	43.40 cent	51.82 cent
Band 2: 1,501–5,500 km	72.64 cent	79.18 cent	90.63 cent
Band 3: 5,501–25,000 km	31.78 cent	31.79 cent	39.22 cent
Band 4: 25,001 km and over	20.56 cent	23.85 cent	25.87 cent

Claims made for journeys undertaken in electric vehicles should use the rates applicable to the middle category of 1,201cc to 1,500cc.

Employer-provided Vehicles

[17.10] On 6 April 2023, Revenue issued *eBrief 093/23* stating TDM Part 05-01-01b has been amended. The main changes relate to the Finance Bill 2023 measures and are outlined below.

A new section 4.1.3 was inserted to outline the measures provided for in the Finance Bill 2023. It confirms that employers can, if they are in a position to do so, apply the new method of calculation of benefit-in-kind ('BIK') prior to enactment of the legislation. Furthermore, they should carry out any necessary adjustments to the BIK calculations in respect of prior-2023 pay periods by way of a current period adjustment and not amend prior-period payroll submissions.

The new rules for the calculation of BIK for 2023 and subsequent years (arising from Finance Act 2019 changes) have been moved from s 10 to s 4.

Section 6—Electric Vehicles, has been updated for the Finance Bill 2023 measures.

The examples have been updated to apply the new rules effective from 1 January 2023, to include the additional Finance Bill 2023 measures.

Returns by Employers in Relation to Reportable Benefits

[17.11] On 21 March 2023, Revenue published *eBrief 141/23* announcing TDM Part 38-03-33 has been created. The manual is called *Returns by Employers in Relation to Reportable Benefits* and provides information in regard to the Finance Act 2022 measures contained in s 897C of the Taxes Consolidation Act 1997 that require employers to report to Revenue details of certain payments/benefits, which are made without the deduction of tax, to employees and/or directors.

The manual provides details of the benefits to be reported and the stakeholder engagement process in regard to the implementation of the measures.

The Provision of Staff Awards

[17.12] On 20 March 2023, Revenue published *eBrief 074/23* stating TDM Part 05-01-01j has been updated to provide additional guidance regarding the tax treatment of the following:

2.3 Examination awards

A cash award made to an employee in recognition of passing an examination or acquiring a qualification is a taxable payment.

However, where the award is a reimbursement of certain of the employee's expenses incurred in studying for and sitting an examination, it may be made without the charge to tax where certain conditions are satisfied.

2.4 Special increments

Special increments of salary awarded on passing an examination are chargeable to tax, as part of the employee's remuneration in the ordinary way.

3 Course and examination fees

Reimbursement by an employer of course or examination fees paid by an employee, or direct payment of course or examination fees by an employer on behalf of an employee, are not regarded as a taxable benefit if the course undertaken is relevant to the business of the employer.

A course is regarded as relevant to the business of an employer where it leads to the acquisition of knowledge or skills which are:

— necessary for the duties of the employment; or
— directly related to increasing the effectiveness of the performance of the present or prospective duties of the office or employment.

4 Other examination expenses

A cash award made to an employee in recognition of passing an examination or acquiring a qualification is a taxable payment.

A payment made to an employee to reimburse him or her for the purchase of laptops or similar technological aids, is regarded as a taxable benefit/perquisite and PAYE, PRSI and USC must be operated on the value of the benefit. The value of the benefit must be calculated in line with the rules set out in TDM Part 05-01-01a.

A payment in regard to certain expenses incurred in studying for and sitting an examination, may be made without the charge to tax where all of the following conditions are satisfied:

- the course/qualification must bear some relationship to the employees duties;
- the amount paid is only a reimbursement of the expenses necessarily incurred;

- the payments can be vouched to receipts; and
- appropriate governance and control mechanisms are in operation together with supporting documentation.

Allowable expenses include the cost of course materials other than those provided as part of the course fees and certain travel expenses.

4.1 Travel expenses

Where the employee begins a journey to the course or exam centre directly from home or returns directly to home, then the expenses of travel that may be reimbursed without deduction of tax are the lesser of those incurred on the journey between:

(a) home and the course/exam centre; or
(b) the normal place of work and the course/exam centre.

The normal place of work is the place where the employee normally performs the duties of their employment. Determining an employee's normal place of work is a question of fact that can only be considered based on the specific circumstances of each case.

4.2 Records to be kept

The guidelines covering any tax-free payment, including the maintenance of records and a proper control system are set out in TDM Part 05-01-06 paragraph 1.3—Records to be kept.

These records can be subject to compliance intervention, in accordance with the Compliance Intervention Framework.

Pensions Manual

[17.13] On 15 March 2023, Revenue issued *eBrief 063/23* confirming amendments have been made to the pension manuals.

A number of updates have been made to the Pensions Manuals following a review and to reflect amendments in Finance Act 2022. The main changes are:

Chapter 7—Lump Sum Benefits and Commutation

This chapter has been updated to include a reference to pan-European personal pension products ('PEPPs') in the context of commuting a pension within 'trivial limits'.

Chapter 10—Benefits on Death-in-Service

This chapter has been updated in section 2 regarding capital acquisitions tax where an individual dies in service and the equivalent pension value is transferred to an approved retirement fund ('ARF').

Chapter 13—Transfer Payments

Section 2 has been updated to provide clarity on availability of transfer payments to a PEPP. It also provides a link to a new Chapter 31.

Chapter 17—Overseas Employers, Overseas Employees and Employees Seconded From Overseas

Section 3 has been updated to state that the section only applies to overseas employment contracts and includes an example clarifying the tax treatment of employees seconded from outside Ireland. It also removes guidance for seconded employees staying more than five years requiring Revenue's written permission.

Section 5 has been updated to include guidance that the treatment as set out in this section applies to both Irish and non-Irish employment contracts.

Section 6 has been updated to state that, in certain circumstances, a non-resident employee may remain in an Irish occupational pension scheme.

Section 7 is updated to provide clarity for overseas employees of Irish employers.

Section 8 has been updated to state that an employee on secondment from an Irish employer for up to five years can be deemed to remain on the payroll.

Section 10 has been updated to include a reference to PEPPs.

Chapter 23—Approved Retirement Benefits

This Chapter has been updated to include references to PEPPs.

Section 4, the specified income requirement, has been removed following the abolition of the approved minimum retirement fund ('AMRF') in the Finance Act 2021.

Section 5, the AMRF, has been updated to include guidance on the previous treatment of this product.

Section 8 has been updated with new contact details for qualified fund managers ('QFM') advising Revenue of the intention to act as a QFM.

Section 9 has been updated regarding capital acquisitions tax where an individual dies in service and the equivalent pension value is transferred to an ARF.

Chapter 24—Personal Retirement Savings Accounts ('PRSAs')

Section 24.2 has updated examples and includes a reference to PEPP.

A new section 24.3 is added which clarifies the position regarding employer contributions to a PRSA, following changes in the Finance Act 2022.

Section 24.7 has been updated to include details on the interaction of PEPP products with a PRSA.

Section 24.9 updates details of transfers from PRSAs to other pension products.

Section 24.14 includes a link to the new Chapter 31—PEPPs.

Chapter 25—Limit on Tax Relieved Pension Funds

Section 4 has been amended:

— to update the circumstances in which a benefit crystallisation event ('BCE') is deemed to occur to include cases where the assets are retained in a PEPP rather than transferred to an ARF;

— to include information on vested PEPPs;

— to include PEPPs within the definition of a 'relevant pension arrangement'.

Section 5 has been updated to include the circumstances in which the holder of a PEPP must provide the PEPP provider/administrator with a declaration relating to a BCE.

The BCE Declaration example within the appendix section has also been updated to allow for declarations relating to a PEPP.

Chapter 27—Taxation of Retirement Lump Sums

Section 3 has been updated to include a lump sum from a PEPP as a lump sum arrangement.

A link has been added to TDM Part 07-01-09A which deals with lump sums from a foreign pension under s 200A of the TCA 1997.

A new section 10 has been inserted to provide information on lump sums paid from a PEPP.

Section 15 has been updated to provide details on amendments to the new s 200A TCA, which deals with the treatment of lump sums from foreign pension arrangements.

Footnote 2 has been updated to include the UK as a country from which an individual can claim migrant member relief on a pre-existing pension arrangement.

Chapter 31—Pan-European Pension Products ('PEPPs')

A new Chapter 31 has been inserted into the Pension Manual which provides guidance relating to the taxation of PEPPs in Ireland.

The topics covered in this Chapter are tax relief, PRSI and USC, benefits on retirement, death benefits, interaction with other pension arrangements, vested PEPPs, transfers between PEPPs and other pension products, migrant member relief and PEPP sub-accounts, imputed distributions, non-residents and vested PEPPs, anti-avoidance, pension adjustment orders, retirement benefits not taken on or before age 75 and non-established PEPP providers.

Exemption from Income Tax in Respect of Certain Payments made under Employment Law

[17.14] On 4 March 2023, Revenue issued *eBrief 059/23* stating TDM Part 07-01-27 has been updated as follows:

1. Paragraph 2 has been amended to update the definitions of both 'relevant Act' and 'relevant authority':

Relevant Act:

— Sick Leave Act 2022 and Parent's Leave and Benefit Act 2019 were added as examples.

— Equal Status Acts 2000–2015 was removed as an example.

Relevant authority:

— A Rights Commissioner, the Director of the Equality Tribunal and an Employment Appeals Tribunal were removed as examples.

2. Paragraph 3 is updated to reflect the expanded opportunities for mediation under the Workplace Relations Act 2015. It now states that:

The Employment Equality Acts 1998 to 2021 and the Workplace Relations Act 2015 contain provisions that allow a dispute between an employee and an employer to be resolved through mediation. Where such mediation results in an agreement acceptable to both parties, the mediator draws up the terms of settlement for signature by both parties. A payment made by an employer in accordance with such a settlement may be treated as a payment made on foot of a recommendation, decision or determination by a relevant authority for the purposes of the exemption.

The exemption afforded by s 192A applies to payments made on foot of a recommendation, decision or determination by a 'relevant authority' (paragraph 2). The exemption also extends to a settlement arrived at under a mediation process provided for in a relevant Act.

3. Appendix 2 has been updated with redrafted examples of how the exemption operates in practice, such as:

Example 1

Michael made a claim under the Employment Equality Act 1998 claiming that he was discriminated against in a recruitment process at work. The WRC held that his employer had discriminated against him on grounds of civil status, family status and age in the manner in which it conducted the selection process for the relevant position. Michael was awarded €20,000 compensation for the distress suffered by him as a result of the discrimination.

Tax Treatment: The payment of €20,000 qualifies for exemption under s 192A of the TCA 1997.

Example 2

Siobhán, a civil servant, made a claim under the Employment Equality Act 1998 claiming that she was discriminated against by her employer when she was excluded from the higher pay scales applicable to senior members of her grade.

The WRC found that Siobhán's employer discriminated against her on age grounds and also found that she was victimised by her employer. She was awarded the higher pay scale payment and compensation of €8,000.

Tax Treatment: The payment of €8,000 awarded for victimisation qualifies for the exemption under s 192A of the TCA 1997. However, the higher scale payment itself is remuneration and chargeable under s 112 of the TCA 1997.

Payments on Termination of an Office or Employment or Removal from an Office or Employment

[17.15] On 14 March 2023, Revenue published *eBrief 057/23* confirming TDM Part 05-05-19—Payments on Termination of an Office or Employment or Removal from an Office or Employment, has been updated.

At paragraph 3.6 reference to Pensions Manual—Appendix V, was inserted, stating detailed guidance on the appropriate method to be used to calculate the present value of the pension lump sum for the purposes of the RCS calculation is available in Appendix V of the Revenue Pensions Manual.

Pensions Manual—Appendix V has also been amended as follows:

- An effective date for this guidance has been included.
- A reference to the use of this guidance for the purposes of the calculation of the increase in basic exemption has been added.

Pensions Manual—Appendix V should be read in conjunction with TDM 05-05-19.

Double Deduction of Tax at Source: Credit through PAYE System for Non-refundable Foreign Tax

[17.16] On 14 March 2023, Revenue published *eBrief 056/23* which noted that TDM Part 42-04-62 has been updated as follows:

- Paragraph 2.1.1 has been amended to reflect updated practice with regard to Irish employment income which is subject to payroll withholding tax in non-DTA jurisdictions, specifically relating to the claiming of unilateral relief in such circumstances.
- Paragraph 6 provides updated guidance on the funding of foreign payroll withholding tax liabilities which may arise when an Irish resident employee exercises duties abroad.
- The examples in Appendices 1 and 2 have been updated.
- The application form (Double Deduction 1) in Appendix 3 has been amended to request details of the intended departure and return dates to the State in respect of the assignment and also the expected work pattern of the employee between the two territories.

Employee Payroll Tax Deductions in Relation to Non-Irish Employments Exercised in the State

[17.17] On 6 March 2023, Revenue issued *eBrief 047/23* stating TDM Part 42-04-65 has been amended. The contents of Chapter 5 of TDM Part 42-04-65 relating to internationally mobile employees and tax equalisation have been removed. More detailed guidance on these matters has been published in TDM Part 02-04-01—Tax Equalisation Arrangements.

PAYE/USC Regulations—Emergency Tax

[17.18] On 27 February 2023, Revenue issued *eBrief 042/23* confirming TDM Part 42-04-24a has been updated to reflect the increase in tax bands introduced by the Finance Act 2022.

In addition, examples throughout the manual have been updated including relevant references to information on the revenue website.

Income Tax (Employments) Regulations 2018

[17.19] On 17 January 2023, Revenue issued *eBrief 011/23* which noted that TDM Part 42-04-71 has been updated to reflect the changes made to the Income Tax (Employments) Regulations 2018[2] as a result of the Income Tax (Employments) Regulations 2022.[3]

These changes, which are operational from 1 January 2023, amend the Income Tax (Employments) Regulations 2018 that prescribe the manner in which the deduction of tax from salaries and wages under the 'Pay As You Earn' system operates.

The changes are as follows:

- Regulation 4(1)(a) is amended to provide that the reliefs from income tax which an employee is entitled to for the year may include reliefs in respect of which a claim has been made, prior to the end of the year of assessment, through such electronic means as Revenue will make available. The amendment also provides clarity that tax relief available under s 469 of the Taxes Consolidation Act 1997 ('Relief for health expenses') may be included on a claim made prior to the end of the year of assessment.
- Regulation 10(1) is amended to provide clarity that an employer is required to send certain information relating to a payment of emoluments to an employee using the prescribed form which is 'a notification', and to provide for the reporting of certain information in respect of employee and employer contributions to a PEPP.

---

2 Income Tax (Employments) Regulations 2018 (SI 345/2018).

3 Income Tax (Employments) Regulations 2022 (SI 690/2022).

— Regulation 11(3) is a technical amendment amending the reference from 'section' to 'Regulation'.
— Regulation 17(2) is amended to provide clarity that an employer is required to send certain information relating to the commencement of a new employee in employment using the prescribed form which is 'a notification'.
— New Regulation 22A, which provides that an employer may, in certain circumstances and where no payment of emolument is made during the last income tax month of the year, make a repayment of tax to an employee during the last income tax month of the year so that the employee can get the benefit of any unused credits at the end of the year under the cumulative PAYE system.
— Regulation 27 is amended to require an employer to correct a return for any pay period when requested to do so by Revenue.
— Regulation 31, which provides for net pay arrangements, is amended in paragraph 1 to include contributions to a PEPP in the meaning of 'allowable contribution'.

EMPLOYMENT TAX CASES

Deductibility of Employee Expenses

[17.20] ***HMRC v Kunjur[4]—Court of Appeal of England and Wales—Cannan, Jonathon & Bacon LJJ—appeal from First-Tier Tribunal—Income Tax (Earnings and Pensions) Act 2003—whether living accommodation rental expenses were incurred wholly exclusively and necessarily in the performance of the doctor's duties of employment.***

This was an appeal by the HMRC against a decision of the First-tier Tribunal ('FTT'), which allowed in part an appeal by Mr Kunjur against income tax assessments and penalties for the tax years 2012–13 to 2016–17.

Mr Kunjur was an experienced dental surgeon who was undertaking further training as a maxillofacial surgeon. To undertake this training, Mr Kunjur took the only available position, which was at a hospital in South London, with occasional duties at another hospital in the same area. His family was based in Southampton:

He claimed a tax deduction for accommodation expenses incurred to avoid unmanageable commutes for employment purposes at a London hospital. HMRC considered that the expenses were not deductible and charged a penalty for carelessly claiming such a deduction. Mr Kunjur claimed he was entitled to relief for that expenditure in his tax return for the relevant tax years.

The FTT held that Mr Kunjur was entitled to relief for a proportion of expenditure. By using the self-employment test in the Income Tax (Trading and Other Income) Act 2005,

4 *Commissioners for HMRC v Kunjur* [2023] UKUT 00154 (TCC). See *Arthur Cox Employment Law Yearbook 2021* at [20.30] for decision of the FTT in *Kunjur v Commissioners for Her Majesty's Revenue and Customs* [2021] UKFTT 362 (TC).

the FTT considered that the portion of expenditure to be allowed was to be determined by reference to the amount of time it considered he spent at the premises performing some of the duties of his employment. The FTT addressed three issues in its decision: (1) whether Mr Kunjur was obliged to incur the expenses as holder of the employment; (2) whether the expenses were incurred wholly and exclusively in the performance of the duties of the employment; and (3) whether the expenses were incurred in the performance of the duties of the employment. The FTT answered all three issues in favour of Mr Kunjur, subject to apportionment of the expenditure according to the time spent on formal and informal on-call duties, research, and article preparation. It recognised that this would be only a 'small proportion' and allowed him to appeal against the penalty; the appeal was allowed in full.

HMRC appealed to the Upper Tribunal (Tax and Chancery Chamber) (the 'UT') on all three grounds. Shortly before the hearing of the appeal, Mr Kunjur withdrew his case on the appeal, citing his concern about his potential liability to costs if HMRC were to succeed. Accordingly, HMRC stated that it would not seek costs against Mr Kunjur if its appeal succeeded.

The UT concluded the FTT erred in law in its approach to all three issues and reached conclusions that were not supported by the relevant authorities or the facts.

The UT's decision highlights the stricter regime for the deductibility of expenses for employees than the regime for the self-employed. The underlying policy rationale for the stricter regime is that employees should be provided by their employers with all the facilities to enable them to carry out their duties and therefore there is little reason for additional expenditure to be incurred by employees. The principal statutory requirement for the self-employed to deduct expenses is that the expenses are incurred 'wholly and exclusively' for the purposes of the business (per s 34 of the Income Tax (Trading and Other Income) Act 2005). For employees, the equivalent statutory provision (s 336(1) of the Income Tax (Earnings and Pensions) Act 2003) requires both that the employee is obliged to incur the expenses as holder of the employment and that the amount claimed is 'incurred wholly, exclusively and necessarily in the performance of the duties of the employment'. This is a cumulative test. Accordingly, the appeal would have succeeded if HMRC succeeded on any of the grounds of appeal, however here the HMRC succeeded on all three grounds.

Whether Mr Kunjur was obliged to incur the expenses as holder of the employment

On the first ground, the UT concluded that the FTT was wrong to suggest that the test of whether an employee was obliged to incur the expenditure as holder of the employment may be a subjective test, and that there was no distinction between offices and employments in this regard. The UT applied the objective test established by the House of Lords in *Ricketts v Colquhoun*[5] and *Owen v Pook*,[6] which required the FTT to consider whether all doctors employed in the same role as Mr Kunjur would be obliged to incur expenditure of that nature, or whether the rental of accommodation was a

5 *Ricketts v Colquhoun* 10 TC 118.
6 *Owen v Pook* [1970] AC 244.

matter of personal choice for Mr Kunjur arising from his personal circumstances. The UT concluded that the reason Mr Kunjur had to incur the expenditure was not because he was obliged to do so by reason of the nature of the employment, but because his family home was in Southampton, which was a matter of personal choice. The UT held that it was therefore irrelevant whether it was reasonable to expect Mr Kunjur to use other accommodation (ie, the student/dorm accommodation) that was available to him, or to uproot his family, as those were factors personal to Mr Kunjur.

Whether the expenses were incurred wholly and exclusively in the performance of the duties of the employment

On the second ground, the UT held that the FTT erred in law in finding that the expenditure could be apportioned to identify an amount that was incurred wholly and exclusively in the performance of the duties. The UT followed the well-established principle that the words 'wholly and exclusively' limit relief in respect of expenditure that serves a dual purpose, and that no deduction is available where the expenditure is required for the performance of the duties but also serves a personal purpose. The UT cited examples of such expenditure from *Bolam v Barlow*[7] and *Hillyer v Leeke*[8] and noted that the position was similar to that of self-employed individuals, as illustrated by *Mallalieu v Drummond*.[9] The UT rejected the FTT's analysis that any personal advantage to Mr Kunjur was merely an effect of the expenditure rather than the object of the expenditure and held that Mr Kunjur's object was clearly to provide himself with living accommodation during his working week for both employment purposes and personal purposes.

Whether the expenses were incurred in the performance of the duties of the employment

On the third ground, the UT held that the FTT erred in law in finding that the expenditure on the accommodation was incurred by Mr Kunjur in the performance of his duties. The UT applied the reasoning of Vinelott J in *Elderkin v Hindmarsh*,[10] who held that expenditure on living allowances for an engineer who had to work away from home was not incurred in the performance of his duties, but simply put him in a position to do the work he was employed to do. The UT also quoted Viscount Cave in *Ricketts v Colquhoun*, who stated that an employee does not, as a rule, eat or sleep while performing his duties, but either before or after their performance. The UT accepted that the accommodation was being used while Mr Kunjur performed his duties but held that the expenditure was not incurred in the performance of the duties but was incidental expenditure that provided Mr Kunjur with accommodation from which he could, among other things, take calls and carry out research.

Analysis

The UT's decision is a clear application of the statutory test in s 336(1) of the Income Tax (Earnings and Pensions) Act 2003 and the relevant caselaw on the deductibility of

7 *Bolam v Barlow* 31 TC 136.
8 *Hillyer v Leeke* [1976] STC 490.
9 *Mallalieu v Drummond* [1983] STC 665.
10 *Elderkin v Hindmarsh* [1988] STC 267.

employee expenses. The UT demonstrated that the FTT had misunderstood or misapplied the test in several respects and had reached conclusions that were not consistent with the authorities or the facts. The UT's decision confirms that the test is a strict and objective one, and that expenditure on living accommodation that serves the dual purpose of enabling an employee to perform the duties of the employment and providing personal comfort and convenience is not deductible from earnings.

Recovery of Tax from Employee

[17.21] ***67TACD2023[11]—PAYE/USC—Tax Appeals Commission—whether the respondent was entitled to proceed to recover from the appellant, the tax under-deducted by his former employers***

This is an appeal against PAYE/USC end-of-year statements issued by the Revenue Commissioners for the tax years 2014–2017, which showed an underpayment of tax totalling €2,505.

The appellant submitted that his former employers failed to remit the correct quantum of tax deducted from his wages to the respondent on his behalf and that his former employers were liable to pay and discharge the outstanding tax. He submitted that he was being subjected to double taxation by the respondent's demand for the outstanding tax, which was unlawful, unfair and contrary to the respondent's code of practice.

The respondent submitted that an underpayment of tax arose as employer tax deductions from the appellant's remuneration were not sufficient, based on the appellant's total income for the relevant tax years of assessment. The respondent's officials assessed the appellant to tax on the basis that the appellant was liable to discharge the outstanding tax in accordance with reg 28(3) of the Income Tax (Employments) (Consolidated) Regulations, 2001.[12] Section 986 (Regulations) of the Taxes Consolidation Act 1997 provides for the making of regulations by the Revenue Commissioners which allow for the collection and recovery of tax from the employee in certain circumstances where the tax should have been deducted by the employer from the employee's emoluments. Regulation 28(3) provides that the Revenue Commissioners may recover the amount of an under-deduction from an employee in certain circumstances, namely, where they are satisfied that the employer took reasonable care to comply with the regulations and that the under-deduction arose due to an error made in good faith.

The respondent submitted that the underpayment of tax arose from the under-deduction of tax by the appellant's employers. One of the employers incorrectly operated the appellant's payroll using a cumulative basis rather than a week 1 basis of calculation and later corrected the error following an investigation by the joint investigations unit in August 2018. However, an underpayment arose in 2014 and 2015 as the amount of tax collected in the employment was insufficient taking into account other employments

---

11 67TACD2023.

12 Income Tax (Employments) (Consolidated) Regulations 2001 (SI 559/2001).

falling within the tax years of assessment. The under-deduction in 2016 and 2017 arose as the appellant's other employer did not operate the updated P2C issued in November 2016. As these errors were made in good faith and the employers took reasonable care to comply with the regulations, the respondent submitted that the appellant was liable to pay the tax in accordance with reg 28(3). Accordingly, the respondent clarified that the underpayments of tax did not arise because of a shortfall in the remittance of taxes by either employer. Instead, the respondent submitted, the appellant received the benefit of the remittances made and there was no shortfall in the sums credited to him by the respondent based on the remittances.

The Commissioner determined that the respondent was entitled to recover the underpayment of tax from the appellant pursuant to reg 28(3), as the respondent was satisfied that the employers met the conditions of the regulation, and that the appellant received the benefit of the remittances made by the employers. The Commissioner rejected the appellant's assertion that his employers failed to remit the tax deducted from his wages.

The Commissioner also rejected the appellant's claim of double taxation, as the underpayment of tax was based on the appellant's total income for each tax year, which exceeded the tax deducted by the employers. The Commissioner upheld the end-of-year statements for 2014 to 2017, subject to any reductions made since the commencement of the appeal.

The Commissioner's determination was based on the facts and figures provided by the respondent, which showed the breakdown of the appellant's income, tax paid, tax liability, and underpayment for each tax year. The Commissioner also relied on the relevant legislation, namely Part 42, Chapter 4 (ss 983–997A) of the Taxes Consolidation Act 1997, which provides for the collection and recovery of income tax on emoluments, and reg 28(3) of the Income Tax (Employments) (Consolidated) Regulations 2001, which allows the respondent to recover the underpayment of tax from the employee in certain circumstances. The Commissioner found that the respondent had applied the legislation correctly and that the appellant had not established any grounds to challenge the respondent's decision.

The case illustrates the operation of the PAYE system and the obligations of both employers and employees in relation to the deduction and remittance of tax. It also demonstrates the scope and limitations of reg 28(3), which gives the respondent discretion to recover the underpayment of tax from the employee rather than the employer, subject to certain conditions. The case highlights the importance of employers' compliance with the regulations and the P2Cs issued by the Revenue Commissioners, as well as employees' awareness of their tax affairs and the impact of their total income on their tax liability.

The relevant statutory provision, reg 28(3) of the Income Tax (Employments) (Consolidated) Regulations 2001, provides that the respondent must be satisfied that the employer took reasonable care to comply with the provisions of the regulation and must be satisfied that the under-deduction was due to an error made in good faith.

Accordingly, the appeal was denied, and the assessments upheld.

Failure to Register Additional Employment

[17.22] ***81TACD2023[13]—PAYE/USC—Tax Appeals Commission—recovery of underpaid tax from employee due to failure to register additional employment***

This appeal concerned a taxpayer's challenge to Statements of Liability issued by the Revenue Commissioner ('Revenue') showing underpayments of PAYE and USC for tax years 2016, 2017 and 2018. The underpayment arose from the appellant's tax credit certificates in 2016, 2017 and 2018 not recording his part-time employment with a different employer to his full-time employer. Revenue made deductions from the appellant's tax credits in subsequent years to discharge the tax due.

The appellant's submissions were primarily focused on the contention that he should not be held liable for a mistake that he believed had been made by Revenue and which had resulted in him being obliged to repay tax. Revenue denied that it was responsible for the error and stated that it had not been properly notified of the appellant's additional part-time employment. The appellant explained in his submissions that the deductions to his tax credits by Revenue placed him and his family under extreme financial pressure.

The Commissioner had regard to the High Court decision in *Menolly Homes Ltd v Appeal Commissioners*[14] and explained that the onus lay on the appellant to demonstrate that the Statements of Liability issued by Revenue were incorrect. The Commissioner was satisfied that the appellant had not so demonstrated; indeed, it seemed to the Commissioner that the appellant was not disputing that the underpayment had arisen.

The appellant contended that the underpayment arose due to an error by Revenue. The Commissioner was satisfied that s 112(1) and s 960C of the TCA 1997, read together, confirmed that the appellant was liable for the tax underpayments, and for the repayment of that liability. Furthermore, while the appellant was unhappy with the manner in which Revenue had sought to recoup the underpayment, the Commissioner considered that this was a matter he did not have jurisdiction to consider in this appeal, which was focused on Revenue's finding that an underpayment had arisen.

The Commissioner agreed with Revenue that the appellant seemed to be seeking to appeal Revenue's management of his tax affairs, and that this was not an appealable matter under the TCA 1997. Section 949A of the TCA 1997 provides that an 'appealable matter' means 'any matter in respect of which an appeal is authorised by the Acts'. The Commissioner was satisfied that the TCA 1997 does not authorise the making of an appeal on the basis of Revenue's management of a taxpayer's tax affairs. Furthermore, the Commissioner accepted the submission of Revenue that it was incumbent on the appellant to check the tax credit certificates issued for 2016 and 2017, and to notify Revenue that one of his employers was not thereon recorded.

Insofar as the appellant submitted that the PAYE system generally was not fit for purpose, and/or that Revenue's management of the PAYE system was generally

13 81TACD2023.

14 *Menolly Homes Ltd v Appeal Commissioners* [2010] IEHC 49.

deficient or unsatisfactory, the Commissioner was satisfied that such arguments were outside his jurisdiction.

Refund of Overpaid Taxes

[17.23] ***87TACD2023[15]—PRSI—Tax Appeals Commission—appeal against the refusal by Revenue to refund overpayments on the ground that repayments were sought outside the statutory timeframe***

This was an appeal brought by the taxpayer against the refusal by Revenue to refund an overpayment of income tax for 2017 in the amount of €3,202.03 on the ground that the repayment was sought outside of the statutory timeframe.

On 7 June 2022, the appellant filed her Form 11 income tax return relating to the chargeable period of 2017. The return showed she had made an overpayment of €3,202.03. On 20 July 2022, the respondent refused the appellant's claim for a repayment as the claim was not made within the prescribed time frame, that is within four years of the chargeable period.

The appellant submitted that, due Covid-19 lockdowns and the closure of offices she had great difficulty in understanding the revenue system and in finding someone she could speak to in person or over the phone in order to better understand the process and timelines required. The Commissioner held that the burden of proof in the appeals process rests with the tax payer and that s 865(2) of the TCA 1997 provides that a person is entitled to a repayment of tax paid where it was not due, however s 865(4) provides that this repayment shall not be allowed unless a claim is made within four years of the end of the chargeable period to which the overpayment relates. The Commissioner noted that the timeframe set out in s 865(4) was not a discretionary timeframe, and neither Revenue nor the Tax Appeals Commission could disapply it or consider any mitigating circumstances. The appeal was denied and the Commissioner held that Revenue was correct in refusing the repayment of an overpayment of tax where it was not claimed within the statutory timeframe.

Deduction of Employee Expenses

[17.24] ***91TACD2023[16]—PAYE—Tax Appeals Commission—appeal against the refusal by Revenue to allow a deduction of the costs of radon remediation in the taxpayer's dwelling while using the home as a workplace due to Covid-19 restrictions***

This was an appeal by the taxpayer of Revenue's decision to refuse the appellant's claim for a deduction from his assessable income for the year 2020 of an amount of €3,355.46. The expense was incurred in respect of the carrying out of radon remediation

---

15 87TACD2023.

16 91TACD2023.

works (the 'works') to his home, which was located in a high radon area, in July 2020, a period during which the appellant was also required to work from home as a result of Covid-19 restrictions.

The appellant's home was located in an area that had high levels of radon as defined by European legislation, which he set out to the Commissioner. The home was purchased in 2020 and the appellant was aware of the radon levels in the area prior to the purchase. The appellant had acquired the services of a radon tester approved by the Environmental Protection Agency ('EPA'), who produced a report on 8 June 2020 finding that the home had high levels of radon throughout. This report strongly recommended that remediation works be carried out on the property to reduce the amount of radon prevalent, for the safety of all its inhabitants. The appellant followed the recommendations in the report and engaged an EPA-approved contractor to carry out those works. The appellant gave evidence that this contractor advised that the cost of the works could likely be claimed back from either his employer, or failing that, as a deduction by way of submission to Revenue of a tax return. The contractor suggested that the government restrictions requiring the appellant to work from home would constitute grounds for claiming the costs of the works as a deduction.

The appellant submitted that, as his employer was under a statutory duty under the Health, Safety and Welfare at Work Act 2005 to provide him with a safe working environment, and under that same legislation he was required as an employee to make reasonable provision for his own safety and welfare by carrying out the works.

The appellant conceded in cross-examination that he always intended to have the works carried out regardless of the move to working from home during 2020, calling the works 'essential' as the health of he and his family would have been endangered had the radon levels not been reduced by the works.

The appellant's employer declined to reimburse the appellant for the works, so on 7 January 2021, the appellant filed a Form12 for the tax year 2020 and claimed a deduction from his assessable income in the amount of €3,355.46 for the cost of the works. This deduction was refused by Revenue on the grounds that the works amounted to renovations and improvements to the family home, which were not expended 'wholly, exclusively and necessarily' in the performance of his duties of employment.

The facts material to the case were not in dispute and so the first matter to be addressed by the Commissioner was the scope of s 114 of the TCA 1997, which provides that, in relation to deductions in respect of Schedule E income where a holder of an office or employment of profit has to incur expenses travelling in the performance of the duties of that office or employment, or otherwise to expend money wholly, exclusively and necessarily in the performance of those duties, a deduction may be made from the emoluments of the office or employment.

Both the appellant and respondent addressed s 114 of the TCA 1997. The appellant submitted that this provision specifically permitted a deduction for work-related expenses and that the interpretation of this provision by the respondent was so restrictive as to make it an unusable provision. The appellant also submitted that *Customs*

Commissioners v Banerjee,[17] which was also cited by the respondent, indicated that the 'exclusively' element of the rule had been overruled in the UK courts and a duality of purpose should not preclude the claim being made.

The respondent submitted that *Revenue Commissioners v Doorley*[18] requires that where a tax is imposed clearly by statute then any exempting provision must be interpreted strictly. On this basis the respondent submitted that the deduction which the appellant sought fell outside what is permitted by s 114. The respondent also disagreed with the appellant's interpretation of *Bannerjee* and submitted that it did not expand the scope of the 'exclusivity' test. The respondent pointed out that *Bannerjee* determined that the expenses deducted in that case were for the sole purpose of the claimant's job at the time, and the judgment contained *obiter* which indicated that if the claimant had had a duality of purpose then the expenses claimed would not have been deductible.

The Commissioner found that the *Bannerjee* test did not indicate a more expansive reading of the 'exclusivity' test was required and did in fact have the effect that any duality of purpose in incurring an expense would be fatal to that test.

The appellant cited Directive 2013/59/EURATOM[19] (the '2013 Directive') which lays down basic safety standards for protections against the dangers arising from exposure to ionising radiation. Article 5 of the 2013 Directive establishes legal requirements and a regulatory regime for all exposure situations to radiation and requires Member States to take measures and identify and evaluate exposure situations and develop a national action plan for long-term risks relating to radon exposure in dwellings and workplaces. The appellant submitted that during the period in which he was required to work from home, part of the performance of his duties was to ensure he had a safe working environment, and as such his employer was under a duty to reimburse him for any expenditure incurred, or alternatively the respondent would have to allow the deduction from the sum of his assessable income. The appellant further submitted that the respondent was failing in its duty to protect the health and safety of the appellant's family by refusing to allow the deduction, thereby breaching directly effective EU law, including the 2013 Directive.

The Commissioner pointed out that the appellant's own evidence was clear that the works would have been carried out irrespective of working from home protocols in place due to his own safety and wellbeing and that of his family being at risk. The Commissioner noted that reimbursement from the appellant's employer remained a matter between them and was not within the Commission's jurisdiction. The Commissioner found that the appellant's argument regarding the direct effect of the 2013 Directive was misconceived and that the function of the Commission was not to determine whether his obligations under that Directive had been met. The Commissioner determined that

17 *Customs Commissioners v Banerjee* [2011] 1 ALL ER 985.

18 *Revenue Commissioners v Doorley* [1993] I.R. 750.

19 Directive 2013/59/EURATOM laying down basic safety standards for protection against the dangers arising from exposure to ionising radiation, and repealing Directives 89/618/Euratom, 90/641/Euratom, 96/29/Euratom, 97/43/Euratom and 2003/122/Euratom.

none of the provisions of European legislation cited by the appellant made any relief in respect of the works cost mandatory.

The appellant also cited various articles in the Charter of Fundamental Rights of the European Union, including those concerning human dignity, the right to life, the right to bodily integrity, the freedom to engage in work, respect for private and family life, the rights of the child, the right to fair and just working conditions, the right to health care, environmental protection, the right to an effective remedy and the right to equality before the law. The appellant submitted that the refusal of the deduction claim was in violation of these articles due to the very serious health concerns relating to radon exposure. The appellant also submitted that refusal to allow the deduction would constitute unequal treatment, and cited examples of employees under the flat rate expenses regime, the e-working expenses regime, those paying annual professional subscriptions, and local councillors. The appellant submitted that he had a legitimate expectation that his claim would be allowed based on the treatment of these other categories of taxpayers which was inconsistent with the scope of s 114 of the TCA 1997. The appellant submitted that the Commission should find in his favour on the grounds of the expenses falling within the 'wholly and exclusively' test on the basis of legitimate expectations as an EU law principle.

The Commissioner found that the relief offered under alternative exemptions were irrelevant to the appeal before him and related to claiming entirely different expenses. He was also unable to see where the appellant had evidenced any breach of his fundamental rights as he was not blocked from carrying out the works.

The Commissioner found that the cost of the works were not incurred wholly and exclusively in the performance of his employment as a civil servant and there was no contravention of directly effective EU law by stringently reading s 114 of the TCA 1997. Consequently, the Commissioner found the respondent was correct in refusing the deduction to be allowed, and the appeal failed.

Payment of Remuneration versus Preferential Loans

[17.25] ***99TACD2023[20]—PAYE, PRSI, USC—Tax Appeals Commission—appeal against Notices of Estimation for years 2012, 2014, 2015 and 2016 in relation to payments made to director, shareholder and employee—whether payments constituted remuneration or preferential loans***

This was an appeal by an unlimited company against certain PAYE/PRSI/USC Notices of Estimation of Amounts Due issued by Revenue in respect of the years 2012, 2014, 2015 and 2016 (each a 'Notice' and together, the 'Notices'). The Notices arose as a result of various untaxed payments made to an employee, director and shareholder of the company (the 'director'). The respondent considered the nature of each payment made to the director to be remuneration chargeable to tax under the PAYE system in

[20] 99TACD2023.

the year of receipt, however the appellant disputed this and considered each to be preferential loans advanced to the director or consideration paid in exchange for goodwill thereby requiring different tax treatment.

Preferential loans would give rise under s 122 of the TCA 1997 to the receipt by the director of perquisites chargeable to tax under s 112 of the TCA 1997, only on the difference between the interest actually paid in respect of each loan and that which would have been paid had the 'specified rate' of 13.5% been paid under s 122 of the TCA 1997.

The 2012 Notice of Estimation

On 13 November 2012, the appellant transferred €1,177,000 to the director's personal account. In the appellant's P35 end-of-year return for 2012 the appellant disclosed that the director was the sole employee and was paid €50,000.00 in emoluments, from which the appropriate deductions of €20,500.00 was deducted under the PAYE system, €2,818.52 was deducted for USC and €2000.04 was deducted for PRSI. The appellant did not dispute that no tax was returned to the respondent in respect of the €1,177,000 paid to the director, and that this payment was not recorded as a loan on the CT1 corporation tax return submitted by the appellant for 2012.

On 12 December 2012 the respondent issued its Notice of Estimation for 2012 in which it had assessed that the €1,177,000 payment was remuneration paid to the director and that an income tax liability of €588,278.52 was due, and, when PRSI was included, the liability was assessed at €612,039.

The appellant appealed this Notice on the grounds that the PAYE figure was 'incorrect and excessive' and that certain expenditure items incurred wholly and exclusively for the purpose of trade were disallowed. The respondent accepted that, while the director had made certain payments to the appellant totalling €210,000 in 2018 or 2019, these were not repayments of a loan and could not retrospectively alter the character of a payment. The appellant submitted that the payment of €1,177,000 should be treated as a loan given at a preferential rate and taxed only as a perquisite. The appellant further asserted that they had not fully understood that irrespective of whether the loan was for a *bona fide* purpose there would be tax implications for the company and so the funds were repaid in a number of instalments between 2018 and 2020. Section 122 of the TCA 1997 in relation to preferential loan arrangements provides that where there is outstanding, for the whole or part of a year, a loan from an employer to a Schedule E employee, the employee will be treated as having a perquisite chargeable to tax under s 112 of the TCA 1997. Section 122 provides that tax will be charged only on the difference between the interest actually paid in respect of each loan and that which would have been paid had the 'specified rate' of 13.5% been paid under s 122(2) of the TCA 1997.

The Commissioner noted that the appellant's notices of appeal were lacking in specificity and while the agent for the appellant who appeared at the Commission gave oral evidence clarifying the appellant's position, no documentary evidence was provided in support of the appellant's case that this 2012 payment was described as a loan.

The respondent refuted that the payment was a loan and cited *TJ v Criminal Assets Bureau*[21] and *Hudson v Hudson (HM Inspector of Taxes)*[22] in submitting that the tax system relies on self-assessment and the burden of proof in an appeal in proving the appellant's tax realities, rested with the appellant as only the taxpayer is in a position to know their own affairs and that as such, the appellant was obligated to proffer some evidence in support of his case. The respondent submitted that no evidence had been produced to support the appellant's assertions that the 2012 payment constituted a loan. The respondent argued that the minimal documentary evidence provided actually ran directly contrary to the suggestion that this was a loan and that any payments made by the director in 2018 and 2019 could not retrospectively change the character of the 2012 payment.

The 2014, 2015 and 2015 Notices of Estimation

In each of the years of assessment for 2014, 2015 and 2015 the respondent issued Notices to the appellant raising an assessment for significant amounts of PAYE/PRSI/USC being payable for each year of assessment. Each of these Notices were appealed by the appellant on the grounds that the PAYE figure was incorrect and overstated and that the liability appeared to be related to a benefit-in-kind arising on a director's loan, the details of which were in dispute with Revenue. The respondent submitted that this could not be accepted as it was not specified as a ground of appeal in the Notice of Appeal and could not be entered orally during the hearing.

It was not disputed that payments were made by the appellant to the director in 2014, 2015 and 2016, totalling €32,733, €77,705 and €31,293 respectively. The respondent took the view that these payments constituted remuneration chargeable to PAYE, PRSI and USC. Tax was assessed on each of those figures, and the remainder of the amounts assessed for each year in the Notices arose from the respondent's decision to treat the aforementioned €1,177,000 payment as an outstanding preferential loan made by the appellant to the director, chargeable as a perquisite. The respondent referred to this proportion of the amounts as 'alternative assessments' which should only stand if the issue in appeal in the 2012 Notice was determined against the respondent.

The appellant clarified in oral arguments that the payments made in 2014, 2015 and 2016 respectively were consideration for the transfer by the director of the goodwill attaching to his practice. The goodwill was valued in the appellant's accounts at €750,000 however this was not paid as consideration and instead the appellant submitted that they had received this amount in the form of a director's loan, repayable over time, and that the aforementioned payments in 2014, 2015 and 2016 respectively were repayments of this loan. The respondent submitted that there was no evidence to support the assertion that those payments constituted preferential loan payments and as such these were assessed as remuneration paid which would be chargeable to PAYE.

The appellant was put on proof to show that goodwill existed and that €750,000 was the open market value following submissions by the respondent that, in correspondence in

21 *TJ v Criminal Assets Bureau* [2008] IEHC 168.

22 *Hudson v Hudson (HM Inspector of Taxes)* 42 TC 380.

2016, the appellant's agent had previously stated to the respondent that no goodwill was being claimed. The agent opted not to proceed with arguments relating to the alleged transfer of goodwill.

The agent observed that if the charges arising as a consequence of the 2012 payment were to stand, this would cause the appellant to be subjected to double taxation and that the Commissioner would need to make adjustments accordingly based on the findings of the issue relating to the 2012 Notice. The respondent agreed.

The Commissioner found that the sole issue to be determined was the characterisation of the 2012 payment and found that the appellant had failed to establish that this was a preferential loan and agreed with the respondent that documentary evidence produced by the appellant suggested the contrary. The Commissioner noted that the appellant would have needed to have given cogent evidence explaining why the supposed loan had not been recorded in the CT1 for corporation tax and that assertions made by the agent for the appellant were not sufficient evidence as they could not be cross-examined.

The Commissioner's view in relation to the 2014, 2015 and 2016 Notices was that an adjustment was required due to the finding that the 2012 payment did not constitute a loan and must be reduced by Revenue.

Finally, the Commissioner assessed whether the 2014, 2015 and 2016 payments made to the director constituted remuneration. He noted that the respondent put the appellant on full proof as to whether any goodwill transaction had occurred and the appellant at hearing abandoned their argument. No evidence was proffered by the appellant that there were any terms attached to these payments requiring repayment by the director and so could not deem them to be preferential loans chargeable to a perquisite, rather than remuneration.

Special Assignee Relief Program (SARP)

[17.26] ***98TACD2023[23]—SARP—Tax Appeals Commission—appeal from decision of Revenue Commissioners—whether the respondent was correct in refusing to grant relief under SARP to the appellant on the grounds Form SARP 1A was not submitted within the prescribed 90-day period of arriving in the State***

This was an appeal against the refusal by the respondent, the Revenue Commissioners, to grant relief under the Special Assignee Relief Programme ('SARP') to the appellant. SARP is a tax relief for employees assigned to work in Ireland by foreign employers or associated companies provided they satisfy certain conditions.

The appellant arrived in Ireland and commenced employment on 13 February 2022. On 18 February the appellant applied for a PPS Number which he received on 4 May 2022. On 12 May he emailed the respondent seeking an appointment to obtain a public services card ('PSC') to assist with accessing a range of public services. On 17 May he

23 98TACD2023.

was informed the earliest appointment would be in August. On 2 June he corresponded again in relation to the PSC and on 17 June he walked into the PSC centre and waited six hours to obtain an appointment. On 24 June he received his PSC and submitted his Form SARP 1A.

On 27 June, the respondent corresponded with the appellant denying the relief on the ground that the application was not submitted to Revenue within 90 days of arrival in the State and therefore the appellant failed meet the qualifying condition set out in s 825C(2A)(e) of the TCA 1997. The appellant wrote back to explain that he could not submit his Form SARP 1A within 90 days, as both his PPSN and PSC took a considerable amount of time to issue, despite the application being made in early course. On 25 August 2022, the respondent issued formal correspondence refusing the appellant SARP relief, which the appellant appealed to the Commission on 20 October.

The appellant submitted that he applied for the PPSN and PSC in a timely manner but faced delays in obtaining them due to the Covid-19 pandemic and the high demand for PSC appointments. He also stated that he had completed the form and returned it to his employer, who certified it, within 90 days, and that his employer was not familiar with the SARP process and did not advise him to send the form by post.

The respondent submitted that the increased timeline of 150 days during the Covid-19 pandemic was not the case at the time of the appellant's application. The respondent advised that no concessions were available here in respect of the 90 days' timeline and that the Form SARP 1A can be submitted without a PPSN but will not be processed until a PPSN is provided.

The Commissioner had to interpret the provisions of s 825C(2A)(e) of the TCA 1997 and decide whether the appellant met the qualifying conditions to be a 'relevant employee' for the purposes of SARP relief. The Commissioner applied the well-established principles of statutory interpretation, as summarised by the High Court in *Perrigo Pharma International Activity Company v McNamara, the Revenue Commissioners, Minister for Finance, Ireland and the Attorney General*.[24] The Commissioner adopted a literal interpretative approach and gave the words of the statutory provision their plain, ordinary and natural meaning. The Commissioner also considered the context of the words, both within the TCA 1997 and the wider purpose and intention of the relief scheme.

The Commissioner found that the word 'certifies' in s 825C(2A)(e) of the TCA 1997 meant that the employer had to attest or confirm in a formal statement, on a form provided by the respondent, that the appellant complied with the other conditions set out in s 825C(2A)(a)–(d) of the TCA 1997, within 90 days of his arrival in the State. The Commissioner noted that the use of commas in the statutory provision indicated that the word 'certifies' was linked with the 90-day time limit, and that the expression 'in such form as the Revenue Commissioners may require' was separate from the verb 'certifies' and the time limit. The Commissioner observed that the statutory provision

24 *Perrigo Pharma International Activity Company v McNamara, the Revenue Commissioners, Minister for Finance, Ireland and the Attorney General* [2020] IEHC 552.

did not specify that the form had to be submitted, delivered or received by the respondent within 90 days, and that it was not for the Commission or the respondent to add words that were not contained in the statutory provision.

The Commissioner was satisfied that the appellant's employer had certified the Form SARP 1A within 90 days of the appellant's arrival in the State, as evidenced by the date on the form, and that the appellant had met the other criteria to be a 'relevant employee' under s 825C(2A)(a)–(d) of the TCA 1997. The Commissioner was not persuaded by the respondent's argument that the form had to 'land on its desk' within 90 days, as this was not in accordance with the wording or the intention of the statutory provision.

The Commissioner was satisfied that the practical application of seeking the relief and the intention of the legislation and the overarching context confirmed that the relief was introduced to assist the economy and attract employees from abroad. Accordingly, it could not be the case that it is impossible to apply for the relief unless one knows that the form can be submitted without a PPSN by paper format. This would negate having a time limit. Moreover, as the respondent confirmed that a form submitted without a PPSN would sit on its desk and not be actioned, this negated any interpretation that the 90-day time limit is critical in terms of receipt of a form.

The Commissioner also considered the practical difficulties faced by the appellant in obtaining a PPSN and a PSC, which were required to submit the form online, and the lack of consistent and clear information provided by the respondent on its website and forms regarding the SARP relief application process. The Commissioner noted that the explanatory notes in the appellant's completed form and the 2022 Form SARP 1A available online, do not reflect the language of the applicable legislative provisions whereas the 2023 Form SARP 1A attempts to mirror the legislation. Moreover, the guidance notes use differing language such as 'certification is required to be made by an employer … within 90 days' and 'Failure to submit a Form SARP 1A within the 90-day time-limit'. The Commissioner stressed the importance of the administrative forms and guidance not assuming a statutory requirement and time limit not set out in legislation.

The Commissioner stated the lack of consistent information was unhelpful for an individual to understand the procedures, particularly an individual arriving into the State from another jurisdiction.

The Commissioner concluded that the respondent was incorrect to refuse the relief sought by the appellant, and that the appellant was entitled to be granted relief under SARP.

[17.27] *107TACD2023[25]—SARP—Tax Appeals Commission—failure to submit Form SARP 1A within 90 days of arrival into the State*

This appeal concerned the Revenue Commissioners ('Revenue') decision to refuse relief to the appellant under the Special Assignee Relief Programme ('SARP') provided for under s 825C of the Taxes Consolidation Act 1997 (the 'TCA 1997').

25 107TACD2023.

The appellant moved to Ireland from the United Kingdom on 14 February 2022 to take up employment by way of a transfer within his existing employer's structure. On 18 October 2022, the appellant's employer in Ireland completed and submitted a Form SARP 1A to Revenue. Revenue replied to the appellant's employer refusing the application for SARP relief on the basis that the application did not satisfy the requirement, set out in s 825C(2a)(e) of the TCA 1997, that in order for a person to be treated as a 'relevant employee' the individual's relevant employer or associated company must certify within 90 days of the employee's arrival into the State that the individual complied with the conditions referred to in s 825C(2a)(a)–(c) of the TCA 1997.

The appellant appealed Revenue's decision. The appellant made several arguments including that the 90-day time limit is not clearly displayed on Revenue's website and the strict application of the time limit undermines the SARP regime and hinders talent attraction into Ireland.

Revenue submitted that SARP is a lucrative relief which, when first introduced by the Finance Act 2012, did not contain any time limit. This changed in the Finance Act 2014, which contained a 30-day time limit. A further change was then introduced by the Finance Act 2018, which extended the time limit contained in s 825C(2A)(e) of the TCA 1997 to 90 days. Revenue submitted that a 90-day time limit contained in s 825C(2A)(e) of the TCA 1997 has applied since that time, save and with the exception of 2020 during the Covid-19 pandemic, when the time limit was extended to 180 days. Revenue asserted that the 180-day time limit expired at the end of 2020 and the 90-day time limit has applied to SARP applications since then.

At issue in the appeal was whether the appellant could be considered a 'relevant employee' within the meaning of s 825C of the TCA 1997. The Commissioner relied on the summary of the fundamental principles of statutory interpretation of McDonald J in *Perrigo Pharma International Activity Company v McNamara, the Revenue Commissioners, Minister for Finance, Ireland and the Attorney General.*[26] Having regard to these principles, the Commissioner found the words contained in s 825C(2A)(e) of the TCA 1997 are plain and their meaning is self-evident.

Section 825C(2A)(e) states as follows:

> 'In this section, in the case of an individual who arrives in the State in any of the tax years 2015 to 2022, "relevant employee" means an individual –
>
> …
>
> (e) in respect of whom the relevant employer or associated company certifies, in such form as the Revenue Commissioners may require, within 90 days from the employee's arrival in the State to perform the duties referred to in paragraph (b), that the individual complies with the conditions set out in paragraphs (a), (b) and (c)'.

The Commissioner found that this wording means that in order for an employee to be a 'relevant employee' for the purposes of qualifying for SARP relief, a relevant employer

26 *Perrigo Pharma International Activity Company v McNamara, the Revenue Commissioners, Minister for Finance, Ireland and the Attorney General* [2020] IEHC 552.

or associated company must certify that the employee complies with the conditions set out in s 825C(2A)(a)–(c) within 90 days from the employee's arrival in the State to perform his or her employment for that employer or to take up employment within the State with an associated company and to perform duties in the State for that company. The Commissioner further considered that, in the context of s 825C(2A)(e) of the TCA 1997, the meaning of the word 'certify' is plain and self-evident and means that a relevant employer or associated company must complete and sign the Form SARP 1A.

The Commissioner further noted that the burden of proof—as in all taxation appeals—lies with the appellant, citing *Menolly Homes v The Appeal Commissioners*.[27]

As the appellant's employer submitted the Form SARP 1A outside the 90-day period, the Commissioner found that the appellant was not a 'relevant employee' within the meaning of s 825C of the TCA 1997. As such, the Commissioner determined that the appellant failed in showing that he was entitled to SARP relief and did not succeed in showing that Revenue's decision to refuse him SARP relief was incorrect.

[17.28] ***118TACD2023[28]—SARP—Tax Appeals Commission—failure to submit Form SARP 1A within 90 days of arrival into the State***

This appeal concerned the Revenue Commissioners ('Revenue') decision to refuse relief to the appellant under the Special Assignee Relief Programme ('SARP') provided for under s 825C of the Taxes Consolidation Act 1997 (the 'TCA 1997').

On 5 April 2022, the appellant relocated to Ireland as part of an internal move within his company of employment, at the request of his employer. On 2 September 2022, the appellant lodged his Form SARP 1A, via Revenue's 'My Enquiries' online portal, to make a claim for SARP relief. The date of the appellant's arrival in the State was listed on the Form SARP 1A as 5 April 2022. In addition, the Form SARP 1A was signed/certified by the appellant's employer on 1 September 2022.

Revenue refused relief on the basis that the submission date was outside the 90-day time limit, in accordance with s 825C(2A)(e) of the TCA 1997.

Correspondence between the appellant and Revenue prior to the appeal raised some practical points. First, Revenue declined the appellant's offer of a letter from his employer explaining the situation, stating that it would not alter the decision. Second, Revenue stated that no concessionary measures could be allowed in this case. Third, the appellant had contacted Revenue to state that his actual date of arrival in the State was 18 June 2022. While the appellant's employment had commenced on 5 April 2022, the appellant enquired if he could resubmit his application with this change of date. Revenue explained that, while changing the date of the commencement of employment would bring it inside the 90-day time limit, taking up the employment and performing the duties of employment prior to arrival in the State would breach the qualifying condition set out in s 825C(2A)(a) of the TCA 1997, which states that a relevant employee

27 *Menolly Homes v The Appeal Commissioners* [2010] IEHC 49.
28 118TACD2023.

means an individual 'who for the whole of the 6 months immediately before his or her arrival in the State was a full time employee of a relevant employer and exercised the duties of his or her employment for that relevant employer outside the State'.

The appellant appealed to the Tax Appeals Commission arguing that he was not aware of the time limit and was not informed of same by his employer; he had to travel back to his country of origin immediately after arriving in Ireland for a few weeks due to an emergency; and following his return to Ireland, he had Covid-19 symptoms and undertook a precautionary self-isolation period.

Revenue submitted that, as the submission date was beyond the 90-day time limit, the appellant was not entitled to SARP relief as he was not a 'relevant employee' within the meaning of s 825C of the TCA 1997.

The Commissioner first noted that, in an appeal before the Commission, the burden of proof rests on the appellant, who must prove on the balance of probabilities that an assessment to tax is incorrect, citing *Menolly Homes v The Appeal Commissioners*.[29]

The Commissioner then confirmed the fundamental rules of statutory interpretation that apply to taxation exemptions, relying on the decision of McDonald J in *Perrigo Pharma International Activity Company v McNamara, the Revenue Commissioners, Minister for Finance, Ireland and the Attorney General*.[30] Applying these principles, the Commissioner was satisfied that the approach to be taken in relation to the interpretation of s 825C(2A)(e) of the TCA 1997 is a literal interpretative approach and that the wording in the Statute must be given a plain, ordinary or natural meaning.

The Commissioner was satisfied that the words of s 825C(2A)(e) are plain and their meaning is self-evident. The Commissioner explained that the section provides for a 'relevant employee' who must meet a number of conditions, *inter alia* that the employer makes a certification within 90 days of an employee's arrival in the State. The Commissioner noted that the operative words of the section state that 'in respect of whom the relevant employer or associated company certifies ... within 90 days from the employee's arrival in the State'.

The Commissioner observed the legislative history of SARP relief and the legislature's intention of reducing the cost of bringing talent to Ireland. The Commissioner stated that while there may have been concessional extensions granted by Revenue to filing deadlines for the year 2020, the Commissioner does not have jurisdiction to consider the manner in which Revenue operates a non-statutory or extra-statutory concession. Citing *Lee v Revenue Commissioners*,[31] *Stanley v The Revenue Commissioners*,[32] *The State (Whelan) v Smidic*,[33] *Menolly Homes Ltd v The Appeal Commissioners*[34] and

29 *Menolly Homes v The Appeal Commissioners* [2010] IEHC 49.

30 *Perrigo Pharma International Activity Company v McNamara, the Revenue Commissioners, Minister for Finance, Ireland and the Attorney General* [2020] IEHC 552.

31 *Lee v Revenue Commissioners* [2021] IECA 18.

32 *Stanley v The Revenue Commissioners* [2017] IECA 279.

33 *The State (Whelan) v Smidic* [1938] 1 I.R. 626.

34 *Menolly Homes Ltd v The Appeal Commissioners* [2010] IEHC 49.

The State (Calcul International Ltd) v The Appeal Commissioners,[35] the Commissioner explained the scope of the jurisdiction of an Appeal Commissioner is confined to the determination of the amount of tax owing by a taxpayer, in accordance with relevant legislation and based on findings of fact adjudicated by the Commissioner or based on undisputed facts, as the case may be. The jurisdiction of the Commission does not extend to the provision of equitable relief, nor to the provision of remedies available in High Court judicial review proceedings. Therefore, insofar as the appellant sought for the Commissioner to set aside a decision of Revenue based on the alleged unfairness, breach of legitimate expectation, or disproportionality, such grounds of appeal did not fall within the jurisdiction of the Commissioner and thus, did not fall to be determined as part of this appeal.

The Commissioner found that they had no authority or discretion to direct that a claim for SARP relief be afforded to the appellant, where the claim for relief fell outside the 90-day time limit specified in s 825C(2A)(e) of the TCA 1997. In addition, the Commissioner noted that the wording of the provision did not provide for extenuating circumstances in which the 90-day time limit might be mitigated.

Tax Treatment of Employee Stock Options

[17.29] ***Hemingway v HMRC*[36]*—appeal to First-Tier Tribunal—whether a payment received by an employee following termination of share options is taxable in full as a payment in connection with the loss of the employee's share options under s 477 of the Income Tax (Earnings and Pensions) Act 2003 or is a payment in respect of the loss of the employee's employment rights and attracts relief under s 401***

This was an appeal to the First-Tier Tribunal (the 'FTT') by the appellant against a closure notice issued by HMRC, denying him relief under s 401 of the Income Tax (Earnings and Pensions) Act 2003 ('ITEPA 2003') for a payment he received following the merger of his employer's parent company.

The appellant was an IT specialist employed by Broadcom UK Ltd. On 2 June 2006 and 3 May 2007, he was granted options over shares in Broadcom Corporation, the parent company, as part of an employee stock option plan. In 2016, Broadcom Corporation was taken over by Avago Technologies, and his stock options were cancelled for a cash payment of £35,228.15, which was subject to tax and national insurance contributions ('NICs') (deductions of £15,619.12), resulting in a net payment of £19,549.03. The joint election provided that Broadcom could deduct employer NICs 'upon the occurrence of a Chargeable event with respect to the cancellation, assignment or release of an Option'. A chargeable event was defined in the election to include: 'Any event with respect to an option or RSU giving rise to a charge under Section 4(4)(a) of the Act (being within sections 439, 476 or 477 of ITEPA 2003)'.

---

35 *The State (Calcul International Ltd) v The Appeal Commissioners* III ITR 577.

36 *Hemingway v HMRC* [2023] UKFTT 749 (TC).

On 12 May 2016, the appellant brought a claim against Broadcom in the employment tribunal, for the unlawful deduction of £4,861.48 of employer NICs from his wages and failure to provide an adequate pay statement under s 11(2) of the Employment Rights Act 1996 ('ERA 1996'). He argued that the joint election permitting Broadcom to deduct employer NICs from payments made to him, did not apply where he had not exercised the share options himself. Moreover, he argued that the cancellation of the share options was not a chargeable event for the purposes of the joint election; the enforced sale was not a cancellation, or a release of the option and the transaction was not tax compliant and therefore ineffective. The tribunal dismissed his claim holding that: (i) the payment was a discretionary payment falling outside the definition of wages for the purposes of s 27 of the ERA 1996; (ii) the payment was a chargeable event for the purposes of the joint election; and (iii) the cancellation or termination of share options was envisaged by clause 3(B) of the election.

On 20 August 2016, the appellant amended his voluntary tax return in respect of tax year 2015–2016 in which he reported the payment as taxable income ('Initial Return') to claim that he was entitled to relief under s 401 of the ITEPA 2003, so the first £30,000 of the payment was exempt from tax. On 16 March 2017, HMRC purported to open an enquiry into the Initial Return under s 9A of the Taxes Management Act 1970 ('TMA 1970') and, on 22 January 2018, HMRC issued a closure notice refusing the appellant relief and asserting that the payment was taxable under s 477 of the ITEPA 2003, which applies to benefits received in connection with employment-related securities option. The appellant appealed to the FTT against the closure notice, but his appeal was struck out on the ground that his voluntary return was not made in accordance with a notice under s 8 of the TMA 1970 and the FTT had no jurisdiction to consider it. He then gave notice under s 711 of the ITEPA 2003, requiring HMRC to issue a notice under s 8 of the TMA 1970 for the year 2015–2016, which they did. He filed a new return, claiming the same relief under s 401 of the ITEPA 2003, and HMRC opened another enquiry and issued another closure notice, reaching the same conclusion as before.

The appellant appealed again to the FTT, raising the substantive issue of whether the payment was taxable under s 401 or s 477 of the ITEPA 2003, and the procedural issue of whether the first closure notice was retrospectively validated by s 12D of the TMA 1970, which was introduced by the Finance Act 2019 and applies where HMRC treats a voluntary return as a return made in accordance with a notice under s 8 of the TMA 1970.

The FTT dismissed his appeal on both issues but declined to make a costs award against the appellant.

On the substantive issue, the FTT agreed with HMRC that the payment was made in connection with the loss of the appellant's stock options, and not for the loss of his employment rights, and therefore fell within s 477 of the ITEPA 2003, which takes priority over s 401 of the ITEPA 2003 by virtue of s 401(3) of the ITEPA 2003. The FTT found that the payment was intended and was most closely connected to the loss of the options, as evidenced by the terms of the merger agreement, the communications from the employer, and the appellant's own concession that he would not have received the payment had he not held the options. It did not matter that the payment was made a month later, rather than the two days promised by the shareholder services email, as it was still clearly made in connection with the loss of the options. The FTT also found that the payment was within s 477(6) of the ITEPA 2003, as a benefit in consideration or in connection with failing to acquire securities.

The FTT did not accept the appellant's argument that the payment was for the loss of the right to participate in the stock option plan, or that the employer had accepted that s 477 of the ITEPA 2003 did not apply by issuing an amended payslip after the appellant objected to the deductions in which the employer did not deduct the employer NICs in accordance with the joint election. The FTT found the deduction of the employer NIC and the operation of the joint election to be insignificant.

On the procedural issue, the FTT rejected the appellant's argument that s 12D of the TMA 1970 retrospectively validated the first closure notice and invalidated the second closure notice. The FTT found that s 12D did not apply for three reasons: (i) the FTT's striking out of the first appeal in 2019 was conclusive and could not be reopened by s 12D of the TMA 1970; (ii) HMRC ultimately did not treat the first return as made in accordance with a valid notice under s 8 of the TMA 1970, as they withdrew that treatment following the appellant's letter of 13 April 2018 as highlighted by HMRC's letter to the appellant on 27 June 2018; and (iii) the appellant's arguments that the first return was still in existence and that the second return was an amendment to it were not supported by the evidence or the relevant legislation. The FTT also rejected the appellant's argument that the notice under s 8 of the TMA 1970 issued by HMRC in 2019 was not valid, as there was no basis for that argument in the document.

Meaning of Deeming Rule in the Employment-Related Securities Rules

[17.30] ***HMRC v Vermilion Holdings Ltd*[37]*—UK Supreme Court—appeal from Inner House of the Court of Session—meaning of the deeming rule in employment-related securities rules which can cause a security to be treated as employment related***

This was an appeal by the HMRC to the UK Supreme Court against the decision of the Inner House of the Court of Session, which upheld the FTT's decision that a securities option granted to Mr Noble's nominee (Quest Advantage Ltd) by Vermilion Holdings Ltd (Mr Noble's employer) was not an employment-related securities option for the purposes of s 471 of the Income Tax (Earnings and Pensions) Act 2003 ('ITEPA 2003'). The Supreme Court had to determine whether Mr Noble was correct when he exercised the option, after novating it to himself, and sought to treat the gain as liable to capital gains tax or whether HMRC were correct in their assessment for income tax and national insurance contributions ('NICs') on the basis that the option was an employment-related securities option under s 471 of the ITEPA 2003.

[37] *HMRC v Vermilion Holdings Ltd* [2023] UKSC 37.

In 2006, Vermilion Holdings Ltd granted a supplier option to Quest Advantage Ltd (a company owned by Mr Noble and another person) in return for their services as external advisers in a funding exercise. In 2007, Vermilion faced financial difficulties and required a rescue funding exercise, which involved Mr Noble becoming its executive chairman and agreeing to a package of measures that reduced the entitlements of existing stakeholders, including Quest Advantage Ltd. As part of the rescue funding exercise, the 2006 option was cancelled and a new option agreement was executed, giving Quest Advantage Ltd an option to subscribe for a new class of shares in Vermilion, representing up to 1.5% of its issued equity share capital. Mr Noble exercised the option in 2016, after novating it to himself, and sought to treat the gain as liable to capital gains tax, rather than income tax. HMRC disagreed and assessed Vermilion for income tax and NICs on the basis that the option was an employment-related securities option under s 471 of the ITEPA 2003. Vermilion appealed those assessments, with an indemnity from Mr Noble for any tax consequences arising from the exercise of the option.

The Supreme Court considered Part 7 of the ITEPA 2003, which concerns income and exemptions relating to securities. Chapter 5 of Part 7 deals with securities options, and s 471 defines the options to which the chapter applies. Section 471(1) sets out a causal test, asking whether the right or opportunity to acquire the securities option is available by reason of an employment of that person or any other person. Section 471(3) sets out a deeming provision, which avoids the causal inquiry where a person's employer, or a person connected with a person's employer, makes available the right or opportunity to acquire a securities option, unless the person is an individual and the right or opportunity is made available in the normal course of the domestic, family or personal relationships of that person. The effect of the deeming provision is to treat the option as an employment-related securities option, which is subject to income tax as employment income under s 476 of the ITEPA 2003. Accordingly, the main issue in this case was the correct interpretation and application of the deeming provision in s 471(3).

The Supreme Court allowed the appeal, finding in favour of HMRC. It held that the deeming provision in s 471(3) applied to the facts and there was no reason to limit its effect by reference to the causal test in s 471(1), or by adopting a realistic view of the underlying causes and economic mechanism of the grant of the option. Accordingly, as Mr Noble was deemed to have acquired the securities option because of his employment as a director of Quest Advantage Ltd and did not fall within the exception to the deeming provision, he was subject to income tax.

The Supreme Court disagreed with the FTT and the majority of the Inner House, which previously held that the application of the deeming provision would produce absurd, anomalous or unjust results, or that the option was not made available by Vermilion as Mr Noble's employer. However, the Court did acknowledge that there is an exception to a literal application of a deeming rule where it would produce an unjust, absurd or anomalous result.

The Supreme Court considered that the approaches of the FTT and Inner House were erroneous, as they either 'put the cart before the horse' by applying the causal test in s 471(1) before the deeming provision in s 471(3), or denied the deeming provision of its substance by looking at the reason why Vermilion conferred the option.

In this regard, the Supreme Court held the grant of a securities option will be subject to income tax where it 'is available by reason of an employment of that person or any other person'. A decision maker must carefully consider the facts to decide whether there is a causal connection between the person's employment and the grant of the option. However, as this analysis often gives rise to disagreements among judges, the Court stated that it is necessary to look first at the bright line rule in s 471(3):

> 'if a person's employer (or a person connected to that person's employer) provides the employee the right or opportunity to acquire a securities option, that right or opportunity is conclusively treated as having been made available by reason of the employment of that person [unless specific exemptions apply, namely that the right is made available by an individual and made in the normal course of their domestic, family or personal relationships]'.

The Supreme Court therefore held that the purpose of the deeming provision is to avoid the need for any decision maker having to carry out the s 471(1) of the ITEPA 2003 causal test 'by reason of' assessment. It is not open to the taxpayer to defend a demand for tax from HMRC by carrying out the s 471(1) exercise to disapply the s 471(3) deeming provision. In this regard, it is important to note s 471(2) states that, for the purposes of s 471(1), 'employment' includes a former or prospective employment whereas s 471(3) only applies where there is an active employee and employer relationship at the time of the award. This was highlighted in Lord Hodge's judgment:

> 'The statutory provision makes clear that if an employer makes available to an employee a securities option, that option will be treated in the employee's hands as an employment-related securities option and taxed accordingly. **Vermilion, which at the relevant time was Mr Noble's employer, made available to his nominee such an option. Vermilion's reason for so doing is irrelevant when ITEPA 2003, s 471(3) applies**' [emphasis added].

The Supreme Court also distinguished *Price v Revenue and Customs Commissioners*,[38] which had been relied on by the FTT and the Inner House, as it concerned a different factual scenario and did not support Vermilion's case.

38 *Price v Revenue and Customs Commissioners* [2013] UKFTT 297 (TC).

Chapter 18

Transfer of Undertakings

INTRODUCTION

[18.01]

Transfer

In *NC*, the ECJ considered whether the transfer by a notary of their activities to another notary amounted to a transfer for the purposes of art 1(1)(a) of Directive 2001/23/EC relating to the safeguarding of employees' rights in the event of a transfer of undertakings.

Share Schemes

In *Ponticelli*, the Court of Session in Scotland considered whether the respondent worker's entitlements under a share scheme transferred under TUPE.

Date of Transfer

The UK EAT in *Rajput* considered what date should be considered the transfer date in a transaction where there are multiple transfers of different batches of a business in two different jurisdictions.

TRANSFER

[18.02] ***NC v BA*[1]*—European Court of Justice—request for preliminary ruling from Spain—Directive 2001/23/EC*[2]*—safeguarding employees' rights in the event***

---

1 *NC v BA* (Case C-583/21).

2 Directive 2001/23/EC on the approximation of the laws of the Member States relating to the safeguarding of employees' rights in the event of transfers of undertakings, businesses or parts of undertakings or businesses.

of transfer of undertakings—declaration as to the unfairness or nullity of the dismissal—determination of seniority—compensation

A number of employees worked in a notary's office in Spain. They had been employed by a number of notaries who had succeeded each other in that practice. The last notary left the office to practice in another city and offered the employees the choice between positions in his new practice or termination of their contracts, with compensation. They chose the latter. A transfer of undertakings occurred, and the employees were dismissed by the new owner. It was maintained that this dismissal had occurred within the probation period. The employees sought declarations from the Spanish Court that their dismissals by the new owner of the business had been unlawful and asked for their seniority to be calculated from the date they began working for the previous notary. The referring Court considered that the employees had been employed continuously by successive notaries in the practice and that their employment period with the new notary had not exceeded the probationary period. The referring Court noted that Spanish notaries are public officials that assume their post having passed a national competition organised by the Ministry for Justice. Where a notary ceases his/her activities due to transfer or retirement, his/her successor is obliged to preserve the predecessor's archives, but the fate of the notary staff employed by the predecessor is not regulated by any specific rule or contractual clause, except in cases of transfer or leave on personal grounds of the notary.

The referring Court asked the European Court of Justice (the 'ECJ'):

> 'Does Article 1(1)(a) of [Directive 2001/23/EC] … apply to a situation in which the notary in post in a notary's office—who is both a public official and also the private-sector employer of the office's employees, with the employment relationship being governed by general employment legislation and by a sectoral collective agreement—succeeds the outgoing post-holder, takes on the previous notary's [records], continues to provide services at the same place of work using the same material facilities, and takes on the staff who had worked for the previous notary who had held that post?'

The new owner and the Spanish Government objected, stating that the question referred for preliminary ruling was inadmissible, since, four months before the applicants were employed by the new owner, their employment relationship with the predecessor had ceased in exchange for compensation. Therefore, it was argued, no rights transferred. The ECJ held that such a possibility resulted from national legislation that did not relate to Directive 2001/23/EC and that the employees asserted that the compensation had been reimbursed. It also noted that the submissions made by the parties to the substantive hearing were for the referring Court to verify. The referred question, therefore, was deemed admissible.

The ECJ noted that, under art 1(1)(c), Directive 2001/23/EC applies to any transfer of undertaking, business, or part of an undertaking or business to another employer as a result of a legal transfer or merger. The language used means that it applies to both public and private undertakings. The Court examined whether the activities of the notaries fell under the heading of 'economic activity' for the purposes of Directive 2001/23/EC. It noted that the definition of 'economic activity' encompasses any activity involving offering goods or services in a given market; however, activities which fall within the exercise of public powers are usually excluded. In this case, the services provided were being offered on the market to clients in return for remuneration. The services required the notaries to assume the financial risks associated with the activities. Accordingly, the services fell within the meaning of 'economic activity' under Directive 2001/23/EC.

The Court held that the activity of a notarial practice depended on the manpower of that practice and that it was capable of retaining its identity after being transferred if a major part of the workforce was also transferred. In the event that a new owner took over the workforce employed by his/her predecessor and continued to require them to carry out the work associated with their positions, it was held that the practice maintained its identity.

Therefore, the Court held that Directive 2001/23/EC must be interpreted as meaning that it is applicable to a situation where a notary takes over the records and staff of his predecessor and continues to carry on the same activities.

SHARE SCHEMES

[18.03] ***Ponticelli Ltd v Gallagher*[3]*—Court of Session—appeal from UK Employment Appeal Tribunal—Transfer of Undertakings (Protection of Employment) Regulations 2006*[4]*—transfer of undertakings—share schemes—share incentive plan—partnership share agreement—scope of the Regulations—contract of employment***

The respondent worker's contract of employment transferred to the appellant company under the Transfer of Undertakings (Protection of Employment) Regulations 2006 ('TUPE'). Before that transfer, the respondent participated in a Share Incentive Plan ('SIP') offered by his former employer. Participation was facilitated by a separate contract, a Partnership Share Agreement, with his employer and the trustees of the SIP. There was no reference to the SIP in his contract of employment. When the appellant acquired the respondent's former employer's business, the respondent's membership of the SIP ended and the shares held on his behalf were transferred to him. The appellant company then wrote to the respondent and indicated that he would receive a further one-off payment as compensation for the fact that it was not going to continue to provide a SIP following the acquisition of the respondent's former employer.

The respondent applied to the employment tribunal seeking a determination that he was entitled to remain a member of a SIP. He claimed that his right to participate in a SIP transferred to the appellant under reg 4(2)(a) of TUPE. The tribunal accepted this. The appellant appealed to the EAT, arguing that the respondent's entitlement arose from a contract which was entirely separate to his contract of employment. As such, it was contended, TUPE did not apply. The UK EAT upheld the first instance decision.

---

3 *Ponticelli Ltd v Gallagher* [2023] CSIH 32. See *Arthur Cox Employment Law Yearbook 2022* at [19.04] for UK EAT decision in *Ponticelli UK Ltd v Gallagher* [2022] EAT 140.

4 Transfer of Undertakings (Protection of Employment) Regulations 2006 (SI 2006/246).

In the Court of Session, the appellant submitted three grounds of appeal. The first ground was that the EAT had erred in rejecting *Chapman v CPS Computer Group*[5] as being relevant. *Chapman*, the appellant submitted, related to TUPE's predecessor, the Transfer of Undertakings (Protection of Employment) Regulations 1981.[6] The appellant argued that in *Chapman*, as in this case, a right to participate did not form part of the relevant contract of employment and did not survive the transfer of undertakings. However, the Court of Session noted that the Court in *Chapman* had expressed the view that the 1981 Regulations had no relevance to the question to be decided in *Chapman*, being whether the employee's employment was terminated by reason of redundancy, and therefore rejected that ground of appeal.

The appellant's second ground of appeal related to the EAT's acceptance of the decision in *Mitie Managed Services Ltd v French*.[7] In *Mitie*, a contractual right had transferred because the profit-sharing scheme in question had formed part of the employee's contractual rights under TUPE. The appellant argued that this was not on all fours with the facts in this case. The Court of Session found that the Court in *Mitie* approved a purposive interpretation of TUPE such that the inability to transfer the rights and entitlements owed prior to a transfer was not a barrier to achieving the objective of ensuring the protection of the employee's full range of remunerative benefits.

The appellant's final ground of appeal was that reg 4(2)(a) of TUPE could not be interpreted as extending the scope of what is transferred beyond what is envisaged by Directive 2001/23/EC.[8] It argued that the rights and entitlements must exist at the point of transfer 'in consequence of' the contract of employment or the 'employment relationship'. It gave the example of an optional non-contractual benefit like a subsidised gym membership and argued that if this was offered by a transferor company in a separate contract to that of the employee's contract of employment, it would not survive a transfer under the Directive.

The Court found that the scope of the language used in TUPE was 'wide enough' to cover a range of obligations not contained within or 'under' the contract of employment. Whether these obligations arose outside of the employment contract or 'in connection with' that contract or 'from the employment relationship', the result would have been the same in this case. It noted that the Partnership Share Agreement specified that contributions to the SIP were done via salary deduction. As such, it was found that the employment tribunal was correct in holding that rights and entitlements under the scheme formed an integral part of the respondent's overall financial package. Taking the gym membership analogy, the Court found that if the membership was part of a range of benefits available to an employee as part of their financial package it would survive a transfer. Otherwise, the analogy was 'inapposite'.

---

5 *Chapman v CPS Computer Group* [1987] IRLR 462.

6 Transfer of Undertakings (Protection of Employment) Regulations 1981 (SI 1981/1794).

7 *Mitie Managed Services Ltd v French* [2002] ICR 1395.

8 Directive 2001/23/EC on the approximation of the laws of the Member States relating to the safeguarding of employees' rights in the event of transfers of undertakings, businesses or parts of undertakings or businesses.

The Court held that the purpose of the Directive is to ensure that the employment relationship continues, after the transfer, to protect workers from being placed in a less favourable position due to the transfer. The restrictive approach submitted by the appellant, it was held, would enable employers to circumvent this protection by creating separate contracts for certain benefits additional to basic salary but which form part of employee's remuneration packages.

The appeal was dismissed.

DATE OF TRANSFER

[18.04] ***Rajput v Commerzbank AG and Société Générale*[9]*—UK Employment Appeal Tribunal—appeal from employment tribunal—Transfer of Undertakings (Protection of Employment) Regulations 2006*[10]*—territorial issues—questions of an essential nature—geographic location—equity markets and commodities—business purchase—batches and sub-batches—date of transfer—date on which the 'essential nature' of the activity carried on by the transferor began to be carried on instead by the transferee***

The claimant was an employee of the first-respondent bank. In 2016 she took maternity leave. She submitted a claim against the respondent in 2017 for discrimination of various kinds. At this time, the first respondent was in talks with the second respondent about the sale of its business. The claim was heard in March 2018. It was appealed in April 2018 by the first respondent. While the appeal was pending, an agreement was reached between the respondents. The appeal partially succeeded and led to remission of some issues. The claimant argued that the first-respondent bank discriminated against her again from February 2018 to March 2020, when the claimant alleged she was unfairly dismissed.

Negotiations continued between the respondents. The transfer was complex and involved the transferring of batches and sub-batches of the business at different times. The business purchase agreement ('BPA') was signed in November 2018. What was ultimately transferred was the equity markets and commodities ('EMC') business of the first respondent. The claimant was assigned to the EMC business at the time and so was assigned to part of the business transferred. The respondent pleaded that the transfer date was 1 October 2019. The claimant argued that the date was May 2020, when the final batch of the business had been transferred. She alleged that the final part was the 'jewel in the crown' and the most important or attractive part of the transfer. The respondents claimed that the EMC business was 'situated immediately before the transfer in the United Kingdom' for the purposes of reg 3(1)(a) of TUPE. However, a substantial part of the transferring business (being the 'Flow' business) was located in Germany. The Flow business only had a small presence in the United Kingdom.

9 *Rajput v Commerzbank AG and Société Générale* [2023] EAT 116.

10 Transfer of Undertakings (Protection of Employment) Regulations 2006 (SI 2006/246).

The matter was considered by the employment tribunal, which held that it was irrelevant how attractive or unattractive the parts of the business were to the transferee. While it acknowledged that it was difficult to pinpoint the exact date of the transfer, it was noted that the majority of batches had been transferred by the end of September 2019 and, out of a total of 97 London employees to be transferred, 87% had been transferred leading up to 1 October 2019. The Court looked at the date on which the 'essential nature' of the activity carried on by the transferor began to be carried on instead by the transferee. On this basis, it accepted that the transfer date was 1 October 2019, as by this date there was an almost complete transfer of assets in London. The tribunal confined itself to the London operation in its decision. The claimant appealed.

The UK EAT held that the tribunal had correctly decided the date of transfer as not necessarily being the date of the final transaction. It held that the tribunal had not materially erred in asking itself the question when the 'essential nature' of the business was first carried out by the second respondent. However, it was held that the tribunal erred in excluding from its consideration a substantial part of the business geographically located outside the UK in Germany. If it had had regard to the German contingent, the tribunal might have concluded that the transfer had occurred later than 1 October 2019, given that it recognised: 'As regards the public distribution business which was mainly concerned with the German market, the part of the transaction which dealt with that, occurred late in the process and ran into 2020'. In this way, the acquisition may not have been fully completed until after the claimant had been dismissed.

The appeal was allowed in part and the question was remitted for further consideration.

Chapter 19

Unfair Dismissal

INTRODUCTION

[19.01]

Dismissal?

The question as to whether a dismissal had in fact occurred was considered by the Labour Court in *Parkboro Developments Ltd* and by the UK EAT in *Jackson.*

The validity of a resignation was considered by the UK EAT in *Omar.*

Capability

Dismissal on the grounds of incapability came before the UK EAT in *Singh.*

Compensation

Both *Scoil Áine Naofa* and *Topp Tiles Plc* concerned the claimant's contributory conduct in assessing compensation.

Conduct

Dismissal on the grounds of conduct was dealt with by the High Court in *An Bord Banistíochta Gaelscoil Moshíológ*; by the Labour Court in *Aldi Stores Ltd, Connect Trade Union, Inspection Services Ireland Ltd, Laois County Council* and *Tesco Ireland Ltd*; and by the UK EAT in *Charalambou*s and *Hewston.*

Constructive Dismissal

Claims of constructive dismissal were considered by the Labour Court in *Allenfield Care Homes Ltd* and *Go-ahead Transport Services (Ireland) Ltd* and by the UK EAT in *The No. 8 Partnership* and *Brooks*.

Health and Safety

Rodgers concerned a claim of automatic unfair dismissal under the Employment Rights Act 1996, as the employee alleged Covid-19 posed a serious and imminent threat to their wellbeing.

Redundancy

Whether the redundancy defence applies was considered by the Labour Court in *Acorn Brokerage Ltd*, and by the UK EAT in *Teixeira*, *Lovingangels Care Ltd* and *De Bank Haycocks*.

DISMISSAL?

[19.02] ***Parkboro Developments Ltd v Witkowski*[1]*—Labour Court—appeal from Workplace Relations Commission—Unfair Dismissals Acts 1977 to 2015, s 8A—whether employee believed he was dismissed***

The claimant worked for the respondent company as a general operative for 10 years until 16 August 2017. He brought complaints under the Redundancy Payments Act 1967 and the Unfair Dismissals Acts 1977 to 2015. The respondent failed to attend the WRC hearing and an Adjudication Officer found that the dismissal was unfair and awarded the claimant €5,000. The respondent appealed that decision and denied that any dismissal had taken place. The claimant cross-appealed the quantum of the award.

Conflicting accounts were given by both parties of an exchange on 16 August 2017 between the claimant and the owner of the respondent company. The claimant stated that the owner shouted at and summarily dismissed him. He believed that there had been a change in attitude towards him following a personal injuries action by him against the respondent. The owner stated that the claimant walked off the job following a row and that he had attempted to re-engage him.

The Court was satisfied that the claimant believed that he had been dismissed. The claimant left the workplace to walk the 10km to his home rather than take the company van. The owner had allowed the claimant to walk home rather than direct him back to his work. The owner had sought to evade his responsibility, whether out of stubbornness

1 *Parkboro Developments Ltd v Witkowski* UDD2338.

or pride, and had apparently hoped that the claimant would re-appear for work. The Court determined that the claimant was dismissed on 16 August 2017. In view of the 'relatively trivial disagreement of the sort described', which did not come anywhere near justifying dismissal, the dismissal was unfair. The award was adjusted to €5,400 for unfair dismissal.

[19.03] ***Omar v Epping Forest District Citizens Advice*[2]*—UK Employment Appeal Tribunal—appeal from employment tribunal—unfair dismissal—validity of a resignation—constructive dismissal—findings of fact—wrongful dismissal—special circumstances—intention—reasons***

The claimant worked at the respondent's citizens advice service. He resigned from his position 'in the heat of the moment' on foot of an altercation with his manager. The claimant alleged that the chief executive officer had offered him an alternative role the next day. However, some days later, the claimant was told that his manager could no longer work with him and his resignation had been accepted. The claimant attempted to revoke his resignation but the respondent refused to accept this. The claimant brought a claim to the employment tribunal arguing that he had been wrongfully dismissed and that this situation fell within the 'special circumstances exceptions' recognised in *Sothern v Franks Charlesly & Co*, ie there may be exceptions to the general rule of resignation in certain circumstances, such as immaturity or decisions taken in the heat of the moment.[3]

The employment tribunal considered whether there were special circumstances that justified making an exception to the general rule. It held that the claimant had clearly intended to resign. This was evidenced by the fact that his resignation was not followed by an immediate revocation. The tribunal made a finding that the claimant had not been offered a new role, but that if he believed he was being offered that role, he had declined to accept it. It concluded that the claimant had resigned and had not been wrongfully dismissed. The claimant appealed to the UK EAT.

The EAT held that the tribunal had not properly directed itself by reference to the principles applicable to the construction of putative notices of dismissal or resignation. It noted that the 'special circumstances' exception did not exist; that the same rules applied in all cases where notice of dismissal or resignation was given. It stated that a notice of resignation or dismissal could not be unilaterally revoked, and that words that could be said to amount to dismissal/resignation had to be construed objectively in accordance with the rules of contractual interpretation. The EAT noted that it had to be objectively clear to a reasonable bystander that one party had used words that expressed immediate dismissal or resignation; words which constitute an intended or future resignation are not sufficient. The words also must be considered to have been seriously meant at the time they were uttered, although there is no requirement that the resignation itself be reasonable.

The EAT held that no time bar applies, the tribunal may take into account any subsequent communication in the relevant period after the words were conveyed. However,

2 *Omar v Epping Forest District Citizens Advice* [2023] EAT 132.
3 *Sothern v Franks Charlesly & Co* [1981] 1 WLUK 382.

the greater the temporal lapse, the less likely it will be that any evidence subsequently relied on would be indicative of the person's intention at the time the words were uttered. The speaker/writer's words may be considered alongside their demeanour, e.g. whether they were angry or acting out of character at the time the words were conveyed. The EAT noted that while these rules apply to both oral and written words, the latter might be treated as more strongly intended, given the lack of immediacy involved.

The EAT stated that, in not having regard to the above principles, the tribunal did not direct itself to the pertinent question of whether, viewed objectively, the claimant had used words that amounted to words of resignation that he truly intended. Instead the tribunal considered whether there were special circumstances that permitted making an exception to the general rule.

The matter was remitted to a fresh tribunal for a full rehearing.

[19.04] ***Jackson v The University Hospitals of North Midlands NHS Trust[4]—UK Employment Appeal Tribunal—appeal from employment tribunal—Employment Rights Act 1996—constructive dismissal—contract of employment—notice—reasons—redundancy payments—termination—variation***

The claimant was an employee of the respondent, working as a specialist research nurse in haematology. Her contract of employment required her to give four weeks' notice of intention to terminate her employment. She was also subject to the so-called 'Agenda for Change' ('AfC') which governed grading and pay for NHS workers. The claimant's role was graded at band 6 of nine pay bands set out in the AfC.

In 2018, following an external review, the respondent decided to restructure, which would lead to a loss of specialist research nurses and the creation of a single team of generic nurses to deal with all disease specialities. Band 6 nurses could become senior research practitioners but the number of said posts would be reduced. Existing band 6 staff would be invited to apply for these reduced positions and undergo an assessment. If unsuccessful, candidates would be reassigned to a new band 5 post as a research practitioner with reduced pay. The claimant applied for a band 6 position but was unsuccessful. She was informed in a letter dated 13 November 2018 that she would be placed into one of the new band 5 roles with effect from 3 December 2018. The role attracted new terms and conditions that the claimant refused to sign. The respondent did not allow the claimant a trial period in her new role to help her decide whether it constituted appropriate alternative employment.

The claimant submitted that the respondent should make her redundant under the circumstances of enhanced AfC terms, which calculated redundancy pay on the basis of one month's pay for each complete year of reckonable service rather than the statutory formula. NHS workers were taken to having forfeited their redundancy pay if they left employment 'before expiry of notice'. The claimant indicated that, if the respondent refused, she would bring unfair dismissal proceedings. The respondent rejected her grievance. She resigned on 28 December 2018. Her notice period ended

4 *Jackson v The University Hospitals of North Midlands NHS Trust* [2023] EAT 102.

on 25 January 2019. The employee appealed against the rejection of her grievance and the respondent upheld that appeal. The appeal letter indicated that if the claimant revoked her resignation, she would be given eight weeks' notice of the termination of her employment by reason of redundancy. The claimant did this on 21 January 2019 and asserted that the eight-week notice period applied retrospectively from 3 December 2018, being the date that she would have been 'slotted into' her new band 5 role.

On 25 January 2019, the respondent indicated that her employment would terminate after eight weeks, the operative date being 22 March 2019. The claimant stated that her resignation on the 28 December 2018 still subsisted and she considered herself constructively dismissed.

The claimant brought a claim to the employment tribunal for unfair dismissal, statutory redundancy pay, and breach of contract. The claimant's breach of contract claim concerned unpaid notice pay and unpaid contractual redundancy pay. While the tribunal upheld the other complaints, it rejected the claimant's breach of contract claim. The tribunal held that the respondent had not dismissed the claimant on *Hogg*[5] grounds. A *Hogg* dismissal is when there is a unilateral variation of a contract of such a degree that it terminates the original contract and replaces it with another. Accordingly, the claimant was not entitled to the enhanced redundancy payment under contract because she had left the respondent's employ by the time that the notice period expired. The claimant appealed this decision.

The UK EAT considered whether the tribunal had erred in its decision that the claimant was not dismissed on *Hogg* grounds on 3 December 2018 when a new band 5 contract was imposed on her. It cited s 95(1) of the Employment Rights Act 1996 and considered the implications of an employee contract being terminated by the employer with or without notice, and a new contract imposed. In such circumstances there would be no mechanism by which the employee could affirm the old contract.

The EAT held that the employment tribunal had erred in law in its conclusion that the claimant had not been dismissed on *Hogg* grounds. It noted that the tribunal had indicated that there was 'no radical change such as to entitle the claimant to regard herself as constructively dismissed'. This, the EAT noted, was not the test to apply. The tribunal was not dealing with a constructive dismissal but an alleged *Hogg* dismissal. In applying *Hogg*, the tribunal had to consider whether the contract of employment here had been terminated and replaced with another.

The EAT was also critical of the tribunal's finding that the employee had not treated the new contract as a dismissal, but instead raised a grievance. The EAT found that this was not relevant to the question to be considered by the tribunal. Indeed, in *Hogg v Dover College*, Mr Hogg remained in employment. The question was not whether employment had ended simpliciter, but whether the old contract had been terminated by the imposition of a new one.

The intentions of the respondent, which were considered by the tribunal, were also held to be irrelevant. What fell to be considered was what effect the new contract, unilaterally imposed, had on employment. The EAT also questioned the tribunal's compliance

5 *Hogg v Dover College* [1988] ICR 39.

with *Meek*. It held that its decision was inadequately reasoned and that a comparison of band 5 and band 6 posts was not done to ascertain whether the old and new terms were sufficiently different to invoke *Hogg*.

It was held by the EAT that the unilateral substitution of new terms and conditions by the respondent meant that it had terminated the claimant's previous contract and replaced it with a new one. This was relevant to its assessment of whether the claimant was entitled to a contractually-enhanced redundancy payment.

The EAT allowed the appeal and remitted the question on entitlement to contractually-enhanced redundancy payment to a different employment tribunal.

CAPABILITY

[19.05] ***Singh v British Airways Plc*[6]*—UK Employment Appeal Tribunal—appeal from employment tribunal—Employment Rights Act 1996—unfair dismissal—band of reasonable responses—breach of contract—capability—date of termination—powers and duties—extensions of time—postponement—right to appeal—sick leave***

The claimant was employed as cabin crew by the respondent in February 1997. The respondent incorporated an Absence Management Policy into the claimant's employment contract. Section 4 thereof stated that where a manager believed on reasonable grounds that the employee's absence or their inability to perform their duties to the standard required was due to a medical incapacity that was likely to be long term, the manager would seek occupational health advice from British Airways Health Services ('BAHS'). Where BAHS advised that the employee was incapacitated and was unable to perform their functions to the standard required in the foreseeable future, a series of actions may be taken, including termination of employment. The Absence Management Policy provided for a right of appeal against a decision to terminate an employee's employment on foot of s 4 of the Employment Rights Act 1996.

The claimant suffered from a physical impairment (diabetes) and a mental impairment (stress, depression and post-traumatic stress disorder). The claimant was dismissed following a lengthy absence as a result of his ill-health on 31 August 2017, having engaged with BAHS. This termination was supposed to take effect on 5 January 2018. At this time, the claimant had been unable to fly for over a year.

The termination date was extended by the respondent on seven different occasions for various reasons. In each case, the choice to postpone the termination date was said to have been made in order to accommodate the claimant, e.g. to allow him to demonstrate his 'ability to sustain [his] commitments on [his] flying roster' with a view to re-engagement as cabin crew; and/or in order to investigate allegations of racism made by the claimant.

In July 2018, the claimant appealed the respondent's letter giving him notice of the third extension. He indicated that he did not believe that the respondent was acting reasonably in treating the adverse effects of his illnesses as reasons for termination

6 *Singh v British Airways Plc* [2023] EAT 97.

his employment. He cited a 'fume event' which allegedly caused his absences and contested the way in which the respondent dealt with the process to date. He suggested that any decision to terminate his employment was a breach of the procedural expectations under the Absence Management Policy. This appeal was not upheld.

The respondent decided not to extend the termination date for an eighth time and marked the effective date of termination as 21 December 2018. The claimant brought a claim to the employment tribunal for, among other things, unfair dismissal.

The employment tribunal held that the claimant's dismissal was fair and also found that the claimant was afforded a fair appeal against the decision to dismiss him in accordance with the Absence Management Policy. It was held that although the Policy did not contain reference to termination dates being postponed, it also did not prohibit same. The claimant appealed to the UK EAT.

The EAT disagreed with the claimant that the extensions in this case amounted to a breach of the Absence Management Policy and therefore a breach of contract. The position would be different, it was held, if the respondent was to act in a way which was positively inconsistent with the Policy, but that was not the case. Although the Policy envisaged a single decision to terminate an employee's employment, it did not prevent the respondent from extending termination for the employee's benefit.

The EAT considered s 98(4) of the Employment Rights Act 1996 and noted that, in order to ascertain whether a dismissal was unfair, regard must be had to whether the employer acted reasonably or unreasonably in treating the reason as sufficient for dismissing the employee. Accordingly, even if the extensions to the termination date amounted to a breach of contract, this was not sufficient to render the dismissal unfair. Rather, the EAT held, the tribunal would need to examine whether the procedure was within the band of reasonable responses in light of all of the relevant facts. It was clear from the tribunal's findings that there was no substantive unfairness.

The EAT disagreed with the claimant's contention that the absence of an appeal from the 21 December 2018 decision was a breach of contract and that the employment tribunal erred in failing to find that the approach the respondent took was outside the band of reasonable responses. The EAT found that the claimant had been afforded, and had availed of, an appeal in July 2018, and that the tribunal lawfully concluded that the additional matters that the claimant wished to challenge in December 2018, had he been permitted another appeal, would have added very little to the discourse.

The appeal was dismissed.

COMPENSATION

[19.06] ***Scoil Áine Naofa v Hughes*[7]*—Labour Court—appeal from Workplace Relations Commission—Protection of Persons Reporting Child Abuse Act***

7 *Scoil Áine Naofa v Hughes* PPD231 and UDD2330.

1998—Unfair Dismissals Acts 1977 to 2015—protected disclosure—appropriate person—natural justice—fair procedures—relationship between the parties had broken down irredeemably

The claimant was employed by the respondent school as a special needs assistant ('SNA') and was dismissed on 14 June 2019. The first set of proceedings[8] concerned the claimant's allegation, under the Protection of Persons Reporting Child Abuse Act 1998, that he had been dismissed for making a protected disclosure to his principal under the Act. The WRC held that the claimant did not make a disclosure as defined by the Act and found against him.

The Labour Court noted that s 3(1) of the Protection of Persons Reporting Child Abuse Act 1998 requires that a disclosure must be made to an 'appropriate person', being a member of An Garda Síochána, a designated officer appointed by Tusla or the HSE. It was acknowledged by the claimant that he did not make the complaint in question to an appropriate person as required by the Act and therefore, the Protection of Persons Reporting Child Abuse Act 1998 did not apply to the case. The finding of the WRC was therefore upheld in this appeal.

The second set of proceedings[9] concerned the claimant's dismissal following a disciplinary investigation into serious misconduct in the form of alleged self-wetting which, it was claimed, was a reaction to the improvement plan put in place for him by the principal, requesting that the claimant utilise designated break times to take his toilet breaks, like the other staff. The disciplinary investigation followed the statutory procedure set out by the Department of Education and Skills in circular letter 72/2011. The procedure required the principal to compile a written report of an investigation into the incident, which was ultimately submitted to the board of management. A disciplinary meeting was held subsequently and the claimant was said to have acted bizarrely. Subsequent to his dismissal, he allegedly presented at the school seeking a reference. He acted 'peculiarly' and the gardaí were called to the scene.

The claimant lodged a complaint under the Unfair Dismissals Acts 1977 to 2015. The WRC held that his dismissal was unfair and awarded him compensation of €10,000. The claimant appealed, seeking reinstatement instead. The respondent also appealed the decision.

The Labour Court heard that, in accordance with the circular letter 72/2011 sent by the Department to the respondent school, the principal conducted an investigation into the claimant's behaviour. However, it transpired that the principal was both the source of the complaint and the chief witness. Therefore, the principal was acting as judge in her own case. She was not asked to set out her own account of events. Rather, she was asked to hold an investigation and to report on same. The input of the claimant was not sought in compiling the report, breaching the right to be heard.

The Court emphasised the respondent's obligation to conduct any disciplinary procedure in accordance with natural justice and fair procedures. It was held that there were

---

8 *Scoil Áine Naofa v Hughes* PPD231.

9 *Scoil Áine Naofa v Hughes* UDD2330.

deficiencies in the circular letter issued by the Department to schools and by following the instructions in that letter, the rules of natural justice were breached by the respondent.

The Court noted that the description of the actions of the claimant subsequent to his dismissal was not challenged and went to remedy. The Court concluded that the relationship between the parties had broken down irredeemably, which made reinstatement or re-engagement impossible. Accordingly, compensation was the most appropriate remedy. There was no documentary evidence of actual loss and the Court was mindful of the claimant's contribution to his own dismissal. The Court described his behaviour as 'so bizarre and disturbing that the board had every reason for serious concern'. Therefore, an award of €2,000 was made.

[19.07] ***Topp Tiles Plc v Hardy*[10]*—UK Employment Appeal Tribunal—appeal from employment tribunal—discrimination arising from disability—compensation for unfair dismissal—causation and proportionality—contributory conduct***

This was an appeal against an employment tribunal's finding that the claimant had been unfairly dismissed by the respondent and that the dismissal had been discriminatory under the Equality Act 2010. The tribunal also determined that the claimant did not contribute to his dismissal.

The claimant was dismissed from his role as a store manager in November 2019, having originally joined the respondent in 2002. The dismissal followed an altercation with an abusive customer in the store. The claimant submitted that he suffered from depression over a period of 20 years, of which the respondent was aware since 2016, but in respect of which the respondent had provided no support.

The employment tribunal concluded that the claimant was a disabled person, that the respondent had the requisite knowledge of the claimant's disability at the material times, and that the dismissal amounted to 'unfavourable treatment'. The tribunal was satisfied that the claimant's depression was 'more than a trivial contributing factor' in his reaction to the customer's 'highly provocative behaviour', and that the claimant was treated unfavourably due to his difficulties in managing his anger in response to a trigger.

The tribunal concluded that dismissal was not a proportionate sanction. It was critical of the respondent's lack of understanding of how the claimant's disability impacted his performance at work, as well as its lack of care in evaluating the specific nature of the customer's allegations, which contained 'obvious contradictions'. The claimant was aged 60 and the tribunal observed that the decision to dismiss him for gross misconduct had the effect of ending his career.

The claimant was found to have been unfairly dismissed. Furthermore, he did not contribute to his dismissal, as a reasonable employer would not have treated the claimant's handling of the altercation, 'faulty though it was, as an act of gross misconduct in the overall circumstances of the case'.

---

10 *Topp Tiles Plc v Hardy* [2023] EAT 56.

On appeal, the UK EAT rejected the respondent's submission that the necessary causative link was missing because, on the tribunal's findings, all or most of the conduct relied upon by the respondent to dismiss the claimant had not in fact occurred. Although the tribunal had made specific factual findings in relation to the claimant's conduct during the altercation, its conclusion was carefully worded, stating that the claimant was treated unfavourably 'because of something arising in consequence of his disability, namely his difficulties in managing his anger in response to a trigger such as an argument with a customer'. This did not refer to any specific aspect of the alleged conduct and the EAT considered that the tribunal reached a permissible conclusion on foot of a proper analysis in accordance with the legal test.

The EAT did not accept the respondent's submission that certain factual findings made by the tribunal rendered its decision on proportionality 'a matter of conjecture such as to amount to an error of law'. Although the claimant did not take up an offer of counselling, it was a reasonable assumption to make that, had he been offered a referral to an occupational health specialist—a 'qualitatively different process'—as an alternative to dismissal, the claimant may have taken the offer more seriously. The tribunal was entitled to conclude that this was an option worth considering. It was further entitled to take into account the particular circumstances of the claimant, including the potential effect of dismissal on the claimant as an individual, given his age and length of service. While the reference to the dismissal 'ending' the claimant's career was, 'perhaps, unhelpfully dramatic', it was within the margin of appreciation for an employment tribunal in its balancing exercise. As the tribunal had yet to make a finding in relation to remedy, the EAT rejected as unfounded a concern that its findings on proportionality would have 'far reaching effects' on the eventual award.

Finally, the EAT found that there was 'just enough' in the tribunal's decision to find that it had made an assessment that there was culpable and blameworthy conduct on the part of the claimant, having briefly described his handling of the episode as 'faulty'. However the tribunal erred in its conclusion that the 'faulty' conduct did not contribute to the dismissal. The EAT accepted that the tribunal had impermissibly focused on the question of whether it had been reasonable for the respondent to treat the conduct as gross misconduct. Even taking the judgment as a whole, the EAT was unable to find another explanation for the tribunal's finding that the claimant's conduct did not contribute to his dismissal, despite being accepted as the effective cause. Accordingly, the tribunal had not applied the correct test and this limb of the appeal succeeded.

CONDUCT

[19.08] ***An Bord Banistíochta Gaelscoil Moshíológ v Labour Court (No 1)*[11]*—High Court—Cregan J—appeal from Labour Court on a point of law—Unfair***

11 *An Bord Banistíochta Gaelscoil Moshíológ v Labour Court (No. 1)* [2023] IEHC 484. See *An Bord Banistíochta Gaelscoil Moshíológ v Labour Court (No 2)* [2023] IEHC 497 at **[19.09]**; see also *Arthur Cox Employment Law Yearbook 2022* at [20.11] for decision of Labour Court in *An Bord Banistíochta Gaelscoil Moshiológ v Ó Súird* UD/18/102.

Dismissals Acts 1977 to 2015—Workplace Relations Commission Act 2015—unfair dismissal—conduct—delay—fair procedures—policies—unreasonable—suppression of evidence—bias—additional allegations

The appellant was the board of management of a school. The principal of the school was put on administrative leave by the employer following an incident concerning a child in 2012. The parents of the child acknowledged to the appellant that this was a 'minor incident' but this was not shared with the principal. Upon investigation, the HSE recommended that the appellant hold its own investigation, however this was not carried out. Instead it began to investigate other issues relating to the principal's involvement in the submission of enrolment figures which were returned to the Department of Education and Skills. The principal was kept on administrative leave. He was put on notice of the allegations against him in this investigation and a number of additional allegations. These additional allegations were not elaborated upon. The principal was suspended in May 2013. A disciplinary hearing was held, which culminated in the principal being dismissed in August 2015. He appealed to the disciplinary appeal panel which upheld the dismissal. The appellant appointed a new, replacement principal. The principal brought an unfair dismissal claim to the WRC and was successful. The appellant appealed to the Labour Court which dismissed the appeal and ordered the principal's re-engagement with effect from 1 September 2017.

The appellant appealed to the High Court on a point of law under s 46 of the Workplace Relations Commission Act 2015, seeking a declaration that the Labour Court erred in law in deciding that the principal was unfairly dismissed and should be re-engaged. It also sought an order setting aside the decision and remitting the matter to the Labour Court.

The High Court looked at the appellant's policies and procedures. Regard was had, in particular, to Department of Education Circular 60/2009, which dealt with the suspension and dismissal of principals. The circular requires that fair procedures and natural justice are applied. The High Court held that such procedures were not followed.

The High Court held that the appellant had been 'biased' as against the principal and had 'prejudged the issue'. It based this on the transcripts provided and emphasised an 'animus' against the principal, which meant that as time went on, the appellant 'became increasingly determined that he would never be allowed back into the school'.

The High Court also considered a number of procedural failings in the investigation and findings of the appellant during its disciplinary hearing and appeal. The Court was critical of the appellant's failure to investigate the original incident relating to the student allegation, which it considered 'unreasonable'. It pointed to the fact that the parents of the child involved in the first incident had characterised it as a 'minor incident' but that this had not been disclosed to the principal in what was a 'deliberate suppression and concealment of evidence'. It was noted that the principal was placed on administrative leave without giving his side of the story.

The High Court was critical of the appellant's decision to keep the principal on administrative leave while the enrolment issue was being investigated; this and the inclusion of additional allegations without further elaboration were also held to be 'unreasonable'.

The High Court found that the appellant's investigation of the enrolment issue was deficient. The principal's evidence had not been seriously considered and the appellant had also failed to interview previous members of the board that had been involved in the enrolment and reporting of student numbers. The report generated on foot of the investigation was held to be 'a mish-mash of allegations, evidence, notification of suspension and procedural arrangements for a disciplinary hearing'. The report therefore fell short of the requirements in Circular 60/2009. The ultimate allegations of fraud and fraudulent misrepresentation were held to be 'manifestly unreasonable'.

The High Court considered the fact that the appellant had decided to adopt a new policy of zero-tolerance on enrolment issues without warning, which the Court described to be 'manifestly unfair and unreasonable'.

The Court was critical of the appellant's delay in the investigation and conclusion of both issues. The result was that the principal was placed on administrative leave and then suspension for years, leading to reputational damage. It held that the decision to appoint a new principal, even though the principal had appealed to the WRC, was a 'blatant attempt to pre-empt the jurisdiction of the WRC, the Labour Court and the High Court'.

The High Court held that the Labour Court was entitled to find that no reasonable member of the board could have decided to dismiss the principal under the circumstances. The decision to dismiss was 'manifestly unreasonable' and disproportionate.

The High Court noted that the Labour Court had recommended re-engagement of the principal with effect from 1 September 2017, with the period from the date of his dismissal to that date being regarded as a period of unpaid suspension in order to maintain his continuity of service. The High Court, however, held that the continued administrative leave of the principal from January 2013 until May 2013 and his suspension from May 2013 until the end of the disciplinary process was 'manifestly unreasonable'. Accordingly, it found that the Labour Court had erred in law in designating the period from the date of the principal's dismissal to 1 September 2017 as unpaid suspension and this should be set aside.

The appeal was dismissed.

[19.09] ***An Bord Banistíochta Gaelscoil Moshíológ v Labour Court (No 2)[12]—High Court—Cregan J—appeal from Labour Court—Unfair Dismissals Acts 1977 to 2015—Workplace Relations Commission Act 2015—unfair dismissal—conduct—terms of the order—appeal dismissed—re-engagement—costs—stay in the event of an appeal to the Supreme Court***

In this second judgment, the High Court considered the parties' submissions on the exact terms of the order that was made in *An Bord Banistíochta Gaelscoil Moshíológ v Labour*

12 *An Bord Banistíochta Gaelscoil Moshíológ v Labour Court (No. 2)* [2023] IEHC 497. See *An Bord Banistíochta Gaelscoil Moshíológ v Labour Court (No 1)* [2023] IEHC 484 at **[19.08]**; see also *Arthur Cox Employment Law Yearbook 2022* at [20.11] for decision of Labour Court in *An Bord Banistíochta Gaelscoil Moshíológ v Ó Súird* UD/18/102.

Court (No. 1).[13] The judgment dealt with the issue of re-engagement, the issue of costs and the appellant's application for a stay on parts of the order in the event of an appeal to the Supreme Court.

In *An Bord Banistíochta Gaelscoil Moshíológ v Labour Court (No. 1)*, the High Court noted that the Labour Court, in its decision, had recommended re-engagement of the principal with effect from 1 September 2017, with the period from the date of his dismissal to that date being regarded as a period of unpaid suspension in order to maintain his continuity of service. The High Court, however, held that the continued administrative leave of the principal from January 2013 until May 2013 and his suspension from May 2013 until the end of the disciplinary process was 'manifestly unreasonable'. Accordingly, it had found that the Labour Court had erred in law in designating the period from the date of the principal's dismissal to 1 September 2017 as unpaid suspension and this should be set aside.

In this judgment, the High Court concluded that the Labour Court erred in law in imposing a period of unpaid suspension and set that part of the decision aside. The appellant argued that this was not a matter for the Court to set aside and that the matter should be remitted to the Labour Court. The High Court held that finality had to be brought to proceedings and that there was 'no good argument either on the facts or on the law as to why this Court should remit the matter'.

The High Court concluded that re-engagement of the principal can only mean re-engagement as principal of the school. The High Court ordered that he be re-engaged with effect from the date of his dismissal, being 30 November 2015, despite the appointment of a new principal in the interim.

The Court ruled that this was an appropriate case to award the principal costs on a legal practitioner and client basis for a number of reasons, including to highlight the Court's disapproval of the appellant's conduct.

With regard to the stay applied for by the appellant, pending a Supreme Court appeal, the Court refused the application. The Court held that the appellant was not bringing the Supreme Court appeal in a *bona fide* manner but rather for tactical reasons. The 'reality' of the appeal was considered in a review of the proposed grounds of appeal. The Court held, upon review, that the appeal was being brought in bad faith and that there was little in reality and in law that substantiated the stated grounds of appeal.

Finally, the Court considered where the balance of justice lay and found that a refusal of a stay would result in no injustice to the appellant. They would have to engage the principal for the duration of the appeal if one was taken, but had already agreed to place him on the payroll. If the appellant was proposing that no engagement occurred and that the principal was to be simply paid in the interim, this would be a 'waste of taxpayers' money'. The stay was therefore refused. The Supreme Court therefore gave leave to appeal on the remedy issue.

13 *An Bord Banistíochta Gaelscoil Moshíológ v Labour Court (No 1)* [2023] IEHC 484.

[19.10] ***Aldi Stores Ltd v Scott*[14]*—Labour Court—appeal from Workplace Relations Commission—Unfair Dismissals Acts 1977 to 2015, s 8A—whether there were substantial grounds to justify employee's dismissal—whether the employer acted reasonably***

The respondent employer appealed against the decision of an Adjudication Officer that the claimant had been unfairly dismissed.

The claimant was employed by the respondent from January 2020 until his summary dismissal in May 2021 for gross misconduct. The uncontested evidence was that on a number of recorded dates the claimant had taken food or drink products from the store without paying for them and, in a meeting with store managers to discuss the matter, he had used abusive language. It was also uncontested that the employee handbook, which was part of the contract of employment, identified 'theft of stock or property, even of the smallest amount' as warranting summary dismissal.

The respondent carried out a disciplinary process, in the course of which the claimant stated that he suffered from mental health conditions. He provided a doctor's note to state that he was on certain medication, a side-effect of which was forgetfulness. He claimed that he had forgotten to pay for the products as a result of his medication. An occupational health examination cast doubt upon this; nor could the store managers recount any issues with the claimant being forgetful at work. The claimant then indicated that it was his condition, rather than his medication, that was contributing to his forgetfulness. A second occupational health examination followed, which did not alter the doctor's opinion. Having been invited to respond to the case against him, in a meeting on 20 May 2021, the claimant was provided with a letter informing him of his dismissal for gross misconduct, to which his reply was, 'I'll see you in f... court', while leaving the room. He was advised of his right to appeal and he did not appeal.

The respondent submitted that there were substantial grounds justifying the dismissal and that it had acted reasonably and fairly in dismissing him.

The claimant submitted that he suffered from a mental health condition for which he was prescribed medication, a side-effect of which was forgetfulness. He submitted further that all four of his shift-mates took goods from the shelves and paid for them later. He felt that the assistant store manager did not like him and was conducting a witch-hunt. He submitted that he had been put on the busiest till during the disciplinary hearings, which was not consistent with a suspicion of theft on his part.

The Court was satisfied that the respondent's actions fell within the range of actions which a reasonable employer would take in the circumstances. The claimant's dismissal was therefore not unfair.

[19.11] ***Connect Trade Union v Douglas*[15]*—Labour Court—appeal from Workplace Relations Commission—Unfair Dismissals Acts 1977 to 2015—recommendation to conduct a disciplinary procedure—endorsement—impartiality—independence***

---

14 *Aldi Stores Ltd v Scott* UD/22/74.

15 *Connect Trade Union v Douglas* UDD238.

The claimant was employed as a trade union official by the respondent on 4 December 2015. The claimant was based in Limerick. In early 2019, the respondent trade union sought to run a new campaign targeting the construction industry in Dublin. All construction officials were to be part of this campaign and were to work out of the Dublin office. The claimant agreed to engage with the campaign and to work in the Dublin office, as a construction official, for a defined period. He later withdrew this agreement for stated reasons. Under the claimant's contract, he was governed by the Rules of the Union, which stated that: 'Full time officials shall be under the control and obey the lawful orders of the General Secretary'. Notwithstanding this, the claimant refused to accept several instructions from the General Secretary to report to the Dublin office in connection with the campaign. The General Secretary initiated a disciplinary procedure by making a complaint. This complaint resulted in an investigation. The investigation resulted in a recommendation to conduct a disciplinary procedure and this was endorsed by a committee which included two persons who had been party to the recommendation. Ultimately the claimant was dismissed for alleged insubordination.

The claimant brought a claim for unfair dismissal to the WRC, alleging that the instruction to relocate to Dublin was beyond the scope of his contract of employment and the respondent did not act reasonably in dismissing him. He also argued that, by initiating the disciplinary process, the General Secretary acted impermissibly, infringing the claimant's rights to natural justice and fair procedures. The respondent referred to s 6 of the Unfair Dismissals Acts 1977 to 2015 and argued that there were 'substantial grounds' justifying the claimant's dismissing given his insubordination. It argued that he was not being instructed to relocate to Dublin but rather to temporarily report to the Dublin office as part of the campaign.

On appeal to the Labour Court, it was held that the claimant was not under instruction to permanently, or for an unspecified period of time, relocate to Dublin. It was also held that the claimant failed to comply with several instructions of the General Secretary and that, given his contract, this amounted to unreasonable conduct on his part.

The Labour Court found that the Rules of the Union contained provisions as regards the powers and obligations of the General Secretary in the conduct of disciplinary procedures and that these did not alter the respondent's general duty to act fairly and in accordance with fair procedures. The fact that two of the parties that recommended the initiation of a disciplinary procedure ultimately also endorsed same offended natural justice and fair procedures. The Court invoked the maxim, *nemo iudex in causa sua.*[16] It was held that the sequence of events which followed the General Secretary's complaint contravened this principle.

The Court acknowledged that the claimant's conduct did lead to his dismissal and indicated that a percentage of 80% accurately described this contribution. The Court also noted the claimant's inadequate efforts to mitigate his losses.

16 *Nemo iudex in causa sua*—no person can be a judge in their own cause.

It was held that the claimant was unfairly dismissed and compensation of €14,152 was awarded to the claimant, taking into consideration his failure to mitigate his losses.

[19.12] ***Inspection Services Ireland Ltd v Krpeta*[17]*—Labour Court—appeal from Workplace Relations Commission—Unfair Dismissals Acts 1977 to 2015—consent—impartiality—small company—disciplinary issue—state of mind—fair procedure—independent investigator***

The claimant was employed in 2004 as a cargo surveyor and later was promoted to operations manager with the respondent company. The company was a small company, with only one person holding a higher position than the claimant, ie the owner of the company, Mr Saarsteiner.

The claimant applied for annual leave for 24 December 2018. He was informed that this would not be possible as Mr Saarsteiner was taking that day off and both could not be on leave at the same time. On the morning of 24 December, Mr Saarsteiner received a phone call from the claimant's wife to inform him that the claimant had a vomiting bug and could not attend work. When Mr Saarsteiner received the company phone bill, it recorded the claimant's phone as 'roaming in the EU' on that day. Mr Saarsteiner organised to meet the claimant to discuss this. In the course of the meeting, the claimant deleted all data from the company phone. The claimant was suspended with pay, pending an investigation. Mr Saarsteiner engaged experts to assess the claimant's phone and laptop and they confirmed that the data had been irreversibly erased. Mr Saarsteiner engaged an independent expert to carry out an investigation into the circumstances surrounding: (a) the claimant's absence on 24 December 2018; (b) the deletion of data from the company phone; and (c) the deletion of data from the company laptop.

Mr Saarsteiner only agreed partially with the findings of the investigator, who upheld two of the three allegations against the claimant. Mr Saarsteiner elected to hold a disciplinary meeting with the claimant to ascertain whether he had anything to say in response to the investigation. Mr Saarsteiner subsequently summarily dismissed the claimant for gross misconduct. The claimant appealed this decision. He was informed of his option to receive a *de novo* hearing, but did not opt for same.

An appeal was carried out by an independent person and the decision to dismiss was upheld. The claimant was dismissed in 2019.

In a hearing in the WRC concerning the fairness of the dismissal, the Adjudication Officer upheld the claimant's claim and the respondent appealed to the Labour Court.

In the Labour Court, the claimant argued that the procedures followed were unfair and that Mr Saarsteiner could not be considered an impartial person in conducting an impartial disciplinary process and coming to a decision to dismiss the claimant.

It was argued by the respondent that, as his was a small company, it was not contrary to fair procedures for Mr Saarsteiner to make the decision to suspend, conduct the

---

17 *Inspection Services Ireland Ltd v Krpeta* UDD234.

disciplinary hearing and ultimately dismiss the claimant. It was argued that because the investigation and appeal were carried out by independent parties and because the claimant was offered a *de novo* appeal, fair procedures were followed and any procedural infirmity was cured.

Mr Saarsteiner admitted in his evidence that he had decided before he met with the claimant that the claimant was lying. Mr Saarsteiner also admitted to rejecting the independent investigator's findings in relation to one of the allegations, and conducted the disciplinary hearing himself to 'see if the [claimant] had anything to say'. Mr Saarsteiner indicated that, prior to this hearing, he believed that the claimant was guilty of gross misconduct.

The Court found that the disciplinary procedure offended the requirements of fair procedure and was not impartial. It held that Mr Saarsteiner's state of mind was fixed and could not be reconciled with the role of impartial decision maker in a disciplinary process. The Court held that the claimant had contributed to his own dismissal to a substantial degree and set that level at 77%.

The Court therefore awarded compensation at 23% of the maximum award available. The appeal was upheld and the Court varied the Adjudication Officer's award.

[19.13] ***Laois County Council v Donegan[18]—Labour Court—appeal from Workplace Relations Commission—Unfair Dismissals Acts 1977 to 2015—conduct—fair procedures and natural justice—involvement of same manager at multiple stages of disciplinary process—appeal of decision to dismiss—contribution to dismissal—failure to mitigate loss***

The claimant was employed as a plumber by the respondent from 2007 until his dismissal in June 2017. The dismissal was on foot of an incident in October 2016. A senior engineer conducted a contemporaneous and summary report on the incident and a decision was made to carry out a full investigation. The director of services of the respondent company, DB, authorised placing the claimant on administrative leave.

A full investigation was carried out and a report issued, which characterised the claimant's behaviour in relation to the incident as being a health and safety risk. The respondent decided to invoke its disciplinary procedure. A disciplinary interview was held by DB, followed by a disciplinary hearing, also convened by DB. DB issued his report and a recommendation that the claimant be dismissed. The claimant was given a right to appeal this recommendation to the chief executive and he did. The recommendation to dismiss was upheld by the chief executive. The claimant was not given the right to appeal the chief executive's decision. The claimant brought an unsuccessful claim to the WRC under s 8A of the Unfair Dismissals Acts 1977 to 2015. The claimant appealed to the Labour Court.

The Court noted that the procedure invoked by the respondent involved DB at multiple stages. The Court disagreed with the respondent that the decision to place the claimant on administrative leave did not amount to a disciplinary act. It held that it was a decision

18 *Laois County Council v Donegan* UDD2336.

of some import. It was noted that after this decision, DB was once again involved, as he held a disciplinary interview. The Court noted that there was no provision in the written policy of the respondent that provided for the disciplinary interview conducted by DB. DB then embarked on a disciplinary process and ultimately recommended dismissal. The Court noted that the respondent organisation was of such a nature that internal and external management level personnel, who had no other involvement of substance in the case, could have been asked to be involved in the disciplinary procedure.

It was found that the claimant was not afforded a right of appeal from the chief executive's decision to dismiss him. It was also noted that no evidence had been offered that the decision maker considered any alternative sanctions.

The Court held that the claimant had not been afforded fair procedures in the disciplinary procedure and therefore the dismissal was unfair.

However, the Court had regard to the findings of the internal investigation and held that, on the balance of probabilities, the claimant, through his behaviour during the incident of October 2016, contributed to his own dismissal.

Further, it was held that the claimant's attempts to find alternative employment elsewhere, thereby mitigating his loss arising from his dismissal, fell short.

The Court held that reinstatement and re-engagement were not appropriate in this case. Taking into consideration the contribution of the claimant to his own dismissal and his failure to mitigate his own loss, the Court set the award at €9,500.

[19.14] ***Tesco Ireland Ltd v Maguire*[19]*—Labour Court—appeal from Workplace Relations Commission—Unfair Dismissals Acts 1977 to 2015—CCTV—breakdown of the relationship of trust and confidence—fair procedures and natural justice—employee record—whether the sanction of dismissal was proportionate and appropriate***

The claimant was an employee of the respondent, working as a customer assistant. Her employment was terminated on the grounds of serious misconduct following an investigation, disciplinary process and appeal. The allegations against her were twofold: that she had kept a sum of money that belonged to a customer for her own personal gain; and that she took a scratch card without paying for it.

The claimant argued that the disciplinary process was fundamentally flawed. She made a number of allegations to substantiate this, for example, that she had not been shown CCTV footage of the alleged incidents. The respondent argued that during the disciplinary process the claimant did not provide satisfactory reasons for her behaviour sufficient to mitigate the seriousness of her actions. It was also claimed that she refused to look at the CCTV footage which was available during the disciplinary process. She also alleged that she had not been informed that her position was at risk. The claimant contested the suitability of her sanction, given her alleged innocence and the fact that she had 11 years' service without incident. The respondent stated that it had considered

---

19 *Tesco Ireland Ltd v Maguire* UDD2326.

the claimant's record as part of the proceedings and did not take the decision to dismiss lightly. The respondent argued that the relationship of trust and confidence had broken down irreparably.

The claimant took a claim for unfair dismissal to the WRC but was unsuccessful; she appealed to the Labour Court.

The Court considered whether the sanction of dismissal was proportionate and appropriate. It rejected the claimant's contentions about the CCTV footage. When asked at trial why she did not watch the footage, the claimant stated: 'I did not see the CCTV footage. I refused to watch it'. The Court held that the decision not to watch the footage was not indicative of an unfair disciplinary procedure but a decision made by the claimant alone. The Court noted that the reasons given by the claimant to justify her alleged behaviour differed from disciplinary meeting to disciplinary meeting and were not such as to mitigate the sanction ultimately arrived at. The Court referred to correspondence sent to the claimant throughout the investigation process advising her that the outcome of the investigation and disciplinary process may include sanctions up to and including dismissal.

It had not been unreasonable for the respondent to conclude that the claimant's behaviour amounted to serious misconduct. It was noted that the claimant had refused to watch the CCTV footage available during the disciplinary hearing or to provide any reasonable justification for her actions. She had been aware that dismissal was a possible sanction under the circumstances. It was held that the relationship of trust and confidence between the parties had been undermined. The Court found that the decision to dismiss the claimant had been justified and was not disproportionate and upheld the decision of the WRC.

[19.15] ***Charalambous v National Bank of Greece[20]—UK Employment Appeal Tribunal—appeal from employment tribunal—Employment Rights Act 1996—disciplinary procedures—misconduct—direct communication with employee—procedural unfairness—internal appeal***

The respondent was a bank which employed the claimant as a relationship manager in its London office. The claimant wrote an email to the UK country manager and a number of other senior managers seeking a promotion to senior relationship manager. The claimant's trade union representative was copied into the email and her lawyer was blind copied. The claimant attached to the email a spreadsheet of all private clients including commissions, turnover, total assets, year-end comparisons, foreign exchange transactions and total asset by currency. The claimant subsequently forwarded the email with its attachment to her external personal email account and copied in her brother, who worked for another bank, at his personal email account. The claimant then forwarded the email to the respondent's HR manager and again copied her trade union representative. The claimant was invited to a meeting with the UK country manager who informed her that she had released confidential information to the trade union representative when she had copied him into her email. The claimant was suspended pending a disciplinary investigation.

20 *Charalambous v National Bank of Greece* [2023] EAT 75.

The claimant maintained that sharing the confidential information had been an innocent oversight and continued to lobby for a promotion. In February 2019, the respondent invited the claimant to a formal disciplinary hearing. The respondent's country risk manager led the hearing and the claimant was accompanied by her trade union representative. This meeting was recorded. It was followed by a further meeting led by the country risk manager. Again, the claimant was represented and the meeting was recorded. At the latter meeting, the claimant was informed that further evidence had come to light that her lawyer had been blind copied on the original email and that she had forwarded the email to her own personal email address and to her brother.

In March 2019, the claimant was summarily dismissed by the UK country manager for gross misconduct. It was found that the explanation offered by the claimant, that the disclosure of confidential information had been a mistake, was unsatisfactory given that publication occurred on three separate occasions. The claimant appealed against this decision to dismiss. The respondent's HR director heard this appeal. The grounds of appeal included the fact that it was unfair that the country risk manager that had conducted the disciplinary meetings was the decision maker. She also alleged that she was being dismissed because of whistleblowing or because of her race. She maintained that dismissal was too severe a penalty. The appeal was dismissed. The claimant brought a claim to the employment tribunal for unfair dismissal.

The employment tribunal found that the first disciplinary meeting was really a further investigatory meeting. It held that the investigation had been reasonable and that the respondent had a reasonable belief that the claimant had misconducted herself and there were reasonable grounds for that belief. It found that dismissal was within the range of reasonable responses open to a reasonable employer.

The claimant appealed to the UK EAT, arguing that the tribunal erred in finding that the dismissal was fair, notwithstanding that the decision maker, being the UK country manager, was not the individual who conducted the disciplinary hearing. *Budgen & Co v Thomas*[21] was relied on, which, it was stated, was authority for the proposition that a dismissal will be unfair if the manager making the decision to dismiss does not hear directly from the employee. It was submitted that the tribunal ought to have held the dismissal was *prima facie* unreasonable and therefore unfair because the decision maker did not conduct the disciplinary hearing and therefore did not hear directly from the claimant.

The EAT rejected this interpretation of *Budgen*. The EAT noted that in *Budgen*, it was held that it was necessary for the employee to be given 'some opportunity of explaining himself'. However, the EAT did not consider that this meant that, in order for a dismissal to be fair, there must be a meeting between the employee and dismissing officer. The EAT stated that this would be 'good practice' only.

It was noted that the claimant had undergone two formally recorded disciplinary meetings and was represented at both. The records of the meeting were given to the UK country manager for use in making his decision. Further, the officer who conducted

21 *Budgen & Co v Thomas* [1976] ICR 344.

the meetings had also given the UK country manager 'in effect a recommendation for dismissal'. It was taken therefore, that the claimant had been given ample opportunity to explain herself and that any explanations were conveyed to the decision maker. The EAT found that the tribunal was entitled to conclude that the respondent's actions were reasonable in the circumstances.

The appeal was dismissed.

[19.16] ***Hewston v Ofsted[22]—UK Employment Appeal Tribunal—appeal from employment tribunal—Employment Rights Act 1996—unfair dismissal—conduct—ACAS Code—contract of employment—wrongful dismissal—misconduct—length of service—performance—wrongful dismissal—physical contact***

The claimant was an employee of the respondent and worked as an inspector. During a school inspection visit, a group of students came in from the rain and the claimant brushed rainwater off one of the student's hair and forehead. He put his hand on the shoulder of another student. The school made a complaint in writing and this complaint was never furnished to the claimant. The child's written account of the event was also not furnished to the claimant. A report was made to the Local Authority Designated Office ('LADO'). An email from a LADO officer stated that:

> 'On balance I feel the proportionate response is for the employer to investigate this matter internally with Andrew with consideration to raising awareness of professional boundaries and any training that may be required in support of this.
>
> The employer is advised of the duty of care to the employee during the investigation process and Andrew's right to know that he has been referred to the LADO service'.

This email was not shared with the claimant. He was suspended and an investigation followed. The claimant was subject to a disciplinary procedure and was ultimately, summarily dismissed. The claimant brought a complaint of unfair dismissal and wrongful dismissal to the employment tribunal.

Before the tribunal, it was not in dispute that there was no written rule or policy to the effect that the conduct in question could be considered liable to merit dismissal. While the respondent argued that inspectors 'should understand that they should not touch a child', it was also acknowledged that there was also no guidance or training to this effect. The tribunal conflated the issue of whether the claimant was aware of whether the touching was inappropriate and whether he was aware of the sanction that it might attract. The tribunal held that the dismissal was fair and that it was not wrongful.

The UK EAT held that, in relation to unfair dismissal, the tribunal failed to give adequate consideration to the fact that it had not been explained to the claimant either by written policy, training or otherwise, that a single incident of physical contact, even if not found sufficient to give rise to a safeguarding issue, could result in dismissal. It was held that the tribunal should have found that there were no clear rules or guidance in place. Although the respondent did not, strictly speaking, breach the ACAS Code, it did have a list of behaviours that would be viewed as gross misconduct, and physical touching

22 *Hewston v Ofsted* [2023] EAT 109.

was not on that list. The EAT stated that it was incumbent on the tribunal to determine whether it was within the band of reasonable responses by the dismissing and appeal officers to conclude that the claimant's conduct was such that he did not need to be specifically forewarned that his actions would be regarded as so serious that they would warrant dismissal. The EAT noted that where the tribunal's judgment contains no error of law it should not interfere with it, but where an error of law is detected, the situation is different. The EAT examined the tribunal's reasoning and held that the tribunal failed to engage with whether the dismissal was unfair because of the lack of notice as to whether this specific conduct would attract dismissal as a sanction.

It also found that the tribunal erred in not finding that the failure to provide the claimant with the text of the school's complaint, the text of the child's statement, and an email listing the LADO documents seen and relied upon by the dismissing officer rendered the dismissal unfair.

It was held that, on the facts, the tribunal could only have properly concluded that the dismissal was unfair and this conclusion was substituted for that of the tribunal.

In relation to the wrongful dismissal claim, the EAT held that the tribunal did not make a clear finding that it objectively considered the evidence before it. It acknowledged that sometimes, where there is a complaint of unfair dismissal accompanied by a claim of wrongful dismissal, the former will take up the majority of the tribunal's time and argument. However, it was not permissible to 'muddle the two reasoning exercises' and treat the latter as a 'mere afterthought'. The decision to dismiss that complaint was quashed.

The appeal was allowed and the matter was remitted to a different tribunal to determine the wrongful dismissal complaint and determine a remedy for unfair dismissal.

CONSTRUCTIVE DISMISSAL

[19.17] ***Allenfield Care Homes Ltd v Clifford*[23]*—Labour Court—appeal from Workplace Relations Commission—Unfair Dismissals Acts 1977 to 2015—garda vetting—protected disclosure—suspension—probationary review—grievance procedure—whether it was reasonable to terminate employment due to the unreasonable conduct of employer***

The claimant was employed by the respondent as a part-time healthcare assistant from November 2017. In April 2018, the claimant reported an incident that she had witnessed at work, which she alleged amounted to elder abuse. This incident was brought to the attention to the appropriate authorities but was found not to amount to a breach of its trust in care obligations. The claimant considered that her reporting of this incident constituted a protected disclosure under the Protected Disclosures Act 2014.

After undergoing a six-month probationary period and following a probationary interview on 28 May 2018, the claimant became a permanent employee. The claimant was

23 *Allenfield Care Homes Ltd v Clifford* UDD235.

required under the Health Act 2007 to obtain Garda vetting clearance. She failed to do so in a timely manner, despite being reminded of the need to do so by the respondent. The claimant was suspended for a short period in May 2018 pending receipt of her Garda vetting certificate. The claimant resigned in May 2018. She brought proceedings in the WRC for constructive dismissal under the Unfair Dismissals Acts 1977 to 2015. The claimant was unsuccessful and appealed to the Labour Court.

The claimant alleged that her suspension amounted to a penalisation for having made the protected disclosure in April 2018. The claimant pointed to other events, which she said illustrated the respondent's negative attitude towards her, including her probationary review meeting, which she described as a process of 'character assassination'. At trial, the respondent's witnesses gave evidence rejecting any such characterisation of the review meeting. The respondent argued that the disclosure had no bearing on its decision to suspend her in May 2018. The respondent contended that the claimant's resignation was triggered by her probationary review meeting, which immediately preceded it. The respondent pointed to clause 13 of the claimant's written contract outlining a grievance procedure, which she did not avail of before her resignation.

The Court emphasised the fact that the claimant bore the burden of proof to establish that it was reasonable for her to terminate her employment due to the unreasonable treatment of her by the respondent. The Court noted that, to invoke the Unfair Dismissals Acts 1977 to 2015, an employee must have one year's continuous service but that, in this case, the claimant alleged that the requirement was not applicable due to the protected disclosure she had made and the detriment she suffered on foot of same.

The Court stated that the claimant did not provide evidence of a kind that would allow the Court to infer a causal link between her resignation and the complaint made. The fact that the claimant returned to work for a brief period following her suspension supported this. The Court questioned the claimant's credibility, describing her as 'evasive in her answers to questions about why she did not progress her Garda vetting application in a timely fashion'. Accordingly, the Court preferred the respondent's witnesses' version of events regarding the probationary review. The Court marked as a 'major infirmity' the fact that the claimant did not avail of the grievance procedure provided for in clause 13 of her contract before resigning. Therefore, it was held that she did not make out her claim of constructive dismissal.

The appeal failed and the decision of the Adjudication Officer was upheld.

[19.18] ***Go-ahead Transport Services (Ireland) Ltd v Shanahan*[24]*—Labour Court—appeal from Workplace Relations Commission—Unfair Dismissals Acts 1977 to 2015—grievance procedures—apology—work-related stress—resignation before utilising the full procedures available to examine grievances—range of reasonable responses***

The claimant worked as a driver for the respondent company. The claimant maintained that, over time, there had been an accumulation of minor and major breaches of his

24 *Go-ahead Transport Services (Ireland) Ltd v Shanahan* LCR22781.

contract of employment by the respondent, which made his continuing working for the company impossible. These included: an incident where the claimant was approached by a manager when he was on a break regarding complaints made against him, culminating in an informal warning. The respondent apologised for this interruption of his break. Another incident related to a paid day off, 17 March, that had been agreed between the claimant and respondent. In this instance, the claimant received a telephone call on the day in question to say that he was expected to work. When he returned to work on 18 March, he discovered that he was marked 'absent' the day before, despite the agreement made. Ultimately, however, the claimant was paid for the proposed paid day off.

The claimant went on sick leave by reason of claimed work-related stress. The claimant raised a formal grievance regarding the numerous alleged breaches. This was acknowledged but no further communication was forthcoming from the respondent. On 12 May 2021, the claimant resigned, arguing that the respondent's behaviour had been so unreasonable that the claimant had lost all trust and confidence in it. The respondent argued that there had been no breach of contract and that the claimant could not rely on unreasonableness on its part as he did not exhaust the grievance processes available to him before resigning. The respondent indicated that it intended to deal with the grievances raised on his return from sick leave but the claimant had resigned before it had an opportunity. The claimant brought a constructive dismissal claim to the WRC. This was rejected by the Adjudication Officer.

The Labour Court applied *Conway v Ulster Bank Ltd*[25] and *Travers v MBNA Ltd*[26] and held that it was 'incumbent for an appellant to utilise all internal remedies'. It was held that the claimant was aware of the grievance procedure, having utilised it previously. It held that it was reasonable to wait until the claimant returned after sick leave to address his grievance. There was nothing before the Court to suggest any reason why the claimant would have considered that the respondent lacked the ability to deal with his grievances. The Court found that the claimant should have given the respondent an opportunity to address his concerns before resigning. The Court therefore held that the claimant had not acted reasonably in resigning without substantially using the respondent's grievance procedure.

The decision of the Adjudication Officer was upheld.

[19.19] ***The No 8 Partnership v Simmons*[27]*—UK Employment Appeal Tribunal—appeal from employment tribunal—Equality Act 2010—Employment Rights Act 1996—unfair dismissal—constructive dismissal—associative discrimination—time off for dependants—disability discrimination—direct discrimination—comparators—perversity***

The claimant worked in the respondent's dental practice as a dental nurse. She worked for the practice two days per week. In March 2020, Covid-19 caused the practice to close and the claimant was placed on furlough. The practice informed the staff that it

---

25 *Conway v Ulster Bank Ltd* UD 475/1981.

26 *Travers v MBNA Ltd* UD 720/2006.

27 *The No. 8 Partnership v Simmons* [2023] EAT 140.

intended to re-open for emergency treatment and asked the claimant to return to work for her regularly scheduled hours from 26 May. The claimant was concerned about returning to work as she was a carer for her elderly father, who had dementia. She asked to remain on furlough until the end of September to continue to care for him. This request was refused. The claimant was asked to confirm by 22 June whether she would return by 25 June. The claimant resigned on 26 June.

She brought a claim to the employment tribunal arguing that the respondent had refused to grant her emergency care leave and had failed to accommodate her care difficulties. The employment tribunal held that the respondent was in breach of an implied term of trust and confidence and that, as the claimant had resigned as a result of this, she was constructively dismissed. The tribunal also found that the respondent had wrongly refused the claimant's request for time off to care for her father under s 57A of the Employment Rights Act 1996, which entitled her to a reasonable amount of time off to make arrangements for a dependant who was unwell. The tribunal used two hypothetical comparators in accordance with s 23 of the Equality Act 2010. One was a carer of a child and the other was a spouse of a cancer victim. The tribunal held that the claimant had been treated less favourably than both comparators on the associative basis of her father's disability.

The respondent sought to appeal the decision to the UK EAT.

The EAT considered whether the facts supported a finding of direct associative disability discrimination and constructive dismissal. In the first instance, it was held that the claimant had not sought to draw any comparisons with actual or hypothetical comparators in the prosecution of her claim. The EAT noted that the tribunal's reliance on comparators was material to its reasoning on both the discrimination and constructive dismissal claims. It was noted that these comparators were not discussed with the parties and therefore the respondent did not have an adequate opportunity to respond to them. This was deemed to be unfair.

Furthermore, the employment tribunal failed to satisfy the like-for-like comparison required by s 13 of the Equality Act 2010. For example, the tribunal had failed to reveal the age of the child in question, in relation to the first comparator or to assess how this employee would have responded to the circumstances. The EAT stated that the tribunal should have considered questions of relative vulnerability as to the frequency and kind of care required in both hypothetical cases. In the absence of a comparator, the EAT noted that the correct approach was to focus on the actions of the respondent. In considering whether the claimant was subject to less favourable treatment because of her father's disability, the tribunal had indicated that the respondent adopted a 'rather dismissive approach' to the care required. It was not clear from this, it was held, how the tribunal arrived at its conclusion that the less favourable treatment occurred because of the father's disability. It appeared to the EAT that the claimant's request to continue to be furloughed would have been met with rejection whether or not her father had a disability.

Insofar as the constructive dismissal claim was dependent on the tribunal's finding of direct discrimination, the EAT held that it could not stand. The tribunal's finding that there was a breach of an implied term was also unsafe, given, for example, that the tribunal had erred in applying the relevant test when ascertaining whether there had been a breach of an implied term. Instead of asking whether the practice had conducted itself in a way that was likely to damage its relationship of trust and confidence with the claimant, the tribunal had simply decided that there had been a breach.

The respondent asked the EAT to substitute its own findings for that of the tribunal: that the claims should be dismissed. However, the EAT held that its function is limited to ascertaining whether the tribunal has erred in its decisions. On the constructive dismissal claim, the tribunal's failure to apply the correct legal test and provide appropriate explanations for its findings did not equate to perversity. Consequently, that matter was remitted to a differently constituted tribunal for rehearing. However, the discrimination claim was held to be perverse and, accordingly, it was dismissed.

The appeal was allowed.

[19.20] ***Brooks v Leisure Employment Services Ltd*[28]*—UK Employment Appeal Tribunal—appeal from employment tribunal—repudiatory breach—constructive dismissal—affirmation of contract of employment—delay in bringing grievance procedure to a conclusion***

The claimant appealed against an employment tribunal's decision to dismiss her claim for constructive dismissal. The respondent cross-appealed against the tribunal's finding that it had acted in repudiatory breach of the claimant's contract of employment.

The claimant had worked for the respondent since 1990, in a call centre selling resort holidays. Most of her remuneration was commission from these sales. In March 2020, the respondent closed its resorts due to Covid-19 restrictions; the claimant continued to be paid in full. The respondent then assembled a team of its most experienced staff, including the claimant, to work from home dealing with customer issues. A WhatsApp group was set up for the home-working team. The claimant raised concerns in relation to her pay while on the home-working team, given that there would be no sales, and therefore no commission, while the resorts were closed. The respondent removed her from the WhatsApp group without explanation.

In April 2020, the claimant submitted a grievance about the respondent's treatment of her, alleging discrimination and breach of implied term of mutual trust and confidence. In email correspondence about the provision of documentation in the grievance procedure, the claimant purported to reserve all of her rights. By late June, the grievance procedure remained ongoing, and, by email, the claimant resigned with immediate effect. Her grievance was dismissed in August.

The claimant submitted in her complaint that her removal from the WhatsApp group was a repudiatory breach of contract. The employment tribunal found that removing her in that manner, with no consultation or explanation, was a breach of the implied terms on the respondent's part—given the claimant's concerns about loss of earnings—and that this was the reason for her resignation. It concluded, however, that she had affirmed the contract by continuing to accept payment for a further three months without resigning, and consequently her constructive dismissal claim was dismissed.

28 *Brooks v Leisure Employment Services Ltd* [2023] EAT 137.

The respondent cross-appealed, submitting that the tribunal's decision on breach of contract was perverse because the claimant's pleaded case was solely based on her removal from the WhatsApp group, whereas the tribunal had considered wider issues. The claimant, in turn, challenged the conclusion that she had affirmed her contract of employment before resigning, and that the tribunal had failed to take into account that her delay in resigning was to see if the grievance procedure would resolve her concerns.

Dismissing the cross-appeal, the EAT concluded that the tribunal had considered the claimant's pleaded case with care. It had clearly understood that the asserted breach was the claimant's removal from the WhatsApp group, but it considered that the removal 'had to be set in the context of it being done after she had raised genuine and serious concerns about her renumeration if she joined the home-working team', and the fact that she was removed without any consultation or explanation. The tribunal was entitled to take that context into account in deciding whether the respondent had breached the employment contract. Its conclusion did not meet the high threshold for perversity.

Turning to the claimant's appeal, the EAT found that the tribunal had not taken into account the fact that the claimant had raised a grievance, which by the time of her resignation had not been completed. It followed that the tribunal had erred in its decision of affirmation. It had not considered the fact that the claimant had purported to reserve all of her rights, but had focused entirely on the fact that she had received her wages during the period of delay between the breach of contract and her resignation.

Accordingly, the matter was remitted to the same tribunal for fresh determination.

HEALTH AND SAFETY

[19.21] ***Rodgers v Leeds Laser Cutting Ltd*[29]*—Court of Appeal of England and Wales—Underhill, Davies & Stuart-Smith LJJ—appeal from UK Employment Appeal Tribunal—Employment Rights Act 1996—unfair dismissal—Covid-19—serious and imminent danger—health and safety***

The appellant was an employee of the respondent working in a large warehouse-type space. At the beginning of the Covid-19 pandemic, in March 2020, the appellant informed his employer that he had elected to stay home until lockdown was lifted, due to his having a child with an underlying health condition. In April 2020, the appellant was dismissed. He argued automatic unfair dismissal under s 100(1)(d) of Employment Rights Act 1996 (the '1996 Act') and claimed that he had not gone back to work because the risk of Covid-19 infection was a serious and imminent one.

The employment tribunal dismissed his claim, holding that his concerns about Covid-19 were general and did not relate specifically to the workplace. The tribunal rejected the contention that the risk of infection was a serious and imminent danger in circumstances where conditions in the warehouse were such that the workers could socially

29 *Rodgers v Leeds Laser Cutting Ltd* [2022] EWCA Civ 1659.

distance and the employer had put in place measures to reduce the risk of infection. The UK EAT upheld this decision.

The matter was appealed to the Court of Appeal of England and Wales, which considered the application of s 100(1)(d) to cases where the 'danger' referred to in the 1996 Act was prospective transmission of the Covid-19 virus.

The Court considered whether the section could be interpreted as requiring a tribunal to decide whether, objectively, there was a danger present and then, separately, whether the appellant reasonably believed said danger to be serious and imminent. The latter had both subjective and objective aspects. The Court held that s 100(1)(d) should be construed purposively rather than literally. In this way it was enough that the employee had a reasonable belief that the danger existed and that it was serious and imminent. The Court also held that the employee must have left the workplace as a result of the perceived danger.

The Court held that, in theory, there was nothing about the risk of infection from Covid-19 which would bring it outside the scope of s 100(1)(d). Accordingly, it fell to the tribunal to consider whether in this case, the risk amounted to a serious and imminent danger. The Court approved the following test used by the employment tribunal:

> '(1) Did the employee believe that there were circumstances of serious and imminent danger at the workplace? If so:
> (2) Was that belief reasonable? If so:
> (3) Could they reasonably have averted that danger? If not:
> (4) Did they leave, or propose to leave or refuse to return to, the workplace, or the relevant part, because of the (perceived) serious and imminent danger? If so:
> (5) Was that the reason (or principal reason) for the dismissal?'

The Court noted that the tribunal had focused on the distinction between appellant's belief that the danger of infection was 'all around' as compared to his believing that the danger was 'specifically present within the workplace'. The appellant argued that the tribunal erred in its interpretation of s 100(1)(d) as relating to dangers which existed only in the workplace and nowhere else. The Court acknowledged that there was nothing in the section that required that the danger be something exclusively found in the workplace. However, it held that on a reading of the tribunal's judgment, it was clear that the tribunal focused on this distinction to highlight that the appellant did not believe that the danger of Covid-19 was serious and imminent in the workplace. The Court noted that even if its reading of the tribunal's judgment was wrong in this respect, its finding on reasonableness was sound.

The appeal was therefore dismissed.

REDUNDANCY

[19.22] ***Acorn Brokerage Ltd t/a Acorn Insurance Brokers v Ahearne*[30]*—Labour Court—appeal from Workplace Relations Commission—Unfair Dismissals Acts***

30 *Acorn Brokerage Ltd t/a Acorn Insurance Brokers v Ahearne* UDD2316.

1977 to 2015—Workplace Relations Act 2015—preliminary issue—jurisdiction—Covid-19—unlawful termination—appeal form—Labour Court Rules 2022—not formally informed of risk of redundancy—unreasonable behaviour—no appeal—no investigation for redeployment purposes

The claimant worked in data entry with the respondent company. The respondent ran trade stands at public events and meeting places where it advertised its insurance and other services. The appellant's role involved inputting data collected at the trade stands into the respondent's systems. When the Covid-19 pandemic occurred, the claimant was asked not to attend work as a health and safety precaution. On 8 April 2020, she was placed on a period of short-term layoff. On 9 July 2020, she was invited to a meeting and informed that the trade stands aspect of the respondent's business was discontinued and accordingly, her role and the role of the trade stands team leader, were redundant.

The claimant brought a claim to the WRC, contending that she was unfairly dismissed. The Adjudication Officer ruled that her complaint was not well founded. The claimant appealed to the Labour Court.

A preliminary issue was raised before the Labour Court relating to the Court's jurisdiction to hear the appeal. It transpired that the claimant had submitted the wrong type of appeal form. She did not correct same within the 42-day limit and did not seek to extend the time for bringing an appeal under s 44(4) of the Workplace Relations Act 2015. The Court held that the claimant's failure to lodge an appeal using the appropriate form did not necessarily deprive the Court of jurisdiction to hear the appeal. The Court cited caselaw in support of the contention that the Court could consider the degree to which the absence of certain information required by the Labour Court Rules 2022 could invalidate a proposed appeal. Ultimately, the Court was satisfied that both the Court and the respondent were made aware of the claimant's intention to appeal and the form used was not so deficient in fundamental respects that it was invalid.

The respondent contended that a genuine redundancy situation arose, that the claimant was the only data enterer employed at the time and that it was not possible to redeploy her. The respondent argued that no alternative roles were available for the purpose of redeployment and that the displacement of other workers by way of redundancy in order to redeploy the claimant was not appropriate. The claimant argued that she was unfairly selected for redundancy and that other employees on temporary contracts were kept on while she was let go.

The Court agreed that a genuine redundancy situation arose here and that no other employees in the company undertook the same type of work as the claimant at the time. However, the Court found that the respondent had acted unreasonably in its approach to the claimant's redundancy for three reasons. First, the Court noted that the claimant's line manager had been informed in April 2020 that the business was under review. However, the claimant only became aware of the possibility that the trade stand business might be discontinued when she was placed on lay off. She was never formally informed that her role was at risk of redundancy.

Second, the claimant was only informed that the trade stand business was ceasing operations at the meeting on 9 July 2020. At this point the decision had been made to cease trading and the respondent was not invited to give input; nor was she afforded representation at the meeting.

Finally, the Court was not satisfied that the respondent gave due consideration to the questions the claimant posed about alternative employment within the company. No such investigation was actually carried out. It could have been, the Court held, that no alternative roles could be identified upon investigation. However, without this exercise having been carried out, this was unknown. Furthermore, no appeal was afforded to the claimant. The Court held that the respondent failed to balance the interests of the claimant with its own interests and this amounted to unreasonable behaviour on the part of the respondent.

As reinstatement and re-engagement were not appropriate here, the Court awarded compensation of €4,000 to the claimant.

The appeal was upheld.

[19.23] ***Teixeira v Zaika Restaurant Ltd*[31]*—UK Employment Appeal Tribunal—appeal from employment tribunal—Employment Rights Act 1996—compensatory awards—information and consultation procedures—redundancy pools—redundancy selection—unfair dismissal—Polkey reduction***

The claimant worked as one of ten chefs at the respondent's restaurant. The other chefs had greater seniority and experience when compared to the claimant. The claimant was the only non-speciality chef in the group. As a result of the Covid-19 pandemic, there was a reduction in work at the restaurant and the claimant was made redundant. None of the other chefs employed by the respondent were made redundant.

The employment tribunal held that the dismissal was unfair because the employer did not operate a redundancy procedure. The tribunal noted, however, that if the employer had a redundancy procedure, the claimant would have found himself in a redundancy selection pool of one, as he was the only non-speciality chef on staff. It held that even if the claimant had been pooled with the other chefs, he would have scored lowest. In this way, the claimant would have been dismissed and the outcome would have been the same. Accordingly, the tribunal reduced the compensatory award to zero.

The UK EAT held that the tribunal had erred in reducing the compensatory award to zero. It held that generally some warning and consultation should take place before redundancies are made, even where the prospective selection pool consists of a single person.

The EAT held that the tribunal had erred in applying the law, and in concluding that the dismissal was inevitable in circumstances where the claimant could reasonably be placed in a pool of one.

Indeed, it was held, that if a consultation had taken place, it may have resulted in a pool of more than one or affected the choice of selection criteria. This outcome could have

31 *Teixeira v Zaika Restaurant Ltd* [2022] EAT 171.

delayed or avoided dismissal of the claimant. The tribunal, it was held, should have considered the requirement for consultation and whether there was a compelling reason why the dismissal was fair, absent a consultation.

The matter was remitted to the tribunal to decide what the outcome would have been if there had been a consultation. If a pool of more than one would have been created, the tribunal would have to consider what the selection criteria would have been and what outcome would follow.

The appeal was allowed.

[19.24] ***Lovingangels Care Ltd v Mhindurwa*[32]*—UK Employment Appeal Tribunal—appeal from employment tribunal—Employment Rights Act 1996—unfair dismissal—redundancy—employment—band of reasonable responses—job retention scheme—carers—Covid-19—reasons***

The claimant worked as a live-in carer for the respondent company, which provided care services to residents in their own homes. In February 2020, a resident that the claimant cared for was moved to a nursing home. Because of the onset of the Covid-19 pandemic, the work available for carers decreased and the claimant was not reassigned to care for another resident by the respondent. The claimant asked to get the benefit of the Coronavirus Job Retention Scheme but the respondent refused to furlough her. It contended that, without alternate work for the claimant to carry out, the respondent would have to make her redundant.

The tribunal found that the respondent had unfairly dismissed the claimant and held that a reasonable employer would have determined whether the worker should be furloughed for a period in order to ascertain whether there was alternative work available. The respondent had not done so in this case and had not explained its reasons for this decision.

The respondent appealed, arguing that the tribunal had erred in his consideration of the furlough scheme, its purpose and its requirements. The respondent contended that a special approach should be taken to those unfair dismissal claims made in the context of the pandemic. The respondent called for specialised guidance from the UK EAT in this regard.

The EAT held that the approach to unfair dismissals should not be altered in light of the pandemic. It was noted that, despite the profound effect that Covid-19 had on industry, the circumstances of individual employers were diverse. Accordingly, specialised guidance from the EAT would not be particularly helpful.

The EAT held that, contrary to the respondent's contentions, the tribunal did not hold that an employer must furlough employees. Rather, the tribunal had held that the respondent had acted unreasonably by not giving proper consideration to the prospect of furloughing the claimant. The respondent had argued that the claimant would not have met the scheme's requirements for furlough; however, there was no evidence

32 *Lovingangels Care Ltd v Mhindurwa* [2023] EAT 65.

that the respondent had given consideration to this prospect or her eligibility for the scheme in general before dismissing her. Finally, the respondent challenged the tribunal's jurisdiction to decide whether the employee was entitled to furlough pay. The EAT noted that this was not what was decided and held that the tribunal was entitled to conclude that the prospect of furlough should have been afforded proper consideration.

The EAT therefore dismissed the respondent's appeal.

[19.25] ***De Bank Haycocks v ADP RPO UK Ltd*[33]*—UK Employment Appeal Tribunal—appeal from employment tribunal—redundancy—failure to consult properly—selection criteria***

The claimant appealed against an employment tribunal's decision that the respondent employer had acted reasonably in dismissing him for redundancy.

The respondent was the UK subsidiary of a US company. The claimant was part of a team that recruited people for Goldman Sachs (the 'client'). During the Covid-19 pandemic, the client's recruitment needs halved, and subsequently the respondent decided to reduce its recruitment workforce. The US parent company provided the respondent with a tool for scoring and selecting employees for retention. The claimant came last in the rankings. In a meeting a few weeks later, the respondent explained to the claimant that redundancies were necessary and that he was welcome to suggest alternative approaches. The respondent did not inform the claimant of where he had ranked in the scoring process. Two weeks later the claimant was dismissed.

The claimant complained that the dismissal was procedurally unfair due to a lack of any meaningful consultation and a subjective scoring process that had ranked him too low. The employment tribunal rejected his criticisms of the selection criteria and redundancy pool. Overall, the tribunal found the redundancy procedure to be fair and reasonable and the claimant could not demonstrate that he should have scored higher.

On appeal, the claimant submitted that the tribunal had failed to properly consider his argument that there had been a failure to consult properly.

The UK EAT observed that what is considered good practice in redundancy situations varies widely, though consultation should generally occur 'at the formative stages' of the process, with employees being given an opportunity to provide input and potentially impact on the decision. Similarly, approaches to good industrial relations vary significantly across nations. For an employer to use US selection criteria, 'solely because the organisation was a global one', would not reflect 'a recognition of good industrial relations in the UK'. By having discussions at the workforce level at an early stage, differences in good practice would probably have emerged and been taken into account.

33 *De Bank Haycocks v ADP RPO UK Ltd* [2023] EAT 129.

Here, there had been a 'clear absence of consultation at the formative stage', with no opportunity for the claimant 'to discuss the prospects of a different approach to any aspect of the redundancy process chosen by the [respondent]'. The tribunal failed to explain why, in the particular circumstances, the decision was reasonable in the absence of the usual standards of good industrial relations. Thus, it had not provided sufficient reasons for its conclusion. There appeared to be no good reason for the omission of a workforce level of consultation. It followed that the dismissal was unfair and the case was remitted to the tribunal to consider remedy.

Chapter 20

Wages

INTRODUCTION

[20.01]

National Minimum Wage

In *Lloyd*, the UK EAT considered a claim of unlawful deductions from wages resulting in a teaching assistant being paid under the national minimum wage.

Payment of Wages Act 1991

The Labour Court heard a number of claims under the Payment of Wages Act 1991. *ESB Networks* concerned a claim that where the employer delayed making overtime payments to the claimant. In *Switzer*, the claimant alleged that reduction imposed on the allowance his employer had indicated he would receive amounted to a deduction from his wages. *Iarnród Éireann* concerned a claim for an unlawful deduction of wages in respect of a loss of earnings payment the employer had agreed to make to certain employees.

NATIONAL MINIMUM WAGE

[20.02] ***Lloyd v Elmhurst School Ltd*[1]*—UK Employment Appeal Tribunal—appeal from employment tribunal—National Minimum Wage Act 1998—National Minimum Wage Regulations 2015*[2]*—Employment Rights Act 1996—wages—basic hours—salaried hours work—assessment—periods of absence—paid holidays—unlawful deduction in wages***

The claimant was an employee of the respondent, working as a part-time teaching assistant. The claimant worked 21 hours (three days) a week during term time and her

---

1 *Lloyd v Elmhurst School Ltd* [2022] EAT 169.

2 National Minimum Wage Regulations 2015 (SI 2015/621).

contract stipulated that she was entitled to the usual school holidays as 'holidays with pay'. The claimant argued that this meant her hours were 21 hours over 52 weeks of the year as the paid school holidays counted for that purpose.

The claimant brought a claim against the respondent to the employment tribunal for unlawful deduction from wages, under the Employment Rights Act 1996, arguing that she had been paid below the level of the national minimum wage. The national minimum wage is a mandatory entitlement under s 17 of the National Minimum Wage Act 1998.

It was accepted that the claimant engaged in 'salaried hours work' for the purpose of the National Minimum Wage Regulations 2015 (the '2015 Regulations'). The employment tribunal held that the claimant's 'basic hours' for the purpose of reg 21(3) were 21 hours over 40 weeks. This was comprised of 36 weeks she worked during term time and four weeks statutory leave under the Working Time Regulations 1998, if she worked during term time only. It was held that although her contract classified 'the usual school holidays as holidays with pay', this did not mean that these holidays could be considered working hours for the purposes of the 2015 Regulations. The tribunal dismissed her claim for unlawful deduction from wages.

The claimant appealed to the UK EAT and argued that the tribunal had erred in its interpretation of 'basic hours' under the 2015 Regulations.

Central to the appeal was the correct interpretation of the 2015 Regulations and whether non-working hours of school holidays counted towards 'basic hours'. The EAT ultimately held that the calculation of 'basic hours' included all hours paid as contractual holiday. It held that the tribunal was incorrect to find that the only periods of absence that counted towards this calculation were those which were absences from days when the employee would be working.

The EAT held that once it was accepted that paid absences could count towards 'basic hours', then reg 21(3) could not be interpreted as providing for a distinction between absences, depending on whether the absence was one which related to a day that would otherwise be worked. Regulation 21(3) did not address or cover the nature of the hours to be considered. Rather, it looked to whether there was entitlement under contract to be paid for a number of hours a year. This was bolstered by reg 21(7). The EAT held that nothing in reg 21(3) indicated that the basic hours ascertained from the contract did not include a holiday period if same had to take place, eg during a period of annual shut down. The EAT held that if 'basic hours' under reg 21(3) were to only include absences which would otherwise be worked, it would have been 'spelt out' in the legislation.

The EAT found that the tribunal erred in focusing on the periods during which the claimant was in fact working and in assuming that only those hours counted as basic hours. Instead, the tribunal ought to have ascertained her 'basic hours' from an examination of her contract.

The EAT concluded that the tribunal had also erred in relying on the decision in *Royal Mencap v Tomlinson-Blake*[3] and reg 27(2) in its interpretation of 'basic hours' under reg 21(3); neither, it was held, were relevant to the interpretation of the term.

3 *Royal Mencap v Tomlinson-Blake* [2021] ICR 497.

The EAT found that the tribunal had wrongly interpreted the amount of leave that the claimant was entitled to under the 2015 Regulations. Her correct entitlement was 5.6 weeks leave as opposed to 4 weeks.

The appeal was allowed and the case was remitted to a different tribunal for consideration.

PAYMENT OF WAGES ACT 1991—DEDUCTIONS

[20.03] ***ESB Networks v O'Grady*[4]*—Labour Court—appeal from Workplace Relations Commission—Payment of Wages Act 1991—deductions—delay in processing payments—online system—error of computation—paper claims—overtime—collective agreement—submitting overtime and other claims through online system***

The claimant worked as a network technician for the respondent company. The respondent introduced a new payroll procedure, which required workers to submit overtime and other claims through a new system, the MyTime app. The claimant argued that his union was excluded from negotiations leading to a collective agreement on this new procedure. The claimant failed, refused or neglected to use the MyTime app and continued to submit his claims manually.

The claimant maintained that he was doing this based on a union instruction not to use the online system. This resulted in a delay in payments being made. The claimant alleged that he was sanctioned for returning his claims manually by having his payments deliberately not processed in a timely manner. The claimant raised a formal grievance. This delay, he alleged, was contrary to s 5(6) of the Payment of Wages Act 1991 (the '1991 Act'), which states that unless non-payment of wages on the date payment falls due occurs as a result of an error of computation, failure to pay on time is a breach of the 1991 Act. He alleged unlawful deductions from his wages. The claimant brought a claim to the WRC under the 1991 Act, but was unsuccessful. He appealed to the Labour Court.

The respondent argued that the claimant's union was not one it recognised. It noted that any engagement with the MyTime app did not affect basic wages. It submitted that the use of the MyTime app was agreed by the respondent's group of unions and that its employees were well informed of the change of procedure. They were also informed that there was no facility for reverting to paper claims and that doing so would result in delays in processing payments. The Court noted that, by letter of 12 November 2021, the claimant's union advised that a refusal to migrate to the online system was not an instruction from the union and was not industrial action. The Court noted that it was common cause that certain payments that were due to the claimant were made at a later date. Accordingly, the Court had to consider whether there was a deduction by the respondent during the cognisable period. The Court held that the delay in payment 'arose from a decision by the [claimant] to revert to a paper-based system, rather than use the new digital system' despite being forewarned that doing so would lead to processing delays. Therefore, the Court held that no deduction contrary to the 1991 Act occurred during the cognisable period.

---

4 *ESB Networks v O'Grady* PWD237.

The decision of the Adjudication Officer was upheld.

[20.04] ***Department of Justice v Switzer*[5]*—Labour Court—appeal from Workplace Relations Commission—Payment of Wages Act 1991—payment of wages—deductions—business case—allowance—knowledge—reasonable expectation***

The claimant was employed by the respondent in a finance role until he transferred to the Immigration Border Management Unit ('BMU') in 2018. He was an officer in the BMU until May 2020. He contended that, prior to moving to the BMU, he had spoken to the head of BMU, WOD, and developed a legitimate expectation that he would receive an allowance of €18,023 per year for assuming the role. He alleged that he had been told that a business case was required to be submitted to the Human Resources Division before the allowance could be progressed and that ultimately sanction would be required from the Department of Public Expenditure and Reform. The Department of Public Expenditure and Reform sanctioned a reduced allowance in March 2020. The claimant alleged that this had been a deduction from his wages.

The Adjudication Officer found the complaint was not well-founded. The respondent appealed to the Labour Court.

The claimant argued that the calculation should have been made on the basis of an allowance of €18,023 per year. It was agreed that this was the amount included in the business case made by WOD to the Human Resources Division in February 2018. Both parties acknowledged that the claimant was aware that a decision would be required on the business case before an allowance could be granted. An application was made to the Department of Public Expenditure and Reform by the respondent in order to sanction the payment of this allowance. The claimant argued that he had a legitimate expectation that a payment based on an allowance of €18,023 per year would be paid to him. He confirmed at the hearing, before the Labour Court, that he did not believe that all requests for sanction were automatically conceded by the respondent.

The Labour Court considered the claimant's knowledge, from 2018, that the allowance was initially subject to a decision by the Human Resources Division on the business case made and his knowledge in 2020 that an application had been made to the Department of Public Expenditure and Reform. It could not conclude from this that he could have reasonably believed that any undertaking had been given to pay the €18,023 per year allowance to him.

The claimant cited discussions with WOD, prior to his taking up the role in the BMU, that included an undertaking that he would be paid the allowance. The respondent denied this. The Court held that where the content of these conversations was contested, neither party had provided evidence, testimonial or otherwise, to assist the Court in establishing the truth of the matter on the balance of probabilities.

The Court concluded that the claimant had not established that he had a legitimate expectation that he was entitled to the allowance during his period in the role of BMU.

---

5 *Department of Justice v Switzer* PWD2325.

PAYMENT OF WAGES—PROPERLY PAYABLE

[20.05] ***Iarnród Éireann v Moroney*[6]*—Labour Court—appeal from Workplace Relations Commission—Payment of Wages Act 1991—wages—payment of wages—properly payable—Covid-19—overtime—booking offices—enhanced voluntary severance scheme—loss of earnings***

The claimant worked for the respondent company as a station manager in the Limerick district. The company was impacted by Covid-19 and had to review the feasibility of opening booking offices on Sundays and Bank Holidays. Ultimately, a decision was made to close them. At first, this was to be a temporary measure, but subsequently it was made permanent. Following a dispute, the Labour Court ultimately recommended a loss of earning payment for the affected workers. While the complaint to the Labour Court concerned both executive and clerical employees, the loss of earnings payment was initially only provided to clerical employees. An agreement was reached with the trade unions on 26 January 2022 that the respondent would provide payment to a number of named executive employees of which the claimant was one. However, the respondent subsequently refused to pay the claimant his loss of earnings on the basis that he had retired on 28 January 2022. The claimant brought a claim to the WRC, which found that he had suffered an unlawful deduction in his wages. The WRC ordered the respondent to pay the claimant €5,000 in compensation,

The respondent appealed to the Labour Court. It relied on a letter from the trade unions dating from July 2009 which set out a policy for considering loss of earnings. It stated that loss of earnings compensation would be available 'where loss of regular rostered/structured earnings over a minimum period of 52 weeks prior to a defined change is determined'. In those circumstances, 'a lump sum payment of compensation will be paid, provided loss is sustained over 26 weeks post change'. The lump sum identified was to be no more than twice the annual loss or €10,000, whichever is the lower.

The respondent also relied on a document entitled 'Voluntary Severance Terms 2012'. This set out a number of conditions in respect of an enhanced voluntary severance scheme including that: '20% of payment will be exempt from recovery, of the remaining 80%, 1/36 will be deducted for each calendar month or part thereof that the period from date of loss to date of exit from service is short 3 calendar years'.

The Court asked the respondent to process the claimant's claim to see if he would qualify for a payment. It transpired that the claimant's losses in the relevant period exceeded €10,000 and therefore if compensation was owing, it would have to be capped at that figure.

The Labour Court referred to the High Court decision in *Marek Balan's v Tesco Ltd*[7] which stated that the Court should look first to 'what was properly payable' by the

6 *Iarnród Éireann v Moroney* PWD2312.
7 *Marek Balan's v Tesco Ltd* [2020] 31 ELR 125.

respondent to the claimant. Here, the respondent had collective agreements in place to deal with loss of earning. In the 2009 letter, it stated that in order to qualify for the payment there had to be a loss of regular rostered overtime for a period of 26 weeks after the change occurred. The overtime in this case stopped in April 2020. Accordingly, the claimant had a loss for at least 26 weeks after the cessation of overtime. He was also employed during the agreed period to measure the loss, being May 2021 to October 2021.

The Court referred to the 2012 agreement, which stated that the terms applied to enhanced voluntary severance terms for a period of time. The Court did not consider that this supplanted the 2009 agreement. Further, by not processing the claimant's complaint, the respondent was not applying the terms of that 2012 agreement, as the agreement permitted 20% of the payment to be exempt from recovery. The respondent had confirmed in the course of the hearing that the clause had only applied where, within three years of receiving loss of earnings compensation, a worker became eligible to receive voluntary redundancy. The claimant became eligible to receive voluntary redundancy. However, it was unable to show where that had happened in the past.

The Court held that the collective agreement was in place at the relevant time.

The appeal failed and the respondent was ordered to pay the claimant €10,000.

Chapter 21

Whistleblowing

INTRODUCTION

[21.01]

Legislation

The Guidance for public sector bodies with reference to protected disclosures was published by the Government in December 2023. This Guidance is noted in Chapter 13. See also the European Union (Protection of Persons Who Report Breaches of Union Law) Regulation 2003, the Protected Disclosures Act 2014 (Disclosure to Prescribed Persons) (Amendment) Order 2023 and the Protected Disclosures Act 2014 (Digital Markets act) (Amendment) Regulations 2023, each of which is also noted in Chapter 13.

European Convention on Human Rights

In *Halet v Luxembourg*, the ECtHR considered whether the criminal conviction of the applicant for disclosure to a journalist of confidential documents protected by professional secrecy amounted to a disproportionate interference with his right to freedom of expression.

Relevant Wrongdoing

The UK EAT considered the question as to what constitutes a relevant wrongdoing in *Westfield Community Development Association.*

Unfair Dismissal

A number of cases before the UK EAT in 2023 concerned claims of unfair dismissal on foot of making a protected disclosure. In *Lyfár-Cissé*, the claimant had previously made protected disclosures and employment claims and was subsequently dismissed following a disciplinary process. *Sellafield Ltd* related to allegations of sexual harassment and the subsequent claim of protected disclosure detriment and victimisation. In *Virgin Active Ltd*, the respondent argued the employment tribunal's delay in producing a judgment risked their entitlement to a fair trial. See also Barrett decision as noted in Chapter 11.

Penalisation

In *Ashton Dog Pound*, the Labour Court focused on the test to establish whether an employee has been penalised for making a protected disclosure.

The UK EAT considered the appropriate remedy for penalisation for bringing a protected disclosure in *Care and Learning Alliance*.

EUROPEAN CONVENTION ON HUMAN RIGHTS

[21.02] ***Halet v Luxembourg*[1]*—European Court of Human Rights (Grand Chamber)—appeal from previous finding of European Court of Human Rights*[2]*—European Convention on Human Rights, art 10—freedom of expression—criminal conviction for disclosing confidential documents to the media—Luxleaks***

The applicant was a former employee of PwC; he alleged that his criminal conviction for the disclosure to a journalist of confidential documents protected by professional secrecy amounted to a disproportionate interference with his right to freedom of expression.

The applicant submitted that, while employed by PwC, he was directly involved in the company's activity, including obtaining the 'best possible treatment' for its clients from the Luxembourg tax authority. The respondent State countered that, at the relevant time, the applicant merely performed the tasks of an administrative employee, dispatching tax returns to clients.

Between 2012 and 2014, hundreds of documents prepared by PwC were leaked to various media outlets (the 'Luxleaks'). These included advance tax agreements and corporate tax returns that revealed highly advantageous tax agreements between the Luxembourg tax authorities and PwC, on behalf of its multinational company clients.

An internal investigation by PwC revealed that some 45,000 pages of confidential documents had been copied by a former employee and handed over to a journalist at the latter's request. Following media coverage of the leaked documents, the applicant too contacted the same journalist and offered to hand over further documents. The journalist agreed to the transfer of 16 documents (including company tax returns) from the applicant, some of which featured in a television programme, and

---

1 *Halet v Luxembourg* (App No 21884/18).

2 See *Arthur Cox Employment Law Yearbook 2021* at [24.14] for previous decision of European Court of Human Rights in *Halet v Luxembourg* (App No 21884/18).

all of which would be posted online by the International Consortium of Investigative Journalists.

The applicant and others were charged and committed for trial before the Luxembourg District Court, which in June 2016 convicted the applicant of 'theft from one's employer (*vol domestique*), fraudulent access to a system for the processing or automatic transmission of data, breach of commercial secrecy, breach of professional secrecy and laundering and possession (*blanchiment-détention*)'. The applicant received a nine-month term of imprisonment, fully suspended, and a €1000 fine.

The applicant appealed against the first-instance judgment and the appellate court dispensed with the prison sentence but upheld the fine. The appellate court refused the applicant the full protection of whistleblower status. It considered that, while the disclosed tax returns were useful to their recipient, they did not provide 'any previously unknown cardinal information capable of relaunching or contributing to the debate on tax evasion'. The applicant had caused damage to his employer, which 'outweighed the general interest' entailed by their disclosure.

The European Court of Human Rights (the 'ECtHR') accepted that the applicant's conviction amounted to an interference with the exercise of his right to freedom of expression. It further accepted that the interference was prescribed by law and pursued one of the legitimate aims under art 10.2 of the European Convention on Human Rights, namely the protection of the reputation or rights of others.

In finding that the interference was not necessary in a democratic society, the ECtHR was critical of the balancing exercise undertaken by the domestic courts. It held that the domestic courts had interpreted the public interest in the disclosed information in an overly restrictive manner, focusing solely on the business and reputational harm sustained by PwC. In doing so, the domestic courts neglected to have regard to the private interests of PwC's clients, the public interest in preventing and punishing theft, and respect for professional secrecy. Accordingly, the domestic courts had failed to take sufficient account of the specific features of the case.

The ECtHR considered that the information disclosed by the applicant was 'undeniably of public interest', and that the public interest in the disclosure of the information 'outweighed all of the detrimental effects'.

Finally, in relation to the severity of the sanction, the ECtHR, having considered the nature, severity and 'chilling effect' of the applicant's conviction, held that there had been a violation of art 10.

RELEVANT WRONGDOING

[21.03] ***Kealy v Westfield Community Development Association*[3]*—UK Employment Appeal Tribunal—appeal from employment tribunal—Employment Rights***

[3] *Kealy v Westfield Community Development Association* [2023] EAT 96.

Act 1996—whistleblowing—relevant wrongdoing—health and safety—constructive dismissal—protected disclosures—detriment—perversity—qualifying disclosures—reasonable belief—Ofsted

The claimant was employed by the respondent community centre. She allegedly made nine protected disclosures about the use of funds for early years teaching and disability access. She made further disclosures regarding the heating of the nursery at the centre, which posed, she argued, a health and safety issue. Some of these disclosures were made to the employer and some to third parties, including Ofsted. The claimant claimed that she was subjected to seven detriments as a result of the disclosures made. The claimant alleged that, as a result of having been subjected to detriments one to six, she had to resign. The seventh detriment was said to have occurred after her resignation. She brought a claim to the employment tribunal asserting protected disclosure detriment and dismissal, dismissal for assertion of a statutory right, and for constructive dismissal.

The employment tribunal found that some of the disclosures made lacked verifying evidence and none were to be considered protected disclosures. It was found that the claimant lacked credibility, that she did not have a reasonable belief that the disclosures were true, and that she had made some of them to undermine the employer. The claimant appealed to the UK EAT.

The EAT held that the tribunal's list of issues failed to identify certain points that arose, for example whether each disclosure was a qualifying one under s 43B of the Employment Rights Act 1996 and, if so, whether it was made to the employer and therefore protected under s 43C, or to a third party but protected under s 43G. It was held that the tribunal had conflated the questions required to ascertain whether a disclosure is a protected disclosure, including whether the disclosures in question were qualifying disclosures and whether same amounted to protected disclosures, depending on who they were made to.

The tribunal had also erred in concluding that, because some of the disclosures were not true, the claimant did not have a reasonable belief in them. The EAT noted that the two were not mutually exclusive and a person could reasonably believe something to be true even if it turned out to not be true. Furthermore, the tribunal erred in applying the 'reasonable belief' test to all of the disclosures, including any that were made to the respondent.

The question of whether the claimant reasonably believed the disclosures were made in the public interest was relevant to deciding if a disclosure was a qualifying disclosure. Despite dealing with this issue, the EAT found the tribunal seemed to have confused the question of whether the claimant's reasonable belief that making the disclosures was in the public interest with her motive for making them.

The tribunal also erred in holding that the seventh detriment did not give rise to a detriment, given the fact that the claimant had already resigned. This was held to be a non-sequitur by the EAT. It was noted that no reasons were given as to why the tribunal so found.

With regard to the constructive dismissal claim, the EAT held that the tribunal had made a sweeping analysis of the claimant's credibility which undermined all of her claims. A key part of that analysis was the conclusion that the claimant had disclosed to Ofsted that the respondent had not done anything to resolve the heating issues. The tribunal stated that the claimant had denied making such a statement to Ofsted but that it did not believe her. Consequently, the tribunal held that the claimant was 'both deliberately undermining her Line Manager and acting against the interests of her employer'. The EAT noted that the tribunal had accepted elsewhere in the judgment that the claimant had submitted a document to Ofsted which set out steps taken by the respondent to deal with the heating issues. On foot of these inconsistent findings, the EAT held that the tribunal's conclusion was perverse.

The EAT found that in dismissing the employee's claim regarding health and safety detriment and dismissal, the tribunal had simply relied on its findings in respect of the constructive dismissal claim. This was an incorrect approach as the statutory tests for such claims were different and s 48(2) placed an onus on the respondent to demonstrate the reason for any act or failure to act.

The appeal was allowed.

UNFAIR DISMISSAL

[21.04] ***Lyfar-Cissé v Western Sussex University Hospitals NHS Foundation Trust*[4]*—UK Employment Appeal Tribunal—appeal from employment tribunal—Employment Rights Act 1996—unfair dismissal—victimisation—whistleblowing—protected disclosures***

The claimant was employed by the second-named respondent as the Associate Director of Transformation, with responsibility for improving race equality for employees and NHS service users. She made several protected disclosures from 2008 onwards and brought a number of employment claims against her employer between 2004 and 2017.

In 2016, the claimant was the subject of disciplinary proceedings based on 19 allegations against her, including: discrimination; breaching confidentiality; bullying; harassment, and victimisation. The claimant received a final written warning on foot of this process.

At the same time, the Care Quality Commission ('CQC') inspected the second-named respondent. Its overall findings were published in a report, which noted that bullying, harassment and discrimination had become 'rife in the organisation'. Further, the CQC rated the second-named respondent as being 'inadequate in the area of leadership'. In response, NHS Improvement placed the first-named respondent in charge of the second-named respondent's management. The fourth-named respondent, Ms Barker, became managing director of the second-named respondent.

4 *Lyfar-Cissé v Western Sussex University Hospitals NHS Foundation Trust* [2022] EAT 193.

Ms Barker was contacted by one of the individuals, who had previously made a complaint about the claimant, expressing disappointment that the claimant had been retained in her leadership role. Ms Barker alerted the CEO of the first and second-named respondents about the complaint, referring to the CQC's findings regarding leadership and the second-named respondent. Ms Barker called into question the claimant's 'ability to have a leadership role on equality issues' and whether 'there are fit and proper person issues that we are required to address'. Ms Barker also referred to reg 5 of the Health and Social Care Act 2008 (Regulated Activities) Regulations 2014,[5] which provides that a director must satisfy certain requirements, including that they be fit and proper persons.

Two meetings were called to discuss the claimant's position. The claimant denied the allegations against her and claimed that she had been victimised. The CEO held that her role fell within the scope of reg 5 and dismissed the claimant. The claimant argued that she had been unfairly dismissed for making protected disclosures and/or that her dismissal was an act of victimisation under s 27 of the Equality Act 2010.

The employment tribunal held that any protected disclosures made did not form part of the claimant's dismissal. Rather, it held that the principal reason for her dismissal was that the CEO felt it was not appropriate for the claimant, who had been found guilty of victimisation, harassment and discrimination, to be the leader in charge of race equality in the second-named respondent trust. The employment tribunal found the reason for dismissal could be characterised as either conduct or 'some other substantial reason' and therefore, was potentially fair under s 98(1) of the Employment Rights Act 1996.

The claimant appealed against the employment tribunal's dismissal of her claims. She argued that the respondent had impermissibly re-opened the disciplinary process which had been completed previously and had impermissibly failed to apply its disciplinary policy. She also submitted that: the tribunal erred in not sufficiently explaining its finding of 'some other substantial reason'; the tribunal wrongly found that it was not put to the CEO that the claimant's dismissal was ordered because of her making protected disclosures; and the tribunal did not deal with the fact that other managers employed by the respondents, but who had not made protected disclosures, had been treated more favourably than the claimant.

The appeal was stayed when the claimant applied for reconsideration due to what she argued was new evidence that had come to light. This evidence was an article that had been published in the *Health Service Journal*, where the CEO had stated that she had inherited a 'very difficult situation' and a 'number of employment tribunal cases' and, to improve the situation, the Trust had to do some 'brave things'. The claimant argued that the reference to those inherited tribunal cases concerned her case. She also argued that the reference to 'brave things' referred to the decision to terminate her employment. The tribunal rejected this application for reconsideration and the claimant also appealed against that decision.

---

5 Health and Social Care Act 2008 (Regulated Activities) Regulations 2014 (SI 2014/2936).

The UK EAT held that re-opening a disciplinary process that had been previously concluded was a unusual step which required proper justification. However it stated that the focus in an unfair dismissal claim had to be on whether the claimant's dismissal was unfair with reference to s 98(4) of the Employment Rights Act 1996.

It was held that the tribunal had focused on the right question, had applied the right test of fairness, and had considered the appropriate authorities. The EAT held that the tribunal had taken into consideration the fact that the claimant had first faced a disciplinary process under the respondent's disciplinary policy and subsequently had to undergo a second process which was not on foot of any policy. However it was held that the tribunal did apply s 98 of the Employment Rights Act 1996 appropriately and without error. The tribunal found a fair reason for dismissal and dealt with the relevant questions of whether the employer had acted reasonably.

With regard to the allegedly fresh evidence, the EAT rejected the argument that the text of the article revealed that the claimant's dismissal was pre-determined. Rather, this article, it was held, supported the respondents' case and not the claimant's case.

Both appeals were therefore dismissed.

[21.05] ***McDermott v Sellafield Ltd*[6]*—UK Employment Appeal Tribunal—appeal from employment tribunal—Employment Rights Act 1996—Equality Act 2010—whistleblowers—penalisation—costs—protected disclosures detriment—reasons—sexual harassment—focus group interviews—victimisation—liability and costs***

The first-named respondent, Sellafield Ltd, operated the Sellafield nuclear power plant in Cumbria. The third-named respondent was the HR director of Sellafield Ltd. The claimant worked as a consultant in equality, diversity, and inclusion, engaged by Sellafield Ltd.

When an anonymous allegation of sexual harassment was made against a member of HR lead team for Sellafield Ltd, the claimant was asked by the HR director to conduct focus group interviews with members of the HR team. The claimant argued that this was intended to 'flush out if there were any issues' regarding the alleged perpetrator of the alleged sexual harassment. The claimant informed the HR director that a formal investigation should be carried out instead. The claimant carried out the focus groups as asked. She created a report on foot of same which detailed, among other issues, allegations of homophobic abuse allegedly made by an employee. The report characterised the team as 'dysfunctional' and reported the alleged concerns of the interviewees. Members of the lead HR team argued that the report did not capture their positive statements and that the questions asked were designed to elicit criticism of the HR director and the lead team. The HR director terminated the claimant's contract.

6 *McDermott v Sellafield Ltd* [2023] EAT 60.

In the employment tribunal, the claimant alleged detrimental treatment by the respondents on the following grounds: their failure to investigate matters brought to their attention; an alleged attempt to pressure the claimant into taking part in a covert investigation; the decision to dismiss her; the fact of dismissal; 'approving, authorising or failing to prevent a dismissal'; and the manner of the claimant's dismissal.

The claimant complained that she had been subject to detriment on the grounds of protected disclosures made, contrary to s 47B of the Employment Rights Act 1996, and victimisation contrary to 27 of the Equality Act 2010. The protected disclosures and/or acts on which she relied included: the fact that she had advised the HR director that an investigation should be carried out into the allegations of sexual harassment at an early stage of proceedings; that she informed the respondents that immediate action should be taken to 'avoid compounding the impression that systemic issues were ignored or mishandled'; that she urged prompt and meaningful actions to investigate how the team had allowed the situation to develop following a concern raised as to the welfare of one of the employees; and the issuing of the report that she drafted on foot of the meetings. The claimant initiated claims of protected disclosure detriment and victimisation to the employment tribunal. The tribunal dismissed all the complaints and awarded the respondents their costs against the claimant.

The claimant appealed to the UK EAT on several grounds. Grounds 1 to 4 all concerned the tribunal's findings as to whether she had made certain protected disclosures. Ground 5 related to alleged detriment in the decision to dismiss and the fact of the dismissal; she also alleged that the tribunal erred in its application of causation. The claimant maintained that her dismissal was 'done on the ground that' the claimant had made disclosures. Ground 6 was that the tribunal erred in law, in failing to find that her disclosures amounted to protected acts. Grounds 8, 9 and 10 were based on the arguments the tribunal failed to engage with the claimant's case, took a fragmented approach to the judgment, and/or produced a decision which did not comply with *Meek*.

The claimant partly succeeded in some of her complaints relating to disclosure. Further, the EAT held that the tribunal erred by not concluding that the fact that she had advised the HR director that an investigation should be carried out into the allegations of sexual harassment at an early stage of proceedings was a protected act. However, overall, the EAT found that the tribunal made 'specific, reasoned findings, that the claimant was not subjected to the detriment of being pressurised to carry out the focus groups … nor dismissed because of it'. The partial success of the claimant, the EAT held, did not undermine these reasoned findings nor the findings that the content of the claimant's report did not amount to protected disclosures or protected acts; nor was she dismissed because of the report. The EAT was critical of the structure of the tribunal's decision, in particular that it did not set out the law and instead referred to counsel's submissions in lieu of the law. However, it held that the tribunal's overall conclusions were well founded and observed that the EAT could only intervene where there had been an error of law on the part of the tribunal that meant its judgment could not stand.

The liability appeal was dismissed. However the EAT held that the tribunal's costs award was unsafe. The EAT acknowledged that there were aspects of the liability decision in respect of which the tribunal erred and held that, while these were not enough to undermine the liability outcome, they were such to render the costs decision unsafe.

The costs appeal only was allowed.

[21.06] ***Virgin Active Ltd v Hughes*[7]*—UK Employment Appeal Tribunal—appeal from employment tribunal—legislation—whistleblowing—ordinary unfair dismissal—direct discrimination—disciplinary proceedings—delay—legal test—race discrimination***

The claimant was a manager at the respondent's fitness club. In April 2017, investigations were carried out by the claimant into three members of staff. Subsequently, disciplinary processes were commenced against said employees. On foot of same, all three members of staff raised grievances against the claimant, which were investigated by the respondent. It was found that the claimant had not provided adequate support to his staff; that he had made a racist comment to one of them during the relevant investigation; that he favoured disciplinary action as a recourse; and that he had treated one of the employees unfairly and sought to influence the disciplinary action against her to bring about her dismissal. The claimant was suspended and informed that he would be investigated.

A disciplinary hearing took place. The claimant complained to the respondent about not having heard back about an earlier grievance he had made. Ultimately, the claimant was summarily dismissed for gross misconduct. His appeal and work-related stress grievance were subsequently dismissed. The claimant brought a claim to the employment tribunal for whistleblowing, unfair dismissal, 'ordinary' unfair dismissal, and direct age, sex and race discrimination. He argued, as part of his direct race discrimination case, that while a racist comment made against him had not been investigated, the alleged racist comment he had made against the employee he was investigating was progressed.

The claimant was partially successful in his claims before the employment tribunal. His claims of direct age and sex discrimination were dismissed.

The respondent appealed to the EAT. Principally, its arguments centred on the tribunal's delay in producing a judgment and the fact that the tribunal erred in applying the wrong legal test to the race discrimination claim. With regard to the delay, the respondent argued that the delay suffered gave rise to a real risk that the respondent was deprived of a right to a fair trial.

The EAT held that determining a direct discrimination claim is 'inherently a comparative exercise' in that the tribunal has to determine whether the claimant was treated less favourably than a person with whom he does not share the protected characteristic was/would be treated, because of race. In this case, the tribunal had treated the three employees under investigation as actual comparators without considering whether

7 *Virgin Active Ltd v Hughes* [2023] EAT 130.

there were material differences between their circumstances and those of the claimant. The EAT allowed this part of the appeal.

The EAT found that there was a lengthy delay in the tribunal's decision being produced. It was noted that the judge had been seriously ill and this justification for the delay was emphasised in the judgment in a detailed manner. The EAT observed that the judge had taken diligent, handwritten notes throughout the hearing that were available to the tribunal at all stages of its deliberations in hard or soft copy. During the deliberations, the judge made recordings of factual findings and important points discussed and the tribunal had supplementary notes taken by lay members.

The EAT held that it had not been established by the respondent that any delay on the part of the tribunal gave rise to a real risk that the respondent was deprived of a right to a fair trial and the appeal on this ground was dismissed.

PENALISATION

[21.07] ***Ashton Dog Pound v Williamson*[8]*—Labour Court—appeal from Workplace Relations Commission—Protected Disclosures Act 2014—whistleblowers—penalisation—on-call duties—complaints—protected disclosure—unsafe procedures—animal cruelty—Facebook comments***

The claimant worked for the respondent as a dog warden since 2017. In July 2020, he emailed the respondent with an allegation of animal abuse. It was common case that this amounted to a protected disclosure. In October 2020, the claimant was informed by the respondent that he was being investigated for refusing to do on-call duties and in respect of comments he made on Facebook contrary to the respondent's social media policy. He was subsequently suspended arising from complaints made by other members of staff against him. Following an investigation of the complaints, he was advised in June 2021 that his final written warning was being extended by 12 months. A few weeks later, the pound was transferred to Dublin City Council and the claimant, along with other staff, was made redundant.

The WRC held that the claimant had been penalised for making a protected disclosure contrary to the Protected Disclosures Act 2014 and awarded compensation of €18,000.

The Labour Court focused on the test to establish whether an employee has been penalised for making a protected disclosure. The Court held that it is necessary to show that the detriment was imposed 'for' having committed the protected act. The Court, in this way, invoked the 'but for' test.

The Court noted that, in sworn evidence, the claimant acknowledged that 'but for' his protected disclosure it could not be said that he would not have received disciplinary action relating to the on-call issue. In this respect, there was no causal link between the claimant's whistleblowing and the detriment suffered.

8 *Ashton Dog Pound v Williamson* PDD232.

The Court also noted that the claimant had accepted that, on receipt of complaints against him, the respondent had an obligation to investigate same. The Court held that the claimant's suspension pending investigation was within the bounds of reasonable behaviour by an employer. The claimant, once again, could not establish a link between the decision to suspend him and the protected disclosure made.

The claimant asserted that there was a concerted effort, between the respondent and those that issued complaints against him, to target him and that there were issues with the process followed by the respondent. The individual that carried out the investigation into the complaints stated in evidence that he found no evidence to support this contention. The Court held that the claimant failed to establish any link between this process and his protected disclosure.

Regarding the decision to extend the claimant's final written warning for a further 12-month period, it was held that the claimant failed to establish a link between this decision and his protected disclosure.

For these reasons the Court held that no penalisation had occurred.

The appeal succeeded.

[21.08] ***McNicholas v Care and Learning Alliance*[9]*—UK Employment Appeal Tribunal—appeal from employment tribunal—penalisation for having made protected disclosure—remedies—damages—novus actus interveniens***

The claimant was an experienced teacher in England. She moved to Inverness in 2016 where she took up employment for the respondent, first providing relief staffing and additional support on a casual basis, before being employed as a family support practitioner.

The claimant alleged that she was subjected to detriments by the respondent as a result of having made protected disclosures. These protected disclosures concerned the care arrangements for a child with autism who attended the respondent's nursery.

The employment tribunal upheld her complaint, identifying five specific detriments, including that the respondent had forced the claimant to resign, and dismissed her in a way that was automatically unfair. The respondent had made a complaint to the General Teaching Council for Scotland (the 'GTCS') about her fitness to teach. The tribunal considered the genuine substance of these complaints to be in doubt, and that the complaints were retaliatory in nature. The claimant's health suffered as a result of the detriments to which she was subjected and she moved back to England.

In its remedies judgment, the tribunal limited awards for future loss, injury to feeling and psychiatric injury to losses arising prior to February 2018, when the GTCS decided to investigate the respondents' complaint. The tribunal reasoned that this decision to investigate was a *novus actus interveniens* and broke the chain of causation between

9 *McNicholas v Care and Learning Alliance* [2023] EAT 127.

the detriment complained of and the claimant's losses. On appeal, the UK EAT found that the tribunal had erred and that this conclusion was not open to it. The GTCS's decision was not an 'independent, supervening cause of loss', but a 'natural and reasonable consequence of the respondents' wrongful act'. The tribunal's finding was inconsistent with its earlier assessment of the substance of the complaints made by the respondents.

The matter was accordingly remitted to the same tribunal for reconsideration.

Chapter 22

Working Time

INTRODUCTION

[22.01]

Annual Leave

There were three cases before the ECJ (*FI, YQ* and *XT*) concerning the right to paid annual leave.

Connor was before the UK EAT and related to the calculation of holiday pay in accordance with the Working Time Regulations. See also the UK Supreme Court decision in the Northern Ireland case, *Agnew*, which is noted in **Chapter 23**.

Public Holiday Pay

In *Waterford City and County Council*, the Labour Court considered the claimant's entitlement to public holiday pay under the Organisation of Working Time Act 1997.

Night Workers

The ECJ, in *OP*, addressed the special position of night workers.

Rest Periods

The ECJ, in *IH*, considered the employers obligations with reference to rest periods.

Sea Fishing

The issue before the High Court in *Elganagy* was whether the plaintiff was entitled to a remedy under Organisation of Working Time Act 1997 arising from the respondent's alleged breach, and to issue proceedings under s 41 of the Workplace Relations Act 2015 for that purpose, notwithstanding that the relevant 2003 Regulations are silent on compensation and redress.

ANNUAL LEAVE

[22.02] ***FI v Bayerische Motoren Werke AG*[1]*—European Court of Justice—request for preliminary ruling from Germany—Directive 2003/88/EC*[2]*—Charter of Fundamental Rights of the European Union—right to be paid annual leave—lapse of that right—progressive retirement scheme—days of annual leave acquired but untaken—incapacity for work—approximation of laws—fundamental rights—free movement of workers—social policy***

The applicant was employed by the respondent company from 1986 to September 2019. The applicant retired on 1 October 2019.

In late 2012, under a progressive retirement scheme, the parties agreed that the applicant would work part-time. This would have the applicant working from 1 February 2013 to 31 May 2016 before his release from work from 1 June 2016 to 30 September 2019. The applicant took leave from 4 to 25 May 2016 to use up his remaining leave for the year. However, he was sick during that period and was unable to take two and two-thirds days of leave before the end of May 2016.

In 2019, the applicant brought proceedings against the respondent for compensation for the leave not taken due to illness. The German Labour Court dismissed the proceedings because the right to leave for 2016 had lapsed on 31 March 2017. The applicant appealed to the High Labour Court but was unsuccessful. He then initiated an appeal on a point of law to the referring Court, the Federal Labour Court. That Court was unclear as to the application of a provision of domestic law on leave, which provides that a worker's untaken leave is to be forfeited at the end of the period when it becomes impossible for the worker to use it due to work release. The Court referred two questions to the European Court of Justice ('ECJ'), to ascertain whether and to what extent the employer gave the applicant an opportunity to exercise his right to leave. In essence, the referring Court asked whether art 7 of Directive 2003/88/EC or art 31(2) of the Charter of Fundamental Rights of the European Union (the 'Charter') preclude a rule of national law under which paid annual leave acquired during the work phase of a progressive retirement scheme, but not taken, may be forfeited if it cannot be taken during the work release period.

The ECJ held that art 7(1) of Directive 2003/88/EC gives protection to the fundamental right to annual paid leave, which is also protected in art 31(2) of the Charter. The former sets out the rules pertaining to the implementation of that right. The ECJ noted, however, that when the employment relationship comes to an end and the worker is

1 *FI v Bayerische Motoren Werke AG* (Case C-192/22).

2 Directive 2003/88/EC concerning certain aspects of the organisation of working time.

not able to take outstanding annual leave, art 7(2) of Directive 2003/88/EC provides for payment in lieu. Limitations may only be imposed on this right in compliance with art 52(1) of the Charter and any derogation must be limited in scope to what is strictly necessary to protect the interests that the derogation is aimed at. It was held that incapacity due to sickness is not foreseeable and is considered to be beyond the worker's control. However, if a worker is unfit for work for several consecutive years, Directive 2003/88/EC does not preclude national provisions limiting, by a carry over period of 15 months at the conclusion of which the right to paid annual leave is lost, the accumulation of entitlements to such leave by a worker. This was not the case here, where the illness was not a long-term absence and accordingly, no such derogation was permissible.

The ECJ further held that art 7 of Directive 2003/88/EC, when read with art 31(2) of the Charter, must be interpreted as disallowing domestic law which provides that the right to paid annual leave acquired by a worker in the context of a progressive retirement scheme will lapse at the end of the holiday year or at a later date where the worker has been prevented from taking leave before the work release due to sickness.

[22.03] ***YQ v Ředitelství silnic a dálnic ČR*[3]*—European Court of Justice—request for preliminary ruling from Czech Republic—Directive 2003/88/EC*[4]*—social policy—protection of the safety and health of workers—organisation of working time—right to be paid annual leave***

The applicant was employed by the respondent under a contract in 2009. She was given notice of dismissal on 23 October 2013. This notice was ruled as invalid by a judgment of a regional Court on 20 December 2016, which became final on 10 January 2017, and the applicant resumed employment with the respondent. During the period between 1 January 2014 and 10 January 2017, the applicant notified the respondent in writing of her wish to work but was not assigned any work. After being reinstated, the applicant inquired about the possibility of taking her unused annual leave, amassed during the period between 1 January 2014 and 10 January 2017. The respondent refused her request. Despite this refusal, the applicant took leave for the dates she requested. The respondent dismissed her on 9 August 2017, due to her absence.

The applicant was unsuccessful before the Brno City Court, and on appeal, in her action for compensation for the annual leave. Under the national law, the period of time during which an employee's dismissal is subject to challenge before the courts is governed by a scheme set out in paragraphs 69 to 72 of the Labour Code. The scheme states that the employee is not entitled to wage compensation where an obstacle to work has occurred and compensation for leave has not been taken. However, the referring Court noted that, in the event that the termination of employment is invalid, national case law provides that the employee is entitled to wage compensation for the duration of the legal proceedings determining the validity of the termination, subject to the employee having notified the employer in writing of their desire to continue employment. However, as

3 *YQ v Ředitelství silnic a dálnic ČR* (Case C-57/22).

4 Directive 2003/88/EC concerning certain aspects of the organisation of working time.

the employee has not actually worked during this time, they do not have the right to paid annual leave. It was apparent from national case law that even where a dismissal was found unlawful, the period between the date of dismissal and the date on which an employee resumed work after proceedings was not considered as forming part of that person's term of employment.

The European Court of Justice considered whether Directive 2003/88/EC was applicable in this case. Having established that the applicant was a 'worker' for the purposes of the Directive, the Court examined whether art 7(1) must be interpreted as precluding national law by virtue of which a worker unlawfully dismissed and then reinstated in accordance with national law, following the overturning of her dismissal by a Court, is not entitled to be paid annual leave for the period between the date of dismissal and the date of reinstatement.

The Court noted that art 7(1) provides a right to be paid annual leave of at least four weeks and that the right to be paid annual leave is also expressly enshrined in art 31(2) of the Charter of Fundamental Rights. This right, it was held, may not be interpreted restrictively. The Court pointed out that, although it is for the Member States to establish conditions for the implementation of the right to annual leave, they cannot make the existence of that right subject to any precondition whatsoever.

Despite the fact that the applicant did not carry out work during the period that her unfair dismissal proceedings were before the Court, it was not permissible to deny her the right to avail of the annual leave amassed during this time. The period between the date of the unlawful dismissal and the applicant's reinstatement, according to national law, must be treated as part of her period of employment. The Member State, it was held, cannot derogate from the right enshrined in art 7.

[22.04] ***XT v Keolis Agen SARL*[5]*—European Court of Justice—request for a preliminary ruling from France—Charter of Fundamental Rights of the European Union, art 31(2)—Directive 2003/88/EC,*[6] *art 7—social policy—organisation of working time—right to paid annual leave—carry over of entitlements to paid annual leave in the event of long-term illness***

The requests were made in proceedings between XT and other applicants, and the respondent, Keolis Agen SARL, a private company holding a public transport delegation, concerning the latter's refusal to allow them to take accrued days of leave (or to pay an allowance in lieu thereof) which they were unable to take because of absences from work due to illness. During the period of their respective employment, the applicants were absent from work for over a year due to illness, which was not work related. They requested the respondent to grant them the days of paid annual leave that they were not able to take during their respective periods of illness and—for those whose contracts had been terminated due to being declared unfit to work—an allowance in lieu of leave not taken. The applicant refused those applications on the ground that the absences lasted for over a year and were not caused by an occupational disease.

5 *XT v Keolis Agen SARL* (Case C-271/22-275/22).

6 Directive 2003/88/EC concerning certain aspects of the organisation of working time.

The applicants brought an action before the Labour Tribunal, Agen, France, the referring Court, which stayed the proceedings and referred three questions to the ECJ for a preliminary ruling.

By its first question, the referring Court asked, in essence, whether art 7 of Directive 2003/88/EC must be interpreted as meaning 'that a worker may rely on the right to paid annual leave against his or her employer, even if the employer is a private undertaking holding a public service delegation'.

It was noted that the right to paid annual leave is, as a principle of EU social law, not only 'particularly important', but expressly laid down in art 31(2) of the Charter of Fundamental Rights of the European Union (the 'Charter'). The right is thus, 'as regards its very existence, both mandatory and unconditional in nature'. EU or national laws are only required to specify the exact duration and (where appropriate) conditions of annual leave. National courts adjudicating on a dispute between a worker and an employer, who is a private individual, must disapply national legislation negating the right to paid annual leave, or an allowance in lieu thereof, at the end of a reference period and/or a carry-over period fixed by national law when the worker has been unable to take his or her leave.

By its second question, the referring Court asked the ECJ to define the length of the carry-over period applicable to the entitlement to paid annual leave in the case of a reference period equal to one year. It was not, however, for the ECJ, when giving a preliminary ruling, to define the length of the carry-over period applicable to the right to paid annual leave since the determination of that period is a matter for the Member State.

By its third question, the referring Court asked, in essence, whether art 7 of Directive 2003/88/EC must be interpreted as precluding national legislation and/or a national practice which allows applications for paid annual leave made by a worker after the end of the reference period in which the entitlement to that leave arose.

In circumstances in which a worker is unable to work for several consecutive reference periods, the ECJ has held that art 7 does not preclude national provisions or practices limiting the accumulation of entitlements to paid annual leave by a carry-over period, provided that the carry-over period ensures, *inter alia*, that the worker can have, 'if need be, rest periods that may be staggered, planned in advance and available in the longer term and that it is substantially longer than the reference period in respect of which it is granted'.

HOLIDAY PAY

[22.05] ***Connor v Chief Constable of the South Yorkshire Police[7]—UK Employment Appeal Tribunal—appeal from employment tribunal—Working***

7 *Connor v Chief Constable of the South Yorkshire Police* [2023] EAT 42.

Time Regulations 1998,[8] reg 14—working time—annual leave—agreements—termination—holiday pay—contractual terms—calculation of final holiday pay

The claimant began working for the respondent in 2002 and went on sick leave with depression and anxiety in February 2019. The claimant's entitlement to sick pay eventually ran out and he made an application to be paid in lieu of holiday pay. He was paid a sum in lieu based on 288 hours. The claimant was dismissed and on termination of his employment the claimant was entitled to be paid holiday pay for holidays not taken (40 hours and 42 minutes) under the Working Time Regulations 1998.

It was a term of his contract that:

> 'Employees may, on termination of employment, be entitled to payment for untaken annual leave or for other accrued time off. Advice on such entitlement obtained from HR Shared Service in the first instance.
>
> Payment will be based on 1/365th of annual salary for each day's leave. Any payment will be subject to the usual statutory reductions'.

The claimant worked a regular 37-hour week and was paid his wages on a monthly basis. His annual salary was £29,064.00 and during his employment he received the equivalent sum for a week of holiday as he would for a week's work. However, when he was dismissed, his unpaid leave was determined in accordance with the aforementioned term and this meant that he was paid less than what he would have been paid had he taken the holiday leave outstanding.

The claimant brought a claim before the tribunal for holiday pay. The tribunal found that the contractual term dictated the method of calculation and, accordingly, the holiday pay had been correctly calculated by the respondent.

The claimant appealed to the UK EAT. The grounds of appeal concerned two questions: whether there is a default method of ascertaining the payment of holiday pay post termination and whether a contract can stipulate that less pay be given to a worker than any default calculation which is established.

The EAT held that it would undermine the purpose of the Working Time Regulations 1998 if the amount of pay to be paid under contract differed to the usual level of pay. The EAT held that reg 14 does not modify the right to annual leave under the Working Time Regulations 1998. The purpose of reg 14 was to provide a way of calculating payment that supports the right to leave. The EAT found that a contract cannot include a calculation that means that a worker is paid less for untaken leave than they would have been paid if they had taken the leave.

The method of calculation was as follows: (A x B) – C, where A is the period of leave, B is the proportion of worker's leave year that had elapsed before the termination date and C is the period of leave taken between the beginning of the leave year and the

8 Working Time Regulations 1998 (SI 1998/1833).

dismissal. Using this calculation, the EAT calculated the amount of pay to which the claimant was entitled.

The appeal was allowed.

PUBLIC HOLIDAY PAY

[22.06] ***Waterford City and County Council v Smith*[9]*—Labour Court—appeal from Workplace Relations Commission—Organisation of Working Time Act 1997—public holiday pay—compensation—working time***

The claimant was a full-time firefighter employed by the respondent. It was claimed that the respondent undercalculated the claimant's public holiday payments for the duration of his employment, insofar as the respondent failed to pay his normal weekly pay plus various allowances (Saturday and Sunday allowances, night duty meal allowance and night hours allowance) when calculating his public holiday pay. He therefore sought retrospective payment from the date when his employment commenced with the respondent. He also sought compensation for breaches of the Organisation of Working Time Act 1997 (the '1997 Act').

The claimant worked a four-shift system, which was comprised of two day shifts, followed by two night shifts and four days off. His average working week was 42 hours. His basic hours per week were 39 hours and he received overtime for working hours in excess of this. In relation to pay arrangement for public holidays for those rostered off, workers would receive eight hours at a basic rate in lieu. The claimant argued that he was entitled to be paid his normal weekly pay to include the average value of premium payments and allowances received by him as payment for public holidays on which he was rostered off. The claimant alleged that because he was rostered off for four and a half of the public holidays each year, he suffered a shortfall of €644.81 per year.

The respondent argued that it had complied with the 1997 Act and with the Organisation of Working Time (Determination of Pay for Holidays) Regulations 1997[10] (the '1997 Regulations'). The respondent also argued that for the purposes of the complaint, the relevant period was 11 December 2020 to 10 June 2021 and could not extend back for the entirety of the claimant's employment. The respondent argued that the claim for inclusion of overtime in public holiday pay was time barred. The respondent also pointed out that the allowances here were not of a regular, weekly type and that the 1997 Regulations state that allowances are payable only where the amount does not vary in relation to work done. In this case, for example, the Saturday and Sunday allowance was only paid if the worker was working on those days. It also argued that the Working Time Directive does not deal with public holidays.

---

9 *Waterford City and County Council v Smith* DWT237.

10 Organisation of Working Time (Determination of Pay for Holidays) Regulations 1997 (SI 475/1997).

The Court noted that a range of similar appeals were currently before the Court, grounded on identical facts. The Court referred to its previous determination in *Waterford City Council v Runcimanand*[11] as being instructive and outlined the formula for the calculation of the rate payable for public holidays for those who are not rostered as per the 1997 Regulations.

The Court found that the hours worked over the basic hours are not encompassed by the 1997 Regulations, referring to the wording of regs 3(2) and 5(1) in this regard and to its previous determination in *MCM Security Ltd v Power*.[12] The Court concluded that the argument that such hours be included in the calculation of public holiday pay was not well founded in this case.

The Court also found that the allowances described were variable and that a worker would be entitled to different allowances depending on the shifts worked each week. Such allowances were not encompassed by the 1997 Regulations and, accordingly, the Court found that the claim for these allowances to be included in the calculation of public holiday pay for the claimant was not well founded.

The Court adopted its own reasoning in *Waterford City Council v Runcimanand* in concluding that the appeal, which was grounded on identical facts, must fail.

The decision of the Adjudication Officer was affirmed.

NIGHT WORKERS

[22.07] ***OP v Glavna direktsia 'Pozharna bezopasnost i zashtita na naselenieto' kam Ministerstvo na vatreshnite raboti[13]—European Court of Justice—request for preliminary ruling from Bulgaria—Directive 2003/88/EC[14]—Directive 89/391/EEC[15]—Charter of Fundamental Rights of the European Union—working time—night workers—social policy—organisation of working time—health and safety of night workers—level of protection for night workers appropriate to the nature of their work—public sector workers—private sector workers***

The claimants were civil servants working for the respondent as firefighters in the Kula district of Bulgaria. On 31 January 2018 and 31 December 2020, the claimants worked 24-hour shifts, calculated on a quarterly basis. During this time, they carried out night work between 22:00pm and 06:00am, which came to eight hours of night work per 24-hour period. Under the Bulgarian Labour Code, the normal length of a night-work shift in a five-day working week was not permitted to exceed seven hours

11 *Waterford City Council v Runcimanand* WTC 22/316.

12 *MCM Security Ltd v Power* DWT 0895.

13 *OP v Glavna direktsia 'Pozharna bezopasnost i zashtita na naselenieto' kam Ministerstvo na vatreshnite raboti* (Cases C-529/21-536/21).

14 Directive 2003/88/EC concerning certain aspects of the organisation of working time.

15 Directive 89/391/EEC on the introduction of measures to encourage improvements in the safety and health of workers at work.

in any 24-hour period. Any time worked beyond this period gave rise to an increase in pay of 50%. Special rules on work laid down by the Ministry of the Interior stated that the normal length of night work was eight hours in any 24-hour period and where overtime was due, a BGN 0.25 per hour supplement would be applied. The claimants argued that their night work constituted overtime because it corresponded to the difference between the normal length of night work applicable to them and the normal length applicable to workers in the private sector, being one hour. The claimants argued that the method of calculating their overtime payment per the special rules laid down by the Ministry of the Interior was discriminatory and that they should be subject to the more favourable general rules. It was noted that the claimants enjoyed certain benefits that those who were governed by the general rules did not enjoy, eg longer paid leave and higher retirement allowances.

The District Court in Kula, Bulgaria referred two questions to the European Court of Justice ('ECJ') for a preliminary ruling:

> '(1) Does Directive [2003/88/EC] apply where characteristics peculiar to certain specific public service activities, such as the armed forces or the police, or to certain specific activities in the civil protection services inevitably conflict with it, given that:
>
> — Article 1(3) of Directive [2003/88/EC] provides that that directive is to apply to all sectors of activity, both public and private, within the meaning of Article 2 of Directive [89/391];
>
> — Article 2(2) of Directive [89/391] provides that that directive is not to be applicable where characteristics peculiar to certain specific public service activities, such as the armed forces or the police, or to certain specific activities in the civil protection services inevitably conflict with it?
>
> (2) When appraising the equivalence of the appropriate [protection facilities] within the meaning of Article 12(b) of Directive [2003/88/EC] of a category of workers who perform night work and whose night working hours are not more than [seven hours in any 24-hour period] by comparison with another category of workers who also perform night work and whose night working hours are not more than [eight hours], but who have advantages such as longer leave, higher retirement allowances and higher additional remuneration for seniority, is it necessary to take the advantages which workers in the second category enjoy into consideration?'.

The ECJ noted that art 1(3) of Directive 2003/88/EC, when read in light of art 2 of Directive 89/391/EEC to which it refers, makes clear that the Directives are to apply to both public and private sectors. It was held that Directive 89/391/EEC must be broad in scope and the exceptions to it construed restrictively. The ECJ found that the criterion in art 2(2) of Directive 89/391/EEC to exclude certain activities from the scope of that Directive and from Directive 2003/88/EC is not based on the fact that workers work in the public sector, but exclusively on the specific nature of certain tasks carried out by the workers referred to in that provision. The ECJ observed that, even if certain services have to deal with situations that are unforeseeable, the tasks carried out by said services in normal conditions and which relate to duties specifically given to said services are able to be ascertained in advance. It was therefore held that it was clear that Directive 2003/88/EC applies to public sector workers who are taken to be night workers insofar as those workers carry out activities under normal circumstances.

The ECJ interpreted the second question as relating to the applicability of the general principle of equal treatment in art 20 of the Charter of Fundamental Rights of the European Union (the 'Charter') in this case, and whether more favourable working conditions set out in the general rules must be applied to those night workers in the public sector under art 12(a) of Directive 2003/88/EC. It was held that it is for the referring Court to make the necessary determinations in order to identify the relevant categories of workers and ascertain whether the requirement of the comparability of the situations is satisfied. The ECJ stated that the assessment of the comparability of the situations at issue here, as between the public and private sectors, should not be made in a 'global and abstract manner' but in a 'specific and concrete manner having regard to all the elements which characterise those situations'. In particular, regard should be given to the purpose of the national legislation which distinguishes between the categories and its objectives. The ECJ acknowledged the extra benefits that the public sector workers enjoyed, but also noted that there was no evidence which specified whether those benefits were directly linked to the nature of the night work carried out. The ECJ held that, when read in light of art 20 of the Charter, art 12 of Directive 2003/88/EC should be interpreted as not precluding the normal length of night work fixed at seven hours in the domestic legislation for workers in the private sector from not applying to public sector workers if they are in a comparable situation and the differences are based on objective and reasonable criteria.

REST PERIODS

[22.08] ***IH v MÁV-START Vasúti Személyszállító Zrt[16]—European Court of Justice—request for preliminary ruling from Hungary—Charter of Fundamental Rights of the European Union, art 31(2)—Directive 2003/88/EC[17]—rest periods—social policy—protection of the safety and health of workers—organisation of working time—daily rest and weekly rest***

The applicant was an employee of the respondent, working as a train driver. He carried out his work exclusively in Hungary and was subject to a collective agreement. His employment was part of a monthly roster with no weekly rest days, but with rest allocation granted by the employer based on a weekly reference period. The applicant was granted, between two periods of work, a daily rest period of 12 hours to which travel time of two 30-minute periods was added. Once a week, he was granted a weekly rest period of at least 48 consecutive hours. If it was not feasible to grant this period of rest, the employer granted the applicant an uninterrupted rest period of at least 42 hours so that he could benefit from an average weekly rest period of at least 48 hours. If the applicant was granted the weekly rest period, he was not entitled to a daily rest period or travel time. This was also the case if he took leave.

16 *IH v MÁV-START Vasúti Személyszállító Zrt* (Case C-477/21).

17 Directive 2003/88/EC concerning certain aspects of the organisation of working time.

The applicant brought an action in the referring Court for unpaid wages, arguing that he was entitled to the daily rest period immediately before or after his weekly rest periods or period of leave. The respondent argued that the daily rest period must be granted between two periods of work in the same 24-hour period only. It could not be granted where no new period of work is scheduled, eg when a weekly rest period was granted and availed of, or leave was taken. These two periods of work must be successive, the rest period being restorative in intention after working a shift. Additionally, during each seven-day period, it was necessary to provide a longer weekly rest period that replaced the daily rest period.

The referring Court noted that, under Directive 2003/88/EC and the Labour Code, the collective agreement was a derogation from the rules on daily rest and weekly rest periods. The derogations in question were in the workers' favour. For example, the minimum daily rest period under art 3 of Directive 2003/88/EC is 11 hours as compared to the period under the collective agreement, which was 12 hours. The referring Court also noted the discrepancies between the Hungarian language version of art 5 of Directive 2003/88/EC and the English, German and French versions. In the Hungarian version, every worker must be entitled to a minimum rest period of 24 hours in every seven-day working period and 'in addition' the 11-hour daily rest period envisaged by art 3 of Directive 2003/88/EC. The other versions used the term 'plus' instead of 'in addition to'. Therefore, confusion arose as to whether, after the 24-hour rest period, it was still necessary to grant an 11-hour daily rest period, or whether the 24-hour period and 11-hour period should be added together to make up the minimum weekly rest period so that a worker received a minimum weekly rest period of 35 consecutive hours. It was noted that the Hungarian legislation set the duration of the weekly rest period at 48 hours, with a minimum of 42 hours, and that the concept of the 'weekly rest period' used in the collective agreement made no reference to the 'daily rest period' or its length. The Court considered whether the daily rest period must be given between the conclusion of a day's work and the beginning of the next shift even if the latter is several days after the former.

The Court referred the following questions to the European Court of Justice ('ECJ'):

'(1) Must Article 5 of Directive [2003/88], read in conjunction with Article 31(2) of the Charter, be interpreted as meaning that the daily rest period provided for in Article 3 of [that] directive forms part of the weekly rest period?

(2) … must Article 5 of Directive [2003/88], read in conjunction with Article 31(2) of the Charter, be interpreted as meaning that, in accordance with the objective pursued by [that] directive, the aforementioned article lays down only the minimum duration of the weekly rest period, which is to say that the weekly rest period must be at least 35 consecutive hours' long, provided that there are no objective, technical or work organisation conditions which preclude this?

(3) Must Article 5 of Directive [2003/88], read in conjunction with Article 31(2) of the Charter, be interpreted as meaning that, where the law of the Member State and the applicable collective agreement provide for the grant of a continuous weekly rest period of at least 42 hours, it is compulsory, following work which has been performed on the working day prior to the weekly rest period, also to grant the 12-hour daily rest period guaranteed along with it under the relevant legislation of that Member State and the

applicable collective agreement, provided that there are no objective, technical or work organisation conditions which preclude this?

(4) Must Article 3 of Directive [2003/88], read in conjunction with Article 31(2) of the Charter, be interpreted as meaning that a worker is entitled to a minimum rest period which must be granted within the course of 24 hours even if, for any reason, he or she does not have to work in the following 24 hours?

(5) If the [fourth question] is answered in the affirmative, must Articles 3 and 5 of Directive [2003/88], read in conjunction with Article 31(2) of the Charter, be interpreted as meaning that the daily rest period must be granted prior to the weekly rest period?'

The ECJ emphasised that the right to rest appears in two provisions in Directive 2003/88/EC: arts 3 and 5. This indicated that these were two autonomous rights which were aimed at two separate objectives, being, in the case of the daily rest period to enable the worker to extract themselves from their work following a working period. The daily rest period must be consecutive and also must immediately follow a working period to be of utility. In the case of the weekly rest period, the aim is to permit the worker to rest during a seven-day working period. The ECJ stated that actions by a Member State to implement the requirements under the Directive 2003/88/EC must not undermine art 31(2) of the Charter of Fundamental Rights of the European Union (the 'Charter') and arts 3 and 5 of Directive 2003/88/EC. For example, an interpretation of the daily rest period that supported a contention that it formed part of the weekly rest period would undermine the right to daily rest under art 3. As such, art 5 provides both a minimum period of weekly rest and also, in addition, a period of daily rest must be given effect to. The ECJ held therefore that the daily rest period in art 3 must be construed as being not in addition to the 24-hour rest period referred to in art 5, but in addition to the weekly rest period, which is separate and autonomous.

The ECJ held that the national legislation in this case set as the 'weekly rest period' a period of 48 hours, and of no less than 42 hours. It noted that the legislation did not contain any reference to the daily rest period. Article 5 of Directive 2003/88/EC did not contain any reference to national legislation and, accordingly, must be applied uniformly across all Member States, irrespective of domestic law. As such, the concept of 'weekly rest period' in the national legislation did not affect the interpretation of art 5. Article 15 of Directive 2003/88/EC allows Member States to introduce more favourable provisions for workers to facilitate collective agreements. The collective agreement in this case stated that the weekly rest period was at least 42 hours, which was in excess of the minimum required in art 5. As such, the weekly rest period was governed by national law in this case. It was noted that, notwithstanding this, workers were still entitled to other rights conferred on them by Directive 2003/88/EC, eg the right to daily rest provided for in art 3.

Finally, the ECJ noted that currently the respondent granted a daily rest period only if a new period of work was scheduled for within 24 hours of the end of a working shift. It was noted again that the utility of daily rest periods was to allow employees to extract themselves from the working environment and that this period must both be consecutive and must immediately follow a period of work to serve any benefit.

The ECJ held that art 5 of Directive 2003/88/EC, read in light of art 31(2) of the Charter, must be interpreted as meaning that the daily rest period provided in art 3 of Directive 2003/88/EC does not form part of the weekly rest period referred to but must be taken as being in addition to it.

Further, it was held that arts 3 and 5 of Directive 2003/88/EC, read in light of art 31(2) of the Charter must be interpreted as meaning that where national legislation provides for weekly rest periods in excess of 35 consecutive hours, the employee must be granted a daily rest period guaranteed by art 3 in addition to the weekly rest period.

Finally, the ECJ held that art 3 of Directive 2003/88/EC, read in light of art 31(2) of the Charter must be interpreted as meaning that where an employee is granted a weekly rest period, they are entitled to a daily rest period before that weekly rest period.

SEA FISHING

[22.09] ***Elganagy v Galopin Trawlers Ltd*[18]*—High Court—Owens J—appeal from Labour Court— European Communities (Workers on Board Seagoing Fishing Vessels) (Organisation of Working Time) Regulations 2003,*[19] *reg 6—whether worker on seagoing vessel entitled to remedy under s 27(1) of Organisation of Working Time Act 1997—jurisdiction to hear complaint***

This was an appeal on a point of law from a decision of the Labour Court. The plaintiff worked on a seagoing fishing vessel for the respondent and owner of the vessel, Galopin Trawlers Ltd. He alleged that he was not given adequate rest while the vessel was operating, and that the respondent had contravened reg 6 of the European Communities (Workers on Board Seagoing Fishing Vessels) (Organisation of Working Time) Regulations 2003 (the '2003 Regulations').

The plaintiff submitted to the WRC, under s 41 of the Workplace Relations Act 2015, that he was not provided with mandatory rest periods under reg 6 of the 2003 Regulations. The WRC and, on appeal, the Labour Court concluded that they lacked jurisdiction to hear the complaint.

The point of law before the High Court was whether the plaintiff was entitled to a remedy under s 27(1) of the Organisation of Working Time Act 1997 (the '1997 Act') arising from the respondent's alleged breach, and to issue proceedings under s 41 of the Workplace Relations Act 2015 (the '2015 Act') for that purpose, notwithstanding that the provisions of the 2003 Regulations are silent on compensation and redress.

The Court held that legislation implementing EU directives on working time 'can and should' be interpreted as encompassing that remedy, and it must be assumed that the State intended to include this remedy in compliance with EU law.

---

18 *Elganagy v Galopin Trawlers Ltd* [2023] IEHC 544.

19 European Communities (Workers on Board Seagoing Fishing Vessels) (Organisation of Working Time) Regulations 2003 (SI 709/2003).

The Court found that, without any indication of contrary intention, regulations such as the 2003 Regulations must be interpreted in a manner which gives full effect to EU directives, sometimes including interpretations that 'imply or supply content'. In this case, reg 6 of the 2003 Regulations must be read together with s 27(1) of the 1997 Act, reflecting the presumed intention of the State to implement Directive 2000/34[20] in full, by providing remedies to workers affected by breaches of reg 6. There was no indication 'from within' the 2003 Regulations that the State made a deliberate choice not to extend the provisions of s 27(1) of the 1997 Act to breaches of reg 6 of the 2003 Regulations. The Court therefore concluded that the plaintiff was entitled to a remedy under s 27(1) of the 1997 Act.

20 Directive 2000/34/EC amending Council Directive 93/104/EC concerning certain aspects of the organisation of working time to cover sectors and activities excluded from that Directive.

Chapter 23

Northern Ireland—2023 in Outline

INTRODUCTION

[23.01] The political stalemate in Northern Ireland, which began in February 2022 over a dispute regarding the Northern Ireland Protocol, continued throughout 2023. As a result, important changes to the local employment law regime that were intended to come into effect have not yet been implemented. For example, the Employment (Zero Hours Workers and Banded Weekly Working Hours) Bill has not yet been enacted, nor has the Employment Act (Northern Ireland) 2016 been fully implemented, including regulations detailing the gender pay gap reporting regime.

The UK Supreme Court delivered its eagerly-awaited decision in *Chief Constable of the Police Service of Northern Ireland v Agnew.*[1] The UK Supreme Court unanimously upheld the decision of the NI Court of Appeal (and that of the NI Industrial Tribunal in the first instance) that police and civilian officers were entitled to underpayments of holiday pay dating back 20 years. Importantly, it affirmed the reasoning of the NI Court of Appeal that a 'series', for the purposes of art 55 of the Employment Rights (Northern Ireland) Order 1996, is a question of fact that must be answered in light of all of the relevant circumstances, and a gap of more than three months between deductions does not necessarily bring a series to an end. This decision is of particular significance to employers in Northern Ireland, especially those who had claims for holiday pay stayed by the NI Industrial Tribunal pending the decision of the UK Supreme Court.

A number of new employment protections have been passed for Great Britain workers in 2023, such as a week's unpaid leave to care for a dependant,[2] parental leave, and pay for up to 12 weeks when a baby requires neonatal care,[3] protections from redundancy for those who are pregnant or a recent returner from parental leave,[4] and prohibiting employers from making deductions to tips.[5] As employment law is a devolved matter, similar changes would have to be ratified by a functioning Stormont

1 *Chief Constable of the Police Service of Northern Ireland v Agnew* [2023] UKSC 33.
2 Carer's Leave Act 2023.
3 Neonatal Care (Leave and Pay) Act 2023.
4 Protection from Redundancy (Pregnancy and Family Leave) Act 2023.
5 Employment (Allocation of Tips) Act 2023.

assembly, meaning that Northern Irish employment law is continuing to fall further behind the rest of the UK. The passing of the Retained EU Law (Revocation and Reform) Act in Westminster in 2023 is likely to lead to a period of further significant developments in Great Britain employment law. This legislation aims to speed up the process of removing and replacing laws derived from the EU, and will enable the introduction of planned employment law reforms to working time, holiday pay, and TUPE. It is unlikely that these changes will be reflected in Northern Irish law. Due to the protections in art 2 of the NI Protocol for EU Directive-based rights in the Good Friday Agreement, it is possible that developments in Northern Irish employment laws with an EU dimension may mirror those in Ireland. This will be subject to the continuing process between the UK and the EU of working out arrangements in Northern Ireland in the post-Brexit era.

HOLIDAY PAY

[23.02] ***Chief Constable of the Police Service of Northern Ireland v Agnew[6]—UK Supreme Court—Hodge, Briggs, Kitchin & Richards LJJ, Rose LJ—appeal from NI Court of Appeal—Employment Rights (Northern Ireland) Order 1996[7]—Working Time Regulations (Northern Ireland) 2016[8]—holiday pay claims can potentially extend back to 1998***

The respondent police and civilian staff brought claims to the Northern Ireland Industrial Tribunal for underpaid holiday pay under regs 30 and 43 of the Working Time Regulations (Northern Ireland) 2016 ('WTR (NI)') and for unlawful deductions from wages under art 55 of the Employment Rights (Northern Ireland) Order 1996 ('ERO (NI)'). The respondents claimed that the appellants had been calculating their holiday pay based on 'basic' renumeration rather than 'normal' renumeration, which would include regular overtime and allowances. The Industrial Tribunal held that the respondents could claim for underpaid holidays back to either the later of 23 November 1998 (being the implementation date of the WTR (NI)) or the date their employment commenced with the appellants. The appeal was dismissed by the NI Court of Appeal, holding that both the police and civilian staff could claim under both the ERO (NI) and the WTR (NI) back to 1998.

The appellants appealed the decision of the NI Court of Appeal to the UK Supreme Court and argued that police officers could not be treated as workers for the purposes of the ERO (NI), meaning they could not benefit from the 'series of deductions' rule under art 55(3). The appellants accepted that civilian staff could claim under both the ERO (NI) and the WTR (NI), but submitted that a 'series' was broken if any two payments

6 *Chief Constable of the Police Service of Northern Ireland v Agnew* [2023] UKSC 33. See *Arthur Cox Employment Law Yearbook 2019* at **[25.02]** for decision of NI Court of Appeal in *Chief Constable of the Police Service of Northern Ireland and Northern Ireland Policing Board v Agnew* [2019] NICA 32.

7 Employment Rights (Northern Ireland) Order 1996 (SI 1996/1919 (NI 16)).

8 Working Time Regulations (Northern Ireland) 2016 (NISR 2016/49).

were separated by more than three months. Lord Kitchin and Lady Rose delivered a unanimous decision dismissing the appeal. The UK Supreme Court found that the NI Court of Appeal had been entirely correct in its analysis of the actions under the ERO (NI) and the WTR (NI) as being similar domestic actions, due to similarities in their objectives, purposes and characteristics. Therefore, the EU principle of equivalence meant that the more favourable limitation period under the ERO (NI) had to apply to claims under the WTR (NI). The Court reasoned that the appellants' interpretation of a 'series' being broken if any two payments were separated by more than three months would impose an unreasonable burden on a worker if the deductions were connected together in a relevant way. On this point, the Court applied the reasoning of the NI Court of Appeal in *Arthur v London Eastern Railway Ltd.*[9] The three-month limit to bringing a claim from the date the last payment was made does not restrict or qualify the meaning of a 'series' of deductions, contrary to the view expressed by the UK EAT in *Bear Scotland v Fulton.*[10] Whether a claim in respect of two or more deductions constitutes a claim in respect of a series of deductions is essentially a question of fact, and in answering that question, all relevant circumstances must be taken into account. In this case, each unlawful deduction was factually linked to its predecessor by the common fault that the holiday pay was calculated by reference to basic pay rather than normal pay.

The appellants argued that police officers were not 'workers' for the purposes of the ERO (NI), and were thus outside the scope of this legislation. Again, the principle of equivalence was cited in rejecting this argument.

The appellants argued that the NI Court of Appeal should have distinguished between the different types of annual leave available to police and civilian staff, and should have held that annual leave based on EU law must be treated as having been taken first, followed by any additional leave not based on EU law. The effect of this reasoning would be that a series of deductions had been interrupted and ended. The UK Supreme Court rejected this argument, primarily because its conclusions would deny the respondents the sums which they ought to have been paid. The NI Industrial Tribunal and the NI Court of Appeal were right to conclude that, where it is not practicable to distinguish between different types of leave, all the leave to which the worker is entitled must form part of a single, composite pot.

The last question addressed by the UK Supreme Court was: if one was required to take a daily rate for overtime that formed part of a worker's normal pay in order to calculate holiday pay, is the lawful approach to divide the number of days in the four weeks' leave period (20) by the number of calendar days in the reference period or the number of working days that period? It was held that the NI Court of Appeal was right to conclude that the number of working days in the reference period should be used. To use calendar days would not be comparing like with like.

9 *Arthur v London Eastern Railway Ltd (t/a One Stansted Express)* [2006] EWCA Civ 1358, [2007] ICR 193.

10 *Bear Scotland v Fulton* [2015] ICR 221.

This decision is binding across the UK; however, the financial consequences will be greatest for employers in Northern Ireland due to the fact that there is no statutory two-year limit on claims for unlawful deductions from wages.

SEXUAL HARASSMENT

[23.03] ***Geraghty v Forose*[11]*—NI Court of Appeal—McCloskey & Horner LJJ, O'Hara J—appeal from NI Industrial Tribunal—Industrial Tribunals and Fair Employment Tribunal (Constitution and Rules of Procedure) Regulations (NI) 2005*[12]*—Industrial Tribunals and Fair Employment Tribunal (Constitution and Rules of Procedure) Regulations (NI) 2020*[13]*—sex discrimination—anonymity order—Risk of Sexual Harm Order***

This case concerned an appeal by Mr Geraghty ('Mr G') against findings made against him by the NI Industrial Tribunal (the 'Tribunal') and the award which followed from those findings. Ms Forose ('Ms F') began working in a shop in March 2017. Later that year she reported to the police that the owner of the shop, Mr G, had sexually harassed her while she was working. Mr G pleaded guilty to a single charge of common assault for which he received a suspended sentence, and he accepted a Risk of Sexual Harm Order ('ROSH'). Ms F's witness statements to police formed part of her evidence to the Tribunal, as did statements by her mother and friend. Ms F provided the police with details of a long list of explicitly sexual verbal harassment and physical behaviour, including inappropriate touching and smacking. The Tribunal found in Ms F's favour and awarded her £41,500 for injury to her feelings, £20,000 for psychiatric injury and £6,000 by way of aggravated damages. Interest on the award was £4,260, leading to a total of £71,860.

When the original claim to the Tribunal was lodged in August 2017, Schedule 1, r 49 of the Industrial Tribunals and Fair Employment Tribunal (Constitution and Rules of Procedure) Regulations (NI) 2005 (the '2005 Regulations') mandated that the names of Ms F and Mr G were anonymised in the Tribunal's judgment because there was an allegation that a sexual offence had been committed. By the time the case was heard by the Tribunal in September 2021, the new Sch 1, r 44 of the Industrial Tribunals and Fair Employment Tribunal (Constitution and Rules of Procedure) Regulations (NI) 2020 had replaced r 49 in the 2005 Regulations. This rule gives tribunals discretion in relation to orders for anonymity, and Ms F asked the Tribunal to revoke the earlier anonymity order as she wanted the truth to be made public and to empower other women. The Tribunal decided to remove anonymity but postponed this until Mr G's appeal could be heard by the NI Court of Appeal. The NI Court of Appeal similarly decided to revoke

11 *Geraghty v Forose* [2023] NICA 2.

12 Industrial Tribunals and Fair Employment Tribunal (Constitution and Rules of Procedure) Regulations (NI) 2005 (NISR 2005/150).

13 Industrial Tribunals and Fair Employment Tribunal (Constitution and Rules of Procedure) Regulations (NI) 2020 (NISR 2020/3).

anonymity, due primarily to the principle of open justice in accordance with art 10 of the ECHR, as well as Ms F's strong desire to remove anonymity.

Despite Mr G not lodging the relevant papers in the Central Office of the Royal Courts of Justice in time, the NI Court of Appeal exercised its discretion under Ord 3 r 5 of the Rules of the Court of Judicature (NI) 1980[14] to extend the time limit, due to Mr G being unrepresented, the lack of prejudice suffered by Ms F, and there being merit in at least one of the grounds of appeal.

On the first ground of appeal, O'Hara J rejected the claim that Mr G was denied a fair hearing by requiring his cross-examination of Ms F to be conducted via the employment judge. This was a special procedure which allowed the case to be heard in the circumstances where Mr G was subject to an ROSH order which prohibited him from communicating directly with Ms F. O'Hara J also rejected the submission that the Tribunal erred in law by taking into account similar fact evidence in respect of previous allegations made against the appellant by equally young girls in 2013.

The Court of Appeal did rule, however, that the award of £61,500 for injury to feelings and psychiatric damage was clearly excessive, and involved an element of double counting. Instead, the Court of Appeal decided to revise this award to £40,000. The award of £6,000 for aggravated damages was left untouched, leaving a total award of £46,000 excluding interest.

PROCEDURAL UNFAIRNESS AT NI INDUSTRIAL TRIBUNAL

[23.04] ***Andrews v Bryson Charitable Group*[15]*—NI Court of Appeal—McCloskey LJ & Scoffield J—procedural unfairness—McKenzie friend—unrepresented litigant—whistleblowing***

Ms Andrews was employed by Bryson Charitable Group (the 'Group') from October 2017 to June 2018 to provide maternity cover on a fixed-term contract. After a short time working at the Group, Ms Andrews became aware of concerning behaviours and decisions of senior managers, and invoked the Group's whistleblowing policy, she also submitted a formal grievance. Ms Andrews argued that the dismissal of her grievance was vitiated by unlawful detriment and/or less favourable treatment. Ms Andrews pursued two claims in the NI Industrial Tribunal (the 'Tribunal'), a wages claim and an unfair dismissal claim. The Tribunal decided that the appellant had failed to establish a *prima facie* case of the detriment or less favourable treatment alleged, observing that her case revolved around bare, unsupported assertion. The outcome of the unfair dismissal claim was challenged by Ms Andrews in the NI Court of Appeal.

Ms Andrews' appeal centred around the assertion that she did not receive a fair hearing at the Tribunal due to: (i) being refused her request to be accompanied by a

14 Rules of the Court of Judicature (NI) 1980 (NISR 1980/346).

15 *Andrews v Bryson Charitable Group* [2023] NICA 26.

McKenzie friend; (ii) the hearing becoming a 'spectator event' for pupil barristers; (iii) Ms Andrews could not represent herself adequately as she suffered two panic attacks during the hearing; (iv) there was unfairness in the way she was provided with hearing bundles; (v) she was not permitted to question witnesses for the Group; and (vi) there was an unbalanced proportion of spectators within the Tribunal weighing favourably for the Group which was grossly intimidating.

The submissions from the Group at the appeal stage did not address a number of these assertions, neither the way in which the provision of hearing bundles to Ms Andrews was handled nor Ms Andrews not being permitted to question witnesses for the Group. Furthermore, McCloskey LJ noted a number of issues with the fact that Ms Andrews' request to have her two witnesses remain in the Tribunal room upon completion of their evidence was rejected. This simple measure, which could have, to a certain extent, addressed the imbalance created by Ms Andrews representing herself against the Group's solicitor, counsel, and witnesses, was not taken. Giving priority for space at the Tribunal to pupil barristers who had nothing to do with the proceedings was inappropriate and 'impinged adversely the appellant's right to a fair hearing'. With regard to the denial of Ms Andrews' request for a *McKenzie* friend, McCloskey LJ noted that Ms Andrews was denied the right to elaborate on the basis of her application; 'there is an allied consideration in this context, namely the judicial duty, of long standing, to provide reasons for decisions. A curt message conveyed through a court clerk is what the appellant got'.

Ms Andrews' complaint of procedural unfairness was upheld, and the NI Court of Appeal remitted the case to a fresh Tribunal for re-hearing.

SOCIAL MEDIA AND CONFLICTING VIEWS IN THE WORKPLACE

[23.05] As the amount of time spent by society viewing and participating in social media increases, so does the risk of reputational damage to employers. Employment tribunals in Great Britain and Northern Ireland are facing a growing number of cases concerning dismissal or disciplinary action as a response to social media posts relating to religious, political, and gender issues.

[23.06] The dangers of social media were highlighted in two related unfair dismissal cases heard by the NI Industrial Tribunal in 2023 concerning an incident in May 2022, where a video was livestreamed from an Orange Hall outside Belfast, which showed a group of people singing a sectarian song that mocked Michaela McAreavey, who had been murdered on her honeymoon. In the first case, Andrew McDade (who had livestreamed the video) was dismissed by his employer, Norman Emerson Group Ltd, for gross misconduct.[16] Mr McDade's Facebook profile stated that he was employed by Norman Emerson Group Ltd, which led to a significant

16 *McDade v Norman Emerson Group Ltd* [2023] NIIT 63140/22.

amount of negative commentary from members of the public and customers after the incident had gone 'viral'. Mr McDade argued that the purpose of recording the live video was to film the bannerettes inside the Orange Hall as an expression of his culture. This argument, as well as the overall claim, were rejected by the NI Industrial Tribunal, stating that it was difficult to see how any reasonable employer could have arrived at a different outcome. The second case concerned Mr McDade's partner, Rhonda Shiels, who was dismissed by the Southern Health and Social Care Trust after liking and sharing the same video on social media.[17] Ms Shiels argued that she had not watched all of the video and had switched it off before the point in which the offensive singing took place. In this case, the NI Industrial Tribunal similarly upheld the fairness of Ms Shiel's dismissal, stating that the behaviour constituted 'an act of recklessness and a clear breach of the social media policy', which had brought her employer into 'serious disrepute'. Both of these cases demonstrate the potential reputational damage that employers may face if their employees engage in offensive or reckless social media behaviour.

[23.07] In Great Britain there has been a number of employment cases involving social media posts related to the expression of 'gender-critical' views, with proponents stating that they do not believe in the concept of gender identity as distinct from biological sex. One prominent example is *Forstater v CGD Europe*,[18] where a researcher working as a visiting fellow and consultant for a not-for-profit think tank was not offered any further work after her colleagues had complained that a number of her tweets had been transphobic. Ms Forstater brought a claim alleging that this had constituted direct discrimination on the grounds of her philosophical beliefs. In a preliminary hearing before the employment tribunal, she unsuccessfully argued that her beliefs were a protected characteristic under the Equality Act 2010; on appeal the UK EAT found that Ms Forstater's tweets were legitimate statements of her protected beliefs and the matter was reverted to the employment tribunal to determine the substantive issue. The tribunal upheld two complaints of direct discrimination and one of victimisation. In July 2023, Ms Forstater was awarded more than £100,000 in compensation for loss of earnings, injury to feelings, aggravated damages, and interest.

[23.08] On the other side of the transgender debate, there has been an increase in the number of employment disputes relating to alleged discrimination against transgender employees.[19] Under the Equality Act 2010, sexual orientation and sex are protected characteristics, with the provisions expressly including those who have undergone or are undergoing gender reassignment. These are sensitive issues, and employers need to be able to demonstrate that they have taken reasonable steps to prevent discrimination from taking place in the workplace. The Equality Act 2010 does not apply in Northern

---

17 *Shiels v Southern Health and Social Care Trust* [2023] NIIT 59765/22.

18 *Forstater v CGD Europe* [2022] ET/2200909/2019. See *Arthur Cox Employment Law Yearbook 2021* at [4.57] for decision of UK EAT in *Forstater v CGD Europe* UKEAT/0105/20/JOJ.

19 See *https://www.personneltoday.com/hr/transgender-employment-tribunal-cases-rise/* [last accessed 31 October 2023].

Ireland, however Great Britain cases under this legislation are likely to be considered influential in Northern Ireland. While cases on this particular topic have not yet reached the decision stage in the NI tribunals, it is expected that they will arise in the near future.

ALTERNATIVE DISPUTE RESOLUTION

[23.09] Judicial assessment and mediation were launched in the NI Industrial Tribunal in March 2023, bringing Northern Ireland in line with Great Britain and offering employers new avenues for alternative dispute resolution. The aim of this development is to encourage parties to settle early in a timely and cost-effective manner in order to avoid protracted hearings and legal cost. It remains to be seen how effective this will be, however early signs indicate that the up-take has been high.

Index

[all references are to paragraph number]